Account Title	Financial Statement	Classification	Permanent or Temporary	Normal Balance
Paid-In Capital in Excess of Par— Preferred	Balance Sheet	Stockholders' Equity	Permanent	Credit
Preferred Stock	Balance Sheet	Stockholders' Equity	Permanent	Credit
Retained Earnings	Retained Earnings Statement;	Stockholders' Equity	Permanent	Credit
	Balance Sheet	Stockholders' Equity	Permanent	Credit
Stock Dividends Distributable	Balance Sheet	Stockholders' Equity	Permanent	Credit
Treasury Stock	Balance Sheet	Contra Stockholders' Equity	Permanent	Debit
Cash Dividends	Retained Earnings Statement	Contra Stockholders' Equity	Temporary	Debit
Stock Dividends	Retained Earnings Statement	Contra Stockholders' Equity	Temporary	Debit
Income Summary	—	Owner's Equity	Temporary	—
(Owner's Name), Drawing	Statement of Owner's Equity	Owner's Equity	Temporary	Debit
Fees Earned	Income Statement	Revenue	Temporary	Credit
Sales	Income Statement	Revenue	Temporary	Credit
Service Revenue	Income Statement	Revenue	Temporary	Credit
Sales Discounts	Income Statement	Contra Revenue	Temporary	Debit
Sales Returns and Allowances	Income Statement	Contra Revenue	Temporary	Debit
Freight In	Income Statement	Cost of Goods Sold	Temporary	Debit
Purchases	Income Statement	Cost of Goods Sold	Temporary	Debit
Purchases Discounts	Income Statement	Contra Purchases	Temporary	Credit
Purchases Returns and Allowances	Income Statement	Contra Purchases	Temporary	Credit
Advertising Expense	Income Statement	Operating Expense	Temporary	Debit
Bad Debts Expense	Income Statement	Operating Expense	Temporary	Debit
Depletion Expense	Income Statement	Operating Expense	Temporary	Debit
Insurance Expense	Income Statement	Operating Expense	Temporary	Debit
Miscellaneous Expense	Income Statement	Operating Expense	Temporary	Debit
Payroll Tax Expense	Income Statement	Operating Expense	Temporary	Debit
Rent Expense	Income Statement	Operating Expense	Temporary	Debit
Repairs Expense	Income Statement	Operating Expense	Temporary	Debit
Salaries Expense	Income Statement	Operating Expense	Temporary	Debit
Utilities Expense	Income Statement	Operating Expense	Temporary	Debit
Inventory Short and Over (Over)	Income Statement	Other Income	Temporary	Credit
Cash Short and Over (Over)	Income Statement	Other Income	Temporary	Credit
Gain from Realization	Income Statement	Other Income	Temporary	Credit
Gain on Disposal of Assets	Income Statement	Other Income	Temporary	Credit
Interest Income	Income Statement	Other Income	Temporary	Credit
Inventory Short and Over (Short)	Income Statement	Other Expenses	Temporary	Debit
Cash Short and Over (Short)	Income Statement	Other Expenses	Temporary	Debit
Interest Expense	Income Statement	Other Expenses	Temporary	Debit
Loss on Disposal of Assets	Income Statement	Other Expenses	Temporary	Debit
Loss from Realization	Income Statement	Other Expenses	Temporary	Debit

PARADIGM

College
ACCOUNTING

FOURTH EDITION

PARADIGM
College
ACCOUNTING
FOURTH EDITION

CHAPTERS 1-12

Robert L. Dansby, Ph.D.
Columbus Technical Institute • Columbus, Georgia

Burton S. Kaliski, Ed.D.
New Hampshire College • Manchester, New Hampshire

Michael D. Lawrence, MBA, CPA, CMA
Portland Community College • Portland, Oregon

Developmental Editor	Christine Hurney
Editorial Assistants	Susan Capecchi and Nancy Sauro
Copy Editor	Pat Lewis
Proofreader	Laura M. Nelson
Art Director	Joan D'Onofrio
Cover & Text Designer	Jennifer Wreisner
Indexer	Terry Casey

Photo Credits—Front Cover, Roy Weinman, Image Bank; **177**, John Maher, Stock Market; **393**, Chuck Savage, Stock Market; **457**, Digital Stock

Paradigm College Accounting, Fourth Edition, Chapters 1–12
 ISBN: 0-7638-0157-7   Order Number: 01322
Paradigm College Accounting, Fourth Edition, Chapters 1–18
 ISBN: 0-7638-0159-3   Order Number: 27322
Paradigm College Accounting, Fourth Edition, Chapters 1–29
 ISBN: 0-7638-0160-7   Order Number: 28322
Paradigm College Accounting, Fourth Edition, Chapters 1–29, *Annotated Instructor's Edition*
 ISBN: 0-7638-0161-5   Order Number: 04322

Library of Congress Cataloging-in-Publication Data
 Dansby, Robert L.
  Paradigm college accounting. Chapters 1–12 / Robert L. Dansby,
 Burton S. Kaliski, Michael D. Lawrence. – 4th ed.
   p.   cm.
  Rev. ed. of: College accounting / Robert L. Dansby, Burton S.
 Kaliski, Michael D. Lawrence. 3rd ed. Cincinnati, Ohio : South-
 Western College Pub., c1996.
  Includes index.
  ISBN 0-7638-0157-7
   1. Accounting. I. Kaliski, Burton S. II. Lawrence, Michael D.
 III. Dansby, Robert L. College accounting. IV. Title.
 HF5635.D198   1999
 657' .044--dc21   98-27081
                                              CIP

© 2000 by Paradigm Publishing Inc.
 Published by **EMC**Paradigm
 875 Montreal Way
 St. Paul, MN 55102
 (800) 328-1452
 E-mail: educate@emcp.com
 Web site: www.emcp.com

Printed in the United States of America.

10 9 8 7 6 5 4 3

BRIEF CONTENTS

CHAPTER 1 The Nature of Accounting · 1

CHAPTER 2 Recording Business Transactions · 37

CHAPTER 3 Starting the Accounting Cycle for a Service Business · 67

CHAPTER 4 The Accounting Cycle Continued—Work Sheet, Financial Statements, and Adjusting Entries · 109

CHAPTER 5 Completing the Accounting Cycle for a Service Business—Closing Entries and the Post-Closing Trial Balance · 145

COMPREHENSIVE REVIEW PROBLEM 1
FRED HAYES PHOTOGRAPHY STUDIO · 177

CHAPTER 6 Cash and the Combined Journal · 179

CHAPTER 7 Accounting for a Merchandising Business—Purchases and Cash Payments · 221

CHAPTER 8 Accounting for a Merchandising Business—Sales and Cash Receipts · 267

CHAPTER 9 Work Sheet and Adjustments for a Merchandising Business · 317

CHAPTER 10 Financial Statements and Closing Entries for a Merchandising Business · 349

COMPREHENSIVE REVIEW PROBLEM 2
MILLS SPORTING GOODS STORE · 393

CHAPTER 11 Accounting for Payroll—Employee Earnings and Deductions · 397

CHAPTER 12 Accounting for Payroll—Employer Taxes and Reports · 427

COMPREHENSIVE REVIEW PROBLEM 3
CARLSON COMPANY · 457

APPENDIX A The Voucher System · 459

CONTENTS

INTRODUCTION — xxiii

- Accounting and Bookkeeping — xxiii
- Careers in Accounting — xxiii
  - Advancement in Accounting Careers — xxiii
  - Moving up the Career Ladder — xxiv
- Accounting as a Profession — xxiv
  - Public Accounting — xxiv
  - Private Accounting — xxv
  - Not-for-Profit Accounting — xxv
- Accounting Concepts and Principles — xxv
- Organizations That Influence Accounting Practice — xxvi
  - American Institute of Certified Public Accountants — xxvi
  - Financial Accounting Standards Board — xxvi
  - Securities and Exchange Commission — xxvi
  - Internal Revenue Service — xxvi
- Computers and Accounting — xxvi

CHAPTER 1 · THE NATURE OF ACCOUNTING — 1

- Accounting Defined — 2
- Users of Accounting Information — 2
- Forms of Business Organization — 2
- Types of Business Operations — 3
- The Elements of Accounting — 4
  - Assets — 4
  - Liabilities — 5
  - Owner's Equity — 5
- The Accounting Equation — 5
- Business Transactions and the Accounting Equation — 6
  - The Dual Effect of Business Transactions — 6
  - Recording the Effect of Transactions on the Accounting Equation — 7
  - Summary of Transactions — 11
- Financial Statements — 13
  - The Income Statement — 13
  - The Statement of Owner's Equity — 15
  - The Balance Sheet — 15
- Internet Assets — 17
- Joining the Pieces — 18
- Concepts and Skills Review — 24
- Case Problems — 27
- Challenge Problems — 32

CHAPTER 2 · RECORDING BUSINESS TRANSACTIONS — 37

- The Account — 38
- Debits and Credits — 39
- Recording Transactions in Asset, Liability, and Owner's Equity Accounts — 40
- Temporary Owner's Equity Accounts — 42
  - Rules of Debit and Credit as Applied to Revenue and Expense Accounts — 43
  - Recording Transactions in Revenue and Expense Accounts — 43

- Owner's Drawing Account — 45
- The Trial Balance — 47
- Normal Balance of Accounts — 49
- Summary of Debit and Credit Rules — 50
- Internet Assets — 51
- Joining the Pieces — 52
- Concepts and Skills Review — 56
- Case Problems — 58
- Challenge Problems — 63

CHAPTER 3 · STARTING THE ACCOUNTING CYCLE FOR A SERVICE BUSINESS — 67

- The Accounting Cycle — 68
- Step 1: Analyze Transactions from Source Documents — 68
- Step 2: Record Transactions in a Journal — 68
  - Making Journal Entries — 69
  - Compound Journal Entry — 73
  - Advantages of Using a Journal — 75
- Step 3: Post from the Journal to the Ledger — 75
  - The Chart of Accounts — 75
  - The Four-Column Ledger Account Form — 76
  - Posting Illustrated — 77
- Step 4: Prepare a Trial Balance of the Ledger — 80
- Summary of the First Four Steps in the Accounting Cycle — 81
- Locating and Correcting Errors — 82
  - Types of Errors — 82
  - Correcting an Error — 82
  - Summary of Error Correction Procedures — 84
- Errors That Do Not Cause the Trial Balance to Be Out of Balance — 85
- Internet Assets — 86
- Joining the Pieces — 87
- Concepts and Skills Review — 94
- Case Problems — 97
- Challenge Problems — 104

CHAPTER 4 · THE ACCOUNTING CYCLE CONTINUED—WORK SHEET, FINANCIAL STATEMENTS, AND ADJUSTING ENTRIES — 109

- Step 5: Determine Needed Adjustments — 111
  - Supplies Used — 112
  - Insurance Expired — 112
  - Depreciation of Office Equipment and Office Furniture — 113
  - Unpaid Salaries — 115
  - The Matching Principle of Accounting — 116
- Step 6: Prepare a Work Sheet — 117
- Step 7: Prepare Financial Statements from a Completed Work Sheet — 120
  - The Income Statement — 120
  - The Statement of Owner's Equity — 120
  - The Balance Sheet — 122
  - Showing Additional Investments on the Statement of Owner's Equity — 122

Step 8: Journalize and Post Adjusting Entries 124
Internet Assets 125
Joining the Pieces 126
Concepts and Skills Review 131
Case Problems 135
Challenge Problems 140

CHAPTER 5 · COMPLETING THE ACCOUNTING CYCLE FOR A SERVICE BUSINESS—CLOSING ENTRIES AND THE POST-CLOSING TRIAL BALANCE   145

Purpose of Closing Entries 146
Step 9: Journalize and Post Closing Entries 146
  Steps in the Closing Process 146
  Journalizing Closing Entries 150
  Diagram of the Closing Process 151
  Posting Closing Entries 152
Step 10: Prepare a Post-Closing Trial Balance 156
Summary of the Steps in the Accounting Cycle 157
Fiscal Period 157
The Bases of Accounting 158
Internet Assets 159
Joining the Pieces 160
Concepts and Skills Review 164
Case Problems 167
Challenge Problems 174

COMPREHENSIVE REVIEW PROBLEM 1
FRED HAYES PHOTOGRAPHY STUDIO   177

CHAPTER 6 · CASH AND THE COMBINED JOURNAL   179

Cash Defined 180
Control of Cash 180
The Combined Journal 181
  Designing a Combined Journal 183
  Recording Business Transactions in a Combined Journal 184
  Proving the Combined Journal 186
  Posting the Combined Journal 186
Accounting for Petty Cash 187
  Establishing the Petty Cash Fund 190
  Making Payments from the Petty Cash Fund 190
  Petty Cash Payments Record 190
  Replenishing the Petty Cash Fund 191
The Change Fund 193
Cash Short and Over 194
Bank Checking Accounts 195
Maintaining a Checking Account 196
  Signature Card 196
  Making Deposits 196
  Endorsements 197
Writing Checks 197
The Bank Statement 198
  Reconciling the Bank Statement 199
  Updating Cash Records 202
  A More Detailed Bank Reconciliation 202
Internet Assets 204
Joining the Pieces 205
Concepts and Skills Review 210
Case Problems 213
Challenge Problems 218

CHAPTER 7 · ACCOUNTING FOR A MERCHANDISING BUSINESS—PURCHASES AND CASH PAYMENTS   221

Merchandising Activity 222
  Purchasing Procedures 222
  Trade Discounts 225
  Cash Discounts 225
Recording Purchases of Merchandise 226
  The Purchases Account 226
  Recording Purchases 227
  The Purchases Journal 228
  Recording Purchases in a Purchases Journal 229
The Accounts Payable Subsidiary Ledger 230
Posting the Purchases Journal 231
  Posting to the Accounts Payable Ledger 232
  Posting to the General Ledger 232
Merchandise Returns and Allowances 234
  Purchases Returns and Allowances 234
  Recording Purchases Returns and Allowances 235
Recording Cash Payments 236
  The Purchases Discounts Account 236
  Cash Payments Journal 237
Posting the Cash Payments Journal 238
  Posting to the Accounts Payable Ledger 238
  Posting Individual Entries in the General Dr. Column to the General Ledger 239
  Posting Special Column Totals to the General Ledger 239
Proving the Accounts Payable Ledger 239
Freight Charges on Incoming Merchandise 243
Purchase Invoices as a Journal 244
Internet Assets 245
Joining the Pieces 246
Concepts and Skills Review 251
Case Problems 254
Challenge Problems 264

CHAPTER 8 · ACCOUNTING FOR A MERCHANDISING BUSINESS—SALES AND CASH RECEIPTS   267

Sales Activity 268
  Terms of Payment 268
  Procedures for Credit Sales 269
  Procedures for Cash Sales 270
Recording Sales of Merchandise 271
  Recording Sales in General Journal Form 272
  Recording Sales in a Sales Journal 272
The Accounts Receivable Ledger 273
Posting from the Sales Journal 274
  Posting to the Accounts Receivable Ledger 274
  Posting to the General Ledger 274
Sales Returns and Allowances 275
Sales Discounts 277
Recording Cash Receipts 278
  Cash Receipts Journal 279
  Posting the Cash Receipts Journal 279
Schedule of Accounts Receivable 282
Accounting for Sales Taxes 283
  Recording Sales Taxes Collected 284
  Recording Sales Tax in a Sales Journal 284
  Sales Returns Involving a Sales Tax 286
Credit Card Sales 287
  Bank Credit Card Sales 287
  Recording Bank Credit Card Sales 287

Recording Private Company Credit Card
Sales 287
Credit Cards Issued by Department Stores 288
Summary of Journals and Ledgers 288
Internet Assets 290
Joining the Pieces 291
Concepts and Skills Review 297
Case Problems 300
Challenge Problems 309

CHAPTER 9 · WORK SHEET AND ADJUSTMENTS FOR A MERCHANDISING BUSINESS — 317

Chart of Accounts for a Merchandising
Business 318
Determining Needed Adjustments 318
Adjustment for Merchandise Inventory 321
Adjustment for Store Supplies Used 322
Adjustment for Office Supplies Used 323
Adjustment for Insurance Expired 323
Adjustment for Depreciation Expense 323
Adjustment for Salaries Owed but Unpaid 325
The End-of-Period Work Sheet 326
The Trial Balance and Adjustments
Columns 326
The Adjusted Trial Balance Columns 326
Financial Statement Columns 328
Completing the Work Sheet 332
Internet Assets 333
Joining the Pieces 334
Concepts and Skills Review 337
Case Problems 340
Challenge Problems 345

CHAPTER 10 · FINANCIAL STATEMENTS AND CLOSING ENTRIES FOR A MERCHANDISING BUSINESS — 349

Preparing Financial Statements for a
Merchandising Business 350
The Classified Income Statement 350
The Completed Income Statement 356
The Statement of Owner's Equity 356
The Classified Balance Sheet 358
Working Capital and the Current Ratio 359
Journalizing Adjusting Entries 361
Closing Entries for a Merchandising Business 361
The Post-Closing Trial Balance 367
Reversing Entries 367
Interim Statements 371
Internet Assets 372
Joining the Pieces 373
Concepts and Skills Review 380
Case Problems 383
Challenge Problems 389

COMPREHENSIVE REVIEW PROBLEM 2
MILLS SPORTING GOODS STORE — 393

CHAPTER 11 · ACCOUNTING FOR PAYROLL— EMPLOYEE EARNINGS AND DEDUCTIONS — 397

Importance of Payroll 398
Employer/Employee Relationships 398
How Employees Are Paid 399
Fair Labor Standards Act 399
Piece-Rate Plans 399
Calculating Gross Earnings 400
Payroll Deductions 401

FICA Tax (Social Security) 401
The OASDI Taxable Wage Base 401
The FICA Tax Rates 401
Federal Income Tax 402
State and Local Income Taxes 403
Other Deductions 406
Calculating Net Earnings (Take-Home Pay) 406
Payroll Record Keeping 407
The Payroll Register 407
Employee's Earning Record 408
Payroll Systems 409
Manual Payroll System 409
Computerized Payroll System 409
Accounting Entry for Employee Earnings
and Deductions 410
Salaries Expense 410
FICA Tax Payable—OASDI and
FICA Tax Payable—HIP 410
Federal Income Tax Payable 411
Other Amounts Withheld 411
Making Payment to Employees 412
Internet Assets 414
Joining the Pieces 415
Concepts and Skills Review 419
Case Problems 421
Challenge Problems 424

CHAPTER 12 · ACCOUNTING FOR PAYROLL— EMPLOYER TAXES AND REPORTS — 427

Employer Identification Number 428
Employer Payroll Taxes 428
FICA Tax 429
Federal Unemployment Tax 429
State Unemployment Tax 429
Recording Employer's Payroll Taxes 430
FICA Tax Payable—OASDI 431
FICA Tax Payable—HIP 432
FUTA Tax Payable 432
SUTA Tax Payable 432
Filing and Making Payroll Tax Payments 432
FICA and Federal Income Taxes 433
Federal Unemployment Taxes 436
State Unemployment Taxes 438
Form W-2: Wage and Tax Statement 438
Form W-3: Transmittal of Wage
and Tax Statements 439
Paying Other Amounts Withheld 439
Workers' Compensation Insurance 441
Internet Assets 443
Joining the Pieces 444
Concepts and Skills Review 449
Case Problems 451
Challenge Problems 454

COMPREHENSIVE REVIEW PROBLEM 3
CARLSON COMPANY — 457

APPENDIX A · THE VOUCHER SYSTEM — 459

Components of a Voucher System 459
Using the Registers 460
End-of-Month Procedures 461

GLOSSARY — 463

INDEX — 481

Contents

PREFACE TO THE STUDENT

Paradigm College Accounting, Fourth Edition presents the fundamentals of accounting in an easy-to-understand and practical manner. Our approach of blending the *why* with the *how* of accounting allows you to easily master accounting procedures (the how) because you understand the underlying theory (the why). Our overall objective is to provide you with a sound basic understanding of the concepts, procedures, and terminology of accounting. The book is designed to prepare you for direct job entry or for further study of accounting and business.

CHAPTER LAYOUT

This book has certain unique features that we believe make accounting easier to learn and to remember. The layout of each chapter follows this pattern:

Chapter Opening

- Learning Objectives, at the beginning of each chapter, list the important concepts or procedures to be mastered in the chapter. They are keyed to the text material and all of the end-of-chapter exercises and problems.
- Each chapter begins with a vignette that quickly and informally introduces you to the chapter topic and explains why it is important.

Chapter Body

Within each chapter are several features that are designed to help you learn the accounting concepts being presented:

- Each major topic is followed by a Review Quiz. By solving these quizzes, you can check your comprehension of key points and procedures as you work through the chapter. Compare your answers to the answers at the end of the chapter. After you complete all of these quizzes successfully, you should be ready to complete the end-of-chapter Concepts Review questions, Skills Review exercises, and Case Problems.
- Note, Remember, and Caution boxes are placed throughout the narrative for emphasis. These helpful boxes are identified by special icons so that you will not miss them.

    - Note boxes highlight issues that may interest you.

    - Remember boxes reinforce concepts or procedures you learned earlier in the text.

    - Caution boxes flag typical student errors.

- Internet Assets boxes precede the end-of-chapter material and describe ways accountants and financial people can use the Internet as a powerful research and reference tool. These boxes are inspired by the chapter content. You can go directly to the sites described, or you can find links to the sites at the *Paradigm Accounting Web Site* at *www.emcp.com*.

- Color is used to help you easily identify the major accounting documents. Throughout the book, the color combinations shown in the following chart are used for journals, ledgers and other accounting rulings, and statements.

Journals	Ledgers and Other Rulings	Statements
General journal	General ledger	Income statement
Combined journal	Trial balance	Balance sheet
Sales journal	Work sheet	Statement of owner's equity
Cash receipts journal	Accounts receivable ledger	Retained earnings statement
Purchases journal	Accounts payable ledger	Statement of cash flows
Cash payments journal	Payroll register	
	Petty cash payments record	
	Schedule of accounts payable	
	Schedule of accounts receivable	
	Employee's earnings record	
	Bank reconciliation statement	

Concept Building Activities

- Joining the Pieces is a visual summary of the major concepts in the chapter. This valuable feature presents an at-a-glance summary of the major concepts, entries, or terms contained in the chapter. By reviewing this summary, you will be able to quickly see what you know and what you need to review from the chapter.
- The Summary/Restatement of Learning Objectives is an important end-of-chapter tool. In this section, we restate each Learning Objective and explain it with detailed examples. You can use this summary both to check that you have indeed met the Learning Objectives stated at the beginning of the chapter and to review the chapter's key concepts.
- Key terms are in boldface type when they are introduced and defined in the text. These terms and their definitions are repeated at the end of each chapter. A complete glossary appears at the back of the book.
- Concepts Review questions at the end of each chapter cover the major topics and accounting theory introduced in the chapter.

End-of-Chapter Activities

- The Skills Review section at the end of each chapter provides exercises that focus on specific topics in the chapter. These exercises are keyed to the chapter-opening Learning Objectives. Exercises progress from simple to complex and can be solved on forms provided in the *Study Guide and Working Papers* booklet.
- Two sets of Case Problems also appear at the end of each chapter: Groups A and B. These problems, which are also keyed to the chapter's Learning Objectives, cover the major topics of the chapter and serve as its basic problems. The specific topic covered is stated in the objective introducing each problem. All problems can be solved on forms provided in the *Study Guide and Working Papers* or on the computer using the appropriate software.
- Each chapter concludes with a set of three Challenge Problems. The first problem, called Problem Solving, asks you to apply the major concepts in the chapter and requires more creative work than the other end-of-chapter activities. Forms to solve this problem are provided in the *Study Guide and Working Papers*.
- The second and third problems, called Communications and Ethics, provide an opportunity for you to write about one or more of the topics discussed in the chapter. These exercises help you to more completely understand many of the reasons for the accounting procedures that you have just learned and should serve as discussion points.

Cumulative Review Material

Comprehensive Review Problems follow each major segment of the book. These problems require you to combine theory and procedures from several chapters. They are longer than the other problems and simulate a real accounting situation. The *Study Guide and Working Papers* includes forms to use to solve these problems, and each of these problems can be solved using the *Paradigm General Ledger Program.*

SUPPLEMENTS AVAILABLE TO STUDENTS

- *Study Guide and Working Papers*, 1–12, 1–18, and 19–29. In addition to providing forms to solve all exercises and problems, the *Study Guide and Working Papers* includes a complete summary of each chapter as well as a practice test with answers. By completing the practice test, you can discover how well you understand the chapter material and identify areas you should review. Each practice test contains a variety of true/false, multiple-choice, fill-in-the-blank, and matching questions.
- *Paradigm Accounting Web Site* at *www.emcp.com.* This site offers direct links to the sites listed in the Internet Assets feature boxes in the textbook, the complete glossary, a study guide for the *Paradigm Interactive Accounting* CD-ROM, as well as other resources for students.
- *Paradigm Interactive Accounting.* This CD-ROM is an interactive, multimedia presentation that uses a conceptual, management-based approach while introducing the accounting equation, financial statements, and generally accepted accounting principles. The online study guide includes a list of objectives, tutorials, points to remember, and section quizzes.
- *Paradigm General Ledger Program.* An easy-to-use general ledger software program is available to complete many Case Problems, Challenge Problems and all of the Comprehensive Review Problems in the book. An icon in the margin identifies those problems.
- *Paradigm Peachtree Accounting* and *Paradigm QuickBooks Accounting.* Peachtree Accounting for Windows and QuickBooks are popular and widely used commercial software packages. These new tutorial supplements are designed to show you how manual accounting procedures can be converted into a computerized environment. These tutorials use problems and exercises similar to those in the textbook to teach the applications.
- *Excel Spreadsheet Templates.* Excel spreadsheet templates are available for working select end-of-chapter exercises and problems throughout the textbook. An icon in the margin identifies those exercises and problems.

PREFACE TO THE INSTRUCTOR

THE PARADIGM ADVANTAGE

Paradigm College Accounting is the only college accounting text that offers the depth of coverage students need with a reading level long regarded as the best on the market. In addition, we know that accuracy is very important to all of our users and have done everything possible to provide a totally accurate and up-to-date text. To this end, the text has been thoroughly reviewed by the authors, independent reviewers, testers, and users.

We provide the flexibility of the service cycle and the merchandising cycle in the first ten chapters. The chapters are arranged so that both cycles can be covered or just the service cycle can be covered in the first course. *Paradigm College Accounting*'s depth of coverage extends to budgets, standard costs, and cost behavior. These topics, like all topics in the book, are presented in a nonthreatening manner that students can easily understand and quickly learn. Your students will benefit from its clarity.

IMPROVEMENTS IN THE FOURTH EDITION

Our valued users provided feedback for improvements in the fourth edition, and we incorporated many of their suggestions to make the book even better.

New Structure

- Two chapters on payroll. The overwhelming majority of our users requested two chapters on payroll. Accordingly, we split the coverage of payroll to include Chapter 11 on employee earnings, taxes, and records and Chapter 12 on employer taxes and records.
- A new chapter on *cost behavior and cost-volume-profit analysis*. Now teachers who wish to provide an overview of management accounting can do so. In keeping with our tradition of being the most comprehensive college accounting text available, we present a new chapter on the basics of cost behavior and cost-volume-profit analysis. Also in keeping with a fundamental tradition of the text, this chapter is presented in a clear and relaxed style.
- Three versions of the text: 1–12, 1–18, and 1–29. With three versions now available, instructors can choose a format that is appropriate for either a semester or a quarter syllabus.
- Two new appendixes: Appendix B: Other Depreciation Methods and Appendix C: Just-in-Time Inventory Systems. Recent surveys reveal that the sum-of-the-years'-digits method of calculating depreciation is rarely used in actual practice. As a result, and at your suggestion, we moved coverage of this method to Appendix B. We also moved ACRS and MACRS to Appendix B because these methods are rarely used for financial reporting. Chapter 16 will now be shorter and easier to cover. We also developed a new appendix (Appendix C) covering just-in-time inventory systems.
- A complete glossary in all three versions of the text to help students learn the vocabulary of accounting.

Special Text Features

- Joining the Pieces illustrative summaries. The end-of-chapter Joining the Pieces visual summary is one of the book's most popular features. Where possible, we expanded and improved these summaries and in some chapters include up to two or three illustrations.
- Student margin notes and boxes. Without cluttering the book or giving it a "too busy" look, we provided notes and reminders in the margin for students to refer to when dealing with a new topic.
- New design. The text's new design effectively uses color and graphics to present the accounting principles and procedures in a clear, unthreatening, and fun way.
- Addition of Ethics cases. The ethical behavior of practitioners has attracted much attention in recent years. Accordingly, we have added an Ethics problem at the end of each chapter.
- Internet Assets feature. The Internet is one of the most powerful informational tools that has ever been developed. Each chapter includes a new feature box that describes a way the accounting student and the accountant can use this powerful tool.

SUPPLEMENTS

- *Annotated Instructor's Edition (AIE).* The AIE contains the complete student text with teaching notes in the margin. Several types of notes are used, including the following:
  - Teaching Tips: Ways to make difficult concepts understandable; strategies to help students learn key points.
  - Typical Student Misconceptions: Common errors that students make and suggestions for helping students avoid or correct these errors.
  - Point to Stress: Key concepts or procedures that need emphasis.
  - Expanding the Text: Information beyond the scope of the chapter; suggestions for giving students a preview of topics they will learn in later chapters, other accounting courses, or in the business world.
  - PIA CD-ROM: References to sections for assignment within the *Paradigm Interactive Accounting CD-ROM* that relate to the text presentation.
  - Check Figure: Key answers to exercises and problems.
- **NEW!** *Paradigm General Ledger Program* software package. A user-friendly, student-oriented general ledger software package is now available for use with all end-of-chapter Case Problems and the six Comprehensive Review Problems. An icon in the text identifies those problems. A complete solutions checker disk is available. Instructors can use this disk to quickly check student work.
- **NEW!** *Paradigm Peachtree Accounting* and *Paradigm QuickBooks Accounting* tutorials. These packages are designed to show students how manual accounting procedures can be converted into a computerized environment. These tutorials use problems and exercises similar to those in the textbook to teach the applications. A combined print solutions and instructor's guide for both programs is also available.
- **NEW!** *Excel Spreadsheet Templates.* Excel spreadsheet templates are available for working select end-of-chapter exercises and problems throughout the textbook. An icon in the text identifies those problems. Instructor solutions are also available.
- **NEW!** *Expanded Paradigm Accounting Web Site* at *www.emcp.com*. The fourth edition continues its popular Web site. The Web site provides direct links to the sites listed in the Internet Assets feature boxes and provides additional resources for students and instructors.

- **NEW!** *Paradigm Interactive Accounting.* Designed to offer students an overview of accounting from a management and financial perspective, this CD-ROM provides students with an interactive, multimedia presentation of the accounting equation, financial statements, and generally accepted accounting principles. The three sections of this CD-ROM can be integrated into your course instruction in one of two ways. You can assign the CD-ROM as part of the students' study as an introduction during the first two or three weeks of the course, or you can assign it as a culminating overview after chapter 5. Margin notes in the Teacher's Annotated Edition identify which sections in the CD-ROM apply to the text discussion. This edition of the CD-ROM has been updated with the new end-of-book glossary.
- *Solutions Manual, Chapters 1–29.* This manual gives the answers to all end-of-chapter Concepts Review questions, Skills Review exercises, Case Problems (Group A and B), Challenge Problems (Problem Solving, Communications, Ethics), and Comprehensive Review Problems. To make your correcting easier, solutions appear on the same forms that the students will use from their *Study Guide and Working Papers* booklet. Estimated completion times for all exercises and problems are included.
- *Solutions Transparencies, Chapters 1–12, 13–29.* Transparencies of the Solutions Manual are provided for classroom presentation.
- *PowerPoint Solutions, Chapters 1–29.* The pages of the *Solutions Manual* are also provided as PowerPoint slides. In addition, the CD-ROM includes all of the Joining the Pieces summary illustrations.
- *Test Bank, Chapters 1–29.* Each chapter of the test bank contains over 2,000 true/false questions, multiple-choice questions, application problems, and communication problems. The entire print test bank is available on the **NEW!** Computerized Test Generator, which allows instructors to create and customize quizzes, chapter tests, and midquarter and final tests and allows you to create multiple versions of the same test quickly and accurately.
- *Achievement Tests, Chapters 1–29.* These are preselected and preprinted tests created from items found within the Test Bank. These tests can be duplicated for distribution within a class. Answer keys come with the master student set.
- *Video, Chapters 1–12.* A video is available to assist in presentations by supplementing analysis of concepts discussed in the text.
- *Instructor's Guide for Paradigm Interactive Accounting.* This guide contains teaching tips on how to integrate the Paradigm Accounting Web site, other Internet resources, and the Paradigm Interactive Accounting CD-ROM into a course.
- *Practice Sets.* The following chart provides information about the available practice sets. Complete printed solutions are available for each practice set.

Practice Set	Use after Chapter	Type of Business	Type of Ownership	Journals Used	Average Hours to Complete
Rock Creek Consulting	6	Service	Proprietorship	Combination	4
Cascade Computers	10	Merchandising	Proprietorship	General, Purchases, Cash payments, Sales, Cash receipts	6
Turn-About Products	26	Manufacturing	Corporation	General	3

ACKNOWLEDGMENTS

We would like to express our sincere thanks to our many academic colleagues who offered excellent suggestions during the review phase of this project. We could not have completed our task so smoothly without their input. Several reviewers also wrote chapter openers, which provide interesting introductions to the topics in each chapter. We greatly appreciate the time, experience, and expertise provided by all of our reviewers, especially those who methodically and carefully tested all of the problems and exercises in the text.

Linda Alford
Reid State Technical College, AL

Jim Arnold
Portland Community College, OR

Janet Carusso
Briarcliff College, NY

F. Kelly Chamberlain
University of Phoenix, AZ
College of Albemarle, NC

Sherry Cohen
New York, NY

Peggy Danowski
Stratton College, WI

Pam Dashiell
DeVry Institute, GA

Paula Day
Okefenokee Tech, GA

Dee Anne Dill
DeKalb Technical Institute, Clarkston Campus, GA

Tom Donahue
University of St. Thomas, MN

Rebecca Drazdowski
Career Preparatory Institute, PA

Niki Fullerton
University of Montana—Missoula College of Technology, MT

Jerry Funk
Brazosport College, TX

Kevin Fura
Allentown Business School, PA

Joseph F. Gallo
Cuyahoga Community College, Metro Campus, OH

Nila Geiger
Griffin Technical College, GA

Jennifer Gill
Griffin Technical College, GA

James S. Halstead
Clatsop Community College, OR

Doug Hamilton
Berkeley College, NJ

Ernest Head
Carroll Technical Institute, GA

Richard D. Hickox
Glendale Career College, CA

Otis E. Hopkins
Heart of Georgia Tech, GA

Hank Hornberg
Stratton College, WI

Fred Jex
Macomb Community College, MI

Richard Jones
Interstate Career College, AZ

Corazon Lacsamana
Taylor Business School, NY

Stan Lawson
Sandersville Regional Technical Institute, GA

Norbert F. Lindskog
Harold Washington College, IL

William P. Logan
Middle Georgia Technical Institute, GA

Gregory K. Lowry
Mercer University Stetson School of Business and Economics, GA

Cora Lytle
NCA School of Business, PA

Kathleen McCabe
John Wesley College, NC

Maki Ohy Gragg
City College of San Francisco, CA

David Payne
North Metro Technical College, GA

Ken Perry
Southwestern Indian Polytechnic Institute, NM

Mark Reddick
DeKalb Technical Institute, Covington-Newton Campus, GA

David Rodriguez
Columbus Technical Institute, GA

Joan Ryan
Clackamas Community College, OR

Marilyn Ryan
St. Paul, MN

Kathy Safley
Kirkwood Community College, IA

John Slodysko
NCA School of Business, PA

Barry Smith
De Anza College, CA

Sondra Smith
Carroll Technical Institute, GA

Al Walczak
Linn-Benton Community College, OR

Scott Wallace
Blue Mountain Community College, OR

William H. Wallace
Rochester Institute of Technology, NY

Philip M. Walter
Belleview Community College, WA

Mary Ann Whitehurst
Griffin Technical College, GA

Paul Winter
St. Paul, MN

Allan Young
DeVry Institute, GA

It takes a large number of people to put together a quality textbook. We thank all those who had a hand in making this book something we are all very proud of. We would especially like to thank Sherry Cohen, Niki Fullerton, Fred Jex, and Paul Winter for their extraordinary job of testing all of the exercises and problems in the text. They have helped us to create a consistent and accurate publication. Norbert Lindskog and Kelly Chamberlain carefully reviewed each chapter of page proofs and we found that their expert suggestions and criticisms were invaluable. Joan Ryan wrote Chapter 29 on government and not-for-profit accounting, adding her expertise to the text. Sondra Smith wrote the new Internet Assets feature boxes.

Profound accolades and thanks are in order for our good friends and valued staff members at Paradigm Publishing who are responsible for publishing this book. Our sincere appreciation goes to Rosemary Fruehling, President of Paradigm, our cherished friend and loyal supporter whom we owe much more than we ever could express. We also wish to thank Mel Hecker, Vice President and Publisher; Sharon Bouchard, Marketing Manager; Jan Johnson, Instructional Design Manager; and Robert Galvin, National Sales Manager. Special thanks are in order for Christine Hurney, our developmental editor, for her enthusiasm, careful attention to detail, and unflagging devotion to the project. Chris is the personification of everything an editor should be, and we greatly appreciate her.

Finally, we would like to recognize the significant contribution of our good friend and professional colleague, Dr. Tom Donahue of Active Learning Systems and the University of St. Thomas. Tom offered many good suggestions and developed the interactive CD-ROM that accompanies the book.

We are also indebted to our families for their love, support, and dedication during this project. To our wives and children, we owe you much.

Wives:	Barbara O'Malley Dansby	
	Janice Graham Kaliski	
	Raynette Lawrence	
Children:	Robert (Champ) Dansby	Kristen Kaliski Cassereau (and son, Luke)
	Allison A. (Alli) Dansby	Karen Kaliski
	Burt Kaliski, Jr. (and spouse,	Michael Kaliski
	Michele; son, Stephen;	Ryan Lawrence
	and daughter, Jessi)	Nicole Lawrence
	John Kaliski	Kevin Lawrence

INTRODUCTION

Welcome to the exciting and challenging world of accounting. You are entering a system of recording and organizing data that keeps the entire Western Hemisphere *in balance*. Without accounting, our modern society, as we know it, could not operate.

Accounting is the *language of business*. Every firm and every individual needs accounting information to make good judgments and sensible business decisions. Only by using this information can owners or managers of businesses know if they are operating successfully.

ACCOUNTING AND BOOKKEEPING

Accounting and bookkeeping are often thought of as being the same. Bookkeeping is, however, only one part of the accounting process; it is the recording part. While bookkeeping focuses on recording accounting data, accounting goes far beyond this and involves classifying, analyzing, and interpreting accounting data.

CAREERS IN ACCOUNTING

Accounting offers many job and career opportunities. Before learning about specific vocational opportunities in accounting, you should understand the difference between a job and a career.

A **job** is an activity that you perform for which you are paid. There are thousands of jobs in our country, ranging from actor to zookeeper. You will probably hold several different jobs in your lifetime, but you should consider whether these jobs will lead to a career. A **career** is a planned sequence of increasingly more challenging and better-paying positions, beginning with an entry-level job.

An **entry-level job** is a paid position that you can obtain because you have had certain educational training; you don't necessarily need previous work experience. Two specific entry-level accounting jobs are those of accounting clerk and bookkeeper, both obtainable with one year of accounting study.

Accounting clerks sort, record, and file accounting data. The high volume of everyday financial events in many organizations requires full-time accounting clerks to maintain up-to-date records, both by hand and in computerized systems. In large organizations, an accounting clerk can specialize in areas such as accounts payable, accounts receivable, inventory, and payroll.

Bookkeepers perform general accounting tasks. Some bookkeepers also participate in the processes of summarizing and analyzing accounting data. The bookkeeper's duties vary depending on the organization's size and the extent to which the organization uses outside accounting services. A *full-charge bookkeeper* is responsible for the entire bookkeeping process and can supervise accounting clerks.

Advancement in Accounting Careers

An entry-level job is only the beginning of a career path. Many entry-level accounting jobs can lead to the job of accountant. **Accountants** plan, summarize, analyze, and interpret accounting information. Accountants have practical experience and usually have college degrees.

Accounting Clerk
Local accounting firm is looking for an accounting clerk to assist in payroll and do bookkeeping tasks. Experience preferred but not required.

Full-Charge Bookkeeper
Talent agency has an opening for a full-charge bookkeeper. Three years' experience required. Working knowledge of Lotus 1-2-3 or EXCEL required. Salary commensurate with experience.

Moving up the Career Ladder

A useful way to discuss a career path is by means of a **career ladder**, a diagram that shows how you can advance in a field. Figure I-1 shows the accounting career ladder of Katherine Spencer, as she envisions it.

FIGURE I-1

The accounting career ladder

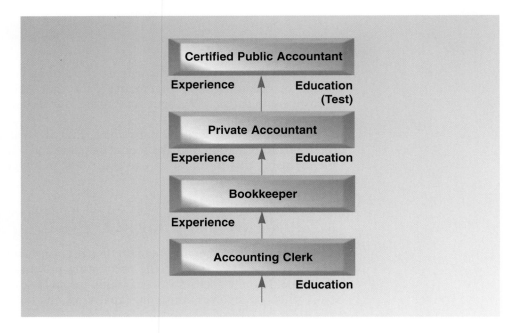

Accountant
Local CPA firm has an immediate opening for an accountant. Duties include accounts payable and general ledger. CPA certification preferred but not required. Salary range is $45,000 to $50,000, depending on experience.

Katherine will start up the career ladder as an accounting clerk, based on her one year's study of accounting. She plans to move up the ladder after a year or two of work experience and become a bookkeeper. Katherine then plans to complete her bachelor's degree in the evenings and advance to the position of accountant. She must then acquire further experience and pass a comprehensive examination to reach her ultimate goal of becoming a **Certified Public Accountant (CPA)**.

The requirements for becoming a CPA vary from state to state. In general, one must be a U.S. citizen, at least 21 years old, and a college graduate with a major concentration in accounting. Additionally, CPA candidates must pass a comprehensive two and one-half day examination in accounting and related subjects, such as law. Katherine plans to use both education and experience, the keys to a successful career, to advance in the profession of accounting.

ACCOUNTING AS A PROFESSION

The word *profession* usually brings to mind medicine, teaching, engineering, and law. These groups have certain common features that lead to their professional status: (1) required education, (2) a thorough and growing body of knowledge, (3) a code of professional ethics, and (4) professional organizations consisting of members of the group. Accounting also has these features, and it too is a profession. The profession of accounting is known as **accountancy**. All professions include fields within the profession. The accounting profession can be divided into three broad fields: (1) public accounting, (2) private accounting, and (3) not-for-profit accounting.

Public Accounting

A **public accountant** is a professional who, for a fee, performs services for individuals or for organizations. A public accountant does not work for any specific company, except as a member of a public accounting firm.

One of the principal services offered by public accountants is auditing. An **auditor** is an accountant who makes an independent review of a company's books to see if proper accounting procedures are being followed. Other services offered by public accountants include management advising, tax advising, and general accounting.

Private Accounting

A **private accountant** is employed by a specific company, such as a department store, a gas company, a manufacturing plant, or a restaurant. This category includes such job titles as *general accountant, industrial accountant, management accountant,* and *controller.* A **controller** is the chief accountant or chief financial officer for an organization.

Some accountants specialize in one aspect of accounting. *Tax accountant, cost accountant,* and *accounting instructor* are among the job titles of these professionals.

Not-for-Profit Accounting

A **not-for-profit accountant** works for a college or university, a public hospital, a public charity, a government (state, local, or federal) agency, or other organization that operates for an objective other than that of earning a profit.

In recent years the not-for-profit sector of our economy has grown considerably. As a consequence, the demand for accounting workers in such organizations has grown.

ACCOUNTING CONCEPTS AND PRINCIPLES

The practice of accounting is guided by **generally accepted accounting principles (GAAP)**, which are rules that govern how accounting personnel measure, process, and report financial information. Figure I-2 shows nine of these rules. Each will be discussed in greater detail in the book.

FIGURE I-2
Generally accepted accounting principles (GAAP)

Principle	Definition
1. Adequate disclosure	Financial reports of a business contain all the information that is needed to determine the business's financial condition.
2. Business entity concept	The financial records of a business are kept separate from the personal financial records of the owner of the business.
3. Consistency	The same accounting procedures are followed from one accounting period to another unless there is valid reason to change.
4. Cost principle	All goods and services acquired by a business are recorded at their actual cost (also called *historical cost*).
5. Going concern concept	Financial reports of a business are prepared with the expectation that the business will remain in operation indefinitely.
6. Matching principle	Revenue (income) earned during an accounting period is recorded in the same period as the expenses associated with earning that revenue.
7. Materiality	Accounting records and reports are prepared according to the guidelines set by GAAP. However, accountants can handle very small amounts (such as the purchase of a screwdriver for $.69) in the easiest and quickest way.
8. Objective evidence	Financial events recorded in accounting records are supported by written source documents.
9. Realization principle	A business earns (realizes) revenue when goods or services are sold to customers, even though cash may not be collected until sometime in the future.

ORGANIZATIONS THAT INFLUENCE ACCOUNTING PRACTICE

Many organizations directly or indirectly influence GAAP. The most important of these organizations are the American Institute of Certified Public Accountants, the Financial Accounting Standards Board, the Securities and Exchange Commission, and the Internal Revenue Service.

American Institute of Certified Public Accountants

The American Institute of Certified Public Accountants (AICPA) is a professional association whose membership is made up of CPAs in public practice, private business, education, and government. Over the years, the AICPA has had a very strong influence on the development of GAAP. From 1938 to 1958, the AICPA's Committee on Accounting Procedures issued a series of pronouncements dealing with the development of accounting standards, principles, and procedures. In 1959, the AICPA organized the Accounting Principles Board (APB) to replace the Committee on Accounting Procedures. From 1959 to 1973, the APB issued a number of opinions that had a strong influence on accounting practice.

Financial Accounting Standards Board

In 1973, the Financial Accounting Standards Board (FASB) was established to develop financial accounting standards for private business and not-for-profit organizations. The FASB is governed by a board of trustees that includes the president of the AICPA and other members who are elected by the AICPA.

Securities and Exchange Commission

The Securities and Exchange Commission (SEC) is an agency of the U.S. government that was established in 1934 to regulate the sale of stock to the public. Although the SEC was given the power to set and enforce accounting practices for companies whose securities are sold to the general public, it has generally relied on the accounting profession to perform these functions. In very few cases has the SEC exercised its legal authority by disagreeing with a position taken by the AICPA or the FASB.

Internal Revenue Service

The Internal Revenue Service (IRS) interprets and enforces the income tax laws and regulations that are passed by Congress. Through these functions, the IRS has a direct effect on accounting practice as it relates to taxes.

COMPUTERS AND ACCOUNTING

Creating both challenge and opportunity, the computer has dramatically influenced the way we process accounting data. The computer has taken over most of the pencil-pushing tasks associated with manual accounting systems, thus freeing accounting workers to do more important tasks.

Regardless of how automated accounting systems become, however, you need a firm foundation in basic accounting principles and procedures. Only by having such a foundation can you understand the accounting process and how information moves through various types of accounting systems. Study the early chapters of this text well; they will form the foundation upon which all your further accounting knowledge will rest.

PARADIGM

COLLEGE

ACCOUNTING

1

THE NATURE

OF

ACCOUNTING

LEARNING OBJECTIVES

After studying Chapter 1, you will be able to:
1. Define *accounting* and related terms.
2. Explain who uses accounting information.
3. Identify three forms of business organizations and three types of business operations.
4. Define and describe the elements of accounting.
5. State the accounting equation.
6. Define *business transaction*.
7. Record business transactions in equation form.
8. Identify four types of transactions that affect owner's equity.
9. Prepare three basic financial statements.

Each of us uses accounting daily in many ways. We rely on accounting information to make decisions about every facet of our personal finances.

For example, we need accounting knowledge to deal with a bank. Accounting helps us understand the summaries of transactions for both savings and checking accounts. We must provide personal financial information to apply for loans for homes, cars, and other goods. We must decide whether to purchase goods by credit or debit cards or for cash.

Understanding accounting information is vital for making investment decisions. Investors must decide what type of investments to make. They must constantly analyze the profitability of their investments to decide if and when to sell them.

— Fred R. Jex, CPA, MBA, Ph.D.
Macomb Community College

On a farm in central Maine, Drew Beedy is counting this year's crop of potatoes. At home in North Dakota, Janice Graham is trying to reach an agreement between her checkbook records and her bank statement for the month. In a clothing factory in southern California, Cathy Owens is trying to keep accurate records of uniforms that are being produced for the armed forces. In an office in Maryland, Ray Clermont is calculating the amount of his take-home pay for the week so he can decide how much to set aside for a new car. All of these individuals, along with millions of other Americans and American organizations, are practicing accounting.

ACCOUNTING DEFINED

LEARNING OBJECTIVE 1

Accounting is the process of recording, summarizing, analyzing, and interpreting financial (money-related) activities to permit individuals and organizations to make informed judgments and decisions. *Recording* means making written records of events. *Summarizing* is the process of combining these written records, at regular intervals, into reports. *Analyzing* means examining these reports by breaking them down in order to determine financial success or failure. *Interpreting* involves the use of financial data to make sound decisions and explain how well a company is meeting its objectives. Accounting combines these four activities—recording, summarizing, analyzing, and interpreting—into a single process and applies this process to financial activities.

USERS OF ACCOUNTING INFORMATION

LEARNING OBJECTIVE 2

A common impression is that accounting is a narrow, specialized field that serves only a part of our society. This impression is incorrect, for every individual and every organization in America needs accounting. Figure 1-1 shows some of the many users of accounting information.

Accounting has often been called the *language of business*. This title is appropriate because a language allows people to communicate to others. In financial terms, accounting is used to communicate information about a business to those who have a need or legal right to know. As Figure 1-1 shows, many individuals and groups use the accounting language in important, decisive ways.

FORMS OF BUSINESS ORGANIZATION

LEARNING OBJECTIVE 3

A private **business** organization operates with the objective of earning a profit. The three major forms of business organizations in this country are the sole proprietorship, the partnership, and the corporation.

FIGURE 1-1
Users of accounting information

Users	Use
Individuals	Individuals, such as Janice Graham and Ray Clermont, must understand accounting to function personally within our society, which is very dependent on financial activities. They—and you—keep checkbooks and other bank records, receive paychecks, pay taxes, use charge cards, borrow money, and purchase a variety of products and services.
Owners	Business owners, such as Drew Beedy and Cathy Owens, must understand accounting to achieve success in their organizations. Very often, the owners do not actually run the business. In such cases, the owners rely on accounting information to determine how well their businesses are being managed.
Managers	Managers use accounting data extensively in deciding on alternatives, such as what to sell, how to price, and when to expand the product line.
Investors	Investors use accounting data for insights on the financial condition of potential investments when deciding whether to invest in a business.
Banks and other lending institutions	Lenders, such as banks, use accounting data in deciding whether to approve a loan.
Governments	Governmental units (federal, state, and local) also record, summarize, analyze, and interpret financial events to operate with limited resources.
Taxing authorities	Tax authorities use accounting data reported to the government in deciding whether a business is complying with tax rules and regulations. Since our country has an extensive taxing system, this is a major use of accounting data.

A **sole proprietorship** is a business owned by one person. This person, called the *proprietor*, receives all profits or losses and is personally liable for the obligations of the business. Sole proprietorships represent the largest number of businesses in the United States; however, most of them are small businesses.

A **partnership** is a form of business that is co-owned by two or more persons. The partners enter into a contract, written or oral, that sets forth how the business will be run and how profits and losses will be divided.

A **corporation** is a form of business that is owned by investors called *stockholders*. Unlike a proprietorship or a partnership, a corporation is legally separate from its owners. This means that the corporation itself, and not the owners, is responsible for its obligations.

TYPES OF BUSINESS OPERATIONS

The most common types of business operations in this country are the service business, the merchandising business, and the manufacturing business.

LEARNING OBJECTIVE 3

A **service business** performs services for customers to earn a profit. Examples of service businesses include doctors, lawyers, engineers, barber shops, beauty salons, and dry cleaners.

A **merchandising business** purchases goods produced by others and then sells these goods to customers. Examples of merchandising businesses include department stores, supermarkets, antique dealers, and media stores.

A **manufacturing business** produces a product to sell to its customers. Examples of manufacturing businesses include automobile manufacturers, toy manufacturers, and bakeries. Figure 1-2 shows some well-known businesses listed according to the type of operation.

FIGURE 1-2
Examples of business operations

Service Businesses	Merchandising Businesses	Manufacturing Businesses
H & R Block	Sears	General Motors
AT&T	Macy's	IBM
Kelly Services	Burger King	Coca-Cola
Merrill Lynch	Montgomery Ward	Harley-Davidson
Walt Disney (theme parks)	Home Depot	Sony
Dun & Bradstreet	J.C. Penney	Ford Motor Co.
Hertz Car Rental	Wal-Mart	General Foods
Viacom (pay TV)	Toys-R-Us	Zenith
Waste Management	K-Mart	Apple Computers
United Parcel Service (UPS)	The Gap	Honda of America

THE ELEMENTS OF ACCOUNTING

LEARNING OBJECTIVE 4

In 1494, an Italian monk named Luca Pacioli published a mathematics text entitled *Summa Mathematica*. For the first time, a complete description was given of a way of keeping business records that had gradually developed over many centuries. The double-entry system described by Pacioli was to become the basis of our modern accounting system. The double-entry system is a simple system based on three elements: *assets*, *liabilities*, and *owner's equity*.

Assets

Assets are items with money value that are owned by a business. This definition contains two key phrases, the first of which is "with money value." An item must have a dollar value to be recorded in accounting records. Therefore, while good health is an asset to you, it is not an asset in accounting, because no definite dollar value can be placed on it.

The second key phrase is "owned by a business." An owner's personal car is not classified as a business asset, because the car is not used for business purposes.

A business has several types—or groupings—of assets, which normally include cash, accounts receivable, equipment, and supplies. The asset **Cash** includes currency (paper money), coins, checks, and money orders made payable to the business. To calculate the value of Cash, the amount of each item is totaled.

Businesses often sell goods or services on credit to customers. On credit means that goods and services are sold with the understanding that payment will be received at a later date. The asset arising from selling goods or services on credit to customers is called **Accounts Receivable**. Stated another way, Accounts Receivable is the dollar amount due from credit customers.

The asset **Equipment** includes the physical assets that a business needs in order to operate. Among these physical assets are office equipment (typewriters and computers), office furniture (desks and chairs), store equipment (cash registers and display cases), and delivery equipment (vans and trucks). Other physical assets include land, buildings, and machinery. These types of assets have several common features: (1) they are **tangible** (capable of being touched); (2) they are expected to be used in the operation of the business, not sold to customers; (3) they are expected to last for at least one year.

The asset **Supplies**, like Equipment, includes physical items needed to operate a business. Unlike Equipment, however, Supplies are usually used up within a year. Common examples of Supplies are office supplies (paper and printer toner), store supplies (string, bags, and wrapping paper), and delivery supplies (boxes, tape, and mailing labels).

Liabilities

Liabilities are debts owed by the business. In our economy it is not always possible, or convenient, to pay cash for everything that is obtained. Thus, it is very common for businesses— even very large and profitable businesses—to regularly purchase goods and services on credit. The liability that results from purchasing goods and services on credit is called **Accounts Payable**. The person or business to whom an account payable is owed is called a **creditor**. An account payable is usually an informal debt that is based on a spoken promise made to the creditor.

Another form of liability is the **Note Payable**, which is a formal written promise to pay a specified amount at a definite future date. A note payable is commonly issued when money is borrowed or when property is mortgaged. We will discuss other forms of liabilities in later chapters. Regardless of the form, however, a liability represents a creditor's claim against the assets of a business.

Owner's Equity

Assets are owned and liabilities are owed. The difference between the two is the part of the business that the owner can claim—the **owner's equity**. Owner's equity is the excess of assets over liabilities. For example, if a business has assets of $30,000 and liabilities of $10,000, the owner's equity is the difference between the two, $20,000. Owner's equity is also called *capital*, *proprietorship*, and *net worth*.

THE ACCOUNTING EQUATION

LEARNING OBJECTIVE 5

The relationship among the accounting elements can be expressed in a simple mathematical form known as the **accounting equation** or the *basic accounting equation*:

Assets = Liabilities + Owner's Equity

or, in symbolic form:

$A = L + OE$

For example, on December 31, 20X2, Jeanette Deese has business assets of $30,000, business liabilities of $10,000, and owner's equity of $20,000. Her accounting equation is:

Asset	=	Liabilities	+	Owner's Equity
$30,000	=	$10,000	+	$20,000

or

$30,000	=	$30,000

Note that the left side of the accounting equation (the asset side) balances with the right side of the equation (the liabilities and owner's equity side). Also note that in the accounting equation, liabilities are placed before owner's equity. This is done because the creditors' claim to assets (liabilities) takes legal priority over the owner's claim to assets (owner's equity).

If two elements of the accounting equation are known, the third can always be found. For example, if assets total $10,000 and liabilities total $6,000, what is the owner's equity? The accounting equation can be rewritten as follows:

Assets	−	Liabilities	=	Owner's Equity

then,

A	−	L	=	OE
$10,000	−	$6,000	=	$4,000

Find the missing element in each of the following:

	A	=	L	+	OE
(a)	$40,000		$25,000		$_____
(b)	$_____		$38,000		$52,000
(c)	$70,000		$_____		$48,000
(d)	$75,000		$ -0-		$_____

CHECK YOUR ANSWERS ON PAGE 34.

BUSINESS TRANSACTIONS AND THE ACCOUNTING EQUATION

LEARNING OBJECTIVE 6

The value of a firm's assets, liabilities, and owner's equity changes constantly as everyday business occurs. Any activity that changes the value of a firm's assets, liabilities, or owner's equity is called a **transaction**. Any event that does not cause such a change is not a transaction. For example, firing an employee does not change the value of any asset, liability, or owner's equity item, so it is not a transaction. Figure 1-3 shows some examples of business transactions.

The last business transaction in Figure 1-3 leads to an important accounting concept. For accounting purposes, the owner of a business and the business itself are considered to be two separate units. The **business entity concept**, one of the many concepts that guide how accounting is done, states that for accounting purposes, a business is a distinct economic entity or unit that is separate from its owner and from any other business. For example, in addition to personal items, Karl Watkins owns a dress shop, a restaurant, and a video arcade. Karl's personal items and each of his three businesses are separate accounting units.

FIGURE 1-3
Examples of business transactions

Example
Purchase of equipment on credit
Cash payment to a creditor
Receipt of cash for services rendered to a customer
Purchase of supplies for cash
Payment of rent for the month
Payment of utility bill
Owner investment of cash in the business

The Dual Effect of Business Transactions

As stated earlier, total assets must always equal liabilities plus owner's equity. In other words, the accounting equation—$A = L + OE$—must always balance. To maintain this balance, transactions are recorded as having a **dual effect** on the basic accounting elements. For example, assume that the O'Malley Company purchased equipment for $3,000 on credit. This transaction has two effects on the accounting elements: (1) since an asset was acquired, assets increase; and (2) since the asset was purchased on credit, liabilities also increase.

Assets	=	Liabilities	+	Owner's Equity
+$3,000		+$3,000		

Assets (on one side of the equation) increased by $3,000, while liabilities (on the other side of the equation) also increased by $3,000, thus maintaining the equation in balance. **Every business transaction has at least two effects on the accounting equation**.

Recording the Effect of Transactions on the Accounting Equation

As we just saw, the effect of business transactions can be stated in terms of changes in the basic elements of the accounting equation. To determine exactly how the equation is affected, each transaction must be *analyzed*, that is, broken down to determine how it affects the accounting elements. After analysis, the changes that result can be recorded. To illustrate, let's look at the transactions completed by Janet Ashley during July 20X3. Janet is an attorney who decided to open her own law practice. The following transactions took place during her first month of operation. Each transaction is analyzed and recorded in an *expanded accounting equation*.

TRANSACTION (A): JANET INVESTED $20,000 CASH TO START HER BUSINESS

LEARNING OBJECTIVE 7

An owner's investment is a contribution of assets to the business. Janet's investment of $20,000 increased the assets of her firm from $0 to $20,000. It also increased her equity in the firm by the same amount because the $20,000 came from Janet, not from a creditor. Thus, both assets and owner's equity increased by $20,000. After this transaction, Janet's accounting equation appears as follows.

	Assets	=	Liabilities	+	Owner's Equity
	Cash	=		+	J. Ashley, Capital
(a)	+ $20,000				+ $20,000

Note that the asset Cash is individually named. Also note that Janet's equity in the business is shown as J. Ashley, Capital. If Janet had invested another asset at the same time, such as equipment, each asset would have been increased, and J. Ashley, Capital would have been increased by the total amount of both assets.

TRANSACTION (B): PURCHASED EQUIPMENT FOR $30,000 ON CREDIT

This transaction caused an increase in an asset and a corresponding increase in a liability. Specifically, the asset Equipment and the liability Accounts Payable were increased by $30,000. The effect on the equation is as follows.

	Assets		=	Liabilities	+	Owner's Equity
	Cash	+ Equipment	=	Accounts Payable	+	J. Ashley, Capital
(a)	+$20,000					+$20,000
(b)		+ $30,000		+ $30,000		
Bal.	$20,000	+ $30,000	=	$30,000	+	$20,000
		$50,000			$50,000	

Note that we subtotaled the items after the second transaction. The subtotals (called *balances*) allow a quick check to see if the equation is still in balance.

TRANSACTION (C): PURCHASED SUPPLIES FOR CASH, $2,000

As a result of this transaction, the firm's supplies increased by $2,000, but the firm's cash decreased by the same $2,000. This is called a **shift in assets**; that is, the individual assets changed, but the total dollar value of assets remained the same. The effect on the equation is as follows.

	Assets			=	Liabilities	+	Owner's Equity
	Cash	+ Supplies	+ Equipment	=	Accounts Payable	+	J. Ashley, Capital
Bal.	$20,000		$30,000		$30,000		$20,000
(c)	− 2,000	+$2,000					
Bal.	$18,000+	$2,000	+ $30,000	=	$30,000	+	$20,000
		$50,000				$50,000	

As you study this recording, note that dollar signs are used only in two circumstances: (1) next to the first entry in a column, and (2) next to the balance. Also note that when a shift in assets occurs, only the asset side of the equation changes.

The assets purchased in Transactions (b) and (c) were recorded at cost, which leads to another fundamental concept of accounting—the **cost principle**. This principle states that, when purchased, all assets are recorded at their actual cost regardless of market value. The actual value of the equipment purchased in Transaction (b) may have been more or less than $30,000. This, however, is not considered when the transaction is recorded. The firm paid $30,000 for the equipment; thus, $30,000 is recorded.

TRANSACTION (D): PERFORMED LEGAL SERVICES FOR CLIENTS AND COLLECTED $900 CASH

Janet operates a service business, the practice of law. Her major activity is service to clients, for which she receives cash. In this transaction, Janet has earned **revenue**—income from carrying out the major activity of a firm—which increases the value of her business. Thus, both the asset Cash and J. Ashley, Capital increased by $900. The effect on the equation is as follows.

	Assets			=	Liabilities	+	Owner's Equity			
					Accounts					
	Cash	+ Supplies	+ Equipment	=	Payable	+	J. Ashley, Capital	+	Revenue	Description
Bal.	$18,000	$2,000	$30,000		$30,000		$20,000			
(d)	+ 900								+ $900	Legal fees
Bal.	$18,900	+ $2,000	+ $30,000	=	$30,000	+	$20,000	+	$900	
		$50,900					$50,900			

Notice that we set up a separate column for recording revenue under the Owner's Equity heading. We did this so that the amount of revenue could easily be determined at any time. Another way to record the revenue would have simply been to add it to the balance of J. Ashley, Capital. Regardless of how we record revenue, however, keep in mind that *revenue always increases owner's equity*.

Other terms may be used to describe certain kinds of revenue, such as *fees earned* for amounts charged by a physician, *fares earned* for amounts received by a taxi service, *sales* for the sale of merchandise by a merchandising business, and *rent income* for amounts received on property that is rented to others.

TRANSACTION (E): PAID SALARIES OF EMPLOYEES, $1,500

Expenses are the costs of operating a business. Unlike the cost of an asset, however, the cost of an expense does not provide a future benefit to the business. Therefore, expenses *decrease* the value of the business. In this transaction, salaries of $1,500 were paid. As shown below, the effect on the equation is a decrease in the asset Cash and a decrease in J. Ashley, Capital.

	Assets		=	Liabilities	+		Owner's Equity		
Cash	**+ Supplies**	**+ Equipment**	**=**	**Accounts Payable**	**+**	**J. Ashley, Capital**	**+ Revenue**	**− Expenses**	*Description*
Bal. $18,900	$2,000	$30,000		$30,000		$20,000	$900		
(e) − 1,500								+$1,500	Salaries ex.
Bal. $17,400 +	$2,000 +	$30,000	=	$30,000	+	$20,000	+ $900	− $1,500	
	$49,400					$49,400			

Notice that, as with revenue, we set up a separate column for recording expenses under the Owner's Equity heading. Notice also that the decrease in owner's equity caused by the expense is shown by increasing an expense entitled Salaries Expense. *An increase in an expense decreases owner's equity.* Another way to record the expense would have been to subtract it directly from the balance of J. Ashley, Capital.

Expenses decrease owner's equity. The decrease is recorded by increasing individual expenses. By increasing expenses, we are simply accumulating the total of expenses incurred during the month so that the total can be subtracted from owner's equity at the end of the month.

TRANSACTION (F): PAID $5,000 OF THE AMOUNT OWED ON EQUIPMENT

A liability is a debt that must be paid. When all or part of a debt is paid, less is owed to creditors. Therefore, Janet's $5,000 payment decreased her liabilities. Since the payment was made in cash, the asset Cash also decreased. The effect on the equation is shown below.

	Assets		=	Liabilities	+		Owner's Equity		
Cash	**+ Supplies**	**+ Equipment**	**=**	**Accounts Payable**	**+**	**J. Ashley, Capital**	**+ Revenue**	**− Expenses**	*Description*
Bal. $17,400	$2,000	$30,000		$30,000		$20,000	$900	$1,500	
(f) − 5,000				− 5,000					
Bal. $12,400 +	$2,000 +	$30,000	=	$25,000	+	$20,000	+ $900	− $1,500	
	$44,400					$44,400			

TRANSACTION (G): JANET WITHDREW $700 CASH FROM THE BUSINESS FOR HER PERSONAL USE

Unlike employees, the owner of a business does not receive a salary. Consequently, it is common for the owner to withdraw cash or other assets for personal use. An owner's **withdrawal**—the removal of business assets for personal use—has the dual effect of decreasing both the asset taken and the value of the business. In this case, Janet withdrew cash. The effect on the equation is a decrease in the asset Cash and a decrease in J. Ashley, Capital.

	Assets			=	Liabilities	+	Owner's Equity			
	Cash	+ Supplies	+ Equipment	=	Accounts Payable	+	J. Ashley, Capital	+ Revenue	− Expenses	Description
Bal.	$12,400	$2,000	$30,000		$25,000		$20,000	$900	$1,500	
(g)	− 700						− 700			Withdrawal
Bal.	$11,700 +	$2,000 +	$30,000	=	$25,000	+	$19,300	+ $900	− $1,500	
		$43,700					$43,700			

Notice that, unlike revenue and expenses, we did not provide a separate column for recording owner withdrawals. As a rule, withdrawals don't occur as frequently as revenue and expenses. As a result, we recorded Janet's withdrawal by subtracting it directly from the balance of owner's equity. Remember that *withdrawals always decrease owner's equity*.

TRANSACTION (H): PERFORMED ADDITIONAL SERVICES FOR CLIENTS, RECEIVING $2,600 CASH

As stated in the analysis of Transaction (d), cash received for services performed increases Cash and owner's equity. The effect on the equation is as follows.

	Assets			=	Liabilities	+	Owner's Equity			
	Cash	+ Supplies	+ Equipment	=	Accounts Payable	+	J. Ashley, Capital	+ Revenue	− Expenses	Description
Bal.	$11,700	$2,000	$30,000		$25,000		$19,300	$900	$1,500	
(h)	+ 2,600							+2,600		Legal fees
Bal.	$14,300 +	$2,000 +	$30,000	=	$25,000	+	$19,300	+ $3,500	− $1,500	
		$46,300					$46,300			

TRANSACTION (I): PAID TWO ADDITIONAL EXPENSES: UTILITIES, $250, AND OFFICE RENT, $600

As stated in the analysis of Transaction (e), expenses decrease owner's equity. And since cash was paid, assets also decrease. Janet's equation now appears as follows.

	Assets			=	Liabilities	+	Owner's Equity			
	Cash	+ Supplies	+ Equipment	=	Accounts Payable	+	J. Ashley, Capital	+ Revenue	− Expenses	Description
Bal.	$14,300	$2,000	$30,000		$25,000		$19,300	$3,500	$1,500	
	− 850								+250	Utilities ex.
(i)									+600	Rent ex.
Bal.	$13,450 +	$2,000 +	$30,000	=	$25,000	+	$19,300	+ $3,500	− $2,350	
		$45,450					$45,450			

Revenue always increases owner's equity. Expenses always decrease owner's equity. Owner withdrawals always decrease owner's equity.

TRANSACTION (J): PERFORMED LEGAL SERVICES FOR A CLIENT ON CREDIT, $500

In this transaction, Janet performed legal services and expects to receive payment in the future. As we discussed earlier, selling goods or services on credit increases the asset Accounts Receivable, which is the measure of cash to be received from credit customers. Selling goods or services on credit also increases owner's equity because revenue is earned. According to the **realization principle**, revenue is recorded when it is earned, even though cash may not be received until later. After recording this transaction, Janet's equation appears as follows.

	Assets			=	Liabilities	+	Owner's Equity			
		Accounts				Accounts					
Cash +	Rec. +	Supplies +	Equipment =		Payable	+	J. Ashley, Capital +	Revenue –	Expenses	Description
Bal. $13,450		$2,000	$30,000		$25,000		$19,300	$3,500	$2,350	
(j)	+$500							+500		Legal fees
Bal. $13,450 +	$500 +	$2,000 +	$30,000 =		$25,000	+	$19,300	+ $4,000	–$2,350	
	⌊———— $45,950 ————⌋					⌊———————— $45,950 ————————⌋				

TRANSACTION (K): RECEIVED $300 CASH AS PARTIAL PAYMENT FOR SERVICES PERFORMED ON ACCOUNT

In this transaction, Janet received cash for services that she had performed on account earlier, in Transaction (j). The effect on her equation is an increase in the asset Cash and a decrease in another asset, Accounts Receivable.

	Assets			=	Liabilities	+	Owner's Equity			
		Accounts				Accounts					
Cash +	Rec. +	Supplies +	Equipment =		Payable	+	J. Ashley, Capital +	Revenue –	Expenses	Description
Bal. $13,450	$500	$2,000	$30,000		$25,000		$19,300	$4,000	$2,350	
(k) + 300	– 300									
Bal. $13,750 +	$200 +	$2,000 +	$30,000 =		$25,000	+	$19,300	+ $4,000 –	$2,350	
	⌊———— $45,950 ————⌋					⌊———————— $45,950 ————————⌋				

When recording the collection of an account receivable, you always increase the asset Cash, and you always decrease the asset Accounts Receivable. No revenue is recorded, because the revenue was recorded when it was earned. *Do not record the same revenue twice.*

After all transactions have been recorded, Janet's equation is still in balance. The total assets ($45,950) equal the total liabilities plus owner's equity ($45,950). With accurate recording, the accounting equation will always balance.

Janet's transactions are those of a service business. However, certain conclusions can be drawn that apply to all forms of business:

- The effect of every business transaction can be stated in terms of increases or decreases (or both) in the basic elements of the accounting equation.
- The effect of recording a business transaction must always leave the two sides of the accounting equation in balance.

Summary of Transactions

The business transactions of Janet Ashley, Attorney, are summarized in tabular form in Figure 1-4.

	Assets				=	Liabilities	+	Owner's Equity			
	Cash	+ Accounts Rec.	+ Supplies	+ Equipment	=	Accounts Payable	+	J. Ashley, Capital	+ Revenue	− Expenses	*Description*
(a)	+$20,000							+$20,000			Investment
(b)				+$30,000		+$30,000					
Bal.	$20,000			$30,000		$30,000		$20,000			
(c)	−2,000		+$2,000								
Bal.	$18,000		$2,000	$30,000		$30,000		$20,000			
(d)	+900								+ $900		Legal fees
Bal.	$18,900		$2,000	$30,000		$30,000		$20,000	$900		
(e)	−1,500									−$1,500	Salaries ex.
Bal.	$17,400		$2,000	$30,000		$30,000		$20,000	$900	$1,500	
(f)	−5,000					− 5,000					
Bal.	$12,400		$2,000	$30,000		$25,000		$20,000	$900	$1,500	
(g)	−700							− 700			Withdrawal
Bal.	$11,700		$2,000	$30,000		$25,000		$19,300	$900	$1,500	
(h)	+2,600								+2,600		Legal fees
Bal.	$14,300		$2,000	$30,000		$25,000		$19,300	$3,500	$1,500	
(i)	−850									+250	Utilities ex.
										+600	Rent ex.
Bal.	$13,450		$2,000	$30,000		$25,000		$19,300	$3,500	$2,350	
(j)		+$500							+500		Legal fees
Bal.	$13,450	$500	$2,000	$30,000		$25,000		$19,300	$4,000	$2,350	
(k)	+300	− 300									
Bal.	$13,750	+ $200	+ $2,000	+ $30,000	=	$25,000	+	$19,300	+ $4,000	− $2,350	

└────────────── $45,950 ──────────────┘   └────────────── $45,950 ──────────────┘

FIGURE 1-4
Business transaction summary

Since Transaction (k) is the last one, each column total is double-ruled; this is a standard accounting practice.

LEARNING OBJECTIVE 8

It should be stressed that the accounting equation includes only business assets and liabilities. The owner's personal assets and liabilities are excluded (as part of the business entity concept we discussed earlier).

As you study the summary of Janet's transactions, note that owner's equity was only *increased* by owner investment and revenue [Transactions (a), (d), (h), and (j)]. Also note that owner's equity was only *decreased* by owner withdrawals and expenses [Transactions (e), (g), and (i)]. We can illustrate the effect of these four types of transactions on owner's equity as shown in Figure 1-5.

FIGURE 1-5
Transactions that affect owner's equity

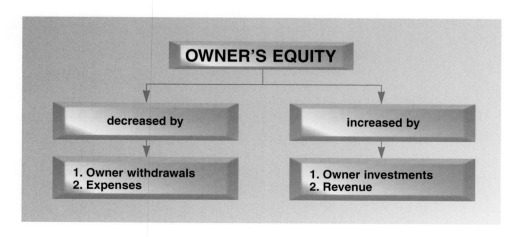

OWNER'S EQUITY

decreased by	increased by
1. Owner withdrawals 2. Expenses	1. Owner investments 2. Revenue

REVIEW QUIZ

1-2

Record the following transactions for Alex Baldwin in an expanded accounting equation with these headings: Cash + Accounts Receivable + Supplies = Accounts Payable + A. Baldwin, Capital + Revenue – Expenses. After recording the last transaction, prove that the equation is in balance.

(a) Alex invested $10,000 cash in the business.
(b) Invested supplies valued at $2,000 in the business.
(c) Paid rent for the month, $600.
(d) Performed services and received cash, $800.
(e) Purchased supplies on credit, $200.
(f) Performed services on credit, $625.
(g) Withdrew cash for personal use, $500.
(h) Received $250 cash as partial payment for services performed on account.

CHECK YOUR ANSWERS ON PAGE 34.

FINANCIAL STATEMENTS

LEARNING OBJECTIVE 9

We have concentrated on the recording function of accounting for most of Chapter 1. The chapter concludes with three summaries prepared by the accountant. Summaries of financial activities are called **financial statements**, which are prepared on a regular basis at the end of an accounting period.

An **accounting period** is typically one year; however, it can be any length of time for which accounting records are maintained. Usually, the minimum length of an accounting period is one month, and the maximum length is one year. Janet Ashley is using an accounting period of one month, as she is interested in what has happened by July 31, 20X3, the end of her first month of operation.

The three basic financial statements are the income statement, the statement of owner's equity, and the balance sheet:

- *Income statement.* A summary of a business's revenue and expenses for a specific period of time, such as a month or a year.
- *Statement of owner's equity.* A summary of the changes that have occurred in owner's equity during a specific period of time, such as a month or a year.
- *Balance sheet.* A listing of a firm's assets, liabilities, and owner's equity at a specific point in time, such as the last day of a month or the last day of a year.

Janet's financial statements for her first month of operation are shown in Figure 1-6. The statements were prepared directly from the information shown on the tabular summary of Janet's July transactions (Figure 1-4).

The Income Statement

As stated above, an **income statement** shows a summary of a business's revenue and expenses for a specific period of time. When revenue exceeds expenses, there is a **net income**. On the other hand, when expenses exceed revenue, there is a **net loss**. Janet's income statement shows a net income of $1,650, because her revenue for the period exceeded her expenses for the same period.

Observe these points about Janet's income statement:

Income Statement
Revenue
– Expenses
Net Income
(or Net Loss)

1. The heading consists of three lines answering the questions *who, what,* and *when. Who* is the name of the firm, not that of the owner (business entity concept). *What* is an income statement. *When* is for the accounting period just ended.

FIGURE 1-6
Financial statements

Income Statement

Janet Ashley, Attorney at Law Income Statement For Month Ended July 31, 20X3			
Revenue:			
Legal fees earned			$4 0 0 0 00
Expenses:			
Salaries expense	$1 5 0 0 00		
Rent expense	6 0 0 00		
Utilities expense	2 5 0 00		
Total expenses		2 3 5 0 00	
Net income		$1 6 5 0 00	

Statement of Owner's Equity

Janet Ashley, Attorney at Law Statement of Owner's Equity For Month Ended July 31, 20X3			
Janet Ashley, capital, July 1, 20X3			$20 0 0 0 00
Net income for the month	$1 6 5 0 00		
Less withdrawals	7 0 0 00		
Increase in capital		9 5 0 00	
Janet Ashley, capital, July 31, 20X3		$20 9 5 0 00	

Balance Sheet

Janet Ashley, Attorney At Law Balance Sheet July 31, 20X3			
Assets			
Cash	$13 7 5 0 00		
Accounts receivable	2 0 0 00		
Supplies	2 0 0 0 00		
Equipment	30 0 0 0 00		
Total assets		$45 9 5 0 00	
Liabilities			
Accounts payable		$25 0 0 0 00	
Owner's Equity			
Janet Ashley, capital		20 9 5 0 00	
Total liabilities and owner's equity		$45 9 5 0 00	

2. *Only* revenue and expenses are placed on the income statement. An owner investment is a contribution of assets to the firm, not revenue. An owner withdrawal is the removal of assets from the firm, not a business expense. Thus, both owner investments and owner withdrawals are stated in terms of changes in owner's equity, not in terms of revenue and expenses. That is why they *do not* appear on the income statement.
3. Net income is the difference between total revenue and total expenses. Janet's revenue is $4,000, and her expenses are $2,350. The difference between the two ($4,000 – $2,350 = $1,650) is the net income for the period. Had expenses exceeded revenue, the words net loss would have been substituted for net income.
4. Expenses are listed in order of size, beginning with the largest; this is a common arrangement.

Other terms used to describe the income statement are *earnings statement*, *operating statement*, and *statement of operations*. Another term less frequently used is *profit and loss statement*, or *P & L statement*.

The Statement of Owner's Equity

Statement of Owner's Equity
Shows the changes that have taken place in owner's equity.

The **statement of owner's equity** is a summary of the changes that have taken place in owner's equity during the accounting period. As you have already learned, four types of transactions affect owner's equity: (1) revenue and (2) owner investments, which increase it; and (3) expenses and (4) withdrawals, which decrease it. All of these items are reflected in a statement of owner's equity, except that two of them (revenue and expenses) are combined into the net income or net loss figure.

Observe these points about Janet's statement of owner's equity:

1. The three-line heading is similar to that of the income statement in that both the income statement and the statement of owner's equity cover a specific period of time.
2. Since this was Janet's first month of operation, her beginning capital balance was her initial investment of $20,000. Next month, she will begin with a balance of $20,950.
3. The net income figure is obtained from the income statement. Therefore, the income statement should be prepared first.
4. The net increase in capital is the difference between Janet's net income for the period and her withdrawals for the period. Had Janet shown a net loss for the period, or if her withdrawals had exceeded her net income, there would have been a net decrease in capital, which would have been *subtracted* from the opening capital balance.

The statement of owner's equity is also called the *capital statement*.

The Balance Sheet

Balance Sheet
Lists assets, liabilities, and owner's equity.

As stated earlier, the **balance sheet** shows a firm's assets, liabilities, and owner's equity at a specific point in time, the end of the accounting period. It is an expanded statement of the accounting equation showing that A = L + OE.

Note these points about Janet's balance sheet, shown in Figure 1-6:

1. It has a three-line heading that differs significantly on the *when* line. While an income statement and a statement of owner's equity describe what happened over a period of time, a balance sheet tells "what is" on a given date. The first two statements have been described as motion pictures. The balance sheet has been described as a snapshot.
2. The figure for J. Ashley, Capital ($20,950) was taken from the statement of owner's equity. Thus, the statement of owner's equity is prepared before the balance sheet.

3. The final, double-ruled totals show balance or equality. A balance sheet shows that A = L + OE.
4. If there had been additional liabilities, the format for the liabilities section would have been the same as that for the assets section.
5. This form of balance sheet, with the liabilities and owner's equity sections presented directly below the assets section, is called the *report form*. Another common arrangement lists the assets on the left and the liabilities and owner's equity on the right. This arrangement is called the *account form of balance sheet* because of its similarity to the account. (The account is a basic accounting record we will study in Chapter 2.) Let's look at Janet's balance sheet in account form. (See Figure 1-7.)

Other terms used to describe the balance sheet are *statement of financial position* and *position statement*.

FIGURE 1-7
Account form of the balance sheet

Janet Ashley, Attorney at Law Balance Sheet July 31, 20X3				
Assets		Liabilities		
Cash	$13 7 5 0 00	Accounts payable	$25 0 0 0 00	
Accounts receivable	2 0 0 00			
Supplies	2 0 0 0 00	Owner's Equity		
Equipment	30 0 0 0 00	Janet Ashley, capital	20 9 5 0 00	
		Total liabilities		
Total assets	$45 9 5 0 00	and owner's equity	$45 9 5 0 00	

REVIEW QUIZ 1-3

John Dee started Dee's Delivery Service on August 1, 20X1. His August transactions are recorded in equation form below. Using these data, prepare: (1) an income statement, (2) a statement of owner's equity, and (3) a balance sheet in report form.

	Assets			=	Liabilities	+	Owner's Equity				
	Cash	+ Supplies	+ Equipment =		Accounts Payable	+	J. Dee,Capital	+ Revenue	− Expenses	Description
(a)	+ $10,000						+$10,000			Investment
(b)	− 1,000	+$1,000								
Bal.	$9,000	$1,000					$10,000			
(c)			+$18,000		+$18,000					
Bal.	$9,000	$1,000	$18,000		$18,000		$10,000			
(d)	− 500								+$500	Rent expense
Bal.	$8,500	$1,000	$18,000		$18,000		$10,000		$500	
(e)	−300								+300	Utilities ex.
Bal.	$8,200	$1,000	$18,000		$18,000		$10,000		$800	
(f)	+1,200							+$1,200		Delivery rev.
Bal.	$9,400	$1,000	$18,000		$18,000		$10,000	$1,200	$800	
(g)	− 200								+200	Salaries ex.
Bal.	$9,200	+ $1,000	+ $18,000	=	$18,000	+	$10,000	+ $1,200	− $1,000	

CHECK YOUR ANSWERS ON PAGE 35.

As you reach the end of your first chapter in accounting, you should now be able to identify the accounting elements, record business transactions in equation form, and prepare the basic financial statements. In other words, you are forming the foundation for the study of accounting. You will use this accounting foundation throughout this course and in all other accounting courses and practices.

INTERNET ASSETS

WHERE CAN I FIND NATIONAL ACCOUNTING ASSOCIATION SITES ON THE INTERNET?

The following sites will help you to do research, get newsletters, and find answers to your accounting questions:

http://weatherhead.cwru.edu/Accounting
The site of the Academy of Accounting Historians. The academy encourages research, publication, teaching, and personal interchanges in all phases of accounting history.

http://www.rutgers.edu/Accounting/raw/aaa
The site of the American Accounting Association. The association is a voluntary organization of persons interested in accounting education and research. Members receive a newsletter (*Accounting Education News*) and at least one of the association's journals: *The Accounting Review*, *Accounting Horizons*, or *Issues in Accounting Education*.

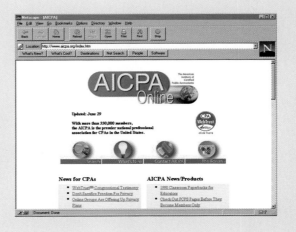

http://www.aicpa.org/index.htm
The site of the American Institute of Certified Public Accountants (AICPA). The AICPA has more than 330,000 members and is one of the premier national professional associations for CPAs in the United States. At this site you can use a search engine and look up accounting topics as well as keep up with the latest news and laws in accounting.

JOINING THE PIECES

THE EXPANDED ACCOUNTING EQUATION

Assets =	**Liabilities** +	**Owner's Equity** +	**Revenue** –	**Expenses**
Anything of value that is OWNED by the business in order to operate.	Debts OWED by the business.	The difference between assets and liabilities.	Inflow of assets (cash and accounts receivable) from operating during the accounting period.	Costs necessary to operate the business.
Examples: Cash Accounts Receivables Supplies Equipment Buildings Land	**Examples:** Accounts Payable Notes Payable Taxes Payable	**Also called:** Capital Net Worth Proprietorship	**Examples:** Service Revenue Accounting Fees Fares Earned Rent Income Medical Fees Earned	**Examples:** Rent Expense Salaries Expense Repairs Expense Utilities Expense

Owner's Withdrawals

The removal of assets from the business for the personal use of the owner.

Dual effect of withdrawal:

1. Decrease in the asset taken
2. Decrease in owner's equity

Income Statement
Summarizes revenue and expenses to determine the amount of net income (or net loss) to be carried to the statement of owner's equity.

Leeds Company
Income Statement
For Year Ended December 31, 20XX

Revenue:		
Service revenue		$10 0 0 0 00
Expenses:		
Salaries expense	$3 0 0 0 00	
Rent expense	2 0 0 0 00	
Utilities expense	1 0 0 0 00	
Total expenses		6 0 0 0 00
Net income		$ 4 0 0 0 00

Statement of Owner's Equity
Summarizes the changes that have taken place in owner's equity and provides an updated capital figure to be carried to the balance sheet.

Leeds Company
Statement of Owner's Equity
For Year Ended December 31, 20XX

Beginning capital		$ 9 0 0 0 00
Net income for period	$4 0 0 0 00	
Less withdrawals	2 0 0 0 00	
Increase in capital		2 0 0 0 00
Ending capital		$11 0 0 0 00

Balance Sheet
A listing of assets, liabilities, and owner's equity as of a certain date.

Leeds Company
Balance Sheet
December 31, 20XX

Assets		
Cash	$3 0 0 0 00	
Accounts receivable	2 0 0 0 00	
Supplies	1 0 0 0 00	
Equipment	6 0 0 0 00	
Total assets		$12 0 0 0 00
Liabilities		
Accounts payable		$ 1 0 0 0 00
Owner's Equity		
Owner, capital		11 0 0 0 00
Total liabilities and owner's equity		$12 0 0 0 00

SUMMARY/RESTATEMENT OF LEARNING OBJECTIVES

1. Define accounting and related terms.

Accounting is the process of recording, summarizing, analyzing, and interpreting financial (money-related) activities to permit individuals and organizations to make informed judgments and decisions. Recording means making written records of transactions and events that have a financial effect on the business. Summarizing is the process of combining these written records, at regular intervals, into reports that owners and managers can use in the decision-making process. Analyzing means examining these reports by breaking them down in order to determine financial success or failure. Interpreting involves the use of financial data to make sound decisions and determine if a company is meeting its plans and objectives.

2. Explain who uses accounting information.

All members of our society use accounting information. Individuals use accounting information to function in a society that is dependent on financial activities. For example, we use accounting information when we analyze our paychecks to determine if the correct amount of taxes has been withheld, when we take out loans, when we buy goods and services, and when we use charge cards.

Owners of businesses use accounting information to help control expenses, monitor revenue, and protect assets. Managers use accounting information to make better business decisions. Investors use accounting information to help them decide if an investment in a particular company would be profitable. Lenders use accounting information to decide if a company has sufficient financial strength to qualify for a loan. Government agencies and taxing authorities use accounting information to operate and to determine how well private businesses are complying with tax rules and regulations.

3. Identify three forms of business organizations and three types of business operations.

The three most popular forms of business in this country are the **sole proprietorship**, the **partnership**, and the **corporation**. A sole proprietorship is a business owned by one person only. A partnership is a business that is co-owned by two or more persons. A corporation is a form of business owned by stockholders.

The three most common types of business operations are the **service business**, the **merchandising business**, and the **manufacturing business**. A service business sells a service to its customers—such as tax assistance provided by H & R Block. A merchandising business buys goods produced by others, and then sells these goods to customers. Examples of merchandising businesses include Sears, Montgomery Ward, and Macy's. A manufacturing business actually produces the goods it sells—such as Ford Motor Company, Coca-Cola, and IBM.

4. Define and describe the elements of accounting.

Assets are items with money value that are owned by a business. This element includes Cash, Accounts Receivable, Equipment, and Supplies. Assets are the money and material with which a business has to work.

Liabilities are debts owed to **creditors**. Creditors are individuals or organizations from which a purchase on credit has been made or a loan of money has been obtained. The most common type of liability is Accounts Payable.

Owner's equity is the dollar value of the claim of the owner to the assets of a business. It is the interest of the owner in the business.

5. State the accounting equation.

The **accounting equation** is:

Assets = Liabilities + Owner's Equity

or, expressed in symbols,

A = L + OE

6. Define business transaction.

A **business transaction** is any activity that changes the value of a firm's assets, liabilities, or owner's equity.

7. Record business transactions in equation form.

Several different business transactions follow, recorded in equation form. For simplicity, we have chosen to put the balances only at the end of June, 20XX.

(a) Walter Collins invested $25,000 in an architectural firm.
(b) Purchased supplies for cash, $750.
(c) Purchased equipment for $2,700, paying $500 cash and owing the balance.
(d) Paid rent for the month, $700.
(e) Performed design services for cash, $1,700.
(f) Paid $1,000 of the amount owed for equipment.
(g) Performed design services on account, $400.
(h) Paid salaries for the month, $600.
(i) Withdrew $300 cash for personal use.
(j) Received $250 as partial payment from services performed on account in Transaction (g).

	Cash	+	Accounts Rec.	+ Supplies	+ Equipment	=	Accounts Payable	+ W.Collins, Capital	+ Revenue	– Expenses	Description
(a)	+$25,000							+$25,000			Investment
(b)	–750			+$750							
(c)	–500				+$2,700		+ $2,200				
(d)	–700									+$700	Rent expense
(e)	+1,700								+$1,700		Design fees
(f)	–1,000						–1,000				
(g)			+$400						+400		Design fees
(h)	–600									+600	Salaries ex.
(i)	–300							– 300			Withdrawal
(j)	+250		–250								
Bal.	$23,100	+	$150	+ $750	+ $2,700	=	$1,200	+ $24,700	+ $2,100	– $1,300	

Assets = Liabilities + Owner's Equity

$26,700 = $26,700

8. Identify four types of transactions that affect owner's equity.

Owner's equity is affected by four types of transactions: (1) owner investments and (2) revenue, which increase it; and (3) expenses and (4) owner withdrawals, which decrease it.

9. Prepare three basic financial statements.

The **income statement**, the **statement of owner's equity**, and the **balance sheet** in Figure 1-8 are prepared from the information used in Objective 7.

FIGURE 1-8
Three basic financial statements

Walter Collins, Architect
Income Statement
For Month Ended June 30, 20XX

Revenue:			
Design fees earned			$2 1 0 0 00
Expenses:			
Rent expense	$7 0 0 00		
Salaries expense	6 0 0 00		
Total expenses		1 3 0 0 00	
Net income		$ 8 0 0 00	

Walter Collins, Architect
Statement of Owner's Equity
For Month Ended June 30, 20XX

Walter Collins, capital, June 1, 20XX			$25 0 0 0 00
Net income for the month	$8 0 0 00		
Less withdrawals	3 0 0 00		
Increase in capital		5 0 0 00	
Walter Collins, capital, June 30, 20XX		$25 5 0 0 00	

Walter Collins, Architect
Balance Sheet
June 30, 20XX

Assets			
Cash	$23 1 0 0 00		
Accounts receivable	1 5 0 00		
Supplies	7 5 0 00		
Equipment	2 7 0 0 00		
Total assets		$26 7 0 0 00	
Liabilities			
Accounts payable		$ 1 2 0 0 00	
Owner's Equity			
Walter Collins, capital		25 5 0 0 00	
Total liabilities and owner's equity		$26 7 0 0 00	

KEY TERMS

accounting The process of recording, summarizing, analyzing, and interpreting financial (money-related) activities to permit individuals and organizations to make informed judgments and decisions.

accounting equation The equation that expresses the relationship between the accounting elements in a simple mathematical form: Assets = Liabilities + Owner's Equity.

accounting period A period that is typically one year; however, it can be any length of time for which accounting records are maintained, often for a month.

accounts payable The liability that results from purchasing goods or services on credit.

accounts receivable The asset arising from selling goods or services on credit to customers.

assets Items with money value that are owned by a business.

balance sheet A listing of a firm's assets, liabilities, and owner's equity at a specific point in time. Other terms used to describe the balance sheet are statement of financial position and position statement.

business An organization that operates with the objective of earning a profit.

business entity concept The principle that states that, for accounting purposes, a business is a distinct economic entity or unit that is separate from its owner and from any other business.

cash The asset Cash includes currency (paper money), coins, checks, and money orders made payable to the business.

corporation A form of business organization that is owned by stockholders.

cost principle The principle that states that, when purchased, all assets are recorded at their actual cost regardless of market value.

creditor A business or person to whom a debt is owed.

dual effect The principle that states that all business transactions are recorded as having *at least* two effects on the basic accounting elements.

equipment The physical assets needed by a business in order to operate.

expenses The costs of operating a business. Unlike the cost of an asset, the cost of an expense does not provide a future benefit to the business. Therefore, its effect is a reduction in owner's equity.

financial statements Summaries of financial activities.

income statement A summary of a business's revenue and expenses for a specific period of time, such as a month or a year. Other terms used to describe the income statement are earnings statement, operating statement, statement of operations, and profit and loss statement.

liabilities Debts owed by the business.

manufacturing business A business that produces a product to sell to its customers.

merchandising business A business that purchases goods produced by others and then sells them to customers to earn a profit.

net income Occurs when revenue earned during an accounting period exceeds the expenses of the same period.

net loss Occurs when expenses exceed revenue during an accounting period.

note payable A formal written promise to pay a specified amount at a definite future date.

owner's equity The excess of assets over liabilities (also called capital, proprietorship, and net worth).

partnership A business co-owned by two or more persons.

realization principle The principle that states that revenue should be recorded when it is earned, even though cash may not be collected until later.

revenue Income earned from carrying out the activities of a firm.

service business A business that performs services for customers to earn a profit.

shift in assets Occurs when one asset is exchanged for another asset, such as when supplies are purchased for cash.

sole proprietorship A business owned by one person.

statement of owner's equity A summary of the changes that have occurred in owner's equity during a specific period of time, such as a month or a year. Another term used to describe the statement of owner's equity is capital statement.

supplies Short-term physical assets needed to operate a business.

tangible All physical assets used by a business are tangible (capable of being touched).

transaction Any activity that changes the value of a firm's assets, liabilities, or owner's equity.

withdrawal The removal of business assets for the owner's personal use.

CONCEPTS AND SKILLS REVIEW

CONCEPTS REVIEW

1. Phil Watson records and summarizes financial data. Is he doing accounting? Explain your answer.
2. Identify some of the users of accounting information.
3. Classify the following businesses as service, merchandising, or manufacturing: (a) car dealer; (b) supermarket; (c) dental office; (d) computer factory; (e) e-mail network provider.
4. Identify and explain each of the basic accounting elements.
5. Why is good health not an asset in accounting?
6. What is the major difference between the assets Equipment and Supplies?
7. Why is firing an employee not considered to be a transaction?
8. Bill Taylor has two businesses. Does the business entity concept state that Bill should combine both businesses into a single entity for accounting purposes? Explain your answer.
9. Which of the following are business transactions? (a) paid salaries, (b) hired an employee, (c) received cash for services performed, (d) the owner paid her home electric bill from her personal checking account.
10. Explain the dual effect in accounting.
11. What four types of transactions affect owner's equity?
12. How does buying an asset for cash differ from paying an expense?
13. Sue Lyon performed legal services for a client today, but agreed to let the client pay her in four equal installments, starting in 30 days. Has Sue earned revenue today or will she earn it when the installments are received? Explain your answer.
14. Why is the balance sheet called a snapshot, while the income statement and the statement of owner's equity are called motion pictures?
15. How does the account form of the balance sheet differ from the report form?

SKILLS REVIEW

(Forms are provided in the *Study Guide and Working Papers* book.)

EXERCISE 1-1

LEARNING OBJECTIVE 5

Objective: To calculate the value of the missing element in the accounting equation

Directions: In each of these examples, find the missing value:

	A	L	OE
(a)	$85,800	$33,900	$_____
(b)	$92,655	$_____	$47,395
(c)	$_____	$66,000	$33,500
(d)	$45,952	$_____	$29,044
(e)	$_____	$44,558	$27,934
(f)	$_____	$44,300	($16,300)

EXERCISE 1-2

LEARNING OBJECTIVE 6

Objective: To indicate the effect of business transactions on the accounting elements

Directions: Using check marks, indicate the effects on the accounting elements for each of the business transactions presented.

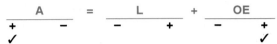

	A	=	L	+	OE
	+ −		− +		− +
Example: Owner invested cash	✓				✓
(a) Purchased equipment on credit					
(b) Bought supplies for cash					
(c) Paid liability for equipment					
(d) Performed services for cash					
(e) Paid operating expenses					
(f) Performed services on credit					
(g) Owner withdrew cash					
(h) Collected on services from (f)					

EXERCISE 1-3

LEARNING OBJECTIVE 7

Objective: To record business transactions in equation form

Directions: Use the transactions from Exercise 1-2 and record them by using plus and minus signs in the expanded equation: Cash + Accounts Receivable + Supplies + Equipment = Accounts Payable + J. Walker, Capital + Revenue − Expenses.

EXERCISE 1-4

LEARNING OBJECTIVE 9

Objective: To prepare an income statement

Directions: From the following data, prepare an income statement in good form for the Twin City Barber Shop for the year ended December 31, 20XX. Use only those items that are needed.

Item	Amount
Salaries Expense	$ 22,800
Rent Expense	18,000
Supplies	3,500
Utilities Expense	9,600
Revenue from Services	138,250
Cash	19,400
Repairs Expense	900
Miscellaneous Expense	700

EXERCISE 1-5

LEARNING OBJECTIVE 9

Objective: To prepare a statement of owner's equity

Directions: Stan Lawson is a financial planner. Prepare his statement of owner's equity for the year ended December 31, 20XX, if he began the year with a capital balance of $42,600, earned a net income of $36,400 during the year, and withdrew $2,000 per month.

Objective: To identify balance sheet items

Directions: From the following list of items from the records of Ace Plumbing Company, identify those items that would appear on the balance sheet:

1. Revenue from Services
2. Cash
3. Land
4. Equipment
5. Miscellaneous Expense
6. Accounts Payable
7. Repairs Expense
8. Notes Payable
9. Supplies
10. Bill Rese, Capital
11. Rent Expense
12. Accounts Receivable

EXERCISE 1-7

Objective: To prepare a balance sheet in report form

Directions: From the following information, prepare a balance sheet in report form for Tidy Maid, a professional maid and janitorial service. The date is December 31, 20XX, and the owner is Phillipe Cassereau.

Item	Amount
Accounts Payable	$17,800
Accounts Receivable	14,000
Cash	13,600
P. Cassereau, Capital, January 1, 20XX	34,200
P. Cassereau, Capital, December 31, 20XX	?
Withdrawals	12,800
Equipment	42,000
Supplies	13,700
Net income for the year	44,100

EXERCISE 1-8

Objective: To prepare a corrected balance sheet

Directions: The following balance sheet was prepared by an inexperienced bookkeeper. Several errors were made. Find and list the errors.

Speedy Repair Shop Balance Sheet For Year Ended December 31, 20XX	
Assets	
Cash	$17 3 0 0 00
Supplies	7 5 0 00
Equipment	21 7 0 0 00
Total assets	$38 7 5 0 00
Liabilities	
Accounts payable	$ 8 4 6 0 00
Owner's Equity	
Speedy Repair Shop, capital	$29 2 9 0 00
Total liabilities and owner's equity	38 7 5 0 00

CASE PROBLEMS

GROUP A

(Forms are provided in the *Study Guide and Working Papers* book.)

LEARNING OBJECTIVE 7

PROBLEM 1-1A

Objective: To record business transactions in an expanded accounting equation

Cynthia Evans opened a tutoring service on January 2, 20XX. During January, the following transactions occurred:

(a)   Cynthia invested $7,000 cash in the firm.
(b)   Purchased office supplies on credit, $1,950.
(c)   Purchased office equipment on credit, $7,000.
(d)   Invested a personal computer, valued at $2,500, into the firm.
(e)   Paid rent, $500.
(f)   Received cash for tutoring fees, $700.
(g)   Paid salary of receptionist, $400.
(h)   Paid $1,000 of the liability for office equipment.
(i)   Received cash for tutoring fees, $1,200.
(j)   Paid utility bill, $390.
(k)   Withdrew $900 cash for personal use.

Directions: Record each of these transactions in an expanded accounting equation with these headings:

Assets	=	Liabilities	+	Owner's Equity		
Cash + Office Supplies + Office Equipment	=	Accounts Payable	+	Cynthia Evans, Capital	+ Revenue	– Expenses

Calculate balances after recording each transaction.

PROBLEM 1-2A

LEARNING OBJECTIVE 7

Objective: To record business transactions in an expanded accounting equation

James Lawrence opened a shoe repair business on April 1, 20XX. During April, he completed the following transactions:

(a)   James invested $9,000 cash in the firm.
(b)   Purchased supplies on credit, $1,450.
(c)   Purchased equipment on credit, $4,800.
(d)   Paid rent for the month of April, $700.
(e)   Received cash for services performed, $425.
(f)   Performed shoe repair services on credit, $650.
(g)   Paid half of the liability for supplies.
(h)   Paid $1,500 on the liability for equipment.
(i)   Received cash for services performed, $390.
(j)   Withdrew $500 cash for personal use.
(k)   Paid utilities expense for April, $350.
(l)   Collected $200 of the revenue earned in Transaction (f).

Directions: Record these transactions in an expanded accounting equation with these headings:

Assets				=	Liabilities	+	Owner's Equity		
Cash +	Accounts Receivable +	Supplies +	Equipment =		Accounts Payable	+	James Lawrence, Capital	+ Revenue –	Expenses

Calculate balances after recording each transaction.

PROBLEM 1-3A

Objective: To record business transactions in an expanded accounting equation

Dee Ann Dill opened a printer and computer repair shop this month. During the month, she completed the following transactions:

(a) Dee Ann invested $7,000 cash and $11,000 worth of equipment in the firm.
(b) Paid cash for office supplies, $425.
(c) Purchased wrapping paper, string, and cash register tape for cash, $395.
(d) Purchased equipment for $1,900, paying $500 down and owing the balance.
(e) Paid rent for the month, $675.
(f) Performed repair services for cash, $450.
(g) Performed repair services on credit, $775.
(h) Returned $40 of defective supplies purchased in Transaction (c), receiving a cash refund.
(i) Received $200 cash for the services performed in Transaction (g).
(j) Paid utilities expense for the month, $380.
(k) Paid half of the amount due on Transaction (d).

Directions: Record Dee Ann's transactions for the month in an expanded accounting equation with these headings:

Assets					=	Liabilities	+	Owner's Equity		
Cash +	Accounts Receivable +	Office Supplies +	Store Supplies +	Equipment =		Accounts Payable	+	Dee Ann Dill, Capital	+ Revenue –	Expenses

Calculate balances after each transaction.

PROBLEM 1-4A

Objective: To prepare three financial statements

The data presented below are for Drug-a-Bug, an insect exterminator, on April 30, 20XX.

Item	Amount
Accounts Payable	$6,310
Accounts Receivable	1,000
Cash	1,700
Bob Dion, Capital, April 1	4,850
Miscellaneous Expense	150
Office Equipment	4,200
Office Supplies	375
Rent Expense	510
Revenue from Services	2,150
Salaries Expense	780
Store Equipment	3,500
Store Supplies	445
Utilities Expense	350
Withdrawals	300

Directions:
1. Prepare an income statement for the month ended April 30, 20XX.
2. Prepare a statement of owner's equity for the month ended April 30, 20XX.
3. Prepare a balance sheet in report form as of April 30, 20XX.

PROBLEM 1-5A

LEARNING OBJECTIVE 7, 8, 9

Objective: To record business transactions and prepare financial statements

Gary Parker, CPA, started his practice on September 1, 20X1. He completed the following transactions during his first month of operations:

(a) Gary invested the following in the firm: cash, $11,400; office supplies, $700; office equipment, $4,500.
(b) Paid rent for the month, $550.
(c) Purchased a word processor for $3,700 on credit.
(d) Purchased a copier for $8,000, paying $500 down and agreeing to pay the balance in three equal installments.
(e) Performed services for cash, $925.
(f) Wrote business checks for Gary's personal bills, $500.
(g) Purchased a printer for cash, $600.
(h) Purchased computer ribbons for cash, $110.
(i) Performed services on credit, $1,200.
(j) Paid utilities for the month, $315.
(k) Paid cash for a new desk for Gary's office, $850.
(l) Collected $750 of the services performed in Transaction (i).
(m) Paid for the word processor purchased in Transaction (c).
(n) Paid salary of part-time employee, $600.
(o) Paid first installment due on the copier purchased in Transaction (d).

Directions:
1. Record Gary's September transactions in an expanded accounting equation with these headings. Use the Description column to provide a brief explanation of each transaction involving owner's equity, such as rent expense, fees earned or withdrawal [calculate balances only after Transaction (o)]:

Assets				=	Liabilities	+	Owner's Equity				
Cash +	Accounts Receivable +	Office Supplies +	Office Equipment	=	Accounts Payable	+	Gary Parker, Capital +	Revenue –	Expenses	Description

2. Prepare an income statement for September.
3. Prepare a statement of owner's equity for September.
4. Prepare a September 30 balance sheet in account form.

GROUP B

(Forms are provided in the *Study Guide and Working Papers* book.)

PROBLEM 1-1B

LEARNING OBJECTIVE 7

Objective: To record business transactions in an expanded accounting equation

Herman Gallegos opened a software design service on January 8, 20XX. During January, the following transactions occurred:

(a) Herman invested $13,000 cash in the business to get it started.
(b) Purchased office supplies on credit, $755.
(c) Purchased office equipment on credit, $3,500.
(d) Invested office equipment, valued at $11,000, in the firm.
(e) Paid rent, $600.

(f) Received cash for services performed, $800.
(g) Paid salary of assistant, $600.
(h) Paid half of the liability for the equipment purchased in Transaction (c).
(i) Received cash for services performed, $500.
(j) Paid telephone bill, $200.
(k) Withdrew $1,000 cash for personal use.

Directions: Record each of these transactions in an expanded accounting equation with these headings:

Assets			=	Liabilities	+	Owner's Equity		
Cash + Office Supplies + Office Equipment			=	Accounts Payable	+	Herman Gallegos, Capital	+ Revenue	− Expenses

Calculate balances after recording each transaction.

PROBLEM 1-2B

LEARNING OBJECTIVE 7

Objective: To record business transactions in an expanded accounting equation

Kevin Slusher opened a shoe repair business on May 1, 20XX. During May, he completed the following transactions:

(a) Kevin invested $7,500 cash in the firm.
(b) Purchased supplies on credit, $1,150.
(c) Purchased equipment on credit, $4,400.
(d) Paid rent for the month of May, $900.
(e) Received cash for services performed, $525.
(f) Performed shoe repair services on credit, $750.
(g) Paid half of the liability for supplies.
(h) Paid $1,600 on the liability for equipment.
(i) Received cash for services performed, $490.
(j) Withdrew cash for personal use, $700.
(k) Paid utilities expense for May, $450.
(l) Collected $300 of the revenue earned in Transaction (f).

Directions: Record these transactions in an expanded accounting equation with these headings:

Assets				=	Liabilities	+	Owner's Equity		
Cash +	Accounts Receivable +	Supplies +	Equipment	=	Accounts Payable	+	Kevin Slusher, Capital	+ Revenue	− Expenses

Calculate balances after recording each transaction.

PROBLEM 1-3B

LEARNING OBJECTIVE 7

Objective: To record business transactions in an expanded accounting equation

Dee Ann Dill opened a printer and computer repair shop this month. During the month, she completed the following transactions:

(a) Dee Ann invested $8,000 cash and $12,000 worth of equipment in the firm.
(b) Paid cash for office supplies, $525.
(c) Purchased wrapping paper, string, and cash register tape for cash, $355.
(d) Purchased equipment for $2,900, paying $700 down and owing the balance.
(e) Paid rent for the month, $775.
(f) Performed repair services for cash, $550.

(g) Performed repair services on credit, $875.
(h) Returned $50 of defective supplies purchased in Transaction (c), receiving a cash refund.
(i) Received $300 cash for the services performed in Transaction (g).
(j) Paid utilities expense for the month, $340.
(k) Paid half of the amount due on Transaction (d).

Directions: Record Dee Ann's transactions for the month in an expanded accounting equation with these headings:

Assets					=	Liabilities	+	Owner's Equity		
Cash +	Accounts Receivable +	Office Supplies +	Store Supplies +	Equipment	=	Accounts Payable	+	Dee Ann Dill, Capital +	Revenue −	Expenses

Calculate balances after each transaction.

PROBLEM 1-4B

LEARNING OBJECTIVE 9

Objective: To prepare three financial statements

The data presented below are for Raise the Roof, a roof repair firm, on May 31, 20XX.

Item	Amount
Accounts Payable	$6,810
Accounts Receivable	1,100
Cash	1,850
Russ Clark, Capital, May 1	4,690
Miscellaneous Expense	190
Office Equipment	4,200
Office Supplies	375
Rent Expense	710
Revenue from Services	3,350
Salaries Expense	880
Store Equipment	3,850
Store Supplies	445
Utilities Expense	450
Withdrawals	800

Directions:
1. Prepare an income statement for the month ended May 31, 20XX.
2. Prepare a statement of owner's equity for the month ended May 31, 20XX.
3. Prepare a balance sheet in report form as of May 31, 20XX.

PROBLEM 1-5B

LEARNING OBJECTIVE 7, 8, 9

Objective: To record business transactions and prepare financial statements

Marilyn Skinner is an attorney who started her own practice on October 1, 20X1. During October, she completed the following transactions:

(a) Marilyn invested the following in the firm: cash, $8,800; office supplies, $600; office equipment, $5,200.
(b) Paid rent for the month, $650.
(c) Purchased a word processor for $2,400 on credit.
(d) Purchased a copier for $10,000, paying $1,000 down and agreeing to pay the balance in three equal installments.
(e) Performed services for cash, $1,250.
(f) Wrote business checks for personal bills, $600.
(g) Purchased a printer for cash, $595.

(h) Purchased computer ribbons for cash, $90.
(i) Performed services on credit, $1,800.
(j) Paid utilities for the month, $295.
(k) Paid cash for a new office desk, $900.
(l) Collected $750 of the services performed in Transaction (i).
(m) Paid for the word processor purchased in Transaction (c).
(n) Paid salary of part-time employee, $600.
(o) Paid first installment due on the copier purchased in Transaction (d).

Directions:
1. Record Marilyn's October transactions in an expanded accounting equation with these headings. Use the Description column to provide a brief explanation of each transaction involving owner's equity, such as rent expense, fees earned, or withdrawal. [Calculate balances only after Transaction (o).]

	Assets			=	Liabilities	+		Owner's Equity			
	Accounts	Office			Accounts		Marilyn Skinner,				
Cash +	Receivable +	Supplies +	Office Equipment	=	Payable	+	Capital +	Revenue –	Expenses		Description

2. Prepare an income statement for October.
3. Prepare a statement of owner's equity for October.
4. Prepare an October 31 balance sheet in account form.

CHALLENGE PROBLEMS

PROBLEM SOLVING

Andi McWhorter is the owner of McWhorter's Bookkeeping and Tax Service, a sole proprietorship that has operated successfully for several years. On January 1, 20X1, the firm had balances as follows:

Item	Balance
Cash	$ 6,600
Accounts Receivable	2,100
Office Supplies	880
Office Furniture	6,500
Office Equipment	11,600
Accounts Payable	2,800
Notes Payable	7,000
Andi McWhorter, Capital	17,880

The following transactions occurred during January and February, 20X1:

January transactions:
(a) Paid rent for the month, $550.
(b) Purchased office supplies on credit, $700.
(c) Paid for repairs to copier, $275.
(d) Purchased an electronic typewriter for cash, $575.
(e) Paid Simmons Company, a creditor, $600 on an account payable.
(f) Received cash from various clients for services performed, $1,725.
(g) Performed services on account for a client, $325.
(h) Purchased two boxes of computer ribbons for cash, $75.
(i) Paid for the office supplies purchased in Transaction (b).
(j) Received cash on account from credit clients, $1,300.
(k) Paid utility bill for the month, $490.
(l) Paid salaries of employees, $2,580.

(m) Received cash from various clients for services performed, $1,840.
(n) Purchased office supplies for cash, $228.
(o) Returned a defective paper cutter purchased in Transaction (n), receiving a cash refund, $40.
(p) Performed services on account for a client, $150.
(q) Withdrew cash for personal use, $1,600.
(r) Received cash from various clients for services performed, $800.
(s) Paid the telephone bill, $165.
(t) Paid $1,100 on a note payable, which was issued when equipment was purchased on credit months earlier.
(u) Received cash from various clients for services performed, $1,000.

February transactions:
(a) Paid rent for the month, $550.
(b) Paid $700 for advertising on a local radio station.
(c) Paid $225 to have advertising leaflets printed.
(d) Received cash from various clients for services performed, $1,760.
(e) Received cash on account from credit clients, $600.
(f) Purchased a desk for use in the reception area, $525.
(g) Withdrew cash for personal use, $1,600.
(h) Paid a personal dental bill using the firm's bank account, $200.
(i) Purchased three filing cabinets for cash, $470.
(j) Received cash from various clients for services performed, $1,980.
(k) Paid $1,100 on a note payable for equipment purchased earlier.
(l) Paid utility bill, $472.
(m) Paid telephone bill, $171.
(n) Paid salaries of employees, $2,500.
(o) Received cash from various clients for services performed, $1,350.
(p) Performed services on account for a customer, $400.
(q) Withdrew cash for personal use, $300.
(r) Purchased land for $6,000 as a future building site, paying $1,000 down and giving a note payable due in two years for the difference.
(s) Received cash on account from credit clients, $330.

Directions:
1. List the following headings at the top of a sheet of paper turned sideways: Cash + Accounts Receivable + Office Supplies + Office Furniture + Office Equipment + Land = Accounts Payable + Notes Payable + Andi McWhorter, Capital + Revenue − Expenses. Place the heading Description next to Expenses.
2. Enter the beginning balance of each item (given above) on the first line under the captions you listed in Direction l.
3. Record the firm's January transactions. Use the Description column to provide a brief explanation of each transaction involving owner's equity, such as rent expsene, fees earned, or withdrawal. Calculate balances only after the last transaction for the month.
4. Prepare financial statements at the end of January.
5. Record the firm's February transactions. Enter balances only after the last transaction.
6. Prepare financial statements at the end of February.

COMMUNICATIONS

As you learned in this chapter, a major reason companies keep good accounting records is to comply with tax rules and regulations. This, however, is only one reason to keep accurate and complete accounting records. Before 1913, there was no Internal Revenue Service. (Congress was given the power to tax our income in 1913 with the Sixteenth Amendment to the Constitution.) Yet, companies have always maintained accounting records.

Write a paragraph offering at least two different reasons why a firm should keep accounting records even if no taxing authority requires these records.

ETHICS

William Collins owns two different businesses—a roof repair firm and a painting company. During the current year, the roofing business made a net income of $75,000 while the painting company lost $50,000. In order to show himself in a less profitable way, William combined the two businesses under a single name—Roof 'n Paint Company. He then reported to all interested parties a $25,000 net income for the year.

Indicate which accounting principle William is violating. Explain why his method of reporting violates this principle.

ANSWERS TO REVIEW QUIZZES

REVIEW QUIZ 1-1

(a) $15,000
(b) $90,000
(c) $22,000
(d) $75,000

REVIEW QUIZ 1-2

		Assets			=	Liabilities	+		Owner's Equity			
	Cash	+	Accounts Rec.	+ Supplies	=	Accounts Payable	+	A. Baldwin, Capital	+ Revenue	− Expenses	Description
(a)	+$10,000							+$10,000			Investment
(b)				+$2,000				+2,000			Investment
Bal.	$10,000			$2,000				$12,000			
(c)	−600									+$600	Rent expense
Bal.	$ 9,400			$2,000				$12,000		$600	
(d)	+800								+ $800		Revenue
Bal.	$10,200			$2,000				$12,000	$800	$600	
(e)				+200		+$200					
Bal.	$10,200			$2,200		$200		$12,000	$800	$600	
(f)			+$625						+625		Revenue
Bal.	$10,200		$625	$2,200		$200		$12,000	$1,425	$600	
(g)	−500							−500			Withdrawal
Bal.	$ 9,700		$625	$2,200		$200		$11,500	$1,425	$600	
(h)	+250		−250								
Bal.	$ 9,950 +		$375 +	$2,200	=	$200	+	$11,500 +	$1,425 −	$600	

$12,525

$12,525

1.

Dee's Delivery Service Income Statement For Month Ended August 31, 20X1			
Revenue:			
Delivery revenue			$1 2 0 0 00
Expenses:			
Rent expense	$ 5 0 0 00		
Utilities expense	3 0 0 00		
Salaries expense	2 0 0 00		
Total expenses			1 0 0 0 00
Net income			$ 2 0 0 00

2.

Dee's Delivery Service Statement of Owner's Equity For Month Ended August 31, 20X1		
John Dee, capital, August 1, 20X1		$10 0 0 0 00
Net income for the month	$ 2 0 0 00	
Less withdrawals	—	
Increase in capital		2 0 0 00
John Dee, capital, August 31, 20X1		$10 2 0 0 00

3.

Dee's Delivery Service Balance Sheet August 31, 20X1		
Assets		
Cash	$ 9 2 0 0 00	
Supplies	1 0 0 0 00	
Equipment	18 0 0 0 00	
Total assets		$28 2 0 0 00
Liabilities		
Accounts payable		$18 0 0 0 00
Owner's Equity		
John Dee, capital		10 2 0 0 00
Total liabilities and owner's equity		$28 2 0 0 00

2

RECORDING

BUSINESS

TRANSACTIONS

LEARNING OBJECTIVES

After studying Chapter 2, you will be able to:
1. Explain the double-entry accounting framework.
2. Describe the standard form of account.
3. Describe the T account.
4. Explain the rules of debit and credit as applied to asset, liability, and owner's equity accounts.
5. Explain the need for temporary owner's equity accounts.
6. Explain the rules of debit and credit as applied to temporary owner's equity accounts.
7. Record business transactions in T accounts and prepare a trial balance.

Chapter 2 introduces you to a manual system of recording transactions using debits and credits. Today, however, many accounting systems are computerized.

Understanding how to record business transactions into a manual accounting system helps you understand how to enter data into a computerized accounting system. Both systems use the same information as the basis of the transactions, the effects of the transaction on the accounting elements are the same, and the purpose of storing financial information for future use does not change.

In Chapter 1, accounting was defined as the process of recording, summarizing, analyzing, and interpreting financial activities. While the computer can save much time in the summarizing process, accounting employees must enter the transactions into the computer before the computer can summarize the data to generate financial statements and reports

— Fred R. Jex, CPA, MBA, Ph.D.
Macomb Community College

LEARNING OBJECTIVE 1

I n Chapter 1, you learned that the elements of accounting are assets, liabilities, and owner's equity. You also learned that every business transaction has at least two effects on the accounting elements. For example, the purchase of equipment for cash causes: (1) an increase in the asset *Equipment*, and (2) a decrease in the asset *Cash*. This dual effect provides the basis for what is commonly called double-entry accounting. **Double-entry accounting** means that each business transaction has at least two effects, both of which are recorded in the accounting records. *It does not mean that business transactions are recorded twice.*

You learned in Chapter 1 that business transactions can be recorded in terms of their effect on the basic elements of the accounting equation. To review, a $500 purchase of supplies on account can be recorded as follows.

Assets	=	Liabilities	+	Owner's Equity
Supplies	**=**	**Accounts Payable**		
+$500		+$500		

Recording transactions in terms of their effect on the accounting equation is easy to understand, and it clearly shows the dual effect. The volume of daily transactions, however, makes this form of recording impractical for an actual accounting system because all transactions are recorded on a single sheet. To prepare reports and statements, accountants must have day-to-day information available for *each* accounting element. Therefore, separate records are needed to show increases and decreases in each asset, each liability, and each aspect of owner's equity. Such a record is called an *account*, which we will discuss next.

THE ACCOUNT

LEARNING OBJECTIVE 2

An **account** is an individual record or form used to record and summarize information related to each asset, each liability, and each aspect of owner's equity. An account can be thought of as a storage bin. As business transactions occur, financial information is recorded and stored in various asset, liability, and owner's equity accounts. In this way, financial information is easily and quickly available for preparing financial statements and reports.

The exact form of an account varies, depending on its use. Some accounts may be bound in book form, others may be in loose-leaf binders, and others may be part of a computer system. Figure 2-1 shows the **standard form of account**, which has three major parts:

❶ The account title and number.
❷ The left side, which is called the **debit** side.
❸ The right side, which is called the **credit** side.

FIGURE 2-1
The standard form of account

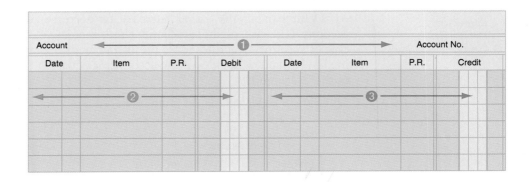

Each account is given an appropriate title to identify it as asset, liability, or owner's equity. Accounts are also assigned numbers to aid in locating and recording. The account title and account number are written on the first horizontal line of the form.

The *Date* column of an account is used to record the date on which a transaction occurs. The *Item* column is used to record a brief description of the entry, if needed. The *P.R.* (Posting Reference) column is discussed in Chapter 3. The **debit** and **credit** columns are money columns used to record the dollar amounts of transactions. Soon we will look at how to record transactions using debits and credits.

Accounts are often grouped together in book form; such a grouping of accounts is called a **ledger**. Thus, accounts are frequently referred to as *ledger accounts*.

The T Account

LEARNING OBJECTIVE 3

The **T account**, so named because it looks like a capital letter T, is a skeleton version of the standard form of account. The T account provides the same basic data as the standard form of account: (1) the account title, (2) the debit side, and (3) the credit side. Because they can be drawn quickly and easily, T accounts are useful for learning purposes. The T account is illustrated below:

Title of Account	
Debit Side	Credit Side

DEBITS AND CREDITS

The left side of *any* account is the debit side. **To debit** an account means to enter an amount on the left, or debit, side. The right side of *any* account is the credit side. **To credit** an account means to enter an amount on the right, or credit, side. To save time, the abbreviation **Dr.** is commonly used for debit; and the abbreviation **Cr.** is commonly used for credit. These abbreviations come from the Latin terms **d**ebe**re** and **c**rede**re**.

The word charge is sometimes used as a synonym for debit. Thus, *to charge* an account means the same as *to debit* an account.

Rules of Debit and Credit

LEARNING OBJECTIVE 4

Let us stress that to debit an account means to enter an amount on the left side of the account, and to credit an account means to enter an amount on the right side of the account. *Do not* think of the terms debit and credit as meaning increase or decrease; **only think of them as meaning left and right**.

Debit can signify *either* increase or decrease, depending on the type of account. Likewise, credit can signify *either* increase or decrease, depending on the type of account. The rules for debiting and crediting are best understood by relating the left and right sides of the accounting equation to the debit and credit sides of the T account:

Left Side of Equation		Right Side of Equation
Assets	=	Liabilities + Owner's Equity

Title of Account	
Left, or Debit Side	Right, or Credit Side

Assets are on the left side of the equation; debit is on the left side of the account. Therefore, asset accounts are increased on the debit side. Liabilities and owner's equity are on the right side of the equation; credit is on the right side of the account. Therefore, liability accounts and the owner's capital account (the name given to the main account for owner's equity) are increased on the credit side.

An account has only two sides; thus, the decrease side is always opposite the increase side. Because asset accounts are increased on the debit side, they are decreased on the credit side. On the other hand, liability and owner's equity accounts are decreased on the debit side, because they are increased on the credit side.

The rules of debit and credit can be shown as follows:

Assets		=	Liabilities		+	Owner's Equity	
Asset Accounts			**Liability Accounts**			**Owner's Capital Account**	
Debit	Credit		Debit	Credit		Debit	Credit
+	−		−	+		−	+

The rules of debit and credit are based on logic and tradition. Since assets are on the left side of the equation and debit is on the left side of the account, it is logical to increase assets on the debit side. The same logic is applied to increasing liability and owner's equity accounts on the credit (right) side, since liabilities and owner's equity are on the right side of the equation. It is possible that the rules of debit and credit could be reversed had the accounting equation developed in reverse order.

REVIEW QUIZ
2-1

Do the terms *debit* and *credit* mean increase or decrease, or may they mean either? Explain.

CHECK YOUR ANSWER ON PAGE 65.

RECORDING TRANSACTIONS IN ASSET, LIABILITY, AND OWNER'S EQUITY ACCOUNTS

For several years, William Taylor worked for a large talent and booking agency. In November 20X1, he decided to go into business for himself. The name of his new business is Taylor and Associates. The following transactions took place and were recorded during his first month of operations. In order to make a proper entry for each transaction, a careful analysis is made to determine:

- The titles of the accounts affected by the transaction.
- Whether the accounts affected were increased or decreased.
- How to increase or decrease (debit or credit) the accounts affected.

For illustration purposes, the following recorded transactions are identified by letters instead of the date on which they occurred.

TRANSACTION (A): MR. TAYLOR INVESTED $10,000 CASH INTO HIS BUSINESS TO GET IT STARTED

Analysis: Cash was received by the business. Therefore, the Cash account must be increased. Cash—an asset account—is increased on the debit side.

Owner investments increase the equity of the business. Therefore, the owner's capital account must be increased. The owner's capital account is increased on the credit side.

Entry:

Cash			William Taylor, Capital	
+	−		−	+
(a) 10,000				(a) 10,000

TRANSACTION (B): PURCHASED OFFICE EQUIPMENT FOR $3,000 ON ACCOUNT

Analysis: The business acquired an asset, office equipment. Therefore, an asset account entitled Office Equipment must be increased. Asset accounts are increased on the debit side.

The business incurred a liability as a result of purchasing office equipment on account. Therefore, a liability account called Accounts Payable is increased. Liability accounts are increased on the credit side.

Entry:

Office Equipment			Accounts Payable	
+	−		−	+
(b) 3,000				(b) 3,000

TRANSACTION (C): PURCHASED OFFICE SUPPLIES FOR CASH, $125

Analysis: The business acquired an asset—office supplies. Therefore, the Office Supplies account must be increased. Office Supplies—an asset account—is increased on the debit side.

Cash was paid. Therefore, the Cash account must be decreased. Cash—an asset account—is decreased on the credit side.

Entry:

Office Supplies			Cash	
+	−		+	−
(c) 125			(a) 10,000	(c) 125

TRANSACTION (D): PAID $500 ON EQUIPMENT PURCHASED IN TRANSACTION (B)

Analysis: Cash was paid. Therefore, the Cash account must be decreased. Cash—an asset account—is decreased on the credit side.

Part of an account payable was paid. Therefore, the Accounts Payable account must be decreased by the amount of the payment. Accounts Payable—a liability account—is decreased on the debit side.

Entry:

	Cash			Accounts Payable	
+		**–**		**–**	**+**
(a) 10,000		(c) 125		**(d) 500**	(b) 3,000
		(d) 500			

Note that in each of the preceding ledger entries, *the debit part of the entry equals the credit part of the entry*. This is an accounting rule that must always hold true. In the double-entry system, a debit recorded in one account must be accompanied by an equal credit recorded in another account. Making equal debits and credits maintains the accounting equation in balance and provides a means of verifying the mathematical accuracy of recorded transactions.

It is the dollar amounts of the debits and credits that must be equal; the actual count of debit transactions and credit transactions does not matter.

On plain paper, draw T accounts and record the following transactions:

(a) Ted Bonner invested $8,000 in a new business to be called Bonner Electronics.
(b) Purchased equipment on account, $1,200.
(c) Purchased office supplies for cash, $500.
(d) Purchased shop supplies on account, $300.
(e) Paid $600 on equipment purchased in Transaction (b).

CHECK YOUR ANSWERS ON PAGE 65.

TEMPORARY OWNER'S EQUITY ACCOUNTS

In Chapter 1, you learned that there are two ways to increase owner's equity: (1) investments of cash or other assets into the business by the owner, and (2) revenue from various sources. You also learned that there are two ways to decrease owner's equity: (1) withdrawals of cash or other assets by the owner, and (2) expenses of operating the business.

It is possible to record all changes in owner's equity directly in the owner's capital account. Expenses and withdrawals reduce owner's equity. Thus, these items would be recorded on the debit side (the decrease side) of the owner's capital account. Investments and revenue increase owner's equity. Thus, these items would be recorded on the credit side (the increase side) of the owner's capital account. The owner's capital account would then appear as follows:

Owner's Capital Account	
Debit	Credit
–	+
Expenses	Owner Investments
Owner Withdrawals	Revenue

The procedure just described is not practical, however. In most businesses, expense and revenue transactions occur constantly, and the owner frequently withdraws assets for personal use. Recording these transactions in the owner's capital account clutters the account and does not yield a separate record for expense items, revenue items, and owner withdrawals. To determine the net income or net loss for an accounting period, the owner's capital account would have to be analyzed very carefully to determine the amount of revenue and expenses.

It is generally considered a better accounting practice to have a separate ledger account for each type of expense, each type of revenue, and withdrawals. These accounts are subdivisions of the owner's capital account and are used to show changes that occur in owner's equity during an accounting period. When the period is over, these accounts will have served their purpose, and their balances will be transferred to the owner's capital account. Thus, expense accounts, revenue accounts, and the owner's drawing account are said to be **temporary owner's equity accounts**.

Rules of Debit and Credit as Applied to Revenue and Expense Accounts

Since revenue and expense accounts are subdivisions of owner's equity, the rules of debit and credit are applied to these accounts based on their relationship to owner's equity. Revenue increases owner's equity. Thus, the rules of debit and credit are the *same* for revenue accounts as they are for the owner's capital account. The owner's capital account is increased on the credit side; revenue accounts are likewise increased on the credit side. The owner's capital account is decreased on the debit side; revenue accounts are likewise decreased on the debit side.

Expenses are the opposite of revenue; they decrease owner's equity. Thus, the increase and decrease sides of expense accounts are *opposite* the increase and decrease sides of the owner's capital account. The owner's capital account is decreased on the debit side; expense accounts are increased on the debit side. The owner's capital account is increased on the credit side; expense accounts are decreased on the credit side.

The relationship of revenue and expense accounts to the owner's capital account can be illustrated as follows:

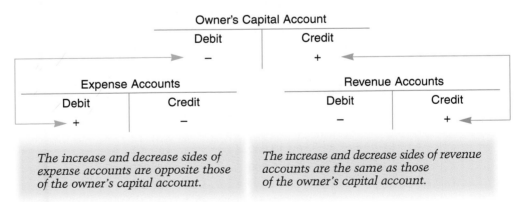

The increase and decrease sides of expense accounts are opposite those of the owner's capital account.

The increase and decrease sides of revenue accounts are the same as those of the owner's capital account.

Recording Transactions in Revenue and Expense Accounts

To illustrate recording expense and revenue transactions, let's continue looking at the first month's transactions of Taylor and Associates.

TRANSACTION (E): PAID FIRST MONTH'S RENT, $400

Analysis: Rent was paid for November. Therefore, an expense account entitled Rent Expense must be increased. Expense accounts are increased on the debit side. Cash was paid. Therefore, the Cash account must be decreased by the amount of the payment. Cash—an asset account—is decreased on the credit side.

Entry:

Rent Expense			Cash	
+	−		+	−
(e) 400			(a) 10,000	(c) 125
				(d) 500
				(e) 400

TRANSACTION (F): PAID FOR REPAIRS TO EQUIPMENT, $50

Analysis: Repairs were made to equipment. Therefore, the Repairs Expense account must be increased. Expense accounts are increased on the debit side. Cash was paid. Therefore, the Cash account must be decreased. Cash—an asset account—is decreased on the credit side.

Entry:

Repairs Expense			Cash	
+	−		+	−
(f) 50			(a) 10,000	(c) 125
				(d) 500
				(e) 400
				(f) 50

TRANSACTION (G): RECEIVED CASH FROM CUSTOMERS FOR SERVICES, $1,800

Analysis: Cash was received from customers. Therefore, the Cash account must be increased. Cash—an asset account—is increased on the debit side. Cash received from services yields revenue to the business. Therefore, a revenue account must be increased. Revenue accounts are increased on the credit side. We will use a revenue account entitled Service Revenue.

Entry:

Cash			Service Revenue	
+	−		−	+
(a) 10,000	(c) 125			(g) 1,800
(g) 1,800	(d) 500			
	(e) 400			
	(f) 50			

TRANSACTION (H): PERFORMED SERVICES ON ACCOUNT, $400

Analysis: Services were performed on credit for customers. Therefore, the Accounts Receivable account must be increased. Accounts Receivable—an asset account—is increased on the debit side. Services performed, whether for cash or on account, yield revenue to the business. Therefore, a revenue account must be increased. Revenue accounts are increased on the credit side.

Entry:

Let us pause for a minute to look at Figure 2-2 which shows a summary of the debit and credit rules we have learned so far.

FIGURE 2-2
Debit and credit rule summary

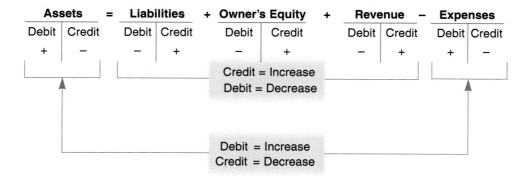

To help remember the rules of debit and credit, think of the position of the accounts within the accounting equation. Assets (to the far left of the equation) and expenses (to the far right of the equation) are handled the same: they are both increased with debits and decreased with credits. On the other hand, the three account classifications in the middle of the equation—liabilities, owner's equity, and revenue—are just the opposite: they are increased with credits and decreased with debits.

Owner's Drawing Account

Owners of businesses frequently withdraw cash or other assets from the business for their personal use. As stated earlier, it is possible to record withdrawals directly in the owner's capital account; however, it is usually considered better practice to have a separate **drawing account**. Since withdrawals decrease owner's equity, the drawing account is increased on the debit side (the decrease side of owner's equity). The relationship of the drawing account to the owner's capital account is as follows:

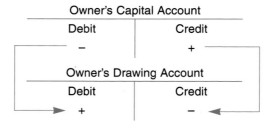

The increase and decrease sides of the owner's drawing account are opposite those of the owner's capital account.

RECORDING OWNER WITHDRAWALS

To illustrate the recording of an owner withdrawal, let's look at the next transaction completed by William Taylor during his first month of operations.

TRANSACTION (I): MR. TAYLOR WITHDREW $800 CASH FROM THE BUSINESS FOR PERSONAL USE

Analysis: Cash was withdrawn from the business. Therefore, the Cash account must be decreased by the amount of the withdrawal. Cash—an asset account—is decreased on the credit side.

Owner withdrawals result in an increase in the owner's drawing account, representing a decrease in owner's equity. The owner's drawing account is increased on the debit side.

Entry:

Cash				William Taylor, Drawing		
+		−		+		−
(a) 10,000		(c) 125		**(i) 800**		
(g) 1,800		(d) 500				
		(e) 400				
		(f) 50				
		(i) 800				

TRANSACTION (J): COLLECTED $100 CASH ON ACCOUNT FROM CREDIT CUSTOMERS IN TRANSACTION (H)

Analysis: Cash was received from credit customers. Therefore, the Cash account must be increased. Cash—an asset account—is increased on the debit side.

Collections on account from credit customers result in a decrease in the Accounts Receivable account. Accounts Receivable—an asset account—is decreased on the credit side.

Entry:

Cash				Accounts Receivable		
+		−		+		−
(a) 10,000		(c) 125		(h) 400		**(j) 100**
(g) 1,800		(d) 500				
(j) 100		(e) 400				
		(f) 50				
		(i) 800				

Now that we have analyzed and recorded all of Mr. Taylor's November transactions, let's review the steps involved in analyzing a transaction.

Before recording each transaction, you should decide:

1. Which accounts are affected by the transaction.
2. Whether there is an increase or decrease in the accounts.
3. How to increase or decrease (debit or credit) the accounts involved.

These steps are so important that you should firmly entrench them in your mind. A careful analysis of a transaction will yield a correct entry. Take Transaction (g), for example, in which Mr. Taylor received $1,800 in cash for services performed. The thought quickly comes to mind, "We have cash." And what is cash? It is an asset. How do you increase an asset account? Assets are increased on the debit side. Now we have the debit part of our entry, and you know that we must also have an equal credit. Cash received from services is revenue to the business. Thus, we need to increase a revenue account. How are revenue accounts increased? They are increased on the credit side. By following these steps, we obtain a debit to the Cash account for $1,800 and a credit to the Service Revenue account for $1,800.

After each entry, *check to make sure that the debit part of your entry equals the credit part*. When all the transactions have been recorded in the accounts, the total of all the debits should be equal to the total of all the credits.

Debits are used to record:	Credits are used to record:
1. increases in asset accounts	1. increases in liability accounts
2. increases in expense accounts	2. increases in the owner's capital account
3. increases in the owner's drawing account	3. increases in revenue accounts
4. decreases in liability accounts	4. decreases in asset accounts
5. decreases in the owner's capital account	5. decreases in expense accounts
6. decreases in revenue accounts	6. decreases in the owner's drawing account

REVIEW QUIZ 2-3

On plain paper, draw T accounts and record the following transactions made by Judy Lyle:

(a) Received cash for services performed, $5,000.
(b) Paid rent for the month, $600.
(c) Paid utility bill, $540.
(d) Paid salaries of employees, $1,800.
(e) Paid for repairs to equipment, $200.
(f) Owner withdrew cash for personal use, $500.

CHECK YOUR ANSWER ON PAGE 65.

THE TRIAL BALANCE

LEARNING OBJECTIVE 7

As we have stressed, total debits must always equal total credits in a double-entry accounting system. To test the equality of debits and credits in the ledger, a trial balance is prepared periodically. A **trial balance** is a listing, as of a certain date, of all ledger accounts with their balances. A trial balance is typically prepared at the end of each month. However, a trial balance can be prepared any time it is felt that the equality of debits and credits should be checked.

The first step in preparing a trial balance is to find the balance of each ledger account. The **balance** of any account is the difference between the total debits and the total credits in that account. Balances are arrived at by **footing** (adding) the debit and credit columns of each account and calculating the difference between the two columns. As an example, the balance of the Cash account of Taylor and Associates is found as follows:

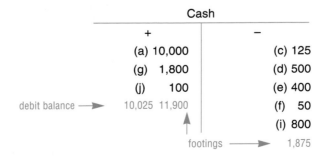

The debit column footing is $11,900. The credit column footing is $1,875. The balance of the account, $10,025, is determined by subtracting the lesser footing from the greater footing. The balance is written on the same line as the greater footing. When the debit footing is greater, as in this case, the account has a **debit balance**; so the balance is written on the debit side. On the other hand, when the credit footing is greater, the account has a **credit balance**; and the balance is written on the credit side.

Manual accounting records are done in ink. However, footings are customarily done in pencil (in case of an arithmetic error). Therefore, footings are also called *pencil footings*.

The ledger accounts of Taylor and Associates are reproduced in Figure 2-2. To show their relationship to the accounting equation, accounts are listed under the headings ASSETS = LIABILITIES + OWNER'S EQUITY. Note that when an account has both debit and credit amounts—as does the Cash account—it is necessary to foot and balance the account. When an account has only one debit amount and one credit amount—as does the Accounts Payable account—it is not necessary to foot the sides because there is only one amount on each side. In this situation, it is only necessary to balance the account. When an account has entries only on one side—as does the Service Revenue account—it is only necessary to foot the account. And when an account has only one entry—as do William Taylor, Drawing; Rent Expense; and Repairs Expense—it is not necessary to calculate a balance since there is only one amount (which is the balance).

FIGURE 2-2
Ledger accounts of Taylor and Associates

| ASSETS | = | LIABILITIES | + | OWNER'S EQUITY |

Cash

+	−
(a) 10,000	(c) 125
(g) 1,800	(d) 500
(j) 100	(e) 400
10,025 11,900	(f) 50
	(i) 800
	1,875

Accounts Receivable

+	−
(h) 400	(j) 100
300	

Office Supplies

+	−
(c) 125	

Office Equipment

+	−
(b) 3,000	

Accounts Payable

−	+
(d) 500	(b) 3,000
	2,500

William Taylor, Capital

−	+
	(a) 10,000

William Taylor, Drawing

+	−
(i) 800	

Service Revenue

−	+
	(g) 1,800
	(h) 400
	2,200

Rent Expense

+	−
(e) 400	

Repairs Expense

+	−
(f) 50	

FIGURE 2-3
A trial balance

Taylor and Associates Trial Balance November 30, 20X1		
Account Title	**Debit**	**Credit**
Cash	10 0 2 5 00	
Accounts Receivable	3 0 0 00	
Office Supplies	1 2 5 00	
Office Equipment	3 0 0 0 00	
Accounts Payable		2 5 0 0 00
William Taylor, Capital		10 0 0 0 00
William Taylor, Drawing	8 0 0 00	
Service Revenue		2 2 0 0 00
Rent Expense	4 0 0 00	
Repairs Expense	5 0 00	
Totals	14 7 0 0 00	14 7 0 0 00

Since the trial balance is not a formal financial statement, no dollar signs are needed.

After each account has been balanced, each account balance is carefully transferred to a two-column sheet, with the debit balances in one column and the credit balances in the other. Each column is then totaled, and the totals are compared.

The trial balance of Taylor and Associates is shown in Figure 2-3. The trial balance was prepared on November 30, 20X1, and this date is entered in the heading.

It should be stressed that a trial balance shows only that total debits equal total credits. A trial balance is not a formal financial statement or report. However, information to prepare formal statements can come directly from the trial balance. A trial balance can be prepared on analysis paper, as we did for Taylor and Associates, or simply by totaling debit and credit balances on an adding machine tape.

NORMAL BALANCE OF ACCOUNTS

An account usually has more increases than decreases. Consequently, the **normal balance** side of an account is always the same as the increase side. Asset, expense, and drawing accounts are increased on the debit side; therefore, they normally have debit balances. Liability, owner's capital, and revenue accounts, on the other hand, are increased on the credit side; thus, they normally have credit balances. Figure 2-4 shows where account balances would normally be listed on a trial balance.

FIGURE 2-4
Normal balances

Account Title	Debit Balance	Credit Balance
Asset Accounts	✓	
Liability Accounts		✓
Owner's Capital Account		✓
Owner's Drawing Account	✓	
Revenue Accounts		✓
Expense Accounts	✓	—
Equal Totals	✓	✓

The ledger of Coastal Realty appears as follows on July 31, 20XX. Determine the balance of each account and prepare a trial balance.

ASSETS	=	LIABILITIES	+	OWNER'S EQUITY

Cash

(a) 18,000	(b) 500
(h) 850	(f) 800
(j) 1,200	(g) 400
	(i) 800
	(k) 960

Office Supplies

(b) 500	

Store Supplies

(c) 900	
(d) 300	

Store Equipment

(e) 2,000	

Accounts Payable

	(c) 900
	(d) 300
	(e) 2,000

Lin Todd, Capital

	(a) 18,000

Lin Todd, Drawing

(i) 800	

Commission Revenue

	(h) 850
	(j) 1,200

Rent Expense

(f) 800	

Utilities Expense

(g) 400	

Travel Expense

(k) 960	

CHECK YOUR ANSWERS ON PAGE 66.

SUMMARY OF DEBIT AND CREDIT RULES

We have studied several rules of debit and credit. These rules can be summarized as shown in the chart in Figure 2-5. Notice that the increase side and the normal balance are the same color. This emphasizes that an account's normal balance is always on the increase side.

FIGURE 2-5
Summary of debit and credit rules

Account	Increase Side	Decrease Side	Normal Balance
Asset	Debit	Credit	Debit
Liability	Credit	Debit	Credit
Owner's Capital	Credit	Debit	Credit
Revenue	Credit	Debit	Credit
Owner's Drawing	Debit	Credit	Debit
Expense	Debit	Credit	Debit

FIGURE 2-6
Expanded basic accounting equation

Let's now tie our rules together and look at an expanded statement of the basic accounting equation as illustrated in Figure 2-6.

Assets	=	Liabilities	+	Owner's Capital	+	Revenue	–	Expenses	–	Owner's Drawing
+ −		− +		− +		− +		+ −		+ −
Left Right		Left Right		Left Right		Left Right		Left Right		Left Right
Debit Credit		Debit Credit		Debit Credit		Debit Credit		Debit Credit		Debit Credit

Why do expense and drawing accounts have debit balances?

CHECK YOUR ANSWER ON PAGE 66.

A Final Note on Debits and Credits

At this point, you may still feel a little unsure about when to debit and when to credit. If you are feeling uncertainty, don't worry, it will pass. When you drive your car, don't you automatically pull onto the right side of the road without having to stop and think? You do this because you have practiced it so much. In accounting, like anything else, you improve when you practice. Study the debit and credit rules closely and continue practicing. You will soon find debits and credits as natural as driving on the right side of the road.

INTERNET ASSETS

HOW CAN THE INTERNET EXPEDITE MY WORK AS AN ACCOUNTANT?

As an accountant, you will find the Internet to be a valuable tool. The Internet is the world's largest computer network; more precisely, it is a network of computer networks. It was initially developed by the Defense Department as a secure means for sending messages between computers without interference or problems with connections. Now the Internet has many applications.

Why has the Internet grown so much in such a short period of time? The Internet allows users to obtain up-to-date information on virtually any subject in a matter of seconds. To be successful in today's world, a business must be able to rapidly assimilate and react to changes in the marketplace. The most effective means of accessing this timely information is through the Internet.

Accountants can use the Internet for a wide variety of purposes. Using the Internet, you can:

1. Communicate instantly with clients via e-mail.
2. Obtain up-to-the-minute financial quotes and other business data in seconds.
3. Market your organization through newsletters, a Web page, and interactive online publicity programs.
4. Get up-to-date world news and business news.
5. Find inexpensive advice on legal, accounting, and computer issues.
6. Obtain instantaneous data on economic events and financial trends.
7. Keep continually abreast of what's occurring in the accounting field through accounting, business, and government periodicals.

TOTAL DEBITS = TOTAL CREDITS

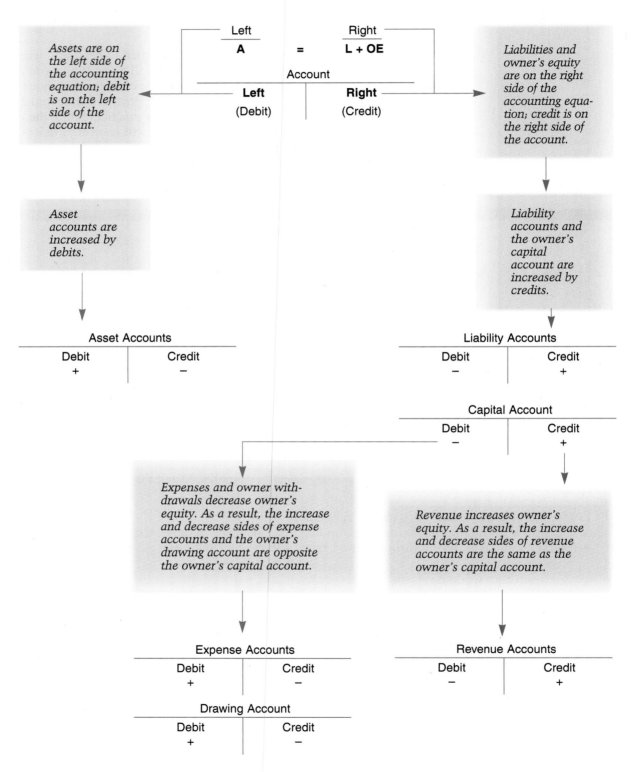

Assets are on the left side of the accounting equation; debit is on the left side of the account.

Liabilities and owner's equity are on the right side of the accounting equation; credit is on the right side of the account.

	Left		Right
	A	**=**	**L + OE**

Account

Left	**Right**
(Debit)	(Credit)

Asset accounts are increased by debits.

Liability accounts and the owner's capital account are increased by credits.

Asset Accounts	
Debit	Credit
+	−

Liability Accounts	
Debit	Credit
−	+

Capital Account	
Debit	Credit
−	+

Expenses and owner withdrawals decrease owner's equity. As a result, the increase and decrease sides of expense accounts and the owner's drawing account are opposite the owner's capital account.

Revenue increases owner's equity. As a result, the increase and decrease sides of revenue accounts are the same as the owner's capital account.

Expense Accounts	
Debit	Credit
+	−

Drawing Account	
Debit	Credit
+	−

Revenue Accounts	
Debit	Credit
−	+

SUMMARY/RESTATEMENT OF LEARNING OBJECTIVES

1. Explain the double-entry accounting framework.

Each business transaction affects the accounting elements in at least two ways. Recording both effects of a transaction is called **double-entry accounting**. The double-entry system provides a means of verifying the mathematical accuracy of recorded transactions. When both effects of a transaction have been recorded, assets equal liabilities plus owner's equity.

2. Describe the standard form of account.

An **account** is an individual record or form used to record increases and decreases in each asset, each liability, and owner's equity. The exact form of account can vary, depending on the use. The **standard form of account** is a basic account form with two amount (or money) columns. The left column is the *Debit* column. The right column is the *Credit* column. These columns are used to record the dollar value of business transactions. The standard form of account also has a *Date* column for recording the date on which transactions occur; an *Item* column for recording a brief description of an entry, if needed; and a *P.R. (Posting Reference)* column, which will be discussed in Chapter 3.

3. Describe the T account.

The **T account** is a skeleton version of the standard form of account. The T account is used mainly for illustrations, since it can be drawn quickly and easily. The T account, so named because it looks like the letter T, has a space for the account title, a left, or debit, side, and a right, or credit, side. The T account is shown here:

```
                Account Title
     _____
        Debit Side    |    Credit Side
                      |
```

4. Explain the rules of debit and credit as applied to asset, liability, and owner's equity accounts.

Transactions are recorded in accounts using the rules of debit and credit. Asset accounts are increased by entering an amount on the debit side. Asset accounts are decreased by entering an amount on the credit side. The reverse is true of liability and the owner's capital accounts. These accounts are increased by entering an amount on the credit side and decreased by entering an amount on the debit side. These rules evolved from the accounting equation Assets = Liabilities + Owner's Equity. By having opposite increase and decrease sides for accounts on the left side of the equation (assets) and accounts on the right side of the equation (liabilities and owner's equity), the equation is maintained in balance.

5. Explain the need for temporary owner's equity accounts.

Owner's equity can be increased in two ways: (1) investments of cash or other assets by the owner, and (2) revenue. Conversely, owner's equity can be decreased in two ways: (1) owner withdrawals of cash or other assets from the business, and (2) expenses of operating the business. These changes could be recorded directly in the owner's capital account. However, this would clutter the account and complicate the determination of net income or net loss. Therefore, it is considered a better practice to maintain separate ledger accounts for revenue, expenses, and owner withdrawals. When the accounting period is over, the balances of these accounts are transferred to the owner's capital account. Thus, these accounts are referred to as **temporary owner's equity accounts**.

NOTE

Investments by the owner usually occur infrequently. Therefore, a separate ledger account is not maintained for owner investments. Instead, investments are recorded directly in the owner's capital account.

6. Explain the rules of debit and credit as applied to temporary owner's equity accounts.

The rules of debit and credit are applied to temporary owner's equity accounts based on their relationship to owner's equity. Revenue increases owner's equity. Consequently, the rules of debit and credit are the same for revenue accounts as they are for the owner's capital account. Revenue accounts are increased on the credit side and decreased on the debit side (the same as the owner's capital account). Expenses and owner withdrawals decrease owner's equity. Thus, the increase and decrease sides of these accounts are opposite the increase and decrease sides of the owner's capital account. Expense accounts and the owner's drawing account are increased on the debit side and decreased on the credit side (the opposite of the owner's capital account).

7. Record business transactions in T accounts and prepare a trial balance.

The Walton Company incurred the following transactions during June, 20X2:

(a) Peyton Walton invested $6,000 in his new cement finishing service.
(b) Purchased supplies for cash, $800.
(c) Invested a used truck, valued at $5,200, in the business.
(d) Purchased office equipment on account, $800.
(e) Received cash for services rendered, $125.
(f) Received cash for services rendered, $250.
(g) Purchased gasoline and truck parts for cash, $68.
(h) Paid salary of assistant, $350.
(i) Received cash for services rendered, $300.
(j) Paid utility bill, $292.
(k) Paid salary of assistant, $350.

Transactions are recorded, T accounts are footed and balanced, and a trial balance is prepared as shown in Figure 2-7.

FIGURE 2-7

Preparation of a trial balance

Cash				Accounts Payable		Peyton Walton, Capital	
(a) 6,000	(b) 800				(d) 800		(a) 6,000
(e) 125	(g) 68						(c) 5,200
(f) 250	(h) 350						11,200
(i) 300	(j) 292						
4,815 6,675	(k) 350						
	1,860						

Supplies		Service Revenue	
(b) 800			(e) 125
			(f) 250
			(i) 300
			675

CONTINUES

FIGURE 2-7
Continues

Office Equipment		Salaries Expense	
(d) 800		(h) 350	
		(k) 350	
		700	

Truck		Truck Expense	
(c) 5,200		(g) 68	

		Utilities Expense	
		(j) 292	

Walton Company
Trial Balance
June 30, 20X2

Account Title	Debit	Credit
Cash	4 8 1 5 00	
Supplies	8 0 0 00	
Office Equipment	8 0 0 00	
Truck	5 2 0 0 00	
Accounts Payable		8 0 0 00
Peyton Walton, Capital		11 2 0 0 00
Service Revenue		6 7 5 00
Salaries Expense	7 0 0 00	
Truck Expense	6 8 00	
Utilities Expense	2 9 2 00	
Totals	12 6 7 5 00	12 6 7 5 00

KEY TERMS

account An individual form or record used to record and summarize information related to each asset, each liability, and each aspect of owner's equity.

balance The balance of an account is determined by footing (adding) the debit side, footing the credit side, and calculating the difference between the two sides.

credit To credit (Cr.) an account means to enter an amount on the right, or credit, side of the account.

credit balance Occurs when the amount on the credit side of an account is greater than the amount on the debit side.

debit To debit (Dr.) an account means to enter an amount on the left, or debit, side of the account.

debit balance Occurs when the amount on the debit side of an account is greater than the amount on the credit side.

double-entry accounting Each business transaction affects the accounting elements in at least two ways. Recording both effects of a transaction is called double-entry accounting.

drawing account A temporary owner's equity account that is used when an owner withdraws cash or other assets from the business for personal use.

footing The total of the debit column or credit column of an account.

ledger A collective grouping of accounts.

normal balance The normal balance of an account is always the same as the increase side of that account; it is where you would expect to find the balance of that account.

standard form of account A form of account with separate debit and credit sides; shown in Figure 2-1.

T account The T account, so named because it looks like a capital letter T, is a skeleton version of the standard form of account.

temporary owner's equity accounts Expense accounts, revenue accounts, and the owner's drawing account are called temporary owner's equity accounts because their balances will be transferred to the owner's capital account at the end of the accounting period.

trial balance A listing of all ledger accounts with their balances to test the equality of debits and credits; it is usually prepared at the end of each month.

CONCEPTS AND SKILLS REVIEW

CONCEPTS REVIEW

1. What is meant by double-entry accounting?
2. What is an account?
3. Why is it better to record business transactions in accounts rather than in equation form?
4. A ledger is sometimes called a book of accounts. Is this always a good description of a ledger? Explain.
5. What is the meaning of the word *debit*? The word *credit*?
6. Explain the rules of debit and credit as applied to asset, liability, and owner's equity accounts.
7. List three reasons for using temporary owner's equity accounts.
8. Explain the rules of debit and credit as applied to temporary owner's equity accounts.
9. How are account balances calculated?
10. What is a footing?
11. Is it possible for an account to have a zero balance if there are entries on both the debit and credit sides of that account? Explain.
12. What is a trial balance?
13. What does a trial balance prove?
14. What is meant by the normal balance of an account?

SKILLS REVIEW

(Forms are provided in the *Study Guide and Working Papers* book.)

EXERCISE 2-1

LEARNING OBJECTIVE 4, 6

Objective: To identify the rules of debit and credit

Directions: Fill in the blanks in the following chart. The first one is done as an example.

	Type of Account	Increase Side	Decrease Side	Normal Balance
Cash	Asset	Debit	Credit	Debit
Equipment				
Joe King, Drawing				
Accounts Payable				
Service Revenue				
Accounts Receivable				
Joe King, Capital				

CONTINUES

	Type of Account	Increase Side	Decrease Side	Normal Balance
Taxes Payable	_____	_____	_____	_____
Fees Earned	_____	_____	_____	_____
Rent Expense	_____	_____	_____	_____

EXERCISE 2-2

Objective: To apply the rules of debit and credit

Directions: Complete the following chart concerning increases and decreases in the accounting elements. The first item is done as an example.

	Recorded on Debit Side	Recorded on Credit Side
(a) Increase in Cash account	✓	_____
(b) Decrease in Accounts Payable account	_____	_____
(c) Increase in owner's drawing account	_____	_____
(d) Increase in owner's capital account	_____	_____
(e) Increase in expense account	_____	_____
(f) Decrease in owner's capital account	_____	_____
(g) Increase in revenue account	_____	_____

EXERCISE 2-3

Objective: To record business transactions in T accounts

Directions: Use a set of T accounts to record each of the following transactions. Identify each transaction by letter.

(a) Bought equipment on account, $600.
(b) Received cash for services performed, $900.
(c) Paid rent for the month, $350.
(d) Paid creditors on account, $400.
(e) Bought equipment for cash, $300.

EXERCISE 2-4

Objective: To analyze a set of transactions

Directions: Read each of the following transactions and write an analysis of how each would be recorded. Use the examples found in this chapter as a guide.

(a) Bought supplies on account.
(b) Performed services for cash.
(c) Paid creditors on account.
(d) Bought equipment on account.
(e) Performed services on credit.
(f) Paid rent for the month.
(g) Paid salaries of employees.
(h) Owner withdrew cash for personal use.
(i) Purchased equipment for cash.
(j) Owner made an additional investment of cash in the firm.

EXERCISE 2-5

Objective: To record business transactions in T accounts

Directions: Set up T accounts with the following titles: Cash; Accounts Receivable; Supplies; Equipment; Accounts Payable; Tom Anderson, Capital; Tom Anderson, Drawing; Revenue from Commissions; Rent Expense; and Utilities Expense. Record the transactions listed on the next page in your accounts, identifying each transaction by letter.

(a) Owner invested $11,000 cash in his real estate firm.
(b) Purchased supplies for cash, $250.
(c) Purchased equipment on account, $950.
(d) Paid rent for the month, $600.
(e) Sold a house and received a commission of $3,900.
(f) Paid $600 on the equipment purchased in Transaction (c).
(g) Sold a house and earned a commission of $4,000 to be received next month.
(h) Withdrew $600 cash for personal use.
(i) Purchased supplies for cash, $355.
(j) Paid utility bill for the month, $320.
(k) Invested a personal computer, valued at $1,200, into the business.

EXERCISE 2-6

LEARNING OBJECTIVE 7

Objective: To prepare a trial balance

Directions: Using your solution to Exercise 2-5, foot the accounts and prepare a trial balance for Tom Anderson Realty as of June 30, 20X1.

CASE PROBLEMS

GROUP A

(Forms are provided in the *Study Guide and Working Papers* book.)

LEARNING OBJECTIVE 4, 7

PROBLEM 2-1A

Objective: To record business transactions in T accounts and prepare a trial balance

On May 5, 20X1, John Distasio started a carpet cleaning business called Best Way Carpet Cleaners. He completed the following transactions during the month:

(a) John transferred $14,500 from his personal savings account to a bank account for the business.
(b) John invested a small truck, which he had owned personally, in the business. The value of the truck was $8,000.
(c) Paid rent on a small office, $625.
(d) Purchased office supplies for cash, $575.
(e) Purchased equipment on account, $4,000.
(f) Received cash for services performed, $150.
(g) Performed services on credit, $350.
(h) Purchased truck supplies on account, $125.
(i) Paid salary of employee, $550.
(j) Paid for repairs to truck, $225.
(k) Received $200 for the services performed in Transaction (g).
(l) Paid utilities, $315.
(m) Paid creditor $75 on the purchase in Transaction (h).
(n) John withdrew cash for personal use, $625.
(o) Paid salary of employee, $575.

Directions: (1) Draw a set of T accounts with the following titles: Cash; Accounts Receivable; Office Supplies; Truck Supplies; Equipment; Truck; Accounts Payable; John Distasio, Capital; John Distasio, Drawing; Cleaning Fees; Rent Expense; Salaries Expense; Truck Expense; and Utilities Expense. (2) Record each of the transactions in the T accounts. (3) Foot and calculate the balance of each account and prepare a trial balance as of May 31, 20X1.

Objective: To describe transactions recorded in T accounts

Directions: For each entry in the following T accounts, describe the transaction (both debit and credit parts) that created the entry:

Cash	
(a) 4,000	(b) 200
	(c) 800
(f) 225	(g) 280
(k) 600	(h) 500
	(i) 200

Equipment	
(c) 800	

B. O'Malley, Drawing	
(h) 500	

Accounts Receivable	
(d) 900	(f) 225

Office Supplies	
(b) 200	
(e) 400	

Accounts Payable	
(i) 200	(e) 400
	(j) 300

Service Revenue	
	(d) 900
	(k) 600

Store Supplies	
(j) 300	

B. O'Malley, Capital	
	(a) 4,000

Delivery Expense	
(g) 280	

PROBLEM 2-3A

Objective: To record business transactions in T accounts and prepare a trial balance

On June 1, 20X1, David Mack established a small business, Century Bookkeeping Service, to keep records for small businesses and to provide tax assistance to businesses and individuals. During June, David completed the following transactions:

(a) David began the business by placing $14,000 into a business checking account.
(b) Purchased office supplies for cash, $450.
(c) Purchased office equipment on account, $3,900.
(d) Purchased a microcomputer system (office equipment) for $4,200, paying $1,100 down and agreeing to pay the balance in 90 days.
(e) Paid first month's rent, $600.
(f) Paid for an advertisement in the local newspaper, $170.
(g) Received cash for services performed, $400.
(h) Purchased a laser printer (office equipment) on account, $600.
(i) Performed services on credit, $425.
(j) Paid salary of part-time employee, $350.
(k) Purchased a case of floppy disks for use with the computer, $160.
(l) Paid utility bill for the month, $299.
(m) Paid telephone bill, $180.
(n) Collected $200 from the services performed in Transaction (i).
(o) Withdrew cash for personal use, $700.
(p) Paid to have the carpet cleaned, $75.
(q) Paid salary of part-time employee, $350.

Directions: (1) Draw a set of T accounts with the following titles: Cash; Accounts Receivable; Office Supplies; Office Equipment; Accounts Payable; David Mack, Capital; David Mack, Drawing; Revenue from Fees; Rent Expense; Salaries Expense; Advertising Expense; Telephone Expense; Utilities Expense; and Miscellaneous Expense. (2) Record the transactions in the T accounts, using the transaction letters to identify the debits and credits. (3) Foot and find the balance of each account and prepare a trial balance dated June 30, 20X1.

LEARNING OBJECTIVE 4, 5, 6, 7

PROBLEM 2-4A

Objective: To record business transactions in T accounts and prepare a trial balance

George Lawson started an air-conditioning and heating repair business on March 1, 20X1, and completed the following transactions during his first month of operations:

(a) George invested $28,000 in his new business known as Lawson Service Company.
(b) Purchased office supplies for cash, $375.
(c) Purchased office equipment on account, $3,200.
(d) Purchased a used automobile for cash, $8,500.
(e) Purchased two light-duty utility trucks, $24,600, paying $6,000 down with the balance on account.
(f) Paid $90 for gasoline and oil.
(g) Paid rent for the month, $800.
(h) Received $110 for repairing an air-conditioning unit at Cody Motel.
(i) Earned $450 for repairs to a heating unit at Cody Motel. Will receive cash later this month.
(j) Paid for repairs to automobile, $75.
(k) Earned $610 for repairing the air-conditioning unit at Central Hospital. Cash is to be received next month.
(l) Paid salaries of employees, $925.
(m) Paid telephone bill, $125.
(n) Paid utility bill, $205.
(o) George withdrew $800 for personal use.
(p) George paid a personal bill using a company check, $75.
(q) Made first payment on the trucks, $575.
(r) Paid $500 on the equipment purchased in Transaction (c).
(s) Received the cash due from Transaction (i).

Directions: (1) Draw a set of T accounts with the following titles: Cash; Accounts Receivable; Office Supplies; Office Equipment; Automobile; Trucks; Accounts Payable; George Lawson, Capital; George Lawson, Drawing; Service Revenue; Rent Expense; Salaries Expense; Gasoline and Oil Expense; Telephone Expense; Utilities Expense; and Miscellaneous Expense. (2) Record George's transactions in the T accounts. (3) Foot and find the balance of each account and then prepare a trial balance dated March 31, 20X1.

PROBLEM 2-5A

LEARNING OBJECTIVE 7

Objective: To prepare a trial balance from a group of alphabetized accounts

Directions: Following is an alphabetized list of the accounts and their balances for Mogren Company on July 31, 20X2. Prepare a trial balance in correct order and form.

Item	Amount
Accounts Payable	$ 9,000
Accounts Receivable	3,000
Building	43,000
Cash	11,500
Equipment	30,500
Linda Mogren, Capital	?
Linda Mogren, Drawing	13,500
Rent Expense	7,000

Item	Amount
Revenue from Services	39,900
Salaries Expense	2,850
Telephone Expense	1,000
Utilities Expense	4,300

GROUP B

(Forms are provided in the *Study Guide and Working Papers* book.)

PROBLEM 2-1B

LEARNING OBJECTIVE 4, 5, 6, 7

Objective: To record business transactions in T accounts and prepare a trial balance

On August 1, 20X1, Dorethia Carter started a food catering service called Al La Foods. She completed the following transactions during the month:

(a) Dorethia transferred $13,500 from her personal savings account to a bank account for the business.
(b) Invested a small truck, which she had owned personally, in the business. The value of the truck was $7,800.
(c) Paid rent on a small office, $475.
(d) Purchased office supplies for cash, $550.
(e) Purchased equipment on account, $3,700.
(f) Received cash for services performed, $190.
(g) Performed services on credit, $330.
(h) Purchased truck supplies on account, $180.
(i) Paid salary of employee, $575.
(j) Paid for repairs to truck, $220.
(k) Received $250 for the services performed in Transaction (g).
(l) Paid utilities, $330.
(m) Paid creditor $85 on the purchase in Transaction (h).
(n) Dorethia withdrew cash for personal use, $650.
(o) Paid salary of employee, $600.

Directions: (1) Draw a set of T accounts with the following titles: Cash; Accounts Receivable; Office Supplies; Truck Supplies; Equipment; Truck; Accounts Payable; Dorethia Carter, Capital; Dorethia Carter, Drawing; Catering Fees; Rent Expense; Salaries Expense; Truck Expense; and Utilities Expense. (2) Record each of the transactions in the T accounts. (3) Foot and calculate the balance of each account and prepare a trial balance as of August 31, 20X1.

PROBLEM 2-2B

LEARNING OBJECTIVE 4, 5, 6

Objective: To describe transactions recorded in T accounts

Directions: For each entry in the following T accounts, describe the transaction (both debit and credit parts) that created the entry:

Cash	
(a) 7,000	(c) 135
	(e) 115
(h) 710	(f) 295
(k) 630	(g) 700
	(i) 250

Equipment	
(b) 475	

R. Sluder, Drawing	
(g) 700	

Accounts Receivable	
(d) 835	(h) 710

Office Supplies	Accounts Payable	Fees Earned
(c) 135	(i) 250 | (b) 475	(d) 835
(j) 365	(j) 365	(k) 630

Store Supplies	R. Sluder, Capital	Delivery Expense
(f) 295	(a) 7,000	(e) 115

PROBLEM 2-3B

LEARNING OBJECTIVE 4, 5, 6, 7 **Objective: To record business transactions in T accounts and prepare a trial balance**

On May 1, 20X1, Elisa Kane established a word processing service called E.K. Business Services. During May, Elisa completed the following transactions:

(a) Elisa began the business by placing $12,000 into a business checking account.
(b) Purchased office supplies for cash, $425.
(c) Purchased office equipment on account, $4,300.
(d) Purchased a microcomputer system (office equipment) for $4,700, paying $1,400 down and agreeing to pay the balance in 90 days.
(e) Paid first month's rent, $550.
(f) Paid for an advertisement in the local newspaper, $175.
(g) Received cash for services performed, $325.
(h) Purchased a laser printer (office equipment) on account, $800.
(i) Performed services on credit, $350.
(j) Paid salary of part-time employee, $375.
(k) Purchased a case of floppy disks for use with the computer, $180.
(l) Paid utility bill for the month, $277.
(m) Paid telephone bill, $226.
(n) Collected $250 from the services performed in Transaction (i).
(o) Withdrew cash for personal use, $800.
(p) Paid to have the company name painted on the door, $90.
(q) Paid salary of part-time employee, $375.

Directions: (1) Draw a set of T accounts with the following titles: Cash; Accounts Receivable; Office Supplies; Office Equipment; Accounts Payable; Elisa Kane, Capital; Elisa Kane, Drawing; Revenue from Fees; Rent Expense; Salaries Expense; Advertising Expense; Telephone Expense; Utilities Expense; and Miscellaneous Expense. (2) Record the transactions in the T accounts, using the transaction letters to identify the debits and credits. (3) Foot and find the balance of each account and prepare a trial balance dated May 31, 20X1.

PROBLEM 2-4B

LEARNING OBJECTIVE 4, 5, 6, 7 **Objective: To record business transactions in T accounts and prepare a trial balance**

Susan Miller started a VCR and CD player repair business on April 1, 20X1, and completed the following transactions during her first month of operations:

(a) Susan invested $21,000 in her new business known as Best Video Repair.
(b) Purchased office supplies for cash, $390.
(c) Purchased office equipment on account, $2,700.
(d) Purchased a used automobile for cash, $7,400.
(e) Purchased two light-duty utility trucks, $25,600, paying $6,500 down with the balance on account.
(f) Paid $85 for gasoline and oil.
(g) Paid rent for the month, $775.
(h) Received $75 for repairing a VCR at Mid-Town Motel.

62   *Paradigm College Accounting* • Chapter 2

(i) Earned $750 for repairs to several items at the Mid-Town Motel. Will receive cash later this month.
(j) Paid for repairs to automobile, $70.
(k) Earned $600 for repairing and cleaning VCRs and tape players at Ochee School District. Cash is to be received next month.
(l) Paid salaries of employees, $875.
(m) Paid telephone bill, $108.
(n) Paid utility bill, $150.
(o) Susan withdrew $825 for personal use.
(p) Susan paid a personal bill using a company check, $85.
(q) Made first payment on the trucks, $625.
(r) Paid $575 on the equipment purchased in Transaction (c).
(s) Received the cash due from Transaction (i).

Directions: (1) Draw a set of T accounts with the following titles: Cash; Accounts Receivable; Office Supplies; Office Equipment; Automobile; Trucks; Accounts Payable; Susan Miller, Capital; Susan Miller, Drawing; Service Revenue; Rent Expense; Salaries Expense; Gasoline and Oil Expense; Telephone Expense; Utilities Expense; and Miscellaneous Expense. (2) Record Susan's transactions in the T accounts. (3) Foot and find the balance of each account and then prepare a trial balance dated April 30, 20X1.

PROBLEM 2-5B

LEARNING OBJECTIVE 7

Objective: To prepare a trial balance from a group of alphabetized accounts

Directions: Following is an alphabetized list of the accounts and their balances for Emerson Company on June 30, 20X2. From this alphabetized list, prepare a trial balance in correct order and form.

Item	Amount
Accounts Payable	$3,900
Accounts Receivable	1,000
Cash	7,200
Delivery Expense	95
Equipment	3,900
Paul Emerson, Capital	?
Paul Emerson, Drawing	800
Rent Expense	650
Revenue from Services	4,750
Salaries Expense	2,590
Truck	8,200
Utilities Expense	375

CHALLENGE PROBLEMS

PROBLEM SOLVING

On August 1, 20X1, David Payne started Fast Track Delivery Company, a local pickup and delivery service. David incurred the following transactions during his first month of operations:

(a) David invested the following assets in the business: cash, $11,000; office supplies, $60; truck supplies, $32; and equipment, $5,000.
(b) Purchased additional office supplies and paid cash, $125.
(c) Purchased a new delivery truck for $19,400, paying $2,500 down and signing a note payable for the balance.

(d)   Paid for gasoline and oil, $70.
(e)   Made deliveries to charge customers, $335.
(f)   Paid rent for the month, $550.
(g)   Made deliveries to cash customers, $228.
(h)   Collected the amount due from the customers in Transaction (e).
(i)   Paid for repairs to truck, $90.
(j)   Purchased truck supplies on account, $75.
(k)   Paid salaries of employees, $900.
(l)   Made deliveries to credit customers, $345.
(m) Purchased a microcomputer system for cash, $2,300.
(n)   Purchased printer ribbons, diskettes, and computer paper for cash, $425.
(o)   As a favor, David sold a printer ribbon at cost, $20, to the owner of the business next door.
(p)   Paid cash for gasoline and oil, $135.
(q)   Discovered that a $40 box of computer diskettes had been stored too close to the heating vent and was ruined.
(r)   Collected $150 of the amount due from Transaction (l).
(s)   Paid $15 to have a flat tire repaired.
(t)   Paid the telephone bill, $148.
(u)   Paid utility bill, $399.
(v)   Paid salaries of employees, $900.
(w) Made deliveries to cash customers, $665.
(x)   Withdrew cash for personal use, $900.

Directions: (1) Set up T accounts with the following titles: Cash; Accounts Receivable; Office Supplies; Truck Supplies; Equipment; Truck; Accounts Payable; Notes Payable; David Payne, Capital; David Payne, Drawing; Delivery Revenue; Rent Expense; Salaries Expense; Gasoline and Oil Expense; Utilities Expense; Telephone Expense; Repair Expense; and Miscellaneous Expense. (2) Record the transactions in the T accounts. (3) Foot and find the balance of the accounts and prepare a trial balance as of August 31, 20X1. (4) Prepare an income statement for the month ending August 31, 20X1. (5) Prepare a statement of owner's equity for the month ending August 31, 20X1. (6) Prepare a balance sheet in report form as of August 31, 20X1.

COMMUNICATIONS

Karen Lewis just completed the second chapter in her college accounting course. After being introduced to debits and credits, Karen wondered why some accounts are increased by debits, while others are decreased by debits. She asks "Why can't all accounts be increased by debits and decreased by credits?"

Provide an answer to Karen's question in a brief paragraph.

ETHICS

John Grimes owns a small appliance repair shop. This month his business's electric bill was $375, and his home electric bill was $125. John wrote a single check to the utility company and debited the Utilities Expense account for the total.

Explain (a) what John has done wrong and (b) why what he did violates proper accounting principles and identify the particular principle he violated.

REVIEW QUIZ 2-1

Either. To asset accounts, debit means increase and credit means decrease. To liability accounts and the owner's capital account, debit means decrease and credit means increase.

REVIEW QUIZ 2-2

Cash	
(a) 8,000	(c) 500
	(e) 600

Accounts Payable	
(e) 600	(b) 1,200
	(d) 300

Office Supplies	
(c) 500	

Ted Bonner, Capital	
	(a) 8,000

Shop Supplies	
(d) 300	

Equipment	
(b) 1,200	

REVIEW QUIZ 2-3

Cash	
(a) 5,000	(b) 600
	(c) 540
	(d) 1,800
	(e) 200
	(f) 500

Judy Lyle, Drawing	
(f) 500	

Service Revenue	
	(a) 5,000

Salaries Expense	
(d) 1,800	

Rent Expense	
(b) 600	

Utilities Expense	
(c) 540	

Repairs Expense	
(e) 200	

Account Title	Debit	Credit
Coastal Realty **Trial Balance** **July 31, 20XX**		
Cash	16590 00	
Office Supplies	500 00	
Store Supplies	1200 00	
Store Equipment	2000 00	
Accounts Payable		3200 00
Lin Todd, Capital		18000 00
Lin Todd, Drawing	800 00	
Commission Revenue		2050 00
Rent Expense	800 00	
Utilities Expense	400 00	
Travel Expense	960 00	
Totals	23250 00	23250 00

REVIEW QUIZ 2-5

Expense accounts and the owner's drawing account are used to record decreases in the owner's capital account. Therefore, the increase and decrease sides of these accounts are opposite those of the owner's capital account. Since the owner's capital account is increased with a credit and decreased with a debit, the expense and drawing accounts are increased with a debit and decreased with a credit.

3

STARTING THE ACCOUNTING CYCLE FOR A SERVICE BUSINESS

LEARNING OBJECTIVES
After studying Chapter 3, you will be able to:
1. Describe the standard form of a two-column journal.
2. Record business transactions in a two-column journal.
3. Prepare a chart of accounts.
4. Post from a two-column journal to ledger accounts.
5. Prepare a trial balance from a ledger after posting.
6. Describe the four-column ledger account form.
7. Describe the procedures for locating and correcting errors in the accounting process.
8. Make entries to correct errors in the ledger.

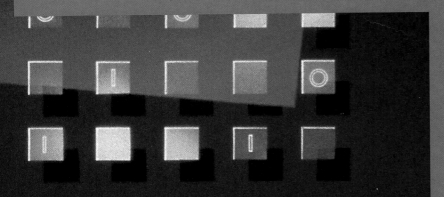

In Chapter 2, you learned the basic rules of debit and credit as you recorded business transactions in T accounts. You also learned that, because of the dual effect, at least two accounts are affected by each business transaction. In addition, you learned how to check the equality of debits and credits in the ledger by preparing a trial balance.

THE ACCOUNTING CYCLE

Having successfully mastered the objectives of Chapter 2, you are now ready to begin studying the series of steps that businesses use to process accounting data. The standard sequence of steps or procedures used by a business to record and summarize accounting data is known as the **accounting cycle**. In Chapter 3, we will study the first four steps in the accounting cycle for a service business. We will then study the next four steps in the accounting cycle in Chapter 4 and conclude our study in Chapter 5. The first four steps in the accounting cycle are:

1. Analyze transactions from source documents.
2. Record transactions in a journal.
3. Post from the journal to the ledger.
4. Prepare a trial balance of the ledger.

STEP 1: ANALYZE TRANSACTIONS FROM SOURCE DOCUMENTS

When business transactions occur, business papers are prepared as evidence of those transactions. Business papers can take the form of check stubs, receipts, sales slips, cash register tapes, invoices, bills or any other document that serves as proof that a business transaction has taken place. These business papers, called **source documents**, are used by the accountant to analyze a transaction into its debit and credit parts. The accounting principle of **objective evidence** states that source documents should form the foundation for recording business transactions.

STEP 2: RECORD TRANSACTIONS IN A JOURNAL

The objective of double-entry accounting is to make equal (and accurate) debit and credit entries in the proper ledger accounts. Recording business transactions in T accounts accomplishes this. However, recording transactions directly in T accounts breaks up the debit and credit parts of an entry since the debit is recorded in one account and the credit is recorded in another. The likelihood of errors is greater when the debit and credit parts of an entry are recorded on separate pages of the ledger. To overcome this problem, an important step in the accounting cycle occurs before recording transactions in T accounts. The first formal record of business transactions is made in a form known as the journal. The **journal** provides a complete record of each transaction in chronological order (by order of date).

LEARNING OBJECTIVE 1

Since the journal is the first place transactions are formally recorded, it is referred to as the **book of original entry**. Various types of journals are used today. The basic form of journal is a two-column journal called the **general journal**. The general journal is an all-purpose journal in which any business transaction can be recorded in chronological sequence from the first transaction of the accounting period to the last. The general journal is shown in Figure 3-1.

FIGURE 3-1
The general journal

	General Journal				**① Page 1**
	② Date	**③ Account Title**	**④ P.R.**	**Debit**	**⑤ Credit**
1					1
2					2
3					3
4					4

Note the following features of the general journal:

❶ Numbered pages, beginning with page 1.
❷ A *Date* column used to record the date on which a transaction occurs.
❸ An *Account Title* column, used to record the accounts affected by a transaction, as well as a brief explanation of the transaction.
❹ A posting reference (*P.R.*) column, which has a special use and is described on page 77.
❺ Two money (or amount) columns, labeled *Debit* and *Credit*, respectively. Each is used to record the dollar amount of transactions.

Making Journal Entries

LEARNING OBJECTIVE 2

The process of recording transactions in a journal is called **journalizing**. Journalizing differs from recording in T accounts in form only; the analysis of the transactions and the accounts used are identical. To illustrate how to make journal entries, we will again look at William Taylor's transactions for Taylor and Associates during November 20X1. (Remember, you studied these in Chapter 2.) This time, however, we will record the transactions in general journal format by the date the transactions occurred, rather than by letters.

REMEMBER

To record a transaction, it must be analyzed into its debit and credit parts. For each transaction, you must decide:
1. Which accounts are affected by the transaction
2. Whether the accounts affected were increased or decreased
3. How to increase or decrease (debit or credit) the accounts affected

TRANSACTION, NOVEMBER 1, 20X1: WILLIAM TAYLOR INVESTED $10,000 CASH IN HIS BUSINESS

Analysis: Cash was received in the business. Therefore, the Cash account, an asset, must be increased. Increases in asset accounts are recorded as debits, so the Cash account is debited for $10,000. Owner investments increase the equity of the business. Therefore, the owner's capital account must be increased. The owner's capital account is increased by a credit, so William Taylor, Capital is credited for $10,000.

Starting the Accounting Cycle for a Service Business

Entry:

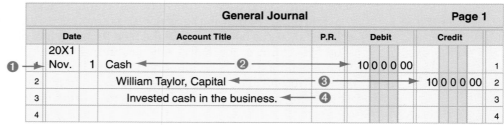

FIGURE 3-2
Sample journal entry

	Date		Account Title	P.R.	Debit	Credit	
❶ → 1	20X1 Nov.	1	Cash ←———— ❷ ————→		10 0 0 0 00		1
2			William Taylor, Capital ←——— ❸ ———→			10 0 0 0 00	2
3			Invested cash in the business. ←— ❹				3
4							4

Note the following features of the journal entry in Figure 3-2.

❶ The date of the entry consists of the year (20X1), the month (Nov.), and the day of the month (1).

❷ The title of the account to be debited (Cash) is written on the first line at the extreme left margin of the Account Title column. The amount of the debit ($10,000.00) is written in the Debit column on the same line. Debits are *always* written before credits. Dollar signs *are not* used in the journal.

❸ The title of the account to be credited (William Taylor, Capital) is written on the second line of the Account Title column and indented one-fourth to one-half inch. The amount of the credit ($10,000.00) is written in the Credit column on the same line.

❹ The explanation of the entry (Invested cash in the business) is written on the third line and indented an additional one-fourth to one-half inch. Some accountants prefer to omit the explanation if the nature of the entry is self-explanatory.

TRANSACTION, NOVEMBER 6: PURCHASED OFFICE EQUIPMENT FOR $3,000 ON ACCOUNT

Analysis: The business acquired an asset, office equipment. Increases in asset accounts are recorded as debits. The Office Equipment account is therefore debited for $3,000. The business incurred a liability as a result of purchasing an asset on credit. Therefore, the liability account Accounts Payable must be increased. Increases in liability accounts are recorded as credits, so the Accounts Payable account is credited for $3,000.

Entry:

5		6	Office Equipment		3 0 0 0 00		5
6			Accounts Payable			3 0 0 0 00	6
7			Purchased equipment on account.				7
8							8

Note that the date is simply listed as 6. It is not necessary to repeat the year or the month until either one changes or a new page in the journal is started.

TRANSACTION, NOVEMBER 9: PURCHASED OFFICE SUPPLIES FOR CASH, $125

Analysis: The business acquired an asset, office supplies. Increases in asset accounts are recorded as debits. The Office Supplies account is therefore debited for $125. Cash, an asset, was paid. Decreases in asset accounts are recorded as credits. The Cash account is therefore credited for $125.

Entry:

9		9	Office Supplies		1 2 5 00			9
10			Cash			1 2 5 00		10
11			Purchased office supplies for cash.					11
12								12

TRANSACTION, NOVEMBER 12: PAID $500 ON THE EQUIPMENT PURCHASED ON NOVEMBER 6

Analysis: Part of an account payable was paid. Therefore, the liability account, Accounts Payable, must be decreased by the amount of the payment. Decreases in liability accounts are recorded as debits, so the Accounts Payable account is debited for $500. The payment decreased Cash, so the Cash account is decreased by a credit of $500.

Entry:

13		12	Accounts Payable		5 0 0 00			13
14			Cash			5 0 0 00		14
15			Made payment on account—Nov. 6.					15
16								16

REVIEW QUIZ
3-1

The following transactions are those of Judy Baxter during March 20XX. Record each transaction in a general journal. Omit the explanations.

Mar. 1 Judy invested $7,000 cash in her business.
4 Purchased supplies on credit, $750.
6 Purchased equipment for cash, $475.
9 Paid half of the amount owed for supplies.

CHECK YOUR ANSWERS ON PAGE 106.

TRANSACTION, NOVEMBER 15: PAID FIRST MONTH'S RENT, $400

Analysis: Rent, an expense, was paid. Therefore, the Rent Expense account must be increased. Increases in expense accounts are recorded as debits, so the Rent Expense account is debited for $400. The payment decreased Cash, so the Cash account is decreased by a credit of $400.

Entry:

17		15	Rent Expense		4 0 0 00			17
18			Cash			4 0 0 00		18
19			Paid first month's rent.					19
20								20

TRANSACTION, NOVEMBER 17: PAID FOR REPAIRS TO EQUIPMENT, $50

Analysis: Equipment was repaired. Therefore, the Repairs Expense account must be increased. Increases in expense accounts are recorded as debits, so the Repairs Expense account is debited for $50. Cash was decreased by the payment, so the Cash account is credited for $50.

Entry:

21		17	Repairs Expense			5 0 00			21
22			Cash				5 0 00		22
23			Paid for equipment repairs.						23
24									24

TRANSACTION, NOVEMBER 18: RECEIVED CASH FROM CUSTOMERS FOR SERVICES PERFORMED, $1,800

Analysis: Cash, an asset, was received from customers. Therefore, the Cash account must be increased. Increases in asset accounts are recorded as debits, so the Cash account is debited for $1,800. Cash received for services performed yields revenue to the business. Therefore, a revenue account must be increased. Revenue accounts are increased by credits, so the Service Revenue account is credited for $1,800.

Entry:

25		18	Cash			1 8 0 0 00			25
26			Service Revenue				1 8 0 0 00		26
27			Performed services for cash.						27
28									28

TRANSACTION, NOVEMBER 20: PERFORMED SERVICES ON ACCOUNT, $400

Analysis: Services were performed on credit for customers. Therefore, the Accounts Receivable account, an asset, must be increased. Increases in asset accounts are recorded as debits, so the Accounts Receivable account is debited for $400. Performing services, whether for cash or on account, increases revenue. Revenue accounts are increased by credits, so the Service Revenue account is credited for $400.

Revenue is recorded when it is earned, no matter when the actual receipt of cash takes place (realization principle).

Entry:

29		20	Accounts Receivable			4 0 0 00			29
30			Service Revenue				4 0 0 00		30
31			Performed services on account.						31
32									32

TRANSACTION, NOVEMBER 27: MR. TAYLOR WITHDREW $800 FROM THE BUSINESS FOR PERSONAL USE

Analysis: Owner withdrawals result in an increase in the owner's drawing account. The owner's drawing account is increased by a debit, so William Taylor, Drawing is debited for $800. The withdrawal also decreased Cash, so the Cash account is credited for $800 to show the decrease.

Entry:

33		27	William Taylor, Drawing			8 0 0 00			33
34			Cash				8 0 0 00		34
35			Withdrew cash for personal use.						35
36									36

TRANSACTION, NOVEMBER 29: COLLECTED $100 ON ACCOUNT

Analysis: Cash was collected from a credit customer. Therefore, the Cash account, an asset, must be increased. Increases in asset accounts are recorded as debits, so the Cash account is debited for $100. Part of an account receivable was collected. Therefore, the Accounts Receivable account, an asset, must be decreased. Decreases in assets are recorded as credits, so the Accounts Receivable account is credited for $100. Assume that this transaction is recorded on page 2 of the journal, so the year and month are listed.

Entry:

		General Journal				Page 2	
	Date	Account Title	P.R.	Debit	Credit		
1	20X1 Nov. 29	Cash		1 0 0 00			1
2		Accounts Receivable			1 0 0 00		2
3		Collected cash on account.					3
4							4

Compound Journal Entry

We have now journalized all of the transactions we introduced for Taylor and Associates in Chapter 2. Each transaction had only one debit and one credit. When only two accounts are affected by the transaction (a debit and a credit), it is often referred to as a simple entry. To record some transactions, however, you will have to use more than one debit or credit. An entry requiring three or more accounts is called a **compound entry**. The following entry shows how to record a compound entry.

TRANSACTION, NOVEMBER 30: MR. TAYLOR PURCHASED OFFICE FURNITURE FOR $2,000, PAYING $500 DOWN, WITH THE BALANCE OWED ON ACCOUNT

Analysis: The business acquired an asset, office furniture. Increases in asset accounts are recorded as debits, so the Office Furniture account is debited for $2,000. Cash was paid. The Cash account is therefore decreased by a credit of $500. The business also incurred a liability as a result of purchasing an asset on credit. Increases in liability accounts are recorded as credits, so the Accounts Payable account is credited for $1,500.

Entry:

5		30	Office Furniture		2 0 0 0 00		5
6			Cash			5 0 0 00	6
7			Accounts Payable			1 5 0 0 00	7
8			Purchase, paying part cash.				8
9							9

Note how the two credits are simply listed, one under the other. A compound entry with two debits would list both debits at the left margin of the account title column, followed by an indented credit. When making compound entries, the total of the debits must always equal the total of the credits—the same as in a simple entry.

The completed journal of Taylor and Associates for the month of November 20X1 is shown in Figure 3-3.

FIGURE 3-3
General journal for Taylor and Associates, November, 20X1

	Date		Account Title	P.R.	Debit	Credit	
	General Journal					Page 1	
1	20X1 Nov.	1	Cash		10 0 0 0 00		1
2			William Taylor, Capital			10 0 0 0 00	2
3			Invested cash in the business.				3
4							4
5		6	Office Equipment		3 0 0 0 00		5
6			Accounts Payable			3 0 0 0 00	6
7			Purchased equipment on account.				7
8							8
9		9	Office Supplies		1 2 5 00		9
10			Cash			1 2 5 00	10
11			Purchased office supplies for cash.				11
12							12
13		12	Accounts Payable		5 0 0 00		13
14			Cash			5 0 0 00	14
15			Made payment on account—Nov. 6.				15
16							16
17		15	Rent Expense		4 0 0 00		17
18			Cash			4 0 0 00	18
19			Paid first month's rent.				19
20							20
21		17	Repairs Expense		5 0 00		21
22			Cash			5 0 00	22
23			Paid for equipment repairs.				23
24							24
25		18	Cash		1 8 0 0 00		25
26			Service Revenue			1 8 0 0 00	26
27			Performed services for cash.				27
28							28
29		20	Accounts Receivable		4 0 0 00		29
30			Service Revenue			4 0 0 00	30
31			Performed services on account.				31
32							32
33		27	William Taylor, Drawing		8 0 0 00		33
34			Cash			8 0 0 00	34
35			Withdrew cash for personal use.				35

It is customary to skip a line after each journal entry.

	Date		Account Title	P.R.	Debit	Credit	
	General Journal					Page 2	
1	20X1 Nov.	29	Cash		1 0 0 00		1
2			Accounts Receivable			1 0 0 00	2
3			Collected cash on account.				3
4							4
5		30	Office Furniture		2 0 0 0 00		5
6			Cash			5 0 0 00	6
7			Accounts Payable			1 5 0 0 00	7
8			Purchase, paying part cash.				8

Remember
The year and the month are rewritten if the page changes.

Advantages of Using a Journal

Now that we have introduced the journal and discussed how transactions are recorded in this type of record, let's review the advantages of using a journal as the book of original entry. Four major advantages of using a journal are:

1. The journal provides a chronological (by order of date) record of transactions. In effect, it is a complete diary of a firm's transactions. Should it become necessary to check an entry, the entire entry can be found by referring to the date the transaction was recorded. When entries are recorded directly in T accounts, it is not possible to find the complete entry in this way.
2. The journal provides a place to make an explanation of an entry, should an explanation be needed.
3. Use of the journal lessens the possibility of a recording error, because both the debit and credit parts of an entry are recorded together. When entries are recorded directly in T accounts, the debit and credit parts of the entry are recorded in separate accounts. This increases the likelihood of omitting the debit part of an entry, omitting the credit part of an entry, or making duplicate debits and credits.
4. Because the journal shows both the debit and credit parts of an entry in one place, it is easier to locate recording errors.

Kyle King's business had the following transactions in June 20X1. Record each transaction in a general journal. Omit explanations.

Jun. 12 Paid utilities expense, $145.
    17 Kyle withdrew cash for personal use, $175.
    22 Received cash for services performed, $950.
    25 Kyle made the following additional investments in his business: office supplies, $75; and a truck, $4,000.

CHECK YOUR ANSWERS ON PAGE 106.

STEP 3: POST FROM THE JOURNAL TO THE LEDGER

As we have emphasized, use of the journal offers the strong advantage of a complete record of transactions in chronological order. The journal, however, does not provide a summary of financial information about each account. If, for example, you were asked to find the balance of the Cash account from the general journal, you would have to go through the entire journal and write down all debits to Cash (the increases) and all credits to Cash (the decreases), and then find the difference between the two. This, obviously, is not practical. So, to provide a summary, we need to transfer the information from the journal to the individual ledger accounts. The process of transferring amounts from the journal to the ledger is called **posting**, which is the third step in the accounting cycle. Before we discuss how to post, however, let's look at a system used to organize and identify accounts in the ledger.

The Chart of Accounts

LEARNING OBJECTIVE 3

In making journal entries and transferring them to the ledger, the accountant needs a directory of accounts available. A directory of accounts available in the ledger is called a **chart of accounts**. The chart of accounts for Taylor and Associates is shown in Figure 3-4.

FIGURE 3-4
Chart of accounts

Taylor and Associates • Chart of Accounts

Assets (100–199)	Owner's Equity (300–399)
111 Cash	311 William Taylor, Capital
112 Accounts Receivable	312 William Taylor, Drawing
113 Office Supplies	
116 Office Equipment	**Revenue (400–499)**
117 Office Furniture	411 Service Revenue
Liabilities (200–299)	**Expenses (500–599)**
211 Accounts Payable	511 Rent Expense
	512 Repairs Expense

The numbering scheme used by Taylor and Associates is a three-digit, five-category plan, with the first digit indicating the category of account (1 = asset, 2 = liability, 3 = owner's equity, 4 = revenue, 5 = expenses), and the second and third digits indicating the position of the individual accounts within their particular classifications. Often a gap is left between account numbers so that new accounts can be added in the future at the appropriate place in the ledger.

Large business firms may use a four-digit or five-digit numbering plan. Additionally, the ledger may be divided into other categories of accounts.

The number of accounts needed by a business depends on the size of the business and the nature of its operations. Small businesses, such as Taylor and Associates, may need relatively few accounts. Large businesses, particularly manufacturing firms, could need hundreds (or thousands) of ledger accounts to provide a summary of operations.

The order of accounts in the ledger usually follows the order of accounts listed on the financial statements, with balance sheet accounts being shown first, followed by income statement accounts. Thus, the usual sequence of accounts in the ledger is *assets, liabilities, owner's equity, revenue,* and *expenses.*

The Four-Column Ledger Account Form

LEARNING OBJECTIVE 6

To this point, the ledger accounts we have worked with have consisted of T accounts and the standard form of account. The T account is a good tool for emphasizing the contrast between debit and credit entries, and some businesses use the standard form of account. However, most businesses use a more practical form of ledger account. This is the **four-column account form** or the **balance form of account**. Look closely at the four-column account form illustrated in Figure 3-5. Notice that there are four amount columns: (1) a *Debit* column, (2) a *Credit* column, (3) a *Debit Balance* column, and (4) a *Credit Balance* column. The debit and credit columns are used to enter debits and credits from the journal. The balance columns are used to enter the balance of the account after each posting.

FIGURE 3-5
The four-column account form

General Ledger						
Account						Account No.
Date	Item	P.R.	Debit	Credit	Balance	
					Debit	Credit

The advantages of the four-column account form include:

1. Only one Date column is needed.
2. You can easily see whether the balance of an account is a debit or a credit.
3. Since the four-column account form shows the balance of the account after each posting, the detail involved in footing and balancing the standard form of account is reduced. As a result, there is less chance of confusion and error when determining account balances.

Now, let's look at how Taylor and Associates' November transactions are posted to the ledger.

Posting Illustrated

LEARNING OBJECTIVE 4

We will first show the five-step process of posting the debit part of an entry and then the five-step process of posting the credit part of an entry. The five steps for posting the debit part of an entry (shown in Figure 3-6) are as follows:

❶ Record the date of the journal entry (Nov. 1, 20X1) in the Date column of the account.
❷ Record the amount of the journal entry ($10,000.00), without a dollar sign or decimal point, in the Debit column of the account.
❸ Record the code GJ (for General Journal) and the page number (1) of the journal in the P.R. (Posting Reference) column of the account. The purpose of this step is to be able to trace the entry back to the journal.
❹ Record the number of the Cash account (111) in the P.R. column of the journal. This step has two purposes: (1) it indicates that posting has been done, and (2) it indicates the account to which posting has been made. After steps 3 and 4 have been completed, a **cross-reference** will be provided between the journal and the ledger. This reference exists because the page number of the journal appears in the P.R. column of the Cash account, and the number of the Cash account appears in the P.R. column of the journal.
❺ Calculate the new balance of the account. You keep a running balance of the account. Since the account had no previous balance, the $10,000 posting becomes the balance. Had there been a previous balance, the posting would have been added to obtain the new balance. A credit posting would be subtracted because the Cash account normally has a debit balance.

FIGURE 3-6
Posting the debit part of an entry

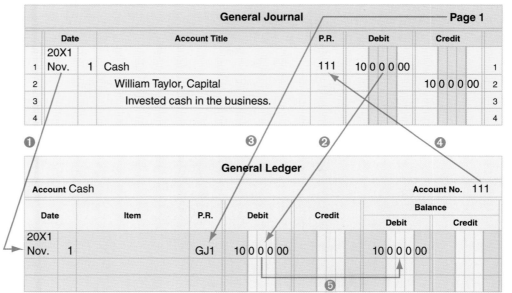

Posting the credit part of an entry is a similar five-step process, shown in Figure 3-7. The five steps for posting the credit part of an entry are as follows:

❶ Record the date of the journal entry (Nov. 1, 20X1) in the Date column of the account.
❷ Record the amount ($10,000.00) in the Credit column of the account.
❸ Record the code GJ1 in the P.R. column of the account.
❹ Record the number of the account (311) in the P.R. column of the journal.
❺ Calculate the new balance of the account.

FIGURE 3-7
Posting the credit part of an entry

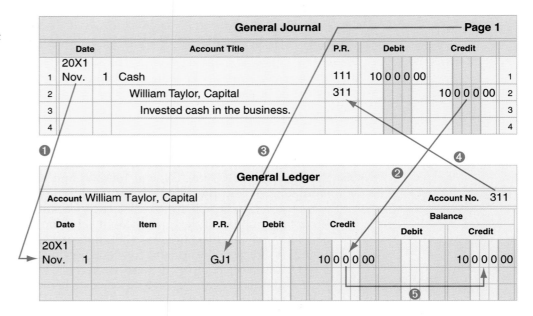

A similar procedure is followed in posting all entries to the ledger. Taylor and Associates' fully posted ledger is shown in Figure 3-8.

FIGURE 3-8
Fully posted ledger of Taylor and Associates

General Ledger								
Account Cash							Account No.	111
Date	Item	P.R.	Debit	Credit	Balance			
					Debit		Credit	
20X1 Nov. 1		GJ1	10 0 0 0 00		10 0 0 0 00			
9		GJ1		1 2 5 00	9 8 7 5 00			
12		GJ1		5 0 0 00	9 3 7 5 00			
15		GJ1		4 0 0 00	8 9 7 5 00			
17		GJ1		5 0 00	8 9 2 5 00			
18		GJ1	1 8 0 0 00		10 7 2 5 00			
27		GJ1		8 0 0 00	9 9 2 5 00			
29		GJ2	1 0 0 00		10 0 2 5 00			
30		GJ2		5 0 0 00	9 5 2 5 00			

Footings are not needed with the four-column account.

CONTINUES

FIGURE 3-8
Continued

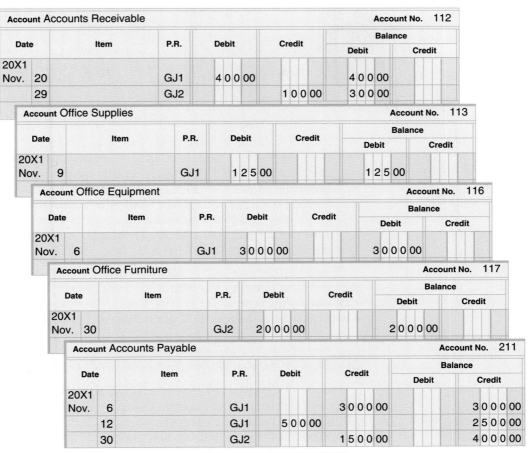

Account Accounts Receivable   **Account No.** 112

Date	Item	P.R.	Debit	Credit	Balance Debit	Balance Credit
20X1 Nov. 20		GJ1	400 00		400 00	
29		GJ2		100 00	300 00	

Account Office Supplies   **Account No.** 113

Date	Item	P.R.	Debit	Credit	Balance Debit	Balance Credit
20X1 Nov. 9		GJ1	125 00		125 00	

Account Office Equipment   **Account No.** 116

Date	Item	P.R.	Debit	Credit	Balance Debit	Balance Credit
20X1 Nov. 6		GJ1	3000 00		3000 00	

Account Office Furniture   **Account No.** 117

Date	Item	P.R.	Debit	Credit	Balance Debit	Balance Credit
20X1 Nov. 30		GJ2	2000 00		2000 00	

Account Accounts Payable   **Account No.** 211

Date	Item	P.R.	Debit	Credit	Balance Debit	Balance Credit
20X1 Nov. 6		GJ1		3000 00		3000 00
12		GJ1	500 00			2500 00
30		GJ2		1500 00		4000 00

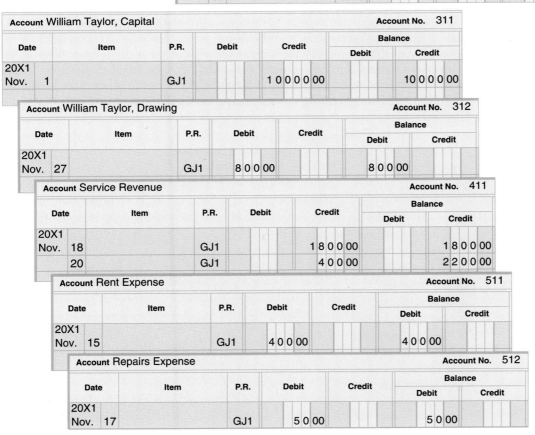

Account William Taylor, Capital   **Account No.** 311

Date	Item	P.R.	Debit	Credit	Balance Debit	Balance Credit
20X1 Nov. 1		GJ1		10000 00		10000 00

Account William Taylor, Drawing   **Account No.** 312

Date	Item	P.R.	Debit	Credit	Balance Debit	Balance Credit
20X1 Nov. 27		GJ1	800 00		800 00	

Account Service Revenue   **Account No.** 411

Date	Item	P.R.	Debit	Credit	Balance Debit	Balance Credit
20X1 Nov. 18		GJ1		1800 00		1800 00
20		GJ1		400 00		2200 00

Account Rent Expense   **Account No.** 511

Date	Item	P.R.	Debit	Credit	Balance Debit	Balance Credit
20X1 Nov. 15		GJ1	400 00		400 00	

Account Repairs Expense   **Account No.** 512

Date	Item	P.R.	Debit	Credit	Balance Debit	Balance Credit
20X1 Nov. 17		GJ1	50 00		50 00	

When calculating a new account balance, add debit postings to debit balances and subtract credit postings from debit balances. Likewise, add credit postings to and subtract debit postings from credit balances.

Note two matters of form in the fully posted ledger:
- As in the journal, the year (20X1) is written only at the top of the Date column, and the month (Nov.) is written only with the first posting of the month to an account. Entries after that are dated with just the number of the day, as on the second line of the Cash account.
- It was assumed that a second journal page was used to record the transactions of November 29 and 30. Thus, GJ2 was written in the P.R. columns of the accounts affected.

Since transactions are recorded first in the journal (the book of original entry) and then transferred to the ledger, the ledger is often referred to as the **book of final entry**. After the ledger is fully posted, the next step in the accounting cycle is to prepare a trial balance to check the equality of debits and credits in the ledger.

STEP 4: PREPARE A TRIAL BALANCE OF THE LEDGER

In Chapter 2, you learned how to test the equality of debits and credits in the ledger by preparing a trial balance. Using a journal for original entries, and then posting to the ledger, increases the importance of this test because two records, the journal and the ledger, are now involved. Preparing a trial balance is the fourth step in the accounting cycle.

LEARNING OBJECTIVE 5

As we explained in Chapter 2, the first step in preparing a trial balance is to find the balance of each account in the ledger. Since Taylor and Associates is using the balance form of account, all accounts were balanced at the time of posting. So, we just need to very carefully transfer the balances to the trial balance form, entering debit balances in one column and credit balances in the other. The November 30, 20X1, trial balance of Taylor and Associates is illustrated in Figure 3-9.

FIGURE 3-9
Trial balance of Taylor and Associates

Taylor and Associates Trial Balance November 30, 20X1				
Account Title		**Debit**	**Credit**
Cash		9 5 2 5 00	
Accounts Receivable		3 0 0 00	
Office Supplies		1 2 5 00	
Office Equipment		3 0 0 0 00	
Office Furniture		2 0 0 0 00	
Accounts Payable			4 0 0 0 00
William Taylor, Capital			10 0 0 0 00
William Taylor, Drawing		8 0 0 00	
Service Revenue			2 2 0 0 00
Rent Expense		4 0 0 00	
Repairs Expense		5 0 00	
Totals		16 2 0 0 00	16 2 0 0 00

REVIEW QUIZ
3-3

From the following list of account balances, use your knowledge of normal balances to prepare a trial balance for Lou's TV Repair Shop on December 31, 20XX. Place accounts in proper order.

Account	Balance
Accounts Payable	$ 7,210
Cash	1,400
Equipment	16,400
Lou Fisher, Capital	14,600
Lou Fisher, Drawing	700
Rent Expense	3,000
Repairs Expense	450
Revenue from Services	16,380
Salaries Expense	2,510
Supplies	3,860
Truck	9,400
Utilities Expense	470

CHECK YOUR ANSWER ON PAGE 107.

SUMMARY OF THE FIRST FOUR STEPS IN THE ACCOUNTING CYCLE

Now that we have discussed the trial balance, let's take a moment to review the first four steps in the *accounting cycle*, as shown in Figure 3-10.

FIGURE 3-10

The first four steps in the accounting cycle

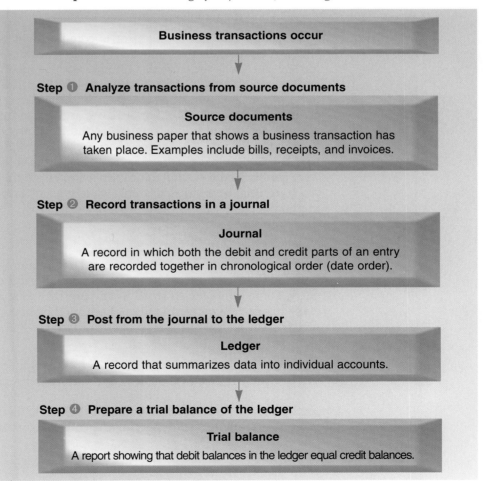

Business transactions occur

Step ❶ Analyze transactions from source documents

Source documents

Any business paper that shows a business transaction has taken place. Examples include bills, receipts, and invoices.

Step ❷ Record transactions in a journal

Journal

A record in which both the debit and credit parts of an entry are recorded together in chronological order (date order).

Step ❸ Post from the journal to the ledger

Ledger

A record that summarizes data into individual accounts.

Step ❹ Prepare a trial balance of the ledger

Trial balance

A report showing that debit balances in the ledger equal credit balances.

LOCATING AND CORRECTING ERRORS

LEARNING OBJECTIVE 7

Accountants and accounting students are all too familiar with the old saying, "To err is human . . .," because, without a doubt, errors will occasionally be made in recording journal entries and posting to the ledger. A good accounting system contains a built-in warning that certain types of errors have been made. That warning is an unbalanced trial balance. If the trial balance does not have equal debit and credit totals, there is an error somewhere in the records. That error can be a math error, a recording error, or a posting error. Each of these is discussed next.

Types of Errors

Math errors are simply errors in adding or subtracting. They are made when balancing accounts or when adding the columns of a trial balance. Math errors are so common that the first thing you should do if your trial balance does not balance is add the columns again.

Recording errors are errors made in journalizing, such as not recording equal debits and credits, or making debits or credits to the wrong account or for an incorrect amount.

Posting errors are errors made in the process of transferring figures from the journal to the ledger. Examples include the following:

- Posting a debit or a credit more than once.
- Posting a debit to the credit side of an account, or vice versa.
- Leaving out the posting of a debit or a credit.
- Posting the wrong amount.

The last type of posting error is common and includes transpositions and slides. A **transposition** is a reversal of digits, such as recording 87 for 78, or 123 for 132. A **slide** is the entry of a number with an incorrectly placed decimal point, such as recording 2,170 for 21,700, or 4,500 for 450. A quick way to check for either a transposition or a slide is to find the difference between the debit and credit column totals of the trial balance and divide this amount by 9. An answer without a remainder indicates that either a transposition or a slide *may* have been made. To find these types of errors, you carefully check all amounts on the trial balance against the ledger account balances to make sure that all balances were correctly copied, and you may need to check the ledger back to the journal.

It is important to determine what type of error has been made, for the method of correcting an error depends on its type.

Correcting an Error

Some errors are corrected by erasure, others by lining out the incorrect information and writing in the correct information, and still others by making a journal entry. Some errors are so small in amount that they are not worth the time and effort involved in correcting them. Each method of correction is described in this section as it relates to the type of error made.

MATH ERRORS

Math errors, if made in pencil, are corrected by erasing the wrong figure—whether it is a total or a footing—and writing the correct figure. If made in ink, math errors are corrected by lining out the wrong figure, initialing the correction (for future reference), and entering the correct figure in ink.

RECORDING ERRORS

How you correct a recording error depends on *when* you find the error. Recording errors discovered *before* posting can be corrected by lining out the incorrect information and entering the correct information. In the following entry, for example, the Utilities Expense account was incorrectly debited for the payment of salaries to employees. We can correct the error as follows.

	Date		Account Title	P.R.	Debit	Credit	
1	20XX Jun.	10	~~Utilities Expense~~ *Salaries Expense* *BSK*		4 0 0 00		1
2			Cash			4 0 0 00	2
3			Paid salaries of employees.				3

General Journal — Page 1

When an error has been made in recording an amount, draw a line through the incorrect amount and write the correct amount immediately above it. In the following entry, for example, a $225 purchase of store supplies was incorrectly recorded as $252.

	Date		Account Title	P.R.	Debit	Credit	
1	20X1 Apr.	8	Store Supplies		*B.D.* *2 2 5 00* ~~2 5 2 00~~		1
2			Cash			*B.D.* *2 2 5 00* ~~2 5 2 00~~	2
3			Purchased store supplies.				3

General Journal — Page 1

Some recording errors may not be discovered until after the error has been posted to the ledger. For example, assume that on June 9, 20X2, a $700 cash purchase of office supplies was incorrectly journalized as a debit to the Office Equipment account (instead of a debit to the Office Supplies account) and a credit to the Cash account. The entry was then posted. The error was then discovered on June 30 as a result of routine tracing of journal entries to the ledger. Since the error now appears in *both* the journal and the ledger, it should not be corrected by lining out the incorrect information and entering the correct information. Instead, you should make a **correcting entry**.

LEARNING OBJECTIVE 8

A good way to make a correcting entry is to set up T accounts both for the incorrect entry that was made and for the correct entry that should have been made. The two sets of T accounts can then be compared, and a proper correcting entry can be prepared. For example, for the recording error stated above, T accounts can be prepared as follows.

TRANSACTION, JUNE 9, 20X2: PURCHASED OFFICE SUPPLIES FOR CASH, $700

Incorrect entry that was made:

Office Equipment		Cash	
+	−	+	−
700			700

Entry that should have been made:

Office Supplies		Cash	
+	−	+	−
700			700

Now, by looking at the two sets of T accounts, we can see that only part of the entry is incorrect. The credit to the Cash account is correct. Therefore, an entry is needed to transfer $700 from the Office Equipment account to the Office Supplies account. The correcting entry follows.

	20X2						
1	Jun.	30	Office Supplies	7 0 0 00			1
2			Office Equipment		7 0 0 00		2
3			To correct error of June 9, in which				3
4			a purchase of office supplies was				4
5			debited to Office Equipment.				5
6							6

POSTING ERRORS

An amount that is correctly entered in the journal, but posted incorrectly to the ledger, can be corrected by drawing a line through the error and writing the correct figure above it. For example, on May 4, 20X1, a $600 receipt of cash for services performed was correctly journalized as a debit to Cash and a credit to Service Revenue. However, it was posted to the ledger as a debit to Cash for $600 and a credit to Service Revenue for $6,000. We can correct the Service Revenue account as follows.

Account Service Revenue						Account No.	411	
						Balance		
Date	Item	P.R.	Debit	Credit		Debit	Credit	
20X1				DH			DH	
May 4		GJ1		6 0 0 00			6 0 0 00	
				6 0 0 0 00			6 0 0 0 00	

As we just saw, you can line out an incorrect amount that has been posted to the correct account. But when a posting is made to the wrong account, you should make a correcting entry. For example, a $75 payment for a repair bill was journalized correctly as a debit to Repairs Expense and a credit to Cash. But the entry was posted as a debit to Rent Expense and a credit to Cash. The error can be corrected by the following entry.

	20X1						
1	Jan.	5	Repairs Expense	7 5 00			1
2			Rent Expense		7 5 00		2
3			To correct error in which Rent				3
4			Expense was debited for a repair.				4
5							5

Suppose the amount of the above error had been only $2. Would such a small correction be worth the time involved in making it? Probably not, but the answer is not a clear yes or no. If the amount of an error is deemed to be small and insignificant, a correction may not be made. On the other hand, if not making the correction would result in a misstatement of net income or financial position, a correction must be made. The accounting concept of **materiality** states that proper procedures must be strictly followed only for items and transactions whose values are significant enough to affect the business's financial statements.

Summary of Error Correction Procedures

We have discussed quite a few ways to correct the various types of errors. Let's pause and look at the summary shown in Figure 3-11.

FIGURE 3-11
Summary of correction procedures

Type of Error	Method of Correction
Math error made in pencil	Erasure
Math error made in pen	Line out the incorrect figure, initial, and enter the correct figure
Recording error discovered before posting	Line out incorrect information, initial, and enter correct information
Recording error that has been posted	Correcting entry
An incorrect amount posted to the correct account	Line out, initial, and enter the correct amount
A correct amount posted to the incorrect account	Correcting entry

Errors That Do Not Cause the Trial Balance to Be Out of Balance

Certain errors cause the trial balance to be out of balance. However, many types of errors will not result in the trial balance being out of balance. Examples of these types of errors include:

1. Failure to record a transaction.
2. Failure to post an entire entry to the ledger.
3. Posting the wrong amount to the debit *and* credit sides of the correct accounts.
4. Posting the debit (or credit) part of an entry to the wrong account, but to the correct side.
5. Recording a transaction twice.
6. Posting a transaction twice.

The point to remember is that a trial balance shows equality of debits and credits. It does not give you absolute certainty that no errors have been made—so work carefully.

Indicate how each of these errors will be corrected:

1. A cash purchase of equipment was recorded as a cash purchase of supplies. The entry has not been posted to the ledger.
2. A journal entry for $470 was posted as $47 in one of the accounts involved.
3. A cash payment of $50 for repairs expense was journalized as a debit to Rent Expense and a credit to Cash. The entry was then posted.
4. In a company with over $6,000,000 in annual sales, it was discovered that the purchase of a $6.40 book of stamps was debited to Advertising Expense, instead of to Postage Expense.

CHECK YOUR ANSWERS ON PAGE 107.

HOW CAN I KEEP UP WITH CURRENT EVENTS BY GETTING ON ACCOUNTING MAILING LISTS?

By getting on accounting mailing lists on the Internet, you can receive current information on tax laws, keep abreast of what's occurring in the accounting field, do research, get advice on accounting-related questions, and read monthly accounting periodicals.

When you subscribe to a listserver through e-mail, you receive a weekly or monthly subscription to select periodicals and articles. This is a way to keep up with the latest news in accounting and to have an ongoing discussion with others on important accounting topics. ANET, an educational accounting consortium, is a mailing service specifically designed for accountants. You can join these groups by sending an e-mail to *listproc@scu.edu.au* and including *"subscribe listname"* in the body of the message, where any of the following listnames appear:

Anews-L   A newsletter concentrating on news of journals, conferences, and other matters of interest to accountants.

AAES-L   American Accounting Association newsletter.

AAATC-L   American Accounting Association Teaching and Curriculum section.

Aacrdn-L   Accounting program accreditation.

AAccSys-L   Accounting information systems. Discusses all matters concerned with accounting information systems theory and practice.

AFinAcc-L   Discusses all aspects of financial accounting.

Astdnt-L   Enables student-to-student contact around the world.

For more information about accounting listservers check out the following sites:

http://www.csu.edu.au/anet/lists/AMGTACC-L/msg00025.html

http://www.asaenet.org/Sections/Finance/listserv.html

http://www.regent.edu/lawlib/lists/ll-t-tax.html

JOINING THE PIECES

THE FIRST FOUR STEPS IN THE ACCOUNTING CYCLE

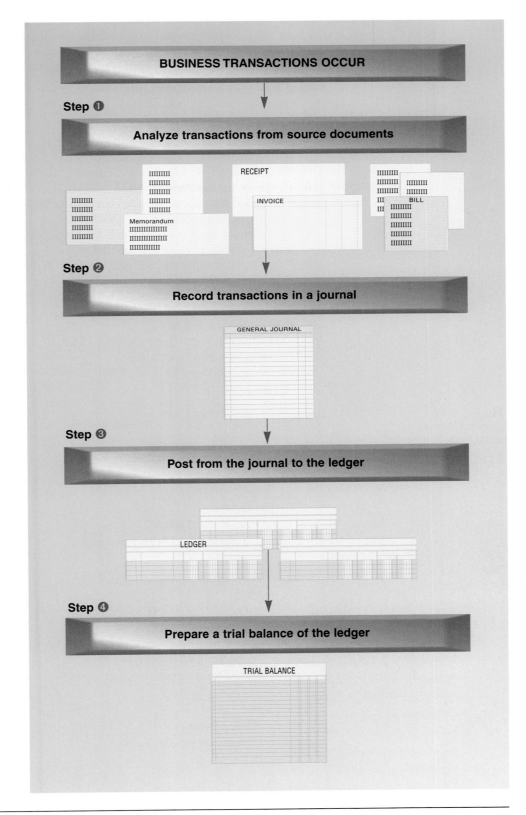

BUSINESS TRANSACTIONS OCCUR

Step ❶   **Analyze transactions from source documents**

RECEIPT

INVOICE

Memorandum

BILL

Step ❷   **Record transactions in a journal**

GENERAL JOURNAL

Step ❸   **Post from the journal to the ledger**

LEDGER

Step ❹   **Prepare a trial balance of the ledger**

TRIAL BALANCE

SUMMARY/RESTATEMENT OF LEARNING OBJECTIVES

1. Describe the standard form of a two-column journal.

The standard form of a two-column journal, or **general journal**, has numbered pages, beginning with page number 1. It contains a *Date* column, used to record the date on which a transaction occurs; an *Account Title* column, used to record the accounts affected by a transaction, as well as a brief description of the transaction; and a *P.R.* column, used to record the numbers of the accounts to which posting has been made. It also contains two money columns, labeled *Debit* and *Credit*, used to record the dollar amounts of transactions.

2. Record business transactions in a two-column journal.

Several business transactions and their journal recordings follow:

20XX

May 1 Peter Klaus started Peter's Furniture Repair, a furniture repair and refinishing business, by investing the following assets into the firm: cash, $5,000; supplies, $2,000; and equipment, $9,000.
   3 Paid rent for the month, $425.
   5 Purchased additional supplies on credit, $480.
   7 Performed services for cash, $990.
   9 Purchased a used pick-up truck for $8,500 by paying $1,000 down and signing a note payable for the difference.
   28 Paid for the supplies purchased on May 5, $480.
   29 Withdrew $600 cash for personal use.
   29 Performed services for cash, $1,075.
   30 Paid utility bill, $360.
   31 Paid telephone bill, $125.
   31 Paid salary of part-time employee, $450.
   31 Paid for repairs to truck, $30.
   31 Performed services for cash, $300.

FIGURE 3-12
General journal recordings

	Date		Account Title	P.R.	Debit	Credit	
	General Journal					**Page 1**	
1	20XX May	1	Cash		5 0 0 0 00		1
2			Supplies		2 0 0 0 00		2
3			Equipment		9 0 0 0 00		3
4			Peter Klaus, Capital			16 0 0 0 00	4
5			Invested assets in the business.				5
6							6
7		3	Rent Expense		4 2 5 00		7
8			Cash			4 2 5 00	8
9			Paid first month's rent.				9
10							10
11		5	Supplies		4 8 0 00		11
12			Accounts Payable			4 8 0 00	12
13			Purchased supplies on credit.				13
14							14
15		7	Cash		9 9 0 00		15
16			Service Revenue			9 9 0 00	16
17			Performed services for cash.				17
18							18

CONTINUES

FIGURE 3-12
Continued

19		9	Truck		8 5 0 0 00			19
20			Cash			1 0 0 0 00		20
21			Notes Payable			7 5 0 0 00		21
22			Purchased a truck, paying					22
23			$1,000 down.					23
24								24
25		28	Accounts Payable		4 8 0 00			25
26			Cash			4 8 0 00		26
27			Paid an account—May 5.					27
28								28
29		29	Peter Klaus, Drawing		6 0 0 00			29
30			Cash			6 0 0 00		30
31			Withdrew cash for personal use.					31
32								32
33		29	Cash		1 0 7 5 00			33
34			Service Revenue			1 0 7 5 00		34
35			Performed services for cash.					35
36								36
37								37
38								38

	General Journal					Page 2	
	Date	**Account Title**	**P.R.**	**Debit**		**Credit**	
1	20XX May 30	Utilities Expense		3 6 0 00			1
2		Cash				3 6 0 00	2
3		Paid utility bill.					3
4							4
5	31	Telephone Expense		1 2 5 00			5
6		Cash				1 2 5 00	6
7		Paid telephone bill.					7
8							8
9	31	Salaries Expense		4 5 0 00			9
10		Cash				4 5 0 00	10
11		Paid salary of employee.					11
12							12
13	31	Repairs Expense		3 0 00			13
14		Cash				3 0 00	14
15		Paid for repairs to truck.					15
16							16
17	31	Cash		3 0 0 00			17
18		Service Revenue				3 0 0 00	18
19		Performed services for cash.					19

3. Prepare a chart of accounts.

A **chart of accounts** for Peter's Furniture Repair is shown in Figure 3-13. The numbering scheme is the three-digit, five-category plan illustrated in the chapter.

FIGURE 3-13
*Chart of accounts
example*

Peter's Furniture Repair • Chart of Accounts

Assets	Owner's Equity	Expenses
111 Cash	311 Peter Klaus, Capital	511 Rent Expense
112 Supplies	312 Peter Klaus, Drawing	512 Salaries Expense
115 Equipment		513 Utilities Expense
116 Truck	**Revenue**	514 Telephone Expense
	411 Service Revenue	515 Repairs Expense
Liabilities		
211 Accounts Payable		
212 Notes Payable		

4. Post from a two-column journal to ledger accounts.

The journal entries recorded in Figure 3-12 by Peter Klaus are posted to the ledger as shown in Figure 3-14. Missing are P.R. marks in the journal, since there is little value in showing the journal again. Look closely at the Accounts Payable account, which shows how you should handle an account with a zero balance.

FIGURE 3-14
*Ledger posting
example*

General Ledger

Account Cash   **Account No. 111**

Date		Item	P.R.	Debit	Credit	Balance Debit	Balance Credit
20XX May	1		GJ1	5 0 0 0 00		5 0 0 0 00	
	3		GJ1		4 2 5 00	4 5 7 5 00	
	7		GJ1	9 9 0 00		5 5 6 5 00	
	9		GJ1		1 0 0 0 00	4 5 6 5 00	
	28		GJ1		4 8 0 00	4 0 8 5 00	
	29		GJ1		6 0 0 00	3 4 8 5 00	
	29		GJ1	1 0 7 5 00		4 5 6 0 00	
	30		GJ2		3 6 0 00	4 2 0 0 00	
	31		GJ2		1 2 5 00	4 0 7 5 00	
	31		GJ2		4 5 0 00	3 6 2 5 00	
	31		GJ2		3 0 00	3 5 9 5 00	
	31		GJ2	3 0 0 00		3 8 9 5 00	

Account Supplies   **Account No. 112**

Date		Item	P.R.	Debit	Credit	Balance Debit	Balance Credit
20XX May	1		GJ1	2 0 0 0 00		2 0 0 0 00	
	5		GJ1	4 8 0 00		2 4 8 0 00	

Account Equipment   **Account No. 115**

Date		Item	P.R.	Debit	Credit	Balance Debit	Balance Credit
20XX May	1		GJ1	9 0 0 0 00		9 0 0 0 00	

CONTINUES

FIGURE 3-14
Continued

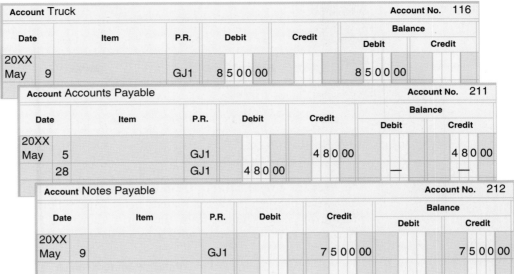

Account Truck   **Account No.** 116

Date	Item	P.R.	Debit	Credit	Balance Debit	Balance Credit
20XX May 9		GJ1	8 5 0 0 00		8 5 0 0 00	

Account Accounts Payable   **Account No.** 211

Date	Item	P.R.	Debit	Credit	Balance Debit	Balance Credit
20XX May 5		GJ1		4 8 0 00		4 8 0 00
28		GJ1	4 8 0 00		—	—

Account Notes Payable   **Account No.** 212

Date	Item	P.R.	Debit	Credit	Balance Debit	Balance Credit
20XX May 9		GJ1		7 5 0 0 00		7 5 0 0 00

Account Peter Klaus, Capital   **Account No.** 311

Date	Item	P.R.	Debit	Credit	Balance Debit	Balance Credit
20XX May 1		GJ1		16 0 0 0 00		16 0 0 0 00

Account Peter Klaus, Drawing   **Account No.** 312

Date	Item	P.R.	Debit	Credit	Balance Debit	Balance Credit
20XX May 29		GJ1	6 0 0 00		6 0 0 00	

Account Service Revenue   **Account No.** 411

Date	Item	P.R.	Debit	Credit	Balance Debit	Balance Credit
20XX May 7		GJ1		9 9 0 00		9 9 0 00
29		GJ1		1 0 7 5 00		2 0 6 5 00
31		GJ2		3 0 0 00		2 3 6 5 00

Account Rent Expense   **Account No.** 511

Date	Item	P.R.	Debit	Credit	Balance Debit	Balance Credit
20XX May 3		GJ1	4 2 5 00		4 2 5 00	

Account Salaries Expense   **Account No.** 512

Date	Item	P.R.	Debit	Credit	Balance Debit	Balance Credit
20XX May 31		GJ2	4 5 0 00		4 5 0 00	

Account Utilities Expense   **Account No.** 513

Date	Item	P.R.	Debit	Credit	Balance Debit	Balance Credit
20XX May 30		GJ2	3 6 0 00		3 6 0 00	

CONTINUES

FIGURE 3-14
Continued

Account Telephone Expense						Account No.	514
						Balance	
Date	Item	P.R.	Debit	Credit		Debit	Credit
20XX May 31		GJ2	1 2 5 00			1 2 5 00	

Account Repairs Expense						Account No.	515
						Balance	
Date	Item	P.R.	Debit	Credit		Debit	Credit
20XX May 31		GJ2	3 0 00			3 0 00	

5. Prepare a trial balance from a ledger after posting.

The trial balance for Peter Klaus's firm, Peter's Furniture Repair, is shown in Figure 3-15. It is taken from the ledger shown in Figure 3-14. Note that the Accounts Payable account, with a zero balance, is omitted.

FIGURE 3-15
Trial balance example

Peter's Furniture Repair Trial Balance May 31, 20XX		
Account Title	**Debit**	**Credit**
Cash	3 8 9 5 00	
Supplies	2 4 8 0 00	
Equipment	9 0 0 0 00	
Truck	8 5 0 0 00	
Notes Payable		7 5 0 0 00
Peter Klaus, Capital		16 0 0 0 00
Peter Klaus, Drawing	6 0 0 00	
Service Revenue		2 3 6 5 00
Rent Expense	4 2 5 00	
Salaries Expense	4 5 0 00	
Utilities Expense	3 6 0 00	
Telephone Expense	1 2 5 00	
Repairs Expense	3 0 00	
Totals	25 8 6 5 00	25 8 6 5 00

6. Describe the four-column ledger account form.

The **four-column ledger account**, like the standard form of account, has a debit and a credit column. However, the four-column account form also has *debit and credit balance columns* to maintain a continuous or running balance of the account. The four-column account form is widely used in practice.

7. Describe the procedures for locating and correcting errors in the accounting process.

The initial step in locating errors is to be aware that an error exists. The built-in warning that an error is present is an unbalanced trial balance. It is then necessary to determine the type of error that has been made.

A **math error** results from incorrect adding or subtracting. Thus, the first way to look for a math error is to add an unbalanced trial balance again. A **recording error** is one made in the journal. A **posting error** results from incorrect transfers of amounts from the journal to the ledger, or from the ledger to the trial balance. Typical posting errors include **transpositions** and **slides**, each of which can be detected by dividing the difference in trial balance totals by the number 9. If the division is without a remainder, either type of error is likely (but not definite).

Only errors made in pencil can be corrected by erasure. Math errors made in ink, recording errors that have not been posted, and errors made by posting an incorrect amount to the right account can be corrected by lining out the incorrect information, initialing, and entering the correct information. Recording errors that have been posted to the ledger and errors made by posting an amount to the wrong account are corrected by correcting entries. We will review **correcting entries** next.

8. Make entries to correct errors in the ledger.

The following two examples illustrate when correcting entries are needed.

Example 1: A $500 payment for a newspaper ad was correctly journalized as a debit to Advertising Expense and a credit to Cash. But when the entry was posted, the debit part of the entry was incorrectly posted to the Advertising Supplies account. We can correct this error as follows:

	20X1					
1	May	12	Advertising Expense	5 0 0 00		1
2			Advertising Supplies		5 0 0 00	2
3			To correct error in which a payment			3
4			for a newspaper ad had been			4
5			debited to Advertising Supplies.			5
6						6

Example 2: A $60 purchase of office supplies was journalized as a debit to Store Supplies and a credit to Cash. The entry was then posted. The error can be corrected by the following entry:

	20X4					
1	Jun.	25	Office Supplies	6 0 00		1
2			Store Supplies		6 0 00	2
3			To correct error in which a purchase			3
4			of office supplies had been debited			4
5			to Store Supplies.			5
6						6

KEY TERMS

accounting cycle The steps involved in the recording and summarizing processes of accounting.

balance form of account A ledger account form with four amount columns that many businesses prefer to use because the balance is always known and it is easy to see whether the balance is a debit or a credit. Also called the **four-column account form**.

book of final entry The ledger is referred to as the book of final entry because amounts are transferred (posted) to the ledger from the journal.

book of original entry The journal is referred to as the book of original entry because it is the first place in which transactions are formally recorded.

chart of accounts A directory or listing of accounts in the ledger.

compound entry An entry requiring three or more accounts.

correcting entry An entry used to correct certain types of errors in the ledger.

cross-reference A way of connecting a journal entry to its corresponding ledger entries so that the transaction can be traced back to its original entry or forward to its final entry.

general journal The basic form of journal that has two money columns.

journal A form in which transactions are recorded in chronological order (by order of date).

journalizing The process of recording transactions in a journal.

math errors Errors made in addition or subtraction.

posting The process of transferring amounts from the journal to the ledger.

posting errors Errors that result from incorrect transfers from the journal to an account or from the ledger to the trial balance.

principle of materiality States that proper accounting procedures have to be strictly followed only for events and transactions that would have an effect on a business's financial statements.

principle of objective evidence States that source documents should form the foundation for recording business transactions.

recording errors Errors made in journal entries.

slide An entry with an incorrectly placed decimal point, such as entering 100 for 1,000 or 24.50 for 245.

source documents Various types of business papers used as a basis for recording business transactions.

transposition The reversal of digits, such as entering 240 for 420.

CONCEPTS AND SKILLS REVIEW

CONCEPTS REVIEW

1. Why can it be difficult to determine the order in which transactions occurred using just a set of T accounts?
2. What are the first two steps in the accounting cycle?
3. Why is a journal called a book of original entry?
4. Describe the procedure for recording a compound entry in the journal.
5. What purpose is served by a chart of accounts?
6. What is the usual sequence of accounts in the ledger?
7. Using the five-category numbering plan shown in this chapter, indicate the first digit for each of the following accounts: (a) Accounts Payable; (b) Service Revenue; (c) William Brown, Drawing; (d) Store Equipment; and (e) Utilities Expense.
8. What is the third step in the accounting cycle?
9. What is the fourth step in posting either a debit or a credit from the journal to the ledger?
10. What is the fourth step in the accounting cycle?
11. Indicate whether each of the following errors is a math error, a recording error, or a posting error.
    a. A purchase of supplies for cash was entered in the journal as a debit to Equipment and a credit to Cash.
    b. A debit to Accounts Payable was correctly journalized for $950, but was posted as $590.
    c. A $500 debit to the Cash account was correctly posted, but the balance of the account was calculated incorrectly.
12. How would you correct each of the errors described in Question 11?
13. Give examples of a transposition and of a slide. Prove that the difference, in each, is evenly divisible by 9.
14. Give three examples of errors that *will not* prevent a trial balance from balancing.

EXERCISE 3-1

LEARNING OBJECTIVE 2

Objective: To record transactions in a general journal

Directions: The following transactions were incurred by Scott Service Company during October 20X1, its first month of operation. Record each of these transactions in a general journal. Use these accounts: Cash; Accounts Receivable; Supplies; Equipment; Accounts Payable; Julie Scott, Capital; Julie Scott, Drawing; Service Revenue; Salaries Expense; Rent Expense.

20X1
Oct. 1 Julie invested $13,000 in cash to start the business.
   2 Paid rent for the month, $550.
   4 Purchased supplies for cash, $575.
   8 Purchased equipment on credit, $3,100.
  10 Performed services for customers and received cash, $600.
  12 Purchased supplies on account, $400.
  15 Performed services for customers on account, $1,300.
  21 Withdrew cash for personal use, $900.
  27 Paid salaries for the month, $950.
  31 Paid $200 on the equipment purchased on October 8.

EXERCISE 3-2

LEARNING OBJECTIVE 2

Objective: To record compound journal entries

Directions: Each of the three situations presented in this exercise requires a compound journal entry. Record each in a general journal.

1. Jeff Olsom invested $8,000 cash and $16,000 worth of equipment in his business.
2. Purchased office supplies, $800, and store supplies, $900, on credit.
3. Purchased $18,500 worth of equipment, paying $3,000 down and owing the balance.

EXERCISE 3-3

LEARNING OBJECTIVE 2

Objective: To determine normal balances and increase sides of accounts

Directions: A list of 15 accounts follows. For each, indicate by check marks the normal balance and the increase side.

Account Title	Normal Balance		Increase Side	
	Dr.	Cr.	Dr.	Cr.
1. Supplies				
2. Owner, Drawing				
3. Accounts Receivable				
4. Truck				
5. Service Revenue				
6. Payroll Taxes Payable				
7. Owner, Capital				
8. Accounts Payable				
9. Miscellaneous Expense				
10. Office Equipment				
11. Rent Expense				
12. Fees Earned				
13. Cash				
14. Rental Revenue				
15. Utilities Expense				

EXERCISE 3-4

LEARNING OBJECTIVE 4

Objective: To post to the four-column account form

Directions: Open four-column ledger accounts for Cash, 111; Supplies, 112; Equipment, 115; Accounts Payable, 211; and Edgar Lester, Capital, 311. Post the following entries:

	Date		Account Title	P.R.	Debit	Credit	
1	20X1 Jul.	6	Cash		13 0 00 00		1
2			Supplies		1 8 00 00		2
3			Equipment		7 0 00 00		3
4			Edgar Lester, Capital			21 8 00 00	4
5			Invested assets to start the				5
6			business.				6
7							7
8		8	Equipment		10 5 00 00		8
9			Accounts Payable			10 5 00 00	9
10			Purchased additional equipment				10
11			on account.				11
12							12
13		9	Supplies		3 2 5 00		13
14			Cash			3 2 5 00	14
15			Purchased additional supplies				15
16			for cash.				16
17							17

General Journal — Page 1

EXERCISE 3-5

LEARNING OBJECTIVE 5

Objective: To prepare a trial balance from account balances

Directions: A list of alphabetized accounts and their balances follows. Prepare a trial balance in proper form for Marshall TV Repair as of June 30, 20X2.

Account	Balance
Accounts Payable	$ 6,390
Accounts Receivable	2,455
Building	62,000
Cash	9,300
Delivery Truck	9,700
Equipment	15,700
Sue Marshall, Capital	?
Sue Marshall, Drawing	1,600
Mortgage Note Payable	56,000
Rent Expense	5,600
Repairs Expense	2,210
Revenue from Services	32,745
Salaries Expense	17,500
Supplies	5,110
Utilities Expense	2,600

EXERCISE 3-6

LEARNING OBJECTIVE 8

Objective: To make correcting entries

Directions: Three situations requiring correcting entries follow. In each situation, record the correcting entry in a general journal.

1. A $700 purchase of office equipment for cash was recorded in the journal as a $700 purchase of store equipment for cash. The entry had already been posted when the error was discovered.
2. A $560 purchase of supplies on credit was recorded in the journal as a $650 purchase of supplies on credit. The entry was then posted.
3. A payment of $600 for the owner's home mortgage was debited to the Rent Expense account, and the entry was posted.

EXERCISE 3-7

LEARNING OBJECTIVE 7

Objective: To determine the effect of errors on the trial balance

Directions: Several errors are listed below. Considering each error individually, state whether the trial balance will balance or not.

1. A $500 debit to Rent Expense was posted to the debit side of Telephone Expense. The credit part of the entry was posted correctly.
2. A $700 payment for utilities was journalized correctly, but never posted.
3. A $60 payment for advertising was posted as a debit to Advertising Expense and a debit to Cash.
4. A $400 payment on account was posted twice to both accounts affected.
5. A $450 cash receipt from a customer on account was correctly journalized but was posted as a debit and a credit of $540.

CASE PROBLEMS

GROUP A

LEARNING OBJECTIVE 2

PROBLEM 3-1A

Objective: To record transactions in a general journal

Arturo Santiago's computer, stereo, and VCR repair shop opened on March 1, 20X2. During March, the following transactions occurred:

20X2
Mar. 1 Arturo invested $7,000 cash in his business.
1 Paid rent for the month, $450.
3 Purchased supplies for cash, $650.
5 Purchased equipment on credit, $3,800.
6 Made repairs and received cash, $210.
7 Made repairs on credit, $250.
15 Hired an assistant at a monthly salary of $900.
17 Invested an additional $2,000 in the business.
20 Purchased supplies on credit, $450.
22 Paid for advertising in a local newspaper, $95.
25 Made repairs and received cash, $775.
28 Paid gas and electric bills for the month, $350.
30 Collected the amount due from March 7.
31 Paid the salary due to the assistant hired on March 15.
31 Made repairs on credit, $295.
31 Paid telephone bill, $105.

Directions: Record these transactions in a general journal. Use these accounts: Cash; Accounts Receivable; Supplies; Equipment; Accounts Payable; Arturo Santiago, Capital; Arturo Santiago, Drawing; Repair Revenue; Rent Expense; Salaries Expense; Advertising Expense; Utilities Expense; and Telephone Expense.

PROBLEM 3-2A

Objective: To make entries, including compound entries, in a general journal

Charles Medlin's new business, Effective Career Planning, opened on April 1, 20X1. The following transactions occurred during the first month of operations:

20X1

Apr. 1 Charles invested the following assets in the business: cash, $3,200; office supplies, $400; and a word processor valued at $2,100.

   1 Paid rent for April, $550.

   3 Purchased additional office supplies, $500, and office equipment, $1,200, paying $600 down with the balance on account.

   7 Paid for repairs to equipment, $230.

   12 Invested an additional $1,600 cash and a car valued at $9,000 in the business.

   16 Paid utility bill for the month, $518.

   19 Paid salary of administrative assistant, $560.

   24 Hired a cleaning service to maintain the property, starting in May, at $750 a month.

   28 Withdrew office supplies for personal use, $175.

   30 Recorded fees earned and received for the month, $2,025.

Directions: Record these transactions in a general journal, using these accounts: Cash; Office Supplies; Office Equipment; Automobile; Accounts Payable; Charles Medlin, Capital; Charles Medlin, Drawing; Professional Fees; Rent Expense; Salaries Expense; Repairs Expense; and Utilities Expense.

PROBLEM 3-3A

Objective: To record transactions, post, and prepare a trial balance

On June 1, 20X2, Lori Lawson began an accounting practice called Lawson and Associates. During the first month of operations, the firm completed the following transactions:

20X2

Jun. 1 Lori invested the following assets in the firm: cash, $2,700; office supplies, $600; and office equipment, $16,500.

   1 Paid rent for the month, $775.

   3 Purchased office supplies for cash, $225.

   5 Purchased an executive desk and chair set, $2,700, paying $600 down and owing the balance.

   8 Received cash for accounting services performed, $3,200.

   11 Withdrew $200 cash for personal use.

   14 Performed accounting services on credit, $2,100.

   17 Paid the liability of June 5.

   20 Paid utilities for the month, $550.

   22 Paid $75 for repairs to equipment.

   25 Purchased additional office supplies for cash, $375.

   27 Discovered that $35 worth of the office supplies purchased on the 25th were of poor quality. The supplies were returned for a cash refund.

   29 Collected $1,300 of the amount due from June 14.

   30 Paid salaries for the month, $1,050.

   30 Paid telephone bill, $195.

   30 Paid miscellaneous expenses, $175.

Directions:

1. Open a ledger of four-column accounts for Lawson and Associates, using the following account titles and numbers: Cash, 111; Accounts Receivable, 112;

Office Supplies, 113; Office Equipment, 118; Accounts Payable, 211; Lori Lawson, Capital, 311; Lori Lawson, Drawing, 312; Accounting Fees Earned, 411; Rent Expense, 511; Salaries Expense, 512; Utilities Expense, 513; Telephone Expense, 514; Repairs Expense, 515; and Miscellaneous Expense, 516.

2. Record the transactions in a general journal.
3. Post the journal entries to the ledger.
4. Prepare a trial balance of the ledger as of June 30, 20X2.

LEARNING OBJECTIVE 8

PROBLEM 3-4A

Objective: To record correcting entries

During a routine audit, the following errors were discovered in the ledger of the Capital Company:

1. A $700 purchase of store supplies for cash was recorded as a purchase of office supplies for cash.
2. A $1,000 credit purchase of store supplies was recorded as a cash purchase.
3. The owner of the business, Joe Turner, used a company check to pay a personal utility bill of $95. The payment had been recorded and posted as a debit to Utilities Expense.
4. A $1,500 purchase of equipment on credit was recorded as $15,000 in both accounts affected.
5. A collection of $500 from credit customers was recorded as a debit to the Cash account and a credit to the Fees Earned account.

Directions: In two-column form, journalize a correcting entry for each of the five errors.

LEARNING OBJECTIVE 2, 4, 5

PROBLEM 3-5A

Objective: To record transactions, post, and prepare a trial balance for an established business

Following is the August 31, 20X1 trial balance of Allan Young, MD:

Allan Young, MD Trial Balance August 31, 20X1		
Account Title	Debit	Credit
111 Cash	10 0 0 0 00	
112 Accounts Receivable	3 0 0 0 00	
113 Office Supplies	2 0 0 0 00	
114 Medical Supplies	3 0 0 0 00	
117 Office Equipment	9 0 0 0 00	
118 Medical Equipment	10 7 0 0 00	
211 Accounts Payable		1 5 0 0 00
311 Allan Young, Capital		25 5 0 0 00
312 Allan Young, Drawing	35 9 0 0 00	
411 Medical Fees Earned		80 8 0 0 00
511 Salaries Expense	23 5 0 0 00	
512 Rent Expense	6 0 0 0 00	
513 Utilities Expense	3 5 0 0 00	
514 Laboratory Fees Expense	1 0 0 0 00	
515 Miscellaneous Expense	2 0 0 00	
Totals	107 8 0 0 00	107 8 0 0 00

Dr. Young completed the following transactions during September:

20X1

Sep. 1 Paid office rent for the month, $1,050.
2 Purchased office equipment on account, $7,000.
3 Collected $2,000 of the amount due from credit patients.
4 Purchased office supplies on account, $700.
6 Paid cash for medical supplies, $1,300.
7 Paid cash for laboratory analysis, $365.
9 Paid salaries of employees, $1,600.
11 Paid cash to creditors on account, $2,100.
12 Paid miscellaneous expenses, $400.
15 Recorded amount received from cash patients, $5,250.
15 Purchased medical equipment on account, $10,000.
17 Discovered that part of the equipment purchased on the 15th had dents and scratches. The seller of the equipment agreed to a price reduction of $1,000.
21 Recorded charges to credit patients, $4,750.
25 Paid cash from the business bank account for a personal bill, $445.
28 Paid electric bill, $2,300.
29 Paid water bill, $65.
29 Paid to have carpet cleaned in the reception room, $190.
30 Paid salaries of employees, $1,600.
30 Paid cash for laboratory analysis, $290.

Directions:

1. Open a four-column account for each account listed in Dr. Young's trial balance. Enter the balances in his accounts, dating them September 1, 20X1, writing the word Balance in the Item column, and placing a check mark (✓) in the P.R. column, as illustrated here for the Cash account.

Account Cash						Account No.	111	
Date	Item	P.R.	Debit	Credit	Balance			
					Debit		Credit	
20X1 Sep. 1	Balance	✓			10 0 0 0 00			

2. Record the September transactions in a two-column journal beginning on page 17.
3. Post the journal entries to the ledger.
4. Prepare a trial balance as of September 30, 20X1.

GROUP B

LEARNING OBJECTIVE 2

PROBLEM 3-1B

Objective: To record transactions in a general journal

Nancy Elsberry's watch and jewelry repair shop opened on May 1, 20X2. During May, the following transactions occurred:

20X2

May 1 Nancy invested $7,500 cash in her business.
1 Paid rent for the month, $500.
3 Purchased supplies for cash, $600.
5 Purchased equipment on credit, $4,100.
6 Made repairs and received cash, $335.

May 7 Made repairs on credit, $390.
  15 Hired an assistant at a monthly salary of $850.
  17 Invested an additional $2,200 in the business.
  20 Purchased supplies on credit, $475.
  22 Paid for advertising in a local newspaper, $105.
  25 Made repairs and received cash, $400.
  28 Paid gas and electric bills for the month, $480.
  30 Collected the amount due from May 7.
  31 Paid the salary due to the assistant hired on May 15.
  31 Made repairs on credit, $305.
  31 Paid telephone bill, $108.

Directions: Record these transactions in a general journal. Use these accounts: Cash; Accounts Receivable; Supplies; Equipment; Accounts Payable; Nancy Elsberry, Capital; Nancy Elsberry, Drawing; Repair Revenue; Rent Expense; Salaries Expense; Advertising Expense; Utilities Expense; and Telephone Expense.

LEARNING OBJECTIVE 2

PROBLEM 3-2B

Objective: To make entries, including compound entries, in a general journal

Thomas Workman's new business, Best Exterminators, opened on November 1, 20X1. The following transactions occurred during the first month of operations:

20X1
Nov. 1 Thomas invested the following assets in the business: cash, $4,200; office supplies, $450; and a word processor valued at $2,200.
  1 Paid rent for November, $600.
  3 Purchased additional office supplies, $600, and office equipment, $1,300, paying $800 down with the balance on account.
  7 Paid for repairs to equipment, $245.
  12 Invested an additional $1,700 cash and a car valued at $11,000 in the business.
  16 Paid utility bill for the month, $427.
  19 Paid salary of administrative assistant, $580.
  24 Hired a cleaning service to maintain the property, starting in December, at $650 a month.
  28 Withdrew office supplies for personal use, $180.
  30 Recorded fees earned and received for the month, $2,725.

Directions: Record these transactions in a general journal, using these accounts: Cash; Office Supplies; Office Equipment; Automobile; Accounts Payable; Thomas Workman, Capital; Thomas Workman, Drawing; Professional Fees; Rent Expense; Salaries Expense; Repairs Expense; and Utilities Expense.

LEARNING OBJECTIVE 2, 4, 5

PROBLEM 3-3B

Objective: To record transactions, post, and prepare a trial balance

On January 2, 20X1, Angelique Chung began an income tax preparation firm called Chung and Associates. During the first month of operations, the firm completed the following transactions:

20X1
Jan. 2 Angelique invested the following assets in the firm: cash, $2,900; office supplies, $550; and office equipment, $15,500.
  2 Paid rent for the month, $675.
  3 Purchased office supplies for cash, $230.

Jan. 5 Purchased an executive desk and chair set, $3,200, paying $800 down and owing the balance.
  8 Received cash for accounting services performed, $3,300.
 11 Withdrew $250 cash for personal use.
 14 Performed accounting services on credit, $2,250.
 17 Paid the liability of January 5.
 20 Paid utilities for the month, $600.
 22 Paid $65 for repairs to equipment.
 25 Purchased additional office supplies for cash, $400.
 27 Discovered that $45 worth of the office supplies purchased on the 25th were of poor quality. The supplies were returned for a cash refund.
 29 Collected $1,200 of the amount due from January 14.
 30 Paid salaries for the month, $1,100.
 31 Paid telephone bill, $224.
 31 Paid miscellaneous expenses, $185.

Directions:

1. Open a ledger of four-column accounts for Chung and Associates, using the following account titles and numbers: Cash, 111; Accounts Receivable, 112; Office Supplies, 113; Office Equipment, 118; Accounts Payable, 211; Angelique Chung, Capital, 311; Angelique Chung, Drawing, 312; Accounting Fees Earned, 411; Rent Expense, 511; Salaries Expense, 512; Utilities Expense, 513; Telephone Expense, 514; Repairs Expense, 515; and Miscellaneous Expense, 516.
2. Record the transactions in a general journal.
3. Post the journal entries to the ledger.
4. Prepare a trial balance of the ledger as of January 31, 20X1.

LEARNING OBJECTIVE 8

PROBLEM 3-4B

Objective: To record correcting entries

During a routine audit, the following errors were discovered in the ledger of the Swanson Company:

1. A $950 purchase of store supplies for cash was recorded as a purchase of office supplies for cash.
2. A $1,300 credit purchase of store supplies was recorded as a cash purchase.
3. The owner of the business, Jan Hopkins, used a company check to pay a personal utility bill of $180. The payment had been recorded and posted as a debit to Utilities Expense.
4. A $1,600 purchase of equipment on credit was recorded as $16,000 in both accounts affected.
5. A collection of $700 from credit customers was recorded as a debit to the Cash account and a credit to the Fees Earned account.

Directions: In two-column form, journalize a correcting entry for each of the five errors.

LEARNING OBJECTIVE 2, 4, 5

PROBLEM 3-5B

Objective: To record transactions, post, and prepare a trial balance for an established business

Following is the October 31, 20X1 trial balance of Michelle Parker, MD:

	Michelle Parker, MD Trial Balance October 31, 20X1		
Account Title		**Debit**	**Credit**
111	Cash	12 0 00 00	
112	Accounts Receivable	3 0 00 00	
113	Office Supplies	3 0 00 00	
114	Medical Supplies	4 0 00 00	
117	Office Equipment	8 5 00 00	
118	Medical Equipment	20 0 00 00	
211	Accounts Payable		2 5 00 00
311	Michelle Parker, Capital		28 0 00 00
312	Michelle Parker, Drawing	32 6 00 00	
411	Medical Fees Earned		88 6 00 00
511	Salaries Expense	24 3 00 00	
512	Rent Expense	5 5 00 00	
513	Utilities Expense	4 0 00 00	
514	Laboratory Fees Expense	1 4 00 00	
515	Miscellaneous Expense	8 00 00	
	Totals	119 1 00 00	119 1 00 00

Dr. Parker completed the following transactions during November:

20X1

Nov. 1 Paid office rent for the month, $1,075.
2 Purchased office equipment on account, $7,800.
3 Collected $2,500 of the amount due from credit patients.
4 Purchased office supplies on account, $650.
6 Paid cash for medical supplies, $1,350.
7 Paid cash for laboratory analysis, $400.
9 Paid salaries of employees, $1,900.
11 Paid cash to creditors on account, $2,600.
12 Paid miscellaneous expenses, $390.
15 Recorded amount received from cash patients, $9,000.
15 Purchased medical equipment on account, $5,205.
17 Discovered that part of the equipment purchased on the 15th had scratches and dents. The seller of the equipment agreed to a price reduction of $900.
21 Recorded charges to credit patients, $4,550.
25 Paid cash from the business bank account for a personal bill, $450.
28 Paid electric bill, $2,500.
29 Paid water bill, $75.
29 Paid to have carpet cleaned in the reception room, $290.
30 Paid salaries of employees, $1,900.
30 Paid cash for laboratory analysis, $305.

Directions:
1. Open a four-column account for each account listed in Dr. Parker's trial balance. Enter the balances in her accounts, dating them November 1, 20X1, writing the word Balance in the Item column, and placing a check mark (✓) in the P.R. column, as illustrated on the next page for the Cash account.

Account Cash						Account No. 111	
Date	Item	P.R.	Debit	Credit	Balance		
					Debit	Credit	
20X1 Nov. 1	Balance	✓			12 0 0 0 00		

2. Record the November transactions in a two-column journal beginning on page 17.
3. Post the journal entries to the ledger.
4. Prepare a trial balance as of November 30, 20X1.

CHALLENGE PROBLEMS

PROBLEM SOLVING

The Georgian Theater is a Victorian-style theater that operated profitably for many years. In recent years, however, it had started to lose money due to intense competition from several multiscreen theaters that had opened in the area. The original owner made several unsuccessful attempts to sell the theater while it was still in operation. Finally, it was closed on January 14, 20X0, and has been vacant since. On April 2, 20X2, Jay Richards entered into a contract with the owner to purchase and restore the theater. He completed the following transactions during April:

20X2
Apr. 2 Jay transferred the balance of his savings account, $12,000, to a bank account for the business.

3 Using the value of his home as security, Jay borrowed $45,000 from a local bank by signing a 5-year note payable.

4 Purchased the Georgian Theater for $175,000, paying $30,000 down with the balance on a 30-year mortgage note payable. Assets of the purchase are allocated as follows: building, $100,000; land, $40,000; projection equipment, $20,000; concession equipment, $15,000.

5 Purchased office equipment on account, $6,000.

5 Entered into a contract with a food vending company to run the concession stand. The contract calls for the concessionaire to pay rent of 10% of the monthly concession sales, with a minimum of $500, which was collected in advance.

5 Purchased office supplies for cash, $245.

6 Paid $2,000 to have all seats and carpets steam cleaned.

6 Paid for a full-page ad in a local newspaper, $900.

7 Opened the theater to the public by offering a free showing.

9 Paid for advertising leaflets, $300.

10 Paid miscellaneous expenses, $225.

12 Cash received from admissions for the week, $4,500.

15 Paid semimonthly wages, $2,540.

17 Purchased office supplies on account, $75.

19 Cash received from admissions for the week, $6,500.

21 Returned a defective printer ribbon (from the April 17 purchase) and received a credit of $12.

21 Purchased six video machines for use in the lobby, $24,500, paying $5,000 down with the balance on account.

23 Paid a personal bill using the business bank account, $40.

27 Cash received from admissions for the week, $7,200.

Apr. 28   Paid water bill, $120.
        29   Paid electricity bill, $2,500.
        29   Paid telephone bill, $95.
        30   Paid film rental expense for the month, $5,500.
        30   Cash received from video machines, $590.
        30   Paid creditors on account, $1,000.
        30   Cash received from admissions for the last three days in the month, $3,600.
        30   Made first payment to the bank for the loan of April 3, $475.
        30   The concessionaire reported sales for the month of $10,500.

Directions: On May 1, you were hired as bookkeeper for the theater. By carefully going through each April transaction, you are to:

1. Develop a complete chart of accounts using a three-digit, five-category plan.
2. Develop a ledger by opening an account for each account title you listed in the chart of accounts.
3. Record the April transactions in a general journal.
4. Post the journal entries to the ledger.
5. Prepare a trial balance as of April 30, 20X2.
6. Prepare an income statement for the month ending April 30, as Jay is very eager to see how well the business did during its first month of operations.

COMMUNICATIONS

Bill Vines, who owns a small business, is taking an accounting course to help him manage his business. After studying the general journal, Bill is wondering if he should set up his books using a journal and a ledger. He reasons that since his business is small, he can just set up ledger accounts and enter his transactions directly into the ledger.

Explain to him in writing why a better accounting system uses both a journal and a ledger.

ETHICS

Jason Walker runs a computer repair service. He has not been very thorough in keeping records of transactions to use as the basis for journal entries, but he is interested in trying to be accurate in what he records. Thus, he asks you, a current student of accounting, to look over his records and give your opinion about the system that he is using.

You immediately find an entry in his journal for the receipt of cash for services performed in the amount of $250, but you find no document to support the entry. When you ask Jason about it, he replies, "That's how I remember it."

Write a brief explanation of what Jason is doing wrong. What accounting principle is he violating and why is he violating it?

REVIEW QUIZ 3-1

	Date		Account Title	P.R.	Debit	Credit	
			General Journal			**Page 1**	
1	20XX Mar.	1	Cash		7 0 0 0 00		1
2			Judy Baxter, Capital			7 0 0 0 00	2
3							3
4		4	Supplies		7 5 0 00		4
5			Accounts Payable			7 5 0 00	5
6							6
7		6	Equipment		4 7 5 00		7
8			Cash			4 7 5 00	8
9							9
10		9	Accounts Payable		3 7 5 00		10
11			Cash			3 7 5 00	11
12							12
13							13

REVIEW QUIZ 3-2

	Date		Account Title	P.R.	Debit	Credit	
1	20X1 Jun.	12	Utilities Expense		1 4 5 00		1
2			Cash			1 4 5 00	2
3							3
4		17	Kyle King, Drawing		1 7 5 00		4
5			Cash			1 7 5 00	5
6							6
7		22	Cash		9 5 0 00		7
8			Service Revenue			9 5 0 00	8
9							9
10		25	Office Supplies		7 5 00		10
11			Truck		4 0 0 0 00		11
12			Kyle King, Capital			4 0 7 5 00	12
13							13
14							14

REVIEW QUIZ 3-3

Lou's TV Repair Shop
Trial Balance
December 31, 20XX

Account Title	Debit	Credit
Cash	1 4 0 0 00	
Supplies	3 8 6 0 00	
Equipment	16 4 0 0 00	
Truck	9 4 0 0 00	
Accounts Payable		7 2 1 0 00
Lou Fisher, Capital		14 6 0 0 00
Lou Fisher, Drawing	7 0 0 00	
Revenue from Services		16 3 8 0 00
Rent Expense	3 0 0 0 00	
Salaries Expense	2 5 1 0 00	
Utilities Expense	4 7 0 00	
Repairs Expense	4 5 0 00	
Totals	38 1 9 0 00	38 1 9 0 00

REVIEW QUIZ 3-4

1. By lining out the title Supplies in the journal and writing the title Equipment above it.
2. By lining out $47 in the ledger account and writing $470 above it.
3. By making the following correcting entry:

1	Repairs Expense	5 0 00		1
2	Rent Expense		5 0 00	2

4. The error could be corrected by the following correcting entry:

1	Postage Expense	6 40		1
2	Advertising Expense		6 40	2

Due to the small amount of this error, however, it may not be corrected, since it would not significantly affect the company's net income figure.

LEARNING OBJECTIVES

After studying Chapter 4, you will be able to:
1. Explain the need for adjusting entries.
2. Make adjusting entries for supplies used, expired insurance, depreciation, and unpaid wages.
3. Complete a work sheet for a service business.
4. Prepare financial statements from a work sheet.
5. Journalize adjusting entries.

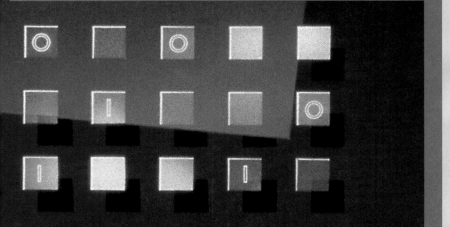

4

THE ACCOUNTING

CYCLE

CONTINUED

Work Sheet, Financial Statements, and Adjusting Entries

Chapter 4 continues with the next four steps in the accounting cycle. This chapter introduces the work sheet as a means of organizing data into a logical form for the preparation of financial statements. The work sheet may be prepared in pencil, and the accountant is usually the only one to see the work sheet. For this reason, the work sheet has been described as the accountant's scratch pad.

If you use a computerized accounting system, the computer prepares the financial statements automatically. Therefore, with a computerized accounting system, a work sheet is not necessary. Even in a computerized accounting system, the accountant must still analyze whether the account balances are current and accurate and determine whether adjusting entries are needed.

— Fred R. Jex, CPA, MBA, Ph.D.
Macomb Community College

Having met the objectives of the first three chapters, you can now (1) use source documents as a basis for recording business transactions, (2) record business transactions in a general journal, (3) post journal entries to a ledger, and (4) take a trial balance of the ledger. In other words, you have learned the first four steps in the accounting cycle. As you will recall, the accounting cycle represents the steps involved in the recording and summarizing processes of accounting.

In Chapter 4, we will study the next four steps in the accounting cycle for a service business:

❺ Determine needed adjustments.
❻ Prepare a work sheet.
❼ Prepare financial statements from a completed work sheet.
❽ Journalize and post adjusting entries.

In Chapter 3, we recorded the November 20X1 transactions of Taylor and Associates in a two-column general journal. After the journal was posted, we took a trial balance of the ledger on November 30. We now look again at the books of Taylor and Associates. It is now December 31, one month later. Many of Taylor and Associates' November transactions (such as the payment of rent and utilities) occurred again in December. Several new transactions also took place in December. One of the December transactions, on December 1, involved payment of cash for a one-year insurance policy, which Mr. Taylor felt he needed to protect his assets. A **premium** (fee) of $240 was paid for this policy, to run from December 1, 20X1 to November 30, 20X2.

Insurance paid in advance can be debited to an asset account entitled Prepaid Insurance, which Mr. Taylor added to his chart of accounts and ledger as account number 114. The following journal entry was made to record the prepayment.

	Date		Account Title	P.R.	Debit	Credit	
			General Journal			**Page 2**	
1	20X1 Dec.	1	Prepaid Insurance	114	2 4 0 00		1
2			Cash	111		2 4 0 00	2
3			Paid insurance premium for one year.				3

Prepaid Insurance	
Debit	Credit
+	−

Remember from Chapter 1 that an asset is any item with money value that the business owns. Insurance paid in advance represents a service that will benefit the business in the future. It is owned and has money value; thus, it is considered an asset.

110   *Paradigm College Accounting* • Chapter 4

Another December event was the hiring of an assistant, Jan Curtis, at a weekly salary of $350. Jan started work on Monday, December 8, and is paid every Friday. Jan's salary will be recorded in an expense account entitled Salaries Expense, which was added to the chart of accounts and ledger as account number 513. This account was debited for $350 on December 12, 19, and 26 for a total of $1,050. On December 31, after all December transactions were recorded and posted, the trial balance shown in Figure 4-1 was prepared.

FIGURE 4-1
Trial balance for Taylor and Associates

Taylor and Associates Trial Balance December 31, 20X1		
Account Title	**Debit**	**Credit**
Cash	8 4 8 5 00	
Accounts Receivable	3 0 0 00	
Office Supplies	2 7 5 00	
Prepaid Insurance	2 4 0 00	
Office Equipment	3 0 0 0 00	
Office Furniture	2 0 0 0 00	
Accounts Payable		3 0 0 0 00
William Taylor, Capital		10 0 0 0 00
William Taylor, Drawing	1 5 0 0 00	
Service Revenue		4 7 0 0 00
Rent Expense	8 0 0 00	
Repairs Expense	5 0 00	
Salaries Expense	1 0 5 0 00	
Totals	17 7 0 0 00	17 7 0 0 00

Now that we know where Taylor and Associates stands at the end of December, it is time for us to look at the next step in the accounting cycle.

STEP 5: DETERMINE NEEDED ADJUSTMENTS

LEARNING OBJECTIVE 1   As we have seen, much of the accounting process involves recording the day-to-day business transactions. Some transactions, however, are not recorded by routine accounting entries. This is not due to error or lack of attention, but is a result of changes in the nature of certain accounts brought about by the passage of time.

For example, the Office Supplies account shows the value of office supplies purchased for use in the business. But office supplies are used constantly in the daily operation of most businesses. Practically every minute, office workers use such items as postage stamps, computer paper, pens, stationery, and paper clips. It would be totally impractical to try to keep up with these items as they are used. Consequently, no regular journal entry is made to record the value of office supplies consumed on a daily basis. Thus, as time passes, the balance of the Office Supplies account does not show the true value of office supplies still on hand.

To illustrate this, let's look again at Taylor and Associates' December 31 trial balance in Figure 4-1. The Office Supplies account shows a balance of $275, which is the result of purchases of office supplies during November and December. On December 31, this balance does not represent the value of office supplies on hand, because some supplies have been used during the past two months. Thus, the Office Supplies account needs to be *adjusted* to reflect the value of supplies used.

The Accounting Cycle Continued

Adjusting entries are made at the end of an accounting period to bring certain accounts up-to-date. Adjusting entries are referred to as **internal transactions** because they do not involve parties outside the business. Taylor and Associates determined that adjustments for the following items were needed as of December 31, 20X1: (1) supplies used, (2) insurance expired, (3) depreciation of office equipment and office furniture, and (4) unpaid salaries.

Supplies Used

LEARNING OBJECTIVE 2

As we stated earlier, the Office Supplies account of Taylor and Associates shows a $275 balance as of December 31. On December 31, Mr. Taylor took an inventory and found $230 worth of office supplies actually left on hand. The amount that should be shown in the Office Supplies account is thus $230; the difference ($275 – $230 = $45) has been used, as shown here:

Amount had	$275	(balance of account)
– Amount left	– 230	(inventory count on December 31)
Amount used	$ 45	(amount used during the period)

The portion of an asset that has been used no longer provides a future benefit to the business; *it becomes an expense*. As a result, we need to take the amount of office supplies used, $45, out of the Office Supplies account and put it into an expense account entitled Office Supplies Expense. Mr. Taylor added this account to the chart of accounts and ledger as account number 514.

Increases in expense accounts are recorded as *debits*, and decreases in asset accounts are recorded as *credits*. Therefore, the entry to adjust the Office Supplies account involves a debit to the Office Supplies Expense account and a credit to the Office Supplies account, as shown below.

Office Supplies Expense	514		Office Supplies	113
+	–		+	–
Adjusting 45			Balance 275	Adjusting 45
			New Balance 230	

Notice that Office Supplies now has a balance of $230, which is equal to the amount of office supplies on hand as of December 31. Thus, this account is up-to-date.

Insurance Expired

As we said earlier, insurance paid in advance is considered to be an asset. As time passes, however, the prepayment gradually expires, and the asset becomes an expense.

On December 31, Mr. Taylor's Prepaid Insurance account shows a balance of $240, which represents a one-year premium paid in advance on December 1. At December 31, one month of the premium has expired, which amounts to $20, as shown below:

$$\frac{\text{Amount of prepayment}}{\text{Number of months prepaid}} = \frac{\$240}{12} = \$20 \text{ per month}$$

The adjusting entry for expired insurance involves transferring the amount that has expired, $20, from the Prepaid Insurance account to the Insurance Expense account, as we see below.

Insurance Expense	515		Prepaid Insurance	114
+	–		+	–
Adjusting 20			Balance 240	Adjusting 20
			New Balance 220	

The Prepaid Insurance account now has a balance of $220, which is the unexpired portion of the premium—the portion that is still an asset.

Depreciation of Office Equipment and Office Furniture

In addition to Office Supplies and Prepaid Insurance, Mr. Taylor's trial balance shows two other assets that need adjusting: Office Equipment and Office Furniture. These assets are referred to as *long-term*, because they are expected to remain useful for several years. As time passes, however, the usefulness of the assets will decline, and eventually they will no longer serve their original purpose. The accounting system must, therefore, reflect the fact that the equipment and furniture will gradually wear out or become obsolete and will have to be replaced.

Depreciation is the term used to describe the expense that results from the loss in usefulness of an asset due to age, wear and tear, and obsolescence. The purpose of depreciation accounting is to spread the cost of an asset over its useful life, rather than treating the asset's cost as an expense in the year it was purchased. In other words, part of the cost of a depreciable asset should be transferred to an expense account during each period the asset is used in producing revenue.

Since it is difficult to determine exactly how long an asset will last, the amount calculated for depreciation is an estimate. On December 31, Mr. Taylor has used his office equipment for two months and his office furniture for one month. Depreciation for the time each was used should be estimated and recorded. There are several acceptable ways to calculate depreciation. Mr. Taylor uses the **straight-line method**, which is a very popular method that yields the same amount of depreciation for each full period an asset is used. Under the straight-line method, the cost of an asset, less any estimated trade-in value, is divided by the number of years the asset is estimated to remain useful, as shown here:

$$\frac{\text{Cost of asset} - \text{Trade-in value}}{\text{Estimated years of usefulness}} = \text{Annual depreciation expense}$$

Mr. Taylor estimates that his $3,000 of office equipment will last for ten years and his $2,000 of office furniture will last for five years. Further, he estimates that the office equipment will not have a trade-in value at the end of its useful life, but that the office furniture will be worth $200. Using these factors, we can calculate Taylor's estimated depreciation expense for 20X1 as follows:

❶ Office Equipment (used for two months in 20X1):

$$\frac{\text{Cost of asset} - \text{Trade-in value}}{\text{Estimated years of usefulness}} = \frac{\$3,000 - \$0}{10 \text{ years}} = \frac{\$3,000}{10} = \$300 \text{ per year}$$

Since the office equipment was used for only two months in 20X1, we further calculate the depreciation as follows:

$$\frac{\$300}{12 \text{ months}} = \$25 \text{ depreciation per month}$$

$$\$25 \times 2 \text{ months} = \$50$$

❷ Office Furniture (used for one month in 20X1):

$$\frac{\text{Cost of asset} - \text{Trade-in value}}{\text{Estimated years of usefulness}} = \frac{\$2,000 - \$200}{5 \text{ years}} = \frac{\$1,800}{5} = \$360 \text{ per year}$$

Since the office furniture was used for only one month in 20X1, we further calculate depreciation as follows:

$$\frac{\$360}{12\ months} = \$30\ depreciation\ per\ month$$

Depreciation is *always* recorded by debiting an expense account entitled *Depreciation Expense*, and crediting an account entitled *Accumulated Depreciation*. When depreciation is recorded for more than one type of asset, it is common to have a depreciation expense account and an accumulated depreciation account for each type of asset. Depreciation on Taylor's long-term assets is recorded as follows.

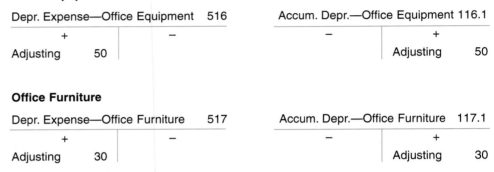

Office Equipment

Depr. Expense—Office Equipment 516		Accum. Depr.—Office Equipment 116.1	
+	−	−	+
Adjusting 50			Adjusting 50

Office Furniture

Depr. Expense—Office Furniture 517		Accum. Depr.—Office Furniture 117.1	
+	−	−	+
Adjusting 30			Adjusting 30

You may be wondering why Accumulated Depreciation is credited instead of the asset itself. Recording the credit in the separate Accumulated Depreciation account allows the original cost of the asset to be shown in the asset account and the related depreciation *accumulated* or summarized in a separate account. This way, the business has a record of the asset's original cost and a separate record of the total amount the asset is estimated to have depreciated.

On the balance sheet, the balance of Accumulated Depreciation is subtracted from the balance of the related asset account, as illustrated in Figure 4-2 on the partial balance sheet of Taylor and Associates. The difference between an asset's cost and its accumulated depreciation is referred to as the asset's **book value**.

FIGURE 4-2
Partial balance sheet

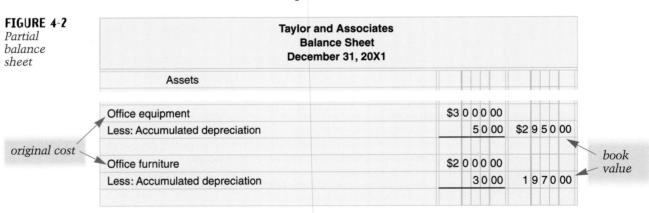

Taylor and Associates Balance Sheet December 31, 20X1		
Assets		
Office equipment	$3 0 0 0 00	
Less: Accumulated depreciation	5 0 00	$2 9 5 0 00
Office furniture	$2 0 0 0 00	
Less: Accumulated depreciation	3 0 00	1 9 7 0 00

original cost

book value

Accumulated Depreciation is an example of a *contra account*. Contra means opposite or offsetting. Thus, the balance of an Accumulated Depreciation account is the opposite of the asset account to which it relates. Since asset accounts normally have debit balances, Accumulated Depreciation will have a credit balance.

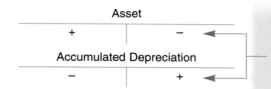

Accumulated Depreciation is a **contra asset account**. A contra asset account is contrary to assets—it has an opposite balance. Assets have debit balances; contra assets have credit balances.

Mr. Taylor assigned account number 116.1 to Accumulated Depreciation—Office Equipment. It is opposite (contra) account number 116, the Office Equipment account. Likewise, account number 117.1 was assigned to Accumulated Depreciation—Office Furniture, to indicate its contra relationship to account number 117, the Office Furniture account. These accounts, along with account number 516 (Depreciation Expense—Office Equipment) and account number 517 (Depreciation Expense—Office Furniture), were added to the chart of accounts and ledger of Taylor and Associates.

Let us stress that only physical, long-lasting assets are depreciated. For Taylor and Associates, this includes only two types of assets. Other depreciable assets include trucks and automobiles, buildings, machinery, fixtures on a building, parking lots, carpeting, cash registers, display cases, computers, and so on. There is, however, one long-term asset that we do not depreciate—land. Land has an unlimited useful life. Consequently, *generally accepted accounting principles (GAAP)* and tax laws do not allow depreciation to be taken on land.

Unpaid Salaries

When Jan Curtis was hired as an assistant on December 8, it was agreed that she would receive a weekly salary of $350, payable every Friday. On December 31, the Salaries Expense account shows a $1,050 balance, representing payments as follows:

Payroll Period	Paid On
Dec. 8–12	Dec. 12
Dec. 15–19	Dec. 19
Dec. 22–26	Dec. 26

The next payroll period is for the week starting on Monday, December 29, 20X1, and ending on Friday, January 2, 20X2. This payroll period is different than the previous three payroll periods in December, however. To see how it is different, let's look at a calendar for December 20X1 (see Figure 4-3).

FIGURE 4-3
Payroll periods

December 20X1						
S	M	T	W	TH.	F	S
	1	2	3	4	5	6
7	8	9	10	11	(12)	13
14	15	16	17	18	(19)	20
21	22	23	24	25	(26)	27
28	**29**	**30**	**31**			

— paydays

The end of the accounting period, December 31, falls in the middle of the payroll period. By stating Jan's salary on a daily basis ($350 ÷ 5 = $70), we determine that she is paid $70 a day. We can illustrate the situation as shown below.

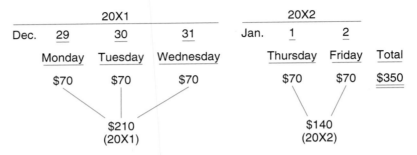

	20X1				20X2		
Dec.	29	30	31	Jan.	1	2	
	Monday	Tuesday	Wednesday		Thursday	Friday	Total
	$70	$70	$70		$70	$70	$350
		$210 (20X1)			$140 (20X2)		

As you can see, the first three days (Monday, Tuesday, and Wednesday) of this payroll period are in 20X1, and the remaining two days are in 20X2. When 20X1 ends, three days of salary expense will not have been paid. These days will not be paid until the next regular payday, which is Friday, January 2, 20X2. However, all expenses of an accounting period should be recorded in that period, even though payment may not have been made. Therefore, on December 31, an adjusting entry is needed to record three days' salary at $70 per day ($70 × 3 = $210).

As illustrated below, the adjusting entry for unpaid salaries involves a debit to the Salaries Expense account and a credit to a liability account entitled Salaries Payable, which Mr. Taylor added to his chart of accounts and ledger as account number 212.

Salaries Expense	513			Salaries Payable	212
+		−		−	+
Balance 1,050					Adjusting 210
Adjusting 210					
New Balance 1,260					

Salaries Expense now shows a balance of $1,260, which is the correct amount of salaries expense for the period. Unpaid salaries always occur when the last day of the accounting period is not the same as the last day of the payroll period.

REMEMBER

Adjusting entries are not caused by errors; they are a planned part of the accounting cycle. For practical reasons, the accounting for internal transactions is postponed until the end of the accounting period.

The Matching Principle of Accounting

The five adjusting entries for Taylor and Associates are based on the **matching principle** of accounting. The matching principle requires that revenue and expenses be recorded in the accounting period in which they occurred. Stated another way, the matching principle states that expenses incurred during an accounting period should be matched with the revenue that was earned during the same period. To match expenses with revenue means to subtract the expenses from revenue to calculate the net income or net loss for the period.

Adjusting entries are needed to properly match expenses and revenue. Had Mr. Taylor not made his adjustments, several expenses would have gone unrecorded for 20X1. Unrecorded expenses result in an understatement of expenses on the income statement. This, in turn, results in an overstatement of net income and owner's equity. Also, assets would be overvalued, as no recognition would have been given to the value of assets used up or expired (supplies and prepaid insurance) or assets depreciated (office equipment and office furniture). Finally, liabilities would be understated, because unpaid salaries at the end of the accounting period would not have been recorded. Although accounts can be adjusted at any time, they are normally adjusted at the end of a month or the end of the year. In relation to the total accounts of a business, only a few generally need adjusting. After you have been through the adjusting process even once, these accounts become easy to recognize.

Now that we have determined the necessary adjustments, we are ready for the next step in the accounting cycle.

REVIEW QUIZ 4-1

Using T accounts, record adjusting entries for the following: (1) the Office Supplies account shows a $900 balance; however, a current count reveals that $750 worth remain on hand; (2) insurance expired, $50; (3) depreciation of trucks, $1,000; (4) unpaid salaries, $150.

CHECK YOUR ANSWERS ON PAGE 143.

STEP 6: PREPARE A WORK SHEET

LEARNING OBJECTIVE 3

The Work Sheet
An accountant's tool

The **work sheet** is an informal working paper that the accountant uses in preparing the financial statements and completing the work of the accounting cycle. The work sheet has been described as the accountant's scratch pad, and it is used to (1) organize data, (2) lessen the possibility of overlooking an adjustment, (3) provide an arithmetical check on the accuracy of work, and (4) arrange data in logical form for the preparation of financial statements. The work sheet is typically prepared in pencil, and usually only the accountant sees it.

The form of the work sheet varies with the needs of the business using it. In completing the accounting cycle for Taylor and Associates, we will use a ten-column work sheet, which is shown in Figure 4-4 on page 118.

Steps in Completing the Work Sheet

The following eight steps are used to complete the work sheet:

❶ **Enter the heading**. The heading consists of the name of the business, the title Work Sheet, and the period of time covered.

❷ **Enter the current trial balance in the Trial Balance columns.** The current trial balance, including accounts without balances—such as those accounts used for adjusting entries—is entered in the Trial Balance columns. The trial balance can be prepared on a separate sheet and copied onto the work sheet, or it can be prepared directly on the work sheet.

❸ **Enter the adjustments in the Adjustments Dr. and Cr. columns.** We now enter the adjustments in the Adjustments columns of the work sheet. Make certain that each adjustment has an equal debit and credit. Each adjustment is labeled as (a), (b), (c), and so on. For example, the first adjustment is a debit to Office Supplies Expense and a credit to Office Supplies. Both the debit and credit are labeled as (a). After all adjustments have been entered, the Adjustments columns are totaled and ruled.

❹ **Complete the Adjusted Trial Balance columns.** Amounts in the Adjustments columns are now combined with account balances in the Trial Balance columns, and the updated amounts are extended to the Adjusted Trial Balance columns. Amounts are extended as follows:

FIGURE 4-4
Ten-column work sheet

Account Title	Trial Balance		Adjustments		Adjusted Trial Balance		Income Statement		Balance Sheet		
	Debit	Credit	Debit	Credit	Debit	Credit	Debit	Credit	Debit	Credit	
1											1
2											2
3											3
4											4
5											5
6											6
7											7
8											8
9											9
10											10
11											11
12											12
13											13
14											14
15											15
16											16
17											17
18											18
19											19
20											20
21											21
22											22
23											23

a. If an account balance *has not* been adjusted, it is simply extended to the same column in the Adjusted Trial Balance section. For example, Cash has a debit balance of $8,485, *and there was no adjustment to this account*. So, the $8,485 balance in the trial balance section is extended directly to the Adjusted Trial Balance Dr. column.

b. If an account has a debit balance and the adjustment is a credit, the *difference* between the two amounts is extended to the Adjusted Trial Balance Dr. column. For example, Office Supplies has a debit balance of $275 and a credit adjustment of $45. The difference between the two amounts, $230, is extended to the Adjusted Trial Balance Dr. column.

c. If an account has a debit balance and the adjustment is also a debit, the two figures are *added*, and the total is moved to the Adjusted Trial Balance Dr. column. For example, the Salaries Expense account has a debit balance of $1,050 and a $210 debit adjustment. The two debits are added, and the total, $1,260, is extended to the Adjusted Trial Balance Dr. column.

d. After all amounts have been extended to the Adjusted Trial Balance columns, total and rule the columns.

❺ **Complete the Income Statement columns.** An income statement summarizes revenue and expenses for an accounting period. Therefore, the balance of the revenue account, Service Revenue, and the balance of each of the expense accounts are extended from the Adjusted Trial Balance columns to the Income Statement columns, following these rules:

a. **A credit remains a credit.** Thus, the $4,700 credit balance of the Service Revenue account is extended to the Income Statement Cr. column.

b. **A debit remains a debit.** Thus, the debit balance of each expense account is extended to the Income Statement Dr. column.

❻ **Complete the Balance Sheet columns.** The remaining account balances—assets, liabilities, owner's capital, and drawing—are extended to the Balance Sheet columns, following these rules:

a. **A debit remains a debit.** Thus, the debit balance of each asset account is extended to the Balance Sheet Dr. column.

b. **A credit remains a credit.** Thus, the credit balance of each accumulated depreciation account and the $10,000 credit balance of the owner's capital account are extended to the Balance Sheet Cr. column.

c. The $1,500 debit balance of the owner's drawing account is extended to the Balance Sheet Dr. column. Notice that the drawing account is not an asset. It is extended to the Balance Sheet Dr. column so that it will be opposite the owner's capital account, which was extended to the Balance Sheet Cr. column.

❼ **Total the Income Statement and Balance Sheet columns.** The Income Statement Dr. and Cr. columns and the Balance Sheet Dr. and Cr. columns are totaled, and each column total is entered directly below the column.

❽ **Determine the amount of net income or net loss and balance the statement columns.** Since the Income Statement Cr. column contains the amount of revenue, and the Income Statement Dr. column contains the amount of expenses, the net income or net loss can be determined by calculating the difference between the two column totals:

Income Statement Cr. column (revenue)	$4,700.00
Income Statement Dr. column (expenses)	− 2,255.00
Net income	$2,445.00

Since revenue exceeded expenses, we have a net income for the period. The term *Net Income* is written in the Account Title column, and the amount of net income is entered under the Income Statement Dr. column and the Balance Sheet Cr. column. The columns are totaled again, as an arithmetic check, and ruled. Had there been a net loss, the amount of the loss would have been entered under the Income Statement Cr. column and the Balance Sheet Dr. column, and described as *net loss* in the Account Title column.

FIGURE 4-5
Placement of items on a work sheet

It should be stressed that the work sheet is not a formal financial statement, but an aid to the accountant. Figure 4-5, which shows the proper placement of items on the work sheet, can be used as a guide when preparing work sheets.

Account Classification	Trial Balance		Adjustments		Adjusted Trial Balance		Income Statement		Balance Sheet	
	Debit	Credit	Debit	Credit	Debit	Credit	Debit	Credit	Debit	Credit
Assets	X				X				X	
Liabilities		X				X				X
Capital		X				X				X
Drawing	X				X				X	
Revenue		X				X		X		
Expenses	X				X		X			

REVIEW QUIZ 4-2

On a completed work sheet, can the amount of net income (or net loss) be obtained by finding the difference between the total of the Balance Sheet Dr. column and the total of the Balance Sheet Cr. column? If so, why?

CHECK YOUR ANSWER ON PAGE 143.

STEP 7: PREPARE FINANCIAL STATEMENTS FROM A COMPLETED WORK SHEET

LEARNING OBJECTIVE 4

Financial statements are usually prepared as soon as possible after the work sheet has been completed. The amounts used to prepare the financial statements are taken directly from the work sheet. An income statement, a statement of owner's equity, and a balance sheet for Taylor and Associates are illustrated in Figure 4-6.

The Income Statement

The income statement is a summary of revenue and expenses, showing net income or net loss for an accounting period. It is prepared directly from data in the Income Statement columns of the work sheet. An income statement is typically prepared at the end of each month, quarter, or year; however, it can be prepared for any period of time.

The Statement of Owner's Equity

The statement of owner's equity summarizes the changes that have occurred in owner's equity during an accounting period, such as a month or a year. It is prepared from the following three pieces of information on the work sheet:

1. The owner's capital balance in the Balance Sheet Cr. column.
2. The owner's drawing account balance in the Balance Sheet Dr. column.
3. The amount of net income or net loss, which is shown at the bottom of the Income Statement section.

FIGURE 4-6
Financial statements

Taylor and Associates
Income Statement
For Two Months Ended December 31, 20X1

Revenue:			
Service revenue			$4 7 0 0 00
Expenses:			
Salaries expense	$1 2 6 0 00		
Rent expense	8 0 0 00		
Repairs expense	5 0 00		
Depreciation expense—office equipment	5 0 00		
Office supplies expense	4 5 00		
Depreciation expense—office furniture	3 0 00		
Insurance expense	2 0 00		
Total expenses		2 2 5 5 00	
Net income		$2 4 4 5 00	

Remember
The dates of the income statement and the statement of owner's equity cover a period of time; the date of the balance sheet is the last day of the accounting period.

Remember
On the income statement, expenses are usually arranged in order of highest to lowest.

Taylor and Associates
Statement of Owner's Equity
For Two Months Ended December 31, 20X1

Capital, November 1, 20X1			$10 0 0 0 00
Net income for period	$2 4 4 5 00		
Less withdrawals	1 5 0 0 00		
Increase in capital		9 4 5 00	
Capital, December 31, 20X1		$10 9 4 5 00	

Taylor and Associates
Balance Sheet
December 31, 20X1

Assets			
Cash		$8 4 8 5 00	
Accounts receivable		3 0 0 00	
Office supplies		2 3 0 00	
Prepaid insurance		2 2 0 00	
Office equipment	$3 0 0 0 00		
Less: Accumulated depreciation	5 0 00	2 9 5 0 00	
Office furniture	2 0 0 0 00		
Less: Accumulated depreciation	3 0 00	1 9 7 0 00	
Total assets		$14 1 5 5 00	
Liabilities			
Accounts payable		$3 0 0 0 00	
Salaries payable		2 1 0 00	
Total liabilities		3 2 1 0 00	
Owner's Equity			
William Taylor, capital		10 9 4 5 00	
Total liabilities and owner's equity		$14 1 5 5 00	

The Balance Sheet

The balance sheet shows that assets = liabilities + owner's equity. Balance sheet data come from the Balance Sheet columns of the work sheet. The up-to-date amount for owner's equity on the balance sheet is taken from the statement of owner's equity.

Notice that Taylor's balance sheet is simply dated December 31, 20X1. As you recall from Chapter 1, the balance sheet—unlike the income statement or the statement of owner's equity—does not show what happened over a period of time. Instead, it shows the financial position of the business at a particular point in time.

Also notice that the accumulated depreciation accounts are subtracted from the related asset accounts. (Remember that depreciation of a long-term asset is not recorded directly in the asset account, but in an accumulated depreciation contra asset account.)

The Balance Sheet column totals of the work sheet ($15,735) *do not* match the totals of the formal balance sheet ($14,155). This is because the Balance Sheet section of the work sheet *is not* a balance sheet; *it is balance sheet data*. We must take the information from the work sheet and arrange it into the correct form for the formal balance sheet. For example, on the work sheet we showed the balance of the drawing account in the Balance Sheet Dr. column. This was done because drawing is opposite owner's equity, which is shown in the Balance Sheet Cr. column. Drawing is not reported on the formal balance sheet; it is reported on the statement of owner's equity. Its effect is reflected in an updated capital figure, which is transferred to the formal balance sheet.

Showing Additional Investments on the Statement of Owner's Equity

The amount listed on the work sheet as owner's capital does not always represent the account balance at the beginning of the accounting period. The owner may have invested additional cash (or other assets) in the business during the period. If this has happened, it will be necessary to refer to the capital account in the ledger to determine the beginning balance and any additional investments made during the period.

To illustrate this, let's use a company other than Taylor and Associates. On January 1, 20X2, James Sean's capital account showed a balance of $12,500. During the year he invested an additional $6,000 cash in the business. His 20X2 income statement shows a profit of $22,600, and he withdrew $15,000 during the year. His statement of owner's equity for the year ended December 31, 20X2, appears in Figure 4-7.

FIGURE 4-7
*Statement of owner's
equity*

James Sean
Statement of Owner's Equity
For Year Ended December 31, 20X2

James Sean, capital, January 1, 20X2		$12 5 0 0 00
Add: Additional investment	$ 6 0 0 0 00	
Net income for the year	22 6 0 0 00	
Total increases	$28 6 0 0 00	
Less withdrawals	15 0 0 0 00	
Increase in owner's equity		13 6 0 0 00
James Sean, capital, December 31, 20X2		$26 1 0 0 00

REVIEW QUIZ
4-3

The financial statement columns of Pace Company's work sheet are shown below. Prepare (1) an income statement, (2) a statement of owner's equity, and (3) a balance sheet.

Pace Company
Work Sheet
For Year Ended December 31, 20X2

	Account Title	Income Statement Debit	Income Statement Credit	Balance Sheet Debit	Balance Sheet Credit	
1	Cash			6 2 0 0 00		1
2	Accounts Receivable			9 2 0 00		2
3	Supplies			6 0 0 00		3
4	Equipment			22 0 0 0 00		4
5	Accumulated Depreciation—Equipment				2 0 0 0 00	5
6	Accounts Payable				1 8 0 0 00	6
7	Joe Pace, Capital				15 9 1 5 00	7
8	Joe Pace, Drawing			18 0 0 0 00		8
9	Service Revenue		52 0 0 0 00			9
10	Salaries Expense	14 3 0 0 00				10
11	Rent Expense	4 2 0 0 00				11
12	Telephone Expense	1 5 7 0 00				12
13	Utilities Expense	2 9 0 0 00				13
14	Depreciation Expense	8 0 0 00				14
15	Office Supplies Expense	2 2 5 00				15
16		23 9 9 5 00	52 0 0 0 00	47 7 2 0 00	19 7 1 5 00	16
17	Net Income	28 0 0 5 00			28 0 0 5 00	17
18		52 0 0 0 00	52 0 0 0 00	47 7 2 0 00	47 7 2 0 00	18

CHECK YOUR ANSWERS ON PAGES 143-144.

STEP 8: JOURNALIZE AND POST ADJUSTING ENTRIES

LEARNING OBJECTIVE 5

The work sheet is not a journal. Thus, the adjustments must be taken from the work sheet and entered on the journal.

Earlier in the chapter, we recorded adjusting entries in T accounts. This was done to introduce adjustments and to show you how they affect the ledger. In actual practice, adjustments are first recorded on the work sheet. However, the work sheet is not a journal, and adjustments are not posted to the ledger from the work sheet. Consequently, adjusting entries must be formally journalized and posted to the ledger so that ledger account balances will be up to date and will agree with the balances reported on the financial statements. Remember that accounting information is not officially a part of the accounting cycle until it is recorded in the general journal—the book of original entry.

The accountant simply copies the adjusting entries from the work sheet to the journal. The heading *Adjusting Entries* is written in the Account Title column above the adjusting entries. No further explanation is needed. Taylor and Associates' adjusting entries are shown in Figure 4-8. Notice that each adjusting entry is dated as of the last day of the accounting period.

FIGURE 4-8
Journalizing adjusting entries

	Date		Account Title	P.R.	Debit	Credit	
			General Journal			**Page 2**	
1			Adjusting Entries				1
2	20X1 Dec.	31	Office Supplies Expense		45 00		2
3			Office Supplies			45 00	3
4							4
5		31	Insurance Expense		20 00		5
6			Prepaid Insurance			20 00	6
7							7
8		31	Depreciation Expense—Office Equip.		50 00		8
9			Accumulated Depr.—Office Equip.			50 00	9
10							10
11		31	Depreciation Expense—Office Furn.		30 00		11
12			Accumulated Depr.—Office Furn.			30 00	12
13							13
14		31	Salaries Expense		2 10 00		14
15			Salaries Payable			2 10 00	15

The source of the information for the adjusting entries is the Adjustments columns of the work sheet. Each adjustment shown on the work sheet affects at least two general ledger accounts. The debit and credit parts of each adjusting entry are found by matching the letters of the adjustments recorded on the work sheet.

After the adjusting entries have been journalized, the next step is to post them to the ledger, thereby bringing the ledger up to date. When posting adjusting entries, you should write the word *Adjusting* in the Item column of the respective ledger account. Figure 4-9 shows the Office Supplies account and the Office Supplies Expense account after the above adjusting entries are posted.

FIGURE 4-9
Office Supplies and
Office Supplies
Expense accounts after
adjusting entries are
posted

General Ledger						
Account Office Supplies						Account No. 113

Date		Item	P.R.	Debit	Credit	Balance	
						Debit	Credit
20X1 Dec.	1	Balance	✓			1 2 5 00	
	5		GJ2	1 5 0 00		2 7 5 00	
	31	Adjusting	GJ2		4 5 00	2 3 0 00	

Account Office Supplies Expense						Account No. 514

Date		Item	P.R.	Debit	Credit	Balance	
						Debit	Credit
20X1 Dec.	31	Adjusting	GJ2	4 5 00		4 5 00	

REVIEW QUIZ
4-4

If adjusting entries are entered on the work sheet, why is it necessary to formally journalize them and post to the ledger?

CHECK YOUR ANSWER ON PAGE 144.

INTERNET ASSETS

HOW CAN I SAFEGUARD THE ACCOUNTING INFORMATION I HAVE STORED ON A COMPUTER?

Protecting your computer data through security measures is a matter of common sense more than anything else. Use a password and change your password on a regular basis. Do not make the password too long, and avoid obvious passwords such as your birthday or name. Mix upper- and lowercase letters with numbers since passwords are often case-sensitive. For network environments, make sure the computer and modem are in a room that can be locked. Do regular, automatic backups in case your data are stolen or corrupted. Keep backups in a separate, secure location—preferably offsite.

If data is sensitive, you can encrypt it or install a "firewall" so that intruders cannot read it. If you need to take these measures, contact your information services professional or your Internet service provider for more information.

The Accounting Cycle Continued

ADJUSTING ENTRIES

SUPPLIES USED

Balance of Supplies account
−   End-of-period inventory count of supplies
Amount of supplies **used** (Supplies Expense)

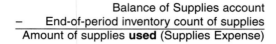

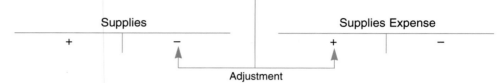

Supplies		Supplies Expense	
+	−	+	−

Adjustment

INSURANCE EXPIRED

$$\frac{\text{Prepaid premium}}{\text{Period of time prepaid}} = \text{Amount } \textbf{expired} \text{ (Insurance Expense)}$$

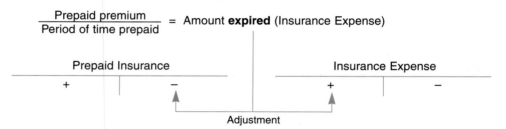

Prepaid Insurance		Insurance Expense	
+	−	+	−

Adjustment

DEPRECIATION OF LONG-TERM ASSETS

$$\frac{\text{Cost of asset} - \text{Trade-in value}}{\text{Estimated years of usefulness}} = \text{Annual } \textbf{depreciation expense}$$

Accumulated Depreciation		Depreciation Expense	
−	+	+	−

Adjustment

UNPAID SALARIES

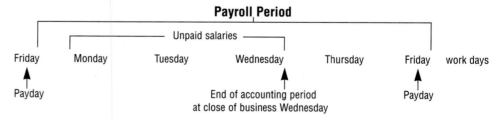

Payroll Period

Unpaid salaries

Friday   Monday   Tuesday   Wednesday   Thursday   Friday   work days

Payday

End of accounting period
at close of business Wednesday

Payday

Salaries earned by employees between the last payday and the end of the accounting period will not be paid until the next payday. However, the amount of unpaid salaries should be recorded to show the proper amount of salaries expense for the period.

Salaries Payable		Salaries Expense	
−	+	+	−

Adjustment

SUMMARY/RESTATEMENT OF LEARNING OBJECTIVES

1. Explain the need for adjusting entries.
Adjusting entries are made to:
- Bring the ledger up-to-date.
- Better match expenses and revenue to more accurately determine the net income (or loss) for the accounting period.
- More accurately state the amount of assets, liabilities, and owner's equity.

2. Make adjusting entries for supplies used, expired insurance, depreciation, and unpaid wages.

R & W Shoe Repair shows the following account balances as of December 31, 20XX:

Account	Balance
Cash	$ 7,755
Supplies	965
Prepaid Insurance	1,800
Equipment	20,000
Accumulated Depreciation—Equipment	4,000
Accounts Payable	7,600
Ray Wilson, Capital	19,780
Ray Wilson, Drawing	2,500
Revenue from Services	62,240
Rent Expense	7,200
Salaries Expense	51,000
Utilities Expense	2,400

Adjustment data are as follows:
(a) Supplies on hand, $750.
(b) Insurance expired, one year of a three-year premium.
(c) Depreciation of equipment. (Equipment has an estimated life of ten years and no trade-in value.)
(d) Salaries unpaid for five days at $200 per day.

Adjustments are prepared as shown below.

(a) Supplies used:

Balance of account	$965
Amount on hand	− 750
Value of supplies used	$215

Adjusting entry:

Supplies Expense			Supplies		
+	−		+	−	
(a) 215			Bal. 965	(a) 215	

(b) Insurance expired: $1{,}800 \times {}^1\!/_3 = \$600$

Adjusting entry:

Insurance Expense			Prepaid Insurance		
+	−		+	−	
(b) 600			Bal. 1,800	(b) 600	

(c)   Depreciation: $20,000 \div 10$ years $= \$2,000$ per year

Adjusting entry:

Depreciation Expense—Equipment			Accumulated Depreciation—Equipment	
+	−		−	+
(c) 2,000				Balance 4,000
				(c) 2,000

(d)   Salaries unpaid: 5 days $\times$ \$200 $= \$1,000$

Adjusting entry:

Salaries Expense			Salaries Payable	
+	−		−	+
Balance 51,000				(d) 1,000
(d) 1,000				

3. Complete a work sheet for a service business.

The information for R & W Shoe Repair is summarized on the work sheet in Figure 4-10 on page 129. Additional accounts needed for adjusting entries have been added at the appropriate places. Note that R & W incurred a net loss for the year.

4. Prepare financial statements from a work sheet.

R & W's income statement, statement of owner's equity, and balance sheet for 20XX are shown in Figure 4-11 on page 130. Each was prepared from the information supplied by R & W's completed work sheet. Notice how the net loss is shown on the first two statements. Also notice that on a statement of owner's equity, withdrawals are added to the net loss.

5. Journalize adjusting entries.

Using the Adjustments columns of R & W's work sheet, adjusting entries are journalized as shown below.

	Date		Account Title	P.R.	Debit	Credit	
			Adjusting Entries				
1	20XX Dec.	31	Supplies Expense		2 1 5 00		1
2			Supplies			2 1 5 00	2
3							3
4		31	Insurance Expense		6 0 0 00		4
5			Prepaid Insurance			6 0 0 00	5
6							6
7		31	Depreciation Expense—Equipment		2 0 0 0 00		7
8			Accumulated Depreciation—Equip.			2 0 0 0 00	8
9							9
10		31	Salaries Expense		1 0 0 0 00		10
11			Salaries Payable			1 0 0 0 00	11
12							12
13							13

General Journal — Page 1

FIGURE 4-10
Work sheet for R & W Shoe Repair

R & W Shoe Repair
Work Sheet
For Year Ended December 31, 20XX

	Account Title	Trial Balance Debit	Trial Balance Credit	Adjustments Debit	Adjustments Credit	Adjusted Trial Balance Debit	Adjusted Trial Balance Credit	Income Statement Debit	Income Statement Credit	Balance Sheet Debit	Balance Sheet Credit	
1	Cash	7 7 5 5 00				7 7 5 5 00				7 7 5 5 00		1
2	Supplies	9 6 5 00			(a) 2 1 5 00	7 5 0 00				7 5 0 00		2
3	Prepaid Insurance	1 8 0 0 00			(b) 6 0 0 00	1 2 0 0 00				1 2 0 0 00		3
4	Equipment	20 0 0 0 00				20 0 0 0 00				20 0 0 0 00		4
5	Accum. Depr.—Equip.		4 0 0 0 00		(c) 2 0 0 0 00		6 0 0 0 00				6 0 0 0 00	5
6	Accounts Payable		7 6 0 0 00				7 6 0 0 00				7 6 0 0 00	6
7	Salaries Payable				(d) 1 0 0 00		1 0 0 00				1 0 0 00	7
8	R. Wilson, Capital		19 7 8 0 00				19 7 8 0 00				19 7 8 0 00	8
9	R. Wilson, Drawing	2 5 0 0 00				2 5 0 0 00				2 5 0 0 00		9
10	Revenue from Services		62 2 4 0 00				62 2 4 0 00		62 2 4 0 00			10
11	Rent Expense	7 2 0 0 00				7 2 0 0 00		7 2 0 0 00				11
12	Salaries Expense	51 0 0 0 00		(d) 1 0 0 0 00		52 0 0 0 00		52 0 0 0 00				12
13	Utilities Expense	2 4 0 0 00				2 4 0 0 00		2 4 0 0 00				13
14	Supplies Expense			(a) 2 1 5 00		2 1 5 00		2 1 5 00				14
15	Insurance Expense			(b) 6 0 0 00		6 0 0 00		6 0 0 00				15
16	Depr. Expense—Equip.			(c) 2 0 0 0 00		2 0 0 0 00		2 0 0 0 00				16
17		93 6 2 0 00	93 6 2 0 00	3 8 1 5 00	3 8 1 5 00	96 6 2 0 00	96 6 2 0 00	64 4 1 5 00	62 2 4 0 00	32 2 0 5 00	34 3 8 0 00	17
18	Net Loss								2 1 7 5 00	2 1 7 5 00		18
19								64 4 1 5 00	64 4 1 5 00	34 3 8 0 00	34 3 8 0 00	19

The Accounting Cycle Continued

FIGURE 4-11
*Financial statements
for R & W Shoe Repair*

R & W Shoe Repair
Income Statement
For Year Ended December 31, 20XX

Revenue:			
Revenue from services			$62 2 4 0 00
Expenses:			
Salaries expense	$52 0 0 0 00		
Rent expense	7 2 0 0 00		
Utilities expense	2 4 0 0 00		
Depreciation expense—equipment	2 0 0 0 00		
Insurance expense	6 0 0 00		
Supplies expense	2 1 5 00		
Total expenses		64 4 1 5 00	
Net loss		($ 2 1 7 5 00)	

R & W Shoe Repair
Statement of Owner's Equity
For Year Ended December 31, 20XX

Capital, January 1, 20XX		$19 7 8 0 00
Net loss for the year	$2 1 7 5 00	
Add: Withdrawals	2 5 0 0 00	
Decrease in capital		4 6 7 5 00
Capital, December 31, 20XX		$15 1 0 5 00

R & W Shoe Repair
Balance Sheet
December 31, 20XX

Assets			
Cash		$ 7 7 5 5 00	
Supplies		7 5 0 00	
Prepaid insurance		1 2 0 0 00	
Equipment	$20 0 0 0 00		
Less: Accumulated depreciation	6 0 0 0 00	14 0 0 0 00	
Total assets			$23 7 0 5 00
Liabilities			
Accounts payable		$ 7 6 0 0 00	
Salaries payable		1 0 0 0 00	
Total liabilities			$ 8 6 0 0 00
Owner's Equity			
R. Wilson, capital			15 1 0 5 00
Total liabilities and owner's equity			$23 7 0 5 00

KEY TERMS

adjusting entries Entries made at the end of an accounting period to bring the balances of certain accounts up to date.

book value The difference between an asset's cost and its accumulated depreciation.

contra asset account An account whose balance is opposite the asset to which it relates. Since asset accounts have debit balances, contra asset accounts (the opposite of assets) have credit balances.

depreciation An allocation process in which the cost of a long-term asset (except land) is divided over the periods in which the asset is used in the production of the business's revenue.

internal transactions Transactions, such as adjustments, that occur within a company and do not affect parties outside the company.

matching principle Requires that revenue earned during an accounting period be offset by the expenses that were necessary to produce that revenue so that the accurate net income or net loss for the period can be reported.

premium A fee paid for insurance coverage that will benefit the business in the future.

straight-line method A popular method of calculating depreciation that yields the same amount of depreciation for each full period an asset is used.

work sheet An informal working paper used by the accountant to organize data for the financial statements and lessen the possibility of overlooking an adjustment.

CONCEPTS AND SKILLS REVIEW

CONCEPTS REVIEW

1. Why do certain accounts need adjusting at the end of an accounting period?
2. Explain why adjustments are referred to as internal transactions.
3. What is the amount of the adjustment for supplies used if $950 worth are on hand and $1,375 is the balance of the Supplies account before adjustment?
4. On June 30, 20X1, Ray Smith paid $1,440 for a three-year insurance policy. Assuming that Ray's accounting period ends on December 31, 20X1, determine how much of the prepayment has expired on that date?
5. Why is depreciation referred to as an allocation process?
6. A long-term asset is purchased on May 1 of the current year. Assuming it has a cost of $70,000, a trade-in value of $10,000, and an estimated life of ten years, what is the depreciation by the straight-line method up to December 31 in the current year? What is the depreciation for the next calendar year the asset is used?
7. What is a contra asset account? What is its normal balance?
8. Weekly salaries are $30,000. Assuming a five-day workweek and a Friday payday, what is the amount of the adjustment for unpaid salaries if the accounting period ends on a Tuesday?
9. Is the work sheet a financial statement? Explain.
10. Describe the process of transferring amounts from the Trial Balance and Adjustments columns of a work sheet to the Adjusted Trial Balance columns.
11. How is the amount of net income or net loss determined from a work sheet?
12. Indicate whether each of the following account balances would appear in the income statement or balance sheet section of a work sheet:
    (a) Cash
    (b) Prepaid Insurance
    (c) Accumulated Depreciation—Office Equipment
    (d) Accounts Payable
    (e) Ray Langford, Capital

(f) Service Revenue
(g) Supplies Expense
(h) Accounts Receivable

13. Why are financial statements prepared as soon as possible after the work sheet is completed?

14. Explain why adjusting entries must be formally journalized and posted to the ledger, even though they already appear on the work sheet.

SKILLS REVIEW

EXERCISE 4-1

LEARNING OBJECTIVE 2

Objective: To record adjusting entries in T accounts

Directions: Five situations follow, each requiring an adjusting entry. Prepare the appropriate entry in T-account form. The last day of the accounting period is December 31 of the current year.

(a) The Supplies account has a balance of $2,650 before adjustment. A count of supplies on hand shows $1,850.

(b) A one-year insurance policy was purchased on October 1 at a $3,600 premium, which was debited to the Prepaid Insurance account.

(c) Equipment for the office was purchased on January 2 for $36,000. It is estimated to have no trade-in value and a useful life of 12 years.

(d) A truck was purchased on July 1 for $30,000. It is expected to be used for six years and have a trade-in value of $6,000.

(e) Salaries for three days are unpaid. Salaries are $50,000 for a five-day week.

EXERCISE 4-2

LEARNING OBJECTIVE 3

Objective: To prepare a work sheet

Directions: From the information that follows, prepare a work sheet for Mogren Financial Services for the year ended December 31, 20X2. Notice that the amounts in this exercise may seem unrealistically small. Our objective is to allow you to do a work sheet without arithmetic getting in the way.

Account	Balance
Cash	$ 60
Accounts Receivable	30
Supplies	40
Prepaid Insurance	30
Equipment	100
Accumulated Depreciation—Equipment	20
Accounts Payable	60
Salaries Payable	—
Linda Mogren, Capital	100
Linda Mogren, Drawing	30
Fees Earned	161
Salaries Expense	11
Rent Expense	40
Supplies Expense	—
Insurance Expense	—
Depreciation Expense—Equipment	—

Adjustment data:
(a) Supplies on hand, $30.
(b) Insurance expired, $10.
(c) Depreciation of equipment, $10.
(d) Unpaid salaries, $10.

EXERCISE 4-3

LEARNING OBJECTIVE 2

Objective: To record adjusting entries for unpaid salaries

Directions: The Flowers Company has a weekly payroll of $42,000, payable every Friday. Journalize the adjusting entry for unpaid salaries, assuming that the last day of the accounting period is on a (a) Monday; (b) Thursday; (c) Wednesday.

EXERCISE 4-4

LEARNING OBJECTIVE 5

Objective: To journalize adjusting entries

Directions: Journalize adjusting entries for the following:

(a) The Prepaid Insurance account shows a balance of $1,200. Of this amount, $690 has expired.
(b) The Repair Supplies account shows a debit balance of $525. A current inventory count reveals that $185 worth remain on hand.
(c) Office equipment is estimated to have depreciated $1,975.
(d) Unpaid and unrecorded salaries total $230.

EXERCISE 4-5

LEARNING OBJECTIVE 5

Objective: To journalize adjusting entries using the Adjustments columns of a work sheet

Directions: Following are the Adjustments columns of Peak Company's work sheet for the year ended December 31, 20X1. Journalize Peak's adjusting entries.

Peak Company
Work Sheet
For Year Ended December 31, 20X1

	Account Title	Adjustments Debit	Adjustments Credit	Adjusted Trial Balance Debit	Adjusted Trial Balance Credit	
1	Cash					1
2	Supplies		(a) 3 0 0 00			2
3	Prepaid Insurance		(b) 6 7 5 00			3
4	Equipment					4
5	Accumulated Depreciation—Equipment		(c) 8 0 0 00			5
6	Accounts Payable					6
7	Salaries Payable		(d) 3 2 5 00			7
8	Jan Dean, Capital					8
9	Jan Dean, Drawing					9
10	Professional Fees					10
11	Rent Expense					11
12	Salaries Expense	(d) 3 2 5 00				12
13	Utilities Expense					13
14	Supplies Expense	(a) 3 0 0 00				14
15	Insurance Expense	(b) 6 7 5 00				15
16	Depreciation Expense—Equipment	(c) 8 0 0 00				16

EXERCISE 4-6

LEARNING OBJECTIVE 4

Objective: To calculate financial statement figures

Directions: A list of several account titles and balances follows. Answer the questions that relate to this list.

Account	Balance
Accounts Payable	$12,000
Accounts Receivable	7,000
Accumulated Depreciation	6,000
Cash	7,000
Depreciation Expense	3,000
Equipment	22,000
Fees Earned	35,110
Insurance Expense	200
Prepaid Insurance	600
Rent Expense	3,200
Bill Rogers, Capital	14,300
Bill Rogers, Drawing	8,000
Salaries Payable	500
Salaries Expense	15,310
Supplies	1,200
Supplies Expense	400

1. What are the total assets?
2. What are the total liabilities?
3. What is the net income or net loss?
4. What is the net increase or net decrease in capital?
5. What is Bill Rogers's end-of-year capital balance?

EXERCISE 4-7

Objective: To prepare financial statements from the financial statement columns of a work sheet

Directions: From the following partial work sheet of the Dave Rodriguez Company, prepare (1) an income statement, (2) a statement of owner's equity, and (3) a balance sheet.

The Dave Rodriguez Company
Work Sheet
For Year Ended June 30, 20XX

	Account Title	Income Statement Debit	Income Statement Credit	Balance Sheet Debit	Balance Sheet Credit	
1	Cash			1 8 0 0 00		1
2	Accounts Receivable			3 0 0 00		2
3	Office Supplies			9 0 0 00		3
4	Prepaid Insurance			8 0 0 00		4
5	Office Equipment			35 5 1 0 00		5
6	Accumulated Depreciation—Office Equipment				1 2 0 0 00	6
7	Accounts Payable				9 0 0 00	7
8	Salaries Payable				8 0 00	8
9	Dave Rodriguez, Capital				13 1 2 0 00	9
10	Dave Rodriguez, Drawing			9 8 0 0 00		10
11	Service Revenue		58 0 0 0 00			11
12	Rent Expense	6 0 0 0 00				12
13	Salaries Expense	9 8 7 0 00				13
14	Utilities Expense	6 2 0 0 00				14
15	Depreciation Expense—Office Equipment	8 0 0 00				15
16	Telephone Expense	5 6 0 00				16
17	Office Supplies Expense	4 0 0 00				17
18	Insurance Expense	3 6 0 00				18
19		24 1 9 0 00	58 0 0 0 00	49 1 1 0 00	15 3 0 0 00	19
20	Net Income	33 8 1 0 00			33 8 1 0 00	20
21		58 0 0 0 00	58 0 0 0 00	49 1 1 0 00	49 1 1 0 00	21

Paradigm College Accounting • Chapter 4

CASE PROBLEMS

GROUP A

LEARNING OBJECTIVE 2

PROBLEM 4-1A

Objective: To determine the amount of adjustments and record the adjustments in general journal form

Bonner Service Company has the following adjustment data on December 31, 20X2:

(a) The Supplies account had a balance of $3,300 on January 1, 20X2. Supplies were purchased on May 1 ($575) and August 6 ($1,600). A year-end inventory shows $2,945 on hand.

(b) The Prepaid Insurance account has a balance of $23,400, representing premiums paid for a three-year policy on March 1, 20X2.

(c) Equipment was purchased for $90,000 in January 20X1. The equipment has an estimated useful life of ten years and an estimated trade-in value of $10,000.

(d) Salaries of $38,000 are paid weekly on Fridays. December 31, 20X2, falls on Wednesday.

Directions: Record each adjusting entry in general journal form.

LEARNING OBJECTIVE 3

PROBLEM 4-2A

Objective: To prepare a work sheet

The following are the account balances of York Enterprises on December 31, 20X2:

Account	Balance	
Cash	$ 4,500	D
Accounts Receivable	3,000	D
Supplies	1,700	D
Prepaid Insurance	1,850	D
Equipment	38,000	D
(contra account) Accumulated Depreciation—Equipment	12,000	C
Accounts Payable	10,600	C
Salaries Payable	—	C
Ben York, Capital	35,770	C
Ben York, Drawing	15,000	D
Fees Earned	91,000	C
Salaries Expense	75,400	D
Rent Expense	7,200	D
Utilities Expense	2,175	D
Repairs Expense	545	D
Supplies Expense	—	D
Insurance Expense	—	D
Depreciation Expense—Equipment	—	D

Adjustment data:
(a) Supplies on hand, $1,500.
(b) Insurance expired, $600.
(c) Depreciation of equipment, $2,600.
(d) Salaries unpaid, $800.

Directions: Prepare a work sheet for York Enterprises for the year ended December 31, 20X2.

The Accounting Cycle Continued

LEARNING OBJECTIVE 4

Objective: To prepare financial statements from a completed work sheet

Directions: Using the work sheet that you completed for York Enterprises in Problem 4-2A, prepare (1) an income statement for the year ended December 31, 20X2; (2) a statement of owner's equity for the year ended December 31, 20X2; (3) a balance sheet dated December 31, 20X2.

PROBLEM 4-4A

LEARNING OBJECTIVE 4

Objective: To prepare financial statements from adjusted account balances

Following is a list of accounts and their adjusted balances from the work sheet of The Powers Group, a management consulting firm, for the six months ended June 30, 20X2:

Account	Adjusted Balance
Accounts Payable	$ 16,650
Accounts Receivable	10,000
Accumulated Depreciation—Automobiles	13,500
Accumulated Depreciation—Office Equipment	4,500
Automobiles	35,000
Auto Supplies	2,575
Auto Supplies Expense	1,620
Cash	12,750
Depreciation Expense—Automobiles	6,200
Depreciation Expense—Office Equipment	1,200
Fees Earned	153,000
Insurance Expense	3,200
Office Equipment	15,000
Office Supplies	8,500
Office Supplies Expense	9,210
Leigh Powers, Capital	60,580
Leigh Powers, Drawing	26,000
Prepaid Insurance	9,600
Rent Expense	4,800
Repairs Expense	575
Salaries Payable	2,000
Salaries Expense	104,000

Directions:
1. Prepare an income statement for the six months ended June 30, 20X2.
2. Prepare a statement of owner's equity for the six months ended June 30, 20X2.
3. Prepare a balance sheet as of June 30, 20X2.

LEARNING OBJECTIVE 2, 3, 4, 5

PROBLEM 4-5A

Objective: To prepare a work sheet and financial statements and journalize adjusting entries

Eddie Broadway, owner of Broadway Photography, prepared the following trial balance on December 31, 20X2:

Broadway Photography
Trial Balance
December 31, 20X2

Account Title	Debit	Credit
Cash	6 1 1 0 00	
Accounts Receivable	2 0 0 0 00	
Office Supplies	6 3 7 5 00	
Photo Supplies	11 6 3 0 00	
Prepaid Insurance	3 7 2 0 00	
Office Equipment	25 0 0 0 00	
Accumulated Depreciation—Office Equipment		5 0 0 0 00
Photo Equipment	40 0 0 0 00	
Accumulated Depreciation—Photo Equipment		12 0 0 0 00
Accounts Payable		25 5 0 0 00
Salaries Payable		—
Eddie Broadway, Capital		52 5 8 5 00
Eddie Broadway, Drawing	17 0 0 0 00	
Photography Revenue		127 2 5 0 00
Rent Expense	6 0 0 0 00	
Office Supplies Expense	—	
Photo Supplies Expense	—	
Insurance Expense	—	
Salaries Expense	102 0 0 0 00	
Depreciation Expense—Office Equipment	—	
Depreciation Expense—Photo Equipment	—	
Utilities Expense	2 5 0 0 00	
Totals	222 3 3 5 00	222 3 3 5 00

Adjustment data:
(a) Office supplies on hand, $5,010.
(b) Photo supplies on hand, $2,610.
(c) Insurance expired during the year, $1,440.
(d) Depreciation of office equipment during the year, $2,500.
(e) Depreciation of photo equipment during the year, $4,000.
(f) Salaries unpaid at the end of the year, $2,000.

Directions:
1. Record the trial balance on a ten-column work sheet and complete the work sheet.
2. Prepare an income statement for the year ended December 31, 20X2.
3. Prepare a statement of owner's equity for the year ended December 31, 20X2.
4. Prepare a balance sheet as of December 31, 20X2.
5. Journalize the December 31, 20X2 adjusting entries.

PROBLEM 4-1B

Objective: To determine the amount of adjustments and record the adjustments in general journal form

Thompson Service Company has the following adjustment data on December 31, 20X2:

(a) The Supplies account had a balance of $3,800 on January 1, 20X2. Supplies were purchased on June 1 ($585) and September 7 ($1,350). A year-end inventory shows $3,445 on hand.

(b) The Prepaid Insurance account has a balance of $23,760, representing premiums paid for a three-year policy on May 1, 20X2.

(c) Equipment was purchased for $130,000 in January 20X1. The equipment has an estimated useful life of ten years and an estimated trade-in value of $10,000.

(d) Salaries of $45,000 are paid weekly on Fridays. December 31, 20X2, falls on Tuesday.

Directions: Record each adjusting entry in general journal form.

PROBLEM 4-2B

Objective: To prepare a work sheet

The following are the account balances of Reid Enterprises on December 31, 20X2:

Account	Balance
Cash	$ 5,500
Accounts Receivable	2,500
Supplies	2,100
Prepaid Insurance	1,760
Equipment	42,000
Accumulated Depreciation—Equipment	10,500
Accounts Payable	8,600
Salaries Payable	—
Vera Reid, Capital	30,970
Vera Reid, Drawing	16,500
Fees Earned	97,000
Salaries Expense	62,800
Rent Expense	8,000
Utilities Expense	5,500
Repairs Expense	410
Supplies Expense	—
Insurance Expense	—
Depreciation Expense—Equipment	—

Adjustment data:
(a) Supplies on hand, $960.
(b) Insurance expired, $750.
(c) Depreciation of equipment, $4,200.
(d) Salaries unpaid, $1,075.

Directions: Prepare a work sheet for Reid Enterprises for the year ended December 31, 20X2.

LEARNING OBJECTIVE 4

Objective: To prepare financial statements from a completed work sheet

Directions: Using the work sheet that you completed for Reid Enterprises in Problem 4-2B, prepare (1) an income statement for the year ended December 31, 20X2; (2) a statement of owner's equity for the year ended December 31, 20X2; (3) a balance sheet dated December 31, 20X2.

PROBLEM 4-4B

LEARNING OBJECTIVE 4

Objective: To prepare financial statements from adjusted account balances

Following is a list of accounts and their adjusted balances from the work sheet of The Stat Team, a consumer research firm, for the six months ended June 30, 20X2:

Account	Adjusted Balance
Accounts Payable	$ 15,600
Accounts Receivable	8,000
Accumulated Depreciation—Office Equipment	5,000
Accumulated Depreciation—Research Equipment	12,400
Cash	21,300
Depreciation Expense—Office Equipment	2,000
Depreciation Expense—Research Equipment	4,200
Fees Earned	140,900
Insurance Expense	3,800
Office Equipment	18,000
Office Supplies	7,200
Office Supplies Expense	6,450
Prepaid Insurance	8,500
Rent Expense	9,600
Repairs Expense	640
Research Equipment	30,600
Research Supplies	3,500
Research Supplies Expense	1,890
Salaries Expense	74,300
Salaries Payable	2,250
Ronald Stephens, Capital	47,830
Ronald Stephens, Drawing	24,000

Directions:
1. Prepare an income statement for the six months ended June 30, 20X2.
2. Prepare a statement of owner's equity for the six months ended June 30, 20X2.
3. Prepare a balance sheet as of June 30, 20X2.

PROBLEM 4-5B

LEARNING OBJECTIVE 2, 3, 4, 5

Objective: To prepare a work sheet and financial statements and journalize adjusting entries

Tom Melon, owner of Speedy Delivery Service, prepared the following trial balance on December 31, 20X2:

Speedy Delivery Service
Trial Balance
December 31, 20X2

Account Title	Debit	Credit
Cash	6 1 0 0 00	
Accounts Receivable	2 1 0 0 00	
Office Supplies	6 2 3 5 00	
Truck Supplies	6 5 0 0 00	
Prepaid Insurance	4 3 5 0 00	
Office Equipment	21 0 0 0 00	
Accumulated Depreciation—Office Equipment		4 0 0 0 00
Trucks	32 0 0 0 00	
Accumulated Depreciation—Trucks		8 4 0 0 00
Accounts Payable		6 0 0 0 00
Salaries Payable		—
T. Melon, Capital		16 4 8 5 00
T. Melon, Drawing	15 0 0 0 00	
Service Revenue		98 8 0 0 00
Rent Expense	4 8 0 0 00	
Office Supplies Expense	—	
Truck Supplies Expense	—	
Insurance Expense	—	
Salaries Expense	33 0 0 0 00	
Depreciation Expense—Office Equipment	—	
Depreciation Expense—Trucks	—	
Utilities Expense	2 6 0 0 00	
Totals	133 6 8 5 00	133 6 8 5 00

Adjustment data:
(a) Office supplies on hand, $5,000.
(b) Truck supplies on hand, $2,650.
(c) Insurance expired during the year, $1,800.
(d) Depreciation of office equipment during the year, $2,800.
(e) Depreciation of trucks during the year, $4,200.
(f) Salaries unpaid at the end of the year, $1,200.

Directions:
1. Record the trial balance on a ten-column work sheet and complete the work sheet.
2. Prepare an income statement for the year ended December 31, 20X2.
3. Prepare a statement of owner's equity for the year ended December 31, 20X2.
4. Prepare a balance sheet as of December 31, 20X2.
5. Journalize the December 31, 20X2 adjusting entries.

CHALLENGE PROBLEMS

PROBLEM SOLVING

Bill Taggart, owner of Taggart Engineering Services, prepared the following trial balance on November 30, 20X2:

Taggart Engineering Services
Trial Balance
November 30, 20X2

	Account Title	Debit	Credit
111	Cash	9 6 0 0 00	
112	Accounts Receivable	6 5 0 0 00	
113	Office Supplies	3 4 0 0 00	
114	Engineering Supplies	6 3 3 0 00	
115	Prepaid Insurance	1 2 0 0 00	
117	Office Equipment	12 4 0 0 00	
117.1	Accumulated Depreciation—Office Equipment		2 8 0 0 00
118	Drafting Equipment	17 5 0 0 00	
118.1	Accumulated Depreciation—Drafting Equipment		3 4 5 0 00
119	Tools	7 2 0 0 00	
119.1	Accumulated Depreciation—Tools		2 2 0 0 00
211	Accounts Payable		1 5 9 0 00
212	Salaries Payable		—
311	Bill Taggart, Capital		33 6 3 0 00
312	Bill Taggart, Drawing	38 0 0 0 00	
411	Professional Fees		118 4 0 0 00
511	Salaries Expense	45 7 0 0 00	
512	Rent Expense	7 2 0 0 00	
513	Depreciation Expense—Office Equipment	—	
514	Depreciation Expense—Drafting Equipment	—	
515	Depreciation Expense—Tools	—	
516	Utilities Expense	3 8 0 0 00	
517	Telephone Expense	2 4 0 0 00	
518	Office Supplies Expense	—	
519	Engineering Supplies Expense	—	
520	Insurance Expense	—	
521	Miscellaneous Expense	8 4 0 00	
	Totals	162 0 7 0 00	162 0 7 0 00

The firm incurred the following transactions during December:

20X2

Dec. 1 Paid rent, $700.

1 Performed services for cash, $2,500.

1 Completed plans for a new office building for Eastway Company. The contract price of the plans was $6,000, with $2,000 to be received when the plans were completed and the balance in 30 days.

4 Purchased office supplies for cash, $500.

5 Purchased engineering supplies on account, $625.

7 Paid salaries of employees, $2,500.

9 Performed services for cash, $800.

10 Performed services for cash, $1,800.

12 Paid telephone bill, $128.

15 Paid salaries of employees, $2,200.

18 Roger Hobbs, a client, paid $500 for blueprints that the firm had done for him on a credit basis in November.

20 Paid cash for a new drafting table, $1,800.

21 Purchased drawing pads, pens, and drafting paper on account, $225.

Dec. 22 Paid cash for two electric pencil sharpeners, $15 each. (Record this as Office Supplies Expense because the accountant decided that, under the materiality concept, the value was insignificant and thus could be expensed directly.)

22 Paid salaries of employees, $2,340.

24 Discovered that one of the pencil sharpeners purchased on December 22 was defective. Returned it for a more expensive model, $25, paying the difference in cash.

26 Paid utility bill, $380.

27 Performed services for cash, $590.

28 Performed services for a client on credit, $350.

29 Paid miscellaneous expenses, $80.

29 Paid salaries of employees, $2,050.

30 Paid cash for engineering supplies, $325.

31 Paid cash for office supplies, $200.

31 Received the amount due from Eastway Company.

31 Prepaid a six-month insurance premium, $1,400.

Directions:

1. Open a ledger account for each account that is listed on Taggart's November 30 trial balance. Use December 1 as the date, and, for each account that has a balance, enter the balance in the appropriate column.

2. Record Taggart's December transactions in a general journal.

3. Post from the journal to the ledger.

4. Prepare a trial balance directly on a ten-column work sheet.

5. Complete the work sheet using the following adjustment data:

   (a) Office supplies on hand, $1,860.

   (b) Engineering supplies on hand, $2,450.

   (c) Insurance expired, $950.

   (d) Depreciation of office equipment, $1,200.

   (e) Depreciation of drafting equipment, $1,450.

   (f) Depreciation of tools, $900.

   (g) Unpaid salaries, $630.

6. Prepare an income statement for the year ended December 31, 20X2.

7. Prepare a statement of owner's equity for the year ended December 31, 20X2.

8. Prepare a balance sheet as of December 31, 20X2.

9. Journalize and post the adjusting entries.

COMMUNICATIONS

Jay Dixon just completed a test on adjusting entries. Even though he did very well on the test, he believes that recording depreciation in a separate contra asset account is redundant and unnecessary. He asks, "Why can't we just record the depreciation as a credit to the asset itself and be done with it?"

Explain to Jay the benefit of recording depreciation in a contra account.

ETHICS

Chad Lott is the owner of a delivery service. Since he has an associate's degree in accounting, he keeps his own records. As you look them over for him, you come to the shocking discovery that there are no adjusting entries. As you explore further, you notice that all prepaid expenses, such as prepaid insurance, are recorded as expenses in their full amounts upon payment. In addition, items such as unpaid salaries are simply not recorded until they are paid in the next accounting period.

When you ask Chad why he does not use adjusting entries, he replies "They are a pain. Besides, we get to the same place after a few days anyway."

Explain to Chad why what he is doing is not appropriate accounting procedure.

ANSWERS TO REVIEW QUIZZES

REVIEW QUIZ 4-1

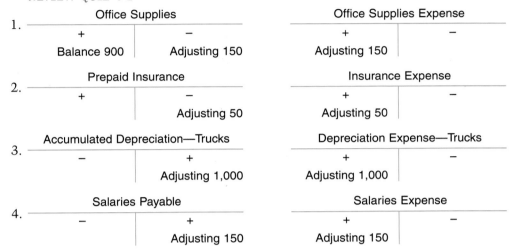

1.

Office Supplies		Office Supplies Expense	
+	−	+	−
Balance 900	Adjusting 150	Adjusting 150	

2.

Prepaid Insurance		Insurance Expense	
+	−	+	−
	Adjusting 50	Adjusting 50	

3.

Accumulated Depreciation—Trucks		Depreciation Expense—Trucks	
−	+	+	−
	Adjusting 1,000	Adjusting 1,000	

4.

Salaries Payable		Salaries Expense	
−	+	+	−
	Adjusting 150	Adjusting 150	

REVIEW QUIZ 4-2

Yes, because differences between revenue and expenses will either increase or decrease capital. The difference between the totals of the Balance Sheet Dr. and Cr. columns of the work sheet reflects the net income or net loss that has not yet been transferred to the owner's capital account.

REVIEW QUIZ 4-3

1.

Pace Company Income Statement For Year Ended December 31, 20X2		
Revenue:		
Service revenue		$52 0 00 00
Expenses:		
Salaries expense	$14 3 00 00	
Rent expense	4 2 00 00	
Utilities expense	2 9 00 00	
Telephone expense	1 5 70 00	
Depreciation expense	8 00 00	
Office supplies expense	2 2 5 00	
Total expenses		23 9 95 00
Net income		$28 0 05 00

2.

Pace Company Statement of Owner's Equity For Year Ended December 31, 20X2				
Capital, January 1, 20X2				$15 9 1 5 00
Net income for period	$28 0 0 5 00			
Less withdrawals	18 0 0 0 00			
Increase in capital				10 0 0 5 00
Capital, December 31, 20X2				$25 9 2 0 00

3.

Pace Company Balance Sheet December 31, 20X2				
Assets				
Cash			$ 6 2 0 0 00	
Accounts receivable			9 2 0 00	
Supplies			6 0 0 00	
Equipment	$22 0 0 0 00			
Less: Accumulated depreciation	2 0 0 0 00		20 0 0 0 00	
Total assets				$27 7 2 0 00
Liabilities				
Accounts payable				$ 1 8 0 0 00
Owner's Equity				
Joe Pace, capital				25 9 2 0 00
Total liabilities and owner's equity				$27 7 2 0 00

REVIEW QUIZ 4-4

It is necessary to make journal entries for adjustments because the work sheet is not a journal. It is an informal document used to organize data and facilitate the work at the end of an accounting period. However, no posting is made from the work sheet. After adjustments have been journalized and posted, the ledger will be up-to-date and will agree with the data presented on the financial statements.

5

COMPLETING THE ACCOUNTING CYCLE FOR A SERVICE BUSINESS

Closing Entries and the Post-Closing Trial Balance

LEARNING OBJECTIVES

After studying Chapter 5, you will be able to:
1. Explain the purpose of the closing process.
2. Journalize and post closing entries.
3. Prepare a post-closing trial balance.

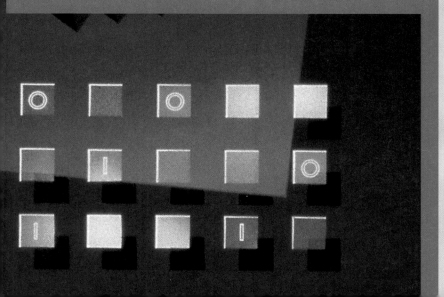

Chapter 5 completes the discussion of the accounting cycle. The chapter shows how to journalize and post closing entries and prepare a post-closing trial balance.

During the closing process, the balances of the temporary accounts are transferred to the capital account so that these accounts can accumulate data for a new accounting period. The ending capital account balance corresponds to the amount presented on the balance sheet.

If you are using a computerized accounting system, the closing process is automatic. The results of both systems are the same.

— Fred R. Jex, CPA, MBA, Ph.D.
Macomb Community College

In Chapter 4, we learned that at the end of an accounting period some accounts normally need adjusting to bring them up to date. We also learned how to prepare a work sheet as an aid in completing the work at the end of the accounting cycle. We used a completed work sheet to prepare financial statements and journalize adjusting entries. In Chapter 5, we will complete our study of the accounting cycle for a service business. Two steps remain to be covered:

⑨ Journalize and post closing entries.
⑩ Prepare a post-closing trial balance.

PURPOSE OF CLOSING ENTRIES

LEARNING OBJECTIVE 1

Revenue and expense accounts and the owner's drawing account are **temporary accounts** (also called **nominal accounts**) used to show changes in owner's equity during a single accounting period. When an accounting period is over, the temporary accounts will have served their purpose for that period. Therefore, their balances are summarized and transferred to the owner's capital account.

The process of transferring the balances of the temporary accounts to the owner's capital account is called the **closing process**. Entries necessary to accomplish the closing process are called **closing entries**.

The closing process has two objectives:

1. To reduce the balances of temporary owner's equity accounts to zero and thus make the accounts ready for entries in the next accounting period. Otherwise, amounts for the next accounting period would be added to amounts from previous accounting periods, which would violate the matching principle.
2. To update the balance of the owner's capital account.

STEP 9: JOURNALIZE AND POST CLOSING ENTRIES

LEARNING OBJECTIVE 2

In the closing process, we will use a new account entitled **Income Summary**. The Income Summary account is a **clearing account** used to summarize the balances of revenue and expense accounts. Use of the Income Summary account avoids the unnecessary detail of closing the balance of each revenue account and each expense account directly into the owner's capital account. The Income Summary account is used only at the end of an accounting period and is opened and closed during the closing process.

Steps in the Closing Process

The closing process consists of four steps:

❶ Close the balance of each revenue account to Income Summary.

② Close the balance of each expense account to Income Summary.
③ Close the balance of Income Summary to the owner's capital account.
④ Close the balance of the owner's drawing account directly to the owner's capital account.

Let's now return to the end-of-period activities of Taylor and Associates and look again at the financial statement columns of Mr. Taylor's December 31 work sheet, as illustrated in Figure 5-1. (The complete work sheet is shown in Chapter 4 on page 118.) The work sheet is very useful when preparing closing entries, because up-to-date balances of all temporary accounts are clearly shown together in one place.

To illustrate closing entries, we will record Taylor's closing entries in T-account form. Later in the chapter we will see how closing entries are formally journalized and posted to the ledger.

FIGURE 5-1
Financial statement columns of the work sheet

Taylor and Associates
Work Sheet
For Two Months Ended December 31, 20X1

	Account Title	Income Statement Debit	Income Statement Credit	Balance Sheet Debit	Balance Sheet Credit	
1	Cash			8 4 8 5 00		1
2	Accounts Receivable			3 0 0 00		2
3	Office Supplies			2 3 0 00		3
4	Prepaid Insurance			2 2 0 00		4
5	Office Equipment			3 0 0 0 00		5
6	Accumulated Depreciation—Office Equipment				5 0 00	6
7	Office Furniture			2 0 0 0 00		7
8	Accumulated Depreciation—Office Furniture				3 0 00	8
9	Accounts Payable				3 0 0 0 00	9
10	Salaries Payable				2 1 0 00	10
11	William Taylor, Capital				10 0 0 0 00	11
12	William Taylor, Drawing			1 5 0 0 00		12
13	Service Revenue		4 7 0 0 00			13
14	Rent Expense	8 0 0 00				14
15	Repairs Expense	5 0 00				15
16	Salaries Expense	1 2 6 0 00				16
17	Office Supplies Expense	4 5 00				17
18	Insurance Expense	2 0 00				18
19	Depreciation Expense—Office Equipment	5 0 00				19
20	Depreciation Expense—Office Furniture	3 0 00				20
21		2 2 5 5 00	4 7 0 0 00	15 7 3 5 00	13 2 9 0 00	21
22	Net Income	2 4 4 5 00			2 4 4 5 00	22
23		4 7 0 0 00	4 7 0 0 00	15 7 3 5 00	15 7 3 5 00	23

STEP 1: CLOSE THE BALANCE OF EACH REVENUE ACCOUNT TO INCOME SUMMARY

As we have seen, all revenue appears in the Income Statement Cr. column of the work sheet. Taylor and Associates' work sheet shows only one revenue account, Service Revenue, with a credit balance of $4,700. To close an account, we must make an entry that will reduce the balance of the account to zero. Thus, the Service Revenue account must be *debited* for its $4,700 *credit* balance. Our credit is to the Income Summary account.

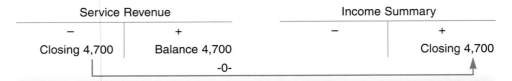

> **Note** *Income Summary is a temporary account that is located in the chart of accounts under owner's equity. It is used only at the end of the accounting period and never appears on the financial statements. And unlike other accounts, Income Summary does not have a normal debit or credit balance.*

STEP 2: CLOSE THE BALANCE OF EACH EXPENSE ACCOUNT TO INCOME SUMMARY

Expenses are shown in the Income Statement Dr. column of the work sheet. Taylor and Associates has seven expense accounts, each with a debit balance. Thus, each must be credited to close it. The Income Summary account could be debited seven times; or, more realistically, there could be one compound debit. This step is shown in Figure 5-2.

FIGURE 5-2
Closing the balance of each expense account to Income Summary

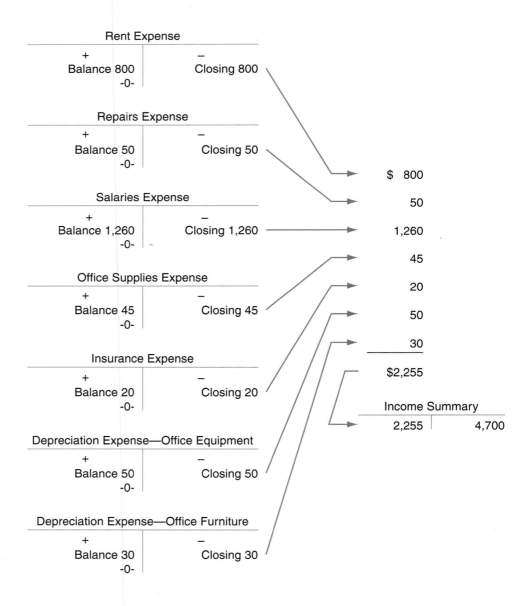

STEP 3: CLOSE THE BALANCE OF INCOME SUMMARY TO THE OWNER'S CAPITAL ACCOUNT

We mentioned at the start of our discussion that the Income Summary account is a clearing account that is opened at the end of an accounting period to summarize and close the balances of revenue and expense accounts. Having closed the balances of revenue and expense accounts in steps 1 and 2, we now close the balance of the Income Summary account into the owner's capital account. The balance of the Income Summary account is found as follows:

Cr. $4,700
Dr.   − 2,255
Bal. $2,445 ◄── balance is a credit

This balance should be a familiar one—it is the net income figure. This is as it should be, since both revenue and expenses have been closed into the Income Summary account. Because this balance is a credit, it is closed by making a debit for the same amount, as shown below.

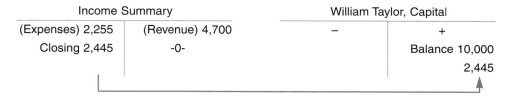

At this stage of the closing process, the Income Summary account will always reflect the amount of net income or net loss. In this case, there is a net income. It is, therefore, transferred to the credit side (the increase side) of the owner's capital account. Had there been a net loss for the period, the entries would have been reversed and the net loss would be transferred to the debit side (the decrease side) of the owner's capital account.

STEP 4: CLOSE THE BALANCE OF THE OWNER'S DRAWING ACCOUNT DIRECTLY TO THE OWNER'S CAPITAL ACCOUNT

The owner's drawing account is not closed to Income Summary.

The balance of the owner's drawing account does not enter into the determination of net income or net loss. Therefore, the drawing account *is not* closed to the Income Summary account. Its balance, instead, is closed directly into the owner's capital account. The drawing account has a debit balance; thus, it is closed by making an equal credit. The amount of drawing is found in the Balance Sheet Dr. column of the work sheet.

William Taylor, Drawing		William Taylor, Capital	
+	−	−	+
Balance 1,500	Closing 1,500	Closing 1,500	Balance 10,000
-0-			2,445

If we now balance William Taylor, Capital, we will find that it has a credit balance of $10,945.

William Taylor, Capital

1,500	Balance 10,000
	2,445
	12,445
	New Bal. 10,945

> **Remember** To balance a T account, find the difference between the two sides: $12,445.00 – $1,500.00 = $10,945.00.

The capital account is now up to date because its balance agrees with the total capital as reported on Taylor's statement of owner's equity, which was illustrated in Chapter 4 on page 121. All revenue, expenses, and owner's drawing accounts have zero balances, as does the Income Summary account. Therefore, the closing process is complete.

Incidentally, the accounts that remain open—assets, contra assets, liabilities, and the owner's capital account—are referred to as **permanent** (or **real**) **accounts**. They are permanent in the sense that their balances will be carried into the next accounting period.

Journalizing Closing Entries

We recorded Mr. Taylor's closing entries in T accounts to illustrate the closing process. In reality, closing entries must be formally journalized and posted to the ledger. The next free line in the journal is used for writing the heading *Closing Entries*. No further explanation is necessary. To illustrate, the closing entries of Taylor and Associates are journalized in Figure 5-3. As with adjusting entries, closing entries are dated as of the last day of the accounting period.

FIGURE 5-3
Closing entries in the general journal

Tip: Only the REID accounts are closed (Revenue, Expenses, Income Summary, and Drawing). ALOC accounts remain open (Assets, Liabilities, and the Owner's Capital account).

	Date		Account Title	P.R.	Debit	Credit	
1	20X1		Closing Entries				1
2	Dec.	31	Service Revenue		4 7 0 0 00		2
3			Income Summary			4 7 0 0 00	3
4							4
5		31	Income Summary		2 2 5 5 00		5
6			Rent Expense			8 0 0 00	6
7			Repairs Expense			5 0 00	7
8			Salaries Expense			1 2 6 0 00	8
9			Office Supplies Expense			4 5 00	9
10			Insurance Expense			2 0 00	10
11			Depr. Expense—Office Equipment			5 0 00	11
12			Depr. Expense—Office Furniture			3 0 00	12
13							13
14		31	Income Summary		2 4 4 5 00		14
15			William Taylor, Capital			2 4 4 5 00	15
16							16
17		31	William Taylor, Capital		1 5 0 0 00		17
18			William Taylor, Drawing			1 5 0 0 00	18

General Journal — Page 3

Diagram of the Closing Process

Now that we have illustrated the closing process, let's summarize the steps in diagram form, as shown in Figure 5-4.

❶ Close the balance of revenue accounts to Income Summary.
❷ Close the balance of expense accounts to Income Summary.
❸ Close the balance of Income Summary to the owner's capital account. After steps 1 and 2, the Income Summary account will show the amount of net income or net loss for the period.
❹ Close the balance of the owner's drawing account to the owner's capital account.

In Figure 5-4, it is assumed that there is a net income for the period; that is, the Income Summary account has a credit balance after expense and revenue accounts are closed. Should a net loss occur, it will appear as a debit balance in the Income Summary account and will be closed to the debit side (the decrease side) of the owner's capital account.

FIGURE 5-4
The four steps of the closing process

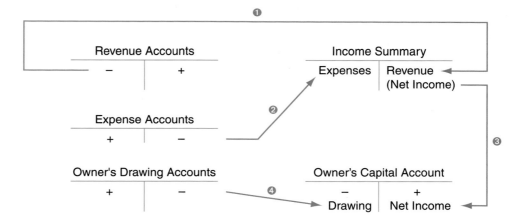

The financial statement columns of Carter Realty's work sheet are shown on the next page. Journalize the entries necessary to close the temporary accounts.

CONTINUES

	Account Title				

Carter Realty Co.
Work Sheet
For Year Ended June 30, 20XX

	Account Title	Income Statement Debit	Income Statement Credit	Balance Sheet Debit	Balance Sheet Credit	
1	Cash			3 0 0 0 00		1
2	Accounts Receivable			1 0 0 0 00		2
3	Office Supplies			8 0 0 00		3
4	Prepaid Insurance			4 0 0 00		4
5	Office Equipment			12 0 0 0 00		5
6	Accumulated Depreciation—Office Equipment				3 0 0 0 00	6
7	Automobiles			26 0 0 0 00		7
8	Accumulated Depreciation—Automobiles				6 0 0 0 00	8
9	Accounts Payable				2 0 0 0 00	9
10	Salaries Payable				4 0 0 00	10
11	Kim Carter, Capital				35 5 0 0 00	11
12	Kim Carter, Drawing			19 0 0 0 00		12
13	Service Revenue		89 6 0 0 00			13
14	Rent Expense	6 0 0 0 00				14
15	Salaries Expense	57 4 0 0 00				15
16	Office Supplies Expense	1 0 0 00				16
17	Telephone Expense	6 0 0 00				17
18	Insurance Expense	2 0 0 00				18
19	Depreciation Expense—Office Equipment	1 0 0 0 00				19
20	Depreciation Expense—Automobiles	2 0 0 0 00				20
21	Utilities Expense	6 3 0 0 00				21
22	Miscellaneous Expense	7 0 0 00				22
23		74 3 0 0 00	89 6 0 0 00	62 2 0 0 00	46 9 0 0 00	23
24	Net Income	15 3 0 0 00			15 3 0 0 00	24
25		89 6 0 0 00	89 6 0 0 00	62 2 0 0 00	62 2 0 0 00	25

CHECK YOUR ANSWERS ON PAGES 174–175.

Posting Closing Entries

After closing entries have been journalized, the next step in the accounting cycle is to post these entries from the general journal to the ledger. After posting has occurred, the permanent accounts will have up-to-date balances and the temporary accounts will have zero balances. To illustrate, the complete ledger of Taylor and Associates is shown in Figure 5-5. Notice that the balances of the permanent accounts (assets, liabilities, and owner's equity) agree with the amounts reported on the financial statements we prepared for Mr. Taylor in Chapter 4. Also notice that we indicate that the temporary accounts are closed by writing the word *Closing* in the Item column of each account and by drawing a line through both the Debit Balance and Credit Balance columns.

FIGURE 5-5
Complete ledger for Taylor and Associates

General Ledger

Account Cash   **Account No.** 111

Date	Item	P.R.	Debit	Credit	Balance Debit	Balance Credit
20X1 Dec. 1	Balance	✓			9 4 2 5 00	
1		GJ2		2 4 0 00	9 1 8 5 00	
5		GJ2		1 5 0 00	9 0 3 5 00	
12		GJ2		3 5 0 00	8 6 8 5 00	
15		GJ2		4 0 0 00	8 2 8 5 00	
19		GJ2		1 0 0 0 00	7 2 8 5 00	
19		GJ2		3 5 0 00	6 9 3 5 00	
20		GJ2	1 0 0 00		7 0 3 5 00	
22		GJ2		7 0 0 00	6 3 3 5 00	
23		GJ2	2 5 0 0 00		8 8 3 5 00	
26		GJ2		3 5 0 00	8 4 8 5 00	

Account Accounts Receivable   **Account No.** 112

Date	Item	P.R.	Debit	Credit	Balance Debit	Balance Credit
20X1 Dec. 1	Balance	✓			3 0 0 00	

Account Office Supplies   **Account No.** 113

Date	Item	P.R.	Debit	Credit	Balance Debit	Balance Credit
20X1 Dec. 1	Balance	✓			1 2 5 00	
5		GJ2	1 5 0 00		2 7 5 00	
31	Adjusting	GJ2		4 5 00	2 3 0 00	

Account Prepaid Insurance   **Account No.** 114

Date	Item	P.R.	Debit	Credit	Balance Debit	Balance Credit
20X1 Dec. 1		GJ2	2 4 0 00		2 4 0 00	
31	Adjusting	GJ2		2 0 00	2 2 0 00	

Account Office Equipment   **Account No.** 116

Date	Item	P.R.	Debit	Credit	Balance Debit	Balance Credit
20X1 Dec. 1	Balance	✓			3 0 0 0 00	

Account Accumulated Depreciation—Office Equipment   **Account No.** 116.1

Date	Item	P.R.	Debit	Credit	Balance Debit	Balance Credit
20X1 Dec. 31	Adjusting	GJ2		5 0 00		5 0 00

CONTINUES

Completing the Accounting Cycle for a Service Business

FIGURE 5-5
Continued

Account Office Furniture — **Account No.** 117

Date		Item	P.R.	Debit	Credit	Balance	
						Debit	Credit
20X1 Dec.	1	Balance	✓			2 0 0 0 00	

Account Accumulated Depreciation—Office Furniture — **Account No.** 117.1

Date		Item	P.R.	Debit	Credit	Balance	
						Debit	Credit
20X1 Dec.	31	Adjusting	GJ2		30 00		30 00

Account Accounts Payable — **Account No.** 211

Date		Item	P.R.	Debit	Credit	Balance	
						Debit	Credit
20X1 Dec.	1	Balance	✓				4 0 0 0 00
	19		GJ2	1 0 0 0 00			3 0 0 0 00

Account Salaries Payable — **Account No.** 212

Date		Item	P.R.	Debit	Credit	Balance	
						Debit	Credit
20X1 Dec.	31	Adjusting	GJ2		2 1 0 00		2 1 0 00

Account William Taylor, Capital — **Account No.** 311

Date		Item	P.R.	Debit	Credit	Balance	
						Debit	Credit
20X1 Dec.	1	Balance	✓				10 0 0 0 00
	31	Closing	GJ3		2 4 4 5 00		12 4 4 5 00
	31	Closing	GJ3	1 5 0 0 00			10 9 4 5 00

Account William Taylor, Drawing — **Account No.** 312

Date		Item	P.R.	Debit	Credit	Balance	
						Debit	Credit
20X1 Dec.	1	Balance	✓			8 0 0 00	
	22		GJ2	7 0 0 00		1 5 0 0 00	
	31	Closing	GJ3		1 5 0 0 00	—	—

Account Income Summary — **Account No.** 313

Date		Item	P.R.	Debit	Credit	Balance	
						Debit	Credit
20X1 Dec.	31	Closing (Revenue)	GJ3		4 7 0 0 00		4 7 0 0 00
	31	Closing (Expenses)	GJ3	2 2 5 5 00			2 4 4 5 00
	31	Closing (Net Income)	GJ3	2 4 4 5 00		—	—

Account Service Revenue — **Account No.** 411

Date		Item	P.R.	Debit	Credit	Balance	
						Debit	Credit
20X1 Dec.	1	Balance	✓				2 2 0 0 00
	23		GJ2		2 5 0 0 00		4 7 0 0 00
	31	Closing	GJ3	4 7 0 0 00		—	—

CONTINUES

FIGURE 5-5
Continued

Account Rent Expense   **Account No.** 511

Date		Item	P.R.	Debit	Credit	Balance Debit	Balance Credit
20X1 Dec.	1	Balance	✓			4 0 0 00	
	15		GJ2	4 0 0 00		8 0 0 00	
	31	Closing	GJ3		8 0 0 00	—	—

Account Repairs Expense   **Account No.** 512

Date		Item	P.R.	Debit	Credit	Balance Debit	Balance Credit
20X1 Dec.	1	Balance	✓			5 0 00	
	31	Closing	GJ3		5 0 00	—	—

Account Salaries Expense   **Account No.** 513

Date		Item	P.R.	Debit	Credit	Balance Debit	Balance Credit
20X1 Dec.	12		GJ2	3 5 0 00		3 5 0 00	
	19		GJ2	3 5 0 00		7 0 0 00	
	26		GJ2	3 5 0 00		1 0 5 0 00	
	31	Adjusting	GJ2	2 1 0 00		1 2 6 0 00	
	31	Closing	GJ3		1 2 6 0 00	—	—

Account Office Supplies Expense   **Account No.** 514

Date		Item	P.R.	Debit	Credit	Balance Debit	Balance Credit
20X1 Dec.	31	Adjusting	GJ2	4 5 00		4 5 00	
	31	Closing	GJ3		4 5 00	—	—

Account Insurance Expense   **Account No.** 515

Date		Item	P.R.	Debit	Credit	Balance Debit	Balance Credit
20X1 Dec.	31	Adjusting	GJ2	2 0 00		2 0 00	
	31	Closing	GJ3		2 0 00	—	—

Account Depreciation Expense—Office Equipment   **Account No.** 516

Date		Item	P.R.	Debit	Credit	Balance Debit	Balance Credit
20X1 Dec.	31	Adjusting	GJ2	5 0 00		5 0 00	
	31	Closing	GJ3		5 0 00	—	—

Account Depreciation Expense—Office Furniture   **Account No.** 517

Date		Item	P.R.	Debit	Credit	Balance Debit	Balance Credit
20X1 Dec.	31	Adjusting	GJ2	3 0 00		3 0 00	
	31	Closing	GJ3		3 0 00	—	—

REVIEW QUIZ

5-2

T-account balances of W. Dee, as of December 31, 20X1, are shown below. Prepare, in general journal form, entries necessary to close the balances of the temporary accounts.

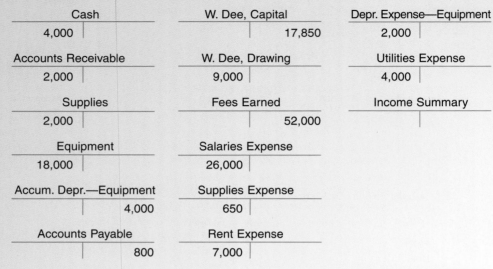

Cash	W. Dee, Capital	Depr. Expense—Equipment
4,000	17,850	2,000

Accounts Receivable	W. Dee, Drawing	Utilities Expense
2,000	9,000	4,000

Supplies	Fees Earned	Income Summary
2,000	52,000	

Equipment	Salaries Expense
18,000	26,000

Accum. Depr.—Equipment	Supplies Expense
4,000	650

Accounts Payable	Rent Expense
800	7,000

CHECK YOUR ANSWERS ON PAGE 175.

STEP 10: PREPARE A POST-CLOSING TRIAL BALANCE

LEARNING OBJECTIVE 3

After closing entries have been posted, you should verify the equality of debits and credits in the accounts that remain open. To do this, you prepare a post-closing trial balance, which is the final step in the accounting cycle. The purpose of the **post-closing trial balance** (also called the **after-closing trial balance**) is to make sure that the ledger will be in balance at the start of the next accounting period. The only accounts appearing on the post-closing trial balance are the permanent accounts, since the balances of all temporary accounts have been reduced to zero. The post-closing trial balance of Taylor and Associates is shown in Figure 5-6.

FIGURE 5-6
The post-closing trial balance

Taylor and Associates Post-Closing Trial Balance December 31, 20X1		
Account Title	**Debit**	**Credit**
Cash	8 485 00	
Accounts Receivable	3 00 00	
Office Supplies	2 30 00	
Prepaid Insurance	2 20 00	
Office Equipment	3 000 00	
Accumulated Depreciation—Office Equipment		50 00
Office Furniture	2 000 00	
Accumulated Depreciation—Office Furniture		30 00
Accounts Payable		3 000 00
Salaries Payable		2 10 00
William Taylor, Capital		10 945 00
Totals	14 235 00	14 235 00

SUMMARY OF THE STEPS IN THE ACCOUNTING CYCLE

We have now completed all the steps in the accounting cycle for a service business, from analyzing source documents to the post-closing trial balance. Let's pause and look at a listing of all the steps we have studied:

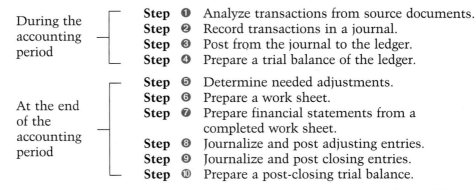

During the accounting period
- **Step ❶** Analyze transactions from source documents.
- **Step ❷** Record transactions in a journal.
- **Step ❸** Post from the journal to the ledger.
- **Step ❹** Prepare a trial balance of the ledger.

At the end of the accounting period
- **Step ❺** Determine needed adjustments.
- **Step ❻** Prepare a work sheet.
- **Step ❼** Prepare financial statements from a completed work sheet.
- **Step ❽** Journalize and post adjusting entries.
- **Step ❾** Journalize and post closing entries.
- **Step ❿** Prepare a post-closing trial balance.

Notice that we divided the accounting cycle into work that is performed *during the accounting period* (steps 1–4), and work that is performed *at the end of the accounting period* (steps 5–10). The greater number of steps to be done at the end of the period may suggest that most of the work of the accounting cycle comes at the end of the accounting period. This, however, is not the case. The routine journalizing and posting that is done during the accounting period takes far more time than the end-of-period work.

Let us stress that most businesses prepare adjusting entries, closing entries, and the post-closing trial balance *only* at the end of a twelve-month accounting period. We used a two-month accounting period for Taylor and Associates—November and December, 20X1. These were the first two months Mr. Taylor was open for business. The next time Mr. Taylor performs the work at the end of the accounting cycle will be for the year ended December 31, 20X2.

We should also emphasize that steps 5 through 10 of the accounting cycle are performed *as of* the last day of the accounting period, not *on* the last day of the accounting period. The accountant will need some time in the new accounting period to assemble the data necessary to complete the work at the end of the preceding period. Thus, it could take several days (or weeks) to complete the work of the previous accounting cycle. Nonetheless, the work sheet, financial statements, adjusting entries, and closing entries are prepared as of the last day of the accounting period.

FISCAL PERIOD

A **fiscal period** is any period of time covering the complete accounting cycle, from the analysis of transactions to the post-closing trial balance. A fiscal period consisting of twelve consecutive months is a **fiscal year**. A fiscal year does not necessarily coincide with the calendar year (from January 1 to December 31). Many businesses have seasonal peaks. For them, it is logical to end the accounting period at the point in the operating cycle in which activity is at its lowest. A fiscal year can thus cover any twelve-month period, starting on the first day of a month and ending twelve months later.

For example, the fiscal year of a ski lodge that is operated only during the snow season may be from July 1 of one year to June 30 of the next year. This way, the ledger would be adjusted and closed as of June 30, which would be the period in which the least amount of business activity is being conducted. A fiscal year ending at a business's lowest point of activity is referred to as a **natural business year**.

THE BASES OF ACCOUNTING

In Chapter 4, we discussed the matching principle, which states that revenue earned during an accounting period should be offset by the expenses that were necessary to generate that revenue. In other words, revenue earned and expenses incurred during any accounting period should be reported (matched) on the income statement for that period.

To apply the matching principle, most accounting systems operate on the **accrual basis of accounting**. As we have already learned, sometimes a transaction occurs in one accounting period, but the cash involved is not received or paid out until a later period. Under the accrual basis, revenue is recorded when it is earned, no matter when cash is received; and expenses are recorded when they are incurred, no matter when cash is paid out. For example, if goods or services are sold on account, in the accrual basis one records revenue at the point of sale, even though the receipt of cash may be in a later period. Likewise, an expense is recorded when it is incurred, even though payment may not be made until a later accounting period. According to GAAP, the accrual basis *must* be used by businesses in which the major activity is the production or trading of goods.

Another basis of accounting is the **cash basis**. With the cash basis, revenue is recorded only when cash is received, and expenses are recorded only when cash is paid out. The cash basis is used mostly by individual taxpayers when filing their personal income tax returns. Here, personal income (wages, salaries, interest, etc.) is reported only when cash has been received; and expenses are reported as personal deductions only when cash has been paid.

Businesses rarely use a strictly cash basis because most companies have some type of equipment, and the Internal Revenue Service requires that equipment be depreciated over a period of years—which results in an expense (depreciation expense) that does not involve cash. As a result, many professional firms and service businesses use the modified cash basis, which is a hybrid of the accrual basis and the cash basis. Under the **modified cash basis**, revenue and expenses are reported only when cash changes hands. However, adjustments must be made for the depreciation of long-term assets. Adjustments must also be made for insurance premiums paid in advance and for purchases of large amounts of supplies.

WHERE CAN I FIND DEFINITIONS OF IRS, GAAP, SEC, EPS, AND OTHER ACCOUNTING TERMS?

If you are having trouble remembering what all of the accounting terms mean, you can find help on the Internet. One place to find the definitions of accounting terms on the Internet is the "Technobabble Dictionary." It is located at

http://www.cpaonline.com/Netscape20/resources.hmx

Another location where you can find virtually every word or acronym in the world of technology is

http://www.whatis.com

Clear explanations, pronunciation guides, and links to other sites for further information make these pages invaluable for both novice and advanced Internet users.

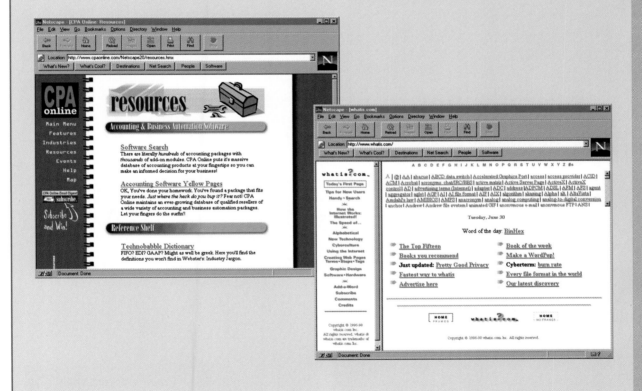

JOINING THE PIECES

STEPS IN THE ACCOUNTING CYCLE FOR A SERVICE BUSINESS

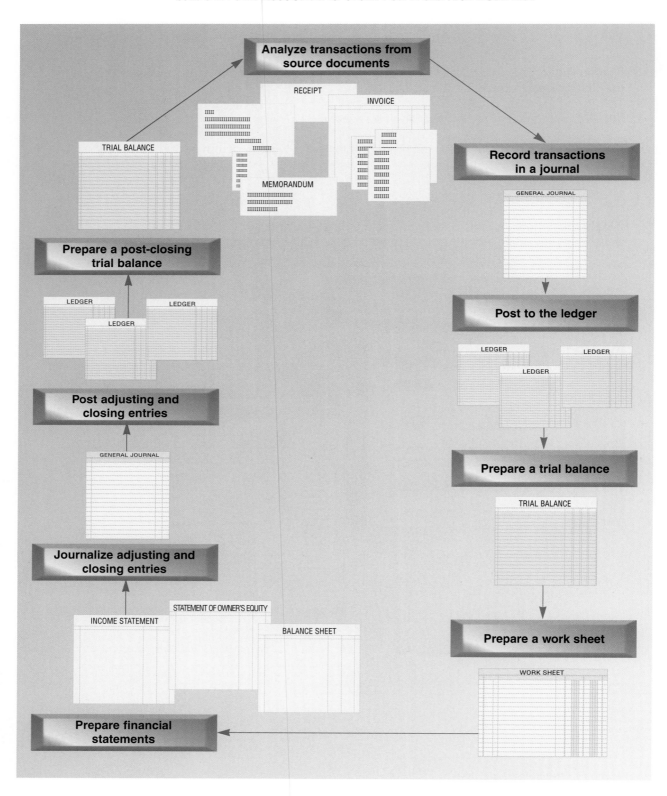

SUMMARY/RESTATEMENT OF LEARNING OBJECTIVES

1. Explain the purpose of the closing process.

Revenue accounts, expense accounts, and the owner's drawing account are **temporary accounts** used to show changes in owner's equity during an accounting period. When the accounting period ends, the temporary accounts will have served their purpose for that period. Therefore, their balances are summarized and transferred to the owner's capital account. The process of transferring the balances of the temporary accounts to the owner's capital account is called the **closing process**. Entries necessary to accomplish the closing process are called **closing entries**. The closing process has two objectives:

- **To reduce the balances of temporary accounts to zero and thus make the accounts ready for entries in the next accounting period.** By starting the new accounting period with zero balances in the temporary accounts, we can accumulate new information about revenue, expenses, and owner withdrawals in the new period.
- **To update the balance of the owner's capital account.** Closing the temporary accounts summarizes their effect on capital and leads to a new capital balance that agrees with the amount reported on the statement of owner's equity.

2. Journalize and post closing entries.

In restating the learning objectives of Chapter 4, we illustrated the work sheet of R & W Shoe Repair. For our review of the closing process, we again use R & W as our illustration. Let's look at the financial statement columns of R & W's work sheet for the year ended December 31, 20XX, as shown in Figure 5-7.

FIGURE 5-7
Financial statement columns of the work sheet

R & W Shoe Repair
Work Sheet
For Year Ended December 31, 20XX

	Account Title	Income Statement Debit	Income Statement Credit	Balance Sheet Debit	Balance Sheet Credit	
1	Cash			7 755 00		1
2	Supplies			7 50 00		2
3	Prepaid Insurance			1 200 00		3
4	Equipment			20 000 00		4
5	Accumulated Depreciation—Equipment				6 000 00	5
6	Accounts Payable				7 600 00	6
7	Salaries Payable				1 000 00	7
8	R. Wilson, Capital				19 780 00	8
9	R. Wilson, Drawing			2 500 00		9
10	Revenue from Services		62 240 00			10
11	Rent Expense	7 200 00				11
12	Salaries Expense	52 000 00				12
13	Utilities Expense	2 400 00				13
14	Supplies Expense	2 15 00				14
15	Insurance Expense	6 00 00				15
16	Depreciation Expense—Equipment	2 000 00				16
17		64 415 00	62 240 00	32 205 00	34 380 00	17
18	Net Loss		2 175 00	2 175 00		18
19		64 415 00	64 415 00	34 380 00	34 380 00	19

The work sheet is the source of all information needed to prepare the closing entries. Current balances of expense and revenue accounts are found in the Income Statement Dr. and Cr. columns, and the balance of the owner's drawing account is found in the Balance Sheet Dr. column.

Four separate journal entries are needed to close the temporary accounts of R & W:

- The balance of the revenue account is transferred to the credit side of the Income Summary account.
- The balances of the expense accounts are transferred to the debit side of the Income Summary account.
- The balance of the Income Summary account is transferred to the owner's capital account.
- The balance of the owner's drawing account is transferred to the debit side of the owner's capital account.

R & W's closing entries are journalized in Figure 5-8.

FIGURE 5-8
Closing the entries in the general journal

	Date		Account Title	P.R.	Debit	Credit	
			General Journal			**Page 2**	
1			Closing Entries				1
2	20XX Dec.	31	Revenue from Services		62 2 4 0 00		2
3			Income Summary			62 2 4 0 00	3
4							4
5		31	Income Summary		64 4 1 5 00		5
6			Rent Expense			7 2 0 0 00	6
7			Salaries Expense			52 0 0 0 00	7
8			Utilities Expense			2 4 0 0 00	8
9			Supplies Expense			2 1 5 00	9
10			Insurance Expense			6 0 0 00	10
11			Depreciation Expense—Equipment			2 0 0 0 00	11
12							12
13		31	R. Wilson, Capital		2 1 7 5 00		13
14			Income Summary			2 1 7 5 00	14
15							15
16		31	R. Wilson, Capital		2 5 0 0 00		16
17			R. Wilson, Drawing			2 5 0 0 00	17

Once closing entries have been journalized, the next step in the accounting cycle is to post the closing entries to the ledger. Since this is a mechanical step, the posting of R & W's closing entries will not be illustrated here.

3. Prepare a post-closing trial balance.

After closing entries have been posted, the accountant should prepare a **post-closing trial balance** (also called an **after-closing trial balance**) to make sure that the ledger is still in balance. As we stated above, R & W's ledger is not illustrated; however, its post-closing trial balance, taken as of December 31, 20XX, appears in Figure 5-9. Notice that only the permanent accounts are shown with balances, as all temporary accounts have been closed.

FIGURE 5-9
The post-closing trial balance

Account Title	Debit	Credit
R & W Shoe Repair		
Post-Closing Trial Balance		
December 31, 20XX		
Cash	7 7 5 5 00	
Supplies	7 5 0 00	
Prepaid Insurance	1 2 0 0 00	
Equipment	20 0 0 0 00	
Accumulated Depreciation—Equipment		6 0 0 0 00
Accounts Payable		7 6 0 0 00
Salaries Payable		1 0 0 0 00
R. Wilson, Capital		15 1 0 5 00
Totals	29 7 0 5 00	29 7 0 5 00

KEY TERMS

accrual basis of accounting The basis of accounting that requires that revenue is recorded when earned, no matter when cash is received, and that expenses are recorded when incurred, no matter when cash is paid.

cash basis of accounting A basis of accounting where revenue is recorded only when cash is received, and expenses are recorded only when cash is paid.

clearing account An account used to summarize the balances of other accounts.

closing entries Entries made at the end of an accounting period to transfer the balances of the temporary accounts to the owner's capital account.

closing process The process of transferring the balances of temporary accounts to the owner's capital account.

fiscal period The period of time that covers a complete accounting cycle. A **fiscal year** is a fiscal period covering twelve months; it does not necessarily coincide with the calendar year.

Income Summary account A clearing account used to summarize the balances of revenue and expense accounts. It is used only at the end of an accounting period and is opened and closed during the closing process.

modified cash basis of accounting A basis of accounting where revenue is recorded only when cash is received and expenses are recorded only when cash is paid. However, adjustments are made for expenditures for items having an economic life of more than one year—such as equipment, prepaid insurance, and large purchases of supplies.

natural business year A fiscal year ending at a business's lowest point of activity.

permanent accounts Assets, liabilities, and owner's capital are permanent accounts in the sense that their balances will be carried into the next accounting period. Permanent accounts are also called **real accounts**.

post-closing trial balance A trial balance prepared after closing entries have been posted. The post-closing trial balance is also called an **after-closing trial balance** and consists only of permanent accounts.

temporary accounts Revenue, expense, and drawing accounts are temporary accounts used to show changes in owner's equity during a single fiscal period. When that period is over, the balances of all temporary accounts are summarized, and the information is transferred to the owner's capital account. Temporary accounts are also called **nominal accounts**.

CONCEPTS REVIEW

1. Why are the balances of certain accounts transferred to the owner's capital account?
2. What are the two objectives of the closing process?
3. What purpose is served by the Income Summary account?
4. Which accounts are closed to the Income Summary account?
5. Identify the steps involved in the closing process.
6. How does the work sheet aid in the closing process?
7. What purpose is served by the post-closing trial balance?
8. Which account balances appear on the post-closing trial balance?
9. The closing process is sometimes referred to as "closing the books." Is this statement totally accurate? Explain.
10. What is meant by a fiscal period?
11. Differentiate between a calendar year and a fiscal year.
12. Why have some businesses adopted a natural business year for fiscal purposes?
13. Differentiate between the accrual basis of accounting and the cash basis of accounting.
14. Why do many professional firms and service businesses use a modified cash basis of accounting?

SKILLS REVIEW

EXERCISE 5-1

LEARNING OBJECTIVE 1

Objective: To classify accounts as permanent or temporary and to indicate the financial statement classification

Directions: Complete the following form. Each line should have two check marks and the word Yes or No. The first one is done as an example.

				Reported On	
Account Title	**Permanent**	**Temporary**	**Closed?**	**Balance Sheet**	**Income Statement**
Cash	✓		No	✓	
Salaries Payable					
Accumulated Depr.					
Fees Earned					
Accounts Receivable					
Supplies Expense					
Owner, Capital					
Accounts Payable					
Rent Expense					
Supplies					
Equipment					

EXERCISE 5-2

LEARNING OBJECTIVE 2

Objective: To journalize closing entries from account balances

The following are adjusted account balances from the work sheet of Smallwood Service Company for the year ended December 31, 20X1:

Account	**Balance**
Service Revenue	$ 51,000
Rent Expense	8,200

Account	Balance
Supplies Expense	1,750
Salaries Expense	27,358
Depreciation Expense—Equipment	4,000
Utilities Expense	2,050
Deana Smallwood, Drawing	15,000
Deana Smallwood, Capital	39,900

Directions: Prepare closing entries in general journal form.

EXERCISE 5-3

LEARNING OBJECTIVE 2

Objective: To journalize closing entries from account balances

As of December 31, 20X1, the ledger of Ingrid Torsay, MD, contained the following balances:

Account	Balance
Ingrid Torsay, Capital	$57,304.25
Ingrid Torsay, Drawing	36,000.00
Medical Fees	79,205.00
Rent Expense	12,000.00
Medical Supplies Expense	2,455.80
Office Supplies Expense	1,235.90
Depreciation Expense—Equipment	3,000.00
Utilities Expense	5,445.35
Miscellaneous Expense	725.80

Directions: Assuming that adjusting entries have been posted and that all accounts have normal balances, journalize the closing entries.

EXERCISE 5-4

LEARNING OBJECTIVE 2

Objective: To analyze and close the Income Summary account

After all revenue and expense accounts of Tim Justice and Associates have been closed, the Income Summary account appears as shown below:

General Ledger								
Account Income Summary						Account No.		313
Date		Item	P.R.	Debit	Credit	Balance		
							Debit	Credit
20X2 Dec.	31	Closing	GJ8		153 0 0 0 00			153 0 0 0 00
	31	Closing	GJ8	89 0 0 0 00				64 0 0 0 00

Directions:
1. Make a journal entry to close the Income Summary account.
2. Total revenue is _____.
3. Total expenses are _____.
4. Net income (or net loss) is _____.

EXERCISE 5-5

LEARNING OBJECTIVE 2

Objective: To make closing entries from a set of T accounts

Directions: Using the T accounts shown on the next page, journalize necessary closing entries as of July 31, 20X0.

Cash		Accounts Payable		T. Lee, Capital	
4,000			1,850		14,550

Supplies				T. Lee, Drawing	
1,800				18,000	

Equipment				Fees Earned	
17,000					44,000

Accum. Depr.—Equipment				Salaries Expense	
	3,200			15,200	

				Rent Expense	
				4,500	

				Utilities Expense	
				2,800	

				Supplies Expense	
				300	

EXERCISE 5-6

LEARNING OBJECTIVE 2

Objective: To journalize closing entries from the Income Statement columns of a work sheet

The following items appear in the Income Statement columns of Jan McCarthy's work sheet for the fiscal year ended July 31, 20X2. Ms. McCarthy is an attorney who withdrew $32,000 during the year.

	Income Statement	
	Debit	**Credit**
Legal Fees Earned		65,000
Salaries Expense	24,000	
Rent Expense	6,000	
Office Supplies Expense	1,350	
Depreciation Expense—Equipment	1,500	
Utilities Expense	1,490	
Miscellaneous Expense	900	
	35,240	65,000

Directions: Journalize Jan McCarthy's closing entries.

EXERCISE 5-7

LEARNING OBJECTIVE 3

Objective: To indicate which accounts will appear on a post-closing trial balance

Directions: Indicate which of the following accounts will appear on a post-closing trial balance by listing the numbers of those accounts:

1. Cash
2. Accounts Payable
3. V. Kelly, Drawing
4. V. Kelly, Capital
5. Insurance Expense

6. Fees Earned
7. Accumulated Depreciation
8. Prepaid Insurance
9. Accounts Receivable
10. Salaries Payable

EXERCISE 5-8

Objective: To arrange the steps in the accounting cycle in proper sequence

Directions: List the following steps of the accounting cycle in the proper sequence:

1. Journalize and post closing entries.
2. Record transactions in a journal.
3. Prepare a post-closing trial balance.
4. Analyze transactions from source documents.
5. Journalize and post adjusting entries.
6. Post from the journal to the ledger.
7. Prepare financial statements from a completed work sheet.
8. Determine needed adjustments.
9. Prepare a work sheet.
10. Prepare a trial balance of the ledger.

CASE PROBLEMS

GROUP A

PROBLEM 5-1A

LEARNING OBJECTIVE 2

Objective: To journalize closing entries from account balances

After the adjusting entries for Richard Hinton, CPA, were posted, his ledger contained the following account balances as of April 30, 20X1:

Account	Balance
Cash	$22,600
Accounts Receivable	3,000
Office Supplies	1,850
Equipment	32,800
Accumulated Depreciation—Equipment	4,000
Accounts Payable	7,800
Salaries Payable	900
Richard Hinton, Capital	39,050
Richard Hinton, Drawing	18,000
Income Summary	—
Accounting Fees Earned	60,500
Salaries Expense	22,600
Rent Expense	5,200
Depreciation Expense—Equipment	1,200
Utilities Expense	3,600
Telephone Expense	900
Office Supplies Expense	500

Directions: Journalize the closing entries.

PROBLEM 5-2A

LEARNING OBJECTIVE 2

Objective: To journalize closing entries from a partial work sheet

The financial statement columns of the work sheet for Don's Carpet Service are shown on the next page.

Completing the Accounting Cycle for a Service Business

Don's Carpet Service
Work Sheet
For Year Ended December 31, 20XX

	Account Title	Income Statement Debit	Income Statement Credit	Balance Sheet Debit	Balance Sheet Credit	
1	Cash			2 680 00		1
2	Office Supplies			980 00		2
3	Delivery Supplies			500 00		3
4	Office Equipment			9 000 00		4
5	Accumulated Depreciation—Office Equipment				3 000 00	5
6	Delivery Equipment			13 000 00		6
7	Accumulated Depreciation—Delivery Equipment				2 000 00	7
8	Accounts Payable				3 200 00	8
9	Salaries Payable				800 00	9
10	Don Graham, Capital				2 320 00	10
11	Don Graham, Drawing			15 000 00		11
12	Income Summary					12
13	Service Revenue		59 000 00			13
14	Salaries Expense	19 000 00				14
15	Rent Expense	6 000 00				15
16	Depreciation Expense—Office Equipment	1 000 00				16
17	Depreciation Expense—Delivery Equipment	1 200 00				17
18	Office Supplies Expense	300 00				18
19	Delivery Supplies Expense	430 00				19
20	Utilities Expense	900 00				20
21	Miscellaneous Expense	330 00				21
22		29 160 00	59 000 00	41 160 00	11 320 00	22
23	Net Income	29 840 00			29 840 00	23
24		59 000 00	59 000 00	41 160 00	41 160 00	24

Directions:
1. Prepare journal entries to close the temporary accounts.
2. What is the balance of the capital account after closing?

LEARNING OBJECTIVE 2

PROBLEM 5-3A

Objective: To prepare a work sheet and journalize adjusting and closing entries

Bethany Pylant, owner of Pylant Software Services, prepared the following trial balance on December 31, 20X2:

Pylant Software Services
Trial Balance
December 31, 20X2

Account Title	Debit	Credit
Cash	10 000 00	
Accounts Receivable	2 000 00	
Office Supplies	2 500 00	
Prepaid Insurance	1 200 00	

Office Equipment	18 0 0 0 00	
Accumulated Depreciation—Office Equipment		3 0 0 0 00
Accounts Payable		2 0 0 0 00
Salaries Payable		—
Bethany Pylant, Capital		15 7 6 0 00
Bethany Pylant, Drawing	25 7 0 0 00	
Service Revenue		77 6 0 0 00
Salaries Expense	22 5 0 0 00	
Rent Expense	12 6 0 0 00	
Advertising Expense	2 4 0 0 00	
Telephone Expense	9 0 0 00	
Office Supplies Expense	—	
Insurance Expense	—	
Depreciation Expense—Office Equipment	—	
Miscellaneous Expense	5 6 0 00	
Totals	98 3 6 0 00	98 3 6 0 00

Adjustment data:
(a) Office supplies on hand, $500.
(b) Insurance expired during the year, $1,000.
(c) Depreciation of office equipment, $1,000.
(d) Unpaid salaries at year end, $255.

Directions:
1. Prepare a work sheet.
2. Journalize adjusting and closing entries.

LEARNING OBJECTIVE 2, 3

PROBLEM 5-4A

Objective: To journalize and post adjusting and closing entries and prepare a post-closing trial balance

The completed work sheet of Comprehensive Management Services is presented in the *Study Guide/Working Papers*.

Directions:
1. Using the Trial Balance section of the work sheet, record all beginning balances in the ledger accounts provided. The Income Summary account, which does not appear on the work sheet, has no balance.
2. Journalize and post the adjusting entries.
3. Journalize and post the closing entries.
4. Prepare a post-closing trial balance.

LEARNING OBJECTIVE 1, 2, 3

PROBLEM 5-5A

Objective: To complete a work sheet and the work of the accounting cycle

Account balances of ABC Enterprises appear as follows on December 31, 20X0:

Number	Account Title	Balance
111	Cash	$ 37,350
112	Accounts Receivable	5,000
113	Office Supplies	19,640
114	Store Supplies	16,110
115	Delivery Supplies	27,500
116	Prepaid Insurance	36,000
117	Office Equipment	90,000
117.1	Accumulated Depreciation—Office Equipment	45,000
118	Store Equipment	75,000

Number	Account Title	Balance
118.1	Accumulated Depreciation—Store Equipment	30,000
119	Truck	40,000
119.1	Accumulated Depreciation—Truck	20,000
211	Accounts Payable	47,500
212	Salaries Payable	—
311	Shirl Mallory, Capital	85,800
312	Shirl Mallory, Drawing	21,200
411	Fees Earned	351,500
511	Rent Expense	12,000
512	Salaries Expense	200,000
513	Office Supplies Expense	—
514	Store Supplies Expense	—
515	Delivery Supplies Expense	—
516	Insurance Expense	—
517	Depreciation Expense—Office Equipment	—
518	Depreciation Expense—Store Equipment	—
519	Depreciation Expense—Truck	—

Adjustment data:
(a) Office supplies on hand, $3,510.
(b) Store supplies on hand, $12,140.
(c) Delivery supplies on hand, $21,900.
(d) Depreciation of office equipment, $9,000.
(e) Depreciation of store equipment, $10,000.
(f) Depreciation of truck, $10,000.
(g) Insurance expired, $6,000.
(h) Salaries unpaid, $5,000.

Directions:
1. Prepare a work sheet for the year ended December 31, 20X0.
2. Prepare an income statement for the year ended December 31, 20X0.
3. Prepare a statement of owner's equity for the year ended December 31, 20X0.
4. Prepare a December 31, 20X0 balance sheet.
5. Journalize the adjusting entries.
6. Journalize the closing entries.

GROUP B

LEARNING OBJECTIVE 2

PROBLEM 5-1B

Objective: To journalize closing entries from account balances

After the adjusting entries for Robert Cooper, MD, were posted, his ledger contained the following account balances as of May 31, 20X1:

Account	Balance
Cash	$25,500
Accounts Receivable	2,500
Office Supplies	2,000
Equipment	34,500
Accumulated Depreciation—Equipment	4,200
Accounts Payable	8,000
Salaries Payable	1,200
Robert Cooper, Capital	44,755
Robert Cooper, Drawing	27,000
Income Summary	—
Medical Fees Earned	74,500

Account	Balance
Salaries Expense	28,300
Rent Expense	6,000
Depreciation Expense—Equipment	1,500
Utilities Expense	3,800
Telephone Expense	980
Office Supplies Expense	575

Directions: Journalize the closing entries.

PROBLEM 5-2B

LEARNING OBJECTIVE 2

Objective: To journalize closing entries from a partial work sheet

The financial statement columns of the work sheet for Mary's Plumbing Company are shown below.

Mary's Plumbing Company
Work Sheet
For Year Ended December 31, 20XX

	Account Title	Income Statement Debit	Income Statement Credit	Balance Sheet Debit	Balance Sheet Credit	
1	Cash			3 0 6 5 00		1
2	Office Supplies			1 6 3 0 00		2
3	Store Supplies			9 8 0 00		3
4	Prepaid Insurance			1 8 0 0 00		4
5	Office Equipment			16 0 0 0 00		5
6	Accumulated Depreciation—Office Equipment				6 0 0 0 00	6
7	Store Equipment			7 5 0 0 00		7
8	Accumulated Depreciation—Store Equipment				4 0 0 0 00	8
9	Accounts Payable				2 7 5 0 00	9
10	Salaries Payable				2 5 0 00	10
11	Mary Lee, Capital				20 8 6 0 00	11
12	Mary Lee, Drawing			1 7 0 0 00		12
13	Revenue from Services		22 6 5 0 00			13
14	Rent Expense	4 0 0 0 00				14
15	Salaries Expense	11 0 0 0 00				15
16	Office Supplies Expense	1 3 7 5 00				16
17	Store Supplies Expense	2 6 1 0 00				17
18	Insurance Expense	9 0 0 00				18
19	Depreciation Expense—Office Equipment	2 0 0 0 00				19
20	Depreciation Expense—Store Equipment	1 0 0 0 00				20
21	Utilities Expense	9 5 0 00				21
22		23 8 3 5 00	22 6 5 0 00	32 6 7 5 00	33 8 6 0 00	22
23	Net Loss		1 1 8 5 00	1 1 8 5 00		23
24		23 8 3 5 00	23 8 3 5 00	33 8 6 0 00	33 8 6 0 00	24

Directions:
1. Prepare journal entries to close the temporary accounts.
2. What is the balance of the capital account after closing?

PROBLEM 5-3B

LEARNING OBJECTIVE 2

Objective: To prepare a work sheet and journalize adjusting and closing entries

Joe Patterson, owner of Patterson Consulting Group, prepared the following trial balance on December 31, 20X1:

Patterson Consulting Group Trial Balance December 31, 20X1		
Account Title	**Debit**	**Credit**
Cash	10 500 00	
Accounts Receivable	2 800 00	
Office Supplies	1 500 00	
Prepaid Insurance	1 200 00	
Office Equipment	21 000 00	
Accumulated Depreciation—Office Equipment		3 800 00
Accounts Payable		2 200 00
Salaries Payable		—
Joe Patterson, Capital		19 440 00
Joe Patterson, Drawing	26 700 00	
Service Revenue		82 900 00
Salaries Expense	24 600 00	
Rent Expense	14 800 00	
Advertising Expense	2 500 00	
Telephone Expense	1 890 00	
Office Supplies Expense	—	
Insurance Expense	—	
Depreciation Expense—Office Equipment	—	
Miscellaneous Expense	850 00	
Totals	108 340 00	108 340 00

Adjustment data:
(a) Office supplies on hand, $650.
(b) Insurance expired during the year, $1,025.
(c) Depreciation of office equipment, $1,150.
(d) Unpaid salaries at year end, $280.

Directions:
1. Prepare a work sheet.
2. Journalize adjusting and closing entries.

LEARNING OBJECTIVE 2, 3

PROBLEM 5-4B

Objective: To journalize and post adjusting and closing entries and prepare a post-closing trial balance

The completed work sheet of DataPlus Bookkeeping Service is presented in the *Study Guide/Working Papers*.

Directions:
1. Using the Trial Balance section of the work sheet, record all beginning balances in the ledger accounts provided. The Income Summary account, which does not appear on the work sheet, has no balance.
2. Journalize and post the adjusting entries.
3. Journalize and post the closing entries.
4. Prepare a post-closing trial balance.

PROBLEM 5-5B

Objective: To complete a work sheet and the work of the accounting cycle

Account balances of ABC Enterprises appear as follows on December 31, 20X0:

Number	Account Title	Balance
111	Cash	$ 30,350
112	Accounts Receivable	4,000
113	Office Supplies	17,640
114	Store Supplies	15,110
115	Delivery Supplies	26,500
116	Prepaid Insurance	24,000
117	Office Equipment	45,000
117.1	Accumulated Depreciation—Office Equipment	22,500
118	Store Equipment	65,000
118.1	Accumulated Depreciation—Store Equipment	26,000
119	Truck	30,000
119.1	Accumulated Depreciation—Truck	15,000
211	Accounts Payable	37,500
212	Salaries Payable	—
311	Shirl Mallory, Capital	38,200
312	Shirl Mallory, Drawing	21,100
411	Fees Earned	351,500
511	Rent Expense	12,000
512	Salaries Expense	200,000
513	Office Supplies Expense	—
514	Store Supplies Expense	—
515	Delivery Supplies Expense	—
516	Insurance Expense	—
517	Depreciation Expense—Office Equipment	—
518	Depreciation Expense—Store Equipment	—
519	Depreciation Expense—Truck	—

Adjustment data:
(a) Office supplies on hand, $2,510.
(b) Store supplies on hand, $11,140.
(c) Delivery supplies on hand, $20,900.
(d) Depreciation of office equipment, $4,500.
(e) Depreciation of store equipment, $6,500.
(f) Depreciation of truck, $7,500.
(g) Insurance expired, $4,000.
(h) Salaries unpaid, $5,000.

Directions:
1. Prepare a work sheet for the year ended December 31, 20X0.
2. Prepare an income statement for the year ended December 31, 20X0.
3. Prepare a statement of owner's equity for the year ended December 31, 20X0.
4. Prepare a December 31, 20X0 balance sheet.
5. Journalize the adjusting entries.
6. Journalize the closing entries.

PROBLEM SOLVING

As of December 31, 20X1, after all revenue and expense accounts have been closed, the Income Summary account in the ledger of Total Accounting Services has a credit balance of $95,000. As of the same date, the Gene Hopkins, Drawing account has a normal balance of $37,000, and the Gene Hopkins, Capital account has a normal balance of $94,500. The firm's income statement reported total expenses of $230,000.

Directions:
1. Journalize the entries necessary to complete the closing process.
2. Prepare a statement of owner's equity for the year ended December 31, 20X1.
3. What was the total revenue for the year?

COMMUNICATIONS

Sometimes related terms are the most difficult to describe. Explain in writing, using examples, the differences among the terms *calendar year*, *fiscal year*, and *natural business year*.

ETHICS

Assume that you work as an assistant loan officer for a bank. You recommend the approval of loans based on the financial standing of an individual or a business. One of your current customers is Gwen Purdue, the owner of a travel service that has just completed its first year of operation and is now asking for a loan of $10,000 to purchase a computer system. The only financial item provided to you is an unadjusted trial balance. Gwen tells you that this list shows that she is in good financial condition, so she should be granted the loan without presenting any additional information.

Explain to Gwen why financial statements are more useful than an unadjusted trial balance and why it is improper for you to recommend approval of a loan based only on what she has provided. Write your explanation in a paragraph or two.

ANSWERS TO REVIEW QUIZZES

REVIEW QUIZ 5-1

	Date		Account Title	P.R.	Debit	Credit	
		General Journal				Page 3	
1			Closing Entries				1
2	20XX Jun.	30	Service Revenue		89 6 0 0 00		2
3			Income Summary			89 6 0 0 00	3
4							4

5		30	Income Summary		74 3 0 0 00		5
6			Rent Expense			6 0 0 0 00	6
7			Salaries Expense			57 4 0 0 00	7
8			Office Supplies Expense			1 0 0 00	8
9			Telephone Expense			6 0 0 00	9
10			Insurance Expense			2 0 0 00	10
11			Depr. Expense—Office Equipment			1 0 0 0 00	11
12			Depr. Expense—Automobiles			2 0 0 0 00	12
13			Utilities Expense			6 3 0 0 00	13
14			Miscellaneous Expense			7 0 0 00	14
15							15
16		30	Income Summary		15 3 0 0 00		16
17			Kim Carter, Capital			15 3 0 0 00	17
18							18
19		30	Kim Carter, Capital		19 0 0 0 00		19
20			Kim Carter, Drawing			19 0 0 0 00	20

REVIEW QUIZ 5-2

			General Journal			Page 1	
	Date		Account Title	P.R.	Debit	Credit	
1			Closing Entries				1
2	20X1 Dec.	31	Fees Earned		52 0 0 0 00		2
3			Income Summary			52 0 0 0 00	3
4							4
5		31	Income Summary		39 6 5 0 00		5
6			Salaries Expense			26 0 0 0 00	6
7			Supplies Expense			6 5 0 00	7
8			Rent Expense			7 0 0 0 00	8
9			Depreciation Expense—Equipment			2 0 0 0 00	9
10			Utilities Expense			4 0 0 0 00	10
11							11
12		31	Income Summary		12 3 5 0 00		12
13			W. Dee, Capital			12 3 5 0 00	13
14							14
15		31	W. Dee, Capital		9 0 0 0 00		15
16			W. Dee, Drawing			9 0 0 0 00	16

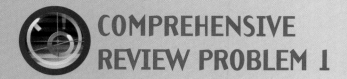

COMPREHENSIVE REVIEW PROBLEM 1

FRED HAYES PHOTOGRAPHY STUDIO

You have reached the end of the first section of this book. The following problem is designed to review and reinforce your knowledge of accounting for a service business.

Fred Hayes has been a photographer since his graduation from high school several years ago. On July 1, 20X1, he decided to open his own photography firm, called Fred's Photos. To start his accounting system, Fred developed the chart of accounts shown in Figure 1.

FIGURE 1
Fred's Photos chart of accounts

Fred's Photos - Chart of Accounts

Assets		Owner's Equity	
111	Cash	311	Fred Hayes, Capital
112	Accounts Receivable	312	Fred Hayes, Drawing
113	Office Supplies	313	Income Summary
114	Photography Supplies	**Revenue**	
115	Prepaid Insurance	411	Photography Revenue
121	Office Equipment	412	Vending Machine Revenue
121.1	Accumulated Depreciation—Office Equipment	**Expenses**	
122	Photography Equipment	511	Salaries Expense
122.1	Accumulated Depreciation—Photography Equipment	512	Advertising Expense
		513	Rent Expense
123	Furniture and Fixtures	514	Repairs Expense
123.1	Accumulated Depreciation—Furniture and Fixtures	515	Insurance Expense
		516	Office Supplies Expense
Liabilities		517	Photography Supplies Expense
211	Accounts Payable	518	Depreciation Expense—Office Equipment
212	Notes Payable	519	Depreciation Expense—Photography Equipment
213	Salaries Payable	520	Depreciation Expense—Furniture and Fixtures
		521	Utilities Expense
		522	Miscellaneous Expense

Fred completed the following transactions during the first month of operations:

20X1
Jul. 1 Fred invested $40,000 cash and photography equipment valued at $20,000 in the business.
  1 Purchased office supplies for cash, $1,300.
  1 Purchased photography supplies on account, $6,700.
  1 Paid July rent, $1,700.
  1 Paid for a newspaper ad, $500.
  2 Purchased office equipment on account, $6,750.
  2 Paid property insurance for the upcoming year, $3,600.

Jul. 3 Purchased a microcomputer system and software, $3,200, by issuing a note payable.
    5 Paid for promotional handouts, $150.
    6 Paid miscellaneous expenses, $175.
    7 Paid salaries of employees, $1,400.
    7 Recorded week's cash receipts for photo work, $1,350.
    8 Paid for carpet cleaning (Miscellaneous Expense), $75.
    9 Recorded photo work done for a customer on account, $855.
    9 Purchased additional photography supplies on account, $3,200.
   10 Purchased additional photography equipment for cash, $3,500.
   10 Entered into a contract with Southside Food Vendors to place vending machines in the waiting room. Fred is to receive 10% of all sales, with a minimum of $200 monthly. Received $200 as an advance payment.
   11 Purchased furniture for the lobby area, $1,700. Paid cash in full.
   12 Paid cash for the installation of overhead lighting fixtures, $900.
   15 Recorded second week's cash receipts for photo work, $2,170.
   15 Paid weekly salaries, $1,400.
   17 Fred withdrew cash for personal use, $800.
   18 Paid for TV ad, $710.
   19 Paid for repair to equipment, $80.
   19 Collected $500 for the photo work done on account on the 9th.
   22 Recorded third week's cash receipts for photo work, $2,045.
   22 Paid weekly salaries, $1,400.
   23 Did a special wedding photo session for a customer on credit, $550.
   28 Recorded fourth week's cash receipts for photo work, $1,995.
   29 Paid salaries of employees, $1,400.
   30 Paid water bill for July, $75.
   30 Paid power bill for July, $1,095.
   31 Made a $500 payment on the note for the microcomputer purchased on July 3.
   31 Made a payment for the office equipment purchased on account, $2,000.
   31 Made a payment on the photography supplies purchased on account, $1,000.
   31 Wrote a business check to pay for Fred's home phone bill, $310.
   31 Southside Food Vendors reported a total of $2,800 of vending machine sales for July. Ten percent of these sales is $280. Since $200 had already been received and recorded in July, Fred was owed $80. Received the $80 check.

Directions:
1. Open an account in the ledger for each account shown in the chart of accounts.
2. Journalize each of the transactions for July, beginning on page 1 of the general journal.
3. Post the journal entries to the ledger.
4. Prepare a trial balance of the ledger in the first two columns of a ten-column work sheet.
5. Complete the ten-column work sheet. Assume for the purposes of this problem that Fred has a one-month accounting period. Data for adjustments are as follows:
   (a) Office supplies on hand, $850.
   (b) Photography supplies on hand, $6,550.
   (c) Insurance expired, $300.
   (d) Salaries unpaid, two days of a five-day week; weekly salaries are $1,400.
   (e) Depreciation of office equipment, $190.
   (f) Depreciation of photography equipment, $275.
   (g) Depreciation of furniture and fixtures, $75.
6. Prepare an income statement for the month ended July 31.
7. Prepare a statement of owner's equity for the month ended July 31.
8. Prepare a balance sheet as of July 31.
9. Journalize adjusting entries from the completed work sheet.
10. Journalize closing entries.
11. Post adjusting and closing entries to the ledger.
12. Prepare a post-closing trial balance.

6

CASH AND

THE COMBINED

JOURNAL

LEARNING OBJECTIVES

After studying Chapter 6, you will be able to:

1. Define cash as it is used in accounting.
2. Describe internal control procedures related to cash.
3. Record transactions in a combined journal, post the combined journal to the ledger, and cross-reference the two records.
4. Describe the purpose of and need for a petty cash fund.
5. Record the establishment of a petty cash fund.
6. Record the replenishment of a petty cash fund.
7. Record the establishment of a change fund.
8. Record cash shortages and overages.
9. Prepare a bank reconciliation.

Flowers need rain and sunshine to flourish. A business needs cash. Such cash must be properly measured in correct amounts and safeguarded from loss. For large businesses, measuring and safeguarding cash is complex. A business usually divides its cash into different funds or accounts for ease of operation and control. Can you think of two funds or accounts that cash might be divided into?

Cash by its very nature is easily subject to loss or theft. To avoid such loss or theft, a business must keep accurate records of cash received and disbursed. Periodically, the actual amount of cash the business owns must be compared to the amount of cash shown by the records of the business. What are some ways that this comparison could be accomplished? How should a business account for cash that has been lost or stolen?

A newly-formed small business, such as a dry cleaning store, might design an accounting system that would be different from that of a large, well-established business. Many newly established small businesses use a special journal called a combined journal to account for their cash transactions. This journal could be maintained on a personal computer or the combined journal could be completed manually. The combined journal would be designed to account for both cash received and cash disbursed. Can you visualize how such a journal might look?

— Allan M. Cross, CPA, MBA
Parks Junior College

In Chapters 1 through 5, we covered the complete accounting cycle for a service business from analyzing source documents to the post-closing trial balance. Throughout the accounting cycle, certain measures are necessary to protect a business's assets from theft, loss, and misuse. Cash is an asset that is particularly vulnerable to such factors. In this chapter, we will study those procedures that are necessary to protect and control cash.

CASH DEFINED

LEARNING OBJECTIVE 1

In a narrow sense, **cash** refers to the amount of currency (paper money) and coin owned by a business or an individual. To most businesses, however, cash has a much broader meaning. In addition to currency and coin, cash usually includes such items as checks made payable to the business, money orders made payable to the business, traveler's checks, cashier's checks, bank drafts, and receipts from credit card sales.

CONTROL OF CASH

LEARNING OBJECTIVE 2

Cash is generally considered the most precious of all assets. Without adequate cash, a business simply cannot survive. For not only is cash needed to pay employees, creditors, expenses, and taxes, cash is also needed for the business to grow and expand.

Special controls are needed to protect cash because almost everyone wants it, and it is easily taken if not protected. Further, it is often easy to conceal that cash has been taken by altering accounting records.

The protection and control of cash are part of the overall system of internal control. **Internal control** refers to the methods and procedures a business uses to internally protect its assets. Some common steps that are used to control and protect cash are:

- Those who physically handle cash (cashiers, clerks, etc.) should not be the same as those who account for cash (bookkeepers, accountants).
- All cash received should be deposited in a bank daily.

- Only a small amount of cash (called petty cash) should be kept on hand.
- All cash payments, except for petty cash, should be made by check.
- Checks should be prenumbered so that it is easy to see what checks have been written and when.
- Only a few properly designated persons should be involved in the receipt, payment, and recording of cash.
- Receipt and payment of cash should be recorded efficiently and accurately.

The last step leads to our next topic of discussion, the combined journal. This type of journal saves journalizing and posting time when recording cash and other transactions.

THE COMBINED JOURNAL

LEARNING OBJECTIVE 3

In many businesses, cash is the most active element, with receipts and payments occurring constantly. So far we have recorded all receipts and payments of cash in a two-column general journal. The two-column journal is a basic journal in which any business transaction, no matter how complex, can be recorded. However, the use of a two-column journal can be extremely time-consuming. Let's look again at an entry in a two-column journal.

	Date		Account Title	P.R.	Debit	Credit	
	20XX		General Journal			Page 6	
1	May	1	Rent Expense	511	5 0 0 00		1
2			Cash	111		5 0 0 00	2
3			Paid rent for the month.				3

In this entry, Rent Expense is debited for $500, and Cash is credited for $500. In addition to writing the amount of the transaction in the Debit and Credit columns, it is necessary to write both account titles in the Account Title column. Additionally, when the entry is posted to the ledger, it is necessary to post an individual debit to the Rent Expense account and an individual credit to the Cash account. If forty business transactions were recorded in a two-column journal during the month, it would be necessary to make forty individual debits, forty individual credits, and eighty postings to the ledger. (Even more postings would be required if some of the entries were compound entries.)

A two-column journal may be all that is needed in a business that has few transactions. When there are many transactions, however, the detail of two-column entries and the numerous posting of debits and credits are very time-consuming. In this situation, errors are more likely to occur.

To save journalizing and posting time, a **combined journal** can be used. A combined journal, also called a **combination journal**, is a multicolumn journal that typically has two special columns for recording cash transactions, various other special columns for recording transactions that occur often, and two general columns for recording transactions that occur less often.

The combined journal is used mainly by small businesses with one bookkeeper. The top portion of the combined journal used by Ann Sherwood, Interior Decorator, is shown in Figure 6-1.

The use of a combined journal saves journalizing time because it is not necessary to write the titles of the accounts when entries are made in special columns. It also saves posting time because special columns are posted by totals rather than item by item.

FIGURE 6-1
Combined journal

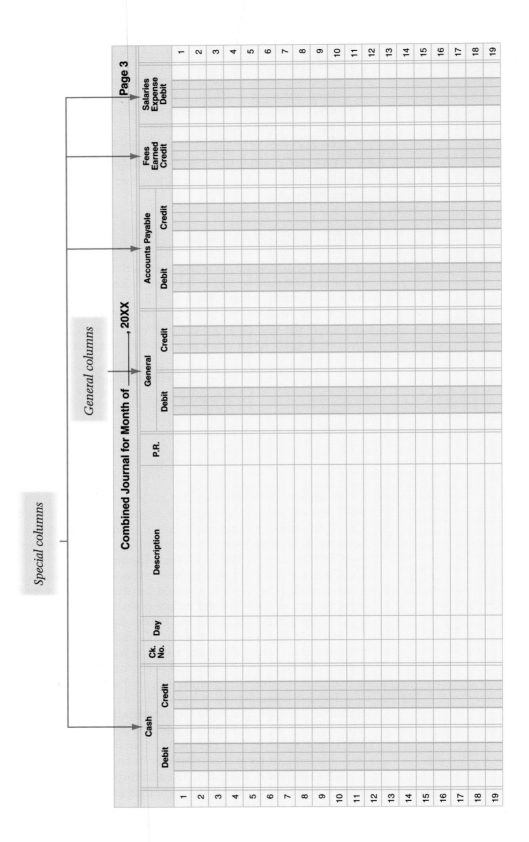

Designing a Combined Journal

The combined journal should be designed to fit the individual needs of the business using it. Special columns should be set up for those accounts that are most often affected by business transactions. Cash, for example, is usually active. Therefore, having special columns only for recording increases and decreases in Cash saves journalizing and posting time. For some businesses, the Accounts Payable account is also very active. For these businesses, special increase and decrease columns for Accounts Payable can be justified.

Within reason, the combined journal can have as many special columns as the business deems practical. Ann Sherwood feels that her needs are met by having a combined journal with General Debit and Credit columns and special columns for Cash Debit and Credit, Accounts Payable Debit and Credit, Fees Earned Credit, and Salaries Expense Debit. Let's look at these column headings in a bit more detail.

CASH DEBIT COLUMN

When Cash is increased, the amount of the increase is recorded in the Cash Debit column. The related credit is recorded in the Accounts Payable Credit column, the Fees Earned Credit column, or the General Credit column.

CASH CREDIT COLUMN

When Cash is decreased, the amount of the decrease is recorded in the Cash Credit column. The related debit is recorded in the Accounts Payable Debit column, the Salaries Expense Debit column, or the General Debit column.

ACCOUNTS PAYABLE DEBIT COLUMN

When payment is made on an account payable, the amount of the payment is recorded in the Accounts Payable Debit column. The related credit is recorded in the Cash Credit column.

ACCOUNTS PAYABLE CREDIT COLUMN

When Accounts Payable is increased, the amount of the increase is recorded in the Accounts Payable Credit column. The related debit is entered in the General Debit column.

FEES EARNED CREDIT COLUMN

Fees Earned is the title Ann Sherwood gave to her revenue account. When she earns revenue, it is recorded in the Fees Earned Credit column. The related debit to Cash is recorded in the Cash Debit column.

SALARIES EXPENSE DEBIT COLUMN

Ann pays employees every week. When payment is made, the amount of the payment is recorded in the Salaries Expense Debit column. The related credit is to Cash, which is recorded in the Cash Credit column.

GENERAL DEBIT AND CREDIT COLUMNS

It is not practical to maintain special columns that will seldom be used. Therefore, the combined journal contains General Debit and Credit columns for recording entries in accounts for which no special column is provided. For example, the electric bill is usually paid only once a month. Thus, a special column entitled Utilities Expense Debit would have only one entry a month. This would not be an efficient use of space. So, when the electric bill is paid, the debit to Utilities Expense is made in the General Debit column.

Recording Business Transactions in a Combined Journal

Let's now turn our attention to how entries are recorded in the combined journal. To illustrate recording transactions in a combined journal, let's look at a narrative of the transactions completed by Ann Sherwood during June 20XX. These transactions are recorded in the combined journal in Figure 6-2. As with any journal, each transaction must be analyzed into its debit and credit parts before recording. To review how to analyze a transaction, the first three transactions are shown with an analysis.

Jun. 1 Issued Check No. 120 for June rent, $600.

The payment of rent causes an increase in Rent Expense and a decrease in Cash. A special column is provided only when it will be used frequently. Rent is paid only once a month. Thus, there is no special column for recording increases in Rent Expense. Instead, the debit is recorded in the General Debit column. The account title, Rent Expense, is written in the Description column. The decrease in Cash is recorded in the Cash Credit column. The number of the check, 120, is written in the Ck. No. (check number) column.

Rent Expense		Cash	
+	–	+	–
600			600

Jun. 1 Received cash for services performed, $400.

This transaction caused an increase in Cash and an increase in revenue. The increase in Cash is recorded in the Cash Debit column. The increase in revenue is recorded in the Fees Earned Credit column. Since both debit and credit amounts are recorded in special columns, it is not necessary to write the title of either account in the Description column. Therefore, a check mark (✓) is placed in the Description column to show that no account title needs to be written.

Cash		Fees Earned	
+	–	–	+
400			400

Jun. 2 Received cash from the sale of old office equipment at cost, $200.

This transaction caused a *shift in assets*. One asset, Cash, was increased while another asset, Office Equipment, was decreased. The increase in Cash is recorded in the Cash Debit column. The decrease in Office Equipment is recorded in the General Credit column because there is no special column entitled Office Equipment Credit.

Cash		Office Equipment	
+	–	+	–
200			200

Following are the remainder of the transactions that occured in June.

Jun. 3 Purchased office supplies on account from Keith Office Supply Company, $250.
5 Received cash for services performed, $800.
5 Issued Check No. 121 for $500 to Timmers Company, a creditor.
7 Purchased decorating supplies on account from Engle Suppliers, $900.
8 Issued Check No. 122 for salary of employee, $325.
9 Issued Check No. 123 for miscellaneous expenses, $75.
10 Purchased office equipment on account, $1,200.
12 Issued Check No. 124 for a six-month prepayment of insurance premiums, $450.

FIGURE 6-2
The combined journal for Ann Sherwood, June 20XX

Combined Journal for Month of June, 20XX
Page 6

#	Cash Debit	Cash Credit	Ck. No.	Day	Description	P.R.	General Debit	General Credit	Accounts Payable Debit	Accounts Payable Credit	Fees Earned Credit	Salaries Expense Debit
1		6 0 0 00	120	1	Rent Expense		6 0 0 00					
2	4 0 0 00			1	✓						4 0 0 00	
3	2 0 0 00			2	Office Equipment			2 0 0 00				
4				3	Office Supplies		2 5 0 00			2 5 0 00		
5	8 0 0 00		121	5	✓						8 0 0 00	
6		5 0 0 00		5					5 0 0 00			
7			122	7	Decorating Supplies		9 0 0 00			9 0 0 00		
8		3 2 5 00		8	✓							3 2 5 00
9		7 5 00	123	9	Miscellaneous Expense		7 5 00					
10				10	Office Equipment		1 2 0 0 00			1 2 0 0 00		
11		4 5 0 00	124	12	Prepaid Insurance		4 5 0 00					
12		3 2 5 00	125	14	✓							3 2 5 00
13		1 0 0 00	126	16	Automobile		1 2 0 0 00					
14					Notes Payable			1 1 0 0 00				
15	2 5 4 6 00			18	✓						2 5 4 6 00	
16		8 0 0 00	127	20	Ann Sherwood, Drawing		8 0 0 00					
17		8 0 00	128	21	Advertising Expense		8 0 00					
18		3 2 5 00	129	21	✓				2 5 0 00			3 2 5 00
19		2 5 0 00	130	23	✓							
20		4 0 00	131	27	Repairs Expense		4 0 00					
21		3 8 0 00	132	29	Utilities Expense		3 8 0 00					
22		3 2 5 00	133	30	✓							3 2 5 00
23	7 5 0 00			30	✓						7 5 0 00	
24		9 0 0 00	134	30	✓				9 0 0 00			
25	4 6 9 6 00	6 3 7 5 00					16 7 7 5 00	11 2 0 00	16 5 0 00	2 3 5 0 00	4 4 9 6 00	13 0 0 00

Jun. 14 Issued Check No. 125 for salary of employee, $325.
   16 Purchased an automobile for use in the business,$12,000. Issued Check No. 126 for the down payment, $1,000, and issued a note payable for the balance.
   18 Received cash for services performed, $2,546.
   20 Ann withdrew $800 for personal use. Issued Check No. 127.
   21 Issued Check No. 128 for an ad in a local newspaper, $80.
   21 Issued Check No. 129 for salary of employee, $325.
   23 Issued Check No. 130 for $250 to Keith Office Supply Company for the supplies purchased on June 3.
   27 Issued Check No. 131 for repair to office equipment, $40.
   29 Issued Check No. 132 for utility bill, $380.
   30 Issued Check No. 133 for salary of employee, $325.
   30 Received cash for services performed, $750.
   30 Issued Check No. 134 for $900 to Engle Suppliers for payment of decorating supplies purchased on June 7.

Proving the Combined Journal

When the month's transactions have been journalized, each column of the combined journal should be totaled and the equality of debits and credits proved. We can do this as follows:

| | Column Totals | |
Column Titles	Debit	Credit
Cash	$ 4,696	$ 6,375
General	16,775	11,200
Accounts Payable	1,650	2,350
Fees Earned		4,496
Salaries Expense	1,300	
Totals	$24,421	$24,421

A less formal way to prove that the combined journal is to use a calculator and enter each debit column total using the plus (+) bar and each credit column total using the minus (–) bar. After all column totals have been entered in this manner, press the Total key, and a zero (0) will appear on the display screen. This procedure is called the **zero proof test**. Zero proof means that equal columns have a zero difference.

```
+    4,696
–    6,375
+   16,775
–   11,200
+    1,650
–    2,350
–    4,496
+    1,300
          
        -0-
```

Posting the Combined Journal

Like posting from the general journal, posting from the combined journal is usually done at the end of each month. Two types of postings are made from the combined journal: (1) individual postings of amounts in the General Debit and Credit columns, and (2) summary postings of amounts in special columns.

POSTING THE GENERAL COLUMNS

The procedure for posting amounts in the General Debit and Credit columns is similar to posting from a two-column journal. Each entry is posted individually to the account identified in the Description column. To illustrate, let's look at Figure 6-3, which shows how the June 1 debit to Rent Expense is posted. The five steps for posting the debit are as follow:

❶ Enter the date of the entry (Jun. 1) in the Date column of the Rent Expense account.
❷ Enter the amount of the entry ($600) in the Debit column of the Rent Expense account.
❸ Calculate the new balance of the Rent Expense account by adding the current posting to the previous balance: $600 + $3,000 = $3,600.

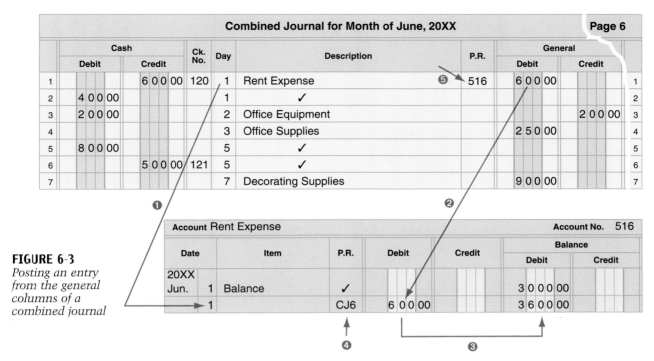

Combined Journal for Month of June, 20XX								Page 6
Cash		Ck. No.	Day	Description	P.R.	**General**		
Debit	Credit					Debit	Credit	
	6 0 0 00	120	1	Rent Expense	⑤ 516	6 0 0 00		1
4 0 0 00			1	✓				2
2 0 0 00			2	Office Equipment			2 0 0 00	3
			3	Office Supplies		2 5 0 00		4
8 0 0 00			5	✓				5
	5 0 0 00	121	5	✓				6
			7	Decorating Supplies		9 0 0 00		7

❶   ❷

Account Rent Expense						Account No. 516	
Date	Item	P.R.	Debit	Credit	**Balance**		
					Debit	Credit	
20XX Jun. 1	Balance	✓			3 0 0 0 00		
1		CJ6	6 0 0 00		3 6 0 0 00		

❹   ❸

FIGURE 6-3
Posting an entry from the general columns of a combined journal

❹ Enter the reference "CJ" and the page number of the combined journal (6) in the P.R. column of the Rent Expense account.

❺ Enter the number of the Rent Expense account (516) in the P.R. column of the combined journal.

POSTING THE TOTALS OF SPECIAL COLUMNS

Special columns are used only for recording debits or credits to specific accounts. For example, only increases in Cash are recorded in the Cash Debit column, and only decreases in Cash are recorded in the Cash Credit column. Thus, at the end of the month, the total of the Cash Debit column is posted to the debit side of the Cash account, and the total of the Cash Credit column is posted to the credit side of the Cash account. All other special columns are posted in the same way. To illustrate, Figure 6-4 shows how the special column totals of Ann Sherwood's combined journal are posted. Notice that the number of each account to which a posting was made is written in parentheses directly below the special column total. The check marks below the General Debit and Credit columns mean that amounts in these columns are posted individually, not by totals.

In this section, we have shown that the combined journal is a useful and time-saving way to record business transactions, especially those involving cash. Let's now turn to specific types of cash transactions. Petty cash is discussed next.

ACCOUNTING FOR PETTY CASH

LEARNING OBJECTIVE 4

To control cash, most businesses use bank checking accounts when making cash expenditures. However, it is not practical to write checks for very small amounts. Suppose that the postal service delivered a package on which $0.30 postage was due. The time and effort involved in writing a check for this small amount cannot be justified. Consequently, most businesses maintain a **petty cash fund**—*petty* meaning small—which is an amount of money kept in the office for making small expenditures.

The amount of the petty cash fund depends on the needs of the individual business. It can be $25, $50, $100, or any amount considered necessary.

FIGURE 6-4
Posting the special columns of a combined journal

When an entry is recorded in special columns, a check mark is entered in the P.R. column to show that the amount is not individually posted.

Special column totals are posted as of the last day of the month.

Combined Journal for Month of June, 20XX — Page 6

	Day	Ck. No.	Cash Debit	Cash Credit	Description	P.R.	General Debit	General Credit	Accounts Payable Debit	Accounts Payable Credit	Fees Earned Credit	Salaries Expense Debit
1	1	120		600 00	Rent Expense	516	600 00					
2	1		40 00		✓	✓					40 00	
3	2		20 00		Office Equipment	118		20 00				
4	3				Office Supplies	114	25 00			25 00		
5	5		80 00		✓	✓					80 00	
18	21	129		325 00	✓	✓						325 00
19	23	130		250 00	✓	✓			250 00			
20	27	131		40 00	Repairs Expense	517	40 00					
21	29	132		380 00	Utilities Expense	518	380 00					
22	30	133		325 00	✓	✓						325 00
23	30		750 00		✓	✓					750 00	
24	30	134		900 00	✓	✓			900 00			
25			4696 00	6375 00			16775 00	11200 00	1650 00	2350 00	4496 00	1300 00
26			(111)	(111)			(✓)	(✓)	(211)	(211)	(411)	(511)

Account Cash   Account No. 111

Date	Item	P.R.	Debit	Credit	Balance Debit	Balance Credit
20XX Jun. 1	Balance	✓			3972 00	
30		6	4696 00		8668 00	
30		6		6375 00	2293 00	

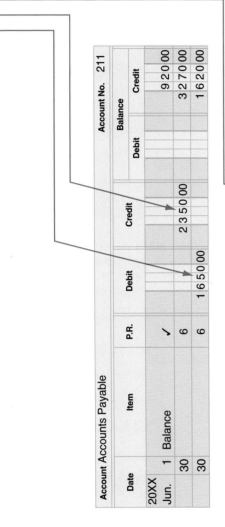

Account Accounts Payable   **Account No.** 211

Date		Item	P.R.	Debit	Credit	Balance Debit	Balance Credit
20XX Jun.	1	Balance	✓				9 2 0 00
	30		6		2 3 5 0 00		3 2 7 0 00
	30		6	1 6 5 0 00			1 6 2 0 00

Account Fees Earned   **Account No.** 411

Date		Item	P.R.	Debit	Credit	Balance Debit	Balance Credit
20XX Jun.	1	Balance	✓				20 0 0 0 00
	30		6		4 4 9 6 00		24 4 9 6 00

Account Salaries Expense   **Account No.** 511

Date		Item	P.R.	Debit	Credit	Balance Debit	Balance Credit
20XX Jun.	1	Balance	✓			6 5 0 0 00	
	30		6	1 3 0 0 00		7 8 0 0 00	

Remember
The general columns are posted individually. Special columns are posted by totals.

Establishing the Petty Cash Fund

The first step in establishing a petty cash fund is to estimate the amount of cash needed in the fund. Then, a check for this amount is written payable to Petty Cash. The check is then cashed, and the money is placed in a box, a drawer, or a safe to be used for the fund. The check is recorded in the journal by debiting the Petty Cash account (an asset) and crediting the Cash account.

For example, on July 2, 20XX, Ann Sherwood wrote Check No. 159 to establish a petty cash fund in the amount of $75. She made the following entry to record this transaction.

	Cash		Ck. No.	Day	Description	P.R.	General	
	Debit	Credit					Debit	Credit
1									1
10		75 00	159	2	Petty Cash		75 00		10

Combined Journal for Month of July, 20XX — Page 7

Making Payments from the Petty Cash Fund

To maintain control over the petty cash fund, the disbursing of money from the fund is usually restricted to one person. This person, often referred to as the **petty cashier**, can be a bookkeeper, a secretary, an office manager, or anyone else who is properly designated.

When a petty cash payment is made, the petty cashier prepares a **petty cash voucher**. The petty cash voucher shows the details of the payment and serves as proof that a payment was made from the fund. A petty cash voucher is shown in Figure 6-5.

FIGURE 6-5
Petty cash voucher

Petty Cash Voucher

No. _2_ Date _July 5, 20XX_

Paid to: _U.S. Postal Service_

Purpose: _Postage due_

Account charged: _Postage Expense_ Amount _1 27_

Payment received by:

Bill Winner Approved by: _A.S._

A properly approved voucher is the petty cashier's authority to make payment out of the fund. The petty cashier should ask the person receiving payment to sign the petty cash voucher. If there is a receipt (as in the case of a retail purchase), it should be attached to the voucher.

Petty Cash Payments Record

Some firms prefer to record all petty cash payments on a single sheet called the **petty cash payments record**. A petty cash payments record is not a journal. Instead, it is an **auxiliary record** used as a basis for making a journal entry. At some point in time, usually at the end of the month, the petty cash payments record is summarized, and the total is entered in the journal.

Ann Sherwood made the following expenditures from her petty cash fund during July, 20XX. These expenditures are recorded in the petty cash payments record shown in Figure 6-6.

20XX
Jul. 3 Issued Voucher 1 for small office supply items, $15.
5 Issued Voucher 2 for postage due on package received, $1.27.
7 Issued Voucher 3 for postage stamps, $3.
9 Issued Voucher 4 for the purchase of a first-aid package, $8.
12 Issued Voucher 5 for a personal cash withdrawal, $10.
18 Issued Voucher 6 for postage stamps, $6.
25 Issued Voucher 7 for the purchase of a one-quarter page advertisement in a local high school annual, $25.
30 Issued Voucher 8 for postage due on package received, $.57.

The petty cash payments record shows that the fund was established on July 2, 20XX. The words *Established Fund* and the amount *$75* are written in the Description column. The formal journal entry to record the establishment of the fund was illustrated on page 190.

All payments made from the petty cash fund are recorded in the Total Amount column. The amount of each payment is then extended to a special column at the right, which identifies the specific type of expense that was paid. Special columns are provided for the expenses most often paid out of petty cash. Ann Sherwood has provided special columns for Office Supplies Expense, Miscellaneous Expense, and Postage Expense. When a transaction occurs that affects an account for which no special column is provided, the title of the account affected is written in the Other Accounts column, and the amount of the payment is entered in the Amount column.

Replenishing the Petty Cash Fund

LEARNING OBJECTIVE 6

To **replenish the petty cash fund** means to put back into the fund the amount that has been paid out of the fund. The petty cash fund is usually replenished at the end of the month. However, it can be replenished any time the fund begins to run low.

To replenish the fund, compare the amount left in the fund with the original amount of the fund. For example, if the original amount of the fund was $50, and there is $3 in the fund at the end of the month, you must put $47 into the fund to bring it back up to its original balance of $50.

The journal entry to record replenishing the petty cash fund involves a debit to *each item* listed in the petty cash payments record and a credit to Cash. To illustrate, refer again to Ann Sherwood's petty cash payments record in Figure 6-6. During July, Ann paid the following items out of petty cash:

Expense	Amount
Office Supplies Expense	$15.00
Miscellaneous Expense	8.00
Postage Expense	10.84
Ann Sherwood, Drawing	10.00
Advertising Expense	25.00
Total	$68.84

Since $68.84 was paid out of the fund during July, it is necessary to put this amount back into the fund. The entry to record replenishment of the fund is shown in the combined journal at the top of page 193.

FIGURE 6-6
Petty cash payments record

Petty Cash Payments for Month of July, 20XX

Day	Description	Vou. No.	Total Amount	Office Sup. Exp.	Misc. Expense	Postage Expense	Other Accounts	Amount
2	Established Fund, $75.00	✓						
3	Office Supplies	1	15 00	15 00				
5	Postage Due	2	1 27			1 27		
7	Stamps	3	3 00			3 00		
9	First-Aid Package	4	8 00		8 00			
12	Owner Withdrawal	5	10 00				Ann Sherwood, Drawing	10 00
18	Stamps	6	6 00			6 00		
25	Advertisement in School Annual	7	25 00				Advertising Expense	25 00
30	Postage Due	8	57			57		
			68 84	15 00	8 00	10 84		35 00
31	Balance in Fund $ 6.16							
	Replenish Fund 68.84							
	Total in Fund $75.00							

Combined Journal for Month of July, 20XX — Page 7

	Cash		Ck. No.	Day	Description	P.R.	General	
	Debit	Credit					Debit	Credit
12		6 8 84	187	31	Office Supplies Expense		1 5 00	12
13					Miscellaneous Expense		8 00	13
14					Postage Expense		1 0 84	14
15					Ann Sherwood, Drawing		1 0 00	15
16					Advertising Expense		2 5 00	16

Let us stress that the journal entry to record the replenishment of the petty cash fund involves a debit to each item listed in the petty cash payments record and a credit to Cash. The petty cash fund is a continuous or revolving fund that, when depleted, is brought back up to its original balance. Thus, the Petty Cash account itself *is not debited* when the fund is replenished. The Petty Cash account is debited *only* when the fund is being established or when the amount in the fund is increased. The Petty Cash account is credited *only* when the amount of the fund is decreased or eliminated completely.

REVIEW QUIZ 6-1

On January 2, 20XX, Tonya Shire established a petty cash fund in the amount of $75. During January, she made the following payments from the fund: office supplies, $10; postage stamps, $18; window cleaning (Miscellaneous Expense), $35; and postage due on package received, $1.25.

(a) In general journal form, record the establishment of the fund on January 2.

(b) In general journal form, record the replenishment of the fund on January 31.

CHECK YOUR ANSWERS ON PAGES 219-220.

REMEMBER

The Petty Cash account is not debited when the fund is replenished. The Petty Cash account is debited only when the fund is established or when the original amount in the fund is increased. The Petty Cash account is credited only when the amount in the fund is decreased or when the fund is eliminated.

THE CHANGE FUND

LEARNING OBJECTIVE 7

Businesses that have many cash transactions usually establish a **change fund**, which is an amount of money that is placed in the cash register drawer and is used to make change for customers who pay in cash. To establish a change fund, two factors must be considered: (1) the amount of money that needs to be in the fund, and (2) the various denominations of bills and coins that are needed.

The establishment of a change fund is recorded by debiting an asset account entitled **Change Fund** and crediting the Cash account. To illustrate this, we will use a business other than Ann Sherwood's, because Ann is an interior decorator and does not have many cash transactions. Let's assume that on March 23,

20X1, Bill Marcus, owner of The Snack Shop, decides to put $125 in a change fund. Bill's entry to record the change fund is shown below.

	20X1						
1	Mar.	23	Change Fund	1 2 5 00			1
2			Cash		1 2 5 00		2
3			Established a change fund.				3

At the close of business each day, Bill will take $125 (in the appropriate denominations) out of the cash register and put it in a safe place, so that it can be put back in the register the next morning. The remaining cash is then deposited in the bank.

The Change Fund account, like the Petty Cash account, is debited only once—when the fund is established. It is left at the initial amount, unless the amount in the fund is increased or decreased.

Let's now look at how to record errors that are made when making change to customers.

CASH SHORT AND OVER

LEARNING OBJECTIVE 8

In many businesses, such as grocery stores and drugstores, cash is exchanged constantly. In such situations, it is hard to avoid errors in receiving cash from customers and making change to customers. Thus, at the end of a business day, it is not uncommon for the amount of cash in the cash register to differ from the cash sales that were rung up on the register. When this happens, there is a *cash shortage* or a *cash overage*, either of which should be investigated.

If the source of the shortage or overage cannot be determined, an account entitled **Cash Short and Over** can be used to bring the cash on hand into agreement with the cash sales. The Cash Short and Over account is used to record *both* shortages and overages. (The Cash Short and Over account can also be used to record shortages and overages in the petty cash fund.) To illustrate, let's look at two different situations. In the first, which we will call Situation A, sales for the day totaled $600. After the change fund was removed, however, there was only $598 in the cash register—a $2 shortage. In the second situation, Situation B, sales for the day totaled $769. But after the change fund was removed, the amount of cash in the register totaled $774—a $5 overage. Journal entries to record these situations follow.

SITUATION A: RECORDING A $2.00 SHORTAGE

1	X	X	Cash	5 9 8 00		1
2			Cash Short and Over	2 00		2
3			Sales Revenue		6 0 0 00	3
4			To record sales revenue and			4
5			a cash shortage.			5

SITUATION B: RECORDING A $5.00 OVERAGE

1	X	X	Cash	7 7 4 00			1
2			Sales Revenue		7 6 9 00		2
3			Cash Short and Over		5 00		3
4			To record sales revenue and				4
5			a cash overage.				5

In Situation A, the Cash Short and Over account is *debited* for the amount of the shortage. In Situation B, the Cash Short and Over account is *credited* for the amount of the overage. After the journal entries are posted, the Cash Short and Over account appears as shown below.

Account Cash Short and Over					Account No. 530		
Date	Item	P.R.	Debit	Credit	Balance		
					Debit	Credit	
X X		GJ3	2 00		2 00		
X		GJ3		5 00		3 00	

Since the cash overage of $5 (the credit side) exceeded the cash shortage of $2 (the debit side), there is a net overage of $3 (the balance of the account). Shortages and overages tend to balance each other out over the course of the accounting period. Therefore, there should only be a small balance in the Cash Short and Over account at the end of the period. How you account for any end-of-period balance in the Cash Short and Over account depends on whether that balance is a debit or a credit. Should the account end up with a debit balance (net shortage), it is reported on the income statement as miscellaneous expense. On the other hand, an end-of-period credit balance (net overage) is reported on the income statement as miscellaneous income. In either case, the balance of the Cash Short and Over account is closed to Income Summary during the closing process.

REMEMBER

The Cash Short and Over account does not have a normal balance because it is a summarizing account. At the end of the month, if its balance is Dr., it is considered an expense; if its balance is Cr., it is considered a revenue.

REVIEW QUIZ 6-2

At the close of business on Tuesday, Tom Snyder, owner of Tom's Great Subs, totaled and cleared his cash register. According to the register, his total sales for the day amounted to $957. However, when he counted the amount of money in the register and subtracted his $100 change fund, he found only $954. Record the sales revenue and the cash shortage in general journal form.

CHECK YOUR ANSWER ON PAGE 220.

BANK CHECKING ACCOUNTS

Earlier in the chapter, we stressed that a very important feature of any good system of internal control is the efficient management of cash. For a business of any size, all cash received during operating hours should be deposited in a bank account at the end of the day. And all payments made by the business—except those made out of petty cash—should be made by check.

Offering convenience as well as protection, the use of a **bank checking account** has become a near universal business practice. Cash that is deposited in a bank is physically protected. And since only authorized persons can write checks, control over cash payments is also provided.

MAINTAINING A CHECKING ACCOUNT

You are probably familiar with how to open a checking account, make deposits, and write checks. Let's review these procedures. In this section, we will discuss signature cards, deposit slips, and endorsements.

Signature Card

A checking account is opened by filling out a short application with the bank, making a deposit, and signing a signature card. A **signature card** lists personal information and contains the signature of the person or persons who are authorized to write checks on the account. The bank keeps the signature card on file as an aid in identifying possible forgeries. When Ann Sherwood opened a checking account with Citizens Bank & Trust Company, she signed the signature card illustrated below in Figure 6-7.

FIGURE 6-7
Bank signature card

Date _5-1-20XX_   Account Number _12 17 860_

Depositor _Ann Sherwood_

Citizens Bank & Trust Company will recognize payment of funds, or other business on this account, only as authorized by the signatures below.

Signature _Ann Sherwood_

Signature _____

Making Deposits

A **deposit slip** or **deposit ticket** is prepared when coin, currency, or checks are deposited in a bank account. It indicates the **depositor's** name and account number and summarizes the amount deposited. The deposit slip prepared by Ann Sherwood on July 15, 20XX, is shown in Figure 6-8.

FIGURE 6-8
Bank deposit slip

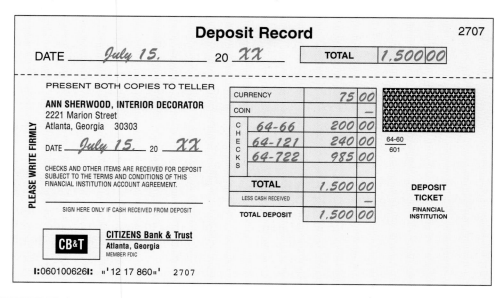

The name, address, and account number of the depositor are usually preprinted on the deposit slip. When making a deposit, the depositor enters both coin and currency on the lines provided. Checks being deposited should also be listed on the lines provided. Each check should be listed according to its American Bankers Association (ABA) transit number. **ABA numbers** are the small numbers located in the upper right corners of checks. (We will discuss the meaning of ABA numbers shortly.)

Endorsements

Checks and money orders must be endorsed before a bank will accept them for deposit. An **endorsement** is a signature or stamp on the back of the check. An endorsement transfers ownership of the check to the bank (or to another business or to an individual). There are three common forms of endorsement: (1) the blank endorsement, (2) the full endorsement, and (3) the restrictive endorsement.

THE BLANK ENDORSEMENT

An endorsement consisting only of the depositor's name signed or stamped on the back of a check is referred to as a **blank endorsement**. A lost or stolen check with this type of endorsement can be cashed by anyone who has possession of it. Therefore, a blank endorsement should be used only when a depositor is in a bank ready to cash the check or make a deposit.

THE FULL ENDORSEMENT

A **full endorsement** specifies the party to whom a check is being transferred. The phrase *Pay to the order of* is written before the name of the person (or business) to whom the check is being transferred. A full endorsement is safer than a blank endorsement because only the person or business named in the endorsement can transfer the check to someone else.

THE RESTRICTIVE ENDORSEMENT

A **restrictive endorsement** specifies the purpose for which the money is to be used. For example, a check endorsed *For Deposit Only* cannot be cashed; it can only be deposited. The restrictive endorsement is popular among businesses because of the protection provided by the restriction of funds.

WRITING CHECKS

A **check** is a written order directing a bank to pay a specified sum of money to a designated person or business. A check is said to be drawn against the account of the person who wrote it. Thus, the person (or business) who writes a check is called the **drawer**. The bank on which a check is drawn is called the **drawee**. And the person (or business) to whom a check is made payable is called the **payee**.

A complete description of all checks written should be made in a **checkbook**, which is the depositor's record of the checking account. A checkbook is a bound book of checks with related **check stubs**. Checks are perforated for easy removal, and the stub remains in the checkbook as a permanent record of the check.

Two checks written by Ann Sherwood during June 20XX, are shown in Figure 6-9. Notice that the check number appears on both the check and the stub. Both the stub and the check also contain the date of the check, the amount of the check, the party to whom the check was written, and the purpose of the expenditure. Since the check stub often serves as a source document for a journal entry, all information on the stub should be filled in before the check is written. Otherwise, the record of the check could be overlooked if one is working under pressure or in a hurry.

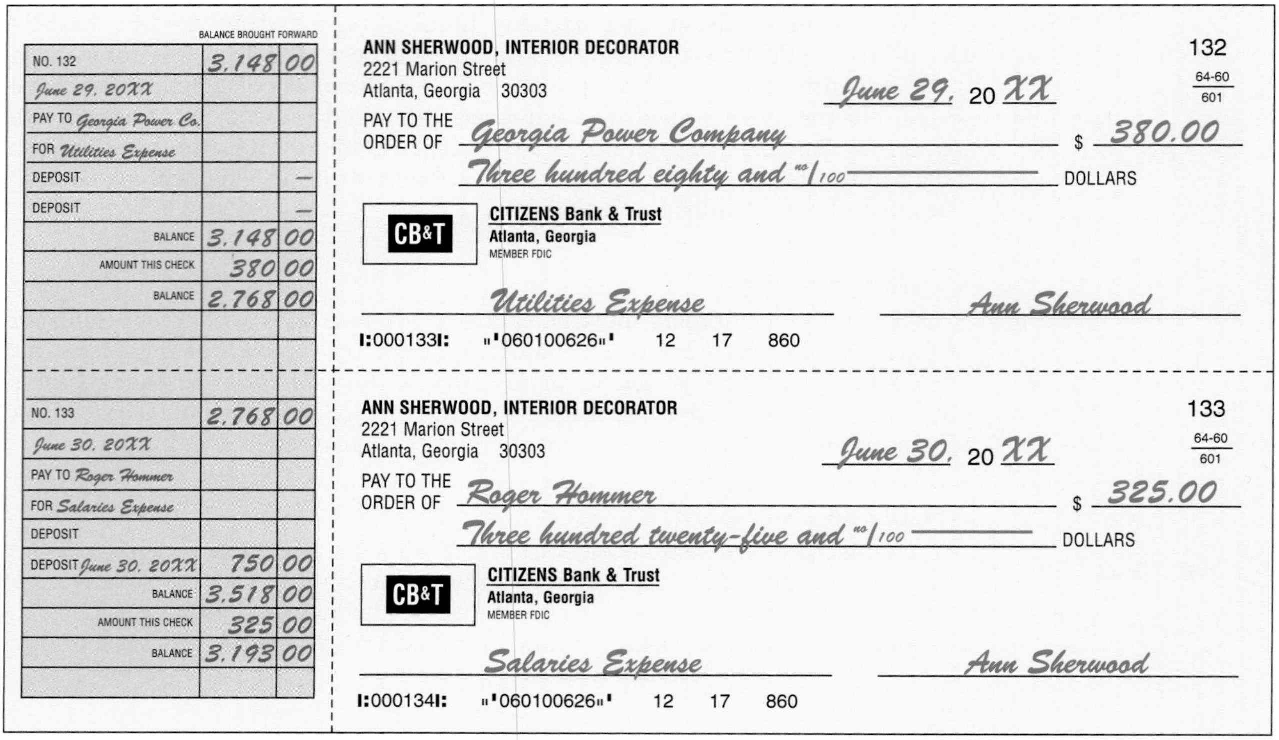

FIGURE 6-9
Checks and stubs

Look at how the amount of a check is written. It is written first in figures. The amount is then restated in words on the line below the name of the payee. The amount of cents is shown as a fraction of a dollar. Thus, 20 cents is written as 20/100. If there are no cents, *00/100* or *no/100* is written. After the amount of the check has been written out in words, a line is drawn to fill in any empty space remaining—to avoid the possibility of the amount being altered.

Some businesses prepare checks mechanically on small machines called checkwriters (or check protectors). Checkwriters are used to write and perforate the amount of a check, making it impossible to alter the dollar amount for which the check is written. Computer-generated checks are also commonly used.

ABA Numbers

A little earlier we mentioned that, for identification purposes, banks are assigned numbers by the American Bankers Association. These ABA numbers are printed in the upper right corner of checks. ABA numbers are often printed on deposit slips as well. The ABA number of Citizens Bank & Trust is $\frac{64-60}{601}$. This number contains three pieces of information:

1. 64 is the number assigned to all banks located in the Atlanta, Georgia area.
2. 60 is the number specifically assigned to Citizens Bank & Trust.
3. 601 is a number used for check routing. This number aids the banking system in routing checks first to the area in which a bank is located and then to the specific bank on which the check is drawn.

THE BANK STATEMENT

Once a month the bank sends each depositor a **bank statement**, which is a report showing the bank's record of the checking account. The bank statement shows the balance of the account at the beginning of the month, the amount of deposits received by the bank during the month, the checks paid by the bank during the month, the service charge or other bank fees, any other additions to or subtractions from the account, and the balance of the account at the end of the month. Also, all checks that are listed on the bank statement are returned with the statement. These are the checks that the bank has paid out of the account. They are referred to as **canceled checks**.

The bank statement received by Ann Sherwood on September 3, 20XX, is shown in Figure 6-10.

FIGURE 6-10
Bank statement

To: Ann Sherwood
2221 Marion Street
Atlanta, Georgia 30303
Account No. 12 17 860

CB&T

CITIZENS Bank & Trust
Atlanta, Georgia
MEMBER FDIC

CHECKS		DEPOSITS	DATE	BEGINNING BALANCE: $6,200
#168	$400		8-01-XX	$5,800
#169	225		8-02-XX	5,575
#170	120		8-05-XX	5,455
#171	80		8-10-XX	5,375
#172	300		8-12-XX	5,075
#174	50	$1,500	8-15-XX	6,525
#175	70		8-16-XX	6,455
#176	80		8-16-XX	6,375
#178	325		8-18-XX	6,050
#179	450		8-23-XX	5,600
#182	25		8-25-XX	5,575
#183	1,825		8-27-XX	3,750
		750	8-29-XX	4,500
#184	150		8-30-XX	4,350
SC	12		8-30-XX	4,338
#185	528		8-30-XX	3,810

ENDING BALANCE: $3,810

Reconciling the Bank Statement

LEARNING OBJECTIVE 9
The bank statement and the checkbook are both records of a depositor's checking account transactions. However, the balance shown on the bank statement and the balance in the checkbook normally do not agree at the end of the month. This lack of agreement is usually not due to errors, but is the result of time lags between the depositor making an entry in the checkbook and the bank making the same entry. Also, the bank often makes deductions from (or additions to) an account that the depositor is unaware of until the statement arrives. Let's look at some common reasons why the bank statement balance may not agree with the checkbook balance:

1. **Outstanding checks**. When a depositor writes a check, the check is immediately entered in the checkbook. However, it may take several days before the check reaches the depositor's bank for payment. If the check appears in the checkbook but not on the statement, it is referred to as **outstanding**.
2. **Deposits in transit**. Certain deposits such as deposits made late in the day, night deposits, deposits by mail, and deposits made to automated teller machines (ATMs) may not reach the bank's accounting department in time to be added to the depositor's account when the statement is being prepared.

Deposits made (and appearing in the checkbook) but not appearing on the bank statement are referred to as **deposits in transit**. Deposits in transit are also called **outstanding deposits**.

3. **Service charges and other bank fees**. In most cases, banks charge a fee for providing checking accounts. This fee, called a **service charge**, is subtracted directly from the depositor's account. The service charge, along with other charges, is shown on the bank statement. Other charges that the bank may make include fees for imprinting checks, fees for collecting money for the depositor, and fees for the use of ATMs.

4. **Errors**. It is not uncommon for depositors to make (1) arithmetic errors when making entries in a checkbook and (2) errors due to transpositions and slides. On occasion, the bank will also make errors. Due to the use of electronic processing equipment, however, the bank is less likely to make errors.

5. **Bank collections**. As a convenience to customers, some banks collect notes or other securities for the depositor and enter these amounts directly in the depositor's account. Such collections appear on the bank statement but not in the checkbook. Also, some checking accounts pay interest, which is calculated by the bank and entered directly into the depositor's account.

6. **NSF (Not Sufficient Funds) checks**. When a check is deposited, it is counted as cash. On occasion, however, some checks that have been deposited turn out to be bad. In other words, the issuers of these checks do not have sufficient funds in their accounts to pay the checks. The bank will notify the depositor of any bad checks. The depositor must in turn make a deduction from the Cash account and the checkbook.

When the bank statement balance and the checkbook balance do not agree, the two must be brought into agreement. The process of making the bank statement balance agree with the checkbook balance is called **bank reconciliation**, or **reconciling the bank statement**. The bank statement is reconciled by the following steps:

❶ Add the amount of deposits in transit to the bank statement balance.
❷ Subtract the amount of outstanding checks from the bank statement balance.
❸ Add to the checkbook balance the amount of any interest earned on the account or any collection made by the bank for the depositor.
❹ Subtract any charges appearing on the bank statement from the checkbook balance.

After making these adjustments, the adjusted balance of the bank statement should agree with the adjusted balance of the checkbook. To illustrate this process, let's look again at Ann Sherwood's bank statement in Figure 6-10. According to the statement, Ann's ending bank balance is $3,810. On the same date, however, Ann's checkbook balance is $2,940. The two records are reconciled as follows:

❶ Ann compares each deposit recorded in the checkbook with that appearing on the bank statement. She discovers that a deposit of $800, made on August 31, has not reached the bank in time to be entered on the bank statement. Thus, the deposit is outstanding.

❷ Ann arranges her canceled checks in numerical order and compares the amount of each check appearing on the bank statement with the amount recorded on her check stubs. A check mark (✓) is placed by each check that appears on both records. Those checks recorded on stubs that have not been checked off are outstanding. Using this process, Ann finds that the following checks are outstanding:

Check No.	Amount
173	$1,200
177	212
180	160
181	140

❸ Ann examines the bank statement for charges made against her account. She finds a $12 service charge.

❹ By comparing the amounts of the canceled checks with the amounts recorded on the check stubs, Ann finds that she wrote a check for $150 but recorded it in the checkbook as $120. This caused her checkbook balance to be overstated by $30.

Based on this analysis, Ann prepared the bank reconciliation statement shown in Figure 6-11. Note that every bank reconciliation begins with two known factors: the balance per bank statement and the balance per checkbook.

FIGURE 6-11
Bank reconciliation statement

Ann Sherwood, Interior Decorator Bank Reconciliation Statement August 31, 20XX		
Balance per bank statement		$3 8 1 0 00
Add: Deposit in transit		8 0 0 00
		$4 6 1 0 00
Deduct: Outstanding checks		
#173	$1 2 0 0 00	
#177	2 1 2 00	
#180	1 6 0 00	
#181	1 4 0 00	1 7 1 2 00
Adjusted bank statement balance		$2 8 9 8 00
Balance per checkbook		$2 9 4 0 00
Deduct:		
Service charge	$1 2 00	
Error in checkbook	3 0 00	4 2 00
Adjusted checkbook balance		$2 8 9 8 00

REVIEW QUIZ
6-3

Todd Baker received his bank statement on October 1, 20XX. According to his statement, Todd has a bank balance of $922. However, Todd's checkbook shows a balance of $870. Closer observation revealed the following:

1. A deposit of $40 was in transit.
2. Check #34 for $41 and Check #38 for $56 were outstanding.
3. A service charge of $4 had been made against Todd's account.
4. Todd wrote Check #36 for $31; however, he entered only $30 in his checkbook.

Prepare a bank reconciliation statement for Todd.

CHECK YOUR ANSWER ON PAGE 220.

Updating Cash Records

All the checkbook adjustments appearing on the bank reconciliation statement should be entered in the checkbook to bring the checkbook balance into agreement with the cash in the bank. Ann's bank reconciliation statement shows two checkbook adjustments: (1) a $12 deduction for a bank service charge, and (2) a $30 deduction due to incorrectly recording a $150 check as $120. The service charge should be entered in the checkbook as a deduction on the next unused check stub. The words *August S.C.* are written on the check stub to identify the amount. The $30 error adjustment should also be entered in the checkbook as a deduction because the checkbook balance is overstated due to recording only $120 for a check that was written for $150.

Journal entries are needed for checkbook adjustments appearing on the bank reconciliation statement.

A journal entry is needed for the $12 service charge because it is a cash payment, even though no check was written. (It was taken directly from the account by the bank.) No journal entry is needed for the $30 error adjustment, because the effect of the error was confined solely to the checkbook. (The check had been written for the correct amount and journalized correctly but entered incorrectly on the check stub.) The entry for the service charge is recorded in the combined journal as follows:

	Cash		Ck. No.	Day	Description	P.R.	General		
	Debit	Credit					Debit	Credit	
16		12 00		3	Miscellaneous Expense*		12 00		16

Combined Journal for Month of September, 20XX — Page 9

An account entitled Bank Service Charge could have been used.

Journal entries *are not* needed for adjustments to the bank statement balance because these amounts relate to the bank's records. However, if the bank has made an error, the bank's accounting department should be notified so that the necessary corrections can be made.

A More Detailed Bank Reconciliation

We were able to reconcile Ann Sherwood's bank statement by following the steps that are somewhat standard in the reconciliation process. Let's take a moment to look at an example that is a little more involved. The accountant for McGreggor Company assembled the following data as of April 30, 20X1:

1. Bank statement balance, $12,900.
2. Checkbook balance, $8,130.
3. Deposit in transit, $950.
4. Checks outstanding (total), $3,160.
5. Bank had charged a $75 check written by McGreggor Lawn Service to the account of McGreggor Company.
6. Bank collected a $3,000 note for McGreggor, charging a $15 collection fee.
7. A $300 check that McGreggor had deposited was returned by the bank because it is a bad (NSF) check.
8. Bill McGreggor made a personal withdrawal at an ATM, $50.

Based on this data, we can prepare McGreggor's bank reconciliation as shown in Figure 6-12.

FIGURE 6-12
Bank reconciliation statement

McGreggor Company Bank Reconciliation Statement April 30, 20X1			
Balance per bank statement			$12 9 0 0 00
Add: Deposit in transit	$ 9 5 0 00		
Error made by bank	7 5 00	1 0 2 5 00	
		$13 9 2 5 00	
Deduct: Outstanding checks		3 1 6 0 00	
Adjusted bank statement balance		$10 7 6 5 00	
Balance per checkbook		$ 8 1 3 0 00	
Add: Note collected		3 0 0 0 00	
		$11 1 3 0 00	
Deduct:			
Collection fee	$ 1 5 00		
NSF check	3 0 0 00		
Cash withdrawal	5 0 00	3 6 5 00	
Adjusted checkbook balance		$10 7 6 5 00	

Remember that when an adjustment is made *to the checkbook balance* in the reconciliation process, a journal entry is needed. The following entries are thus needed to update McGreggor's books. Notice that the $300 NSF check is debited to the Accounts Receivable account. This is because the amount is still owed by the customer, even though the check bounced. The $300 will remain in Accounts Receivable until it is collected, at which time it will be debited to Cash and credited to Accounts Receivable.

	20X1					
1	Apr.	30	Cash	3 0 0 0 00		1
2			Notes Receivable		3 0 0 0 00	2
3			Note collected by bank.			3
4						4
5		30	Miscellaneous Expense	1 5 00		5
6			Cash		1 5 00	6
7			Bank collection fee.			7
8						8
9		30	Accounts Receivable	3 0 0 00		9
10			Cash		3 0 0 00	10
11			NSF check returned by bank.			11
12						12
13		30	Bill McGreggor, Drawing	5 0 00		13
14			Cash		5 0 00	14
15			Owner withdrew cash using ATM.			15

HOW CAN I USE REMOTE BANKING?

Remote banking and electronic banking will play a major role in the future of banking. Remote banking software, available from most banks, allows you to make fund transfers, check balances, pay bills, and download bank statements from home. CheckFree, the nation's leading provider of bill-paying services, offers options for banking by phone or by personal computer. Many of these services allow you to obtain a debit card, cash card, or guarantee card.

Search the following sites for more information about how to bank online:

http://www.checkfree.com

http://www.wiso.gwdg.de/ifbg/bank_1.html

http://www.magicline.com/Home.html

http://www.mkn.co.uk/bank

http://www.chase.com/tx/retail/online.html

http://www.comerica.com/homebank/quin.html

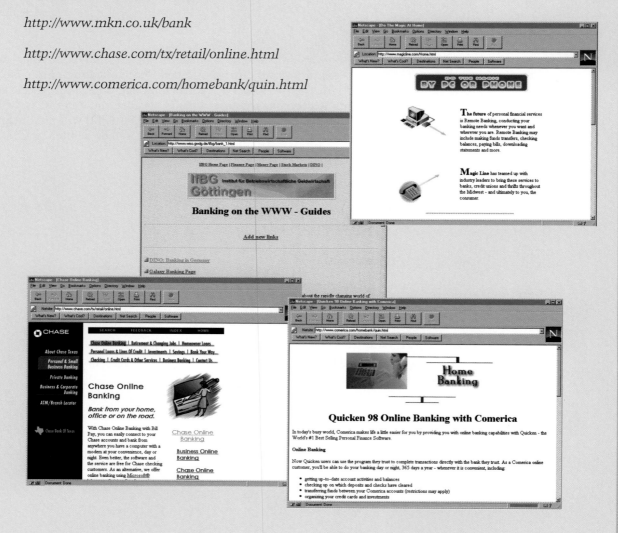

STEPS TO RECONCILE THE BANK STATEMENT

Bank Statement Balance				Checkbook Balance			
Balance per bank statement		$XXX		Balance per checkbook			$XXX
Add:				Add:			
Deposits in transit	$XXX			Bank collections	$XXX		
Bank errors that understate statement balance	XXX	XXX		Interest earned	XXX		
				Recording errors that understate balance	XXX	XXX	
Deduct:				Deduct:			
Outstanding checks	$XXX			Recording errors that overstate balance	$XXX		
Bank errors that overstate statement balance	XXX	XXX		Service charges	XXX		
				Imprinting check charges	XXX		
				NSF checks	XXX		
				Other bank charges	XXX	XXX	
Adjusted bank statement balance		$XXX		Adjusted checkbook balance			$XXX

SUMMARY/RESTATEMENT OF LEARNING OBJECTIVES

1. Define cash as it is used in accounting.

In a narrow sense, **cash** refers to the amount of currency and coins owned by a business or individual. However, items such as traveler's checks, money orders, and checks made payable to the business are also included in cash.

2. Describe internal control procedures related to cash.

Internal control is defined as the procedures and measures used by a business to protect its assets from theft, loss, and misuse. Typical measures taken to protect and control cash include the following:

- Cashiers, clerks, and others who actually handle cash (i.e., by operating cash registers, maintaining cash drawers, receiving payments from customers, etc.) should not make journal entries to record the receipt and payment of cash.
- All cash receipts should be deposited daily in a bank account.
- Only a small amount of cash (called **petty cash**) should be kept on hand.
- All cash payments, except for petty cash, should be made by check.
- Checks should be prenumbered so that it is easy to see what checks have been written and when.
- Only a few properly designated persons should be involved in the receipt, payment, and recording of cash.
- Receipt and payment of cash should be recorded efficiently and accurately.

3. Record transactions in a combined journal, post the combined journal to the ledger, and cross-reference the two records.

A **combined journal** is a multicolumn journal designed to save journalizing and posting time. Typically, a combined journal has two special columns for recording increases and decreases in cash, various other special columns for recording transactions that occur often, and two general columns for recording transactions that are not recorded in special columns. The use of a combined journal saves journalizing time because it is not necessary to write account titles when making entries in special columns. The combined journal is illustrated in Figure 6-2. Posting from the combined journal is illustrated in Figures 6-3 and 6-4.

4. Describe the purpose of and need for a petty cash fund.

To aid in the control of cash, most businesses use a **bank checking account**. Making all payments by check, however, would mean that someone authorized to write checks must always be available. This is not always practical. Nor is it practical to write checks for very small amounts. Each working day, business firms are confronted with transactions that involve the immediate payment of cash, such as postage due on packages, overnight deliveries, coffee and doughnuts, a birthday card for a customer, small items of office supply, and the like. Making these payments by check would be costly and time-consuming. Consequently, an office fund known as the **petty cash fund** (*petty* means small) is usually maintained for making small expenditures.

5. Record the establishment of a petty cash fund.

The first step in establishing a petty cash fund is to estimate how much cash is needed in the fund. An entry is then made debiting the Petty Cash account and crediting the Cash account. For example, on March 2, 20XX, Herb McQuaig, owner of Herb's Pawn Shop, estimated that his business needed $75 in a petty cash fund. Herb's entry to record the establishment of the fund is shown in general journal form below.

	20XX																			
1	Mar.	2	Petty Cash			7	5	00										1
2			Cash									7	5	00	2
3			Established petty cash fund.												3

6. Record the replenishment of a petty cash fund.

On March 31, 20XX, the following expenses had been paid from the petty cash fund of Herb's Pawn Shop:

Expense	Amount
Postage Expense	$10.00
Office Supplies Expense	15.00
Window Cleaning (Miscellaneous Expense)	25.00
Contributions Expense	12.50
Total	$62.50

Since $62.50 has been paid out of the fund, this amount must be placed back in the fund to bring it back to its balance on March 2. The entry to record the replenishment of the fund is shown next in general journal form.

	20XX																	
1	Mar.	31	Postage Expense			1	0	00						1
2			Office Supplies Expense			1	5	00						2
3			Miscellaneous Expense			2	5	00						3
4			Contributions Expense			1	2	50						4
5			Cash							6	2	50	5
6			Replenished petty cash fund.										6

7. Record the establishment of a change fund.

Businesses that have frequent cash transactions usually establish a **change fund** in order to make change for customers. The change fund is established by first determining how much is needed in the fund and then deciding what denominations of currency and coin are needed. A journal entry is then made debiting the Change Fund account (an asset) and crediting the Cash account. For example, Sharon Joyner is getting ready to open a gift shop. On July 2, 20X2, Sharon established a change fund in the amount of $75. Her general journal entry to record the fund is shown below.

	20X2						
1	Jul.	2	Change Fund	7 5 00			1
2			Cash		7 5 00		2
3			Established a change fund.				3

8. Record cash shortages and overages.

Example 1—A cash shortage: A cash register reading indicated that sales for the day totaled $600. However, there was only $596 cash in the register after the change fund was removed. The entry to record the sales revenue and the $4 cash shortage is shown below in general journal form.

The shortage is considered an expense.

	X	X	Cash	5 9 6 00		
1						1
2			Cash Short and Over	4 00		2
3			Sales Revenue		6 0 0 00	3
4			Recorded sales revenue and			4
5			a cash shortage.			5

Example 2—A cash overage: A cash register reading indicated that sales for the day totaled $525. However, the cash in the register totaled $528 after the change fund was removed. The entry to record the sales revenue and the $3 overage is shown below in general journal form.

The overage is considered a revenue.

	X	X	Cash	5 2 8 00		
1						1
2			Sales Revenue		5 2 5 00	2
3			Cash Short and Over		3 00	3
4			Recorded sales revenue and			4
5			a cash overage.			5

9. Prepare a bank reconciliation.

Regularly, usually once a month, the bank will send each **depositor** a **bank statement**, which is a copy of the bank's record of the checking account. Although the bank statement and the **checkbook** are both records of the depositor's account transactions, their balances rarely agree at the time the statement is prepared. This difference is usually due to time lags between the same entry being recorded on both records. When the bank statement and the checkbook do not agree, their balances must be reconciled (brought into agreement). For example, James Weeks is a plumbing contractor. His October bank statement shows a balance of $1,600. However, Mr. Weeks's checkbook shows a balance of $1,301. Further investigation revealed the following:

- The bank had not received an October 31 deposit, $400.
- The following checks were **outstanding**:

Check No.	Amount
143	$200
151	30
153	120

- The bank had collected a note receivable of $300 plus interest of $35 and had credited Mr. Weeks's account.

- A bank service charge of $13 was made against Mr. Weeks's account.
- Mr. Weeks had written a check for $225, but had entered $252 in his checkbook.

Mr. Weeks's bank reconciliation is shown below.

James Weeks Bank Reconciliation Statement October 31, 20XX			
Balance per bank statement			$1 6 0 0 00
Add: Deposit in transit			4 0 0 00
			$2 0 0 0 00
Deduct: Outstanding checks			
#143		$2 0 0 00	
#151		3 0 00	
#153		1 2 0 00	3 5 0 00
Adjusted bank statement balance			$1 6 5 0 00
Balance per checkbook			$1 3 0 1 00
Add: Note and interest collected		$3 3 5 00	
Error in checkbook		2 7 00	3 6 2 00
			1 6 6 3 00
Deduct: Service charge			1 3 00
Adjusted checkbook balance			$1 6 5 0 00

KEY TERMS

ABA (American Bankers Association) numbers Numbers printed on checks and deposit slips that contain information as to the bank, the area in which it is located, and the like.

auxiliary record A business record that is not essential but is helpful in maintaining records that are essential; an example is the petty cash payments record.

bank checking account An amount of cash on deposit with a bank that the bank must pay at the written order of the depositor.

bank reconciliation Making the bank statement balance agree with the checkbook balance.

bank statement A monthly report showing the bank's record of the checking account.

blank endorsement An endorsement consisting only of a signature on the back of a check. A check with this kind of endorsement can be cashed or transferred to another by anyone who has possession of it.

canceled checks Checks that have been paid by the bank out of the depositor's account.

cash In its most basic meaning, cash is currency (paper money) and coin. The definition in a business context also includes checks, money orders, traveler's checks, cashier's checks, bank drafts, and receipts from credit card sales.

Cash Short and Over An account used to bring the Cash account into agreement with the actual amount of cash on hand. This account is used in businesses that have many cash transactions and thus often have small amounts of cash over or under what the cash register shows.

change fund An amount of money that is maintained in the cash register for making change for cash customers.

Change Fund account An asset account in which the amount of the change fund is recorded.

check A written order directing a bank to pay a specified sum of money to a designated person or business.

checkbook A bound book of checks with stubs; the depositor's record of the checking account.

check stub Part of a check that remains in the checkbook as a permanent record of the check.

combined journal A multicolumn journal used by small businesses to help save journalizing and posting time. It has two special columns for recording debits and credits to cash, various other special columns for recording transactions that occur often, and two general columns for recording transactions that occur less often. Also called a **combination journal**.

depositor The business or person under whose name a checking account is opened.

deposits in transit Deposits made and appearing in the checkbook but not appearing on the bank statement. Also called **outstanding deposits**.

deposit slip A form that is prepared when coin, currency, or checks are deposited in a bank account. It indicates the depositor's name and account number and summarizes the amount deposited. Also called **deposit ticket**.

drawee The bank on which a check is drawn.

drawer The business or person who writes a check.

endorsement A signature or stamp on the back of a check that transfers ownership of the check to the bank or another person.

full endorsement Uses the phrase *Pay to the order of*, followed by the name of the business or person to whom the check is being transferred. Only the specified business or person can cash the check.

internal control The procedures used within a company to protect its assets.

NSF check (nonsufficient funds check) A check drawn against an account in which there are *nonsufficient funds*; a bad check.

outstanding check A check that was recorded in the checkbook but does not appear on the bank statement. In other words, a check that has been written and entered in the checkbook but has not reached the bank's accounting department.

payee The business or person to whom a check is made payable.

petty cash fund A small amount of cash kept in the office for making small payments for items such as postage and office supplies.

petty cashier The person designated to disburse money from the petty cash fund.

petty cash payments record An auxiliary record, one that is used to record payments from the petty cash fund. At the end of the month, the record is summarized and used as a basis for a journal entry.

petty cash voucher A voucher used when payment is made from the petty cash fund. It shows the amount of the payment, the purpose, and the account to be debited.

replenishing the petty cash fund *Replenish* means to fill up. When applied to the petty cash fund, this term means to bring the amount of the fund back up to the level it was at the beginning of the month.

restrictive endorsement An endorsement on the back of a check that specifies the purpose for which the money is to be used. *For deposit only* is a common one. It means that the check cannot be cashed—it can only be deposited.

service charges Charges or fees by the bank that are subtracted directly from the depositor's account and appear on the bank statement. Also called **bank charges**.

signature card Lists personal information and contains the signature of the person(s) authorized to write checks on a bank account. The bank keeps these cards on file to help identify possible forgeries.

zero proof test A test performed using the plus and minus bars of a calculator— *zero proof* means that two equal columns have a zero difference.

CONCEPTS AND SKILLS REVIEW

CONCEPTS REVIEW

1. Why are special controls necessary to protect cash?
2. Identify three methods of internal control for cash that you think are important.
3. Why should cash transactions be handled by more than one person?
4. What factors should be considered when designing a combined journal?
5. What is the purpose of special columns in a combined journal?
6. How are the special columns of a combined journal posted?
7. How are the general columns of a combined journal posted?
8. Cash in a petty cash fund is not subjected to the same measures of control as cash in a bank account. How is this practice justified?
9. What is meant by *establishing* a petty cash fund?
10. What information should be shown on a petty cash voucher?
11. Is a petty cash payments record a type of journal? Explain your answer.
12. What is meant by an *auxiliary* record?
13. How often is a petty cash fund replenished?
14. What is a change fund?
15. What is the purpose of the Cash Short and Over account?
16. What is the normal balance of the Cash Short and Over account? Explain your answer.
17. How does a bank checking account provide both physical and internal protection of cash?
18. Why do banks require a new depositor to fill out a signature card?
19. What information is shown on the bank statement?
20. The bank statement and the checkbook are both records of a depositor's checking account transactions. Why, then, do they rarely agree at the end of a month?

SKILLS REVIEW

EXERCISE 6-1

LEARNING OBJECTIVE 1

Objective: To determine which items are classified as cash

Directions: For each item listed, place a check mark in the Yes column if the item is classified as cash or a check mark in the No column if it is not classified as cash.

Item	Classified as Cash Yes	No
(a) Checks made payable to the business		
(b) Money orders		
(c) Postage stamps		
(d) Savings bonds due to mature in ten years		
(e) Currency		
(f) Cashier's check		
(g) Coin		
(h) Traveler's check		
(i) Petty cash		
(j) Change fund		
(k) Amount on deposit in a bank checking account		

EXERCISE 6-2

LEARNING OBJECTIVE 5

Objective: To record the establishment of and an increase in a petty cash fund

On May 1, 20XX, Jon Fischer established a petty cash fund in the amount of $200. On July 1, he increased the fund to $250.

Directions: Record both transactions in general journal form.

EXERCISE 6-3

LEARNING OBJECTIVE 6

Objective: To record replenishment of a petty cash fund

During May 20X0, James Flaherty paid the following expenses from his petty cash fund:

Postage Expense	$50
Miscellaneous Expense	23
Supplies Expense	25
Advertising Expense	15
James Flaherty, Drawing	25

Directions: In general journal form, record the replenishment of the fund on May 31.

EXERCISE 6-4

LEARNING OBJECTIVE 5, 6

Objective: To record petty cash transactions in a general journal

Allie Sterling is a design engineer. During June 20X1, she incurred the following petty cash transactions:

(a)   Established a petty cash fund in the amount of $75.
(b)   Replenished the fund for expenditures as follows: postage expense, $17; office supplies expense, $14; design supplies expense, $20; miscellaneous expense, $15.50.
(c)   Increased the fund by an additional $25.

Directions: Record the above transactions in general journal form.

EXERCISE 6-5

LEARNING OBJECTIVE 7

Objective: To record the establishment of and a decrease in a change fund

On June 15, 20X1, Lynn Sapp established a change fund in the amount of $150 for her new catering service. On July 5, she decreased the fund to $125. (Hint: A reverse of the first entry.)

Directions: Record both transactions in general journal form.

EXERCISE 6-6

LEARNING OBJECTIVE 8

Objective: To record cash shortages and overages

Directions: Record the following cash sales and cash shortages and overages in general journal form.

May 1, 20X1: Cash in cash register totaled $672. Sales for the day totaled $672.
May 2, 20X1: Cash in cash register totaled $455. Sales for the day totaled $461.
May 3, 20X1: Sales for the day totaled $789. Cash in cash register totaled $793.

EXERCISE 6-7

LEARNING OBJECTIVE 9

Objective: To classify items for a bank reconciliation

Directions: Identify each item in the following list as (a) added to the bank statement balance, (b) subtracted from the bank statement balance, (c) added to the checkbook balance, or (d) subtracted from the checkbook balance.

1. Deposits in transit
2. Outstanding checks
3. Service charge
4. NSF check charge

5. Deposit on bank statement but not in checkbook
6. Charge for printing checks

EXERCISE 6-8

Objective: To determine the true balance of cash

The Itasca Company's Cash account shows a balance of $5,150 as of March 31, 20XX. The balance shown on the bank statement of the same date is $7,014. The bookkeeper found the following:

Deposit in transit, $1,200
Outstanding checks, $1,815
Note collected by bank for Itasca, $1,270
Service charge, $21

Directions: Calculate the adjusted bank statement balance and the true cash balance as of March 31.

EXERCISE 6-9

Objective: To prepare a bank reconciliation statement

Todd Camp received his bank statement dated September 1, 20XX. According to the statement, Todd has a bank balance of $2,250. On the same date, however, Todd's checkbook indicates a balance of $2,074. Closer observation revealed the following facts:

(a) A $60 deposit made on August 31 was not on the bank statement.
(b) Check Nos. 76 ($25) and 79 ($78) were outstanding.
(c) The bank had collected $140 from a customer of Todd's and entered it directly in his account.
(d) The bank charged $7 for service and deducted it from Todd's account.

Directions: Prepare a bank reconciliation statement.

EXERCISE 6-10

Objective: To make journal entries from a bank reconciliation statement

Directions: From the following bank reconciliation statement of Lanier Company, prepare journal entries needed to update the Cash account.

Lanier Company Bank Reconciliation Statement June 30, 20X5		
Balance per bank statement		$10 2 0 0 00
Add: Deposit in transit		1 4 0 0 00
		$11 6 0 0 00
Deduct: Outstanding checks		
#122	$ 1 1 8 00	
#125	2 2 5 00	
#129	9 2 00	4 3 5 00
Adjusted bank statement balance		$11 1 6 5 00
Balance per checkbook		$ 9 6 9 0 00
Add: Collection of note		1 5 0 0 00
		$11 1 9 0 00
Deduct: Service charge		2 5 00
Adjusted checkbook balance		$11 1 6 5 00

CASE PROBLEMS

GROUP A

LEARNING OBJECTIVE 3

PROBLEM 6-1A

Objective: To record business transactions in a combined journal

The following transactions were incurred by Japan Holmes Company during May, 20X2:

20X2

May 1 Issued Check No. 41 for May rent, $900.
1 Issued Check No. 42 for the purchase of office supplies, $180.
2 Issued Check No. 43 for the purchase of a new printer, $550 (Office Equipment).
4 Received cash for services performed, $550.
5 Purchased office supplies on account from G. Blake, $110.
6 Received cash for services performed, $910.
7 Issued Check No. 44 for salaries of employees, $900.
8 Received cash for services performed, $75.
9 Issued Check No. 45 for phone bill, $121 (Utilities Expense).
10 Issued Check No. 46 for repairs to office equipment, $140.
12 Received cash for services performed, $780.
14 Issued Check No. 47 for salaries of employees, $900.
16 Received cash for services performed, $326.
17 Issued Check No. 48 for office supplies, $175.
21 Received cash for services performed, $400.
21 Issued Check No. 49 for salaries of employees, $900.
22 Purchased office supplies on account from P. White, $420.
23 Purchased a new calculator on account from Ace Suppliers, $159.
25 Issued Check No. 50 for utility bill, $528.
27 Received cash for services performed, $105.
28 Issued Check No. 51 to G. Blake in payment of office supplies purchased on May 5.
29 Received cash for services performed, $340.
31 Issued Check No. 52 to Ace Suppliers in payment of the calculator purchased on May 23.
31 Issued Check No. 53 for salaries of employees, $900.
31 Received cash for services performed, $400.

Directions:
1. Record these transactions in a combined journal similar to the one illustrated in this chapter.
2. Total, prove, and rule the journal.

LEARNING OBJECTIVE 3

PROBLEM 6-2A

Objective: To open ledger accounts, journalize transactions in a combined journal, post to the ledger, and prepare a trial balance

The following is the May 31, 20X1 trial balance of the Torbet Service Company.

		Torbet Service Company Trial Balance May 31, 20X1				
	Account Title		**Debit**		**Credit**	
111	Cash		3 0 5 0 00			
114	Office Supplies		4 0 0 00			
115	Advertising Supplies		6 0 0 00			
125	Office Equipment		1 8 0 0 00			
211	Accounts Payable				9 8 0 00	
215	Notes Payable				2 5 0 0 00	
311	Dan Torbet, Capital				3 3 9 0 00	
312	Dan Torbet, Drawing		1 2 0 0 00			
411	Fees Earned				2 4 1 0 00	
511	Rent Expense		8 0 0 00			
512	Salaries Expense		9 0 0 00			
513	Repairs Expense		5 0 00			
514	Utilities Expense		4 0 0 00			
518	Miscellaneous Expense		8 0 00			
	Totals		9 2 8 0 00		9 2 8 0 00	

Torbet incurred the following transactions during June:

20X1

Jun. 1 Issued Check No. 14 for June rent, $400.

1 Issued Check No. 15 to Jay Smith in partial payment of an account payable, $250.

2 Received cash for services performed, $900.

3 Received cash for services performed, $175.

5 Purchased office supplies on account from Walsh Company, $420.

6 Purchased a microcomputer system for $5,000. Issued Check No. 16 for a $1,000 down payment and issued a note payable for the balance.

7 Received cash for services performed, $189.

8 Issued Check No. 17 for the monthly phone bill, $95 (Utilities Expense).

10 Issued Check No. 18 in payment of employees' salaries, $450.

11 Received cash for services performed, $600.

12 Issued Check No. 19 for an owner withdrawal, $600.

15 Issued Check No. 20 for window cleaning, $75.

18 Received cash for services performed, $600.

19 Issued Check No. 21 in partial payment of a note payable, $185.

21 Issued Check No. 22 in payment of employees' salaries, $475.

25 Received cash for services performed, $130.

26 Received cash for services performed, $800.

30 Issued Check No. 23 to Walsh Company in payment of the office supplies purchased on June 5.

30 Issued Check No. 24 in payment of employees' salaries, $480.

Directions:

1. Open a ledger account and enter the balance, as of June 1, of each account on the trial balance.

2. Record the transactions in a combined journal like the one illustrated in the chapter.

3. Total, prove, and rule the combined journal and post to the ledger.

4. Prepare a trial balance as of June 30.

LEARNING OBJECTIVE 5, 6

PROBLEM 6-3A

Objective: To record journal entries to establish and replenish a petty cash fund and to record petty cash payments in a petty cash record

On March 1, 20X3, Daniel Myers established a petty cash fund. The following petty cash transactions occurred during the month:

Mar. 1 Daniel established the petty cash fund in the amount of $60.
   2 Issued Voucher No. 1 for postage due on a package, $3.
   3 Issued Voucher No. 2 for postage due on a package, $3.50.
   8 Issued Voucher No. 3 to have a spot removed from the carpet, $15 (Miscellaneous Expense).
   15 Issued Voucher No. 4 for the purchase of pens for the office, $9.45.
   19 Issued Voucher No. 5 for the purchase of a box of staples, $2.95.
   20 Issued Voucher No. 6 for the owner's personal use, $5.
   23 Issued Voucher No. 7 for the purchase of office supplies, $7.50.
   30 Issued Voucher No. 8 for postage due on a package, $0.74.
   31 Replenished the fund.

Directions:
1. Journalize the entry to establish the petty cash fund.
2. Record the disbursements from the fund in a petty cash payments record.
3. Complete the petty cash payments record—total, rule, and set up for the new month.
4. Journalize the entry to replenish the fund.

LEARNING OBJECTIVE 9

PROBLEM 6-4A

Objective: To reconcile a bank statement and journalize necessary entries

The following data relate to the checking account of Susan Sheppard as of July 31, 20X1:

Balance per bank statement		$7,600
Balance per checkbook		6,000
Deposit in transit		75
Outstanding checks:		
#122	$400	
#126	50	
#129	125	
#130	200	775
Bank service charge		13
Imprinting check charge		18
Note receivable collected by bank		
and entered in Susan's account		931

Directions:
1. Prepare a statement to reconcile Susan's checkbook with her July bank statement.
2. Journalize any entries needed to bring the Cash account into agreement with the adjusted checkbook balance.

GROUP B

LEARNING OBJECTIVE 3

PROBLEM 6-1B

Objective: To record business transactions in a combined journal

The following transactions were incurred by Weston Company during July, 20X2:

20X2
Jul. 1 Issued Check No. 321 for July rent, $900.
     1 Issued Check No. 322 for office supplies, $95.
     3 Received cash for services performed, $190.
     5 Purchased office supplies on account from D. Evans, $299.
     7 Received cash for services performed, $285.
     8 Issued Check No. 323 for salaries, $900.
     9 Issued Check No. 324 for the purchase of a new computer, $2,800.
    11 Received cash for services performed, $400.
    13 Issued Check No. 325 for electric bill, $355.
    15 Purchased a calculator on account from Fox Supplies, $140.
    17 Received cash for services performed, $105.
    19 Issued Check No. 326 for equipment repairs, $60.
    20 Issued Check No. 327 to D. Evans to pay for the purchase of the 5th.
    21 Received cash for services performed, $205.
    22 Issued Check No. 328 for automobile supplies, $75.
    23 Issued Check No. 329 for salaries, $935.
    25 Received cash for services performed, $250.
    25 Issued Check No. 330 for telephone bill, $230.
    28 Received cash for services performed, $800.
    29 Purchased office equipment on account from E. Foster, $325.
    30 Issued Check No. 331 to Fox Supplies to pay for the purchase of July 15.
    31 Issued Check No. 332 for salaries, $890.
    31 Received cash for services performed, $180.

Directions:
1. Record Weston's transactions in a combined journal similar to the one illustrated in this chapter.
2. Total, prove, and rule the journal.

LEARNING OBJECTIVE 3

PROBLEM 6-2B

Objective: To open ledger accounts, journalize transactions in a combined journal, post to the ledger, and prepare a trial balance

The following is the June 30, 20X2 trial balance of the Citizens Service Company.

Citizens Service Company Trial Balance June 30, 20X2		
Account Title	Debit	Credit
111 Cash	1 2 5 0 00	
114 Office Supplies	6 4 0 00	
115 Advertising Supplies	6 0 0 00	
125 Office Equipment	4 8 0 0 00	
211 Accounts Payable		7 8 0 00
215 Notes Payable		1 2 9 0 00
311 Bill Willis, Capital		5 4 5 0 00
312 Bill Willis, Drawing	1 6 5 0 00	
411 Fees Earned		4 7 1 5 00
511 Rent Expense	1 0 5 0 00	
512 Salaries Expense	1 5 9 0 00	
513 Repairs Expense	5 0 00	
514 Utilities Expense	4 6 0 00	
518 Miscellaneous Expense	1 4 5 00	
Totals	12 2 3 5 00	12 2 3 5 00

The following transactions were incurred during July.

20X2

Jul. 1 Received cash for services performed, $700.
   3 Issued Check No. 24 for July rent, $750.
   5 Issued Check No. 25 to R. Sawyer in partial payment on an account payable, $300.
   6 Received cash for services performed, $600.
   8 Purchased office supplies, $275, and advertising supplies, $90, on account from Acme Company.
  10 Issued Check No. 26 for a utility bill, $120.
  11 Bill Willis, the owner, invested an additional $1,000 cash in the business.
  12 Received cash for services performed, $1,400.
  15 Issued Check No. 27 for salaries, $575.
  15 Issued Check No. 28 for office cleaning, $65.
  17 Issued Check No. 29 for owner withdrawal, $400.
  19 Received cash for services performed, $350.
  22 Issued Check No. 30 for office equipment, $560.
  26 Received cash for services performed, $900.
  29 Issued Check No. 31 to Acme Company for the purchase of July 8.
  30 Issued Check No. 32 in partial payment of a note payable, $1,000.
  31 Received cash for services performed, $400.
  31 Issued Check No. 33 for salaries, $595.

Directions:
1. Open a ledger account and enter the balance, as of July 1, of each account on the trial balance.
2. Record the transactions in a combined journal like the one illustrated in the chapter.
3. Total, prove, and rule the combined journal and post to the ledger.
4. Prepare a trial balance as of July 31.

LEARNING OBJECTIVE 5, 6

PROBLEM 6-3B

Objective: To record journal entries to establish and replenish a petty cash fund and to record petty cash payments in a petty cash record

On October 1, 20XX, Norlida Mohd Noor established a petty cash fund. The following petty cash transactions occurred during October:

Oct. 1 Norlida established a petty cash fund in the amount of $90.
   2 Issued Voucher No. 1 for postage due, $3.75.
   5 Issued Voucher No. 2 for cab fare, $10.
   9 Issued Voucher No. 3 for purchase of flowers for an employee's birthday, $15.
  14 Issued Voucher No. 4 for purchase of small items of office supply, $30.
  20 Issued Voucher No. 5 for postage due, $2.25.
  22 Issued Voucher No. 6 for owner's personal use, $17.
  29 Issued Voucher No. 7 for postage due, $1.97.
  31 Replenished the fund.

Directions:
1. Journalize the entry to establish the petty cash fund.
2. Record the disbursements from the fund in a petty cash payments record.
3. Complete the petty cash payments record—total, rule, and set up for the new month.
4. Journalize the entry to replenish the fund.

PROBLEM 6-4B

Objective: To reconcile a bank statement and journalize necessary entries

The following data relate to the checking account of Robert Evans as of August 31, 20X1:

Balance per bank statement		$7,455
Balance per checkbook		7,546
Deposit in transit		650
Outstanding checks:		
#103	$ 85	
#107	110	
#111	96	
#112	103	394
Bank service charge		15
Imprinting check charge		10
Collection of a note receivable		190

Directions:

1. Prepare a statement to reconcile Robert's checkbook with his August bank statement.
2. Journalize any entries needed to bring the Cash account into agreement with the adjusted checkbook balance.

CHALLENGE PROBLEMS

PROBLEM SOLVING

Lakewood Realty Company's bank statement just arrived. To reconcile the statement, Lakewood's accounting clerk gathered the following data:

1. The statement, dated June 30, 20X1, shows a balance of $4,845.18.
2. The bank statement shows the following deposits:

Date	Amount
Jun. 7	$5,315.75
10	1,345.69
14	2,456.75
25	3,456.80

3. Lakewood's checkbook shows the following deposits:

Date	Amount
Jun. 5	$5,315.75
9	1,345.69
12	2,456.75
25	3,456.80
29	1,500.00

4. The bank statement includes two charges for returned checks. One is an NSF check in the amount of $80 from Jan Lee, a client. The other is a $400 check from David Wiche that was returned with the imprint "Account Closed."
5. The following checks are outstanding:

Number	Amount
418	$521.50
510	314.67
512	76.90
521	125.40
525	98.10

6. Jason Marshall, a client, owed Lakewood $595.65. He paid this amount directly to Lakewood's bank on June 15, and it was entered into Lakewood's account. The bank charged a $15 collection fee for this service.
7. The bank statement shows the following ATM withdrawals for the personal use of the owner. None has been recorded by the owner.

Date	Amount
Jun. 14	$30.00
18	25.00
23	45.00
30	10.00

8. The bank statement lists a $12.80 service charge.
9. The bank statement lists a $255 check drawn by Lakeside Rental Company. Lakewood notified the bank of this error.
10. Lakewood's Cash account shows a balance of $5,485.76 on June 30.

Directions:
1. Prepare a bank reconciliation statement for Lakewood as of June 30.
2. Journalize any entries needed in Lakewood's records to bring the balance of the Cash account into agreement with the adjusted checkbook balance.

COMMUNICATIONS

John Huey uses a checkbook for all payments, except for petty cash, in his lawn care business. However, John does not take time to reconcile his bank statement. He figures that since his bank uses electronic equipment, its records must be correct. He thus accepts that the balance shown on his bank statement is his true balance of cash.

Explain why a bank reconciliation is always needed.

ETHICS

Paula Day is the manager and bookkeeper of E. Dozier's Appliance Company. Paula also fills in as cashier when one of the regular cashiers is on break, out ill, or on vacation. In addition to keeping up with all cash transactions and funds, Paula also does the company's data entry, ordering, inventory, and the monthly bank reconciliation.

Paula is an honest, ethical person. However, the system at E. Dozier's Appliance Company allows for all kinds of ethical violations. Discuss the potential for dishonesty at the firm. Indicate which internal controls are missing in its structure.

ANSWERS TO REVIEW QUIZZES

REVIEW QUIZ 6-1
(a)

	20XX									
1	Jan.	2	Petty Cash		7 5 00					1
2			Cash				7 5 00			2
3			Established petty cash fund.							3

(b)

1		31	Office Supplies Expense				1 0	00					1
2			Postage Expense				1 9	25					2
3			Miscellaneous Expense				3 5	00					3
4			Cash							6 4	25		4
5			Replenished petty cash fund.										5

REVIEW QUIZ 6-2

1	X	X	Cash			9 5 4	00						1
2			Cash Short and Over			3	00						2
3			Sales Revenue						9 5 7	00		3

REVIEW QUIZ 6-3

Todd Baker Bank Reconciliation Statement October 1, 20XX							
Balance per bank statement					$ 9 2 2	00
Add: Deposit in transit					4 0	00
					$ 9 6 2	00
Deduct: Outstanding checks						
#34	$ 4 1	00				
#38	5 6	00			9 7	00
Adjusted bank statement balance					$ 8 6 5	00
Balance per checkbook					$ 8 7 0	00
Deduct:						
Service charge	$ 4	00				
Error in checkbook	1	00			5	00
Adjusted checkbook balance					$ 8 6 5	00

7

ACCOUNTING

FOR A

MERCHANDISING

BUSINESS

Purchases and Cash Payments

LEARNING OBJECTIVES

After studying Chapter 7, you will be able to:
1. Describe the procedures and forms used in purchasing merchandise.
2. Record credit purchases in a general journal and a purchases journal, and post to the accounts payable ledger and the general ledger.
3. Record purchases returns and allowances.
4. Record purchases discounts.
5. Record cash payments in a cash payments journal and post to the accounts payable ledger and the general ledger.
6. Prepare a schedule of accounts payable.
7. Record freight charges on incoming merchandise.

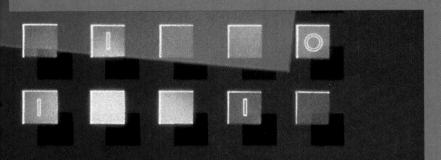

When designing accounting systems, accountants have two primary objectives. One is that the system is effective and the other is that the recording methods used are efficient. This means that transactions are recorded accurately with minimal effort.

In the first five chapters, the accounting system was designed for you to record transactions in a two-column general journal and a general ledger. The transactions that you recorded were for a firm that provided personal services.

In this chapter and the next three chapters, you will be using an accounting system designed for a merchandising business—a firm that buys goods for resale. You will use four special journals, the general journal, two subsidiary ledgers, and the general ledger to record these transactions. The use of special journals and subsidiary ledgers reduces work involved in journalizing and posting transactions. In each special journal and subsidiary ledger, only one type of transaction is recorded.

In this chapter, you will record transactions in two special journals—the purchases journal and the cash payments journal. The purchases journal is used to record the purchase of goods (merchandise inventory) on account, and the cash payments journal is used to record all cash payments. You will also learn to maintain records for individual creditors in the accounts payable subsidiary ledger.

— Janice H. Kelly, CPA
St. Louis Community College at Forest Park

In Chapters 1–6, we studied accounting procedures suitable to businesses that perform personal services for their customers, such as legal services and interior decorating. You learned how to record business transactions in a two-column general journal and a combined journal. You also learned how to post from these journals to the ledger, prepare a trial balance, and complete the work at the end of the accounting cycle. In Chapter 7, your accounting horizons will expand in three directions: (1) you will move to a different form of business, merchandising; (2) you will use two additional journals; and (3) you will learn how to operate an accounting system with more than one ledger.

MERCHANDISING ACTIVITY

A **merchandising business**, also called a **trading business**, is a business that earns its revenue by buying goods and then reselling these goods to customers. Goods that are to be sold to customers are called **merchandise**, **merchandise inventory**, or **stock in trade**.

Merchandising can take place at two levels—retail and wholesale. **Retail businesses**, such as grocery stores, drugstores, and restaurants, sell directly to consumers. **Wholesalers** purchase goods in bulk from manufacturers and sell them to retailers, other wholesalers, schools and other nonprofit institutions, and, at times, directly to consumers. For our study of merchandising, we will use the example of Lakeside Electronics, a wholesaler. However, the procedures we will cover are also used in retail businesses.

Purchasing Procedures

LEARNING OBJECTIVE 1

There are two sides to merchandising: (1) purchasing and (2) selling. Each requires formal documents and control procedures. In Chapter 7, we are concerned with purchasing procedures; in Chapter 8, we will deal with selling procedures.

The purchasing procedures used by a company depend on the size of the business and the nature of its operations. In a smaller merchandising business, one person could be responsible for all purchases. This person would usually be the store manager or the owner. In large retail and wholesale concerns, the purchasing function is usually performed by a *purchasing agent* who heads the purchasing department.

Let's take a moment to preview the steps in the purchasing procedure:

❶ Managers identify goods needed and request them by preparing a purchase requisition, which is sent to the purchasing department.
❷ The purchasing department chooses the seller (vendor) and sends an order.
❸ The seller receives the order and prepares an invoice (bill), which is shipped with the goods or a few days after the goods.
❹ When the merchandise is received by the buyer, it is checked against the invoice and payment is approved.

The purchasing process begins with a department head or manager identifying the goods needed and sending the firm's purchasing agent a purchase requisition. The **purchase requisition** is a written request for goods to be ordered; an example is shown in Figure 7-1.

FIGURE 7-1
Purchase requisition

Purchase Requisition	
No.: **237**	Date: **October 25, 20X1**
To: **Purchasing** Department	
From: **Electrical** Department	
Order:	

Quantity	Description
1,000 feet	**Galvanized copper cable, #4443-6**

Date Needed: **November 15, 20X1**	
Requested by: **B.K.**	

The purchasing department has the responsibility of determining the best source of supply and the best possible price. Once the decision to buy has been made, the purchasing department prepares a **purchase order**. The purchase order is prepared with at least three copies and distributed as follows:

• The original is sent to the seller (vendor).
• One copy is kept in the purchasing department (for its records).
• One copy is sent to the firm's accounting department (for comparison with the seller's invoice, which will arrive later).
• One copy is sent to the receiving department. This copy is often a blind copy (one without quantities) to encourage the receiving department to make an independent count of the goods when they arrive.

The flow of the purchase order is shown in Figure 7-2. The purchase order form used by Lakeside Electronics appears in Figure 7-3.

FIGURE 7-2
The flow of the purchase order

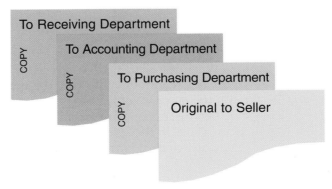

To Receiving Department
To Accounting Department
To Purchasing Department
Original to Seller

FIGURE 7-3
Purchase order

Lakeside Electronics 1200 San Palo Road Los Angeles, CA 90099			Purchase Order No.: __199__	

To: **Key Suppliers** Date: **October 25, 20X1**

__**Redville, CA 90362**__

_____

Enter our order for:

Quantity	Description		Unit Price	Total	
1,000 feet	**Galvanized copper cable #4443-6**		.575	575	00

Fill by:_____ Ship via: **Truck**

Ordered by: **M.L.** Requisition No.: **237**

Upon receipt of the purchase order, the seller prepares an invoice to send with the goods (or a few days after the goods). An **invoice** is a business document that shows the names and addresses of the buyer and the seller, the date and terms of the sale, a description of the goods, the price of the goods and total owed, and the mode of transportation for delivery.

The same invoice serves as both a sales invoice and a purchase invoice. To the seller, it is a **sales invoice**; to the buyer, who gets a copy, it is a **purchase invoice**. Figure 7-4 shows the invoice sent to Lakeside Electronics by Key Suppliers for the purchase order of October 25. Lakeside has assigned its own control number (101) to the invoice.

FIGURE 7-4
Purchase invoice

K KEY SUPPLIERS Redville, CA 90362	*Invoice Control No. 101* Invoice No.: __3329__

Sold to: **Lakeside Electronics** Date: __**November 2, 20X1**__

__**1200 San Palo Road**__ Ship Via: __**Truck**__

__**Los Angeles, CA 90099**__ Your Order No.: **199**

Terms: __**2/10,n/30**__

Quantity	Description		Unit Price	Total	
1,000 feet	**Galvanized copper cable #4443-6**		.575	575	00

When the merchandise arrives, the firm's receiving department prepares a **receiving report** to verify that the quantities received, and other details agree with the purchase order.

Our discussion of merchandising has now taken us from the decision to purchase goods to the actual receipt and verification of those goods. Our next step is to make a journal entry to record the cost of merchandise purchased. Before discussing accounting procedures for merchandise, however, we need to discuss merchandise discounts. Discounts are important in merchandising because they result in a decrease in the cost of merchandise purchased. Often the decision to buy from a particular supplier will depend on what discounts are available. There are two common types of discounts on merchandise: (1) trade discounts and (2) cash discounts. Both are discussed next.

Trade Discounts

Sellers usually print catalogs that show the **list price** of their merchandise. The actual price charged for identical items, however, may vary because of the class of the buyer (schools, hospitals, retailers, wholesalers, etc.), the quantity of the items sold, and general price changes. For example, a processor of food products may sell to schools and public hospitals at one price, but to restaurants and motels at a higher price.

It would be expensive for sellers to print a new catalog each time there was a price changed. To permit price changes without having to print new catalogs, many businesses offer **trade discounts**—a percentage reduction from the list price of merchandise. For example, merchandise could be listed in a seller's catalog at $800, but offered for sale less a 10% trade discount. Trade discounts are often printed on separate sheets and made available (or not made available) to buyers. When there is an overall price increase on merchandise, the increase can be shown by reducing the discounts or eliminating them altogether.

Trade discounts *are not* recorded in the accounting records of the buyer or the seller. The buyer always records goods at their actual cost. (Remember the *cost principle* from Chapter 1.) The seller records items sold at their actual selling price. For example, Hollis & Sons had merchandise listed for sale at $2,000 less a 10% trade discount. Hise Company purchased the merchandise subject to these terms. The amount of the trade discount is $200 ($2,000 × 10%). Therefore, the amount recorded for the sale by Hollis & Sons is $1,800 ($2,000 − $200); and the amount recorded for the purchase by Hise Company is $1,800. The fact that the goods were listed for $2,000 is immaterial. The actual contract price was $1,800; thus, $1,800 is recorded by both the buyer and the seller.

Cash Discounts

Manufacturers and wholesalers often offer a cash discount to their credit customers. A **cash discount** is a discount offered to encourage prompt and early payment by a buyer. Unlike trade discounts, cash discounts *are recorded* in the accounting records of both the seller and the buyer. The seller refers to cash discounts as **sales discounts**; the buyer refers to them as **purchases discounts**.

A common expression of a cash discount is 2/10,n/30 (read *two ten, net thirty*). This means that a 2% discount can be taken from the invoice price of merchandise if the invoice is paid within 10 days of the date on the invoice. If payment is not made within 10 days, the total amount of the invoice is due within 30 days of the invoice date. For example, let's assume that on January 1 merchandise with a cost of $600 is purchased subject to terms of 2/10,n/30. If the buyer pays for the goods within 10 days of January 1 (by January 11), a discount of $12 can be taken, as we see here:

Invoice total	$600	Invoice total	$600
Discount rate	× .02	Discount amount	− 12
Discount amount	$ 12	Amount to be paid	$588

The buyer would thus pay $588 in full settlement of the invoice. If payment is not made within 10 days, the full $600 invoice price must be paid within 30 days (by January 31).

NOTE

If no cash discount is offered, the terms are often stated as n/30. (Net amount is due within 30 days.)

In Chapter 8, we will see how the seller accounts for a cash discount. Later in this chapter, we will record a cash discount for the buyer. For now, let's turn our attention to recording the cost of merchandise purchased.

REMEMBER

The discount period starts with the date of the invoice, not with the date goods are received.

REVIEW QUIZ 7-1

What is the net amount due on each of the following invoices?

	Invoice Price	Date of Invoice	Terms	Date Paid
(a)	$1,200	Jun. 10	2/10,n/30	Jun. 19
(b)	800	Aug. 28	2/10,n/30	Sep. 5
(c)	900	Jul. 6	1/10,n/30	Jul. 31
(d)	980	Dec. 2	3/10,2/20,n/30	Dec. 18
(e)	400	Jul. 8	n/30	Aug. 7

CHECK YOUR ANSWERS ON PAGE 265.

RECORDING PURCHASES OF MERCHANDISE

LEARNING OBJECTIVE 2

In general use, the word *purchase* refers to the act of buying any product or service. In merchandising, however, the term *purchases*, unless stated otherwise, refers *only* to the purchase of merchandise intended for resale to customers. In this section, we will look at how the purchase of merchandise is recorded and work with a new account entitled Purchases.

The Purchases Account

The cost of all merchandise purchased during an accounting period is debited to a temporary owner's equity account entitled **Purchases**. (More exact titles, such as **Merchandise Purchases** or **Purchases of Merchandise** can be used; however, the briefer title is customary.)

The *sole* purpose of the Purchases account is to keep a record of the cost of merchandise purchased for resale during an accounting period. The cost of assets that are not stock in trade, such as equipment and supplies, is recorded in the appropriate asset account, *not* in Purchases. In final analysis, there are only two classes of buying that a merchandising firm enters into: (1) assets for operating the business and (2) purchases of merchandise for resale.

To better understand the function of the Purchases account, let's look at its placement in the expanded accounting equation.

Assets		=	Liabilities		+	Owner's Equity		+	Revenue		−	Expenses	
Debit	Credit		Debit	Credit		Debit	Credit		Debit	Credit		Debit	Credit
+	−		−	+		−	+		−	+		+	−

												Purchases	
												Debit	Credit
												+	−

The Purchases account is debited for the cost of merchandise purchased for resale.

The Purchases account falls under the category of cost accounts. **Cost accounts** are like expense accounts in that both are presented on the income statement and enter into the calculation of net income (or net loss). They differ, however, in that expense accounts are used to record the cost of items necessary to operate the business (salaries of employees, rent, utilities, repairs, etc.), and cost accounts are used *only* to determine the cost of merchandise sold to customers. We will discuss how to determine the cost of merchandise sold in Chapter 10. Our task now is to record a purchase of merchandise.

Recording Purchases

Recall from Chapter 3 that source documents are used as a basis for making journal entries because they provide written evidence that a transaction has taken place. The source document for recording a purchase of merchandise is the purchase invoice. No journal entry is made from the purchase requisition or the purchase order because, at the time they are prepared, no goods have changed hands. To illustrate recording a purchase of merchandise, let's look again at the invoice sent to Lakeside Electronics by Key Suppliers (Figure 7-4). The debit portion of Lakeside's entry is to Purchases, since merchandise was purchased. The credit portion of the entry is to Accounts Payable, since the merchandise was purchased on credit.

	20X1							
1	Nov.	2	Purchases			5 7 5 00		1
2			Accounts Payable—Key Suppliers	/			5 7 5 00	2
3			Purchased merchandise on account.					3

Had the merchandise in this transaction been purchased with cash, the credit would have been to the Cash account. Most merchandise, however, is bought on credit. Buying goods on credit often gives a business time to sell the goods and generate revenue before actually paying for the goods.

REMEMBER

The Purchases account is used only to record the cost of merchandise intended for resale. If the firm buys anything else, it is recorded in the appropriate asset account, not Purchases.

The Purchases Journal

In Chapter 6, you learned how to use a combined journal. It was introduced as a way for smaller businesses to save time in both journalizing and posting. Along the same line of reasoning, a business that makes purchases often can save journalizing and posting time by using a purchases journal.

The **purchases journal** is used to record only credit purchases, since most purchases are made on credit. The actual design of a purchases journal is tailored to the needs of the business. Some businesses design their purchases journal to record only credit purchases of merchandise. Other businesses design their purchases journal to record all credit purchases. The purchases journal we will be working with is that of John Graham, owner of Lakeside Electronics—a wholesale distributor of TVs, radios, stereo equipment, electrical supplies, and electronic toys. John's purchases journal is shown in Figure 7-5.

FIGURE 7-5
Purchases journal

	Date		Invoice No.	Account Credited	P.R.	Purchases Dr. Accts. Pay. Cr.	
1	20X1 Nov.	2	101	Key Suppliers		5 7 5 00	1
2		5	102	Master Aerials		2 8 5 0 00	2
3		12	103	Pantech Corporation		6 3 0 0 00	3
4		19	104	Key Suppliers		4 1 0 00	4
5		26	105	Pantech Corporation		3 7 5 00	5
6		28	106	Master Aerials		2 8 0 00	6
7		29	107	Wilks Company		2 4 0 0 00	7
8		29	108	Williams Electrical Company		4 0 0 0 00	8
9		30		Total		17 1 9 0 00	9

Purchases Journal — Page 1

Lakeside's purchases journal is designed to record only credit purchases of merchandise. Notice that it has only one money column, entitled Purchases Dr./Accounts Payable Cr. One money column is enough, because *all* credit purchases of merchandise involve a debit to the Purchases account and a credit to the Accounts Payable account.

The standard Date and P.R. columns are included in Lakeside's purchases journal. Two additional nonmoney columns are also included: (1) an Invoice No. column for writing the number of the invoice for each purchase, and (2) an Account Credited column for recording the names of suppliers from whom credit purchases are made.

The purchases journal is one of a variety of special journals (also called **special purpose journals**) used by many businesses, particularly larger businesses. A **special journal** is a journal used to record transactions that are similar in nature. Special journals not only save time in recording specialized transactions, but they also allow for a delegation of work because individual accountants or bookkeepers can be assigned to specific journals.

In addition to credit purchases, special journals are commonly used to record cash payments, sales of merchandise, and cash receipts. We will work with each of these special journals in this and the next chapter. For now, let's concentrate on the purchases journal.

Recording Purchases in a Purchases Journal

To illustrate the use of a purchases journal, let's look at the credit purchases of merchandise made by Lakeside Electronics during November 20X1:

20X1
Nov. 2 Purchased copper cable from Key Suppliers, $575; terms, 2/10,n/30.
     5 Purchased antennas from Master Aerials, $2,850; terms, 2/10,n/30.
    12 Purchased TV sets from Pantech Corporation, $6,300; terms, 2/10,n/30.
    19 Purchased TV stands from Key Suppliers, $410; terms, n/30.
    26 Purchased receivers from Pantech Corporation, $375; terms, 2/10,n/30.
    28 Purchased tape players from Master Aerials, $280; terms, n/30.
    29 Purchased electronic toys from Wilks Company, $2,400; terms, 2/10,n/30.
    29 Purchased various items from Williams Electrical Company, $4,000; terms, 2/10,n/30.

Starting with Invoice No. 101, these purchases are recorded in the purchases journal in Figure 7-5. Notice that each entry is recorded on one horizontal line. Also notice that the name of each supplier is written in the Account Credited column, and the number of the invoice related to each purchase is entered in the Invoice No. column. After the last entry on November 29, the journal is totaled.

For control purposes, Lakeside Electronics consecutively numbers each purchase invoice when it is received. Some firms use the number assigned to the invoice by the supplier.

The following credit purchases were made by Lockman Used Cars during May 20X8:

20X8
May 2 Purchased office supplies from Ace Suppliers, $200.
     8 Purchased office equipment from Ace Suppliers, $800.
    12 Purchased automobiles for resale from Tower Auction, $12,400. Invoice No. 48.
    18 Purchased a microcomputer for use in the office from King Co., $4,500.
    20 Purchased automobiles for resale from Tower Auction, $57,300. Invoice No. 49.
    28 Purchased automobiles for resale from Tower Auction, $60,000. Invoice No. 50.
    30 Purchased automobiles for resale from Burr Motors, $45,000. Invoice No. 51.
    30 Purchased a van for resale from Clyde Wright, $11,200. Invoice No. 52.

Record these credit purchases using a one-column purchases journal and a two-column general journal. Total the purchases journal.

CHECK YOUR ANSWERS ON PAGE 266.

THE ACCOUNTS PAYABLE SUBSIDIARY LEDGER

The Accounts Payable account, as we have seen, is a liability account that represents debts owed to the creditors of a business. When a business has only a few creditors, it is possible to maintain a separate Accounts Payable account for each creditor. If a business has many creditors, which is often the case, having an individual ledger account for each creditor could result in a very large and unwieldy ledger. Imagine, for example, that a business makes credit purchases from 200 different creditors. Then envision the size of its ledger if, in addition to all other accounts, a separate account were maintained for each creditor. A single ledger would be too large to handle efficiently and would make it difficult to prepare a trial balance or the financial statements.

To overcome these problems, accounts for creditors are often set up in a *separate* ledger. A separate ledger containing only one type of account is called a **subsidiary ledger**. A subsidiary ledger containing only creditors' accounts is called an **accounts payable ledger** or a **creditors' ledger**. When subsidiary ledgers are used, the main ledger is called the **general ledger**.

Accounts in the accounts payable ledger are designed to show the balance owed to each creditor. The three-column account form, as shown in Figure 7-6, is usually used.

FIGURE 7-6
The three-column account form

Accounts Payable Ledger						
Name						
Address						
Date	Item	P.R.	Debit	Credit	Balance	

Liability accounts normally have credit balances. Therefore, with rare exceptions, creditors' accounts will have credit balances. Thus, the three-column account form shown above is more suited for creditors' accounts than the four-column account form commonly used in the general ledger.

Accounts in the accounts payable ledger are usually not assigned numbers. Instead, they are arranged in alphabetical order to make it easy to add new accounts and remove inactive accounts.

The balances of creditors' accounts in the accounts payable ledger are summarized by the Accounts Payable account in the general ledger. That is, when all posting is complete, the balance of the Accounts Payable account will equal the sum of the balances of the creditors' accounts. Thus, the Accounts Payable account is said to *control* the accounts payable ledger. A **controlling account** is an account in the general ledger that summarizes accounts in a related subsidiary ledger.

To illustrate the controlling account/subsidiary ledger relationship, let's look at the amounts owed by Jan Watkins, a health and beauty supplies distributor, on March 31, 20X9.

Creditor	Balance Owed
Bibb Cosmetics	$ 250
Davis Office Supply	200
Superior Natural Foods	400
Twin City Beauty Supplies	800
Total	$1,650

FIGURE 7-7

Relationship between the accounts payable ledger and the controlling account in the general ledger

Jan maintains an accounts payable subsidiary ledger, which is summarized by an Accounts Payable controlling account in her general ledger. Figure 7-7 shows the relationship between the two.

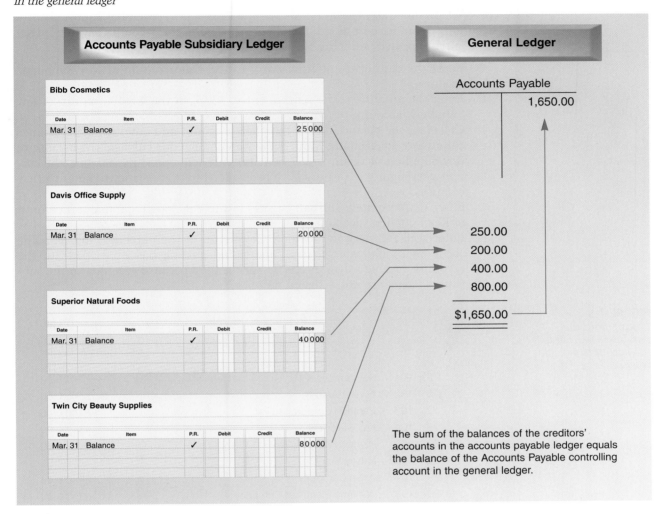

POSTING THE PURCHASES JOURNAL

The process of posting from the purchases journal, or any special journal, is very similar to the procedures that you learned in Chapter 6 for posting the combined journal. However, extra care is required because postings are made to *both* the subsidiary ledger and the general ledger. To illustrate, let's look again at Lakeside Electronics' purchases journal (shown in Figure 7-5). Two types of postings are made from Lakeside's purchases journal:

1. Posting of individual credits to creditors' accounts in the accounts payable ledger. To keep the accounts payable ledger current, posting is usually done on a daily basis.
2. Posting the total of the money column to the general ledger as a debit to the Purchases account and a credit to the Accounts Payable account. Since this total represents total credit purchases for the month, it is posted at the end of the month.

Posting to the Accounts Payable Ledger

Each entry in the purchases journal represents a purchase on account and requires an individual posting to the subsidiary ledger account of the creditor from whom the purchase was made. Posting to creditors' accounts is a five-step process. To illustrate, Figure 7-8 shows how Lakeside's November 2 journal entry recording a purchase from Key Suppliers is posted to the accounts payable ledger. The entry is posted using the following steps:

1. Enter the date of the journal entry in the Date column of Key Suppliers' account.
2. Enter the amount of the journal entry, $575, in the Credit column of Key Suppliers' account.
3. Calculate the balance of Key Suppliers' account and enter it in the Balance column of the account. Since there was no previous balance, the balance of Key Suppliers' account is $575. Had there been a previous balance, the current posting of $575 would have been added to that balance to obtain a new balance.
4. Enter P1 (*p*urchases journal, page *1*) in the P.R. (posting reference) column of Key Suppliers' account.
5. Enter a check mark (✓) in the P.R. column of the purchases journal. The check mark indicates that an individual posting has been made to the accounts payable ledger. A check mark is used because accounts in the subsidiary ledger are not assigned numbers.

FIGURE 7-8
Posting from the purchases journal to the accounts payable ledger

Purchases Journal — **Page 1**

	Date		Invoice No.	Account Credited	P.R.	Purchases Dr. Accts. Pay. Cr.	
	20X1						
1	Nov.	2	101	Key Suppliers	⑤ ✓	575 00	1
2		5	102	Master Aerials		2,850 00	2
3		12	103	Pantech Corporation		6,300 00	3
4		19	104	Key Suppliers		410 00	4
5		26	105	Pantech Corporation		375 00	5
6		28	106	Master Aerials		280 00	6
7		29	107	Wilks Company		2,400 00	7
8		29	108	Williams Electrical Company		4,000 00	8
9		30		Total		17,190 00	9

Accounts Payable Ledger

Name Key Suppliers
Address Redville, CA 90362

Date		Item	P.R.	Debit	Credit	Balance
20X1						
Nov.	2		P1		575 00	575 00

Posting to the General Ledger

Though the purchases journal has only one money column, the total of the column is posted *twice* to the general ledger; once as a debit to the Purchases account, and once as a credit to the Accounts Payable account. This, too, is a five-step process. Let's look at Figure 7-9 to see how it is done for Lakeside Electronics on November 30, 20X1.

① Enter the last day of the month, November 30, in the Date columns of the Purchases and Accounts Payable accounts.
② Enter the total of the money column, $17,190, on the debit side of the Purchases account and the credit side of the Accounts Payable account.
③ Calculate the new balance of the accounts by adding the current posting to the previous balance.
④ Enter P1 in the P.R. columns of the accounts.
⑤ Enter the numbers of the accounts, 211 and 511, directly below the column total in the purchases journal to indicate that the amounts have been posted.

FIGURE 7-9
Posting from the purchases journal to the general ledger

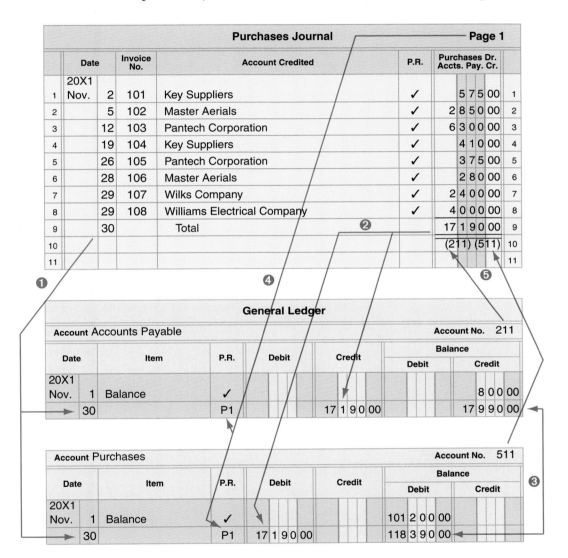

We should note two other points concerning the posting of the purchases journal:

1. The Purchases account is numbered 511. Purchases and related accounts are numbered in the 500 series, which we will use for cost accounts.
2. Even though individual postings were made to each creditor's account in the accounts payable ledger, the total of the money column is still posted to the Accounts Payable controlling account in the general ledger. Remember that the balance of the Accounts Payable controlling account at the end of the month must equal the total of the balances of the creditors' accounts in the accounts payable subsidiary ledger.

MERCHANDISE RETURNS AND ALLOWANCES

In merchandising, a *return* occurs when a customer returns to the seller part (or all) of the items purchased. An *allowance* occurs when the seller grants a customer a price reduction on items due to some factor, such as damaged or defective goods.

Almost all merchandising concerns encounter the problem of merchandise returns and allowances. Goods may have been damaged while in shipment, may have been shipped in the wrong size or color, or may not suit the specific needs of the customer. Items purchased as gifts may be the wrong size and thus returned for a refund.

The seller refers to merchandise returns or allowances as sales returns and allowances; the purchaser refers to merchandise returns or allowances as **purchases returns and allowances**. In this chapter, we are concerned with purchases returns and allowances. In Chapter 8, we will learn the proper accounting treatment for sales returns and allowances.

Purchases Returns and Allowances

The effect of a purchase return or allowance is a decrease in the cost of merchandise purchased. The amount of returns and allowances could be *credited* directly to the Purchases account. (Recall that Purchases is *debited* when merchandise is purchased.) This practice, however, would not provide a separate record of purchases returns and allowances. To provide for better control, the amount of returns and allowances is usually recorded in a contra account entitled the Purchases Returns and Allowances account.

The Purchases Returns and Allowances account is contra to the Purchases account. Thus, the Purchases Returns and Allowances account has a normal credit balance, which is opposite the debit balance of the Purchases account. This is illustrated by the following T accounts.

Purchases	511	Purchases Returns and Allowances 511.1	
Debit	Credit	Debit	Credit
+	–	–	+
To record the cost of merchandise purchased for resale.			To record the cost of merchandise returned and allowances received.

Purchases Returns and Allowances is a deduction from Purchases. Its balance is thus opposite the balance of Purchases.

The balance of the Purchases Returns and Allowances account is shown on the income statement as a reduction in the balance of the Purchases account. The account number, 511.1, assigned to Purchases Returns and Allowances indicates that it is contra to account number 511, the Purchases account.

Recording Purchases Returns and Allowances

LEARNING OBJECTIVE 3

When a return or allowance on merchandise is needed, the buyer must inform the seller of the details surrounding the return or allowance. The buyer often does this by sending a debit memorandum. A **debit memorandum** is the buyer's written request to the seller for credit. The buyer maintains an accounts payable ledger account for each creditor. Creditors' accounts in the accounts payable ledger have normal *credit* balances. When a return or allowance is made, part (or all) of the balance in the creditor's account will not be paid. Consequently, the buyer *debits* (decreases) the creditor's account for the amount of the return or allowance; thus, the term *debit memorandum*. The debit memorandum in Figure 7-10 was issued to Master Aerials by Lakeside Electronics on December 2, 20X1.

FIGURE 7-10
Debit memorandum

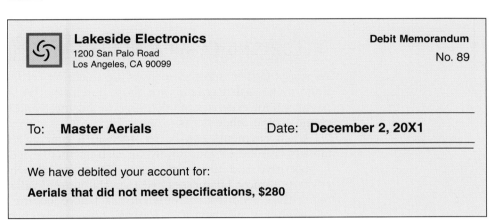

The seller usually issues a **credit memorandum** after receiving the buyer's debit memorandum. (Credit memorandums will be discussed further in Chapter 8.) The buyer can use a copy of the debit memorandum as a source document for recording the return or wait for confirmation from the seller and use the credit memorandum as a source document. Lakeside used the above debit memorandum as a source document to make the following general journal entry.

	20X1						
1	Dec.	2	Accounts Payable—Master Aerials	211/✓	2 8 0 00		1
2			Purchases Returns and Allowances	511.1		2 8 0 00	2
3			Returned merchandise for credit.				3

Notice that the debit part of this entry involved Accounts Payable (a controlling account) and Master Aerials (a creditor's account). Debits or credits to the controlling account require a posting to *both* the controlling account in the general ledger and the creditor's account in the accounts payable ledger. To indicate that this dual posting is necessary, a diagonal line is drawn in the P.R. column of the journal at the time of journalizing. In the journal entry above, the diagonal line signifies that a $280 debit posting needs to be made to both the Accounts Payable controlling account in the general ledger and the Master Aerials account in the accounts payable subsidiary ledger.

Posting is usually made to the general ledger at the end of the month, but it is usually made daily to the subsidiary ledger. When the above entry was posted to the subsidiary ledger, a small check mark (✓) was made to the right of the diagonal line. When posting was made to the Accounts Payable controlling account, the account number of Accounts Payable (211) was written to the left of the diagonal line.

The following selected transactions were completed by Danny Ellis, owner of the Ellis Company, during June 20X9. Record each transaction in a general journal.

20X9
Jun. 5 Purchased office supplies on account from B. Spence Suppliers, $300.
      9 Purchased merchandise for cash, $800.
     15 Purchased merchandise on account from Wilks Co., $1,200.
     16 Returned $30 of office supplies for credit to B. Spence Suppliers.
     21 Returned $200 of merchandise for credit to Wilks Co.

CHECK YOUR ANSWERS ON PAGE 266.

RECORDING CASH PAYMENTS

As stated earlier, most purchases are made on credit. Eventually, however, we must make cash payments for those purchases. We also commonly make cash payments for expenses of operating the business and for cash purchases of merchandise and other assets.

Cash payments can be recorded in a general journal, which is a process already familiar to you. Recording cash payments in a general journal, however, is repetitive and time-consuming. To more efficiently record and post cash payments, most businesses use a special journal called the *cash payments journal* or the *cash disbursements journal*. Before looking at how cash payments are recorded in a cash payments journal, however, we need to take a minute to discuss how cash payments are handled when payment is made in time to take advantage of a purchases discount.

The Purchases Discounts Account

LEARNING OBJECTIVE 4

Earlier in this chapter we learned that some sellers offer a cash discount to the buyer if payment for merchandise is made promptly. The effect of a purchases discount is a reduction in the cost of merchandise purchased. As such, purchases discounts could be recorded on the credit side (the reduction side) of the Purchases account. It is considered a better practice, however, to use a separate account that is contra to Purchases. This account is entitled **Purchases Discounts**. The nature of the Purchases Discounts account can be illustrated as shown below.

Purchases Discounts	511.2
Debit	Credit
−	+
	To record discounts received for prompt payment of merchandise.

To illustrate how to record a purchases discount, let's look at one of Lakeside's November cash payments. On November 12, 20X1, Lakeside issued a check for $563.50 to Key Suppliers in payment of a November 2 invoice for $575 less a 2% discount ($575 × .02 = $11.50; $575 − $11.50 = $563.50). In general journal form, this entry appears as shown on the next page.

		20X1																		
1		Nov.	12	Accounts Payable—Key Suppliers	211/✓		5	7	5	00										1
2				Purchases Discounts	511.2										1	1	50			2
3				Cash	111										5	6	3	50		3
4				Paid for Nov. 2 purchase.																4

Now, let's look at how cash payments are recorded in a cash payments journal.

Cash Payments Journal

LEARNING OBJECTIVE 5 A **cash payments journal** (or **cash disbursements journal**) is a special journal used for recording all disbursements of cash. The source document for entries in the cash payments journal is a completed check stub, which you studied in Chapter 6. As with all special journals, the cash payments journal is designed to meet the needs of the business using it. For Lakeside Electronics, John Graham uses a standard cash payments journal (shown in Figure 7-11) with four money columns entitled Cash Cr., Purchases Discounts Cr., Accounts Payable Dr., and General Dr.

A Cash Cr. column is always necessary in a cash payments journal because all cash payments involve a credit to the Cash account. The Purchases Discounts Cr. column is used to record discounts received for paying invoices within the discount period. The Accounts Payable Dr. column is used for recording payments to creditors. And the General Dr. column is used for recording debits to accounts other than Accounts Payable. Firms with many frequently occurring expenses or many cash purchases may have other special debit columns.

John's cash payments journal also has a Date column, an Account Debited column, and a P.R. column. John also uses a Ck. No. (check number) column for recording the numbers of the source documents. To illustrate the use of the cash payments journal, let's look at Lakeside's cash payments for the month of November, 20X1:

20X1
Nov. 2 Issued Ck. No. 126 for November rent, $675.
12 Issued Ck. No. 127 for $563.50 to Key Suppliers in payment of November 2 invoice, less 2% discount.
15 Issued Ck. No. 128 for $2,793 to Master Aerials in payment of November 5 invoice, less 2% discount.
22 Issued Ck. No. 129 for $6,174 to Pantech Corporation in payment of November 12 invoice, less 2% discount.
25 Issued Ck. No. 130 for the cash purchase of merchandise, $800.
27 Issued Ck. No. 131 for payment of the November power bill, $620.
28 Issued Ck. No. 132 for payment of employee salaries for the month, $2,250.
30 Issued Ck. No. 133 for payment of telephone bill, $240.
30 John Graham issued Ck. No. 134 to himself for personal use, $1,500.

Starting with Ck. No. 126, John's November cash payments are recorded in his cash payments journal, as shown in Figure 7-11. The cash payments journal must be in balance before posting to the general ledger. The proof follows Figure 7-11.

	Cash Payments Journal						Page 3		

	Date	Ck. No.	Account Debited	P.R.	General Dr.	Accounts Payable Dr.	Purchases Discounts Cr.	Cash Cr.	
1	20X1 Nov. 2	126	Rent Expense		675 00			675 00	1
2	12	127	Key Suppliers			575 00	11 50	563 50	2
3	15	128	Master Aerials			2850 00	57 00	2793 00	3
4	22	129	Pantech Corporation			6300 00	126 00	6174 00	4
5	25	130	Purchases		800 00			800 00	5
6	27	131	Utilities Expense		620 00			620 00	6
7	28	132	Salaries Expense		2250 00			2250 00	7
8	30	133	Telephone Expense		240 00			240 00	8
9	30	134	John Graham, Drawing		1500 00			1500 00	9
10	30		Totals		6085 00	9725 00	194 50	15615 50	10

FIGURE 7-11
Cash payments journal

Proof:

	Debit Columns	Credit Columns
General	$ 6,085.00	
Accounts Payable	9,725.00	
Purchases Discounts		$ 194.50
Cash		15,615.50
Totals	$15,810.00	$15,810.00

POSTING THE CASH PAYMENTS JOURNAL

Posting the cash payments journal follows some of the same procedures you learned for posting the purchases journal. To illustrate, let's look again at Lakeside's November cash payments journal. Three different types of postings are made:

1. Posting of individual debits to creditors' accounts in the accounts payable ledger. As stated earlier, posting to the accounts payable ledger is usually done on a daily basis.
2. Posting of individual debits to appropriate general ledger accounts from the General Dr. column. Amounts in this column can be posted on a daily, weekly, or monthly basis.
3. Posting of special column totals to the appropriate general ledger accounts. Summary posting of special column totals is done at the end of the month.

Each type of posting is discussed and illustrated next.

Posting to the Accounts Payable Ledger

Each amount in the Accounts Payable Dr. column is posted daily to the specific creditor's account in the accounts payable ledger, as shown in Figure 7-12 on pages 240–241.

To indicate that a posting has been made to the accounts payable ledger, a check mark (✓) is entered in the P.R. column of the cash payments journal next to the name of the creditor. To complete the cross-reference, the code CP and the page number of the cash payments journal are entered in the P.R. column of the creditor's account to which a posting was made. Notice that the debit postings from the cash payments journal reduce the balances of the creditors' accounts. Remember that creditors' accounts represent liabilities; thus, they normally have credit balances. Consequently, a debit posting results in a reduction in the account.

Posting Individual Entries in the General Dr. Column to the General Ledger

Each amount appearing in the General Dr. column is posted individually to the general ledger account named in the Account Debited column, as shown in Figure 7-12. The notation CP with a page number is entered in the P.R. column of each general ledger account to which a posting was made, and the appropriate account number is entered in the P.R. column of the cash payments journal. A check mark (✓) is entered under the General Dr. column total to indicate that a summary posting is not made; the amounts have already been posted individually. Notice that the date used for posting is the *date of the journal entry*, even if posting is made at the end of the month.

Posting Special Column Totals to the General Ledger

Special column totals are posted to the general ledger at the end of the month, as shown in Figure 7-12.

As you have already learned, account numbers are entered below special column totals to indicate summary postings. To complete the cross-reference, the code CP with a page number is entered in the P.R. column of the ledger accounts affected. Notice that the date used for summary posting is November 30, the last day of the month.

PROVING THE ACCOUNTS PAYABLE LEDGER

Let's now look at Figure 7-13 to see the complete accounts payable ledger of Lakeside Electronics, as it appears on November 30.

Schedule of Accounts Payable

LEARNING OBJECTIVE 6
From the accounts payable ledger, we can prepare a **schedule of accounts payable**, which is simply a listing of the balances in the accounts payable ledger. Figure 7-14 shows Lakeside's schedule of accounts payable as of November 30, 20X1.

The accounts payable ledger shows the amounts owed to individual creditors, and the Accounts Payable controlling account shows the total amount owed to *all* creditors. Thus, when all posting has been completed, the total of the schedule of accounts payable should agree with the balance of the Accounts Payable account. This is easy to check by comparing the schedule of accounts payable with the balance of the Accounts Payable account, which is shown in Figure 7-15, fully posted.

FIGURE 7-12

*Posting the cash
payments journal to the
general ledger and the
accounts payable ledger*

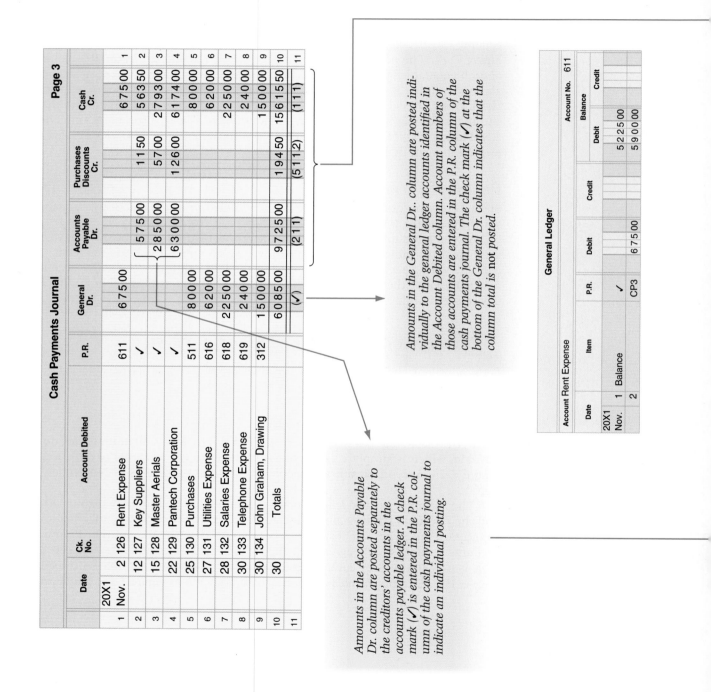

Cash Payments Journal — Page 3

	Date	Ck. No.	Account Debited	P.R.	General Dr.	Accounts Payable Dr.	Purchases Discounts Cr.	Cash Cr.	
1	20X1 Nov. 2	126	Rent Expense	611	675 00			675 00	1
2	12	127	Key Suppliers	✓		575 00	11 50	563 50	2
3	15	128	Master Aerials	✓		2850 00	57 00	2793 00	3
4	22	129	Pantech Corporation	✓		6300 00	126 00	6174 00	4
5	25	130	Purchases	511	800 00			800 00	5
6	27	131	Utilities Expense	616	620 00			620 00	6
7	28	132	Salaries Expense	618	2250 00			2250 00	7
8	30	133	Telephone Expense	619	240 00			240 00	8
9	30	134	John Graham, Drawing	312	1500 00			1500 00	9
10	30		Totals		6085 00	9725 00	194 50	15615 50	10
11					(✓)	(211)	(5112)	(111)	11

*Amounts in the General Dr. column are posted indi-
vidually to the general ledger accounts identified in
the Account Debited column. Account numbers of
those accounts are entered in the P.R. column of the
cash payments journal. The check mark (✓) at the
bottom of the General Dr. column indicates that the
column total is not posted.*

*Amounts in the Accounts Payable
Dr. column are posted separately to
the creditors' accounts in the
accounts payable ledger. A check
mark (✓) is entered in the P.R. column of the cash payments journal to
indicate an individual posting.*

General Ledger

Account Rent Expense — Account No. 611

Date		Item	P.R.	Debit	Credit	Balance Debit	Balance Credit
20X1 Nov.	1	Balance	✓			5225 00	
	2		CP3	675 00		5900 00	

The totals of special columns are posted to the general ledger accounts identified in the headings of the columns. Account numbers are entered under the column totals to indicate that a summary posting has been made.

General Ledger

Account Cash   **Account No.** 111

Date	Item	P.R.	Debit	Credit	Balance Debit	Balance Credit
20X1						
Nov. 1	Balance	✓			21400 00	
30		CP3		15615 50	5784 50	

Account Accounts Payable   **Account No.** 211

Date	Item	P.R.	Debit	Credit	Balance Debit	Balance Credit
20X1						
Nov. 1	Balance	✓				8000 00
30		P1		17190 00		17990 00
30		CP3	9725 00			8265 00

Account Purchases Discounts   **Account No.** 511.2

Date	Item	P.R.	Debit	Credit	Balance Debit	Balance Credit
20X1						
Nov. 1	Balance	✓				2321 00
30		CP3		194 50		2515 50

Accounts Payable Ledger

Name Key Suppliers
Address Redville, CA 90362

Date	Item	P.R.	Debit	Credit	Balance
20X1					
Nov. 2		P1		575 00	575 00
12		CP3	575 00		—

Name Master Aerials
Address 17 Tulane Way, Sacramento, CA 95816

Date	Item	P.R.	Debit	Credit	Balance
20X1					
Nov. 5		P1		2850 00	2850 00
15		CP3	2850 00		—

Name Pantech Corporation
Address 4460 Riverfront Dr., Columbus, OH 43206

Date	Item	P.R.	Debit	Credit	Balance
20X1					
Nov. 12		P1		6300 00	6300 00
22		CP3	6300 00		—

FIGURE 7-13

Complete accounts payable ledger

Accounts Payable Ledger

Name Key Suppliers
Address Redville, CA 90362

Date		Item	P.R.	Debit	Credit	Balance
20X1 Nov.	2		P1		5 7 5 00	5 7 5 00
	12		CP3	5 7 5 00		—
	19		P1		4 1 0 00	4 1 0 00

Name Master Aerials
Address 17 Tulane Way, Sacramento, CA 95816

Date		Item	P.R.	Debit	Credit	Balance
20X1 Nov.	5		P1		2 8 5 0 00	2 8 5 0 00
	15		CP3	2 8 5 0 00		—
	28		P1		2 8 0 00	2 8 0 00

Name Pantech Corporation
Address 4460 Riverfront Dr., Columbus, OH 43206

Date		Item	P.R.	Debit	Credit	Balance
20X1 Nov.	12		P1		6 3 0 0 00	6 3 0 0 00
	22		CP3	6 3 0 0 00		—
	26		P1		3 7 5 00	3 7 5 00

Name Wilks Company
Address 1211 12th Ave. West, Los Angeles, CA 90012

Date		Item	P.R.	Debit	Credit	Balance
20X1 Nov.	29		P1		2 4 0 0 00	2 4 0 0 00

Name Williams Electrical Company
Address 1718 54th St., Los Angeles, CA 90038

Date		Item	P.R.	Debit	Credit	Balance
20X1 Nov.	1	Balance	✓			8 0 0 00
	29		P1		4 0 0 0 00	4 8 0 0 00

FIGURE 7-14

Schedule of accounts payable

Lakeside Electronics
Schedule of Accounts Payable
November 30, 20X1

Key Suppliers	4 1 0 00
Master Aerials	2 8 0 00
Pantech Corporation	3 7 5 00
Wilks Company	2 4 0 0 00
Williams Electrical Company	4 8 0 0 00
Total	8 2 6 5 00

Only accounts with open balances are included on the schedule of accounts payable.

FIGURE 7-15
Accounts Payable after
end-of-month posting

Account	Accounts Payable							Account No.	211
Date	Item	P.R.	Debit	Credit	Balance				
					Debit		Credit		
20X1 Nov. 1	Balance	✓					8 0 0 00		
30		P1		17 1 9 0 00			17 9 9 0 00		
30		CP3	9 7 2 5 00				8 2 6 5 00		

FREIGHT CHARGES ON INCOMING MERCHANDISE

FOB Shipping Point
Buyer pays freight

FOB Destination
Seller pays freight

The terms of a sale should always specify who—the buyer or the seller—bears the costs of transporting the goods to the buyer. If the terms are **FOB (free on board) shipping point**, the buyer is responsible for all freight costs while the goods are in transit. Under these terms, the seller pays the freight only to the shipping point; the buyer must pay the freight costs from the shipping point to the point of destination. On the other hand, if the goods are shipped **FOB destination**, the seller is responsible for all freight costs until the goods reach their destination.

When the buyer is responsible for freight costs (FOB shipping point), the entire invoice price of goods, including freight, can be debited to the Purchases account. Or the charges for freight can be debited to a separate account entitled **Freight In** or **Transportation In**. For example, Lakeside Electronics maintains a separate account for freight charges on incoming merchandise. On December 2, 20X1, Lakeside purchased merchandise costing $700 on account from Pantech Corporation. The goods were shipped *FOB shipping point*, and there was a $30 transportation charge. The general journal entry to record the purchase is shown below.

	20X1						
1	Dec.	2	Purchases		7 0 0 00		1
2			Freight In		3 0 00		2
3			Accounts Payable—Pantech Corp.	/		7 3 0 00	3
4			Purchased merchandise on account.				4

Since most of Lakeside's purchases are shipped FOB destination (seller pays the freight), Lakeside records such freight charges in a general journal. However, if a firm frequently buys merchandise FOB shipping point, the purchases journal can be expanded to three columns to record the freight charge. Let's assume for a moment that Lakeside uses such a purchases journal. The above entry would then be recorded as shown below.

Purchases Journal								Page 2
Date	Account Credited	Invoice No.	Terms	P.R.	Accts. Pay. Cr.	Freight In Dr.	Purchases Dr.	
20X1 Dec. 2	Pantech Corporation	113	2/10,n/30	✓	7 3 0 00	3 0 00	7 0 0 00	1

The balance of the Freight In account is not treated as an operating expense. Rather, its balance is shown on the income statement as an addition to the Purchases account, to obtain the delivered cost of purchases. We will discuss this further in Chapter 10 when we look at the income statement for a merchandising business.

We should stress that the Freight In account is used *only* to record freight on incoming merchandise. Freight paid on assets purchased for use in the business is debited to the asset account itself, *not* Freight In.

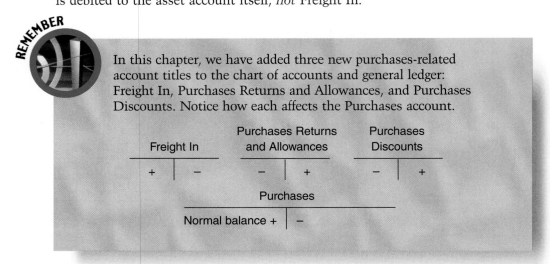

In this chapter, we have added three new purchases-related account titles to the chart of accounts and general ledger: Freight In, Purchases Returns and Allowances, and Purchases Discounts. Notice how each affects the Purchases account.

Freight In	Purchases Returns and Allowances	Purchases Discounts
+ | –	– | +	– | +

Purchases

Normal balance + \| –

PURCHASE INVOICES AS A JOURNAL

We have stressed that the actual design of a special journal is tailored to the needs of the business using it. Thus, it naturally follows that there are many variations in the appearance and use of special journals. One variation involves using purchase invoices as a purchases journal. Using this method, posting is made to the accounts payable ledger directly from individual invoices. As a posting reference, invoice numbers are entered in the P.R. columns of creditors' accounts.

At the end of the month, the invoices are totaled, and a summarizing entry is made in the general journal. To illustrate this method, let's use the example of SaveWay Market, a small independent grocery store. At the end of August 20X3, SaveWay's bookkeeper sorts the month's invoices and finds that the totals are as follows: purchases of merchandise, $12,400; freight in, $288; store supplies, $212; office supplies, $190; and office equipment, $495. The bookkeeper then makes a summarizing entry, as shown below.

	20X3					
1	Aug.	31	Purchases	12 4 0 0 00		1
2			Freight In	2 8 8 00		2
3			Store Supplies	2 1 2 00		3
4			Office Supplies	1 9 0 00		4
5			Office Equipment	4 9 5 00		5
6			Accounts Payable		13 5 8 5 00	6
7			Recorded purchases for August.			7

WHAT ARE BOOKMARKS AND HOW ARE THEY USED?

Web browsers offer a feature called Bookmarks or Favorite Sites that allow you to store Web site addresses or URLs, that you use most frequently. Bookmarks eliminate the need to look up and type the address each time you want to visit one of these sites on the Internet. Bookmarks make it easy for you to find your favorite sites without having to memorize their location. Most browsers have a Bookmark menu that allows you to add or delete an address from the Bookmark list.

For more information on Bookmarks or to learn how to create one, look at the following Web sites:

http://www.ulst.ac.uk/library/training/netscape/index.htm

http://www.cs.uri.edu/students/grad/corcoran/netscape_tutorial/book.html

http://infopeople.berkeley.edu:8000/bkmk/index.html

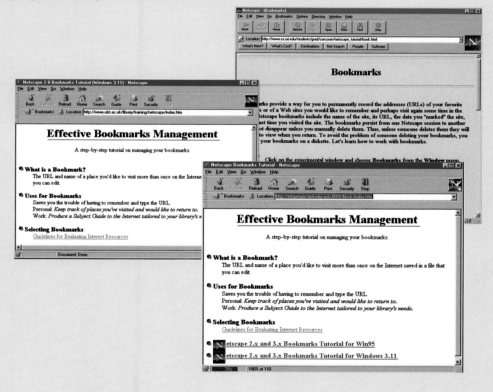

Accounting for a Merchandising Business

PROCEDURES FOR POSTING THE PURCHASES JOURNAL

The total of the money column is posted to the debit side of the Purchases account and to the credit side of the Accounts Payable account. The numbers of these accounts are written under the column total.

Each entry in the money column is posted individually to a creditor's account in the accounts payable ledger. A check mark (✓) is made in the P.R. column to indicate that an individual posting has been made.

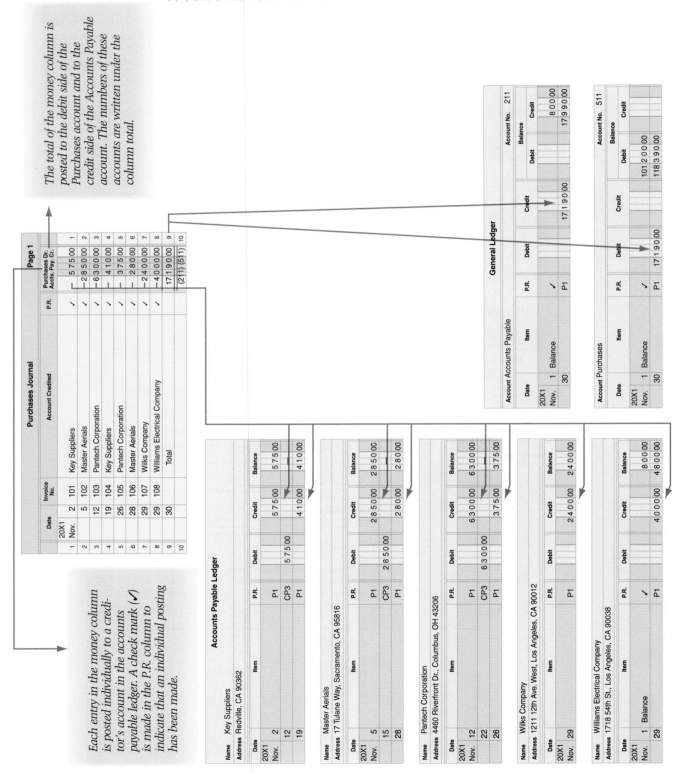

Cash Payments Journal — Page 3

Date	Ck. No.	Account Debited	P.R.	General Dr.	Accounts Payable Dr.	Purchases Discounts Cr.	Cash Cr.	
20X1 Nov. 2	126	Rent Expense	611	675 00			675 00	1
12	127	Key Suppliers	✓		575 00	11 50	563 50	2
15	128	Master Aerials	✓		2850 00	57 00	2793 00	3
22	129	Pantech Corporation	✓		6300 00	126 00	6174 00	4
25	130	Purchases	511	800 00			800 00	5
27	131	Utilities Expense	616	620 00			620 00	6
28	132	Salaries Expense	618	2250 00			2250 00	7
30	133	Telephone Expense	619	240 00			240 00	8
30	134	John Graham, Drawing	312	1500 00			1500 00	9
30		Totals		6085 00	9725 00	194 50	15615 50	10
				(✓)	(211)	(511.2)	(111)	11

Totals of special columns are posted to the general ledger at the end of the month. As a posting reference, account numbers are entered directly below column totals.

Amounts in the General Dr. column are posted individually to the general ledger accounts identified in the Account Debited column. Accounts numbers of the respective accounts are entered in the P.R. column.

Amounts in the Accounts Payable Dr. column are posted separately to creditors' accounts in the accounts payable ledger. A check mark (✓) is entered in the P.R. column to indicate an individual posting.

General Ledger accounts

Account	No.	Balance
John Graham, Drawing	312	1,500
Purchases	511	800
Rent Expense	611	675
Salaries Expense	618	2,250
Utilities Expense	616	620
Telephone Expense	619	240
Cash	111	15,615.50
Accounts Payable	211	9,725
Purchases Discounts	511.2	194.50

Accounts Payable Ledger

Name Key Suppliers
Address Redville, CA 90362

Date	Item	P.R.	Debit	Credit	Balance
20X1 Nov. 2		P1		575 00	575 00
12		CP3	575 00		—
19		P1		410 00	410 00

Name Master Aerials
Address 17 Tulane Way, Sacramento, CA 95816

Date	Item	P.R.	Debit	Credit	Balance
20X1 Nov. 5		P1		2850 00	2850 00
15		CP3	2850 00		—
28		P1		280 00	280 00

Name Pantech Corporation
Address 4460 Riverfront Dr., Columbus, OH 43206

Date	Item	P.R.	Debit	Credit	Balance
20X1 Nov. 12		P1		6300 00	6300 00
22		CP3	6300 00		—
26		P1		375 00	375 00

SUMMARY/RESTATEMENT OF LEARNING OBJECTIVES

1. Describe the procedures and forms used in purchasing merchandise.

Just as there is a great variety in the types and sizes of merchandising firms, there is also a great variety in the procedures used to buy goods to be resold. In a small retail firm, the owner may do all the buying. In large retail and wholesale concerns, purchasing begins with the preparation of a **purchase requisition** by any department in the firm. This form is sent to the purchasing department where a **purchase order** is prepared and sent to a supplier. Upon receipt and acceptance of the purchase order, the supplier prepares an **invoice**, which is a form that describes the goods and the details of the purchase. The invoice is sent to the buyer with the goods or a few days later. When the buyer receives the goods, a **receiving report** is prepared by the receiving department.

2. Record credit purchases in a general journal and a purchases journal, and post to the accounts payable ledger and the general ledger.

The Yogurt Shoppe made the following credit purchases during July 20XX:

20XX
Jul.   1   Merchandise from Alder Co., $750; terms, 2/10,n/30.
      7   Merchandise from Beeler Co., $900; terms, 2/10,n/30.
    16   Equipment from Caldwell Co., $2,500; terms, n/30.
    22   Supplies from Lamont Suppliers, $400; terms, n/30.
    28   Merchandise from Beeler Co., $500; terms, 2/10,n/30.
    29   Merchandise from Alder Co., $400; terms, 2/10,n/30.

These transactions are recorded in the general journal and **purchases journal** that follow. Remember that only credit purchases of merchandise are recorded in a one-column purchases journal. Credit purchases of nonmerchandise items are recorded in the general journal. Posting references are shown in the purchase journal; however, the ledger accounts themselves are not shown since numerous examples are shown in the chapter.

	20XX								
1	Jul.	16	Equipment		2 5 0 0 00				1
2			Accounts Payable—Caldwell Co.	/			2 5 0 0 00		2
3									3
4		22	Supplies		4 0 0 00				4
5			Accounts Payable—Lamont Suppliers	/			4 0 0 00		5

			Purchases Journal			**Page 1**	
	Date	Invoice No.	Account Credited	P.R.	Purchases Dr. Accts. Pay. Cr.	
1	20XX Jul. 1	1	Alder Co.	✓	7 5 0 00	1
2	7	2	Beeler Co.	✓	9 0 0 00	2
3	28	5	Beeler Co.	✓	5 0 0 00	3
4	29	6	Alder Co.	✓	4 0 0 00	4
5	31		Total		2 5 5 0 00	5
6					(211) (511)	6

3. Record purchases returns and allowances.

On December 14, 20XX, Turner's Imported World purchased merchandise costing $5,800 on account from North American Importers. On December 19, upon receipt of the merchandise, Turner discovered that an oriental rug costing $500 was not the one ordered. The item was returned for credit. In general journal form, entries to record the purchase and the return are shown on the next page.

	20XX						
1	Dec.	14	Purchases		5 8 0 0 00		1
2			Accts. Payable—No. American Importers	/		5 8 0 0 00	2
3			Purchased merchandise on account.				3
4							4
5		19	Accts. Payable—No. American Importers	/	5 0 0 00		5
6			Purchases Returns and Allowances			5 0 0 00	6
7			Returned merchandise for credit.				7

4. Record purchases discounts.

A **cash discount** is a discount offered by a seller to encourage prompt payment by a buyer. To the seller, the cash discount is a **sales discount**; to the buyer, it is a **purchases discount**. A common expression of a cash discount is 2/10,n/30, which means that a 2% discount can be deducted if merchandise is paid for within 10 days of the date of the invoice.

To review how to record purchases discounts (sales discounts are discussed in Chapter 8), assume that on June 12, 20X3, Jeanette Register purchased $500 worth of merchandise, with terms of 2/10,n/30, from Joe Lewis Company. The following entry was made to record Jeanette's payment for the goods on June 22.

	20X3						
1	Jun.	22	Accounts Payable—Joe Lewis Co.	/	5 0 0 00		1
2			Purchases Discounts ($500 × .02)			1 0 00	2
3			Cash			4 9 0 00	3
4			Paid for June 12 purchase.				4

5. Record cash payments in a cash payments journal and post to the accounts payable ledger and the general ledger.

The Yogurt Shoppe made the following cash expenditures during July 20XX:

20XX
Jul. 1 Paid rent, $450.
 5 Purchased merchandise for cash, $820.
 9 Paid Alder Company amount owed, $750, less 2% discount.
 17 Paid Beeler Company amount owed, $900, less 2% discount.
 25 Paid Caldwell Company amount owed, $890, no discount.
 30 Paid utility bill for the month, $625.
 31 Paid salaries for the month, $1,200.

These payments are recorded in the **cash payments journal**. Posting references are shown in the P.R. column and below the money column totals; however, the ledgers are not shown since they are illustrated in the chapter.

Cash Payments Journal									Page 2	
	Date	Ck. No.	Account Debited	P.R.	General Dr.	Accounts Payable Dr.	Purchases Discounts Cr.	Cash Cr.		
1	20XX Jul. 1	1	Rent Expense	611	4 5 0 00			4 5 0 00	1
2	5	2	Purchases	511	8 2 0 00			8 2 0 00	2
3	9	3	Alder Company	✓		7 5 0 00	1 5 00	7 3 5 00	3
4	17	4	Beeler Company	✓		9 0 0 00	1 8 00	8 8 2 00	4
5	25	5	Caldwell Company	✓		8 9 0 00		8 9 0 00	5
6	30	6	Utilities Expense	614	6 2 5 00			6 2 5 00	6
7	31	7	Salaries Expense	618	1 2 0 0 00			1 2 0 0 00	7
8	31		Totals		3 0 9 5 00	2 5 4 0 00	3 3 00	5 6 0 2 00	8
9					(✓)	(2 1 1)	(5 1 1.2)	(1 1 1)	9

6. Prepare a schedule of accounts payable.

A **schedule of accounts payable** is a listing of all account balances in the **accounts payable subsidiary ledger**. The total of the schedule is compared with the balance of the **Accounts Payable controlling account** (in the general ledger) to verify the posting accuracy of the subsidiary ledger. After all postings are complete, the total of the schedule of accounts payable should agree with the balance of the Accounts Payable account.

7. Record freight charges on incoming merchandise.

When merchandise is shipped **FOB shipping point**, the buyer is responsible for paying freight (to destination) charges. There are two ways of accounting for freight charges on incoming merchandise: (1) the freight charge can be debited to the Purchases account along with the cost of the merchandise purchased, or (2) the freight charge can be debited to a separate account entitled **Freight In**. To illustrate the use of the Freight In account, assume that on March 18, 20X4, Lee Drug Company purchased merchandise costing $800 on account from Central Supply Company. Terms of shipment were FOB shipping point, and there was a $40 freight charge. The purchase is recorded in general journal form as follows.

	20X4						
1	Mar.	18	Purchases		8 0 0 00		1
2			Freight In		4 0 00		2
3			Accts. Payable—Central Supply Co.	/		8 4 0 00	3
4			Purchased merchandise on account.				4

KEY TERMS

accounts payable ledger A subsidiary ledger that lists the individual accounts of creditors. Also called the **creditors' ledger**.

cash discounts Discounts offered by a seller to encourage early payment by a buyer. To the seller, cash discounts are **sales discounts**; to the buyer, cash discounts are **purchases discounts**.

cash payments journal A special journal used for recording all disbursements of cash. Also called the **cash disbursements journal**.

controlling account An account in the general ledger that summarizes accounts in a related subsidiary ledger.

cost accounts Accounts that are presented on the income statement; used to determine the cost of goods sold to customers.

credit memorandum A written statement that indicates a seller's willingness to reduce the amount owed by a buyer.

debit memorandum The buyer's written request to a seller for credit for a merchandise return or allowance.

FOB destination A shipping term that means that the seller is responsible for all freight costs until the goods reach their destination.

FOB shipping point A shipping term that means that the buyer is responsible for all freight costs while the goods are in transit.

Freight In account A general ledger account in which charges for freight on incoming merchandise are recorded. Also called **Transportation In**.

general ledger A ledger containing the financial statement accounts.

invoice A business document that contains the names and addresses of the buyer and the seller, the date and terms of the sale, a description of the goods, the price of the goods, and the mode of transportation used to ship the goods. The seller calls the invoice a **sales invoice**; the buyer calls it a **purchase invoice**.

list price The price appearing in a price catalog issued by the seller.

merchandise (or merchandise inventory) Goods held for sale to customers. Also called **stock in trade**.

merchandising business A business that earns its revenue by buying goods and then reselling those goods. Also called a **trading business**.

purchase order A written order from a buyer of goods to the seller, listing items needed and a description of the goods.

purchase requisition A written request for goods to be purchased. It is usually prepared by a department head or manager and sent to a firm's purchasing department.

Purchases account A temporary owner's equity account that is used to record the cost of merchandise purchased for resale. Other possible titles include **Merchandise Purchases** or **Purchases of Merchandise**.

Purchases Discounts account A contra purchases account that records discounts received for prompt payment of merchandise (purchases discounts).

purchases journal A special journal used only to record credit purchases of merchandise. (Some businesses design a multicolumn purchases journal that is used to record all credit purchases, not just merchandise.)

Purchases Returns and Allowances account A contra purchases account that is used to record returns and allowances on merchandise purchases.

receiving report A report prepared by the receiving department to indicate what goods were received and in what quantity.

retail businesses Those who own businesses such as grocery stores, drugstores, and restaurants, which sell directly to consumers.

schedule of accounts payable A listing of the individual creditor balances in the accounts payable ledger.

special journals Journals used by businesses to record transactions that are similar in nature; examples are the purchases journal and the cash payments journal. Also called **special-purpose journals**.

subsidiary ledgers Ledgers that contain only one type of account; the example in this chapter is the accounts payable ledger.

trade discount A percentage reduction from the list price of merchandise.

wholesalers Those who purchase goods in bulk from manufacturers and sell them to retailers, other wholesalers, schools and other not-for-profit institutions, and, at times, directly to consumers.

CONCEPTS AND SKILLS REVIEW

CONCEPTS REVIEW

1. How can a computer be classified as equipment in one business but as merchandise in another?
2. What is the difference between merchandising activity on the retail level and that on the wholesale level?
3. How are trade discounts shown on the accounting records?
4. How does a cash discount differ from a trade discount?
5. How can one discount be both a sales discount and a purchases discount?
6. State the meaning of the following credit terms: (a) n/30; (b) 2/10,n/30; and (c) 3/10,2/20,n/30.
7. Why is the Purchases account an owner's equity account?
8. What form is used as a source document to record a purchase?
9. How does a special journal save time in both recording and posting?
10. Are all purchases recorded in the purchases journal? Explain your answer.
11. Why is a subsidiary ledger considered to be a secondary ledger?

12. Explain why posting an entry both to an individual creditor's account and to the Accounts Payable account does not cause an imbalance in the general ledger.
13. How does a merchandise allowance differ from a merchandise return?
14. Compare a debit memo with a credit memo by stating (a) who prepares each form and (b) what its purpose is.
15. How does the purchaser of goods account for a cash discount?
16. What is the function of the General Dr. column in the cash payments journal?
17. What three types of postings are made from the cash payments journal?
18. How is the accuracy of posting to a subsidiary ledger checked?
19. a. What is meant by transportation terms?
    b. Identify two common transportation terms.
20. Identify two ways to account for freight on incoming merchandise.
21. How can purchase invoices be used in place of a purchases journal?

SKILLS REVIEW

EXERCISE 7-1

LEARNING OBJECTIVE 1

Objective: To calculate net prices when trade discounts are used

Directions: For each letter, calculate the price to be recorded in the accounting records:

	List Price	Trade Discount Rate
(a)	$ 900	40%
(b)	1,650	35%
(c)	3,375	18%
(d)	9,860	30%
(e)	1,980	12½%

EXERCISE 7-2

LEARNING OBJECTIVE 4

Objective: To calculate amounts to be paid

Directions: Calculate the amount due on each of the following invoices:

	Invoice Price	Date of Invoice	Terms	Date Paid
(a)	$1,900	July 6	2/10,n/30	July 14
(b)	800	October 30	2/10,n/30	November 9
(c)	880	May 12	1/10,n/30	May 27
(d)	925	June 27	3/10, 2/20,n/30	July 13
(e)	1,450	August 24	n/60	October 12

EXERCISE 7-3

LEARNING OBJECTIVE 2

Objective: To record purchases in general journal form

Directions: Citizens Drugstore made the following credit purchases during March 20X1. Record each in a two-column general journal.

20X1
Mar. 3 Assorted medicines from Central Laboratories, $8,500.
     7 Filing cabinets for use in the office from Allied Office Equipment Company, $1,095.
    12 Hair care appliances from Ace Products, $3,220.
    16 Candies and gums from Wholesale Distributors, $1,950.

Mar. 22 Computer paper and stationery for use in the office from Office
Stationers, $355.

27 A used delivery truck from Acme Auto, $8,600.

EXERCISE 7-4

LEARNING OBJECTIVE 2, 3 **Objective: To record purchases in a purchases journal and a general journal**

Directions: Record the transactions from Exercise 7-3 in a purchases journal
(page 1) and a general journal (page 1). Number invoices starting with 1.

EXERCISE 7-5

LEARNING OBJECTIVE 2, 3 **Objective: To record purchases, returns, and allowances in general journal form**

Directions: Record each of the following transactions in general journal form:

(a) Purchased merchandise on credit from Allard Corporation, $600.
(b) Returned $60 of the merchandise purchased in Transaction (a), receiving credit.
(c) Purchased merchandise for cash, $675.
(d) Discovered that a $50 item purchased in Transaction (c) was defective. It was returned and a cash refund was received.
(e) Purchased store supplies on credit from Krystal Suppliers, $950.
(f) Discovered that some wrapping paper purchased in Transaction (e) was water stained. An allowance of $45 was granted.
(g) Purchased office equipment on credit, $8,800, from Stallard Equipment Company.
(h) An item of the equipment purchased in Transaction (g) was found to not work properly. It was returned and credit was granted for $2,000.

EXERCISE 7-6

LEARNING OBJECTIVE 3 **Objective: To record cash payments in general journal form**

Directions: Stark's Variety Store made the following cash disbursements during
April 20XX. Record each cash payment in general journal form.

20XX
Apr. 1 Paid rent for the month, $700.
4 Paid Weaver Co. for an invoice of March 26, $475 less a 2% discount.
9 Purchased merchandise for cash, $250.
15 Paid Reed Co. for an $875 purchase of merchandise on April 5. The purchase carried terms of 2/10,n/30.
22 Purchased office equipment for cash, $950.
27 Paid utility bill, $250.
30 Paid monthly salaries, $2,560.

EXERCISE 7-7

LEARNING OBJECTIVE 5 **Objective: To record cash payments in a cash payments journal**

Directions: Record the cash payments from Exercise 7-6 in a cash payments journal like the one illustrated in the chapter. Number checks starting with 94. Total and rule the cash payments journal.

EXERCISE 7-8

LEARNING OBJECTIVE 2 **Objective: To record a summary entry from purchases invoices**

Directions: At the end of October 20X1, the bookkeeper for The Sandwich
Shoppe sorted the firm's invoices for the month and found that the totals are as

---

follows: merchandise, $5,600; freight in, $145; store supplies, $165; office supplies, $120; store equipment, $750. Record these purchases in general journal form.

EXERCISE 7-9

LEARNING OBJECTIVE 3

Objective: To make journal entries to correct errors

Directions: Make entries in general journal form to correct each of the following errors:

(a) A $150 return of store supplies was credited to the Purchases Returns and Allowances account.
(b) A bill of $95 for freight charges on a cash register purchased for use in the store was debited to the Freight In account.
(c) A $725 purchase of computer ribbons intended for resale was debited to the Office Supplies account.

CASE PROBLEMS

GROUP A

LEARNING OBJECTIVE 2, 3

PROBLEM 7-1A

Objective: To record purchases and returns

The following transactions were completed by Davis Company during May 20X2:

20X2
May 1   Purchased merchandise on account from Clark Co., $995, Invoice No. 1.
     6   Purchased office supplies on account from Ellis Co., $240, Invoice No. 2.
     7   Purchased merchandise on account from Puan Co., $780, Invoice No. 3.
    11   Returned merchandise to Puan Co., receiving a $45 credit.
    12   Received a credit memorandum from Ellis Co. for a shortage on the purchase of May 6, $30.
    18   Purchased merchandise for cash, $875.
    22   Returned defective merchandise purchased on May 18, receiving a $50 cash refund.
    25   Purchased store equipment for $1,000, paying $400 down and owing Astor Co. the balance, Invoice No. 4.
    27   Purchased merchandise on account from Wilson Co., $850, Invoice No. 5.
    29   Received an allowance of $85 on the purchase of May 25 because the equipment was damaged during shipment.

Directions: Record these transactions in a two-column general journal and a one-column purchases journal.

PROBLEM 7-2A

LEARNING OBJECTIVE 2, 3, 6

Objective: To record purchases and returns, post to two ledgers, and prepare a schedule of accounts payable

Credit purchases and related returns and allowances completed by Campus Bookstore during September 20X2 are as follows:

20X2

Sep. 1 Purchased merchandise on account from Lang Co., $2,550.

4 Purchased merchandise on account from MidWest Publishing Co., $6,890.

7 Purchased merchandise on account from Clothing Wholesalers, $1,256.25, less a 20% trade discount.

10 Purchased merchandise on account from Lang Co., $975.

11 Purchased office supplies on account from Regents Supply Co., $245.80.

14 Purchased office equipment on account from Hamer Equipment Co., $13,500.

15 Purchased merchandise on account from Addington Co., $700.

16 Received a credit memorandum from Regents Supply Co. for office supplies returned, $60.

18 Purchased merchandise on account from MidWest Publishing Co., $4,700.

21 Purchased store supplies on account from Hamer Equipment Co., $530.

25 Received a credit memorandum from MidWest Publishing Co. as an allowance for damaged goods, $110.

28 Purchased merchandise on account from Addington Co., $950.

30 Purchased office supplies on account from Regents Supply Co., $65.

Directions:

1. Open the following accounts in the general ledger and enter the balances as of September 1:

	Account	Balance
113	Store Supplies	$ 675.90
114	Office Supplies	345.75
121	Office Equipment	12,956.00
211	Accounts Payable	9,600.00
511	Purchases	98,568.35
511.1	Purchases Returns and Allowances	1,450.00

2. Open the following accounts in the accounts payable ledger and enter these balances as of September 1:

Account	Balance
Addington Co.	$1,400.00
Clothing Wholesalers	1,250.00
Hamer Equipment Co.	2,500.00
Lang Co.	1,810.00
MidWest Publishing Co.	960.00
Regents Supply Co.	1,680.00

3. Record the September transactions in a two-column general journal and a one-column purchases journal, posting to the accounts payable ledger after each entry. Number invoices starting with 126.

4. Total the purchases journal. Make all postings from the general journal to the general ledger at the end of the month. Then post the column total from the purchases journal.

5. Prepare a schedule of accounts payable as of September 30.

6. Compare the balance of the Accounts Payable controlling account as of September 30 with the total of the schedule of accounts payable. The two amounts should be the same.

PROBLEM 7-3A

LEARNING OBJECTIVE 2, 6, 7 **Objective: To record and post purchases and freight charges**

Home Appliance and Supply Company is located in Albuquerque, New Mexico. The following credit purchases were made by the firm during June 20XX:

Accounting for a Merchandising Business

20XX

Jun. 1 Refrigerators from Allard Co., $7,790, Inv. No. 211, freight, $425, FOB Albuquerque.

5 Microwave ovens and toasters from Technical Products Co., $8,800, Inv. No. 212, freight, $510, FOB Birmingham, Alabama.

8 Ceiling fans from Buena Vista Co., $1,900, Inv. No. 213, freight, $88, FOB Las Cruces, New Mexico.

10 Space heaters from Alamogordo Co., $1,050, Inv. No. 214, freight, $77.50, FOB Alamogordo, New Mexico.

12 Office equipment from Thompson Suppliers, $5,500, Inv. No. 215, freight, $212, FOB Albuquerque.

18 Store equipment from Carlsbad Co., $4,800, Inv. No. 216, freight, $228, FOB Carlsbad, New Mexico.

24 Freezers from Allard Co., $6,980, Inv. No. 217, freight, $418, FOB Albuquerque.

30 Blenders and mixers from Technical Products Co., $4,500, Inv. No. 218, freight, $100, FOB Birmingham.

Directions:

1. Open the following accounts in the general ledger and record the balances of June 1:

	Account	Balance
118	Office Equipment	$ 12,900
119	Store Equipment	25,900
211	Accounts Payable	15,955
511	Purchases	125,800
512	Freight In	2,410

2. Open the following accounts in the accounts payable ledger and enter the balances as of June 1:

Account	Balance
Alamogordo Co.	$4,355
Allard Co.	2,510
Buena Vista Co.	875
Carlsbad Co.	2,590
Technical Products Co.	5,625
Thompson Suppliers	-0-

3. Record the June purchases in a two-column general journal and a three-column purchases journal like the one illustrated in the chapter. Post to the accounts payable ledger after each entry.

4. Total the purchases journal. Make all postings from the general journal to the general ledger at the end of the month. Then post the column totals from the purchases journal.

5. Prepare a schedule of accounts payable and compare its total to the balance of the Accounts Payable controlling account.

LEARNING OBJECTIVE 2, 4, 5, 6, 7

PROBLEM 7-4A

Objective: To record purchases and cash payments, post them, and prepare a schedule of accounts payable

The following selected transactions were completed by Barney's Sports Shop during February 20X1:

20X1

Feb. 1 Issued Check No. 113 for February rent, $900.

2 Issued Check No. 114 to All-American Co. for the balance of the account, less a 2% discount.

Feb. 3 Issued Check No. 115 to Best Equipment Co. for the balance of the account, less a 2% discount.

3 Purchased merchandise from All-American Co., $1,550, terms, 2/10,n/30, Invoice No. 109.

4 Purchased merchandise from Al's Sports Wholesalers, $2,850, terms, 2/10,n/30, Invoice No. 110.

7 Issued Check No. 116 for the cash purchase of merchandise, $745.

9 Issued Check No. 117 in payment of a three-year insurance policy, $850.

11 Barney James, the owner, issued Check No. 118 for his home phone bill, $275.

13 Issued Check No. 119 in full payment of the purchase of February 3.

15 Issued Check No. 120 for the cash purchase of office supplies, $325.

17 Purchased display cases from Best Equipment Co., $1,650, terms, 3/10,n/30, Invoice No. 111.

22 Purchased office supplies from Office Suppliers, $820, terms, n/30, Invoice No. 112.

25 Issued Check No. 121 to Al's Sports Wholesalers for payment on account, $1,000.

27 Issued Check No. 122 for the purchase of February 17.

28 Issued Check No. 123 for monthly salaries, $1,500.

28 Issued Check No. 124 for freight charges on merchandise, $295.

Directions:

1. Open the following accounts in the general ledger and enter these balances as of February 1:

	Account	Balance
111	Cash	$16,000
112	Office Supplies	980
113	Prepaid Insurance	75
116	Store Equipment	15,600
211	Accounts Payable	10,810
312	Barney James, Drawing	1,200
511	Purchases	9,500
511.2	Purchases Discounts	345
512	Freight In	128
612	Salaries Expense	1,500
613	Rent Expense	900

2. Open the following accounts in the accounts payable ledger and record these balances as of February 1:

Account	Balance
All-American Co.	$3,710
Al's Sports Wholesalers	2,350
Best Equipment Co.	3,000
Office Suppliers	1,750

3. Record the February transactions in a two-column general journal, a one-column purchases journal, and a cash payments journal like the one illustrated in the chapter. Post to the accounts payable ledger after each entry.

4. Total the special journals. Make all individual postings from the cash payments journal and the general journal to the general ledger at the end of the month. Then post the column totals from the special journals.

5. Prepare a schedule of accounts payable.

6. Compare the balance of the Accounts Payable controlling account with the total of the schedule of accounts payable.

PROBLEM 7-5A

Objective: To record purchases, returns, and cash payments, and prepare a schedule of accounts payable

Diamond Jewelers, owned by Lisa Richardson, has been in business for several years. On July 1, 20X1, the firm's accounts payable ledger contains the following accounts and balances:

Account	Balance
Best Diamond Co.	$1,540.00
Carter's Supplies	720.15
Modern Equipment Co.	2,675.00
Nash Jewelers	1,355.00
Wilson's Gems	725.60

The following transactions were completed during July:

20X1

Jul. 1 Issued Check No. 796 for July rent, $1,100.

5 Issued Check No. 797 to Wilson's Gems for the balance of the account, less a 2% discount.

7 Purchased merchandise from Best Diamond Co., $2,650, Invoice No. 621, terms, 2/10,n/30.

8 Returned merchandise to Best Diamond Co., receiving a $75 credit memorandum.

9 Issued Check No. 798 to Carter's Supplies for the balance of the account, less a 2% discount.

12 Purchased $2,100 worth of merchandise from Wilson's Gems by issuing Check No. 799 for $700, with the balance of $1,400 owed on account, Invoice No. 622. (Hint: You need to use two journals to record this entry.)

15 Purchased display cases from Modern Equipment Co., $875.50, Invoice No. 623, terms, n/30.

17 Issued Check No. 800 to Best Diamond Co. for the purchase of July 7 less the credit of July 8.

18 Issued Check No. 801 for a three-year insurance premium, $2,220.

25 Purchased office supplies, $675, and store supplies, $820, from Carter's Supplies, Invoice No. 624, terms, n/30.

27 Returned damaged office supplies to and received credit from Carter's Supplies, $85.

28 Issued Check No. 802 to Nash Jewelers as a payment on account, $200.

29 Issued Check No. 803 to Modern Equipment Co. for the July 1 balance of the account, with no discount.

30 Issued Check No. 804 to Carter's Supplies for a cash purchase of store supplies, $95.

30 Issued Check No. 805 to Wall Company for the purchase of a new cash register, $3,782.

30 Issued Check No. 806 to Beal Supply Co. for a cash purchase of merchandise, $3,900.

31 Issued Check No. 807 to Northern Transport Co. for freight charges on the July 30 delivery of merchandise, $210.

Directions:

1. Open an account in the accounts payable ledger for each creditor listed at the beginning of the problem. Enter balances as of July 1.
2. Open general ledger accounts and enter these July 1 balances:

	Account	Balance
111	Cash	$19,267.75
115	Office Supplies	475.30
116	Store Supplies	946.20
117	Prepaid Insurance	320.00
121	Office Equipment	3,750.00
122	Store Equipment	11,500.00
211	Accounts Payable	7,015.75
511	Purchases	60,000.00
511.1	Purchases Returns and Allowances	4,000.00
511.2	Purchases Discounts	1,200.00
512	Freight In	800.00
613	Rent Expense	6,600.00

3. Record the July transactions in a one-column purchases journal (as shown in Figure 7-5), a cash payments journal (as shown in Figure 7-11), and a general journal. Post to the accounts payable ledger after each entry.
4. Total the special journals. Make all individual postings from the cash payments journal and the general journal to the general ledger. Then post the column totals from the special journals.
5. Prepare a schedule of accounts payable and compare the total with the balance of the Accounts Payable controlling account.

GROUP B

LEARNING OBJECTIVE 2, 3

PROBLEM 7-1B

Objective: To record purchases and returns

The following transactions were completed by Kinsaul Company during May 20X1:

20X1
May 1 Purchased merchandise on account from Hicks Co., $950, Invoice No. 1.
6 Purchased office supplies on account from Reese Co., $290, Invoice No. 2.
7 Purchased merchandise on account from Kane Co., $585, Invoice No. 3.
11 Returned merchandise to Kane Co., receiving a $50 credit.
12 Received a credit memorandum from Reese Co. for a shortage on the purchase of May 6, $38.
18 Purchased merchandise for cash, $930.
22 Returned defective merchandise purchased on May 18, receiving a $55 cash refund.
25 Purchased store equipment for $1,300, paying $500 down and owing King Co. the balance, Invoice No. 4.
27 Purchased merchandise on account from Lincoln Co., $975, Invoice No. 5.
29 Received an allowance of $90 on the purchase of May 25 because the equipment was damaged during shipment.

Directions: Record these transactions in a two-column general journal and a one-column purchases journal.

LEARNING OBJECTIVE 2, 3, 6

PROBLEM 7-2B

Objective: To record purchases and returns, post to two ledgers, and prepare a schedule of accounts payable

Credit purchases and related returns and allowances completed by The Pro Shop during June 20X1 are as follows:

Accounting for a Merchandising Business

259

20X1
Jun. 1 Purchased merchandise on account from Lesan Co., $3,550.
      5 Purchased merchandise on account from Tamms, Inc., $5,800.
      7 Purchased merchandise on account from Southern Wholesalers, $1,692.73 less a 25% trade discount.
     12 Purchased office supplies on account from Central Supply Co., $285.60.
     13 Purchased office equipment on account from Drummer Equipment Co., $11,900.
     16 Purchased merchandise on account from Arrington Co., $900.
     17 Received a credit memorandum from Central Supply Co. for office supplies returned, $70.
     18 Purchased merchandise on account from Southern Wholesalers, $1,500.
     22 Purchased store supplies on account from Drummer Equipment Co., $600.
     25 Received a credit memorandum from Southern Wholesalers as an allowance for damaged goods, $135.
     28 Purchased merchandise on account from Arrington Co., $925.
     30 Purchased office supplies on account from Central Supply Co., $75.

Directions:

1. Open the following accounts in the general ledger and enter the balances as of June 1:

	Account	Balance
113	Store Supplies	$ 643.75
114	Office Supplies	435.68
121	Office Equipment	12,975.00
211	Accounts Payable	13,155.00
511	Purchases	89,568.15
511.1	Purchases Returns and Allowances	1,255.00

2. Open the following accounts in the accounts payable ledger and enter these balances as of June 1:

Account	Balance
Arrington Co.	$1,845.00
Central Supply Co.	2,455.00
Drummer Equipment Co.	3,590.00
Lesan Co.	3,585.00
Southern Wholesalers	-0-
Tamms, Inc.	1,680.00

3. Record the June transactions in a two-column general journal and a one-column purchases journal, posting to the accounts payable ledger after each entry. Number invoices starting with 224.
4. Total the purchases journal. Make all postings from the general journal to the general ledger at the end of the month. Then post the column total from the purchases journal.
5. Prepare a schedule of accounts payable as of June 30.
6. Compare the balance of the Accounts Payable controlling account as of June 30 with the total of the schedule of accounts payable. The two amounts should be the same.

PROBLEM 7-3B

LEARNING OBJECTIVE 2, 6, 7 **Objective: To record and post purchases and freight charges**

Saben Appliance and Home Center is located in Waterloo, Iowa. The following credit purchases were made by the firm during May 20XX:

20XX
May 1 Washers and dryers from Hanson Co., $6,975, Inv. No. 318, freight, $690, FOB Iowa Falls, Iowa.

Paradigm College Accounting • Chapter 7

May 5   Refrigerators from Schendel Co., $9,500, Inv. No. 319, freight, $540, FOB Webster City, Iowa.

    7   Upright freezer units from Hurley Products Co., $7,595, Inv. No. 320, freight, $325, FOB Conway, South Carolina.

  11   Window fans from Fort Dodge Products Co., $1,345, Inv. No. 321, freight, $100, FOB Waterloo.

  19   Office equipment from Webster Supply, $3,800, Inv. No. 322, freight, $312, FOB Ottumwa, Iowa.

  20   Store equipment from Ankeny Co., $2,800, Inv. No. 323, freight, $318, FOB Waterloo.

  28   Freezers from Schendel Co., $9,675, Inv. No. 324, freight, $775, FOB Webster City.

  31   Various small kitchen appliances from Lakeworth Co., $4,595, Inv. No. 325, freight, $175, FOB La Porte, Indiana.

Directions:

1. Open the following accounts in the general ledger and record the balances of May 1:

	Account	Balance
118	Office Equipment	$ 15,600
119	Store Equipment	26,500
211	Accounts Payable	18,498
511	Purchases	138,900
512	Freight In	3,518

2. Open the following accounts in the accounts payable ledger and enter the balances as of May 1:

Account	Balance
Ankeny Co.	$5,450
Fort Dodge Products Co.	1,850
Hanson Co.	1,560
Hurley Products Co.	4,588
Lakeworth Co.	2,250
Schendel Co.	-0-
Webster Supply	2,800

3. Record the May purchases in a two-column general journal and a three-column purchases journal like the one illustrated in the chapter. Post to the accounts payable ledger after each entry.

4. Total the purchases journal. Make all postings from the general journal to the general ledger at the end of the month. Then post the column totals from the purchases journal.

5. Prepare a schedule of accounts payable and compare its total to the balance of the Accounts Payable controlling account.

LEARNING OBJECTIVE 2, 4, 5, 6, 7

PROBLEM 7-4B

Objective: To record purchases and cash payments, post them, and prepare a schedule of accounts payable

The following selected transactions were completed by All Seasons Natural Food Store during March 20X2:

20X2

Mar. 1   Issued Check No. 205 for March rent, $1,300.

    1   Issued Check No. 206 to Peachtree Foods for the balance of the account, less a 2% discount.

    2   Issued Check No. 207 to Lumpkin Equipment Co. for the balance of the account, less a 2% discount.

Mar. 3 Purchased merchandise from Peachtree Foods, $3,600, terms, 2/10,n/30, Invoice No. 205.

4 Purchased merchandise from Aiken Food Co., $3,860, terms, 2/10,n/30, Invoice No. 206.

8 Issued Check No. 208 for the cash purchase of merchandise, $692.

11 Issued Check No. 209 in payment of a two-year insurance policy, $1,070.

12 Nancy Kinner, the owner, issued Check No. 210 for her home electric bill, $225.

13 Issued Check No. 211 in full payment of the purchase of March 3.

15 Issued Check No. 212 for the cash purchase of office supplies, $418.

17 Purchased display cases from Lumpkin Equipment Co., $1,900, terms, 3/10,n/30, Invoice No. 207.

22 Purchased office supplies from Office Equipment Co., $480, terms, n/30, Invoice No. 208.

26 Issued Check No. 213 to Aiken Food Co. for payment on account, $2,000.

27 Issued Check No. 214 for the purchase of March 17.

29 Issued Check No. 215 for monthly salaries, $1,500.

30 Issued Check No. 216 for freight charges on merchandise, $325.

Directions:

1. Open the following accounts in the general ledger and enter these balances as of March 1:

	Account	Balance
111	Cash	$20,900
112	Office Supplies	684
113	Prepaid Insurance	130
116	Store Equipment	12,900
211	Accounts Payable	10,180
312	Nancy Kinner, Drawing	1,500
511	Purchases	12,450
511.2	Purchases Discounts	392
512	Freight In	150
612	Salaries Expense	3,000
613	Rent Expense	2,600

2. Open the following accounts in the accounts payable ledger and record these balances as of March 1:

Account	Balance
Aiken Food Co.	$ -0-
Lumpkin Equipment Co.	5,000
Office Equipment Co.	2,900
Peachtree Foods	2,280

3. Record the March transactions in a two-column general journal, a one-column purchases journal, and a cash payments journal like the one illustrated in the chapter. Post to the accounts payable ledger after each entry.

4. Total the special journals. Make all individual postings from the cash payments journal and the general journal to the general ledger at the end of the month. Then post the column totals from the special journals.

5. Prepare a schedule of accounts payable.

6. Compare the balance of the Accounts Payable controlling account with the total of the schedule of accounts payable.

PROBLEM 7-5B

Objective: To record purchases, returns, and cash payments, and prepare a schedule of accounts payable

Diamond Jewelers, owned by Lisa Richardson, has been in business for several years. On July 1, 20X1, the firm's accounts payable ledger contains the following accounts and balances:

Account	Balance
Best Diamond Co.	$4,090.00
Carter's Supplies	2,155.00
Modern Equipment Co.	1,275.50
Nash Jewelers	1,255.00
Wilson's Gems	1,700.00

The following transactions were completed during July:

20X1

Jul. 1 Issued Check No. 801 for July rent, $1,200.

5 Issued Check No. 802 to Wilson's Gems for the balance of the account, less a 2% discount.

7 Purchased merchandise from Best Diamond Co., $3,600, Invoice No. 601, terms, 2/10,n/30.

8 Returned merchandise to Best Diamond Co., receiving a $70 credit memorandum.

9 Issued Check No. 803 to Carter's Supplies for the balance of the account, less a 2% discount.

12 Purchased $2,200 worth of merchandise from Wilson's Gems by issuing Check No. 804 for $700, with the balance of $1,500 owed on account, Invoice No. 602. (Hint: You need to use two journals to record this entry.)

15 Purchased display cases from Modern Equipment Co., $779.50, Invoice No. 603, terms, n/30.

17 Issued Check No. 805 to Best Diamond Co. for the purchase of July 7 less the credit of July 8.

18 Issued Check No. 806 for a three-year insurance premium, $2,520.

25 Purchased office supplies, $700, and store supplies, $812, from Carter's Supplies, Invoice No. 604, terms, n/30.

27 Returned damaged office supplies to and received credit from Carter's Supplies, $70.

28 Issued Check No. 807 to Nash Jewelers as a payment on account, $250.

29 Issued Check No. 808 to Modern Equipment Co. for the July 1 balance of the account, with no discount.

30 Issued Check No. 809 to Carter's Supplies for a cash purchase of store supplies, $105.

30 Issued Check No. 810 to Wall Company for the purchase of a new cash register, $3,982.

30 Issued Check No. 811 to Beal Supply Co. for a cash purchase of merchandise, $4,300.

31 Issued Check No. 812 to Northern Transport Co. for freight charges on the July 30 delivery of merchandise, $225.

Directions:

1. Open an account in the accounts payable ledger for each creditor listed at the beginning of the problem. Enter balances as of July 1.

2. Open general ledger accounts and enter these July 1 balances:

	Account	Balance
111	Cash	$22,737.00
115	Office Supplies	1,160.30
116	Store Supplies	1,666.20
117	Prepaid Insurance	2,240.00
121	Office Equipment	4,000.00
122	Store Equipment	12,275.50

	Account	Balance
211	Accounts Payable	$10,475.50
511	Purchases	52,000.00
511.1	Purchases Returns and Allowances	4,100.00
511.2	Purchases Discounts	1,750.00
512	Freight In	1,490.00
613	Rent Expense	7,200.00

3. Record the July transactions in a one-column purchases journal (as shown in Figure 7-5), a cash payments journal (as shown in Figure 7-11), and a general journal. Post to the accounts payable ledger after each entry.

4. Total the special journals. Make all individual postings from the cash payments journal and the general journal to the general ledger. Then post the column totals from the special journals.

5. Prepare a schedule of accounts payable and compare the total with the balance of the Accounts Payable controlling account.

CHALLENGE PROBLEMS

PROBLEM SOLVING

Bob Kessler recently completed a course in college accounting and accepted a job as accounting clerk at Handy Hardware. During Bob's first four weeks on the job, he worked under the careful supervision of the company's accountant. Bob is now through his training period and has assumed the responsibility of recording all purchases, returns, and payments. He is also responsible for posting to the accounts payable ledger and to the general ledger.

During April 20X2, Bob's first month of working independently, he had very little trouble with day-to-day purchases, returns, and payments. The following transactions, however, did require Bob to consult the accountant for help:

20X2

Apr. 12 Paid a $7,000 invoice for office equipment that was purchased from the Lowe Company on April 2 with terms of 2/10,n/30.

15 Discovered that $5,500 worth of lumber that had been purchased on April 4 was of the wrong grade. The purchase carried terms of 3/10, n/30, and payment had been made on April 14 in time to take advantage of the cash discount. The supplier was notified of the error and immediately issued a cash refund.

16 Received a credit memorandum from Lang Company for a defect in store equipment, $95.

18 Discovered that a $99 freight charge on office equipment had been recorded in the Freight In account.

21 Paid an invoice for merchandise that had been purchased on April 11 from the Todd Company. The merchandise was listed for $7,000, but carried a 20% trade discount and terms of 2/10,n/30.

25 Discovered that $4,000 worth of merchandise that had been fully paid for was of inferior quality. Instead of giving a cash refund, the supplier, Tanglewood Products Company, gave Handy Hardware credit against future purchases.

30 When preparing a schedule of accounts payable, Bob discovered that a $700 credit purchase from B. Merrill Company had been posted in the accounts payable ledger to the account of Merrill Supply Company. The entry was journalized correctly and had been posted correctly to the general ledger.

Directions: Assume that you are the accountant. Prepare the general journal entries needed to record each of these situations.

COMMUNICATIONS

In earlier chapters, you learned that the accuracy of posting is checked by preparing a trial balance. That rule seems to have changed in this chapter, as you have learned that the accuracy of posting is checked by preparing a schedule of accounts payable.

Write an explanation of this seeming contradiction. Discuss why it is not a contradiction at all.

ETHICS

Art's Department Store is a successful small retail firm. The company is well managed and seems to have a good accounting system. In fact, the head bookkeeper takes advantage of all cash discounts even when bills are paid after the last date for discount. Art Hall, the owner, has started to investigate the bill-paying practice after receiving complaints from two creditors that they had been paid a couple of days after the cash discount date. Art discovers that it has been common practice to take these discounts late.

Write a brief paragraph explaining what Art should say to the head bookkeeper about this practice.

ANSWERS TO REVIEW QUIZZES

REVIEW QUIZ 7-1

(a) $1,176.00
(b) $784.00
(c) $900.00
(d) $960.40
(e) $400.00

REVIEW QUIZ 7-2

	20X2						
1	Mar.	1	Supplies	4 0 0 00			1
2			Cash		4 0 0 00		2
3							3
4		5	Equipment	9 0 0 00			4
5			Accounts Payable—E & H Co.		9 0 0 00		5
6							6
7		8	Purchases	1 2 0 0 00			7
8			Accounts Payable—C. Medlin Co.		1 2 0 0 00		8
9							9
10		18	Purchases	3 0 0 00			10
11			Cash		3 0 0 00		11
12							12
13		25	Supplies	2 5 0 00			13
14			Cash		2 5 0 00		14

REVIEW QUIZ 7-3

		Date		Invoice No.	Account Credited	P.R.	Purchases Dr. Accts. Pay. Cr.	
			Purchases Journal				**Page 1**	
1	20X8 May	12		48	Tower Auction		12 4 0 0 00	1
2		20		49	Tower Auction		57 3 0 0 00	2
3		28		50	Tower Auction		60 0 0 0 00	3
4		30		51	Burr Motors		45 0 0 0 00	4
5		30		52	Clyde Wright		11 2 0 0 00	5
6		30			Total		185 9 0 0 00	6

		Date		Account Title		Debit	Credit	
			General Journal				**Page 1**	
1	20X8 May	2	Office Supplies			2 0 0 00		1
2				Accounts Payable—Ace Suppliers			2 0 0 00	2
3								3
4		8	Office Equipment			8 0 0 00		4
5				Accounts Payable—Ace Suppliers			8 0 0 00	5
6								6
7		18	Office Equipment			4 5 0 0 00		7
8				Accounts Payable—King Co.			4 5 0 0 00	8

REVIEW QUIZ 7-4

		Date		Account Title		Debit	Credit	
1	20X9 Jun.	5	Office Supplies			3 0 0 00		1
2				Accounts Payable—B. Spence Suppliers			3 0 0 00	2
3								3
4		9	Purchases			8 0 0 00		4
5				Cash			8 0 0 00	5
6								6
7		15	Purchases			1 2 0 0 00		7
8				Accounts Payable—Wilks Co.			1 2 0 0 00	8
9								9
10		16	Accounts Payable—B. Spence Suppliers			3 0 00		10
11				Office Supplies			3 0 00	11
12								12
13		21	Accounts Payable—Wilks Co.			2 0 0 00		13
14				Purchases Returns and Allowances			2 0 0 00	14

ACCOUNTING

FOR A

MERCHANDISING

BUSINESS

Sales and Cash Receipts

LEARNING OBJECTIVES

After studying Chapter 8, you will be able to:
1. Describe procedures and forms used in selling merchandise.
2. Record sales of merchandise in a sales journal and post to the general ledger and the accounts receivable ledger.
3. Record sales returns and allowances.
4. Record sales discounts.
5. Record cash receipts in a cash receipts journal and post to the general ledger and the accounts receivable ledger.
6. Prepare a schedule of accounts receivable.
7. Record credit card sales.

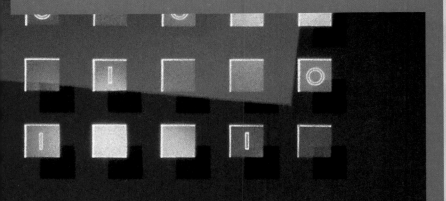

In the last chapter, you learned that a merchandising business engages in repetitive transactions for buying and selling goods. You also learned to record transactions in special journals for buying goods and making cash payments.

Now you will learn to record transactions for the sale of merchandise and cash receipts in two more special journals—the sales journal and the cash receipts journal. In addition to learning to record in these two journals, you will learn to maintain records for credit customers in the accounts receivable subsidiary ledger.

The sales journal is used to record credit sales. Remember, a credit sale is a transaction that requires you to debit Accounts Receivable and to credit Sales. All transactions that require you to debit Cash (incoming cash) are recorded in the cash receipts journal.

— Janice H. Kelly, CPA
St. Louis Community College at Forest Park

In Chapter 7, we started our study of merchandising by examining purchases and cash payments. We learned how to use two special journals and how to post to two separate ledgers. In Chapter 8, our study of merchandising will continue as we look at sales of merchandise and cash receipts. We will work with two more special journals—one for sales of merchandise and one for cash receipts. And we will work with another subsidiary ledger, one designed for the accounts of credit customers.

SALES ACTIVITY

Just as merchandising businesses follow certain procedures to process and record purchases, they follow certain procedures to process and record sales. The exact forms and procedures used for sales transactions depend on the type and size of the business. A small retail business may only use cash register tapes as source documents for recording sales; large retail and wholesale businesses may use very precise forms and follow very precise steps to process and record merchandise sales. To explore further, let's look at some of the procedures used by many businesses to record and process sales of merchandise.

Terms of Payment

The buyer and the seller should always have a definite understanding concerning the terms of payment for merchandise. Some businesses sell only on a cash basis. In such cases, no credit is allowed, and the terms of the sale are *cash* or *net cash*. Other businesses offer **credit terms** that allow customers a certain period of time (the **credit period**) in which to make payment.

Many retailers, for example, sell goods on **revolving charge plans** that allow customers to pay a percentage of their account plus finance charges on a monthly basis. Many manufacturing businesses and wholesalers sell on 30 days' credit. As we learned in Chapter 7, such credit terms are said to be n/30 (net thirty), which means that the invoice price of goods must be paid within 30 days of the date on the invoice.

Another common credit term is *n/EOM*, which means that payment for goods must be made by the end of the month in which the credit purchase was made. As we discussed in Chapter 7, some businesses offer credit terms that allow cash discounts if goods are paid for well in advance of the final date for payment (such as 10 days from the date of the invoice). Look at Figure 8-1 to review common payment terms.

FIGURE 8-1
Common payment terms

Net cash	No credit is allowed by the seller. Payment must be made by the buyer at the time of purchase.
n/30	The amount of an invoice must be paid within 30 days of the date of the invoice.
2/10,n/30	A discount of 2% is allowed if an invoice is paid within 10 days of the date of the invoice. If payment is not made within 10 days, the total must be paid within 30 days of the date of the invoice.
n/EOM	Payment for goods must be made by the end of the month in which the goods were purchased.
C.O.D.	*Cash on delivery.* Under these terms, payment for goods must be made when goods are delivered to the buyer.
FOB shipping point	*Free on board shipping point.* Under these terms, the buyer is responsible for all freight charges from the point of shipment to the point of destination.
FOB destination point	*Free on board destination.* Under these terms, the seller is responsible for freight charges to the point of destination.

Procedures for Credit Sales

LEARNING OBJECTIVE 1

Sales on credit start in one of two ways: (1) receipt of a purchase order from a customer, or (2) preparation of a **sales order** by one of the firm's salespersons. Actually, it is a common practice to write up a sales order in all cases, even after receipt of a purchase order. The sales order serves as an additional record of the sale and identifies the salesperson who handled the sale. The sales order in Figure 8-2 was prepared by Lakeside Electronics upon receipt of a purchase order for two televisions from Andy's Motel on November 2, 20X1.

FIGURE 8-2
Sales order

Sales Order
No.: __710__

Purchase Order No.: __199__   Date: __November 2, 20X1__
Ship to: __Andy's Motel__   Salesperson: __J. Diaz__
         __61 Front Street__   Ship Via: __Truck__
         __Riverside, CA 92502__

Quantity	Description
1	19-inch color, Model No. 12-24457
1	25-inch color, Model No. 12-28378

By: __R.S.__

A copy of the sales order is sent to the credit department for approval. Once approved, it is sent to the billing department, where the **sales invoice** is prepared. Sales invoices are prepared with several copies. One copy is sent to the customer, and another copy is sent to the accounting department to use as a source document for recording the sale. Also, copies are usually sent to the credit department and the shipping department. Figure 8-3 shows how Lakeside Electronics distributes copies of the sales invoice.

FIGURE 8-3
*Distribution of sales
invoice copies*

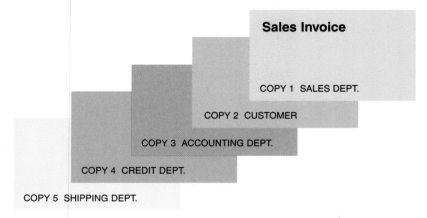

Now, let's look at an example of a sales invoice. The sales invoice prepared when Lakeside Electronics received the order from Andy's Motel on November 2 is shown in Figure 8-4. Shortly, we will use a copy of this invoice to record the credit sale. But first, we need to discuss the procedures for cash sales.

FIGURE 8-4
Sales invoice

Lakeside Electronics
1200 San Palo Road
Los Angeles, CA 90099

Invoice

No.: __277__

Ship to: **Andy's Motel**

61 Front Street

Riverside, CA 92502

Date: __November 2, 20X1__

Order No.: __199__

Shipped by: **Truck**

Terms: __2/10,n/30__

Quantity	Description	Unit Price	Amount
1	19-inch color, Model No. 12-24457	$175.00	$175.00
1	25-inch color, Model No. 12-28378	275.00	275.00
	Total		$450.00

Procedures for Cash Sales

Cash sales are handled in a slightly different manner than credit sales. A commonly used form for cash sales is the **sales ticket** or **sales slip**, which is a form prepared by the seller at the time of sale. A sample sales ticket is shown in Figure 8-5.

A copy of the sales ticket is given to the customer. Another copy is kept in the department that made the sale. And a third copy is sent to the accounting department as a source document for recording the sale.

A variation of the sales ticket is the **cash register tape**. A firm may ring up all cash sales on a cash register. At the end of each day, the register is totaled, and the total of the tape serves as the source document for later journal entries.

Businesses with many cash sales, such as grocery stores and department stores, often use electronic cash registers. Electronic cash registers are on-line with the firm's computer. That is, there is direct communication between the cash register and the firm's computer system. Sales rung up by sales clerks provide the information for the computer to update the firm's accounting records.

FIGURE 8-5
Sales ticket

MERRITT *TV* SALES				
Manchester, NH 03104				
Date: *1-21-XX*			No.: *1280*	
Sold to: *C. Wilson*				
114 West Street				
Hartford, CT				

Quantity	Description		Unit Price	Amount
2	*T.V. Stands*		*$15.00*	*$30.00*
1	*Aerial*		*40.00*	*40.00*
	Total			*$70.00*

RECORDING SALES OF MERCHANDISE

LEARNING OBJECTIVE 2

A sale of merchandise causes an increase in revenue, which increases owner's equity. In earlier chapters, you learned how to record revenue earned from services performed for cash. We used account titles such as Service Revenue and Fees Earned to make journal entries such as the following:

	20XX							
1	May	1	Cash	111	8 0 0 00			1
2			Service Revenue	411			8 0 0 00	2
3			Performed services for cash.					3

In this chapter, you will learn how to record sales of merchandise for cash and on credit, using a revenue account entitled Sales. The **Sales account**, like all revenue accounts, is a temporary account with a normal credit balance. The Sales account is used only to record sales of merchandise. It can be illustrated as follows:

Sales	411
Debit	Credit
–	+
	To record the price of merchandise sold to customers.

Recording Sales in General Journal Form

CASH SALES

A cash sale of merchandise is recorded by debiting the Cash account and crediting the Sales account. For example, refer to the sales ticket for Merritt TV (Figure 8-5). The following general journal entry can be made to record Merritt's cash sale.

	20XX							
1	Jan.	21	Cash		7 0 00			1
2			Sales			7 0 00		2
3			Sold merchandise for cash.					3

CREDIT SALES

Credit sales of merchandise are recorded by debiting the Accounts Receivable account and crediting the Sales account. **Accounts Receivable** is an asset account that shows the total dollar amount due from credit customers. To illustrate, let's look again at the invoice in Figure 8-4 that Lakeside Electronics prepared when an order was received from Andy's Motel. Lakeside can record the sale in general journal form as follows:

	20X1							
1	Nov.	2	Accounts Receivable—Andy's Motel	/	4 5 0 00			1
2			Sales			4 5 0 00		2
3			Sold merchandise on credit.					3

REVIEW QUIZ 8-1

Record the following sales in general journal form:

(a) Sold merchandise for cash, $400.
(b) Sold merchandise on account, $1,200.
(c) Sold equipment (at cost) that was no longer needed by the business, $800.
(d) Sold supplies at cost to a competitor, $200.

CHECK YOUR ANSWERS ON PAGE 313.

Recording Sales in a Sales Journal

To more efficiently record a large volume of credit sales, many businesses use a sales journal. The **sales journal** is a special journal used only to record credit sales of merchandise.

As with any special journal, the design of the sales journal is tailored to the needs of the business using it. Lakeside Electronics uses the sales journal shown in Figure 8-6, which is a common form.

Notice that the sales journal has only one money column, entitled *Accounts Receivable Dr.* and *Sales Cr.* One money column is enough, as all credit sales of merchandise involve a debit to the Accounts Receivable account and a credit to the Sales account.

Only credit sales of merchandise are recorded in the sales journal.

Lakeside's sales journal also has the standard Date and P.R. columns. Additionally, an Invoice No. column is included for writing the number of the sale, and a column entitled Customer's Name is used for identifying credit customers.

To illustrate the use of the sales journal, let's look at Lakeside's credit sales for the month of November, 20X1:

20X1
Nov. 2 Sold two TVs to Andy's Motel, $450.
       8 Sold 40 TVs to Champ's TV Sales, $7,290.
       9 Sold four aerials to Larry's Pub, $160.
      14 Sold 25 AM radios to Dawson's TV and Appliance Co., $261.
      18 Sold various electronic toys to Toyland, $2,400.
      24 Sold 14 AM/FM radios to Andy's Motel, $400.

Each of the above credit sales, starting with Invoice No. 277, is recorded in the sales journal in Figure 8-6. Notice the ease of recording compared to recording sales in general journal form.

FIGURE 8-6
Sales journal

	Date		Invoice No.	Customer's Name	P.R.	Accts. Rec. Dr. Sales Cr.	
1	20X1 Nov.	2	277	Andy's Motel		450 00	1
2		8	278	Champ's TV Sales		7 290 00	2
3		9	279	Larry's Pub		160 00	3
4		14	280	Dawson's TV and Appliance Co.		261 00	4
5		18	281	Toyland		2 400 00	5
6		24	282	Andy's Motel		400 00	6
7		30		Total		10 961 00	7

Sales Journal — Page 14

THE ACCOUNTS RECEIVABLE LEDGER

In Chapter 7, you learned that businesses with many creditors often set up a separate account for each creditor in an accounts payable subsidiary ledger. Individual balances of creditors' accounts in the accounts payable ledger are summarized by the Accounts Payable controlling account, which remains in the general ledger. Along the same line of reasoning, businesses with many credit customers often set up an account for each customer in an **accounts receivable ledger**, or a **customers' ledger**.

The accounts receivable ledger is also a subsidiary ledger and has a controlling account—the Accounts Receivable account. Thus, the balance owed to a business by *each* credit customer is shown in the accounts receivable ledger; and the *total* amount owed by all credit customers is shown in the Accounts Receivable account.

As in the accounts payable ledger, accounts in the accounts receivable ledger are arranged in alphabetical order to make it easier to add new accounts and remove inactive accounts. Since the Accounts Receivable account is an asset with a normal debit balance, customers' accounts in the accounts receivable ledger will—with rare exceptions—have *debit* balances.

POSTING FROM THE SALES JOURNAL

The process of posting special journals is a familiar one to you. In Chapter 7, you learned how to post from the purchases journal and from the cash payments journal to both the accounts payable ledger and the general ledger. Posting the sales journal follows the same procedure. To review, let's look at how Lakeside's November sales journal is posted.

Posting to the Accounts Receivable Ledger

Each entry in the sales journal is posted separately to the accounts receivable ledger. To maintain current and up-to-date balances in customers' accounts, posting is usually done on a daily basis. Having current balances is helpful when answering customer inquiries, considering requests for additional credit, and sending out statements.

To illustrate posting to the accounts receivable ledger, the account of Andy's Motel is posted as shown in Figure 8-7.

FIGURE 8-7

Posting an entry from the sales journal to the accounts receivable ledger

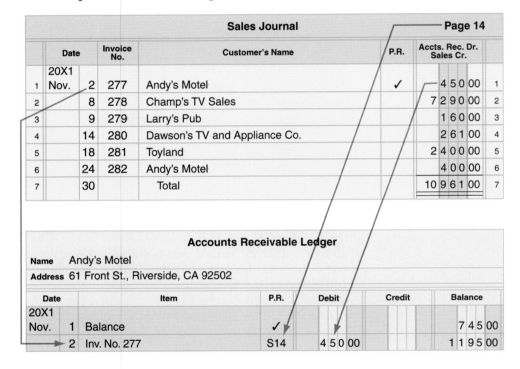

As you have already learned, a check mark (✓) is entered in the P.R. column of the sales journal to indicate that a separate posting has been made. To complete the cross-reference, the code S14 (*Sales journal, page 14*), is entered in the P.R. column of the Andy's Motel account. Other customers' accounts are posted in the same way.

Posting to the General Ledger

At the end of each month, the money column of the sales journal is totaled, and the total is posted twice: (1) as a debit to the Accounts Receivable account and (2) as a credit to the Sales account. The account numbers of these accounts are then written in parentheses directly below the column total. To complete the cross-reference, the code S14 is entered in the P.R. column of the respective accounts. This procedure is shown in Figure 8-8.

FIGURE 8-8

Posting from the sales journal to the general ledger

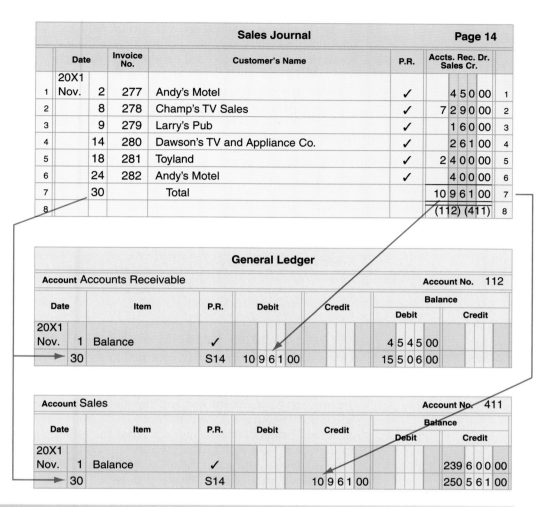

Sales Journal — **Page 14**

	Date		Invoice No.	Customer's Name	P.R.	Accts. Rec. Dr. Sales Cr.	
1	20X1 Nov.	2	277	Andy's Motel	✓	4 5 0 00	1
2		8	278	Champ's TV Sales	✓	7 2 9 0 00	2
3		9	279	Larry's Pub	✓	1 6 0 00	3
4		14	280	Dawson's TV and Appliance Co.	✓	2 6 1 00	4
5		18	281	Toyland	✓	2 4 0 0 00	5
6		24	282	Andy's Motel	✓	4 0 0 00	6
7		30		Total		10 9 6 1 00	7
8						(112) (411)	8

General Ledger

Account Accounts Receivable — **Account No.** 112

Date	Item	P.R.	Debit	Credit	Balance Debit	Balance Credit
20X1 Nov. 1	Balance	✓			4 5 4 5 00	
30		S14	10 9 6 1 00		15 5 0 6 00	

Account Sales — **Account No.** 411

Date	Item	P.R.	Debit	Credit	Balance Debit	Balance Credit
20X1 Nov. 1	Balance	✓				239 6 0 0 00
30		S14		10 9 6 1 00		250 5 6 1 00

REVIEW QUIZ 8-2

The following sales on account were made by Bob Hiller during May 20X5:

20X5
May 1 Sold merchandise on account to Bill French, $300; Invoice No. 1.
　　3 Sold merchandise for cash to David Mack, $500.
　　8 Sold merchandise on account to Lee Smith, $800; Invoice No. 2.
　　12 Sold merchandise for cash to Betty Carson, $670.
　　18 Sold merchandise on account to Leah King, $590; Invoice No. 3.
　　25 Sold store equipment at cost, $4,000.
　　30 Sold merchandise on account to Charles Swift, $500; Invoice No. 4.

Record these sales in a sales journal and a two-column general journal. Then total the sales journal.

CHECK YOUR ANSWERS ON PAGE 313.

SALES RETURNS AND ALLOWANCES

In Chapter 7, we discussed merchandise returns and allowances from the standpoint of the purchaser. We learned that a *return* results when a buyer returns part, or all, of a purchase to the seller. An *allowance* results when a buyer decides to keep damaged or defective goods, but at a reduction from the original price.

On the books of the seller, a return or allowance is recorded as a reduction in sales revenue. Since the Sales account normally has a credit balance, returns and allowances could be recorded on the debit side (the reduction side) of the Sales account. To provide a better record, however, returns and allowances are often recorded in a separate account entitled Sales Returns and Allowances.

Sales Returns and Allowances is a contra revenue account. It thus has a debit balance that is opposite the credit balance of the Sales account. This can be illustrated as follows:

Sales Returns and Allowances 411.1		Sales	411
Debit	**Credit**	**Debit**	**Credit**
+	−	−	+
To record returns from and allowances to customers.			To record the price of merchandise sold to customers.

Contra

Recording Sales Returns and Allowances

LEARNING OBJECTIVE 3

Goods sold on credit are often returned to the seller with the understanding that the customer's account will be credited (reduced) by the amount of the return. The seller usually issues a **credit memorandum** to the customer which shows the amount of credit granted and the reason for the return. On the books of the seller, the customer's Accounts Receivable account has a *debit* balance. Thus, the term *credit* memorandum indicates that the seller has decreased the customer's account and does not expect payment. (Recall from Chapter 7 that the buyer often requests credit from the seller by issuing a *debit memorandum*.)

To illustrate, Lakeside Electronics issued the credit memorandum shown in Figure 8-9 to Champ's TV Sales for the return of a 19-inch color television that proved to be defective.

FIGURE 8-9
Credit memorandum

This credit memorandum serves as a source document for the following general journal entry.

	20X1														
1	Dec.	4	Sales Returns and Allowances	411.1		3	8	9	00						1
2			Accounts Rec.—Champ's TV Sales	112/✓							3	8	9	00	2
3			Granted credit to a customer.												3

The credit part of this entry involves both a controlling account (Accounts Receivable) in the general ledger and a customer's account (Champ's TV Sales) in the accounts receivable subsidiary ledger. As we have learned, debits or credits to a controlling account require a dual posting to the controlling account in the general ledger and to the customer's account in the accounts receivable ledger. To indicate that this dual posting is necessary, a diagonal line is drawn in the P.R. column of the journal at the time the journal entry is made.

When the above entry was posted to the accounts receivable ledger, a small check mark (✓) was made to the right of the diagonal line. When posting was made to the Accounts Receivable controlling account, the account number of Accounts Receivable (112) was written to the left of the diagonal line.

If a cash refund is made because of a sales return or allowance, the Sales Returns and Allowances account is debited and the Cash account is credited. Cash refunds are recorded in the cash payments journal.

REVIEW QUIZ 8-3

In general journal form, record the following transactions for Vivian Carney International:

(a) Sold merchandise on account to Camp Company, $800.
(b) Issued a credit memorandum for $200 to Camp Company for merchandise damaged while in transit.
(c) Issued a cash refund to Rossi and Sons, $400.
(d) Received the balance of Camp Company's account.

CHECK YOUR ANSWERS ON PAGE 314.

SALES DISCOUNTS

We have learned that a cash discount is offered by a seller to encourage a buyer to make prompt payment for a credit purchase. We have also learned that a common form of cash discount is 2/10,n/30. In Chapter 7, we recorded cash discounts as purchases discounts on the books of the buyer. In this chapter, we are concerned with cash discounts as they affect the seller of merchandise.

For the seller, a cash discount is referred to as a **sales discount** and is recorded as a reduction in sales revenue. Sales discounts could thus be recorded on the debit side (the reduction side) of the Sales account. To provide a separate record, however, sales discounts are usually recorded in a contra revenue account entitled **Sales Discounts**. The Sales Discounts account can be illustrated as follows:

Sales Discounts	411.2
Debit	Credit
+	−
To record cash discounts granted to credit customers for prompt payment.	

The Sales Discounts account is a contra revenue account with a normal debit balance. The amount of a sales discount is not recorded until payment is received from a customer.

Recording Sales Discounts

To illustrate recording a sales discount, let's look at one of Lakeside's credit sales during November 20X1. On November 2, Lakeside issued Invoice No. 277 to Andy's Motel for the sale of two TVs for $450, with terms of 2/10,n/30. If Andy's Motel pays the invoice within 10 days (by November 12), $9 of the invoice price (.02 × $450 = $9) can be deducted, and the difference, $441, can be remitted to Lakeside Electronics in full settlement of the debt. To record the cash receipt, Lakeside will debit the Cash account for the actual amount of cash received, $441; debit the Sales Discounts account for the amount of discount granted, $9; and credit Accounts Receivable and the customer's account for the full invoice amount of $450. This entry is illustrated below in general journal form.

	20X1															
1	Nov.	12	Cash					4 4 1	00							1
2			Sales Discounts					9	00							2
3			Accounts Receivable—Andy's Motel	/							4 5 0	00				3
4			Received cash on account.													4

It should be stressed that even though the invoice price of the goods is $450, the receipt of a $441 payment within 10 days completely settles the debt because the customer complied with the terms of payment (2/10,n/30). Thus, the customer's account is credited for the full amount, $450.

On June 10, 20X2, Langford Company purchased goods costing $8,000 from Rodriguez Company. The terms of payment were 3/10,n/30. Langford made payment on June 19, 20X2. In general journal form, record the following transactions:

(a) The purchase and cash payment by Langford Company.
(b) The sale and cash receipt by Rodriguez Company.

CHECK YOUR ANSWERS ON PAGE 314.

RECORDING CASH RECEIPTS

In a merchandising business, cash is received from cash sales, collections on account from credit customers, and various other sources. Lakeside Electronics' cash receipts for November 20X1 are as follows:

20X1
Nov. 4 Received $730.10 from Andy's Motel for the previous balance owed, $745, less 2% discount.
   5 Received $200 on account from Larry's Pub, no discount.
   8 As an accommodation, sold store supplies at cost to a competitor, $50.
   9 Received $2,254 from Dawson's TV and Appliance Co. for the balance owed, $2,300, less 2% discount.
 12 Received $441 from Andy's Motel for the balance owed, $450, less 2% discount.
 15 Recorded cash sales for the first half of the month, $4,910.
 21 Received an $800 cash refund for the return of merchandise that proved to be defective.
 24 Received $700 from Larry's Pub for the balance owed, no discount.
 30 Recorded cash sales for the second half of the month, $5,140.

Cash Receipts Journal

All transactions that increase the amount of cash are recorded in a special journal called the **cash receipts journal**. The source documents for entries in the cash receipts journal are checks received, cash register tapes, and sales tickets.

Because the cash receipts journal is designed to record all receipts of cash, it must contain a *Cash Dr.* column. The number and title of other special columns are determined by the accounts most often affected by cash receipts. Lakeside Electronics uses a cash receipts journal (Figure 8-10) that, in addition to a Cash Dr. column, has special columns for *Sales Discounts Dr.*, *Accounts Receivable Cr.*, and *Sales Cr.* A *General Cr.* column is also included for making credits to accounts for which no special column is provided.

To illustrate the use of a cash receipts journal, let's look again at Lakeside's November cash receipts (page 278). These receipts are recorded in the cash receipts journal shown in Figure 8-10.

FIGURE 8-10
Cash receipts journal

	Date		Account Credited	P.R.	General Cr.	Sales Cr.	Accounts Rec. Cr.	Sales Discounts Dr.	Cash Dr.	
	20X1									
1	Nov.	4	Andy's Motel				7 45 00	14 90	7 30 10	1
2		5	Larry's Pub				2 00 00		2 00 00	2
3		8	Store Supplies		50 00				50 00	3
4		9	Dawson's TV and Appl.				2 3 00 00	46 00	2 2 54 00	4
5		12	Andy's Motel				4 50 00	9 00	4 41 00	5
6		15	Cash Sales			4 9 10 00			4 9 10 00	6
7		21	Purch. Ret. and Allow.		8 00 00				8 00 00	7
8		24	Larry's Pub				7 00 00		7 00 00	8
9		30	Cash Sales			5 1 40 00			5 1 40 00	9
10		30	Totals		8 50 00	10 0 50 00	4 3 95 00	69 90	15 2 25 10	10

Posting the Cash Receipts Journal

Three types of postings are made from the cash receipts journal:

1. Amounts appearing in the Accounts Receivable Cr. column are posted separately to the subsidiary ledger accounts of the customers who made the payments. As we have seen, posting is usually made to the subsidiary ledger on a daily basis.
2. Amounts in the General Cr. column are posted separately to the general ledger accounts identified in the Account Credited column. For example, on November 8, the Store Supplies account was credited for $50. Since there is no special column for credits to Store Supplies, the credit was entered in the General Cr. column. Thus, a $50 credit posting must be made to the Store Supplies account. Such a posting can be made on a daily, weekly, or monthly basis.
3. Special column totals are posted to the general ledger at the end of the month.

Now let's look at Figure 8-11, which shows how the cash receipts journal is posted.

Accounting for a Merchandising Business

FIGURE 8-11
*Posting the cash
receipts journal*

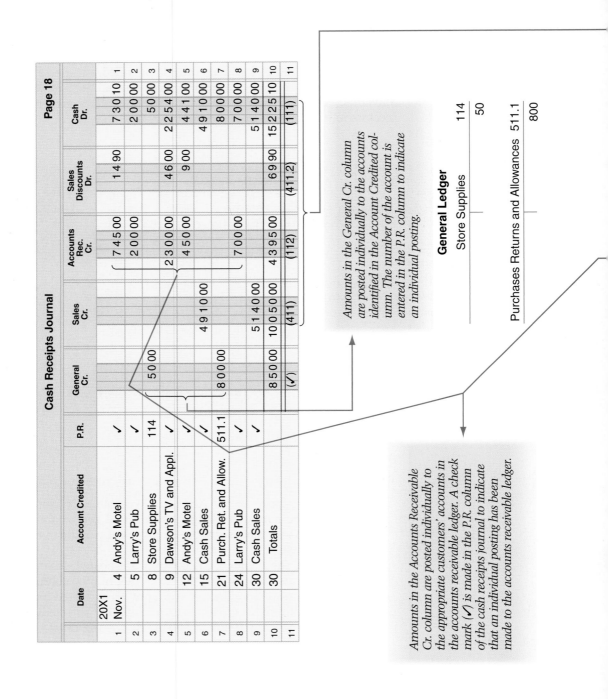

Cash Receipts Journal Page 18

Date		Account Credited	P.R.	General Cr.	Sales Cr.	Accounts Rec. Cr.	Sales Discounts Dr.	Cash Dr.	
20X1									
Nov.	4	Andy's Motel	✓			7 4 5 00	1 4 90	7 3 0 10	1
	5	Larry's Pub	✓			2 0 0 00		2 0 0 00	2
	8	Store Supplies	114	5 0 00				5 0 00	3
	9	Dawson's TV and Appl.	✓			2 3 0 0 00	4 6 00	2 2 5 4 00	4
	12	Andy's Motel	✓			4 5 0 00	9 00	4 4 1 00	5
	15	Cash Sales	✓		4 9 1 0 00			4 9 1 0 00	6
	21	Purch. Ret. and Allow.	511.1	8 0 0 00				8 0 0 00	7
	24	Larry's Pub	✓			7 0 0 00		7 0 0 00	8
	30	Cash Sales	✓		5 1 4 0 00			5 1 4 0 00	9
	30	Totals		8 5 0 00	1 0 0 5 0 00	4 3 9 5 00	6 9 90	1 5 2 2 5 10	10
				(✓)	(411)	(112)	(411.2)	(111)	11

Amounts in the General Cr. column are posted individually to the accounts identified in the Account Credited column. The number of the account is entered in the P.R. column to indicate an individual posting.

Amounts in the Accounts Receivable Cr. column are posted individually to the appropriate customers' accounts in the accounts receivable ledger. A check mark (✓) is made in the P.R. column of the cash receipts journal to indicate that an individual posting has been made to the accounts receivable ledger.

General Ledger

Store Supplies   114

50

Purchases Returns and Allowances 511.1

800

Accounts Receivable Ledger

Name Andy's Motel

Date		Item	P.R.	Debit	Credit	Balance
20X1 Nov.	1	Balance	✓			745 00
	2	Inv. No. 277	S14	450 00		1195 00
	4		CR18		745 00	450 00
	12		CR18		450 00	—
	24	Inv. No. 282	S14	400 00		400 00

Name Dawson's TV and Appliance

Date		Item	P.R.	Debit	Credit	Balance
20X1 Nov.	1	Balance	✓			2300 00
	9		CR18		2300 00	—
	14	Inv. No. 280	S14	261 00		261 00

Name Larry's Pub

Date		Item	P.R.	Debit	Credit	Balance
20X1 Nov.	1	Balance	✓			900 00
	5		CR18		200 00	700 00
	9	Inv. No. 279	S14	160 00		860 00
	24		CR18		700 00	160 00

Special column totals are posted to the general ledger at the end of the month. The account number of the account is written directly under the column total.

General Ledger

Cash	111
15,225.10	

Sales Discounts	411.2
69.90	

Accounts Receivable	112
	4,395.00

Sales	411
	10,050.00

REVIEW QUIZ
8-5

Referring to the cash receipts journal used by Lakeside Electronics, identify the meaning of the check marks located in each of the following positions: (a) under the General Cr. column total; (b) in the P.R. column on the line on which a customer's account is credited; (c) in the P.R. column on the line on which the Sales account is credited (on November 30).

CHECK YOUR ANSWERS ON PAGE 314.

SCHEDULE OF ACCOUNTS RECEIVABLE

LEARNING OBJECTIVE 6

After all posting has been completed, the posting accuracy of the accounts receivable ledger is checked by preparing a **schedule of accounts receivable**. The total of the schedule is then compared with the balance of the Accounts Receivable controlling account in the general ledger.

Lakeside Electronics' complete accounts receivable ledger is shown in Figure 8-12. The balance of each customer's account is listed on the schedule of accounts receivable shown in Figure 8-13.

FIGURE 8-12
Lakeside Electronics' complete accounts receivable ledger

Name Andy's Motel
Address 61 Front St., Riverside, CA 92502

Date		Item	P.R.	Debit	Credit	Balance
20X1						
Nov.	1	Balance	✓			7 4 5 00
	2	Inv. No. 277	S14	4 5 0 00		1 1 9 5 00
	4		CR18		7 4 5 00	4 5 0 00
	12		CR18		4 5 0 00	—
	24	Inv. No. 282	S14	4 0 0 00		4 0 0 00

Name Champ's TV Sales
Address 211 Weems Road, Los Angeles, CA 90010

Date		Item	P.R.	Debit	Credit	Balance
20X1						
Nov.	8	Inv. No. 278	S14	7 2 9 0 00		7 2 9 0 00

Name Dawson's TV and Appliance
Address 6111 Nature Trail, Riverside, CA 92506

Date		Item	P.R.	Debit	Credit	Balance
20X1						
Nov.	1	Balance	✓			2 3 0 0 00
	9		CR18		2 3 0 0 00	—
	14	Inv. No. 280	S14	2 6 1 00		2 6 1 00

CONTINUES

FIGURE 8-12
Continued

Name	Larry's Pub					
Address	1136 West 8th, Los Angeles, CA 90017					

Date		Item	P.R.	Debit	Credit	Balance
20X1 Nov.	1	Balance	✓			9 0 0 00
	5		CR18		2 0 0 00	7 0 0 00
	9	Inv. No. 279	S14	1 6 0 00		8 6 0 00
	24		CR18		7 0 0 00	1 6 0 00

Name	Toyland					
Address	2810 Glendale Dr., Los Angeles, CA 90018					

Date		Item	P.R.	Debit	Credit	Balance
20X1 Nov.	1	Balance	✓			6 0 0 00
	18	Inv. No. 281	S14	2 4 0 0 00		3 0 0 0 00

FIGURE 8-13
Schedule of accounts receivable

Lakeside Electronics Schedule of Accounts Receivable November 30, 20X1	
Andy's Motel	4 0 0 00
Champ's TV Sales	7 2 9 0 00
Dawson's TV and Appliance	2 6 1 00
Larry's Pub	1 6 0 00
Toyland	3 0 0 0 00
Total	11 1 1 1 00

The total of the schedule agrees with the balance of the Accounts Receivable controlling account, which is shown fully posted in Figure 8-14.

FIGURE 8-14
Accounts Receivable controlling account with totals posted from sales journal and cash receipts journal at end of month

Account	Accounts Receivable						Account No. 112

Date		Item	P.R.	Debit	Credit	Balance Debit	Balance Credit
20X1 Nov.	1	Balance	✓			4 5 4 5 00	
	30		S14	10 9 6 1 00		15 5 0 6 00	
	30		CR18		4 3 9 5 00	11 1 1 1 00	

ACCOUNTING FOR SALES TAXES

Most state governments and some county and city governments in our country levy a tax on the retail price of goods and services sold. This tax, called a **sales tax**, is collected from customers by the seller and later paid to the appropriate tax official in the state government.

Rates charged for sales taxes range from a low of 3% to a high of 11%, depending on the state. To illustrate how to account for sales taxes, we will use Dave Marris, who owns the Surf-N-Sand Shop, located on Tybee Island, Georgia. The sales tax rate on Tybee Island is 6%. Thus, when Dave recently sold a $200 surfboard, he collected a sales tax of $12 (.06 × $200). Accordingly, the customer paid Dave $212 for a $200 purchase. The following general journal entry records the sale.

1	X	X	Cash			2 1 2	00			1
2			Sales Tax Payable					1 2	00	2
3			Sales					2 0 0	00	3
4			Recorded cash sale.							4

Had this sale been on credit, the entry would be the same, except that the debit would have been to the Accounts Receivable account and the individual customer's account, instead of to the Cash account.

Reporting Sales Taxes Collected

Most states require that sales taxes collected during the month be sent to the appropriate state official by the middle of the following month. To record this, a debit is made to the Sales Tax Payable account (to decrease the merchant's liability for these taxes), and a credit is made to the Cash account.

To illustrate, we will continue with our example of the Surf-N-Sand Shop. During July 20X0, the store had total sales of $60,000. Since the sales tax rate in the area was 6%, $3,600 (.06 × $60,000) in sales taxes were collected on these sales. In Georgia, sales taxes collected one month must be sent to the State Department of Revenue by the 20th day of the next month. Dave Marris, the owner, thus prepared the sales tax report illustrated in Figure 8-15 and made the following entry to record payment of the taxes.

	20X0									
1	Aug.	20	Sales Tax Payable			3 6 0 0	00			1
2			Miscellaneous Income					3 7 5	00	2
3			Cash					3 2 2 5	00	3
4			Recorded cash sale.							4

Notice that Dave was allowed to keep a small percentage of the sales taxes collected as his fee for collecting the taxes and sending them in. He records this fee ($375) as miscellaneous income. Had Dave been in a state that did not allow the merchant keep to a portion of the taxes as a fee, his entry would have been as follows:

	20X0									
1	Aug.	20	Sales Tax Payable			3 6 0 0	00			1
2			Cash					3 6 0 0	00	2
3			Sent in sales taxes for July.							3

Recording Sales Tax in a Sales Journal

As we have seen, credit sales subject to a sales tax can be recorded in a general journal. If the volume of credit sales is large, however, a more efficient use of journalizing and posting time can be made by expanding a one-column sales journal to three columns: (1) Accounts Receivable Dr., (2) Sales Cr., and (3) Sales Tax Payable Cr. The total amount to be received from a sale (selling price plus sales tax) is entered in the Accounts Receivable Dr. column. The amount of the sale is entered in the Sales Cr. column. And the amount of sales tax charged on the sale is entered in the Sales Tax Payable Cr. column.

To illustrate the use of a three-column sales journal, we will use the example of a company other than Lakeside Electronics because Lakeside is a wholesale firm and thus is not required to collect retail sales taxes. The March 20X5 sales journal of Jarvis Gift Shop, a retailer, is presented in Figure 8-16.

FIGURE 8-15
Monthly sales tax report

GEORGIA DEPARTMENT OF REVENUE
SALES AND USE TAX DIVISION
P. O. BOX 105296
ATLANTA, GEORGIA 30348-5296

SEE INSTRUCTIONS FOR PREPARING
THIS REPORT, TAX BULLETIN AND
SALES TAX UPDATE INFORMATION.

0797030111

Surf-N-Sand
1200 Beach Road
Tybee Island, GA

USE BLACK INK ONLY   COMMODITY CODE _____

SALES AND USE TAX REPORT FOR CALENDAR MONTH OR OTHER AUTHORIZED PERIOD OF *July 20X0*

PART I.A.

			TAX RATE	PART I.B. TAX COLUMN
1. Total Sales	60,000.00			☐ EFT Filer
2. Total Use	-0-			☐ AMENDED RETURN (If Applicable)
3. Total Sales and Use	60,000.00			

COMPLETE EXEMPTION WORKSHEET AND ENTER TOTALS BELOW

		TAX RATE	TAX COLUMN
4. Taxable State Sales and Use (Line 3 minus Total State exemption Line A)	60,000.00	X .04 =	2,400.00
5. Taxable State Sales and Use on Motor Fuel (Line 3 minus Total 1% Motor Fuel exemption Line B)	-0-	X .01 =	
6. Taxable 2nd Motor Fuel Sales and Use (Line 3 minus Total 2nd Motor Fuel exemption Line C)	-0-	X .03 =	
7. Taxable MARTA Sales and Use (Fulton & Dekalb Only) (Line 3 minus Total MARTA exemption Line D)	-0-	X .01 =	
8. Taxable Local Option Sales and Use (Line 3 minus Total Local Option exemption Line E)	60,000.00	X .01 =	600.00
9. Taxable Towns County 2nd Local Option Sales and Use (Line 3 minus Total Towns County 2nd L.O. exemption Line F)	60,000.00	X .01 =	600.00
10. Taxable Special Purpose Sales and Use (Line 3 minus Total Special Purpose exemption Line G)	-0-	X .01 =	
11. Taxable Educational Sales and Use (Line 3 minus Total Educational exemption Line H)	-0-	X .01 =	
12. Taxable Homestead Sales and Use (Line 3 minus Total Homestead exemption Line I)	-0-	X .01 =	
13. Total Tax from Tax Column (Lines 4 - 12 of Part I.B.)	3,600.00	← TOTAL	3,600.00

14. Excess Tax: factor amount	+	
15. Total Tax Due		3,600.00
16. Vendor's Compensation. If timely filed and paid (Use Vendor's Compensation Worksheet)	-	375.00
17. Penalty (Use penalty worksheet)	+	
18. Interest (1% per month or fraction thereof)	+	
19. Estimated Tax Paid Last Month	-	
20. Estimated Tax Due This Month	+	
21. Credit Memo	-	
22. Remit This Amount		3,225.00

This return must be filed and paid by the 20th of the month following the period for which the tax is due to avoid loss of vendor's compensation and the payment of penalty and interest. DEALERS AND CONTRACTORS MUST FILE A TIMELY RETURN EVEN THOUGH NO TAX IS DUE. DO NOT SEND CASH BY MAIL.

Remittance by Electronic Funds Transfer (EFT) must be completed by 3:00 p.m. on the 19th. If the 20th is on a Saturday, Sunday, Monday or a Federal Holiday the EFT must be completed before 3:00 p.m., on the preceding Friday.

☐ IF THERE IS ANY CHANGE IN TRADE NAME, ADDRESS, OWNERSHIP OR TELEPHONE NUMBER, CHECK BOX AND INDICATE THE CHANGE IN THE SPACE ON BACK.

STATE USE ONLY
POSTMARK DATE

MONTH	DAY	YEAR

CORR. CODE ☐   REFUND ☐   AGENT CODE ☐

PART II   SCHEDULE OF TOTAL SALES AND USE EXEMPTIONS FROM EXEMPTION WORKSHEET

A. Total State		F. Total Towns County 2nd L/O
B. Total 1% Motor Fuel		G. Total Special Purpose
C. Total 2nd Motor Fuel		H. Total Educational
D. Total MARTA		I. Total Homestead
E. Total Local Option		

PART III   I certify that this return, including the accompanying schedules or statements, has been examined by me and is, to the best of my knowledge and belief, a true and complete return made in good faith for the period stated. This *20th* day of *August* , 20 *X0*

Return Prepared By _____   Signature *David Marris*   *Owner*
Title (Owner, Partner, Corp. Officer)

FIGURE 8-16
*Multicolumn sales
journal*

	Date	Invoice No.	Customer's Name	P.R.	Accounts Receivable Dr.	Sales Cr.	Sales Tax Payable Cr.	
	20X5							
1	Mar. 1	102	Clyde James	✓	3 1 8 00	3 0 0 00	1 8 00	1
2	3	103	Faye Jerrell	✓	7 9 50	7 5 00	4 50	2
3	5	104	Kyle Sharp	✓	1 3 2 50	1 2 5 00	7 50	3
4	9	105	Lisa Chadwick	✓	3 4 45	3 2 50	1 95	4
5	14	106	River Road School	✓	8 4 8 00	8 0 0 00	4 8 00	5
6	17	107	Bill Edwards	✓	1 0 6 00	1 0 0 00	6 00	6
7	25	108	Clyde James	✓	6 8 90	6 5 00	3 90	7
8	31	109	Beth Todd	✓	3 3 0 72	3 1 2 00	1 8 72	8
9	31		Totals		1 9 1 8 07	1 8 0 9 50	1 0 8 57	9
10					(112)	(411)	(212)	10

Notice the account numbers written in parentheses directly below the column totals. This, as you remember, shows that these column totals were posted to the general ledger. The check marks in the P.R. column mean that the individual amounts were posted to customers' accounts in the accounts receivable ledger.

Sales Returns Involving a Sales Tax

If a customer returns merchandise on which a sales tax was charged, the amount of sales tax must also be returned to the customer. To illustrate this, look again at the sales journal of Jarvis Gift Shop. On March 12, Lisa Chadwick returned merchandise she bought on March 9 for $32.50 plus $1.95 sales tax. The following general journal entry was made to record the return.

	20X5						
1	Mar.	12	Sales Returns and Allowances		3 2 50		1
2			Sales Tax Payable		1 95		2
3			Accounts Receivable—Lisa Chadwick	/		3 4 45	3
4			Granted credit to a customer.				4

REVIEW QUIZ
8-6

Willie Loeb is the owner of The Petite Boutique, which is located in a state with a 6% sales tax on the price of retail items. During the first two weeks in August 20X1, Willie had the following sales-related transactions. Record each transaction in general journal form.

20X1
Aug. 1 Sold merchandise for cash, $400.
   4 Sold merchandise on account to Eve Li, $200.
   6 Sold merchandise for cash, $600.
   10 Sold merchandise on account to Max Leatherwood, $1,400.
   12 Max Leatherwood returned $50 worth of merchandise and was given credit for the return.
   15 Paid sales taxes collected in July 20X1, $940.

CHECK YOUR ANSWERS ON PAGE 315.

Each day in this country millions of people use credit cards to purchase goods and services. There are three basic types of credit cards: (1) those issued by banks (referred to as *bank credit cards*), such as VISA and MasterCard; (2) those issued by private companies (referred to as *nonbank cards*), such as American Express and Diners Club; and (3) those issued by department stores and oil companies, such as Sears and Exxon.

Bank Credit Card Sales

Most retail businesses accept bank credit cards. There are a number of reasons for this. First, the bank that issues the card takes the credit application from the user of the card, thus saving the merchant this task. Additionally, a merchant who accepts bank credit cards is able to make immediate bank deposits of credit card receipts, thereby receiving cash quickly. And the bank that issued the card is responsible for collection of the amount due. So, if a customer fails to make payment, the bank—not the merchant—absorbs the loss.

Recording Bank Credit Card Sales

Bank credit card sales are recorded as *cash sales* because credit card receipts can be deposited in a bank immediately. The bank deducts a discount (fee) that ranges from 3% to 7%. The difference between the receipt total and the discount is credited to the depositor's account.

To illustrate, assume that on June 5, 20XX, Jeans & Company sold merchandise for $100, plus $5 sales tax, to Joe Todd, who used his VISA card. The sale was written up by a sales clerk, and Joe was given a copy of the receipt.

This sale turned out to be the only bank credit card sale Jeans & Company made for the day. Therefore, the one receipt was taken to the bank for deposit at the end of the day. The bank that issued the card, National Bank and Trust, charges a discount rate of 4%, which is applied to the receipt total. A discount of $4.20 ($105 × .04) is thus computed by the bank. The difference between the credit card receipt and the discount ($105 – $4.20 = $100.80) is entered in the bank account of Jeans & Company. The discount is recorded in an expense account entitled **Credit Card Expense**. The entry to record the sale is made in general journal form as follows:

	20XX							
1	Jun.	5	Cash	1 0 0 80				1
2			Credit Card Expense	4 20				2
3			Sales			1 0 0 00		3
4			Sales Tax Payable			5 00		4
5			Recorded bank credit card sale.					5

Recording Private Company Credit Card Sales

A sales receipt from a nonbank credit card (such as American Express) generally cannot be deposited in a bank. Instead, the merchant summarizes sales receipts and submits them to the private card company for payment. The private card company, in turn, makes collection from the card user. This type of sale, unlike a bank credit card sale, is not treated as a cash sale; rather, it is recorded as a sale on account. However, the receivables generated by these sales should be kept separate from other receivables, since it is the credit card company—not the merchant—that is responsible for collection. An account entitled **Accounts Receivable—Credit Cards** can be used.

To illustrate recording nonbank credit card sales, let's assume that, in addition to the bank credit card sale we recorded earlier, Jeans & Company sold $500 of merchandise (plus 5% sales tax) and accepted an American Express card in payment. Assuming that American Express charges a 6% discount rate ($525 × .06 = $31.50), the following general journal entry can be made to record the sale.

	20XX					
1	Jun.	5	Accounts Receivable—Credit Cards	4 9 3 50		1
2			Credit Card Expense	3 1 50		2
3			Sales		5 0 0 00	3
4			Sales Tax Payable		2 5 00	4
5			Recorded nonbank credit card sale.			5

If sales of this type are frequent, the sales journal can be designed so that such sales can be recorded more efficiently. Let's look at how this entry would be recorded in a specially designed sales journal.

Sales Journal									
	Date	Sale No.	Customer	P.R.	Accounts Rec. Dr.	Accounts Rec. Credit Cards Dr.	Credit Card Expense Dr.	Sales Cr.	Sales Tax Payable Cr.
1	20XX Jun. 5		American Express			4 9 3 50	3 1 50	5 0 0 00	2 5 00	1

Credit Cards Issued by Businesses

Many large department stores and oil companies—and some airlines—issue their own credit cards. This type of card usually can be used only in outlets of the company that issued the card. Sales from such cards are recorded as regular credit sales, since the company that issues the card does its own billing.

REVIEW QUIZ 8-7

Robert Sterling accepts both bank credit cards and nonbank credit cards in his retail clothing business. The following credit card sales were made on April 8, 20X2. Record each sale in general journal form. Robert's business is located in an area with a 6% sales tax rate.

(a) Sold merchandise, $900, and accepted a VISA card (assume a discount rate of 4%).

(b) Sold merchandise, $400, and accepted a nonbank credit card (assume a discount rate of 5%).

CHECK YOUR ANSWERS ON PAGE 315.

SUMMARY OF JOURNALS AND LEDGERS

In Chapters 7 and 8, you have added four special journals and two subsidiary ledgers to your accounting repertoire. Figure 8-17 summarizes the uses of the four special journals and the general journal, which you learned about previously.

FIGURE 8-17
Summary of journals

Journal	Used for
Purchases	All credit purchases of merchandise
Cash Payments	All payments of cash
Sales	All credit sales of merchandise
Cash Receipts	All receipts of cash
General	All transactions not in a special journal

What kinds of transactions does this leave for the general journal? There are not many, but here is a list of some of them:

1. Credit purchases of items other than merchandise.
2. Credit sales of assets other than merchandise.
3. Owner investments of assets other than cash.
4. Performance of services on credit.
5. Owner withdrawal of assets other than cash.
6. Correcting entries.
7. Adjusting entries.
8. Closing entries.

There are now three ledgers—two subsidiary and one general. The uses of these ledgers are summarized in Figure 8-18.

FIGURE 8-18
Summary of ledgers

Ledger	Used for
Accounts Payable (subsidiary)	Creditors' accounts
Accounts Receivable (subsidiary)	Customers' accounts
General	Financial statement accounts (asset, liability, owner's equity, revenue, cost, and expense) which are listed in the chart of accounts

The general ledger includes two controlling accounts—Accounts Payable and Accounts Receivable—which summarize the balances of the respective subsidiary ledgers.

REVIEW QUIZ
8-8

Identify the journal in which each of the following transactions would be recorded: (a) cash sale of merchandise; (b) credit purchase of equipment; (c) owner withdrawal of cash; (d) credit sale of merchandise; (e) receipt of cash from a customer; (f) adjusting entries; (g) cash sale of supplies; (h) closing entries; (i) cash purchase of merchandise.

CHECK YOUR ANSWERS ON PAGE 315.

HOW CAN I USE MULITMEDIA TO PRESENT INFORMATION?

Whether you are a student or an employee, on some occasions you will need to make a presentation. The best way to get a point across may be to use visual aids.

Multimedia software allows you to combine video, audio, and graphics applications in your presentation. With a projecting system, you can display graphics from the computer onto a screen. If your artistic ability is limited, you can still add graphics to your presentation by using clip art—predrawn, ready-to-use drawings in a wide variety of subjects. Check out the following Web sites:

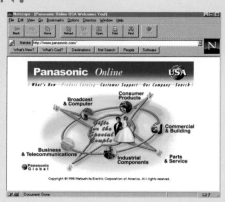

Multimedia Software

Freelance	*http://www.lotus.com/home.nsf/welcome/freelance*
Harvard Graphics	*http://www.spco.com*
PowerPoint	*http://www.microsoft.com/powerpoint/default.asp*

Projecting Systems

Epson	*http://www.epson.com*
Panasonic	*http://www.panasonic.com*
Sony	*http://www.sony.com*

Clip Art

Corel Corp.	*http://www.corel.com*
Nova Development Corp.	*http://www.novadevcorp.com*

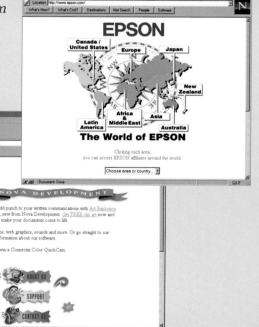

MERCHANDISING TRANSACTIONS

Transaction: On April 3, 20X0, Daughtry Department Store purchased merchandise costing $3,000 on account from Ford Supply Company. Terms of the sale were 2/10,n/30 and payment was made within the discount period.

The Purchaser

On the books of Daughtry Department Store:

	20X0				
1	Apr.	3	Purchases	3 0 0 0 00	1
2			Accounts Payable		3 0 0 0 00	2
3						3

Purchases

Debit	Credit
+	−
Cost of merchandise bought to resell to customers	

	20X0				
1	Apr.	13	Accounts Payable	3 0 0 0 00	1
2			Purchases Discounts		60 00	2
3			Cash		2 9 40 00	3

Purchases Discounts

Debit	Credit
−	+
	Discounts received for prompt payment.

The Seller

On the books of Ford Supply Company:

	20X0				
1	Apr.	3	Accounts Receivable	3 0 0 0 00	1
2			Sales		3 0 0 0 00	2
3						3

Sales

Debit	Credit
−	+
	Price of merchandise sold to customers.

	20X0				
1	Apr.	13	Cash	2 9 40 00	1
2			Sales Discounts	60 00	2
3			Accounts Receivable		3 0 0 0 00	3

Sales Discounts

Debit	Credit
+	−
Discounts given to customers for prompt payment.	

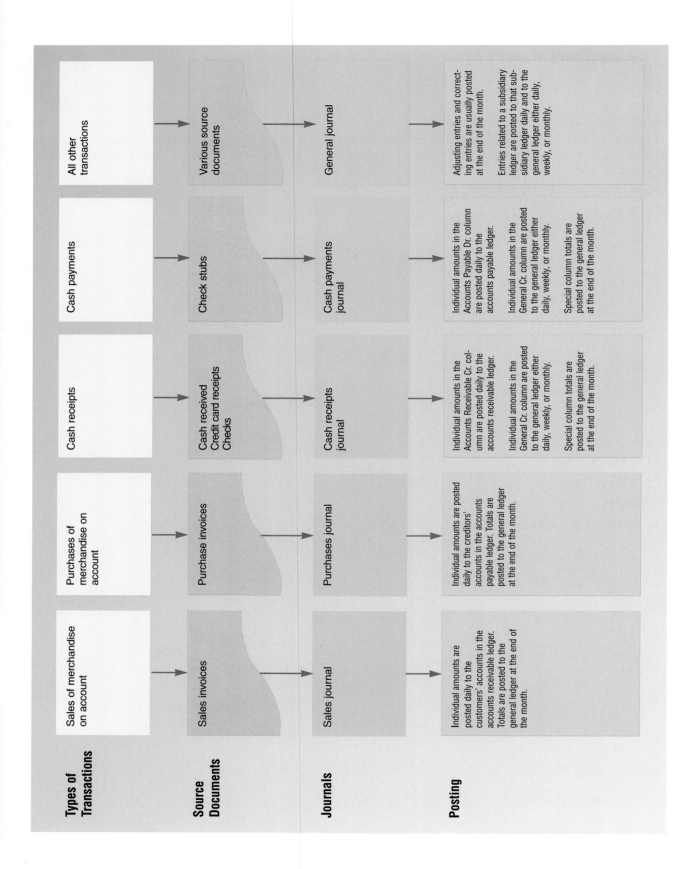

Types of Transactions	Sales of merchandise on account	Purchases of merchandise on account	Cash receipts	Cash payments	All other transactions
Source Documents	Sales invoices	Purchase invoices	Cash received Credit card receipts Checks	Check stubs	Various source documents
Journals	Sales journal	Purchases journal	Cash receipts journal	Cash payments journal	General journal
Posting	Individual amounts are posted daily to the customers' accounts in the accounts receivable ledger. Totals are posted to the general ledger at the end of the month.	Individual amounts are posted daily to the creditors' accounts in the accounts payable ledger. Totals are posted to the general ledger at the end of the month.	Individual amounts in the Accounts Receivable Cr. column are posted daily to the accounts receivable ledger. Individual amounts in the General Cr. column are posted to the general ledger either daily, weekly, or monthly. Special column totals are posted to the general ledger at the end of the month.	Individual amounts in the Accounts Payable Dr. column are posted daily to the accounts payable ledger. Individual amounts in the General Cr. column are posted to the general ledger either daily, weekly, or monthly. Special column totals are posted to the general ledger at the end of the month.	Adjusting entries and correcting entries are usually posted at the end of the month. Entries related to a subsidiary ledger are posted to that subsidiary ledger daily and to the general ledger either daily, weekly, or monthly.

SUMMARY/RESTATEMENT OF LEARNING OBJECTIVES

1. Describe procedures and forms used in selling merchandise.

Sales on credit are initiated either when a purchase order is received from a customer or when a salesperson responds to a customer's request and prepares a **sales order**. In practice, many firms routinely write up sales orders in all cases, even after the receipt of a purchase order. A copy of the sales order often is used to prepare a **sales invoice**, which is sent to the buyer with the goods, a few days in advance of the goods, or after the goods. The sales invoice is the source document for recording the sale.

Cash sales are evidenced by a **sales ticket** or **sales slip**, which is a form prepared at the time of the sale. A copy of the sales ticket is given to the customer, another copy is sent to the accounting department as a source document for recording the sale, and a third copy usually remains with the salesperson who made the sale. A variation of the sales ticket is the **cash register tape**.

2. Record sales of merchandise in a sales journal and post to the general ledger and the accounts receivable ledger.

The July 20XX sales transactions of Tyler Company are shown below. Each is recorded in the accompanying **sales journal**. Complete posting marks are included in the journal. However, posting is not shown at this point.

20XX
Jul. 5 Sold merchandise to West Company, $700; terms, 2/10,n/30.
    7 Sold merchandise to Watson, Inc., $400; terms, 2/10,n/30.
  12 Sold merchandise to Hall Company, $500; terms, n/30.
  26 Sold merchandise to Watson, Inc., $600; terms, 2/10,n/30.
  30 Sold merchandise to Hall Company, $250; terms, n/30.

	Date		Invoice No.	Customer's Name	P.R.	Accts. Rec. Dr. Sales Cr.	
	Sales Journal					**Page 1**	
1	20XX Jul.	5	1	West Company	✓	7 0 0 00	1
2		7	2	Watson, Inc.	✓	4 0 0 00	2
3		12	3	Hall Company	✓	5 0 0 00	3
4		26	4	Watson, Inc.	✓	6 0 0 00	4
5		30	5	Hall Company	✓	2 5 0 00	5
6		31		Total		2 4 5 0 00	6
7						(112) (411)	7

3. Record sales returns and allowances.

On March 23, 20XX, Waller Company sold $500 worth of merchandise on account to Ben Taylor. On March 26, Ben returned $200 worth of the merchandise because of damage. The sale and the return are recorded in general journal form as follows:

1	20XX Mar.	23	Accounts Receivable—Ben Taylor	/	5 0 0 00		1
2			Sales			5 0 0 00	2
3			Recorded sale on account.				3
4							4
5		26	Sales Returns and Allowances		2 0 0 00		5
6			Accounts Receivable—Ben Taylor	/		2 0 0 00	6
7			Accepted return of merchandise from				7
8			a customer.				8
9							9

4. Record sales discounts.

A **sales discount** is a cash discount that is sometimes offered by a seller to encourage a buyer to make prompt payment for a credit purchase. To review, assume that on March 2, 20X4, Sigma Smith, owner of Sigma Products Company, sold merchandise with an invoice price of $800 to Lynn Sapp. The invoice carried terms of 2/10,n/30, and it was paid in full on March 12, 20X4. Sigma Products Company made the following entry to record the receipt.

	20X4							
1	Mar.	12	Cash		7 8 4 00			1
2			Sales Discounts		1 6 00			2
3			Accounts Receivable—Lynn Sapp	/		8 0 0 00		3
4			Received cash on account.					4
5								5

5. Record cash receipts in a cash receipts journal and post to the general ledger and the accounts receivable ledger.

The cash receipts of Tyler Company for July 20XX are as follows:

20XX

Jul.   1   James Tyler invested $5,000 cash in the business.
     5   Sold merchandise for cash, $400.
     8   Sold office supplies at cost to a neighboring business, $90.
     8   Collected balance owed on Hall Company's account, $900, less 2% discount.
   10   Sold merchandise for cash, $1,400.
   14   Received payment on account from West Company, $700, less 2% discount.
   17   Received payment on account from Watson, Inc., $400, less 2% discount.
   31   Sold merchandise for cash, $1,080.

These transactions are recorded in the **cash receipts journal** shown in Figure 8-19. Complete posting marks are included in the journal. The **accounts receivable ledger** (Figure 8-20) and the **Accounts Receivable controlling account** (Figure 8-21) are shown as well.

FIGURE 8-19
Cash receipts journal

		Cash Receipts Journal								Page 4	
	Date	Account Credited	P.R.	General Cr.	Sales Cr.	Accounts Rec. Cr.	Sales Discounts Dr.	Cash Dr.	
	20XX								
1	Jul. 1	James Tyler, Capital	311	5 0 0 0 00				5 0 0 0 00	1
2	5	Cash Sales	✓		4 0 0 00			4 0 0 00	2
3	8	Office Supplies	113	9 0 00				9 0 00	3
4	8	Hall Company	✓			9 0 0 00	1 8 00	8 8 2 00	4
5	10	Cash Sales	✓		1 4 0 0 00			1 4 0 0 00	5
6	14	West Company	✓			7 0 0 00	1 4 00	6 8 6 00	6
7	17	Watson, Inc.	✓			4 0 0 00	8 00	3 9 2 00	7
8	31	Cash Sales	✓		1 0 8 0 00			1 0 8 0 00	8
9	31	Totals		5 0 9 0 00	2 8 8 0 00	2 0 0 0 00	4 0 00	9 9 3 0 00	9
10				(✓)	(411)	(112)	(411.2)	(111)	10
11									11

FIGURE 8-20
Accounts receivable ledger

Accounts Receivable Ledger

Name Hall Company
Address 14 Greystoke Ln., Columbus, OH 43201

Date		Item	P.R.	Debit	Credit	Balance
20XX Jul.	1	Balance	✓			9 00 00
	8		CR4		9 00 00	—
	12	Inv. No. 3	S1	5 00 00		5 00 00
	30	Inv. No. 5	S1	2 50 00		7 50 00

Name Watson, Inc.
Address 5000 Delmar Blvd., St. Louis, MO 63108

Date		Item	P.R.	Debit	Credit	Balance
20XX Jul.	7	Inv. No. 2	S1	4 00 00		4 00 00
	17		CR4		4 00 00	—
	26	Inv. No. 4	S1	6 00 00		6 00 00

Name West Company
Address 431 Highway South, Troy, AL 36081

Date		Item	P.R.	Debit	Credit	Balance
20XX Jul.	5	Inv. No. 1	S1	7 00 00		7 00 00
	14		CR4		7 00 00	—

FIGURE 8-21
Accounts Receivable controlling account

General Ledger

Account Accounts Receivable   **Account No.** 112

Date		Item	P.R.	Debit	Credit	Balance Debit	Balance Credit
20XX Jul.	1	Balance	✓			9 00 00	
	31		S1	2 4 50 00		3 3 50 00	
	31		CR4		2 0 00 00	1 3 50 00	

6. Prepare a schedule of accounts receivable.

From the account balances in Tyler Company's accounts receivable ledger, the following **schedule of accounts receivable** was prepared. Note that the total of the schedule agrees with the balance of the Accounts Receivable controlling account shown in the preceding section.

Tyler Company
Schedule of Accounts Receivable
July 31, 20XX

Hall Company	7 50 00
Watson, Inc.	6 00 00
West Company	—
Total	1 3 50 00

7. Record credit card sales.

The Willoughby Men's Shop accepts two types of credit cards, VISA and American Express. On November 22, 20XX, VISA card sales totaled $400 and American Express sales totaled $300. The business is located in an area with a 6% retail sales tax. The discount rate charged on the VISA sales is 4%, and the discount rate charged on the American Express sales is 6%. These sales are recorded as follows. (Remember that VISA sales are recorded as cash sales and American Express sales are recorded as sales on account.)

To record the VISA sales: $400 × .06 (6% tax) = $24; $424 ($400 + $24) × .04 (4% discount rate) = bank discount of $16.96; $424 − $16.96 = $407.04 (amount of cash received).

	20XX						
1	Nov.	22	Cash	4 0 7	04		1
2			Credit Card Expense	1 6	96		2
3			Sales			4 0 0 00	3
4			Sales Tax Payable			2 4 00	4
5			Recorded VISA card sales.				5

To record the American Express sale: $300 × .06 (6% tax) = $18; $318 ($300 + $18) × .06 (6% discount rate) = discount of $19.08; $318 − $19.08 = $298.92 (amount of cash to be received).

	20XX						
1	Nov.	22	Accounts Receivable—Credit Cards	2 9 8	92		1
2			Credit Card Expense	1 9	08		2
3			Sales			3 0 0 00	3
4			Sales Tax Payable			1 8 00	4
5			Recorded American Express sales.				5

KEY TERMS

Accounts Receivable An asset account that shows the total dollar amount due from credit customers.

Accounts Receivable—Credit Cards An asset account showing the amount due from nonbank credit card sales.

accounts receivable ledger A subsidiary ledger containing only accounts of credit customers; also called the *customers' ledger.*

cash receipts journal A special journal used to record all receipts of cash, regardless of the source.

cash register tape A variation of the sales ticket; the total of the tape serves as the source document for later journal entries.

C.O.D. (cash on delivery) Terms set by the seller that call for payment when the goods are delivered.

Credit Card Expense An expense account that is used to record discounts paid when receipts for credit card sales are deposited with the bank that issued the card (such as VISA or MasterCard) or with the credit card company that issued the card (such as American Express).

credit memorandum A document issued to the customer showing the amount of credit granted and the reason for the return.

credit period The amount of time a seller allows a credit customer to pay for a purchase.

credit terms The terms for payment set by a seller of goods or services; includes the amount of time before payment is due and the rate of discount (if any) for paying early.

revolving charge plan Payment system in which customers pay a percentage of their account plus finance charges on a monthly basis.

Sales account A revenue account used only to record sales of merchandise.

sales discount A cash discount on the books of the seller, which is recorded as a reduction of sales revenue.

Sales Discounts account A contra revenue account with a normal debit balance. It is used to record cash discounts granted to credit customers for prompt payment.

sales invoice Document prepared by a seller of goods and shipped with the goods (or a few days after the goods). It describes the goods and identifies credit terms, price, and the mode of transportation.

sales journal A special journal used only to record credit sales of merchandise.

sales order A document prepared when an order is received from a customer.

Sales Returns and Allowances A contra revenue account with a normal debit balance. It is used to record returns from and allowances to customers.

sales tax A tax on the retail price of goods sold. It is collected by the merchant and paid to the governmental body that levies the tax.

sales ticket A form prepared by the seller when a cash sale is made. It describes the goods sold, identifies the customer, and serves as a source document for recording the sale.

schedule of accounts receivable A listing of the balances in the accounts receivable ledger.

CONCEPTS AND SKILLS REVIEW

CONCEPTS REVIEW

1. What is the source document for recording (a) credit sales; (b) cash sales?
2. Why is the Sales account an owner's equity account?
3. Which account is credited for a cash receipt from (a) a sale of merchandise; (b) sale of supplies; (c) a credit customer paying on account?
4. Compare the accounts receivable ledger with the accounts payable ledger. Which accounts are contained in each ledger?
5. What two types of postings are made from the sales journal?
6. Why is it a common practice to record sales returns in the Sales Returns and Allowances account rather than in the Sales account?
7. What type of balance does the Sales Returns and Allowances account have? What is the relationship of this account to the Sales account?
8. How does the seller of goods account for a cash discount?
9. What three types of postings are made from the cash receipts journal?
10. How does a schedule of accounts receivable serve as a check on the accuracy of the accounts receivable ledger?
11. Who is responsible for the collection and payment of sales tax?
12. What purpose is served by a three-column sales journal?
13. Why are bank credit card sales recorded as cash sales?
14. Who is responsible for the billing of customers in (a) nonbank credit card sales; (b) department store credit card sales?

SKILLS REVIEW

EXERCISE 8-1

LEARNING OBJECTIVE 2 **Objective: To record credit sales in a sales journal and post**

Rogers Company made the following credit sales during June 20X2:

20X2
Jun.   5   Adams Co., $700.
       10   Heard, Inc., $500.
       12   Brown Co., $525.
       17   Heard, Inc., $1,060.
       19   Brown Co., $1,175.
       26   Mallory, Inc., $610.
       30   Adams Co., $565.

Directions: Starting with Invoice No. 477, record these sales on page 1 of a sales journal. Post to the subsidiary ledger after each entry. Total the sales journal and post to the general ledger at the end of the month.

EXERCISE 8-2

LEARNING OBJECTIVE 2, 3

Objective: To record merchandise transactions in general journal form

Directions: Record the following transactions of Sterling Company in general journal form:

(a)   Sold merchandise on account to Smith Co., $7,000.
(b)   Sold merchandise for cash, $3,500.
(c)   Purchased merchandise on credit from Sutton Co., $4,500.
(d)   Issued a credit memorandum to Paul Jones for the return of damaged merchandise, $200.
(e)   Issued a check to Tami Owens for the return of merchandise that was the wrong model, $125.
(f)   Returned merchandise to B & M Manufacturing Co. and received credit, $3,800.
(g)   Returned merchandise to Mobley Co. and received a cash refund, $900.

EXERCISE 8-3

LEARNING OBJECTIVE 5

Objective: To record cash receipts in general journal form

Directions: Melinda Brooks's cash receipts for November 20X1 follow. Record each in general journal form. All credit sales carry terms of 2/10,n/30.

Date		Amount	Received from	For
20X1				
Nov.	1	$11,000	Owner	Cash investment
	3	500	Hall Co.	Cash sale
	7	200	Thomas Co.	Sale of Oct. 28
	10	350	Walk-in customers	Cash sales
	15	700	James Smith	Sale of Nov. 5
	20	850	Rosser Co.	Sale of Oct. 25
	26	225	Wells Co.	Sale of our supplies
	28	800	Speer, Inc.	Sale of Nov. 18

EXERCISE 8-4

LEARNING OBJECTIVE 5

Objective: To record cash receipts in a cash receipts journal

Directions: Record the cash receipts listed in Exercise 8-3 in a cash receipts journal like the one illustrated in the chapter. Total the journal, and prove the equality of the debits and credits in the column totals. Then rule the journal.

EXERCISE 8-5

LEARNING OBJECTIVE 2, 4, 5

Objective: To record merchandise sales and sales discounts in general journal form

The following selected transactions were completed by Twin City Products Company during July 20XX:

20XX
Jul. 3   Sold merchandise for cash, $6,200.
      5   Sold merchandise to Parkside Grocery, $9,500, terms, n/30.
      6   Sold merchandise to Derrek's Quick Stop Grocery, $900, terms, 2/10,n/30.
      8   Sold merchandise to Bronson's Grocery Company, $2,100, terms, 2/10,n/30.
     16   Received payment from Derrek's Quick Stop Grocery for the sale of July 6.
     25   Received payment from Bronson's Grocery Company for the sale of July 8.
     29   Received $1,000 on account from Parkside Grocery.

Directions: Record these transactions in general journal form.

EXERCISE 8-6

LEARNING OBJECTIVE 3

Objective: To record returns and allowances

Directions: Record the following transactions in general journal form:

(a)   Issued a credit memorandum for the return of merchandise sold on account to Lawson Company, $1,650.
(b)   Received a credit memorandum for the return of equipment purchased on account from Zayer Equipment Company, $1,600.
(c)   Issued a check for $225 to Glen Justice as a cash refund for damaged merchandise.
(d)   Received a credit memorandum for the return of merchandise purchased on account from Morton Supply Company, $900.
(e)   Issued a credit memorandum for an allowance made to Susan Watson for defective merchandise sold on account, $400.

EXERCISE 8-7

LEARNING OBJECTIVE 2

Objective: To calculate and record sales tax

Mario's Restaurant is located in an area with a 5% retail sales tax. For the month just ended, Mario reported cash sales of $22,120.

Directions:
1. Calculate the amount of sales tax collected.
2. In general journal form, record a summary entry for the month's cash sales and sales tax collected.
3. In general journal form, record the entry to pay the sales tax to the taxing authority.

EXERCISE 8-8

LEARNING OBJECTIVE 2

Objective: To record retail sales in a three-column sales journal

The Pro Ski Shop is a small ski and accessory shop that sells merchandise on credit to its regular customers. The following credit sales were made during December 20X2. All sales carry terms of n/30 and are subject to a 6% sales tax.

20X2
Dec. 1   Sold skis to Walter Waddell, $338.
      3   Sold a sweater and gloves to Aida Rodriguez, $195.
     12   Sold skis to Mitch Worrell, $330.
     21   Sold an overcoat to Kay Rodgers, $259.95.
     28   Sold various items to Karen Kilmer, $280.
     31   Sold a helmet and gloves to Martin Choi, $190.

Directions:

1. Record these sales in a three-column sales journal like the one illustrated in the chapter. Number sales starting with 225.
2. Total and rule the journal.

EXERCISE 8-9

LEARNING OBJECTIVE 7

Objective: To record credit card sales

Directions: Record the following credit card sales of O'Malley Company. All sales are subject to a 6% retail sales tax.

(a) Sold merchandise, $900, and accepted VISA. The discount rate is 4%.
(b) Sold merchandise, $300, and accepted a nonbank credit card. The discount rate is 5%.

EXERCISE 8-10

LEARNING OBJECTIVE 2, 3, 4

Objective: To identify journals in which transactions are recorded

Directions: A form and several transactions follow. Use a check mark in your working papers to indicate the journal in which each transaction should be recorded, assuming that four special journals and the general journal are used.

Transaction	P	S	CR	CP	G
(a) Collected cash on account					
(b) Purchased supplies for cash					
(c) Owner invested several noncash assets					
(d) Paid a creditor on account					
(e) Purchased merchandise for cash					
(f) Owner withdrew merchandise					
(g) Performed services on credit					
(h) Sold merchandise for cash					
(i) Corrected an error					
(j) Purchased equipment on credit					
(k) Paid utilities expense					
(l) Sold merchandise on credit					
(m) Purchased merchandise on credit					
(n) Adjusted for supplies used					
(o) Performed services for cash					

CASE PROBLEMS

GROUP A

PROBLEM 8-1A

LEARNING OBJECTIVE 2, 3, 6

Objective: To record credit sales and sales returns, post them, and prepare a schedule of accounts receivable

Bayside Supply Company opened on November 12, 20X2. Its credit sales and related returns and allowances for the remainder of the month are as follows. Terms of all sales were 2/10,n/30, FOB destination.

20X2
Nov. 15 Sold merchandise on account to Horton Co., $3,100, Invoice No. 1.
    18 Sold merchandise on account to Duffy Co., $2,550, Invoice No. 2.

Nov. 24 Sold merchandise on account to J. D. Wells Co., $4,400, Invoice No. 3.
25 Issued Credit Memorandum No. 1 for $400 to Horton Co. for merchandise returned.
26 Sold merchandise on account to Trent Co., $4,100, Invoice No. 4.
27 Sold merchandise on account to Zernik, Inc., $900, Invoice No. 5.
28 Sold merchandise on account to Duffy Co., $3,100, Invoice No. 6.
30 Issued Credit Memorandum No. 2 for $250 to Duffy Co. for merchandise returned.
30 Issued Credit Memorandum No. 3 for $150 to Zernik, Inc., for damages to merchandise caused by improper packing.
30 Sold merchandise on account to Trent Co., $1,300, Invoice No. 7.

Directions:
1. Open the following accounts in the accounts receivable ledger: Duffy Co.; Horton Co.; Trent Co.; J. D. Wells Co.; Zernik, Inc.
2. Open the following accounts in the general ledger: Accounts Receivable, 112; Sales, 411; Sales Returns and Allowances, 411.1.
3. Record the November transactions in a one-column sales journal (page 1) and a general journal (page 1). Post to the accounts receivable ledger after each transaction.
4. Total the sales journal, and post the column total to the general ledger. Then, post from the general journal to the general ledger.
5. Prepare a schedule of accounts receivable.
6. Compare the balance of the Accounts Receivable controlling account with the total of the schedule of accounts receivable.

LEARNING OBJECTIVE 2

PROBLEM 8-2A

Objective: To record sales in a three-column sales journal, total, and post to the accounts receivable and general ledgers

Champagne's Department Store opened on December 1, 20XX, and made the following sales during the month. The amounts do not include the 6% sales tax charged on each sale.

Date	Customer	Amount
20XX		
Dec. 3	Baker Co.	$ 730
7	Jane Cote	675
12	Milton Arlen	1,520
16	Mid-Island Store	2,455
22	Jane Cote	620
27	Milton Arlen	1,060
29	Baker Co.	410
30	Jane Cote	345
31	Milton Arlen	810

Directions:
1. Open an account in the accounts receivable ledger for each credit customer to whom a sale was made.
2. Open the following accounts in the general ledger: Accounts Receivable, 112; Sales Tax Payable, 212; Sales, 411.
3. Record each sale on page 1 of a three-column sales journal. Begin with Invoice No. 1. Post to the accounts receivable ledger after making each entry.
4. Total and rule the sales journal, and post the column totals to the general ledger.
5. Prepare a schedule of accounts receivable and verify its total against the balance of the Accounts Receivable account.

PROBLEM 8-3A

TIVE 5

Objective: To record cash receipts in a cash receipts journal and complete the journal

The cash receipts of Boyd's Variety Store for September 20X1 follow:

20X1
CRJ — Sep. 2 Collected $720 from Phil Williams on account.
GJ — 5 Jerry Boyd, the owner, invested an additional $2,000 in the business.
CRJ — 9 Collected the amount due from Edna Hansen for the sale of August 16, $285, less a 1% cash discount.
CRJ — 12 Collected $397.50 from Jean Evans on account.
CRJ — 15 Cash sales for the first half of the month amounted to $1,076.45.
GJ — 19 Received a cash refund for an overcharge on a purchase of equipment, $35.
CRJ — 22 Collected the amount due from Avco Co. for the sale of September 12, $410, less a 2% cash discount.
GJ — 23 Sold old equipment for cash, $375.
CRJ — 27 Collected the amount due from Sylvia Portland, $442.75, less a 3% cash discount.
GJ — 29 Received a cash refund for the return of defective merchandise purchased this week, $75.
CRJ — 30 Cash sales for the second half of the month amounted to $2,692.98.

Directions:
1. Record these transactions in a cash receipts journal like the one illustrated in the chapter. Use page 19 of the journal.
2. Total the journal and prove the equality of the debits and credits in the column totals. Then rule the journal.

PROBLEM 8-4A

LEARNING OBJECTIVE 2, 3, 4, 5, 6

Objective: To record sales-related transactions in special journals, post to the accounts receivable and general ledgers, and prepare a schedule of accounts receivable

Deluth Enterprises, a wholesale dealer of personal care supplies, opened for business on January 2, 20X1. Following are the sales-related transactions completed by the firm during its first month of operations. All sales carry terms of 2/10,n/30. Number both sales invoices and credit memorandums starting with 101.

20X1
Jan. 2 Sold merchandise on account to Linda Sayers, $245.
4 Sold merchandise on account to Marion Parks, $340.
5 Issued a credit memorandum to Marion Parks for damaged merchandise, $50.
9 Sold merchandise on account to Dave Langlin, $560.
11 Received a check from Linda Sayers for the amount due today.
12 Sold merchandise on account to Klasic Kuts, $500.
14 Received a check from Marion Parks for the balance due on her account.
15 Recorded cash sales for the first half of the month, $5,565.
18 Sold merchandise on account to Dave Langlin, $605.
19 Issued a credit memorandum to Dave Langlin for a shortage on the sale of the 18th, $80.
19 Received a check from Dave Langlin in payment of the amount due on the sale of the 9th.
20 Sold merchandise on account to Klasic Kuts, $500.
21 Sold merchandise on account to Scissors Palace, $750.
22 Received a check from Klasic Kuts in payment of the amount due on the sale of the 12th.

Jan. 23 Sold merchandise on account to Marion Parks, $400.

24 Issued a credit memorandum to Marion Parks as an allowance for damaged merchandise due to faulty packaging, $70.

27 Sold merchandise on account to Scissors Palace, $300.

28 Received a check from Dave Langlin for the balance due on his account.

28 Sold merchandise on account to Michelle's, $600.

31 Sold merchandise on account to Michelle's, $250.

31 Recorded cash sales for the second half of the month, $6,170.

Directions:

1. Open the following accounts in the accounts receivable ledger: Klasic Kuts, 411 Herbison Drive, Riverside, GA 30301; Dave Langlin, 4101 Madison Road, Atlanta, GA 30303; Marion Parks, 211 Fourth Place South, Marietta, GA 31101; Michelle's, 511 Warm Springs Loop, Morrow, GA 30302; Linda Sayers, 31 Third Avenue, Atlanta, GA 30330; Scissors Palace, 102 Shannon Mall Shopping Center, Atlanta, GA 30330.

2. Open the following accounts in the general ledger: Cash, 111; Accounts Receivable, 112; Sales, 411; Sales Returns and Allowances, 411.1; Sales Discounts, 411.2.

3. Record Deluth's January transactions in a one-column sales journal, a five-column cash receipts journal, and a general journal. Use page 1 of each journal. Post to the accounts receivable ledger after each entry.

4. Total and rule the special journals, and post the column totals to the general ledger. Post the individual entries from the general journal to the general ledger.

5. Prepare a schedule of accounts receivable as of January 31 and compare its total with the balance of the Accounts Receivable controlling account.

PROBLEM 8-5A

LEARNING OBJECTIVE 2, 3, 4, 5, 6

Objective: To complete a comprehensive problem using five journals and three ledgers

The following transactions were completed by Superior Food Company during October 20X1. All credit sales carry terms of 2/10,n/30.

20X1

Oct. 1 Paid October rent, $1,250.

1 Received the balance of Bill Fahey's account, less a 2% discount.

2 Paid for radio advertising, $1,080.

3 Received the balance of B. Craven's account, less a 2% discount.

3 Sold merchandise on account to Hardy's Food World, $3,900.

3 Purchased office equipment for cash, $3,100.

4 Paid S. Sanchez Co. for the October 1 balance; no discount.

6 Made the following credit purchases from S. Sanchez Co.: store supplies, $450; office supplies, $220; merchandise, $1,060; terms, n/30.

6 Sold merchandise on account to Southside Grocery, $2,600.

7 Recorded cash sales for the week, $4,690.

7 Purchased merchandise on account from Belk's, $8,000; terms, 1/10,n/30.

7 Paid Zachary Products Co. for the October 1 balance, less a 2% discount.

8 Due to damage during shipment, the following items were returned for credit to S. Sanchez Co.: office supplies, $20; store supplies, $40; merchandise, $60.

8 Paid Belk's for the October 1 balance, less a 2% discount.

9 Issued a check to a cash customer for the return of damaged merchandise, $85.

9 Purchased store equipment on account from Baker Supply Co., $6,620; terms, 2/10,n/30.

Oct. 10 Received the balance owed by Adams Co., less a 2% discount.
13 Received full payment from Hardy's Food World for the sale of October 3.
15 Recorded cash sales for the week, $6,010.
15 Paid salaries for the first half of the month, $2,100.
16 Received payment from Southside Grocery for the sale of October 6.
17 Paid Belk's the amount due on the purchase of October 7.
18 Purchased merchandise on account from Engel Co., $3,600; terms, 2/10,n/30.
19 Returned defective merchandise to Engel Co. and received credit, $350.
21 Purchased merchandise for cash, $1,000.
22 Sold at cost a computer printer that was no longer needed, $1,500.
22 Recorded cash sales for the week, $6,495.
23 Paid for miscellaneous expenses, $225.
25 Paid for repairs to delivery truck, $250.
26 Paid gas and oil expense, $125.
27 Purchased merchandise on account from Belk's, $4,000.
28 Paid Engel Co. for the purchase of October 18, less the return of October 19.
30 Sold merchandise on account to Southside Grocery, $1,350.
31 Recorded cash sales for the week, $9,600.
31 Paid salaries for the second half of the month, $2,200.
31 Paid utility bill, $872.

Directions:

1. Open the following accounts in the general ledger and enter the balances as of October 1:

	Account	Balance
111	Cash	$ 9,300
112	Accounts Receivable	11,500
113	Store Supplies	3,500
114	Office Supplies	1,890
121	Store Equipment	18,750
122	Office Equipment	8,560
211	Accounts Payable	19,700
411	Sales	118,400
411.1	Sales Returns and Allowances	3,300
411.2	Sales Discounts	3,940
511	Purchases	46,700
511.1	Purchases Returns and Allowances	5,400
511.2	Purchases Discounts	3,000
611	Rent Expense	3,750
612	Salaries Expense	36,700
613	Utilities Expense	7,800
614	Repairs Expense	890
615	Advertising Expense	3,200
616	Gas and Oil Expense	1,500
618	Miscellaneous Expense	936

2. Open the following accounts in the accounts receivable ledger and enter the balances as of October 1:

Account	Balance
Adams Co.	$4,100
B. Craven	4,500
Bill Fahey	2,900
Hardy's Food World	-0-
Southside Grocery	-0-

3. Open the following accounts in the accounts payable ledger and enter the balances as of October 1:

Account	Balance
Baker Supply Co.	$ -0-
Belk's	6,500
Engel Co.	-0-
S. Sanchez Co.	4,300
Zachary Products Co.	8,900

4. Record the October transactions in a sales journal (page 8), a cash receipts journal (page 7), a purchases journal (page 14), a cash payments journal (page 10), and a general journal (page 5). Post to the subsidiary ledgers after each entry. Start sales invoices with No. 377, purchases invoices with No. 364, and checks with No. 419. Remember that all credit sales carry terms of 2/10,n/30.

5. Post the individual entries from the general journal to the general ledger. Total, rule, and post the special journals.

6. Prepare schedules of accounts receivable and accounts payable and verify the totals.

GROUP B

LEARNING OBJECTIVE 2, 3, 6

PROBLEM 8-1B

Objective: To record credit sales and sales returns, post them, and prepare a schedule of accounts receivable

Gulf Supply Company opened on December 10, 20X2. Its credit sales and related returns and allowances for the remainder of the month are as follows. Terms of all sales were 2/10,n/30, FOB destination.

20X2
Dec. 12 Sold merchandise on account to McCullum Co., $4,100, Invoice No. 1.
    15 Sold merchandise on account to Carbone Co., $2,450, Invoice No. 2.
    18 Sold merchandise on account to Goorbin, Inc., $5,300, Invoice No. 3.
    21 Issued Credit Memorandum No. 1 for $350 to McCullum Co. for merchandise returned.
    25 Sold merchandise on account to Burke Co., $4,300, Invoice No. 4.
    28 Sold merchandise on account to Stone Ridge Co., $1,050, Invoice No. 5.
    29 Sold merchandise on account to Carbone Co., $3,300, Invoice No. 6.
    30 Issued Credit Memorandum No. 2 for $275 to Carbone Co. for merchandise returned.
    30 Issued Credit Memorandum No. 3 for $160 to Stone Ridge Co. for damages to merchandise caused by improper packing.
    31 Sold merchandise on account to Burke Co., $3,350, Invoice No. 7.

Directions:
1. Open the following accounts in the accounts receivable ledger: Burke Co.; Carbone Co.; Goorbin, Inc.; McCullum Co.; Stone Ridge Co.
2. Open the following accounts in the general ledger: Accounts Receivable, 112; Sales, 411; Sales Returns and Allowances, 411.1.
3. Record the December transactions in a one-column sales journal (page 1) and a general journal (page 1). Post to the accounts receivable ledger after each transaction.
4. Total the sales journal, and post the column total to the general ledger. Then, post from the general journal to the general ledger.
5. Prepare a schedule of accounts receivable.
6. Compare the balance of the Accounts Receivable controlling account with the total of the schedule of accounts receivable.

PROBLEM 8-2B

Objective: To record sales in a three-column sales journal, total, and post to the accounts receivable and general ledgers

Wilkinson's Department Store opened on August 1, 20XX, and made the following sales during the month. The amounts do not include the 6% sales tax charged on each sale.

Date		Customer	Amount
20XX			
Aug.	6	Sean Walsh	$1,060
	10	Kris Cassereau	275
	12	Juan Baez	955
	15	Melody Meyer	1,620
	19	Kris Cassereau	865
	21	Melody Meyer	2,145
	24	Sean Walsh	930
	27	Juan Baez	810
	30	Melody Meyer	1,605

Directions:
1. Open an account in the accounts receivable ledger for each credit customer to whom a sale was made.
2. Open the following accounts in the general ledger: Accounts Receivable, 112; Sales Tax Payable, 212; Sales, 411.
3. Record each sale on page 1 of a three-column sales journal. Begin with Invoice No. 1. Post to the accounts receivable ledger after making each entry.
4. Total and rule the sales journal, and post the column totals to the general ledger.
5. Prepare a schedule of accounts receivable and verify its total against the balance of the Accounts Receivable account.

PROBLEM 8-3B

Objective: To record cash receipts in a cash receipts journal and complete the journal

The cash receipts of Garland's Department Store for November 20X1 follow:

20X1
GJ — Nov. 3 Received a cash refund for the return of defective merchandise purchased this week, $295.75.
CRJ — 6 Collected the amount due from Wade Martin for the sale of October 24, $675.10, less a 1% cash discount.
CRJ — 8 Collected $247.95 from Jane Gillis for the sale of September 17.
GJ — 10 Paul Garland, the owner, invested an additional $1,800 in the business.
CRJ — 12 Collected the amount due from Dana Kelly, $550, less a 3% cash discount.
CRJ — 15 Cash sales for the first half of the month amounted to $912.65.
CRJ — 20 Received $1,100 on account from A-One Resort.
GJ — 22 Sold office supplies at cost, $165.
GJ — 24 Received a cash refund for an overcharge on a purchase of equipment, $175.
CRJ — 29 Collected the amount due from Paul Arlen for the sale of November 9, $627.90, less a 2% cash discount.
CRJ — 30 Cash sales for the second half of the month amounted to $1,936.57.

Directions:
1. Record these transactions in a cash receipts journal like the one illustrated in the chapter. Use page 19 of the journal.
2. Total the journal, and prove the equality of the debits and credits in the column totals. Then rule the journal.

PROBLEM 8-4B

LEARNING OBJECTIVE 2, 3, 4, 5, 6

Objective: To record sales-related transactions in special journals, post to the accounts receivable and general ledgers, and prepare a schedule of accounts receivable

Davenport Enterprises, a wholesale dealer of soft drinks, opened for business on March 1, 20X1. Following are the sales-related transactions completed by the firm during its first month of operations. All sales carry terms of 2/10,n/30. Number both sales invoices and credit memorandums starting with 101.

20X1

Mar. 1 Sold merchandise on account to Brenda Myers, $345.

3 Sold merchandise on account to Marvin Stark, $390.

5 Issued a credit memorandum to Marvin Stark for damaged merchandise, $35.

9 Sold merchandise on account to Bob Lawford, $600.

11 Received a check from Brenda Myers for the amount due today.

12 Sold merchandise on account to Country Corner Grocery, $600.

13 Received a check from Marvin Stark for the balance due on his account.

15 Recorded cash sales for the first half of the month, $6,300.

18 Sold merchandise on account to Bob Lawford, $595.

19 Issued a credit memorandum to Bob Lawford for a shortage on the sale of the 18th, $85.

19 Received a check from Bob Lawford in payment of the amount due on the sale of the 9th.

20 Sold merchandise on account to Country Corner Grocery, $625.

22 Sold merchandise on account to Grand Rapids Produce Company, $990.

23 Received a check from Country Corner Grocery in payment of the amount due on the sale of the 12th.

23 Sold merchandise on account to Marvin Stark, $420.

24 Issued a credit memorandum to Marvin Stark as an allowance for damaged merchandise due to faulty packaging, $95.

27 Sold merchandise on account to Grand Rapids Produce Company, $400.

28 Received a check from Bob Lawford for the balance due on his account.

28 Sold merchandise on account to Michael's Foods, $1,000.

31 Sold merchandise on account to Michael's Foods, $540.

31 Recorded cash sales for the second half of the month, $7,780.

Directions:

1. Open the following accounts in the accounts receivable ledger: Country Corner Grocery, 415 East Fulton, Grand Rapids, MI 49503; Grand Rapids Produce Company, 14 Rangeline Road, Grand Rapids, MI 49503; Bob Lawford, 12 Shimmel Road, Centerville, MI 49032; Michael's Foods, 144 Bostwick NE, Grand Rapids, MI 49503; Brenda Myers, 512 East Greenwood, Grand Rapids, MI 49503; Marvin Stark, 312 Bankers Loop, Grand Rapids, MI 49503

2. Open the following accounts in the general ledger: Cash, 111; Accounts Receivable, 112; Sales, 411; Sales Returns and Allowances, 411.1; Sales Discounts, 411.2.

3. Record Davenport's March transactions in a one-column sales journal, a five-column cash receipts journal, and a general journal. Use page 1 of each journal. Post to the accounts receivable ledger after each entry.

4. Total and rule the special journals, and post the column totals to the general ledger. Post the individual entries from the general journal to the general ledger.

5. Prepare a schedule of accounts receivable as of March 31, and compare its total with the balance of the Account Receivable controlling account.

Accounting for a Merchandising Business

PROBLEM 8-5B

Objective: To complete a comprehensive problem using five journals and three ledgers

The following transactions were completed by Bi-City Distributing Company during May 20X1. All credit sales carry terms of 2/10,n/30.

20X1

May 1 Paid May rent, $1,100.
  1 Received the balance of Will Facson's account, less a 2% discount.
  2 Paid for advertising in the local paper, $610.
  4 Received the balance of T. Tarven's account, less a 2% discount.
  4 Sold merchandise on account to Harry's Restaurant, $2,600.
  4 Purchased office equipment for cash, $5,300.
  5 Paid Rojas Co. for the May 1 balance; no discount.
  5 Made the following credit purchases from Rojas Co.: store supplies, $490; office supplies, $330; merchandise, $950; terms, n/30.
  6 Sold merchandise on account to Eastway Foods, $3,500.
  7 Recorded cash sales for the week, $2,300.
  7 Purchased merchandise on account from Prago Co., $9,100; terms, 3/10,n/30.
  7 Paid Zenith Products Co. for the May 1 balance, less a 2% discount.
  8 Due to damage during shipment, the following items were returned for credit to Rojas Co.: office supplies, $22; store supplies, $38; merchandise, $66.
  8 Paid Prago Co. for the May 1 balance, less a 2% discount.
  9 Issued a check to a cash customer for the return of damaged merchandise, $55.
  9 Purchased store equipment on account from Tyler Supply Co., $6,860; terms, n/30.
  10 Received the balance owed by Aims Co., less a 2% discount.
  14 Received full payment from Harry's Restaurant for the sale of May 4.
  15 Recorded cash sales for the week, $2,520.
  15 Paid salaries for the first half of the month, $4,600.
  16 Received payment from Eastway Foods for the sale of May 6.
  17 Paid Prago Co. for the purchase of May 7.
  18 Purchased merchandise on account from Ingalls Co., $4,100; terms, 2/10, n/30.
  19 Returned defective merchandise to Ingalls Co. and received credit, $450.
  21 Purchased merchandise for cash, $1,300.
  22 Sold at cost a computer that was no longer needed, $690.
  22 Recorded cash sales for the week, $2,495.
  23 Paid for miscellaneous expenses, $195.
  25 Paid for repairs to office copier, $65.
  26 Paid gas and oil expense, $110.
  27 Purchased merchandise on account from Prago Co., $2,900; terms, 2/10,n/30.
  28 Paid Ingalls Co. for the purchase of May 18 less the return of May 19.
  30 Sold merchandise on account to Eastway Foods, $4,420.
  31 Recorded cash sales for the week, $2,555.
  31 Paid salaries for the second half of the month, $4,600.
  31 Paid utility bill, $948.

Directions:

  1. Open the following accounts in the general ledger and enter the balances as of May 1:

	Account	Balance
111	Cash	$ 26,600
112	Accounts Receivable	11,800
113	Store Supplies	3,900
114	Office Supplies	1,950
121	Store Equipment	22,500
122	Office Equipment	11,320
211	Accounts Payable	22,200
411	Sales	112,400
411.1	Sales Returns and Allowances	2,400
411.2	Sales Discounts	3,460
511	Purchases	47,600
511.1	Purchases Returns and Allowances	1,810
511.2	Purchases Discounts	700
611	Rent Expense	4,400
612	Salaries Expense	36,800
613	Utilities Expense	3,500
614	Repairs Expense	540
615	Advertising Expense	450
616	Gas and Oil Expense	390
618	Miscellaneous Expense	512

2. Open the following accounts in the accounts receivable ledger and enter the balances as of May 1:

Account	Balance
Aims Co.	$4,600
Eastway Foods	-0-
Will Facson	3,300
Harry's Restaurant	-0-
T. Tarven	3,900

3. Open the following accounts in the accounts payable ledger and enter the balances as of May 1:

Account	Balance
Ingalls Co.	$ –0–
Prago Co.	7,500
Rojas Co.	5,300
Tyler Supply Co.	–0–
Zenith Products Co.	9,400

4. Record the May transactions in a sales journal (page 6), a cash receipts journal (page 9), a purchases journal (page 12), a cash payments journal (page 8), and a general journal (page 3). Post to the subsidiary ledgers after each entry. Start sales invoices with No. 395, purchases invoices with No. 314, and checks with No. 515. Remember that all credit sales carry terms of 2/10,n/30.

5. Post the individual entries from the general journal to the general ledger. Total, rule, and post the special journals.

6. Prepare schedules of accounts receivable and accounts payable and verify the totals.

CHALLENGE PROBLEMS

PROBLEM SOLVING

H. H. Sapp Company started its new fiscal period on July 1, 20X2, and completed the following transactions during July. (All credit sales are subject to terms of 2/10,n/30.)

20X2

Jul. 1 Issued Check No. 720 for July rent, $900.

1 Received a check from Xavier Corp. in payment of balance due, less 2% discount.

2 Issued Check No. 721 for the cash purchase of office supplies, $325.

2 Issued Check No. 722 to Dwyar Products Co. for the balance owed, less 1% discount.

2 Received a check from Illinois Central Products Co. in payment of balance due, less 2% discount.

3 Purchased store equipment on account from Allan Co., $3,800.

3 Purchased merchandise on account from Faulk Co., $24,250; terms, 2/10,n/30.

5 Sold merchandise on account to Leland Co., $3,290; Sales Invoice No. 821.

7 Received a check from Tom Larkin in payment of balance due, less 2% discount.

7 Recorded cash sales, $15,800.

8 Received a check from Hanks Co. in payment of balance due, less 2% discount.

8 Issued Check No. 723 in payment of miscellaneous expenses, $235.

8 Sold merchandise on account to McFarland Co., $5,680; Sales Invoice No. 822.

9 Issued Check No. 724 to Thompson Suppliers for the balance owed, less 2% discount.

9 Purchased merchandise on account from Dunlop Co., $5,000; terms, 2/10,n/30.

10 Issued Check No. 725 to Adams Inc. for the balance owed, no discount.

11 Sold merchandise on account to Leland Co., $5,900; Sales Invoice No. 823.

11 Issued Check No. 726 for the cash purchase of store supplies, $428.

12 Issued Check No. 727 in payment of the telephone bill, $89.

13 Issued Check No. 728 to Faulk Co. for the purchase of July 3.

14 Sold merchandise on account to Illinois Central Products Co., $4,690; Sales Invoice No. 824.

15 Sold merchandise on account to Aims Corp., $5,200; Sales Invoice No. 825.

15 Received a check from Leland Co. for the sale of July 5.

16 Issued Credit Memorandum No. 12 to Illinois Central Products Co. for damaged merchandise, $80.

16 Recorded cash sales, $12,900.

17 Purchased merchandise on account from Elgin Co., $12,500; terms, 1/10,n/30.

18 Received a check from McFarland Co. for the sale of July 8.

19 Issued Check No. 729 to Dunlop Co. for the purchase of July 9.

19 Returned damaged merchandise to Elgin Co., receiving credit, $130.

20 Issued Check No. 730 for the cash purchase of merchandise, $2,500.

20 Received a check from Leland Co. for the sale of July 11.

21 Recorded cash sales, $11,900.

22 Issued Check No. 731 for the payment of repairs expense, $75.

23 Issued Check No. 732 for carpet cleaning, $50.

24 Received a check from Illinois Central Products Co. for the sale of July 14 less the return of July 16.

25 Purchased merchandise on account from Elgin Co., $8,600; terms, 1/10,n/30.

25 Sold merchandise on account to Aims Corp., $2,800; Sales Invoice No. 826.

25 Received a check from Aims Corp. for the sale of July 15.

26 Issued Check No. 733 in payment of the power bill, $967.

Jul. 27 Issued Check No. 734 to Elgin Co. for the balance due on the purchase of July 17 less the return of July 19.

27 Issued Credit Memorandum No. 13 to Aims Corp. for a shortage on the sale of July 25, $30.

28 Purchased merchandise on account from McFadden Co., $6,000; terms, n/30.

29 Returned defective merchandise to McFadden Co., receiving credit, $230.

29 Issued Check No. 735 for advertising, $1,500.

30 Issued Check No. 736 to Allan Co. in payment of the July 3 purchase, no discount.

30 Issued Check No. 737 for the cash purchase of merchandise, $5,200.

30 Purchased the following on account from Wall Supply Inc.: store equipment, $2,000; store supplies, $525; office supplies, $318.

31 Received check for return of damaged merchandise that had been purchased for cash on July 30, $225.

31 Recorded cash sales, $12,500.

31 Issued Check No. 738 in payment of monthly salaries, $5,300.

31 Issued Check No. 739 in payment of transportation charges for merchandise purchased during the month, $390.

31 Sold merchandise on account to Leland Co., $8,500; Sales Invoice No. 827.

31 Sold merchandise on account to Aims Corp. $3,450; Sales Invoice No. 828.

31 Returned damaged store supplies purchased on July 30 and received credit, $50.

31 H. H. Sapp, the owner, issued Check No. 740 to himself as a personal withdrawal, $2,000.

31 Sold merchandise on account to Tom Larkin, $1,280; Sales Invoice No. 829.

Directions:

1. Open the following accounts in the general ledger, entering the balances as of July 1:

	Account	Balance
111	Cash	$12,500
112	Accounts Receivable	31,150
113	Store Supplies	1,800
114	Office Supplies	790
115	Prepaid Insurance	1,200
119	Store Equipment	22,400
119.1	Accumulated Depreciation—Store Equipment	4,500
120	Office Equipment	12,900
120.1	Accumulated Depreciation—Office Equipment	3,200
211	Accounts Payable	18,420
312	H. H. Sapp, Capital	56,620
313	H. H. Sapp, Drawing	—
411	Sales	—
411.1	Sales Returns and Allowances	—
411.2	Sales Discounts	—
511	Purchases	—
511.1	Purchases Returns and Allowances	—
511.2	Purchases Discounts	—
512	Freight In	—
611	Salaries Expense	—
612	Rent Expense	—
613	Utilities Expense	—
614	Advertising Expense	—
615	Telephone Expense	—
616	Repairs Expense	—
622	Miscellaneous Expense	—

2. Open the following accounts in the accounts receivable ledger, entering the balances as of July 1:

Account	Balance
Aims Corp.	$ —
Hanks Co.	6,400
Illinois Central Products Co.	7,850
Leland Co.	—
McFarland Co.	—
Tom Larkin	4,600
Xavier Corp.	12,300

3. Open the following accounts in the accounts payable ledger, entering the balances as of July 1:

Account	Balance
Adams Inc.	$6,900
Allan Co.	—
Dunlop Co.	—
Dwyar Products Co.	4,200
Elgin Co.	—
Faulk Co.	—
McFadden Co.	—
Thompson Suppliers	7,320
Wall Supply Inc.	—

4. Record the July transactions in a purchases journal (page 6), a cash payments journal (page 9), a cash receipts journal (page 7), a sales journal (page 11), and a general journal (page 14). Post to the subsidiary ledgers after each entry.
5. Total, prove (where needed), and rule each special journal.
6. Post to the general ledger.
7. Prepare a trial balance.
8. Prepare a schedule of accounts receivable.
9. Prepare a schedule of accounts payable.
10. Verify the agreement of the subsidiary ledgers with the related controlling accounts.

COMMUNICATIONS

You have been asked by Mayhew Company, a new small business, to take a look at their accounting system. You discover that Mayhew is using a general journal to record all transactions. The company does, however, have three separate ledgers—general, customers', and creditors' ledgers.

Write a brief memo to Mayhew explaining why it would be of value to them to use special journals rather than a single journal. Focus on the advantages of special journals.

ETHICS

Thrift-Mart is a large discount department store located in a heavily populated area. The store has a total of 15 cash registers, each of which is on-line with the company's computer system.

Judy McCutcheon, a new employee who is also studying computer science at the local community college, commented, "On-line cash registers double as computer terminals." This led you, the store manager, to realize that all cash register operators have access to all information in the company's computer system.

What are the dangers of this type of access? What kind of safeguard(s) can be designed to keep cashiers from accessing other company information?

REVIEW QUIZ 8-1

1	(a)	Cash	4 0 0 00		1
2		Sales		4 0 0 00	2
3					3
4	(b)	Accounts Receivable	1 2 0 0 00		4
5		Sales		1 2 0 0 00	5
6					6
7	(c)	Cash	8 0 0 00		7
8		Equipment		8 0 0 00	8
9					9
10	(d)	Cash	2 0 0 00		10
11		Supplies		2 0 0 00	11

REVIEW QUIZ 8-2

		Sales Journal			Page 1	
	Date	Invoice No.	Customer's Name	P.R.	Accts. Rec. Dr. Sales Cr.	
1	20X5 May 1	1	Bill French		3 0 0 00	1
2	8	2	Lee Smith		8 0 0 00	2
3	18	3	Leah King		5 9 0 00	3
4	30	4	Charles Swift		5 0 0 00	4
5	30		Total		2 1 9 0 00	5

		General Journal				Page 1	
	Date	Account Title	P.R.	Debit		Credit	
1	20X5 May 3	Cash		5 0 0 00			1
2		Sales				5 0 0 00	2
3							3
4	12	Cash		6 7 0 00			4
5		Sales				6 7 0 00	5
6							6
7	25	Cash		4 0 0 0 00			7
8		Store Equipment				4 0 0 0 00	8

REVIEW QUIZ 8-3

1	(a)	Accounts Receivable—Camp Co.	/	8 00 00			1
2		Sales			8 00 00		2
3							3
4	(b)	Sales Returns and Allowances		2 00 00			4
5		Accounts Receivable—Camp Co.	/		2 00 00		5
6							6
7	(c)	Sales Returns and Allowances		4 00 00			7
8		Cash			4 00 00		8
9							9
10	(d)	Cash		6 00 00			10
11		Accounts Receivable—Camp Co.	/		6 00 00		11
12							12
13							13

REVIEW QUIZ 8-4

(a) On the books of Langford Company:

	20X2					
1	Jun.	10	Purchases		8 0 00 00		1
2			Accounts Payable—Rodriguez Co.	/		8 0 00 00	2
3				/			3
4		19	Accounts Payable—Rodriguez Co.		8 0 00 00		4
5			Purchases Discounts			2 40 00	5
6			Cash			7 7 60 00	6

(b) On the books of Rodriguez Company:

	20X2					
1	Jun.	10	Accounts Receivable—Langford Co.	/	8 0 00 00		1
2			Sales			8 0 00 00	2
3							3
4		19	Cash		7 7 60 00		4
5			Sales Discounts		2 40 00		5
6			Accounts Receivable—Langford Co.	/		8 0 00 00	6
7							7

REVIEW QUIZ 8-5

(a) Means that the column total is not posted.
(b) Means that a posting is made to the customer's account in the accounts receivable ledger.
(c) Means that an individual posting is not necessary; the amount will be posted as part of the column total.

REVIEW QUIZ 8-6

	Date		Account Title	P.R.	Debit	Credit	
1	20X1 Aug.	1	Cash		4 2 4 00		1
2			Sales Tax Payable			2 4 00	2
3			Sales			4 0 0 00	3
4							4
5		4	Accounts Receivable—Eve Li	/	2 1 2 00		5
6			Sales Tax Payable			1 2 00	6
7			Sales			2 0 0 00	7
8							8
9		6	Cash		6 3 6 00		9
10			Sales Tax Payable			3 6 00	10
11			Sales			6 0 0 00	11
12							12
13		10	Accounts Receivable—Max Leatherwood	/	1 4 8 4 00		13
14			Sales Tax Payable			8 4 00	14
15			Sales			1 4 0 0 00	15
16							16
17		12	Sales Returns and Allowances		5 0 00		17
18			Sales Tax Payable		3 00		18
19			Accounts Rec.—Max Leatherwood	/		5 3 00	19
20							20
21		15	Sales Tax Payable		9 4 0 00		21
22			Cash			9 4 0 00	22

General Journal — Page 10

REVIEW QUIZ 8-7

	Date		Account Title	P.R.	Debit	Credit	
1	20X2 Apr.	8	Cash		9 1 5 84		1
2			Credit Card Expense		3 8 16		2
3			Sales			9 0 0 00	3
4			Sales Tax Payable			5 4 00	4
5							5
6		8	Accounts Receivable—Credit Cards	/	4 0 2 80		6
7			Credit Card Expense		2 1 20		7
8			Sales			4 0 0 00	8
9			Sales Tax Payable			2 4 00	9
10							10

REVIEW QUIZ 8-8

(a) Cash receipts journal
(b) General journal
(c) Cash payments journal
(d) Sales journal
(e) Cash receipts journal
(f) General journal
(g) Cash receipts journal
(h) General journal
(i) Cash payments journal

9

WORK SHEET

AND ADJUSTMENTS

FOR A

MERCHANDISING

BUSINESS

LEARNING OBJECTIVES

After studying Chapter 9, you will be able to:
1. Make adjustments to the Merchandise Inventory account.
2. Make other needed adjustments and complete a work sheet for a merchandising business.

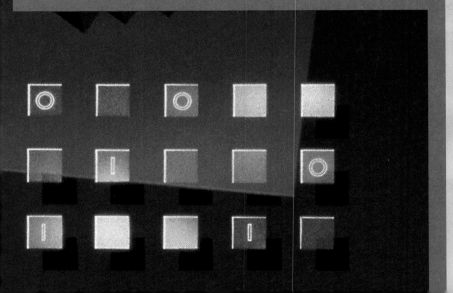

In Chapters 9 and 10, you will learn to perform the year-end accounting activities for a merchandising business. In this chapter, you will learn the first of these activities—to complete the work sheet. Remember from Chapter 4, the work sheet is an informal working paper that the accountant uses for preparing financial statements, journalizing and posting adjusting entries, and journalizing and posting closing entries. In Chapter 10, you will use this work sheet for these end-of-the-accounting-cycle activities.

On the work sheet, you will be required to make adjustments just as you did in Chapter 4; however, there is one major difference. This difference is that you must make adjustments for the beginning and ending balances for merchandise inventory.

— Janice H. Kelly, CPA
St. Louis Community College at Forest Park

O ur study of merchandising has taken us through purchasing and selling procedures, special journals, subsidiary ledgers, controlling accounts, returns and allowances, discounts, and transportation costs. We now reach the end-of-period summarizing and reporting procedures for a merchandising business. End-of-period activities for a merchandising business are similar to the end-of-period activities we studied for a service business in Chapters 4 and 5. In a merchandising business, however, consideration must be given to the amount of merchandise inventory on hand at the beginning and end of the accounting period. Additionally, the use of three ledgers—a general ledger and two subsidiary ledgers—means special checking (i.e., schedules of accounts receivable and accounts payable) that often is not done in service businesses.

CHART OF ACCOUNTS FOR A MERCHANDISING BUSINESS

Before embarking on our study of end-of-period activities for a merchandising business, let's look at the account titles with which we will be working. The full chart of accounts for Lakeside Electronics, as it appears on December 31, 20X1, is shown in Figure 9-1.

Now that we have Lakeside's chart of accounts, the first step in the end-of-period activities is to prepare a trial balance of the general ledger and determine which accounts need adjusting.

As you recall, the trial balance is a form that shows the title and balance of each account in the general ledger. On December 31, 20X1, after all posting has been done, the trial balance of Lakeside appears as shown in Figure 9-2. You may notice that some accounts did not have balances when the trial balance was prepared; they are included because they will be needed during the adjusting process, which we will discuss next.

DETERMINING NEEDED ADJUSTMENTS

Remember that the trial balance shows us that total debits in the ledger equal total credits. But also remember that a few accounts listed on the trial balance will need adjusting to bring their balances up-to-date. As we discussed in Chapter 4, adjustments are needed because certain changes occur during the accounting period, and it is usually not practical to attempt to keep up with these changes as they occur. For example, a prepaid item, such as supplies or insurance, is recorded as an asset when purchased. As time passes, however, the value of the asset is consumed in the business, and therefore its cost gradually becomes an expense. Consequently, an adjustment must be made to record the portion of the prepayment that has been used up or has expired.

FIGURE 9-1
*Chart of accounts for a
merchandising business*

Lakeside Electronics
Chart of Accounts
December 31, 20X1

Assets

111	Cash
112	Accounts Receivable
113	Merchandise Inventory
114	Store Supplies
115	Office Supplies
116	Prepaid Insurance
119	Store Equipment
119.1	Accumulated Depreciation— Store Equipment
120	Office Equipment
120.1	Accumulated Depreciation— Office Equipment
121	Delivery Equipment
121.1	Accumulated Depreciation— Delivery Equipment

Liabilities

211	Accounts Payable
212	Salaries Payable
215	Notes Payable

Owner's Equity

311	John Graham, Capital
312	John Graham, Drawing
313	Income Summary

Revenue

411	Sales
411.1	Sales Returns and Allowances
411.2	Sales Discounts

Cost of Goods Sold

511	Purchases
511.1	Purchases Returns and Allowances
511.2	Purchases Discounts
512	Freight In

Expenses

Selling Expenses:

611	Sales Salaries Expense
612	Advertising Expense
613	Store Supplies Expense
614	Depreciation Expense— Store Equipment
619	Miscellaneous Selling Expense

General Expenses:

711	Rent Expense
712	Office Salaries Expense
713	Insurance Expense
714	Depreciation Expense— Office Equipment
715	Depreciation Expense— Delivery Equipment
716	Utilities Expense
717X	Office Supplies Expense
720	Interest Expense
721	Miscellaneous General Expense

FIGURE 9-2
Trial balance

Lakeside Electronics Trial Balance December 31, 20X1		
Account Title	**Debit**	**Credit**
Cash	6 2 0 0 00	
Accounts Receivable	9 6 8 9 00	
Merchandise Inventory	66 0 0 0 00	
Store Supplies	2 0 1 5 00	
Office Supplies	6 6 7 00	
Prepaid Insurance	7 2 0 00	
Store Equipment	11 3 8 5 00	
Accumulated Depreciation—Store Equipment		4 5 0 0 00
Office Equipment	10 2 0 0 00	
Accumulated Depreciation—Office Equipment		7 1 0 0 00
Delivery Equipment	56 0 0 0 00	
Accumulated Depreciation—Delivery Equipment		13 8 0 0 00
Accounts Payable		14 0 2 5 00
Salaries Payable		
Notes Payable		26 0 0 0 00
John Graham, Capital		75 5 8 1 00
John Graham, Drawing	18 0 0 0 00	
Income Summary		
Sales		304 6 0 0 00
Sales Returns and Allowances	5 2 3 0 00	
Sales Discounts	3 4 6 1 00	
Purchases	144 9 1 8 00	
Purchases Returns and Allowances		6 6 9 2 00
Purchases Discounts		2 9 1 0 00
Freight In	1 1 6 0 00	
Sales Salaries Expense	68 2 0 0 00	
Advertising Expense	5 8 4 0 00	
Store Supplies Expense		
Depreciation Expense—Store Equipment		
Miscellaneous Selling Expense	2 1 0 0 00	
Rent Expense	5 7 0 0 00	
Office Salaries Expense	30 4 5 3 00	
Insurance Expense		
Depreciation Expense—Office Equipment		
Depreciation Expense—Delivery Equipment		
Utilities Expense	6 2 4 0 00	
Office Supplies Expense		
Interest Expense	1 3 0 00	
Miscellaneous General Expense	9 0 0 00	
Totals	455 2 0 8 00	455 2 0 8 00

Additionally, there are usually other items—such as depreciation of long-term assets and unpaid salaries—that must be recorded to match revenue and expenses properly and to state the amount of assets and liabilities accurately.

The accountant for Lakeside Electronics determined that adjustments were needed for the following items as of December 31, 20X1: merchandise inventory, store supplies used, office supplies used, insurance expired, depreciation of equipment, and unpaid salaries.

To illustrate these adjustments, we will first record them in T accounts. T accounts, as you recall, are an excellent way to organize data and collect one's thoughts. We will then enter the adjustments on a work sheet. In the next chapter, we will discuss financial statements, journalizing the adjustments, and closing entries.

Adjustment for Merchandise Inventory

LEARNING OBJECTIVE 1

The cost of merchandise purchased during an accounting period is debited to the Purchases account. However, the Purchases account shows only the cost of merchandise purchased—not the value of merchandise on hand at the end of the accounting period. To determine the value of the goods on hand, it is necessary to take an **inventory**—a physical count to determine how much merchandise is unsold at the end of a period. The value of the goods on hand is then recorded in an *asset* account entitled **Merchandise Inventory**.

During the year, Lakeside constantly purchases, sells, and replaces merchandise. Rather than trying to keep up with this constant change in its inventory, Lakeside waits until the end of the year, takes an inventory of merchandise, and then adjusts the Merchandise Inventory account to show the value of the current inventory.

The adjustment for Merchandise Inventory is relatively simple. The Merchandise Inventory account is decreased by the value of the **beginning merchandise inventory** (the inventory at the beginning of the period), and it is increased by the value of the **ending merchandise inventory** (the inventory at the end of the period). To explore further, in Lakeside's trial balance (Figure 9-2), the Merchandise Inventory account shows a balance of $66,000. Since Lakeside adjusts the Merchandise Inventory account only at year-end, this figure does not represent the value of the goods currently on hand; it represents the value of the goods that were on hand when the period started.

A current count of merchandise (as of December 31) reveals that $72,400 worth of goods remain on hand. This is the up-to-date inventory, the amount we wish to show in the Merchandise Inventory account, and the amount we wish to list on the balance sheet.

How can we make the Merchandise Inventory account show the value of the latest inventory? A popular way is to simply remove the old inventory figure from the Merchandise Inventory account and, in its place, record the new inventory figure. This is accomplished in two steps, as described below.

STEP 1: TRANSFER THE BEGINNING INVENTORY FIGURE FROM MERCHANDISE INVENTORY TO INCOME SUMMARY

Analysis: Merchandise Inventory is an asset account, so it has a normal debit balance. Therefore, to decrease the account, we will credit the account for its balance. Our debit is to the Income Summary account. This adjustment is as follows.

Remember The Income Summary account does not have a normal debit or credit balance.

STEP 2: RECORD THE ENDING INVENTORY FIGURE IN THE MERCHANDISE INVENTORY ACCOUNT

Analysis: The current inventory figure is $72,400. The Merchandise Inventory account should be increased by this amount. The Merchandise Inventory account—an asset—is increased on the debit side. Our credit is to the Income Summary account.

Merchandise Inventory		Income Summary	
+	–		
Balance 66,000	Adjustment 66,000	Adjustment 66,000	**Adjustment 72,400**
Adjustment 72,400			

To adjust the Merchandise Inventory account, take out the old and put in the new.

The old inventory figure, $66,000, has been removed from the Merchandise Inventory account; and the new inventory figure, $72,400, has been recorded in the Merchandise Inventory account. This two-step procedure to adjust the Merchandise Inventory account is generally preferred by accountants because both the beginning and ending inventory figures appear on the income statement, which is prepared directly from the Income Statement columns of the work sheet. (We will discuss the income statement at greater length in the next chapter.) We could have accomplished the same result by adjusting the Merchandise Inventory account for the difference between the beginning and ending inventory figures ($72,400 – $66,000 = $6,400). Under this method, we would have increased the Merchandise Inventory account by $6,400 (because the ending inventory was higher than the beginning), thus bringing its balance to $72,400—the amount of the ending inventory. This method, however, is considered less meaningful because the difference between the inventory figures, $6,400, does not appear as a separate figure on the income statement.

REVIEW QUIZ 9-1

Before adjustment on December 31, 20XX, the Merchandise Inventory account of Tricia's Boutique shows a debit balance of $94,000. A current inventory count (as of December 31), however, shows that the new inventory figure is $97,000. Draw T accounts and make the adjusting entries to (a) remove the balance of the beginning inventory from the Merchandise Inventory account, and (b) record the value of the inventory on hand in the Merchandise Inventory account.

CHECK YOUR ANSWERS ON PAGE 347.

Adjustment for Store Supplies Used

LEARNING OBJECTIVE 2

Lakeside's remaining adjustments are very similar to those we made for Taylor and Associates in Chapter 4. Our next adjustment is for the amount of store supplies used during the period. Referring to Lakeside's trial balance (page 320), we see that the Store Supplies account has a $2,015 balance. This balance represents the cost of supplies on hand at the beginning of the year, plus the cost of supplies purchased during the year. An inventory count on December 31 revealed that $500 worth of store supplies remain on hand. The difference between the balance of the Store Supplies account and the ending inventory of store supplies ($2,015 – $500 = $1,515) is the value of store supplies consumed during the year. The value of store supplies consumed is no longer an asset; it has become an expense. Therefore, the adjustment for the store supplies used involves a debit to the Store Supplies expense account and a credit to the Store Supplies account, as illustrated in the T accounts at the top of the next page.

Store Supplies Expense			Store Supplies		
+	−		+		−
Adjustment 1,515			Balance 2,015		Adjustment 1,515

Adjustment for Office Supplies Used

The adjustment for office supplies used is determined in the same manner as the adjustment for store supplies used. Again, we refer to Lakeside's trial balance and see that the Office Supplies account has a $667 balance. However, an inventory count on December 31 revealed that only $250 worth remain on hand. Thus, $417 ($667 − $250) is the value of office supplies consumed. Our adjusting entry involves a debit to the Office Supplies Expense account and a credit to the Office Supplies account, as shown below.

Office Supplies Expense			Office Supplies		
+	−		+		−
Adjustment 417			Balance 667		Adjustment 417

Adjustment for Insurance Expired

In Chapter 4, we learned that insurance paid in advance is considered an asset because it provides a benefit—insurance protection—that the company will receive in the future. As time passes, however, the prepayment expires and the asset becomes an expense. At the end of the accounting period, we must make an adjustment for the value of insurance expired during the period.

On December 31, Lakeside's Prepaid Insurance account shows a $720 balance. This balance represents a two-year prepayment, made on October 1, for comprehensive (fire, theft, etc.) coverage on merchandise and equipment. The amount of the adjustment at December 31 is determined as follows:

$$\frac{\$720}{24 \text{ months}} = \$30 \text{ monthly expiration}$$

Oct. 1 to Dec. 31 = 3 months

$30 × 3 mo. = $90 insurance expired

The adjusting entry for insurance expired involves a debit to the Insurance Expense account and a credit to the Prepaid Insurance account. This entry is illustrated as follows:

Insurance Expense			Prepaid Insurance		
+	−		+		−
Adjustment 90			Balance 720		Adjustment 90

Adjustment for Depreciation Expense

As you recall, long-term physical assets—such as equipment, buildings, machinery, and furniture—are purchased for use in the business. To match the cost of these assets against the revenue they produce (according to the *accrual basis* of accounting), a part of their cost should be transferred to an expense account during each period the assets are used. This is accomplished by debiting the Depreciation Expense account and crediting the Accumulated Depreciation account.

1. Under the accrual basis of accounting, revenue is recorded when it is earned, regardless of when cash is received; and expenses are recorded when they are incurred, regardless of when they are paid.

2. The Accumulated Depreciation account is a *contra asset account* used to summarize the amount of depreciation recorded over the life of the asset to which it relates. It has a normal credit balance that is opposite the debit balance of the asset account.

Lakeside has three types of depreciable assets: (1) store equipment, (2) office equipment, and (3) delivery equipment. Lakeside uses the *straight-line method* to figure depreciation. This means that the same amount of depreciation is recorded for each full period the asset is used. In prior years, Lakeside's accountant determined the straight-line amount for each type of asset. Since some new equipment was purchased during 20X1, the depreciation amounts were refigured. They are as follows:

Asset	Cost	Depreciation Recorded in Prior Years	Depreciation for 20X1
Store Equipment	$11,385	$ 4,500	$ 900
Office Equipment	10,200	7,100	820
Delivery Equipment	56,000	13,800	9,200

Lakeside's adjusting entries for depreciation are recorded below in T accounts.

Store Equipment

Depreciation Expense—Store Equipment		Accumulated Depreciation—Store Equipment	
+	−	−	+
Adjustment 900			Balance 4,500
			Adjustment 900

Office Equipment

Depreciation Expense—Office Equipment		Accumulated Depreciation—Office Equipment	
+	−	−	+
Adjustment 820			Balance 7,100
			Adjustment 820

Delivery Equipment

Depreciation Expense—Delivery Equipment		Accumulated Depreciation—Delivery Equipment	
+	−	−	+
Adjustment 9,200			Balance 13,800
			Adjustment 9,200

In each case, the Depreciation Expense account did not have a balance before recording the adjusting entry; the Accumulated Depreciation account did have a balance. This is because the Depreciation Expense account shows a cost only for a particular period; and when that period is over, the balance of the account is closed to the Income Summary account (along with all other expenses). The account balance is thus reduced to zero, and the account is ready to record depreciation at the end of the next period. The Accumulated Depreciation account does *not* relate to a single period. It is a contra account used to *accumulate* depreciation over the life of the asset to which it relates.

Adjustment for Salaries Owed but Unpaid

Under the accrual basis of accounting, all salary expense incurred in an accounting period should be recorded in that period, even though payment may not have been made. Thus, at the end of an accounting period, a liability should be recorded for all salaries earned by employees but not yet paid by the employer. The liability for unpaid salaries is determined by calculating the salaries earned by employees from the last payday to the end of the accounting period. Accountants refer to these unpaid salaries as **accrued salaries** or **accrued wages**.

Lakeside's accounting year ends on December 31, 20X1. It is Lakeside's policy to pay employees every other Friday. The last payday was Friday, December 19. Therefore, at the close of business on December 31, eight workdays have passed since employees were last paid. This period can be illustrated as shown in Figure 9-3.

FIGURE 9-3

Calculating the adjustment for unpaid salaries

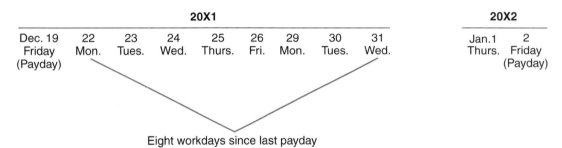

According to payroll records maintained by Lakeside's accountant, sales personnel earned $900 and office personnel earned $700 in the eight days between the last payday and the end of the period. Although these amounts will not be paid until the next regular payday (January 2, 20X2), they are an expense of 20X1. The use of the accrual basis, therefore, requires that they be recorded in 20X1. The adjusting entry involves debits to the expense accounts and a credit to the Salaries Payable account, as follows:

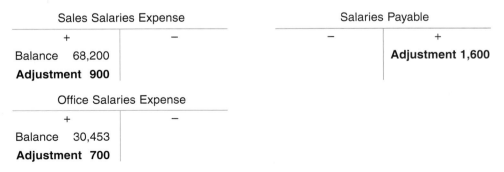

In addition to salaries, other expenses may be unpaid (and unrecorded) at the end of the accounting period. Utilities, for example, may have been used at the end of a period, but payment may not be due until sometime in the next period. These unpaid utilities need to be recorded to show the proper amount of utilities expense for the period.

Watkins Company ends its accounting year on December 31, 20XX. The accounting records showed the following data as of that date:

1. Merchandise Inventory: January 1 (beginning), $24,300; December 31 (ending), $25,600.
2. Balance of Store Supplies account, $600; inventory of store supplies on December 31, $250.
3. A three-year insurance policy for $3,600 was prepaid on November 1, 20XX.
4. Accrued (unpaid) salaries at December 31, $2,300.

Record Watkins's adjusting entries in general journal form.

CHECK YOUR ANSWERS ON PAGE 347.

THE END-OF-PERIOD WORK SHEET

LEARNING OBJECTIVE 2

As you learned in Chapter 4, the work sheet is an informal working paper used by the accountant to organize data and make end-of-period work easier. It is not a financial statement, and it will never be published. Nevertheless, it is an excellent tool that is widely used, particularly by large businesses that could have hundreds of adjustments.

In Chapter 4, we prepared a ten-column work sheet for Taylor and Associates. Now we will prepare a ten-column work sheet for Lakeside Electronics. As you remember from Chapter 4, the work sheet is completed one section at a time. Let's see how it is done for a merchandising business.

The Trial Balance and Adjustments Columns

You start the work sheet by entering the heading; then you enter the trial balance in the first two columns. Your next step is to enter the adjustments in the Adjustments columns. We have seen each adjustment needed by Lakeside Electronics in T-account form. Let's now enter Lakeside's December trial balance and the adjustments on the work sheet, as shown in Figure 9-4. Each adjustment, as you have already learned, is labeled starting with (a). After all adjustments have been entered, the Adjustments columns are totaled to check the equality of debits and credits. The column totals are then ruled.

The Adjusted Trial Balance Columns

The adjustments are now combined with the account balances in the Trial Balance columns, and the updated amounts are moved over to the Adjusted Trial Balance columns, as illustrated in Figure 9-5 on page 329. To avoid confusion, each account is moved in order, starting with the Cash account and proceeding downward line by line. Amounts are moved over as follows:

❶ If an account does not have an adjustment, simply carry over the Trial Balance figure to the appropriate Adjusted Trial Balance column. For example, the Cash account has a debit balance of $6,200. Since this amount was not adjusted, it is moved directly to the Adjusted Trial Balance Dr. column. Remember that a debit remains a debit.

FIGURE 9-4
Trial Balance and Adjustments columns of the work sheet

Lakeside Electronics
Work Sheet
For Year Ended December 31, 20X1

	Account Title	Trial Balance Debit	Trial Balance Credit	Adjustments Debit	Adjustments Credit	
1	Cash	6 2 0 0 00				1
2	Accounts Receivable	9 6 8 9 00				2
3	Merchandise Inventory	66 0 0 0 00		(b) 72 4 0 0 00	(a) 66 0 0 0 00	3
4	Store Supplies	2 0 1 5 00			(c) 1 5 1 5 00	4
5	Office Supplies	6 6 7 00			(d) 4 1 7 00	5
6	Prepaid Insurance	7 2 0 00			(e) 9 0 00	6
7	Store Equipment	11 3 8 5 00				7
8	Accumulated Depreciation—Store Equipment		4 5 0 0 00		(f) 9 0 0 00	8
9	Office Equipment	10 2 0 0 00				9
10	Accumulated Depreciation—Office Equipment		7 1 0 0 00		(g) 8 2 0 00	10
11	Delivery Equipment	56 0 0 0 00				11
12	Accumulated Depreciation—Delivery Equipment		13 8 0 0 00		(h) 9 2 0 0 00	12
13	Accounts Payable		14 0 2 5 00			13
14	Salaries Payable		—		(i) 1 6 0 0 00	14
15	Notes Payable		26 0 0 0 00			15
16	John Graham, Capital		75 5 8 1 00			16
17	John Graham, Drawing	18 0 0 0 00				17
18	Income Summary	—	—	(a) 66 0 0 0 00	(b) 72 4 0 0 00	18
19	Sales		304 6 0 0 00			19
20	Sales Returns and Allowances	5 2 3 0 00				20
21	Sales Discounts	3 4 6 1 00				21
22	Purchases	144 9 1 8 00				22
23	Purchases Returns and Allowances		6 6 9 2 00			23
24	Purchases Discounts		2 9 1 0 00			24
25	Freight In	1 1 6 0 00				25
26	Sales Salaries Expense	68 2 0 0 00		(i) 9 0 0 00		26
27	Advertising Expense	5 8 4 0 00				27
28	Store Supplies Expense	—		(c) 1 5 1 5 00		28
29	Depreciation Expense—Store Equipment	—		(f) 9 0 0 00		29
30	Miscellaneous Selling Expense	2 1 0 0 00				30
31	Rent Expense	5 7 0 0 00				31
32	Office Salaries Expense	30 4 5 3 00		(i) 7 0 0 00		32
33	Insurance Expense	—		(e) 9 0 00		33
34	Depreciation Expense—Office Equipment	—		(g) 8 2 0 00		34
35	Depreciation Expense—Delivery Equipment	—		(h) 9 2 0 0 00		35
36	Utilities Expense	6 2 4 0 00				36
37	Office Supplies Expense	—		(d) 4 1 7 00		37
38	Interest Expense	1 3 0 00				38
39	Miscellaneous General Expense	9 0 0 00				39
40		455 2 0 8 00	455 2 0 8 00	152 9 4 2 00	152 9 4 2 00	40

Work Sheet and Adjustments for a Merchandising Business

327

❷ The Merchandise Inventory account has a $66,000 debit balance in the Trial Balance Dr. column. However, a $66,000 credit adjustment was made to the account in the Adjustments columns. The $66,000 debit balance is balanced out by the $66,000 credit adjustment. Thus, the amount moved to the Adjusted Trial Balance is the amount of the debit adjustment, $72,400.

❸ If an account has a debit balance, and the adjustment is a credit, the difference between the two amounts is entered in the Adjusted Trial Balance Dr. column. For example, the Store Supplies account has a debit balance of $2,015 and a credit adjustment of $1,515. Thus, the difference between the two amounts, $500, is entered in the Adjusted Trial Balance Dr. column.

❹ If an account has a debit balance, and the adjustment is also a debit, add the two figures and move the total to the Adjusted Trial Balance Dr. column. For example, the Sales Salaries Expense account has a debit balance of $68,200 and a $900 debit adjustment. The two debits are added, and the total, $69,100, is entered in the Adjusted Trial Balance Dr. column.

❺ If an account has a credit balance, and the adjustment is also a credit, add the two figures and enter the total in the Adjusted Trial Balance Cr. column. For example, the Accumulated Depreciation—Store Equipment account has a credit balance of $4,500 and a credit adjustment of $900. The two credits are added, and the total, $5,400, is entered in the Adjusted Trial Balance Cr. column.

❻ If an account does not have a balance in the Trial Balance columns, but there is an adjustment, the amount of the adjustment becomes the balance. It is carried over to the appropriate Adjusted Trial Balance column. For example, the Salaries Payable account did not have a balance. However, there was a $1,600 credit adjustment. Thus, $1,600 is moved to the Adjusted Trial Balance Cr. column.

❼ *Both* the $66,000 debit adjustment and the $72,400 credit adjustment to the Income Summary account are moved over to the Adjusted Trial Balance columns. We do this because both figures will appear on the income statement, which is prepared directly from the completed work sheet.

Income Summary is the only account for which you do not combine the debit and credit figures. Instead, you move both to the Adjusted Trial Balance as two distinct figures.

After all amounts have been moved over, the Adjusted Trial Balance columns are totaled to prove the equality of debits and credits. The column totals are then ruled. Lakeside's work sheet through the Adjusted Trial Balance is shown in Figure 9-5.

When extending amounts to the Adjusted Trial Balance columns, "likes" are added and "dislikes" are subtracted. If there are two debits or two credits, you add. If there is one debit and one credit, you subtract.

Financial Statement Columns

Now that the Adjusted Trial Balance columns are complete, our next step is to move the updated amounts over to the appropriate financial statement columns, as shown in Figure 9-6 on pages 330–331. It is possible to complete one set of financial statement columns at a time. For a business with a large number of

FIGURE 9-5
Work sheet through the adjusted trial balance

Lakeside Electronics
Work Sheet
For Year Ended December 31, 20X1

	Account Title	Trial Balance Debit	Trial Balance Credit	Adjustments Debit	Adjustments Credit	Adjusted Trial Balance Debit	Adjusted Trial Balance Credit	
1	Cash	6 200 00				6 200 00		1
2	Accounts Receivable	9 689 00				9 689 00		2
3	Merchandise Inventory	66 000 00		(b) 72 400 00	(a) 66 000 00	72 400 00		3
4	Store Supplies	2 015 00			(c) 1 515 00	500 00		4
5	Office Supplies	667 00			(d) 417 00	250 00		5
6	Prepaid Insurance	720 00			(e) 90 00	630 00		6
7	Store Equipment	11 385 00				11 385 00		7
8	Accum. Depr.—Store Equip.		4 500 00		(f) 900 00		5 400 00	8
9	Office Equipment	10 200 00				10 200 00		9
10	Accum. Depr.—Off. Equip.		7 100 00		(g) 820 00		7 920 00	10
11	Delivery Equipment	56 000 00				56 000 00		11
12	Accum. Depr.—Del. Equip.		13 800 00		(h) 9 200 00		23 000 00	12
13	Accounts Payable		14 025 00				14 025 00	13
14	Salaries Payable		—		(i) 1 600 00		1 600 00	14
15	Notes Payable		26 000 00				26 000 00	15
16	John Graham, Capital		75 581 00				75 581 00	16
17	John Graham, Drawing	18 000 00				18 000 00		17
18	Income Summary	—	—	(a) 66 000 00	(b) 72 400 00	66 000 00	72 400 00	18
19	Sales		304 600 00				304 600 00	19
20	Sales Returns and Allow.	5 230 00				5 230 00		20
21	Sales Discounts	3 461 00				3 461 00		21
22	Purchases	144 918 00				144 918 00		22
23	Purchases Ret. and Allow.		6 692 00				6 692 00	23
24	Purchases Discounts		2 910 00				2 910 00	24
25	Freight In	1 160 00				1 160 00		25
26	Sales Salaries Expense	68 200 00		(i) 900 00		69 100 00		26
27	Advertising Expense	5 840 00				5 840 00		27
28	Store Supplies Expense	—		(c) 1 515 00		1 515 00		28
29	Depr. Exp.—Store Equip.	—		(f) 900 00		900 00		29
30	Miscellaneous Selling Exp.	2 100 00				2 100 00		30
31	Rent Expense	5 700 00				5 700 00		31
32	Office Salaries Expense	30 453 00		(i) 700 00		31 153 00		32
33	Insurance Expense	—		(e) 90 00		90 00		33
34	Depr. Exp.—Office Equip.	—		(g) 820 00		820 00		34
35	Depr. Exp.—Delivery Equip.	—		(h) 9 200 00		9 200 00		35
36	Utilities Expense	6 240 00				6 240 00		36
37	Office Supplies Expense	—		(d) 417 00		417 00		37
38	Interest Expense	130 00				130 00		38
39	Miscellaneous General Exp.	900 00				900 00		39
40		455 208 00	455 208 00	152 942 00	152 942 00	540 128 00	540 128 00	40
41	Net Income							41

FIGURE 9-6
Completed work sheet

	Account Title	Trial Balance Debit	Trial Balance Credit	Adjustments Debit	Adjustments Credit	
1	Cash	6 200 00				1
2	Accounts Receivable	9 689 00				2
3	Merchandise Inventory	66 000 00		(b) 72 400 00	(a) 66 000 00	3
4	Store Supplies	2 015 00			(c) 1 515 00	4
5	Office Supplies	667 00			(d) 417 00	5
6	Prepaid Insurance	720 00			(e) 90 00	6
7	Store Equipment	11 385 00				7
8	Accumulated Depreciation—Store Equipment		4 500 00		(f) 900 00	8
9	Office Equipment	10 200 00				9
10	Accumulated Depreciation—Office Equipment		7 100 00		(g) 820 00	10
11	Delivery Equipment	56 000 00				11
12	Accumulated Depreciation —Delivery Equipment		13 800 00		(h) 920 00	12
13	Accounts Payable		14 025 00			13
14	Salaries Payable		—		(i) 1 600 00	14
15	Notes Payable		26 000 00			15
16	John Graham, Capital		75 581 00			16
17	John Graham, Drawing	18 000 00				17
18	Income Summary		—	(a) 66 000 00	(b) 72 400 00	18
19	Sales		304 600 00			19
20	Sales Returns and Allowances	5 230 00				20
21	Sales Discounts	3 461 00				21
22	Purchases	144 918 00				22
23	Purchases Returns and Allowances		6 692 00			23
24	Purchases Discounts		2 910 00			24
25	Freight In	1 160 00				25
26	Sales Salaries Expense	68 200 00		(i) 900 00		26
27	Advertising Expense	5 840 00				27
28	Store Supplies Expense	—		(c) 1 515 00		28
29	Depreciation Expense—Store Equipment	—		(f) 900 00		29
30	Miscellaneous Selling Expense	2 100 00				30
31	Rent Expense	5 700 00				31
32	Office Salaries Expense	30 453 00		(i) 700 00		32
33	Insurance Expense	—		(e) 90 00		33
34	Depreciation Expense—Office Equipment	—		(g) 820 00		34
35	Depreciation Expense—Delivery Equipment	—		(h) 920 00		35
36	Utilities Expense	6 240 00				36
37	Office Supplies Expense	—		(d) 417 00		37
38	Interest Expense	130 00				38
39	Miscellaneous General Expense	900 00				39
40		455 208 00	455 208 00	152 942 00	152 942 00	40
41	Net Income					41
42						42

Lakeside Electronics
Work Sheet
For Year Ended December 31, 20X1

#	Adjusted Trial Balance Debit	Adjusted Trial Balance Credit	Income Statement Debit	Income Statement Credit	Balance Sheet Debit	Balance Sheet Credit	#
1	6 2 0 0 00				6 2 0 0 00		1
2	9 6 8 9 00				9 6 8 9 00		2
3	72 4 0 0 00				72 4 0 0 00		3
4	5 0 0 00				5 0 0 00		4
5	2 5 0 00				2 5 0 00		5
6	6 3 0 00				6 3 0 00		6
7	11 3 8 5 00				11 3 8 5 00		7
8		5 4 0 0 00				5 4 0 0 00	8
9	10 2 0 0 00				10 2 0 0 00		9
10		7 9 2 0 00				7 9 2 0 00	10
11	56 0 0 0 00				56 0 0 0 00		11
12		23 0 0 0 00				23 0 0 0 00	12
13		14 0 2 5 00				14 0 2 5 00	13
14		1 6 0 0 00				1 6 0 0 00	14
15		26 0 0 0 00				26 0 0 0 00	15
16		75 5 8 1 00				75 5 8 1 00	16
17	18 0 0 0 00				18 0 0 0 00		17
18	66 0 0 0 00	72 4 0 0 00	66 0 0 0 00	72 4 0 0 00			18
19		304 6 0 0 00		304 6 0 0 00			19
20	5 2 3 0 00		5 2 3 0 00				20
21	3 4 6 1 00		3 4 6 1 00				21
22	144 9 1 8 00		144 9 1 8 00				22
23		6 6 9 2 00		6 6 9 2 00			23
24		2 9 1 0 00		2 9 1 0 00			24
25	1 1 6 0 00		1 1 6 0 00				25
26	69 1 0 0 00		69 1 0 0 00				26
27	5 8 4 0 00		5 8 4 0 00				27
28	1 5 1 5 00		1 5 1 5 00				28
29	9 0 0 00		9 0 0 00				29
30	2 1 0 0 00		2 1 0 0 00				30
31	5 7 0 0 00		5 7 0 0 00				31
32	31 1 5 3 00		31 1 5 3 00				32
33	9 0 00		9 0 00				33
34	8 2 0 00		8 2 0 00				34
35	9 2 0 0 00		9 2 0 0 00				35
36	6 2 4 0 00		6 2 4 0 00				36
37	4 1 7 00		4 1 7 00				37
38	1 3 0 00		1 3 0 00				38
39	9 0 0 00		9 0 0 00				39
40	540 1 2 8 00	540 1 2 8 00	354 8 7 4 00	386 6 0 2 00	185 2 5 4 00	153 5 2 6 00	40
41			31 7 2 8 00			31 7 2 8 00	41
42			386 6 0 2 00	386 6 0 2 00	185 2 5 4 00	185 2 5 4 00	42

accounts, however, it is less confusing to start with the Cash account and move downward, line by line, extending each amount to the appropriate statement column. Amounts are moved as follows:

❶ Assets and the owner's drawing account are moved to the Balance Sheet Dr. column.

❷ Accumulated depreciation, liabilities, and the owner's capital account are moved to the Balance Sheet Cr. column.

❸ Both amounts shown for the Income Summary account are moved to the Income Statement columns. Thus, $66,000 is moved to the Income Statement Dr. column; and $72,400 is moved to the Income Statement Cr. column.

❹ Revenue and contra purchases accounts (Purchases Returns and Allowances and Purchases Discounts) are moved to the Income Statement Cr. column.

❺ Expenses, Purchases, and contra sales accounts (Sales Returns and Allowances and Sales Discounts) are moved to the Income Statement Dr. column.

Before looking at how amounts are actually moved to the financial statement columns, let's take a moment to summarize the steps above in diagram form:

Income Statement		Balance Sheet	
Debit	**Credit**	**Debit**	**Credit**
Income Summary	Income Summary	Assets	Accumulated
Sales Returns	Sales	Drawing	Depreciation
and Allowances	Purchases Returns		Liabilities
Sales Discounts	and Allowances		Capital
Purchases	Purchases Discounts		
Freight In			
Expenses			

Now look at Figure 9-6 and, starting with the Cash account, trace how each amount is moved from the Adjusted Trial Balance to the appropriate financial statement column.

Completing the Work Sheet

Having extended all amounts to the appropriate financial statement columns, we can now complete the work sheet as follows:

❶ Total the Income Statement Dr. and Cr. columns.

❷ Total the Balance Sheet Dr. and Cr. columns.

❸ Determine the amount of net income (or net loss) by finding the difference between the Income Statement Cr. column and the Income Statement Dr. column. If the Income Statement Cr. column (revenue) is greater than the Income Statement Dr. column (costs and expenses), there is a net income. On the other hand, if the Income Statement Dr. column is greater than the Income Statement Cr. column, there is a net loss.

❹ Write the words Net income (or Net loss) in the Account Title column.

❺ Enter the net income figure under the Income Statement Dr. column and the Balance Sheet Cr. column. If a net loss exists, the net loss figure is entered under the Income Statement Cr. column and the Balance Sheet Dr. column.

❻ Retotal the Income Statement columns and the Balance Sheet columns as an arithmetic check.

❼ Double rule the column totals.

Lakeside's completed work sheet is shown in Figure 9-6.

REVIEW QUIZ 9-3

The totals of the Income Statement columns and Balance Sheet columns of Massey Company's June 30 work sheet are as follows:

Income Statement		Balance Sheet	
Debit	Credit	Debit	Credit
22,300	40,400	61,000	42,900

Using a separate sheet of paper, balance the columns and state the amount of net income (or net loss) for the period.

CHECK YOUR ANSWERS ON PAGE 347.

INTERNET ASSETS

WHERE CAN I FIND ANSWERS TO ACCOUNTING QUESTIONS ON THE INTERNET?

A good place to look for answers to accounting questions is the AICPA's site at *http://www.aicpa.org/forums/index.htm*. The AICPA's site includes many forums such as general accounting, auditing, taxation, and information technology. A forum is essentially an ongoing electronic conversation on a specialized topic. This location is user-friendly and gives extensive directions for first-time users.

This forum provides an invaluable service to the accounting world. You can pose a question or post a message, and accountants around the world will respond and offer suggestions. One enormous time-saver is the notification option: whenever a message you have posted receives a response, an e-mail will automatically go out notifying you of the response. With this option, you will not have to log on and off continually to check for responses.

Check out the Paradigm Interactive Web Site at *http://www.emcp.com/collgdiv* for answers to your accounting questions. In the Electronic Resource Center you can ask questions of the textbook's authors, other students, and instructors from around the country.

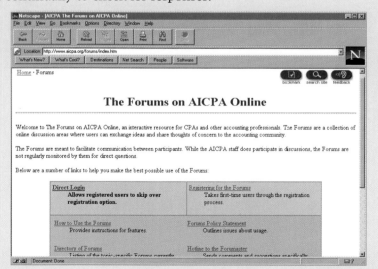

PROCEDURES FOR ADJUSTING THE MERCHANDISE INVENTORY ACCOUNT

Beginning inventory (January 1) = $66,000
Ending inventory (December 31) = $72,400

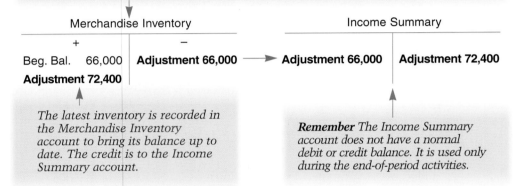

The Merchandise Inventory account must be reduced by the amount of the beginning inventory to make the account ready to record the ending inventory. The debit is to the Income Summary account.

Merchandise Inventory				Income Summary	
+		−			
Beg. Bal. 66,000	**Adjustment 66,000**	→	**Adjustment 66,000**	**Adjustment 72,400**	
Adjustment 72,400					

The latest inventory is recorded in the Merchandise Inventory account to bring its balance up to date. The credit is to the Income Summary account.

Remember *The Income Summary account does not have a normal debit or credit balance. It is used only during the end-of-period activities.*

SUMMARY/RESTATEMENT OF LEARNING OBJECTIVES

1. Make adjustments to the Merchandise Inventory account.

The Rose Bowl is a retail florist. On June 30, 20X1, the end of the Rose Bowl's accounting year, the Merchandise Inventory account had a balance of $46,000. However, a current count revealed that only $42,000 worth of merchandise remained on hand. The adjustment for merchandise is shown below in T-account form.

Merchandise Inventory		Income Summary	
Bal. 46,000	**Adj. 46,000**	**Adj. 46,000**	**Adj. 42,000**
Adj. 42,000			

2. Make other needed adjustments and complete a work sheet for a merchandising business.

The Rose Bowl's June 30, 20X1, trial balance is shown in Figure 9-7.

In addition to the merchandise inventory adjustment presented in the preceding section, The Rose Bowl had the following adjustment data on June 30:

1. A current count revealed that $400 worth of store supplies were on hand.
2. Estimated depreciation on store equipment, $1,000.
3. Estimated depreciation on trucks, $3,000.
4. Accrued (unpaid) salaries, $400.

Using The Rose Bowl's trial balance and the above adjustment data, the work sheet shown in Figure 9-8 was prepared.

FIGURE 9-7
Trial balance for the Rose Bowl

The Rose Bowl Trial Balance June 30, 20X1		
Account Title	**Debit**	**Credit**
Cash	3 1 0 0 00	
Accounts Receivable	6 8 0 0 00	
Merchandise Inventory	46 0 0 0 00	
Store Supplies	6 0 0 00	
Store Equipment	25 0 0 0 00	
Accumulated Depreciation—Store Equipment		3 0 0 0 00
Trucks	38 0 0 0 00	
Accumulated Depreciation—Trucks		7 0 0 0 00
Accounts Payable		4 9 0 0 00
Sales Tax Payable		1 1 0 0 00
Salaries Payable		—
Karen Grimes, Capital		83 5 0 0 00
Karen Grimes, Drawing	25 0 0 0 00	
Income Summary	—	—
Sales		177 1 9 0 00
Sales Returns and Allowances	8 0 0 00	
Purchases	77 8 0 0 00	
Purchases Returns and Allowances		1 2 0 0 00
Purchases Discounts		6 0 0 00
Sales Salaries Expense	32 0 0 0 00	
Advertising Expense	4 8 0 0 00	
Depreciation Expense—Store Equipment	—	
Miscellaneous Selling Expense	8 0 0 00	
Store Supplies Expense	—	
Rent Expense	4 8 9 0 00	
Repairs Expense	6 0 0 00	
Transportation Expense	9 0 0 00	
Depreciation Expense—Trucks	—	
Utilities Expense	9 6 0 0 00	
Miscellaneous General Expense	1 8 0 0 00	
Totals	278 4 9 0 00	278 4 9 0 00

FIGURE 9-8
Work sheet for The Rose Bowl

The Rose Bowl
Work Sheet
For Year Ended June 30, 20X1

#	Account Title	Trial Balance Debit	Trial Balance Credit	Adjustments Debit	Adjustments Credit	Adjusted Trial Balance Debit	Adjusted Trial Balance Credit	Income Statement Debit	Income Statement Credit	Balance Sheet Debit	Balance Sheet Credit
1	Cash	3100.00				3100.00				3100.00	
2	Accounts Receivable	6800.00				6800.00				6800.00	
3	Merchandise Inventory	46000.00		(b) 42000.00	(a) 46000.00	42000.00				42000.00	
4	Store Supplies	600.00			(c) 200.00	400.00				400.00	
5	Store Equipment	25000.00				25000.00				25000.00	
6	Acc. Depr.—Store Equip.		3000.00		(d) 1000.00		4000.00				4000.00
7	Trucks	38000.00				38000.00				38000.00	
8	Accum. Depr.—Trucks		7000.00		(e) 3000.00		10000.00				10000.00
9	Accounts Payable		4900.00				4900.00				4900.00
10	Sales Tax Payable		1100.00				1100.00				1100.00
11	Salaries Payable		—		(f) 400.00		400.00				400.00
12	Karen Grimes, Capital		83500.00				83500.00				83500.00
13	Karen Grimes, Drawing	25000.00				25000.00				25000.00	
14	Income Summary	—	—	(a) 46000.00	(b) 42000.00	46000.00	42000.00	46000.00	42000.00		
15	Sales		177190.00				177190.00		177190.00		
16	Sales Ret. & Allow.	800.00				800.00		800.00			
17	Purchases	77800.00				77800.00		77800.00			
18	Purchases Ret. & Allow.		1200.00				1200.00		1200.00		
19	Purchases Discounts		600.00				600.00		600.00		
20	Sales Salaries Expense	32000.00		(f) 400.00		32400.00		32400.00			
21	Advertising Expense	4800.00				4800.00		4800.00			
22	Depr. Exp.—Store Equip.	—		(d) 1000.00		1000.00		1000.00			
23	Misc. Selling Expense	800.00				800.00		800.00			
24	Store Supplies Expense	—		(c) 200.00		200.00		200.00			
25	Rent Expense	4890.00				4890.00		4890.00			
26	Repairs Expense	600.00				600.00		600.00			
27	Transportation Expense	900.00				900.00		900.00			
28	Depr. Expense—Trucks	—		(e) 3000.00		3000.00		3000.00			
29	Utilities Expense	960.00				960.00		960.00			
30	Misc. General Expense	1800.00				1800.00		1800.00			
31		278490.00	278490.00	92600.00	92600.00	324890.00	324890.00	184590.00	220990.00	140300.00	103900.00
32	Net Income							36400.00			36400.00
33								220990.00	220990.00	140300.00	140300.00

KEY TERMS

accrued salaries (accrued wages) Salaries that are unpaid (and unrecorded) at the end of an accounting period.

beginning merchandise inventory The dollar value of merchandise that is on hand at the beginning of an accounting period.

ending merchandise inventory The dollar value of merchandise that is on hand at the end of an accounting period.

inventory A count taken of the merchandise on hand at the end of an accounting period.

Merchandise Inventory An asset account that shows the value of goods (inventory) on hand at a given moment (usually at the beginning or end of the accounting period).

CONCEPTS AND SKILLS REVIEW

CONCEPTS REVIEW

1. Why are adjustments needed?
2. The Purchases account shows only the cost of merchandise purchased—not what is on hand at the end of the accounting period. Explain.
3. Why is it necessary to adjust the Merchandise Inventory account at the end of an accounting period?
4. For which merchandise inventory—beginning or ending—is the Income Summary account debited? For which is it credited?
5. If the Supplies account shows a balance of $850 before adjustment and $300 is calculated to be on hand, what is (a) the amount of the adjustment for supplies used; (b) the amount of supplies expense to be reported on the income statement; and (c) the amount of supplies to be reported on the balance sheet?
6. What type of account is the Accumulated Depreciation account?
7. If salaries are paid weekly, payday is Friday, and the accounting period ends on a Wednesday, how many days' salary are accrued at the end of that accounting period?
8. Identify the column on the work sheet to which you extend the amounts of (a) assets; (b) contra assets; (c) liabilities; (d) revenue; (e) expenses.
9. How do adjustments for a merchandising business differ from those for a service business?

SKILLS REVIEW

EXERCISE 9-1

LEARNING OBJECTIVE 2

Objective: To calculate the amount of expired insurance

Directions: Information about three insurance policies follows. Complete the table shown here and reproduced in your working papers. All policies were purchased on March 1, 20XX. It is now December 31, 20XX.

Policy Number	Premium	Term (Years)	Monthly Expiration	Expense for 20XX
(1)	$ 288	1	$_____	$_____
(2)	1,440	3	$_____	$_____
(3)	2,160	2	$_____	$_____

Work Sheet and Adjustments for a Merchandising Business

EXERCISE 9-2

Objective: To calculate the amount of the adjustment for accrued salaries

Directions: Wright Company pays salaries of $144,000 on Monday for the preceding week. Calculate the amount of the adjustment for accrued salaries on December 31 if that day falls on (a) Tuesday; (b) Thursday; (c) Saturday. Assume a five-day workweek and the accounting period ending on December 31.

EXERCISE 9-3

Objective: To record adjustments in T accounts

Directions: In separate pairs of T accounts, record each of the following adjustments. When beginning balances are given, insert them in the proper T accounts before making the adjustments.

(a) The Supplies account shows a balance of $1,290 prior to adjustment. Supplies of $470 are on hand.
(b) The Prepaid Insurance account shows a balance of $900 prior to adjustment. Of this amount, $300 has expired.
(c) Accrued salaries amount to $575.
(d) Depreciation of office equipment is $1,075.

EXERCISE 9-4

Objective: To record adjustments in T accounts

Directions: In separate pairs of T accounts, record each of the following adjustments. When beginning balances are given, insert them in the proper T accounts before making the adjustments.

(a) Merchandise inventory (beginning), January 1, $48,000.
Merchandise inventory (ending), December 31, $51,510.
(b) Store supplies on hand, $16,410; balance of Store Supplies account prior to adjustment, $72,450.
(c) Office supplies on hand, $3,125; balance of Office Supplies account prior to adjustment, $21,355.
(d) Insurance expired, $1,000.
(e) Depreciation of office equipment, $35,000.
(f) Weekly salaries of $60,000, unpaid for three days.

EXERCISE 9-5

Objective: To identify work sheet columns

Directions: For each account listed, indicate whether it is extended to the (a) Income Statement Dr. column; (b) Income Statement Cr. column; (c) Balance Sheet Dr. column; or (d) Balance Sheet Cr. column.

1. Purchases Returns and Allowances
2. Accumulated Depreciation—Office Equipment
3. Accounts Payable
4. Sales Discounts
5. Owner, Drawing
6. Rent Expense
7. Prepaid Insurance
8. Merchandise Inventory
9. Freight In
10. Accounts Receivable
11. Owner, Capital
12. Purchases

LEARNING OBJECTIVE 1, 2   **Objective: To prepare a work sheet**

Directions: The December 31, 20XX trial balance of Melvin Company follows. Using the adjustment data that are also listed, prepare a work sheet. The amounts are small so that you can concentrate on how to prepare a work sheet without arithmetic getting in the way.

Melvin Company Trial Balance December 31, 20XX		
Account Title	**Debit**	**Credit**
Cash	9 00	
Accounts Receivable	4 00	
Merchandise Inventory	10 00	
Supplies	7 00	
Prepaid Insurance	3 00	
Equipment	15 00	
Accumulated Depreciation—Equipment		6 00
Accounts Payable		4 00
Salaries Payable		—
James Melvin, Capital		40 00
James Melvin, Drawing	4 00	
Income Summary	—	—
Sales		38 00
Sales Returns and Allowances	2 00	
Purchases	20 00	
Purchases Returns and Allowances		1 00
Rent Expense	3 00	
Salaries Expense	10 00	
Supplies Expense	—	
Insurance Expense	—	
Depreciation Expense—Equipment	—	
Miscellaneous Expense	2 00	
Totals	89 00	89 00

Adjustment data:

(a) and (b) Merchandise inventory at December 31, $9.
     (c) Supplies on hand, $2.
     (d) Insurance expired, $1.
     (e) Accrued salaries, $3.
     (f) Depreciation of equipment, $3.

CASE PROBLEMS

GROUP A

PROBLEM 9-1A

LEARNING OBJECTIVE 2

Objective: To calculate amounts of adjustments

Directions: In each of the following situations, calculate the amount of the adjustment needed as of December 31, the end of the current accounting period.

(a) The Office Supplies account shows a balance of $7,295 on January 1 and a purchase of $16,755 on July 1. The December 31 inventory is $11,210.

(b) The Store Supplies account shows a balance of $11,475 on January 1 and purchases of $35,640 and $19,570 during the year. The December 31 inventory is $5,775.

(c) The Prepaid Insurance account shows a debit balance of $3,240, representing a three-year premium paid on March 1 of the current year.

(d) Salaries of $72,000 are paid weekly on Monday for the preceding week. This year, December 31 fell on a Tuesday.

PROBLEM 9-2A

LEARNING OBJECTIVE 1, 2

Objective: To record adjustments in T accounts

Directions: In each of the following unrelated transactions, record in T accounts opening balances, purchases, and adjustments as of December 31 of the current year.

(a) Merchandise inventory (beginning) on January 1 was $91,645.
Merchandise inventory (ending) on December 31 is $87,365.

(b) The Office Supplies account shows a January 1 balance of $8,145, a July 1 purchase of $17,510, and a December 31 inventory of $5,175.

(c) The Store Supplies account shows a January 1 balance of $7,250, a March 1 purchase of $15,595, and a December 31 inventory of $8,165.

(d) The Prepaid Insurance account shows a payment for a two-year policy on October 1 of this year in the amount of $1,800.

(e) Salaries of $18,000 are paid weekly on Monday for the preceding week. This year, December 31 fell on a Tuesday.

(f) Depreciation expense on office equipment is $15,000.

PROBLEM 9-3A

LEARNING OBJECTIVE 1, 2

Objective: To prepare a work sheet

Account balances and adjustment data for Montrose Carpet Shop follow:

Account	Balance
Cash	$ 6,725
Accounts Receivable	9,450
Merchandise Inventory (January 1)	13,165
Office Supplies	16,210
Store Supplies	14,575
Prepaid Insurance	2,400
Office Equipment	36,000
Accumulated Depreciation—Office Equipment	9,000
Store Equipment	84,000
Accumulated Depreciation—Store Equipment	25,200

Account	Balance
Delivery Equipment	27,000
Accumulated Depreciation—Delivery Equipment	13,500
Accounts Payable	16,510
Salaries Payable	—
George Montrose, Capital	88,220
George Montrose, Drawing	24,000
Income Summary	—
Sales	469,600
Sales Returns and Allowances	21,540
Sales Discounts	9,310
Purchases	301,240
Purchases Returns and Allowances	19,565
Purchases Discounts	6,110
Freight In	14,590
Sales Salaries Expense	30,000
Store Supplies Expense	—
Advertising Expense	4,500
Depreciation Expense—Store Equipment	
Depreciation Expense—Delivery Equipment	
Rent Expense	12,000
Office Salaries Expense	15,000
Office Supplies Expense	—
Utilities Expense	6,000
Insurance Expense	—
Depreciation Expense—Office Equipment	—

Here are the adjustment data:

(a) and (b) Merchandise inventory, December 31, $13,410.
(c) Office supplies on hand, $3,190.
(d) Store supplies on hand, $4,175.
(e) Insurance expired, $800.
(f) Salaries accrued: office, $180; sales, $360.
(g) Depreciation of office equipment, $3,600.
(h) Depreciation of store equipment, $8,400.
(i) Depreciation of delivery equipment, $9,000.

Directions: Prepare a work sheet for the year ended December 31, 20X1.

LEARNING OBJECTIVE 1, 2

PROBLEM 9-4A

Objective: To prepare a work sheet

The June 30, 20X2 trial balance of Coosa Valley Technical Products Co. follows:

Coosa Valley Technical Products Co. Trial Balance June 30, 20X2		
Account Title	**Debit**	**Credit**
Cash	3 0 0 0 00	
Accounts Receivable	8 4 0 0 00	
Merchandise Inventory (July 1, 20X1)	38 9 0 0 00	
Store Supplies	1 5 4 0 00	
Office Supplies	1 3 6 0 00	
Prepaid Insurance	1 8 0 0 00	
Store Equipment	11 0 9 5 00	
Accumulated Depreciation—Store Equipment		2 6 5 0 00
Office Equipment	10 5 0 0 00	
Accumulated Depreciation—Office Equipment		4 5 6 0 00

Work Sheet and Adjustments for a Merchandising Business

341

	Debit	Credit
Delivery Equipment	47 8 0 0 00	
Accumulated Depreciation—Delivery Equipment		12 3 0 0 00
Building	85 7 0 0 00	
Accumulated Depreciation—Building		18 3 5 0 00
Land	38 8 0 0 00	
Accounts Payable		7 4 0 0 00
Salaries Payable		—
Notes Payable		42 0 0 0 00
Jim Wallace, Capital		150 3 0 3 00
Jim Wallace, Drawing	25 0 0 0 00	
Income Summary	—	—
Sales		202 5 0 0 00
Sales Returns and Allowances	3 5 9 0 00	
Sales Discounts	1 7 0 0 00	
Purchases	71 4 0 0 00	
Purchases Returns and Allowances		2 4 5 0 00
Purchases Discounts		4 6 7 9 00
Sales Salaries Expense	38 0 0 0 00	
Advertising Expense	8 9 8 0 00	
Depreciation Expense—Store Equipment	—	
Store Supplies Expense	—	
Miscellaneous Selling Expense	1 2 1 5 00	
Office Salaries Expense	26 7 0 0 00	
Delivery Expense	7 8 4 0 00	
Utilities Expense	8 9 0 0 00	
Depreciation Expense—Office Equipment	—	
Depreciation Expense—Delivery Equipment	—	
Depreciation Expense—Building	—	
Repairs Expense	3 5 6 0 00	
Office Supplies Expense	—	
Insurance Expense	—	
Miscellaneous General Expense	1 4 1 2 00	
Totals	447 1 9 2 00	447 1 9 2 00

Directions: Prepare a work sheet for the year ended June 30, 20X2. Use the following adjustment data:

(a) and (b) Merchandise inventory, June 30, 20X2, $36,710.
(c) Store supplies on hand, $955.
(d) Office supplies on hand, $915.
(e) Insurance expired, $875.
(f) Depreciation of store equipment, $2,400.
(g) Depreciation of office equipment, $2,000.
(h) Depreciation of delivery equipment, $4,000.
(i) Depreciation of building, $3,000.
(j) Accrued salaries: sales, $1,230; office, $810.

GROUP B

PROBLEM 9-1B

LEARNING OBJECTIVE 2

Objective: To calculate amounts of adjustments

Directions: In each of the following situations, calculate the amount of the adjustment needed as of December 31, the end of the current accounting period.

(a) The Office Supplies account shows a balance of $5,575 on January 1 and a purchase of $17,210 on March 1. The December 31 inventory is $7,720.

(b) The Store Supplies account shows a balance of $12,675 on January 1 and purchases of $18,220 and $11,505 during the year. The December 31 inventory is $7,145.

(c) The Prepaid Insurance account shows a debit balance of $1,920, representing a two-year premium paid on June 1 of the current year.

(d) Salaries of $80,000 are paid weekly on Monday for the preceding week. This year, December 31 fell on a Thursday.

PROBLEM 9-2B

LEARNING OBJECTIVE 1, 2

Objective: To record adjustments in T accounts

Directions: In each of the following unrelated transactions, record in T accounts opening balances, purchases, and adjustments as of December 31 of the current year.

(a) Merchandise inventory (beginning) on January 1 was $85,240.
Merchandise inventory (ending) on December 31 is $89,610.

(b) The Office Supplies account shows a January 1 balance of $5,370, an October 1 purchase of $17,210, and a December 31 inventory of $3,945.

(c) The Store Supplies account shows a January 1 balance of $15,175, a March 18 purchase of $28,410, and a December 31 inventory of $17,555.

(d) The Prepaid Insurance account shows a payment for a three-year policy on June 1 of this year in the amount of $7,200.

(e) Salaries of $36,000 are paid weekly on Monday for the preceding week. This year, December 31 fell on a Monday.

(f) Depreciation expense on store equipment is $50,000.

PROBLEM 9-3B

LEARNING OBJECTIVE 2

Objective: To prepare a work sheet

Account balances and adjustment data for Grant's Variety Store follow.

Account	Balance
Cash	$ 9,165
Accounts Receivable	15,210
Merchandise Inventory (January 1)	27,895
Office Supplies	12,910
Store Supplies	16,805
Prepaid Insurance	3,600
Office Equipment	54,000
Accumulated Depreciation—Office Equipment	10,800
Store Equipment	72,000
Accumulated Depreciation—Store Equipment	21,600
Delivery Equipment	20,000
Accumulated Depreciation—Delivery Equipment	8,000
Accounts Payable	19,575
Salaries Payable	—
Alice Grant, Capital	121,045
Alice Grant, Drawing	9,600
Income Summary	—
Sales	421,000
Sales Returns and Allowances	15,210
Sales Discounts	7,900
Purchases	270,000
Purchases Returns and Allowances	13,975
Purchases Discounts	5,100

Account	Balance
Freight In	$ 4,100
Sales Salaries Expense	26,000
Store Supplies Expense	—
Advertising Expense	4,700
Depreciation Expense—Store Equipment	—
Depreciation Expense—Delivery Equipment	—
Rent Expense	12,000
Office Salaries Expense	32,000
Office Supplies Expense	—
Utilities Expense	8,000
Insurance Expense	—
Depreciation Expense—Office Equipment	—

Here are the adjustment data:

(a) and (b) Merchandise inventory, December 31, $32,455.
(c) Office supplies on hand, $3,750.
(d) Store supplies on hand, $4,557.
(e) Insurance expired, $1,200.
(f) Salaries accrued: office, $350; sales, $300.
(g) Depreciation of office equipment, $5,400.
(h) Depreciation of store equipment, $7,200.
(i) Depreciation of delivery equipment, $4,000.

Directions: Prepare a work sheet for the year ended December 31, 20X1.

PROBLEM 9-4B

LEARNING OBJECTIVE 1, 2

Objective: To prepare a work sheet

The December 31, 20X4 trial balance of Spencer Company follows:

Spencer Company Trial Balance December 31, 20X4		
Account Title	**Debit**	**Credit**
Cash	4 0 0 0 00	
Accounts Receivable	9 2 0 0 00	
Merchandise Inventory (January 1)	41 3 0 0 00	
Store Supplies	1 4 5 6 00	
Office Supplies	1 2 8 0 00	
Prepaid Insurance	2 5 8 0 00	
Store Equipment	12 4 9 5 00	
Accumulated Depreciation—Store Equipment		3 2 1 6 00
Office Equipment	11 3 4 8 00	
Accumulated Depreciation—Office Equipment		3 8 9 0 00
Delivery Equipment	42 3 0 0 00	
Accumulated Depreciation—Delivery Equipment		5 1 2 0 00
Building	84 6 0 0 00	
Accumulated Depreciation—Building		16 9 0 0 00
Land	15 6 0 0 00	
Accounts Payable		8 3 0 0 00
Salaries Payable		—

Account		Debit		Credit
Notes Payable				38 0 0 0 00
Anna Spencer, Capital				92 3 0 4 00
Anna Spencer, Drawing		28 0 0 0 00		
Income Summary		—		—
Sales				279 8 0 0 00
Sales Returns and Allowances		3 8 9 0 00		
Sales Discounts		2 3 4 5 00		
Purchases		90 8 0 0 00		
Purchases Returns and Allowances				2 5 6 0 00
Purchases Discounts				4 2 3 0 00
Sales Salaries Expense		49 5 0 0 00		
Advertising Expense		9 4 5 0 00		
Depreciation Expense—Store Equipment		—		
Store Supplies Expense		—		
Miscellaneous Selling Expense		1 4 5 6 00		
Office Salaries Expense		24 6 9 0 00		
Delivery Expense		6 7 8 5 00		
Utilities Expense		8 6 5 5 00		
Depreciation Expense—Office Equipment		—		
Depreciation Expense—Delivery Equipment		—		
Depreciation Expense—Building		—		
Repairs Expense		1 3 5 5 00		
Office Supplies Expense		—		
Insurance Expense		—		
Miscellaneous General Expense		1 2 3 5 00		
Totals		454 3 2 0 00		454 3 2 0 00

Directions: Prepare a work sheet for the year ended December 31, 20X4. Use the following adjustment data:

(a) and (b) Merchandise inventory, December 31, 20X4, $33,500.
     (c) Store supplies on hand, $910.
     (d) Office supplies on hand, $945.
     (e) Insurance expired, $1,450.
     (f) Depreciation of store equipment, $2,200.
     (g) Depreciation of office equipment, $1,890.
     (h) Depreciation of delivery equipment, $4,800.
     (i) Depreciation of building, $3,800.
     (j) Accrued salaries: sales, $1,840; office, $1,215.

CHALLENGE PROBLEMS

PROBLEM SOLVING

Nichols' Apparel Shop's accounts follow in alphabetical order. Also shown are the adjustment data. Missing from the list are the accounts needed for adjusting entries.

Account	Balance
Accounts Payable	$37,300
Accounts Receivable	21,545
Accumulated Depreciation—Office Equipment	16,000

Account	Balance
Accumulated Depreciation—Store Equipment	$ 16,800
Advertising Expense	2,940
Linda Nichols, Capital	71,535
Linda Nichols, Drawing	15,200
Cash	11,110
Freight In	9,125
Merchandise Inventory (January 1)	19,465
Office Equipment	42,000
Office Salaries Expense	37,600
Office Supplies	8,420
Prepaid Insurance	1,620
Purchases	252,300
Purchases Discounts	5,100
Purchases Returns and Allowances	12,300
Rent Expense	14,000
Sales	412,700
Sales Discounts	8,100
Sales Returns and Allowances	15,700
Sales Salaries Expense	41,200
Store Equipment	56,000
Store Supplies	11,710
Utilities Expense	3,700

Adjustment data:

(a) and (b) Merchandise inventory, December 31, $18,340.
  (c) Office supplies on hand, $2,075.
  (d) Store supplies on hand, $3,975.
  (e) Insurance expired: the balance in the Prepaid Insurance account represents the premium paid on August 1, 20X1, for a three-year policy.
  (f) Accrued salaries: sales, $550; office, $490.
  (g) Depreciation of office equipment, $4,000.
  (h) Depreciation of store equipment, 10% of cost.

Directions:

1. Arrange accounts in the proper order and prepare a trial balance. Be sure to add the additional accounts that you will need in the proper place.
2. Complete a work sheet for the year ended December 31, 20X1.

COMMUNICATIONS

Francis Polite is the chief accountant at Asher Company. When training a new employee to make adjustments, Francis was asked why it is necessary to adjust the Merchandise Inventory account for the value of the latest inventory. The employee reasoned that since all purchases of merchandise are recorded in the Purchases account, the balance of that account would show the cost of merchandise on hand at the end of the accounting period.

Explain why and how the Merchandise Inventory account shows the cost of merchandise on hand at the end of the accounting period.

ETHICS

Charles Williams is the accounting supervisor at Albany Products. Among his responsibilities are preparation of adjustments, completion of the work sheet, and preparation of financial statements. You are a new accounting clerk who is working along with Charles. As you look over his adjusting entries, you notice that there is no adjustment for unpaid salaries. You ask Charles about this, and he replies that since salaries will be paid next week, why bother? Besides, with less expense, our profit will be higher, and since our firm shares profits with employees, we will all be better off. Explain to Charles that he is following an unethical practice.

ANSWERS TO REVIEW QUIZZES

REVIEW QUIZ 9-1

Merchandise Inventory		Income Summary	
Bal. 94,000	(a) Adj. 94,000	(a) Adj. 94,000	(b) Adj. 97,000
(b) Adj. 97,000			

REVIEW QUIZ 9-2

1			Adjusting Entries				1
2	20XX Dec.	31	Income Summary	24 3 0 0 00			2
3			Merchandise Inventory		24 3 0 0 00		3
4		31	Merchandise Inventory	25 6 0 0 00			4
5			Income Summary		25 6 0 0 00		5
6		31	Store Supplies Expense	3 5 0 00			6
7			Store Supplies		3 5 0 00		7
8		31	Insurance Expense	2 0 0 00			8
9			Prepaid Insurance		2 0 0 00		9
10		31	Salaries Expense	2 3 0 0 00			10
11			Salaries Payable		2 3 0 0 00		11

REVIEW QUIZ 9-3

	Income Statement		Balance Sheet	
	Dr.	Cr.	Dr.	Cr.
	$22,300	$40,400	$61,000	$42,900
Net Income	18,100			18,100
	$40,400	$40,400	$61,000	$61,000

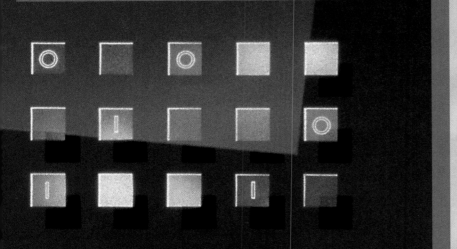

10

FINANCIAL STATEMENTS AND CLOSING ENTRIES FOR A MERCHANDISING BUSINESS

LEARNING OBJECTIVES

After studying Chapter 10, you will be able to:

1. Prepare financial statements for a merchandising business.
2. Journalize adjusting and closing entries for a merchandising business.
3. Prepare a post-closing trial balance.
4. Make reversing entries for accrued (unpaid) salaries.

Have you ever walked through a shopping mall and thought about all of the different businesses there? What do most of those businesses have in common? They are selling merchandise. Even though each store is unique in itself, all of these merchandising businesses have a common accounting situation: accounting for their merchandise inventory.

If you owned one of those businesses, how would you know how much merchandise was sold and how much of that merchandise was later returned by your customers? How would you know the amount of inventory in your store and if your store was earning a profit? The answers to these questions are found in the financial statements prepared for your store.

Accounting is the language of business. The financial statements are the translator of the numbers from accounting records into useful information for the owner of the business.

— Allan M. Cross, CPA, MBA
Parks Junior College

 n the last chapter, we discussed the end-of-period adjustments necessary for a merchandising business, and we prepared a work sheet for Lakeside Electronics. In this chapter, we will prepare financial statements, journalize and post adjusting and closing entries, and prepare a post-closing trial balance.

PREPARING FINANCIAL STATEMENTS FOR A MERCHANDISING BUSINESS

LEARNING OBJECTIVE 1

As we discussed in Chapter 4, a completed work sheet supplies all the information we need to prepare financial statements. This information, however, must be recast into an appropriate format. In this section, we will use the financial statement columns of Lakeside's work sheet to prepare a classified income statement, a statement of owner's equity, and a classified balance sheet. Figure 10-1 shows the financial statement columns of the work sheet for Lakeside Electronics that we presented in Chapter 9.

Financial statements are prepared in this order: (1) the income statement, (2) the statement of owner's equity, and (3) the balance sheet.

- The income statement summarizes revenue and expenses and shows the amount of net income (or net loss) for an accounting period.

- The statement of owner's equity summarizes the changes in owner's equity during the accounting period.

- The balance sheet lists a firm's assets, liabilities, and owner's equity as of a certain date.

The Classified Income Statement

An income statement summarizes revenues and expenses and shows how much net income (or net loss) a firm has for an accounting period. Up to this point, we have shown nonclassified income statements, which simply contain a listing of revenues and expenses. A nonclassified income statement is better suited to the needs of a service business. Determining net income or net loss for a merchandising business is a more involved process. Consequently, it is easier to under-

FIGURE 10-1
Financial statement columns of a work sheet

Lakeside Electronics
Work Sheet
For Year Ended December 31, 20X1

	Account Title	Income Statement Debit	Income Statement Credit	Balance Sheet Debit	Balance Sheet Credit	
1	Cash			6 2 0 0 00		1
2	Accounts Receivable			9 6 8 9 00		2
3	Merchandise Inventory			72 4 0 0 00		3
4	Store Supplies			5 0 0 00		4
5	Office Supplies			2 5 0 00		5
6	Prepaid Insurance			6 3 0 00		6
7	Store Equipment			11 3 8 5 00		7
8	Accumulated Depreciation—Store Equipment				5 4 0 0 00	8
9	Office Equipment			10 2 0 0 00		9
10	Accumulated Depreciation—Office Equipment				7 9 2 0 00	10
11	Delivery Equipment			56 0 0 0 00		11
12	Accumulated Depreciation—Delivery Equipment				23 0 0 0 00	12
13	Accounts Payable				14 0 2 5 00	13
14	Salaries Payable				1 6 0 0 00	14
15	Notes Payable				26 0 0 0 00	15
16	John Graham, Capital				75 5 8 1 00	16
17	John Graham, Drawing			18 0 0 0 00		17
18	Income Summary	66 0 0 0 00	72 4 0 0 00			18
19	Sales		304 6 0 0 00			19
20	Sales Returns and Allowances	5 2 3 0 00				20
21	Sales Discounts	3 4 6 1 00				21
22	Purchases	144 9 1 8 00				22
23	Purchases Returns and Allowances		6 6 9 2 00			23
24	Purchases Discounts		2 9 1 0 00			24
25	Freight In	1 1 6 0 00				25
26	Sales Salaries Expense	69 1 0 0 00				26
27	Advertising Expense	5 8 4 0 00				27
28	Store Supplies Expense	1 5 1 5 00				28
29	Depreciation Expense—Store Equipment	9 0 0 00				29
30	Miscellaneous Selling Expense	2 1 0 0 00				30
31	Rent Expense	5 7 0 0 00				31
32	Office Salaries Expense	31 1 5 3 00				32
33	Insurance Expense	9 0 00				33
34	Depreciation Expense—Office Equipment	8 2 0 00				34
35	Depreciation Expense—Delivery Equipment	9 2 0 0 00				35
36	Utilities Expense	6 2 4 0 00				36
37	Office Supplies Expense	4 1 7 00				37
38	Interest Expense	1 3 0 00				38
39	Miscellaneous General Expense	9 0 0 00				39
40		354 8 7 4 00	386 6 0 2 00	185 2 5 4 00	153 5 2 6 00	40
41	Net Income	31 7 2 8 00			31 7 2 8 00	41
42		386 6 0 2 00	386 6 0 2 00	185 2 5 4 00	185 2 5 4 00	42

stand the income statement if we classify it into sections. A **classified income statement** is divided into sections, as follows:

1. Revenue
2. Cost of Goods Sold
3. Operating Expenses
4. Income from Operations
5. Other Income and Expenses

We will discuss the content of each of these sections shortly. Before we do that, however, let's talk in general terms about the format of the income statement for a merchandising business. The following is a skeleton outline used when the income statement is prepared:

```
    Net Sales for the Period
 –      Cost of Goods Sold
                Gross Profit
 –      Operating Expenses
    Income from Operations
 +           Other Income
 –          Other Expenses
                  Net Income
```

This outline is so important to fully understanding the income statement of a merchandising business that you should firmly entrench it in your mind. It will be followed each time we prepare an income statement.

You should fully understand the concepts of *gross* and *net*. **Gross profit** is the profit before subtracting the expenses of doing business. It results from subtracting the cost of items sold (the **cost of goods sold**) from their net sales price. **Net sales** is obtained by subtracting the amount of sales returns and allowances and the amount of sales discounts from the amount of sales. When expenses are subtracted from gross profit, we obtain the amount of **income from operations**. Then we add other (nonoperating) income and subtract other (nonoperating) expenses to find the net income.

Let's now closely examine the sections of the classified income statement. (Remember, the data you need to prepare Lakeside's income statement can be found on the partial work sheet shown in Figure 10-1 on page 351.)

THE REVENUE SECTION

The revenue section provides a figure for net sales, which is the balance of the Sales account, less the balances of the contra sales accounts (Sales Returns and Allowances and Sales Discounts), as shown in Figure 10-2.

FIGURE 10-2
Net sales

Lakeside Electronics Income Statement For Year Ended December 31, 20X1			
Revenue from sales:			
Sales		$304 600 00	
Less: Sales returns and allowances	$5 230 00		
Sales discounts	3 461 00	8 691 00	
Net sales			$295 909 00

THE COST OF GOODS SOLD SECTION

The cost of merchandise sold to customers during a period is subtracted from the net sales figure for the same period to get the amount of *gross profit*. In most merchandising businesses, the volume of sales is too large to permit a determination of the cost of items as they are being sold. Consequently, a simple formula is generally used. The formula to calculate cost of goods sold is:

```
  Beginning Merchandise Inventory
+    Net Purchases of Merchandise
= Cost of Goods Available for Sale
-    Ending Merchandise Inventory
=              Cost of Goods Sold
```

Notice that to calculate cost of goods sold, you will need both the beginning and ending inventory figures, and you will need the net purchases for the period. You can find the inventory figures in the Income Statement columns of the work sheet. (The beginning inventory will be the debit to the Income Summary account, and the ending inventory will be the credit to the Income Summary account.) You calculate the amount of net purchases as follows:

```
            Total Purchases
- Purchases Returns and Allowances
-         Purchases Discounts
+                     Freight In
=                 Net Purchases
```

Notice that Purchases Returns and Allowances and Purchases Discounts decrease the cost of purchases; the amount of Freight In increases the cost of purchases.

Continuing with our example of Lakeside Electronics, the cost of goods sold section of the income statement appears as shown in Figure 10-3.

FIGURE 10-3
Cost of goods sold

Lakeside Electronics Income Statement For Year Ended December 31, 20X1			
Net sales			$295 909 00
Cost of goods sold:			
Merch. inventory, Jan. 1, 20X1		$ 66 000 00	
Purchases	$144 918 00		
Less: Purchases ret. and allow. $6 692 00			
Purchases discounts 2 910 00	9 602 00		
	$135 316 00		
Add: Freight in	1 160 00		
Net purchases		136 476 00	
Goods available for sale		$202 476 00	
Less: Merchandise inventory,			
December 31, 20X1		72 400 00	
Cost of goods sold			130 076 00
Gross profit			$165 833 00

Notice that the Cost of goods sold is subtracted from net sales to get the gross profit for the period: $295,909 – $130,076 = $165,833.

Cost data related to three businesses are shown below. Calculate the cost of goods sold for each company.

(a)	Beginning Merchandise Inventory	$30,000
	Amount of Purchases during the Period	70,000
	Purchases Returns and Allowances	2,800
	Purchases Discounts	1,450
	Ending Merchandise Inventory	32,000

(b)	Beginning Merchandise Inventory	-0-
	Amount of Purchases during the Period	$90,000
	Purchases Discounts	2,400
	Ending Merchandise Inventory	26,000

(c)	Beginning Merchandise Inventory	$88,000
	Amount of Purchases during the Period	99,400
	Freight In	3,400
	Purchases Returns and Allowances	4,200
	Purchases Discounts	900
	Ending Merchandise Inventory	61,000

CHECK YOUR ANSWERS ON PAGE 389.

THE OPERATING EXPENSES SECTION

Operating expenses, as the name implies, are the regular expenses of operating the business. Lakeside Electronics has broken down its operating expenses into *selling expenses* and *general expenses*. This is a common practice that allows closer analysis and monitoring of the types of expenses. Let's look at these groups in a little more detail.

1. **Selling expenses** are all expenses directly related to the sale of merchandise, such as:
   - Sales Salaries Expense
   - Advertising Expense
   - Store Supplies Expense
   - Depreciation Expense—Store Equipment
   - Miscellaneous Selling Expense

2. **General expenses** (also called **administrative expenses**) are expenses related to the business's office, the overall administration of the business, or any other operating expense that cannot be tied directly to sales activity, such as:
   - Office Salaries Expense
   - Rent Expense
   - Depreciation Expense—Office Equipment
   - Depreciation Expense—Delivery Equipment
   - Utilities Expense
   - Office Supplies Expense
   - Insurance Expense
   - Miscellaneous General Expense

Now let's look at the operating expenses section of Lakeside's income statement shown in Figure 10-4.

THE INCOME FROM OPERATIONS SECTION

Gross profit, minus total operating expenses, equals income from operations. **Income from operations** (also called **operating income**) is a measure of a firm's ongoing operations, or its regular operations. Lakeside's income from operations section is shown in Figure 10-5.

FIGURE 10-4
Operating expenses

Lakeside Electronics
Income Statement
For Year Ended December 31, 20X1

Gross profit			$165 833 00
Operating expenses:			
Selling expenses:			
Sales salaries expense	$69 100 00		
Advertising expense	5 840 00		
Store supplies expense	1 515 00		
Depreciation exp.—store equip.	900 00		
Miscellaneous selling expense	2 100 00		
Total selling expenses		$79 455 00	
General expenses:			
Rent expense	$ 5 700 00		
Office salaries expense	31 153 00		
Insurance expense	900 00		
Depreciation exp.—office equip.	820 00		
Depreciation exp.—delivery equip.	9 200 00		
Utilities expense	6 240 00		
Office supplies expense	417 00		
Miscellaneous general expense	900 00		
Total general expenses		54 520 00	
Total operating expenses			$133 975 00

FIGURE 10-5
Income from operations

Lakeside Electronics
Income Statement
For Year Ended December 31, 20X1

Gross profit	$165 833 00
Total operating expenses	133 975 00
Income from operations	$ 31 858 00

Had operating expenses exceeded gross profit, there would have been a loss from operations.

THE OTHER INCOME AND EXPENSE SECTION

Some businesses have income and expenses that are not a part of normal operations. Food stores, for example, often receive income from vending machine sales and video games. Since this income is not a part of regular operations, it should not be included as part of their regular sales of merchandise. Instead, it is listed at the bottom of the income statement under the heading **Other Income**.

Expenses that are not part of the regular expenses of operating the business should not be listed with the operating expenses. These expenses should be shown in a separate section entitled **Other Expenses**. A common example of a nonoperating expense is interest expense—interest is an expense of borrowing money, not of operating the business.

Lakeside did not have any nonoperating income; however, the firm incurred interest expense of $130 related to a note payable. Since this expense is not a part of normal operations, it is presented on the income statement as shown in Figure 10-6.

FIGURE 10-6
Other expense

Lakeside Electronics Income Statement For Year Ended December 31, 20X1		
Income from operations		$31 8 5 8 00
Other expenses:		
Interest expense		1 3 0 00
Net income		$31 7 2 8 00

REVIEW QUIZ 10-2

The following data are for the Tasty World Ice Cream Factory:

Account	Balance
Sales	$69,500
Sales Returns and Allowances	300
Beginning Merchandise Inventory	9,000
Purchases	22,000
Purchases Discounts	600
Ending Merchandise Inventory	9,500
Operating Expenses (Total)	18,200
Interest Expense (Other Expense)	1,400

Determine the following:

(a) The amount of net sales
(b) The cost of goods sold
(c) The amount of gross profit
(d) The amount of income (or loss) from operations
(e) The amount of net income (or net loss)

CHECK YOUR ANSWERS ON PAGE 389.

The Completed Income Statement

Now let's now look at Lakeside's completed income statement, which is shown in Figure 10-7.

The Statement of Owner's Equity

Using the partial work sheet presented in Figure 10-1, we can find all the data we need to complete the statement of owner's equity. The statement of owner's equity has been called the link between the income statement and the balance sheet. This is because the net income (or net loss) figure from the income statement is entered on the statement of owner's equity, as a necessary part of updating the owner's capital; and the updated capital figure is then entered on the balance sheet. Figure 10-8 shows Lakeside's statement of owner's equity, for the year ended December 31, 20X1.

FIGURE 10-7
Completed income statement

Lakeside Electronics Income Statement For Year Ended December 31, 20X1				
Revenue from sales:				
Sales			$304 600 00	
Less: Sales returns and allowances	$ 5 230 00			
Sales discounts	3 461 00	8 691 00		
Net sales				$295 909 00
Cost of goods sold:				
Merch. inventory, Jan. 1, 20X1			$ 66 000 00	
Purchases	$144 918 00			
Less: Purchases ret. and allow.	$6 692 00			
Purchases discounts	2 910 00	9 602 00		
		$135 316 00		
Add: Freight in		1 160 00		
Net purchases			136 476 00	
Goods available for sale			$202 476 00	
Less: Merch. inv., Dec. 31, 20X1			72 400 00	
Cost of goods sold				130 076 00
Gross profit				$165 833 00
Operating expenses:				
Selling expenses:				
Sales salaries expense		$ 69 100 00		
Advertising expense		5 840 00		
Store supplies expense		1 515 00		
Depr. expense—store equip.		900 00		
Miscellaneous selling expense		2 100 00		
Total selling expenses			$ 79 455 00	
General expenses:				
Rent expense		$ 5 700 00		
Office salaries expense		31 153 00		
Insurance expense		900 00		
Depr. expense—office equip.		820 00		
Depr. expense—delivery equip.		9 200 00		
Utilities expense		6 240 00		
Office supplies expense		417 00		
Miscellaneous general expense		900 00		
Total general expenses			54 520 00	
Total operating expenses				133 975 00
Income from operations				$ 31 858 00
Other expenses:				
Interest expense				130 00
Net income				$ 31 728 00

FIGURE 10-8
Statement of owner's equity

Lakeside Electronics Statement of Owner's Equity For Year Ended December 31, 20X1		
John Graham, capital, January 1, 20X1		$75 5 8 1 00
Net income for period	$31 7 2 8 00	
Less: Withdrawals	18 0 0 0 00	
Increase in capital		13 7 2 8 00
John Graham, capital, December 31, 20X1		$89 3 0 9 00

The Classified Balance Sheet

The principal objective of the balance sheet is to present the reader with as much information as possible about the financial condition of a business at a particular point in time. Until now, the balance sheets we have prepared have been divided into three sections: (1) assets, (2) liabilities, and (3) owner's equity. By grouping items into classifications within these sections, we can prepare a **classified balance sheet**, which presents the reader with more detail.

ASSETS

On the balance sheet, assets are usually classified as either *current* or *plant*. **Current assets** are cash and any other assets that are expected to be realized in cash, sold, used up, or expire within one year. Examples of current assets, other than cash, include accounts receivable, merchandise inventory, supplies, and prepaid insurance. Current assets are listed on the balance sheet according to their **liquidity**, that is, how quickly they will be turned into cash, or how quickly they will be used up or expire. Therefore, cash is listed first and usually is followed by accounts receivable, merchandise inventory, supplies, and prepaid items.

Plant assets are assets that are expected to be used in the business for more than one year. Examples of plant assets include land, buildings, machinery, furniture, computers, and automobiles. Plant assets are usually listed on the balance sheet according to their **stability** (how long they will last). Less stable assets (such as office equipment) are listed first, followed by more stable assets. Land is the most stable asset; therefore, it is typically listed last. Plant assets are also referred to as **fixed assets** or **property, plant, and equipment** or **long-term assets**.

LIABILITIES

Liabilities are presented on the balance sheet as *current* and *long-term*. A **current liability** is a debt that is due for payment within one year. Examples usually include accounts payable, salaries payable, sales tax payable, and short-term notes payable.

A **long-term liability** is one that will not come due for payment within one year. Examples include long-term notes payable and mortgages payable.

OWNER'S EQUITY

The balance sheet also requires an up-to-date amount for the owner's capital. This amount will be supplied by the statement of owner's equity.

When we combine this information (assets, liabilities, and owner's equity), we get Lakeside's balance sheet, dated as of December 31, 20X1, as shown in Figure 10-9.

Now that we have presented each of Lakeside's financial statements, let's pause to look at some key figures on Lakeside's balance sheet.

FIGURE 10-9
Classified balance sheet

Remember *The balance sheet is dated as of the last day of the fiscal period.*

Lakeside Electronics Balance Sheet December 31, 20X1				
Assets				
Current assets:				
Cash			$ 6 2 0 0 00	
Accounts receivable			9 6 8 9 00	
Merchandise inventory			72 4 0 0 00	
Store supplies			5 0 0 00	
Office supplies			2 5 0 00	
Prepaid insurance			6 3 0 00	
Total current assets				$ 89 6 6 9 00
Plant assets:				
Store equipment	$11 3 8 5 00			
Less: Accumulated depreciation	5 4 0 0 00	$ 5 9 8 5 00		
Office equipment	$10 2 0 0 00			
Less: Accumulated depreciation	7 9 2 0 00	2 2 8 0 00		
Delivery equipment	$56 0 0 0 00			
Less: Accumulated depreciation	23 0 0 0 00	33 0 0 0 00		
Total plant assets				41 2 6 5 00
Total assets				$130 9 3 4 00
Liabilities				
Current liabilities:				
Accounts payable	$14 0 2 5 00			
Salaries payable	1 6 0 0 00			
Total current liabilities		$15 6 2 5 00		
Long-term liabilities:				
Notes payable		26 0 0 0 00		
Total liabilities				$ 41 6 2 5 00
Owner's Equity				
John Graham, capital				89 3 0 9 00
Total liabilities and owner's equity				$130 9 3 4 00

Working Capital and the Current Ratio

The balance sheet alone tells us much about the financial condition of a business. Most accountants, however, perform certain analyses so that the balance sheet will be of maximum benefit as a decision-making tool. We will deal with financial statement analysis in detail in a later chapter. For now, we are interested in two important questions about the business:

1. Does the business have enough capital to operate and continue growing?
2. Can the business meet its debts as they fall due?

To help answer these questions, it is common to look at a firm's *working capital* and its *current ratio*, both of which can easily be determined by looking at a classified balance sheet.

WORKING CAPITAL

Working capital is the amount of current assets minus the amount of current liabilities. We can state this in a simple formula, as follows:

Working capital = Current assets – Current liabilities

As we discussed in the preceding section, current assets consist of cash and other assets that will be realized in cash within one year, and current liabilities are debts to be paid within one year. Sufficient current assets must be available to pay current liabilities as they fall due. Thus, working capital represents the funds available to replace inventory and to acquire credit. The larger the working capital, the better able the business is to pay its debts. For Lakeside Electronics, we can calculate working capital as follows:

	Current assets	$89,669
–	Current liabilities	15,625
=	Working capital	$74,044

Remember that capital (or owner's equity) is the difference between total assets and total liabilities. Working capital can be thought of as a current version of total capital.

Total assets – Total liabilities = Owner's capital

Current assets – Current liabilities = Working capital

To be of maximum benefit, working capital should be computed at the end of each period, and any significant change should be subjected to close scrutiny by management. Without adequate working capital, a business can fail. This point is well illustrated by the failure of W.T. Grant Corporation in 1977. W.T. Grant was a large chain of discount department stores that, at the time of its closing, was earning a profit and had millions of dollars in long-term assets. However, the company had insufficient working capital and was forced out of business.

CURRENT RATIO

Closely tied in with working capital is the **current ratio**, which is the ratio of current assets to current liabilities. The current ratio gives an indication of the ability of a business to pay its current liabilities; it is calculated as follows:

$$\text{Current ratio} = \frac{\text{Current assets}}{\text{Current liabilities}}$$

We can calculate Lakeside's current ratio as follows:

$$\frac{\text{Current assets}}{\text{Current liabilities}} = \frac{\$89,669}{\$15,625} = 5.7:1$$

Lakeside's current ratio is 5.7:1, which is read as *5.7 to 1*. This means that Lakeside has approximately $5.70 in current assets for each $1 in current liabilities. While it is difficult to say exactly what is a good current ratio (because of differences in the financial makeup of businesses), a current ratio of 2:1 is generally considered acceptable. Since Lakeside's current ratio is much better than this, it is likely that the firm will be able to pay its debts as they fall due.

REVIEW QUIZ
10-3

Selected data from the classified balance sheet of Glendale Company follow:

Account	Balance
Cash	$ 9,000
Accounts Receivable	12,000
Merchandise Inventory	64,000
Prepaid Insurance	1,000
Store Supplies	800
Store Equipment	18,000
Display Equipment	32,000
Computer	7,800
Accounts Payable	5,800
Sales Tax Payable	1,400
Salaries Payable	800
Note Payable Due in 5 Years	9,400

What is the (a) amount of current assets, (b) amount of current liabilities, (c) working capital, and (d) current ratio? Does it seem that the firm will be able to pay its current liabilities as they fall due? Explain.

CHECK YOUR ANSWERS ON PAGE 392.

JOURNALIZING ADJUSTING ENTRIES

LEARNING OBJECTIVE 2

You will recall from Chapter 4 that the work sheet is a useful tool for accountants. However, the work sheet is not a journal, and no posting is ever made from it to the ledger. Therefore, to get the adjusting entries into the ledger, formal journal entries must be made. This is a simple process, however, because the adjustments already appear on the work sheet. You simply copy them into the journal. In Figure 10-10, we have reproduced the Adjustments columns of Lakeside's work sheet. Starting with the first adjustment—adjustment (a)—very carefully copy each adjustment into the journal, as shown in Figure 10-11.

CLOSING ENTRIES FOR A MERCHANDISING BUSINESS

LEARNING OBJECTIVE 2

In Chapter 5, we discussed closing entries for a service business. As we noted there, the objectives of the closing process are as follows:

1. To reduce the balances of the temporary accounts to zero and thus make the accounts ready for entries in the next accounting period.
2. To update the balance of the owner's capital account.

Remember that with the exception of the owner's drawing account, *all* temporary accounts are income statement accounts. Therefore, to start the closing process, let's refer to the Income Statement columns of Lakeside's work sheet (Figure 10-1 on page 351). The first amounts shown are those in the Income Summary account. These amounts are the beginning and ending inventory figures; they were entered in the Income Statement columns because they are needed in the calculation of cost of goods sold. *Since these figures are a part of the adjusting process, they are not considered when closing.* Therefore, we start with the next account listed—the Sales account—and proceed downward, line by line, closing each account to Income Summary.

FIGURE 10-10
Trial balance and adjustments columns of the work sheet

Remember
The work sheet is not a journal or a ledger. Therefore, adjustments must be formally journalized and posted to the ledger.

To journalize the adjusting entries, carefully copy each adjustment, starting with adjustment (a), on the next free line of the general journal.

Lakeside Electronics
Work Sheet
For Year Ended December 31, 20X1

	Account Title	Trial Balance Debit	Trial Balance Credit	Adjustments Debit	Adjustments Credit	
1	Cash	6 2 0 0 00				1
2	Accounts Receivable	9 6 8 9 00				2
3	Merchandise Inventory	66 0 0 0 00		(b) 72 4 0 0 00	(a) 66 0 0 0 00	3
4	Store Supplies	2 0 1 5 00			(c) 1 5 1 5 00	4
5	Office Supplies	6 6 7 00			(d) 4 1 7 00	5
6	Prepaid Insurance	7 2 0 00			(e) 9 0 00	6
7	Store Equipment	11 3 8 5 00				7
8	Accum. Depr.—Store Equipment		4 5 0 0 00		(f) 9 0 0 00	8
9	Office Equipment	10 2 0 0 00				9
10	Accum. Depr.—Office Equipment		7 1 0 0 00		(g) 8 2 0 00	10
11	Delivery Equipment	56 0 0 0 00				11
12	Accum. Depr.—Delivery Equipment		13 8 0 0 00		(h) 9 2 0 0 00	12
13	Accounts Payable		14 0 2 5 00			13
14	Salaries Payable		—		(i) 1 6 0 0 00	14
15	Notes Payable		26 0 0 0 00			15
16	John Graham, Capital		75 5 8 1 00			16
17	John Graham, Drawing	18 0 0 0 00				17
18	Income Summary	—	—	(a) 66 0 0 0 00	(b) 72 4 0 0 00	18
19	Sales		304 6 0 0 00			19
20	Sales Returns and Allowances	5 2 3 0 00				20
21	Sales Discounts	3 4 6 1 00				21
22	Purchases	144 9 1 8 00				22
23	Purchases Returns and Allowances		6 6 9 2 00			23
24	Purchases Discounts		2 9 1 0 00			24
25	Freight In	1 1 6 0 00				25
26	Sales Salaries Expense	68 2 0 0 00		(i) 9 0 0 00		26
27	Advertising Expense	5 8 4 0 00				27
28	Store Supplies Expense	—		(c) 1 5 1 5 00		28
29	Depr. Expense—Store Equipment	—		(f) 9 0 0 00		29
30	Miscellaneous Selling Expense	2 1 0 0 00				30
31	Rent Expense	5 7 0 0 00				31
32	Office Salaries Expense	30 4 5 3 00		(i) 7 0 0 00		32
33	Insurance Expense	—		(e) 9 0 00		33
34	Depr. Expense—Office Equipment	—		(g) 8 2 0 00		34
35	Depr. Expense—Delivery Equipment	—		(h) 9 2 0 0 00		35
36	Utilities Expense	6 2 4 0 00				36
37	Office Supplies Expense	—		(d) 4 1 7 00		37
38	Interest Expense	1 3 0 00				38
39	Miscellaneous General Expense	9 0 0 00				39
40		455 2 0 8 00	455 2 0 8 00	152 9 4 2 00	152 9 4 2 00	40
41	Net Income					41

FIGURE 10-11
Adjusting entries

	Date		Account Title	P.R.	Debit	Credit	
1			Adjusting Entries				1
2	20X1 Dec.	31	Income Summary		66 0 0 0 00		2
3			Merchandise Inventory			66 0 0 0 00	3
4							4
5		31	Merchandise Inventory		72 4 0 0 00		5
6			Income Summary			72 4 0 0 00	6
7							7
8		31	Store Supplies Expense		1 5 1 5 00		8
9			Store Supplies			1 5 1 5 00	9
10							10
11		31	Office Supplies Expense		4 1 7 00		11
12			Office Supplies			4 1 7 00	12
13							13
14		31	Insurance Expense		9 0 00		14
15			Prepaid Insurance			9 0 00	15
16							16
17		31	Depreciation Expense—Store Equip.		9 0 0 00		17
18			Accumulated Depr.—Store Equip.			9 0 0 00	18
19							19
20		31	Depreciation Expense—Office Equip.		8 2 0 00		20
21			Accumulated Depr.—Office Equip.			8 2 0 00	21
22							22
23		31	Depreciation Expense—Delivery Equip.		9 2 0 0 00		23
24			Accumulated Depreciation—Del. Equip.			9 2 0 0 00	24
25							25
26		31	Sales Salaries Expense		9 0 0 00		26
27			Office Salaries Expense		7 0 0 00		27
28			Salaries Payable			1 6 0 0 00	28

As we discussed in Chapter 5, the closing process is accomplished in four steps, as follows:

❶ *Close the Sales account and other income statement accounts with credit balances to Income Summary.*

Lakeside has three income statement accounts with credit balances: (1) Sales, (2) Purchases Returns and Allowances, and (3) Purchases Discounts. The credit balance of each account is closed by making an equal debit. Our credit is to the Income Summary account. This entry appears as shown below.

Remember *Closing entries are dated as of the last day of the accounting period.*

	Date		Account Title		Debit	Credit	
1			Closing Entries				1
2	20X1 Dec.	31	Sales		304 6 0 0 00		2
3			Purchases Returns and Allowances		6 6 9 2 00		3
4			Purchases Discounts		2 9 1 0 00		4
5			Income Summary			314 2 0 2 00	5
6							6

Remember
You only close the REID accounts:
Revenue
Expenses
Income Summary
Drawing

❷ *Close each expense account and other income statement accounts with debit balances to the Income Summary account.*

Financial Statements and Closing Entries for a Merchandising Business

All amounts remaining on the income statement are debits. Therefore, to close, we make equal credits. To balance the entry, we will make a compound debit to the Income Summary account. This entry follows.

7		31	Income Summary	288 8 7 4 00			7
8			Sales Returns and Allowances		5 2 3 0 00		8
9			Sales Discounts		3 4 6 1 00		9
10			Purchases		144 9 1 8 00		10
11			Freight In		1 1 6 0 00		11
12			Sales Salaries Expense		69 1 0 0 00		12
13			Advertising Expense		5 8 4 0 00		13
14			Store Supplies Expense		1 5 1 5 00		14
15			Depreciation Expense—Store Equip.		9 0 0 00		15
16			Miscellaneous Selling Expense		2 1 0 0 00		16
17			Rent Expense		5 7 0 0 00		17
18			Office Salaries Expense		31 1 5 3 00		18
19			Insurance Expense		9 0 00		19
20			Depreciation Expense—Office Equip.		8 2 0 00		20
21			Depreciation Expense—Delivery Equip.		9 2 0 0 00		21
22			Utilities Expense		6 2 4 0 00		22
23			Office Supplies Expense		4 1 7 00		23
24			Interest Expense		1 3 0 00		24
25			Miscellaneous General Expense		9 0 0 00		25

❸ *Close the Income Summary account to the owner's capital account.*

Remember that when revenue and expenses have been closed to the Income Summary account, this account will show the amount of net income or net loss for the period. We can see this if we pause at this point and draw a T account for Income Summary.

Income Summary

Adj. 66,000	Adj. 72,400
(Expenses) 288,874	(Revenue) 314,202

Remember *The first amounts in the Income Summary account will be the beginning inventory ($66,000) and the ending inventory ($72,400) figures that were recorded during the adjusting process.*

Now, if we balance the Income Summary account, we will find a familiar figure—the amount of net income:

Dr. Column:
$ 66,000
288,874

$354,874

Cr. Column:
$ 72,400
314,202

$386,602

$386,602
– 354,874

$ 31,728 ◄— credit balance = net income

NOTE

Had the Dr. column total exceeded the Cr. column total, a net loss would have been incurred.

The Income Summary account has now served its purpose for this accounting period. All revenue, cost, and expense accounts have been closed. The account was also used to adjust the Merchandise Inventory account to reflect the ending inventory. Therefore, we now close the Income Summary account. Since the balance of the account is a credit (net income), we close it by making an equal debit. Our credit is to John Graham, Capital. Remember that net income increases capital. Thus, we transfer the amount of net income to the credit side (increase side) of the owner's capital account. This entry appears as shown below.

| 26 | | 31 | Income Summary | | 31 7 2 8 00 | | 26 |
| 27 | | | John Graham, Capital | | | 31 7 2 8 00 | 27 |

❹ *Close the balance of the owner's drawing account to the owner's capital account.*

The owner's drawing account is used to record owner withdrawals during a single accounting period. When that period is over, the drawing account has served its purpose. Therefore, its balance is closed to the owner's capital account. Since the drawing account has a debit balance, it is closed by making an equal credit. Our debit is to the owner's capital account.

| 29 | | 31 | John Graham, Capital | | 18 0 0 0 00 | | 29 |
| 30 | | | John Graham, Drawing | | | 18 0 0 0 00 | 30 |

We have now closed all temporary accounts in the ledger of Lakeside Electronics. After these closing entries are posted, the only accounts that will have balances are assets, contra assets, liabilities, and the owner's capital account. The balances of these accounts will be up to date and will agree with the amounts reported on the financial statements. The temporary accounts will have zero balances and will be ready for entries in the next accounting period. The balance of the owner's capital account will correspond exactly to the capital figure reported on the statement of owner's equity. Let's take a quick look at how the John Graham, Capital account looks at this moment.

Account John Graham, Capital						Account No. 311	
Date	Item	P.R.	Debit	Credit	Balance		
					Debit	Credit	
20X1 Jan. 1	Balance	✓				75 5 8 1 00	
Dec. 31	Closing	GJ4		31 7 2 8 00		107 3 0 9 00	
31	Closing	GJ4	18 0 0 0 00			89 3 0 9 00	

If we now compare the balance of John's capital account with the total of the statement of owner's equity (Figure 10-8), we will find that the two amounts agree. This completes the closing process.

Summary of Steps in the Closing Process

Now that we have walked through the steps in the closing process for a merchandising business, let's look at a summary of those steps, shown in Figure 10-12.

FIGURE 10-12
Steps in the closing process

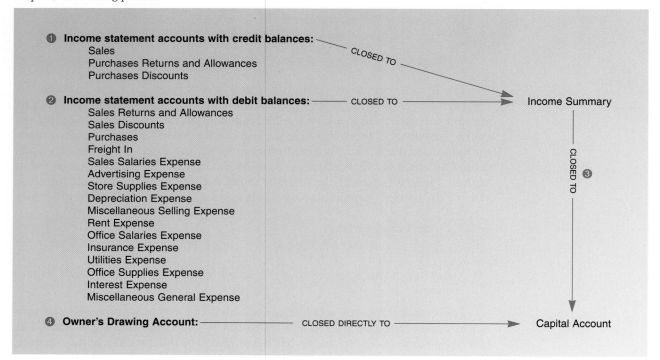

1 Income statement accounts with credit balances:
    Sales
    Purchases Returns and Allowances
    Purchases Discounts
    CLOSED TO

2 Income statement accounts with debit balances: —— CLOSED TO ——
    Sales Returns and Allowances
    Sales Discounts
    Purchases
    Freight In
    Sales Salaries Expense
    Advertising Expense
    Store Supplies Expense
    Depreciation Expense
    Miscellaneous Selling Expense
    Rent Expense
    Office Salaries Expense
    Insurance Expense
    Utilities Expense
    Office Supplies Expense
    Interest Expense
    Miscellaneous General Expense

Income Summary

CLOSED TO **3**

4 Owner's Drawing Account: ———— CLOSED DIRECTLY TO ————→ Capital Account

REVIEW QUIZ
10-4

The partial work sheet of T. Massey International is shown below. Journalize the closing entries as of July 31, 20XX.

	Account Title	Income Statement Debit	Income Statement Credit	Balance Sheet Debit	Balance Sheet Credit	
15	T. Massey, Drawing			12 0 0 0 00		15
16	Income Summary	20 0 0 0 00	21 2 0 0 00			16
17	Sales		70 0 0 0 00			17
18	Sales Returns and Allowances	8 0 0 00				18
19	Sales Discounts	1 2 0 0 00				19
20	Purchases	38 0 0 0 00				20
21	Purchases Discounts		2 9 0 00			21
22	Rent Expense	4 0 0 0 00				22
23	Salaries Expense	9 0 0 0 00				23
24	Depreciation Expense	8 0 0 00				24
25	Supplies Expense	9 5 00				25
26	Telephone Expense	1 9 5 00				26
27	Utilities Expense	1 4 0 0 00				27
28	Miscellaneous Expense	1 2 6 00				28
29		75 6 1 6 00	91 4 9 0 00			29

CHECK YOUR ANSWERS ON PAGE 392.

THE POST-CLOSING TRIAL BALANCE

After the adjusting and closing entries have been posted, another trial balance should be prepared to prove that the ledger is still in balance. Lakeside's post-closing trial balance is shown in Figure 10-13.

FIGURE 10-13
The post-closing trial balance

Lakeside Electronics Post-Closing Trial Balance December 31, 20X1		
Account Title	**Debit**	**Credit**
Cash	6 2 0 0 00	
Accounts Receivable	9 6 8 9 00	
Merchandise Inventory	72 4 0 0 00	
Store Supplies	5 0 0 00	
Office Supplies	2 5 0 00	
Prepaid Insurance	6 3 0 00	
Store Equipment	11 3 8 5 00	
Accumulated Depreciation—Store Equipment		5 4 0 0 00
Office Equipment	10 2 0 0 00	
Accumulated Depreciation—Office Equipment		7 9 2 0 00
Delivery Equipment	56 0 0 0 00	
Accumulated Depreciation—Delivery Equipment		23 0 0 0 00
Accounts Payable		14 0 2 5 00
Salaries Payable		1 6 0 0 00
Notes Payable		26 0 0 0 00
John Graham, Capital		89 3 0 9 00
Totals	167 2 5 4 00	167 2 5 4 00

The only accounts appearing on the post-closing trial balance are the permanent accounts (assets, liabilities, and owner's equity) because the temporary accounts (revenue, expenses, and drawing) have been closed.

REVERSING ENTRIES

Remember that an unpaid expense (or an accrued expense) occurs because the accounting period ends before the expense is due for payment. In Chapter 4 and again in Chapter 9, we made an adjusting entry for salaries that were unpaid when the accounting period ended. In both cases, we debited Salaries Expense (to show the proper amount of expense for the period), and we credited Salaries Payable—because the salaries will be paid in the next accounting period. But what entry do we make when the salaries are paid in the next accounting period?

To answer this question, let's look back at the adjusting entry we made for accrued salaries in Chapter 9. We learned that on December 31, 20X1, Lakeside Electronics had $900 in sales salaries and $700 in office salaries that were unpaid. We made the following adjusting entry to record these amounts.

	20X1		Adjusting Entries					1
2	Dec.	31	Sales Salaries Expense	9 0 0 00				2
3			Office Salaries Expense	7 0 0 00				3
4			Salaries Payable			1 6 0 0 00		4

This entry was then posted to the ledger, and the proper amount of expenses were reported on the income statement. The balance sheet showed the liability for unpaid salaries. The next regular payday was on the following Friday—January 2, 20X2. On that date, Lakeside made payment for the payroll period. However, this payroll period is different than regular payroll periods because part of the salaries were earned by employees in the last accounting period (20X1), and part in the new accounting period (20X2). We can break this down as shown in Figure 10-14. (To simplify the example, let's not worry about office salaries for the moment.)

FIGURE 10-14
Payroll period for sales salaries

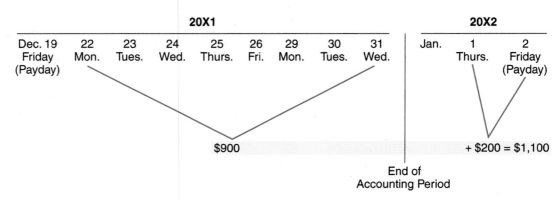

To show the proper amount of sales salaries for each accounting period, we must split the $1,100 sales payroll that is now being paid between the $900 that was accrued at the end of 20X1 and the $200 that was incurred during the first two days of 20X2. The entry to do this appears as shown below.

	20X2							
1	Jan.	2	Sales Salaries Expense	2 0 0 00				1
2			Salaries Payable	9 0 0 00				2
3			Cash			1 1 0 0 00		3

After this entry is posted, the ledger accounts appear as shown in Figure 10-15.

FIGURE 10-15
General ledger accounts showing payment of sales salaries

General Ledger							
Account Salaries Payable						**Account No.** 212	
Date	Item	P.R.	Debit	Credit	Balance		
					Debit	Credit	
20X1 Dec. 31	Adjusting	GJ3		9 0 0 00		9 0 0 00	
20X2 Jan. 2		GJ4	9 0 0 00		—	—	

CONTINUES

Paradigm College Accounting • Chapter 10

FIGURE 10-15
Continued

Account Sales Salaries Expense							Account No. 611
						Balance	
Date	Item	P.R.	Debit	Credit		Debit	Credit
20X1 Dec. 1	Balance	✓				68 2 0 0 00	
31	Adjusting	GJ3	9 0 0 00			69 1 0 0 00	
31	Closing	GJ4		69 1 0 0 00		—	—
20X2 Jan. 2		GJ4	2 0 0 00			2 0 0 00	

The Sales Salaries Expense account shows a $200 balance on January 2, 20X2, which is the correct amount of expense as of this date. The balance of the Salaries Payable account is zero because the liability for payment ended when the January 2 payroll was paid.

In making the above entry, the accountant had to look back in the records to find out how much of the $1,100 sales payroll applied to the current accounting period, and how much was accrued at the end of the last period. This may seem like a simple task, but think of the problems the accountant could have if the company had many employees who were paid on different schedules, such as weekly, monthly, or bimonthly.

Is there anything the accountant can do so that an entry such as this does not have to be split between the two periods? The answer is yes. Use of a technique called reversing entries allows the accountant to make the same entry to record the payment of accrued expenses that would have been made had two separate accounting periods not been involved. **Reversing entries** are made on the first day of the next accounting period, and they are the exact opposite (the reverse) of the adjusting entries made to record the accrued expenses. To illustrate, let's assume that Lakeside decided to use reversing entries. Accordingly, the following entry was made on January 1, 20X2.

1			Reversing Entries				1
2	20X2 Jan.	1	Salaries Payable	9 0 0 00			2
3			Sales Salaries Expense		9 0 0 00		3

Reversing entries are always made as of the first day of the new accounting period.

After this entry is posted, the ledger accounts appear as shown in Figure 10-16.

FIGURE 10-16
General ledger accounts showing reversing entries

General Ledger

Account Salaries Payable							Account No. 212
						Balance	
Date	Item	P.R.	Debit	Credit		Debit	Credit
20X1 Dec. 31	Adjusting	GJ3		9 0 0 00			9 0 0 00
20X2 Jan. 1	Reversing	GJ4	9 0 0 00			—	—

Account Sales Salaries Expense							Account No. 611
						Balance	
Date	Item	P.R.	Debit	Credit		Debit	Credit
20X1 Dec. 1	Balance	✓				68 2 0 0 00	
31	Adjusting	GJ3	9 0 0 00			69 1 0 0 00	
31	Closing	GJ4		69 1 0 0 00		—	—
20X2 Jan. 1	Reversing	GJ4		9 0 0 00			9 0 0 00

Notice that the reversing entry eliminated the credit balance of the Salaries Payable account, and a *credit* balance was created in the Sales Salaries Expense account. In effect, the balance of the liability account has been transferred to the Sales Salaries Expense account. So, on Friday, January 2, we can make our regular payroll entry, as shown below.

				Debit	Credit	
1	20X2 Jan.	2	Sales Salaries Expense	1 1 0 0 00		1
2			Cash		1 1 0 0 00	2

Now look at what happens to the Sales Salaries Expense account when this entry is posted.

Account Sales Salaries Expense						Account No. 611	
						Balance	
Date		**Item**	**P.R.**	**Debit**	**Credit**	**Debit**	**Credit**
20X1 Dec.	1	Balance	✓			68 2 0 0 00	
	31	Adjusting	GJ3	9 0 0 00		69 1 0 0 00	
	31	Closing	GJ4		69 1 0 0 00	—	—
20X2 Jan.	1	Reversing	GJ4		9 0 0 00		9 0 0 00
	2		GJ5	1 1 0 0 00		2 0 0 00	

As we can see, the Sales Salaries Expense account now has a $200 debit balance, which is the proper amount of expense for the January 2, 20X2 payroll. Why did this happen when we did not split the entry? In effect, the reversing entry transferred the $900 unpaid expense for 20X1 to the credit side of the Sales Salaries Expense account. Thus, when the $1,100 debit was posted, the $900 credit balance offset the debit posting and created the proper balance in the account ($200 debit).

You may be thinking, "How do I remember which adjusting entries to reverse?" This is simple. Most adjusting entries are not reversed. The *only* adjusting entry we have studied thus far that would be reversed is for accrued expenses—*none of the other adjusting entries would be reversed.*

Now let's look at Lakeside's reversing entry for both types of salaries.

				Debit	Credit	
1			Reversing Entries			1
2	20X2 Jan.	1	Salaries Payable	1 6 0 0 00		2
3			Sales Salaries Expense		9 0 0 00	3
4			Office Salaries Expense		7 0 0 00	4
5						5

REMEMBER

1. Reversing entries are optional journal entries that are intended to simplify the bookkeeping for transactions that involve accrued expenses.

2. Reversing entries are always made as of the first day of the next accounting period—never on the last day of the period.

3. In this chapter, the only adjusting entry that requires reversal is the one for accrued expenses (unpaid salaries).

Mobley Company made the following adjusting entries as of December 31, 20X3:

			Adjusting Entries			
1			Adjusting Entries			1
2	20X3 Dec.	31	Income Summary	42 0 0 0 00		2
3			Merchandise Inventory		42 0 0 0 00	3
4						4
5		31	Merchandise Inventory	43 2 0 0 00		5
6			Income Summary		43 2 0 0 00	6
7						7
8		31	Insurance Expense	8 0 0 00		8
9			Prepaid Insurance		8 0 0 00	9
10						10
11		31	Supplies Expense	6 9 0 00		11
12			Supplies		6 9 0 00	12
13						13
14		31	Salaries Expense	8 1 0 00		14
15			Salaries Payable		8 1 0 00	15

Make the appropriate reversing entry.

CHECK YOUR ANSWER ON PAGE 392.

INTERIM STATEMENTS

Let us stress that the fiscal period for most businesses consists of 12 consecutive months. At the end of the fiscal period, financial statements are prepared and the adjusting and closing entries are posted to the ledger. But owners and managers do not want to wait until the end of the year to see how well the company is doing financially. Consequently, many businesses prepare **interim statements**, which are statements that are prepared during the fiscal year for periods of *less* than 12 months—such as monthly, quarterly, and semiannually. For example, Coca Cola, like most other large corporations, issues quarterly reports to its stockholders. These statements provide up-to-date information about the results of operations for the period covered by the statements.

To prepare interim statements, the accountant assembles adjustment data for the interim period. The adjustments are then entered on a work sheet, and the interim statements are prepared from the completed work sheet. However, adjusting and closing entries are not journalized, and thus are not entered in the ledger. These entries are recorded only at the end of the fiscal year.

WHERE ON THE INTERNET CAN I FIND RESOURCES TO IMPROVE MY SUPERVISORY SKILLS?

Several sites on the Internet offer advice on developing management and supervisory skills. You may find the following sites helpful:

http://www.prismltd.com/leader.htm
At this site, you will find an article discussing leadership as an interpersonal influence process based on the well-known Hensey-Blanchand framework.

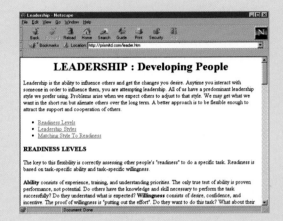

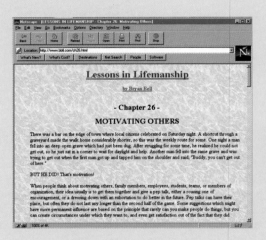

http://bbll.com/ch26.html
This site includes "Lessons in Lifemanship"— practical advice on how to motivate others.

http://www.hardatwork.com/Stump/ME/ME.html
This location addresses common motivational problems.

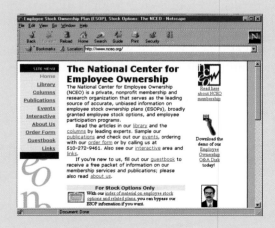

http://www.nceo.org
This site discusses management and supervisory skills needed by owner-employers.

STEPS IN THE ACCOUNTING CYCLE FOR A MERCHANDISING BUSINESS

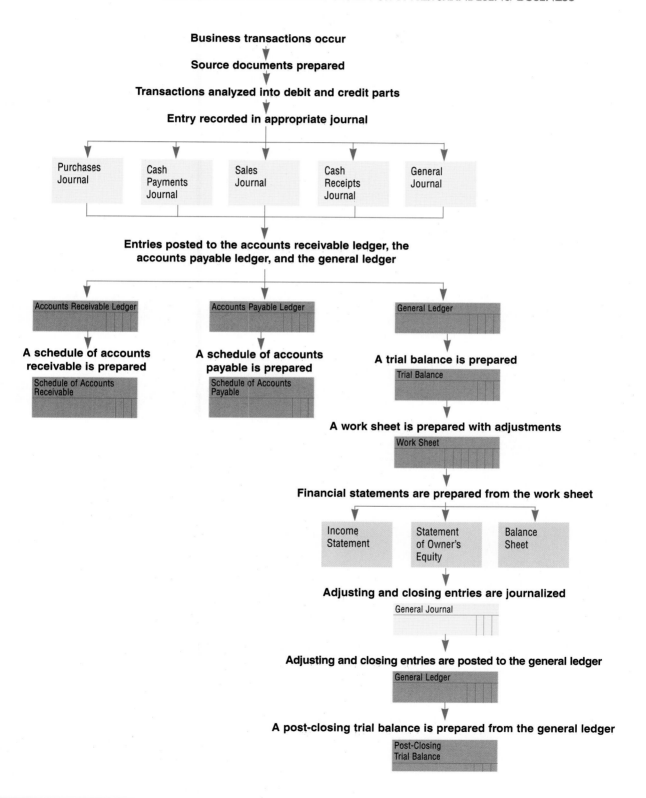

Business transactions occur

Source documents prepared

Transactions analyzed into debit and credit parts

Entry recorded in appropriate journal

| Purchases Journal | Cash Payments Journal | Sales Journal | Cash Receipts Journal | General Journal |

Entries posted to the accounts receivable ledger, the accounts payable ledger, and the general ledger

Accounts Receivable Ledger

Accounts Payable Ledger

General Ledger

A schedule of accounts receivable is prepared

Schedule of Accounts Receivable

A schedule of accounts payable is prepared

Schedule of Accounts Payable

A trial balance is prepared

Trial Balance

A work sheet is prepared with adjustments

Work Sheet

Financial statements are prepared from the work sheet

| Income Statement | Statement of Owner's Equity | Balance Sheet |

Adjusting and closing entries are journalized

General Journal

Adjusting and closing entries are posted to the general ledger

General Ledger

A post-closing trial balance is prepared from the general ledger

Post-Closing Trial Balance

Financial Statements and Closing Entries for a Merchandising Business

SUMMARY/RESTATEMENT OF LEARNING OBJECTIVES

1. Prepare financial statements for a merchandising business.

In the Summary/Restatement of Learning Objectives for Chapter 9, we prepared a work sheet for The Rose Bowl. The financial statement columns of The Rose Bowl's work sheet are reproduced in Figure 10-17.

FIGURE 10-17

The Rose Bowl's work sheet

The Rose Bowl
Work Sheet
For Year Ended June 30, 20X1

	Account Title	Income Statement Debit	Income Statement Credit	Balance Sheet Debit	Balance Sheet Credit	
1	Cash			3 1 0 0 00		1
2	Accounts Receivable			6 8 0 0 00		2
3	Merchandise Inventory			42 0 0 0 00		3
4	Store Supplies			4 0 0 00		4
5	Store Equipment			25 0 0 0 00		5
6	Accumulated Depreciation—Store Equipment				4 0 0 0 00	6
7	Trucks			38 0 0 0 00		7
8	Accumulated Depreciation —Trucks				10 0 0 0 00	8
9	Accounts Payable				4 9 0 0 00	9
10	Sales Tax Payable				1 1 0 0 00	10
11	Salaries Payable				4 0 0 00	11
12	Karen Grimes, Capital				83 5 0 0 00	12
13	Karen Grimes, Drawing			25 0 0 0 00		13
14	Income Summary	46 0 0 0 00	42 0 0 0 00			14
15	Sales		177 1 9 0 00			15
16	Sales Returns and Allowances	8 0 0 00				16
17	Purchases	77 8 0 0 00				17
18	Purchases Returns and Allowances		1 2 0 0 00			18
19	Purchases Discounts		6 0 0 00			19
20	Sales Salaries Expense	32 4 0 0 00				20
21	Advertising Expense	4 8 0 0 00				21
22	Depreciation Expense—Store Equipment	1 0 0 0 00				22
23	Miscellaneous Selling Expense	8 0 0 00				23
24	Store Supplies Expense	2 0 0 00				24
25	Rent Expense	4 8 9 0 00				25
26	Repairs Expense	6 0 0 00				26
27	Transportation Expense	9 0 0 00				27
28	Depreciation Expense—Trucks	3 0 0 0 00				28
29	Utilities Expense	9 6 0 0 00				29
30	Miscellaneous General Expense	1 8 0 0 00				30
31		184 5 9 0 00	220 9 9 0 00	140 3 0 0 00	103 9 0 0 00	31
32	Net Income	36 4 0 0 00			36 4 0 0 00	32
33		220 9 9 0 00	220 9 9 0 00	140 3 0 0 00	140 3 0 0 00	33

The following **classified income statement** (Figure 10-18), statement of owner's equity (Figure 10-19), and **classified balance sheet** (Figure 10-20) were prepared from The Rose Bowl's work sheet.

FIGURE 10-18
Classified income statement

The dates of the income statement and statement of owner's equity cover a specific period of time.

The Rose Bowl
Income Statement
For Year Ended June 30, 20X1

Revenue from sales:				
Sales			$177 1 9 0 00	
Less: Sales returns and allow.			8 0 0 00	
Net sales				$176 3 9 0 00
Cost of goods sold:				
Merch. inventory, July 1, 20X0			$ 46 0 0 0 00	
Purchases		$77 8 0 0 00		
Less: Purchases returns and allow.	$1 2 0 0 00			
Purchases discounts	6 0 0 00	1 8 0 0 00		
Net purchases			76 0 0 0 00	
Goods available for sale			$122 0 0 0 00	
Less: Merch. inv., June 30, 20X1			42 0 0 0 00	
Cost of goods sold				80 0 0 0 00
Gross profit				$ 96 3 9 0 00
Operating expenses:				
Selling expenses:				
Sales salaries expense		$32 4 0 0 00		
Advertising expense		4 8 0 0 00		
Depr. expense—store equip.		1 0 0 0 00		
Misc. selling expense		8 0 0 00		
Store supplies expense		2 0 0 00		
Total selling expenses			$ 39 2 0 0 00	
General expenses:				
Rent expense		$ 4 8 9 0 00		
Repairs expense		6 0 0 00		
Transportation expense		9 0 0 00		
Depr. expense—trucks		3 0 0 0 00		
Utilities expense		9 6 0 0 00		
Misc. general expense		1 8 0 0 00		
Total general expenses			20 7 9 0 00	
Total operating expenses				59 9 9 0 00
Net income				$ 36 4 0 0 00

FIGURE 10-19
Statement of owner's equity

The Rose Bowl Statement of Owner's Equity For Year Ended June 30, 20X1		
Karen Grimes, capital, July 1, 20X0		$83 5 0 0 00
Net income for period	$36 4 0 0 00	
Less: Withdrawals	25 0 0 0 00	
Increase in capital		11 4 0 0 00
Karen Grimes, capital, June 30, 20X1		$94 9 0 0 00

FIGURE 10-20
Classified balance sheet

> The balance sheet is dated as of the last day of the accounting period.

The Rose Bowl Balance Sheet June 30, 20X1			
Assets			
Current assets:			
Cash		$ 3 1 0 0 00	
Accounts receivable		6 8 0 0 00	
Merchandise inventory		42 0 0 0 00	
Store supplies		4 0 0 00	
Total current assets			$ 52 3 0 0 00
Plant assets:			
Store equipment	$25 0 0 0 00		
Less: Accumulated depreciation	4 0 0 0 00	$21 0 0 0 00	
Trucks	$38 0 0 0 00		
Less: Accumulated depreciation	10 0 0 0 00	28 0 0 0 00	
Total plant assets			49 0 0 0 00
Total assets			$101 3 0 0 00
Liabilities			
Current liabilities:			
Accounts payable		$ 4 9 0 0 00	
Sales tax payable		1 1 0 0 00	
Salaries payable		4 0 0 00	
Total liabilities			$ 6 4 0 0 00
Owner's Equity			
Karen Grimes, capital			94 9 0 0 00
Total liabilities and owner's equity			$101 3 0 0 00

2. Journalize adjusting and closing entries for a merchandising business.

The adjusting and closing entries shown in Figure 10-21 and Figure 10-22 were prepared from The Rose Bowl's work sheet.

FIGURE 10-21
Adjusting entries

General Journal — **Page 5**

	Date		Account Title	P.R.	Debit	Credit	
1			Adjusting Entries				1
2	20X1 Jun.	30	Income Summary		46 0 0 0 00		2
3			Merchandise Inventory			46 0 0 0 00	3
4							4
5		30	Merchandise Inventory		42 0 0 0 00		5
6			Income Summary			42 0 0 0 00	6
7							7
8		30	Store Supplies Expense		2 0 0 00		8
9			Store Supplies			2 0 0 00	9
10							10
11		30	Depreciation Expense—Store Equipment		1 0 0 0 00		11
12			Accumulated Depr.—Store Equipment			1 0 0 0 00	12
13							13
14		30	Depreciation Expense—Trucks		3 0 0 0 00		14
15			Accumulated Depreciation—Trucks			3 0 0 0 00	15
16							16
17		30	Sales Salaries Expense		4 0 0 00		17
18			Salaries Payable			4 0 0 00	18

FIGURE 10-22
Closing entries

General Journal — **Page 6**

	Date		Account Title	P.R.	Debit	Credit	
1			Closing Entries				1
2	20X1 Jun.	30	Sales		177 1 9 0 00		2
3			Purchases Returns and Allowances		1 2 0 0 00		3
4			Purchases Discounts		6 0 0 00		4
5			Income Summary			178 9 9 0 00	5
6							6
7		30	Income Summary		138 5 9 0 00		7
8			Sales Returns and Allowances			8 0 0 00	8
9			Purchases			77 8 0 0 00	9
10			Sales Salaries Expense			32 4 0 0 00	10
11			Advertising Expense			4 8 0 0 00	11
12			Depreciation Expense—Store Equip.			1 0 0 0 00	12
13			Miscellaneous Selling Expense			8 0 0 00	13
14			Store Supplies Expense			2 0 0 00	14
15			Rent Expense			4 8 9 0 00	15
16			Repairs Expense			6 0 0 00	16
17			Transportation Expense			9 0 0 00	17
18			Depreciation Expense—Trucks			3 0 0 0 00	18
19			Utilities Expense			9 6 0 0 00	19
20			Miscellaneous General Expense			1 8 0 0 00	20
21							21
22		30	Income Summary		36 4 0 0 00		22
23			Karen Grimes, Capital			36 4 0 0 00	23
24							24
25		30	Karen Grimes, Capital		25 0 0 0 00		25
26			Karen Grimes, Drawing			25 0 0 0 00	26

3. Prepare a post-closing trial balance.

A post-closing trial balance is a trial balance of the ledger prepared after adjusting and closing entries have been posted. Figure 10-23 shows the trial balance that was prepared after The Rose Bowl's adjusting and closing entries were posted. Notice that only the permanent accounts are shown, as all temporary accounts have been closed.

FIGURE 10-23
Post-closing trial balance

The Rose Bowl Post-Closing Trial Balance June 30, 20X1		
Account Title	**Debit**	**Credit**
Cash	3 1 0 0 00	
Accounts Receivable	6 8 0 0 00	
Merchandise Inventory	42 0 0 0 00	
Store Supplies	4 0 0 00	
Store Equipment	25 0 0 0 00	
Accumulated Depreciation—Store Equipment		4 0 0 0 00
Trucks	38 0 0 0 00	
Accumulated Depreciation—Trucks		10 0 0 0 00
Accounts Payable		4 9 0 0 00
Sales Tax Payable		1 1 0 0 00
Salaries Payable		4 0 0 00
Karen Grimes, Capital		94 9 0 0 00
Totals	115 3 0 0 00	115 3 0 0 00

4. Make reversing entries for accrued (unpaid) salaries.

Reversing entries are entries made at the beginning of the next accounting period, and they are the exact reverse of certain adjusting entries made at the end of the preceding period. Reversing entries are not required as part of the accounting cycle, and they should be prepared only when they will save time in the next accounting period. In this chapter, we worked with only one type of adjusting entry that should be reversed—accrued (unpaid) salaries. Accrued salaries are salaries incurred at the end of one period that will not be paid until the next accounting period. When unpaid salaries are paid in the next accounting period, the entry will have to be split between the part of the payment that pertains to the preceding period (salaries payable) and the part that pertains to the current period (salaries expense). Reversing the adjusting entry for accrued salaries (and all accrued expenses) allows the accountant to make routine entries when the expense is paid. That is, the entry does not have to be split between two amounts. The Rose Bowl had only one accrued expense, unpaid salaries in the amount of $400. We can save time when this amount is paid in the next accounting period by making the following reversing entry.

1			Reversing Entries						1
2	20X1 Jul.	1	Salaries Payable		4 0 0 00				2
3		▲	Sales Salaries Expense				4 0 0 00		3

Remember *Reversing entries are made as of the first day of the new accounting period.*

KEY TERMS

classified balance sheet A balance sheet that divides the assets and liabilities sections into the following subsections: current assets and plant assets, and current liabilities and long-term liabilities.

classified income statement An income statement divided into the following sections: revenue, cost of goods sold, operating expenses, and other income and expenses.

cost of goods sold The cost of merchandise sold to customers during the accounting period. The formula used to find cost of goods sold is:

	Beginning Merchandise Inventory
+	Net Purchases of Merchandise
=	Cost of Goods Available for Sale
−	Ending Merchandise Inventory
=	Cost of Goods Sold

current assets Cash and any other assets that will be realized in cash, used up, sold, or expire within one year. Examples include accounts receivable, merchandise inventory, supplies, and prepaid insurance.

current liabilities Debts that are due for payment within one year. Examples are accounts payable, salaries payable, sales tax payable, and the current portion of notes payable.

current ratio The ratio obtained by dividing current assets by current liabilities. It is an indicator of a firm's ability to pay its short-term debts as they become due.

general expenses Expenses related to (1) running a firm's office or (2) any other operating activities that do not involve the sale of merchandise. Also called **administrative expenses**.

gross profit The profit before we subtract the expenses of doing business; it is obtained by subtracting cost of goods sold from net sales.

income from operations Gross profit minus operating expenses. Also called **operating income**.

interim statements Statements that are prepared during the fiscal year for periods of less than 12 months—such as monthly, quarterly, and semiannually.

liquidity Refers to how quickly an asset can be turned into cash, used up, or expire; used in reference to assets, which are listed on the balance sheet in the order of their liquidity.

long-term liabilities Debts that will not come due for payment within one year. Examples are long-term notes payable and mortgages payable.

net sales The amount obtained by subtracting the amount of sales returns and allowances and the amount of sales discounts from the amount of sales.

operating expenses Expenses incurred in the normal operation of the business.

other income or expenses Income or expenses that are not directly associated with the normal operation of the business, such as vending machine sales, interest income, and interest expense.

plant assets Assets that are expected to be used in the business for more than one year. Examples are land, buildings, machinery, furniture, and automobiles. Also called **fixed assets** or **property, plant, and equipment** or **long-term assets**.

reversing entries A technique that allows the accountant to make the same entry to record the payment of accrued expenses that would have been made had two separate accounting periods not been involved.

selling expenses Operating expenses related to the sale of a firm's merchandise.

stability Refers to how long an asset will last. Plant assets are usually listed on the balance sheet according to their stability.

working capital The excess of a firm's current assets over its current liabilities. A strong working capital means that the firm is likely to be able to carry on its current operations.

CONCEPTS AND SKILLS REVIEW

CONCEPTS REVIEW

1. What are the sections of the classified income statement?
2. Explain the difference between gross profit and net income.
3. Identify each of the following as either a selling expense or a general expense: (a) store supplies expense; (b) depreciation expense—office equipment; (c) rent expense; (d) advertising expense; (e) insurance expense; (f) utilities expense.
4. Explain how the statement of owner's equity serves as a link between the income statement and the balance sheet.
5. Explain the order of the current assets on the balance sheet.
6. What are terms for "plant assets"?
7. How does time distinguish between current and long-term liabilities?
8. "The calculations for working capital and the current ratio use the same information, but in different ways." Explain this statement.
9. Are all temporary accounts income statement accounts? Explain.
10. What figures appearing in the Income Summary account are not the result of closing entries?
11. What is the purpose of a post-closing trial balance?
12. How does the use of reversing entries make accounting for accrued expenses easier?
13. Are all adjusting entries reversed? Explain.
14. What is an interim statement?

SKILLS REVIEW

EXERCISE 10-1

LEARNING OBJECTIVE 1

Objective: To calculate cost of goods sold

Directions: From the following data, calculate Richardson Company's cost of goods sold for 20X1.

Item	Amount
Beginning merchandise inventory	$ 47,610
Purchases during the period	114,750
Freight in	3,375
Purchases returns and allowances	14,875
Purchases discounts	3,145
Ending merchandise inventory	37,910

EXERCISE 10-2

LEARNING OBJECTIVE 1

Objective: To calculate income statement amounts

Directions: From the following data, calculate (a) net sales; (b) cost of goods sold; (c) gross profit; (d) net income or net loss.

Item	Amount
Sales	$437,600
Sales returns and allowances	21,600
Sales discounts	9,520
Beginning merchandise inventory	37,510
Purchases	307,300
Ending merchandise inventory	42,710
Operating expenses	82,450

EXERCISE 10-3

Objective: To calculate missing financial statement items

Directions: Calculate the missing items in the following table:

	Sales	Sales Returns and Allowances	Net Sales	Beginning Inventory	Net Purchases	Goods Available for Sale	Ending Inventory	Cost of Goods Sold	Gross Profit
(a)	$122,000	_____	$118,900	_____	$ 72,100	$ 98,600	$19,000	_____	_____
(b)	_____	$900	110,400	$38,000	65,200	_____	32,000	_____	_____
(c)	87,500	_____	81,230	_____	118,000	145,000	_____	$73,400	_____

EXERCISE 10-4

Objective: To prepare financial statements and journalize closing entries

Directions: The financial statement columns of the December 31, 20X4 work sheet for Ingram Company are shown below. Prepare (1) an income statement, (2) a statement of owner's equity, (3) a balance sheet, and (4) journalize closing entries.

Ingram Company
Work Sheet
For Year Ended December 31, 20X4

	Account Title	Income Statement Debit	Income Statement Credit	Balance Sheet Debit	Balance Sheet Credit	
1	Cash			8 7 2 5 00		1
2	Accounts Receivable			9 4 5 0 00		2
3	Merchandise Inventory			12 4 1 0 00		3
4	Office Supplies			6 9 6 5 00		4
5	Office Equipment			147 0 0 0 00		5
6	Accumulated Depreciation—Office Equipment				68 7 0 0 00	6
7	Accounts Payable				16 5 1 0 00	7
8	Salaries Payable				5 4 0 00	8
9	Ray Ingram, Capital				90 2 2 0 00	9
10	Ray Ingram, Drawing			24 0 0 0 00		10
11	Income Summary	13 1 6 5 00	12 4 1 0 00			11
12	Sales		469 6 0 0 00			12
13	Sales Returns and Allowances	21 5 4 0 00				13
14	Sales Discounts	9 3 1 0 00				14
15	Purchases	301 2 4 0 00				15
16	Freight In	14 5 9 0 00				16
17	Purchases Returns and Allowances		19 5 6 5 00			17
18	Purchases Discounts		6 1 1 0 00			18
19	Sales Salaries Expense	30 3 6 0 00				19
20	Advertising Expense	4 5 0 0 00				20
21	Rent Expense	12 0 0 0 00				21
22	Office Salaries Expense	15 1 8 0 00				22
23	Office Supplies Expense	25 4 2 0 00				23
24	Utilities Expense	6 8 0 0 00				24
25	Depreciation Expense—Office Equipment	21 0 0 0 00				25
26		475 1 0 5 00	507 6 8 5 00	208 5 5 0 00	175 9 7 0 00	26
27	Net Income	32 5 8 0 00			32 5 8 0 00	27
28		507 6 8 5 00	507 6 8 5 00	208 5 5 0 00	208 5 5 0 00	28

EXERCISE 10-5

LEARNING OBJECTIVE 1

Objective: To prepare a statement of owner's equity

Directions: From the following data, prepare a statement of owner's equity for Gallaraga Trading Company, owned by Jane Gallaraga, for the year ended December 31, 20XX.

Item	Amount
Capital, January 1, 20XX	$110,610
Net income for the year	47,360
Withdrawals for the year	36,500

EXERCISE 10-6

LEARNING OBJECTIVE 1

Objective: To classify balance sheet items

Directions: Classify each of the items in this exercise as one of the following: (a) current asset; (b) plant asset; (c) current liability; or (d) long-term liability.

1. Notes Payable (due in six months)
2. Store Supplies
3. Accounts Payable
4. Prepaid Insurance
5. Accumulated Depreciation—Store Equipment
6. Salaries Payable
7. Office Equipment
8. Notes Payable (due in five years)
9. Accounts Receivable
10. Merchandise Inventory

EXERCISE 10-7

LEARNING OBJECTIVE 1

Objective: To calculate working capital and the current ratio

Directions: From the following data, calculate (a) working capital, and (b) the current ratio.

Account	Amount
Cash	$ 6,200
Accounts Receivable	5,200
Merchandise Inventory	17,000
Prepaid Insurance	750
Supplies	250
Office Equipment	17,900
Accounts Payable	11,200
Salaries Payable	2,800
Notes Payable (due in three years)	11,300

EXERCISE 10-8

LEARNING OBJECTIVE 2

Objective: To place items on the correct side of the Income Summary account

Directions: Set up a T account for Income Summary. Enter the following data on the correct side of the account. Do you need all of the items?

Item	Amount
Revenue for the period	$157,500
Beginning merchandise inventory	13,900
Expenses for the period	95,700
Owner's withdrawals	10,600
Ending merchandise inventory	17,300
Owner's beginning capital balance	107,500

CASE PROBLEMS

GROUP A

PROBLEM 10-1A

LEARNING OBJECTIVE 1

Objective: To prepare a classified income statement from account balances

The following are account balances after adjustments for B. Logan Clothing Store for the year ended December 31, 20XX:

Account	Balance
Advertising Expense	$ 6,100
Depreciation Expense—Office Equipment	13,000
Depreciation Expense—Store Equipment	16,000
Freight In	5,200
Insurance Expense	7,000
Merchandise Inventory, December 31	37,600
Merchandise Inventory, January 1	42,400
Office Salaries Expense	28,300
Office Supplies Expense	4,750
Purchases	219,550
Purchases Returns and Allowances	13,465
Purchases Discounts	6,300
Rent Expense	25,200
Sales	395,140
Sales Returns and Allowances	15,505
Sales Discounts	7,400
Sales Salaries Expense	23,000
Store Supplies Expense	5,300
Utilities Expense	5,800

Directions: Prepare a classified income statement.

PROBLEM 10-2A

LEARNING OBJECTIVE 1

Objective: To prepare and analyze a classified balance sheet

Adjusted account balances for Wills's Variety Store appear as follows on December 31, 20X1:

Account	Adjusted Balance
Accounts Payable	$16,025
Accounts Receivable	11,819
Accumulated Depreciation—Office Equipment	11,455
Accumulated Depreciation—Store Equipment	16,805
Cash	4,750
Merchandise Inventory	32,600
Notes Payable (due within this year)	7,000
Notes Payable (due beyond this year)	17,000
Office Equipment	37,625
Office Supplies	3,725
Prepaid Insurance	4,500
Salaries Payable	3,600
Store Equipment	42,595
Store Supplies	5,180
James Wills, Capital	70,909

Directions:
1. Prepare a classified balance sheet.
2. Calculate the firm's (a) working capital and (b) current ratio (to the nearest tenth).

PROBLEM 10-3A

Objective: To prepare financial statements from a work sheet

The financial statement columns of Wilson Company's December 31, 20XX work sheet follow:

Wilson Company
Work Sheet
For Year Ended December 31, 20XX

	Account Title	Income Statement Debit	Income Statement Credit	Balance Sheet Debit	Balance Sheet Credit	
1	Cash			5 8 9 5 00		1
2	Accounts Receivable			6 2 5 5 00		2
3	Merchandise Inventory			11 2 7 0 00		3
4	Store Supplies			3 7 1 0 00		4
5	Office Supplies			5 1 6 5 00		5
6	Prepaid Insurance			1 2 0 0 00		6
7	Store Equipment			21 0 0 0 00		7
8	Accum. Depr.—Store Equip.				6 3 0 0 00	8
9	Office Equipment			12 0 0 0 00		9
10	Accum. Depr.—Office Equip.				5 0 0 0 00	10
11	Accounts Payable				8 2 4 5 00	11
12	Salaries Payable				6 0 0 00	12
13	Peggy Wilson, Capital				37 4 9 0 00	13
14	Peggy Wilson, Drawing			7 0 0 0 00		14
15	Income Summary	12 5 4 0 00	11 2 7 0 00			15
16	Sales		194 3 7 5 00			16
17	Sales Returns and Allowances	14 5 0 5 00				17
18	Sales Discounts	3 1 7 5 00				18
19	Purchases	110 5 4 0 00				19
20	Freight In	2 5 5 0 00				20
21	Purchases Returns and Allowances		9 3 1 0 00			21
22	Purchases Discounts		2 1 4 0 00			22
23	Store Supplies Expense	9 4 2 5 00				23
24	Sales Salaries Expense	12 0 0 0 00				24
25	Depr. Expense—Store Equip.	2 1 0 0 00				25
26	Rent Expense	4 8 0 0 00				26
27	Office Supplies Expense	18 0 0 0 00				27
28	Office Salaries Expense	10 0 0 0 00				28
29	Depr. Expense—Office Equip.	1 0 0 0 00				29
30	Insurance Expense	6 0 0 00				30
31		201 2 3 5 00	217 0 9 5 00	73 4 9 5 00	57 6 3 5 00	31
32	Net Income	15 8 6 0 00			15 8 6 0 00	32
33		217 0 9 5 00	217 0 9 5 00	73 4 9 5 00	73 4 9 5 00	33

Directions:
1. Prepare a classified income statement for the year ended December 31, 20XX.
2. Prepare a statement of owner's equity for the year ended December 31, 20XX.
3. Prepare a classified balance sheet as of December 31, 20XX.

PROBLEM 10-4A

LEARNING OBJECTIVE 2

Objective: To prepare closing entries from a work sheet

Directions: From the work sheet in Problem 10-3A, prepare closing entries on page 1 of a general journal.

PROBLEM 10-5A

LEARNING OBJECTIVE 2

Objective: To prepare closing entries from account balances

The following are adjusted account balances of Gregrich's Wallpaper Store as of December 31, 20X5. Beginning merchandise inventory is $19,300; ending is $21,400.

Account	Adjusted Balance
Advertising Expense	$ 4,100
Depreciation Expense—Office Equipment	12,000
Depreciation Expense—Store Equipment	7,000
Robert Gregrich, Capital	180,450
Robert Gregrich, Drawing	13,600
Insurance Expense	5,200
Office Salaries Expense	24,600
Office Supplies Expense	3,275
Purchases	92,600
Purchases Returns and Allowances	5,942
Purchases Discounts	2,520
Rent Expense	36,000
Sales	229,300
Sales Returns and Allowances	8,345
Sales Discounts	2,150
Sales Salaries Expense	37,600
Store Supplies Expense	3,675
Utilities Expense	4,920

Directions: Prepare closing entries on page 4 of a general journal.

PROBLEM 10-6A

LEARNING OBJECTIVE 2, 4

Objective: To record adjusting and reversing entries

Directions:
1. In each of the following unrelated situations, record the appropriate adjusting entry as of December 31, 20X2:
    (a) The Office Supplies account shows a balance before adjustment of $15,300. Office supplies of $7,900 are on hand.
    (b) The Prepaid Insurance account shows a payment of $3,780 on October 1, 20X2, for a three-year policy.
    (c) Salaries of $48,000 are paid on Monday for the preceding week. This year, December 31 fell on a Tuesday.
2. Prepare reversing entries as needed.
3. Record the weekly salary payment on Monday, January 6, 20X3, for the week ended January 3, 20X3.
4. Assuming that the company does not use reversing entries, prepare the entry to pay the salaries on January 6, 20X3.

PROBLEM 10-1B

LEARNING OBJECTIVE 1

Objective: To prepare a classified income statement from account balances

The following are the account balances after adjustments for Gresham Department Store for the year ended December 31, 20XX.

Account	Balance
Advertising Expense	$ 7,100
Depreciation Expense—Office Equipment	16,000
Depreciation Expense—Store Equipment	21,000
Freight In	6,200
Insurance Expense	6,100
Merchandise Inventory, December 31	17,200
Merchandise Inventory, January 1	19,600
Office Salaries Expense	31,500
Office Supplies Expense	5,610
Purchases	275,100
Purchases Returns and Allowances	13,400
Purchases Discounts	6,100
Rent Expense	29,200
Sales	445,100
Sales Returns and Allowances	21,350
Sales Discounts	8,900
Sales Salaries Expense	43,200
Store Supplies Expense	7,155
Utilities Expense	7,000

Directions: Prepare a classified income statement.

PROBLEM 10-2B

LEARNING OBJECTIVE 1

Objective: To prepare and analyze a classified balance sheet

Adjusted account balances for Krause Company appear as follows on December 31, 20XX:

Account	Adjusted Balance
Accounts Payable	$27,350
Accounts Receivable	18,210
Accumulated Depreciation—Office Equipment	15,350
Accumulated Depreciation—Store Equipment	10,600
Cash	9,450
Interest Payable	350
T. Krause, Capital	66,710
Merchandise Inventory	27,110
Notes Payable (due in three years)	8,600
Office Equipment	36,500
Office Supplies	5,145
Prepaid Insurance	2,710
Salaries Payable	3,800
Store Equipment	28,600
Store Supplies	5,035

Directions:
1. Prepare a classified balance sheet.
2. Calculate the firm's (a) working capital; (b) current ratio (to the nearest tenth).

PROBLEM 10-3B

Objective: To prepare financial statements from a work sheet

The financial statement columns of Dusenski Company's December 31, 20XX work sheet follow:

Dusenski Company
Work Sheet
For Year Ended December 31, 20XX

	Account Title	Income Statement Debit	Income Statement Credit	Balance Sheet Debit	Balance Sheet Credit	
1	Cash			3 7 2 5 00		1
2	Accounts Receivable			11 6 8 0 00		2
3	Merchandise Inventory			16 9 1 0 00		3
4	Store Supplies			4 5 0 0 00		4
5	Office Supplies			3 7 5 0 00		5
6	Prepaid Insurance			6 0 0 00		6
7	Store Equipment			85 0 0 0 00		7
8	Accumulated Depreciation—Store Equipment				36 0 0 0 00	8
9	Office Equipment			45 0 0 0 00		9
10	Accumulated Depreciation—Office Equipment				15 0 0 0 00	10
11	Accounts Payable				21 4 5 0 00	11
12	Salaries Payable				2 0 0 0 00	12
13	Ted Dusenski, Capital				116 3 2 0 00	13
14	Ted Dusenski, Drawing			12 0 0 0 00		14
15	Income Summary	12 4 0 0 00	16 9 1 0 00			15
16	Sales		196 5 0 0 00			16
17	Sales Returns and Allowances	11 1 1 0 00				17
18	Sales Discounts	3 1 2 0 00				18
19	Purchases	98 5 0 0 00				19
20	Freight In	2 5 0 0 00				20
21	Purchases Returns and Allowances		6 3 7 0 00			21
22	Purchases Discounts		2 1 0 0 00			22
23	Store Supplies Expense	5 1 2 5 00				23
24	Sales Salaries Expense	36 0 0 0 00				24
25	Depreciation Expense—Store Equipment	12 0 0 0 00				25
26	Rent Expense	6 0 0 0 00				26
27	Office Supplies Expense	6 2 5 0 00				27
28	Office Salaries Expense	31 0 0 0 00				28
29	Depreciation Expense—Office Equipment	5 0 0 0 00				29
30	Insurance Expense	4 8 0 00				30
31		229 4 8 5 00	221 8 8 0 00	183 1 6 5 00	190 7 7 0 00	31
32	Net Loss		7 6 0 5 00	7 6 0 5 00		32
33		229 4 8 5 00	229 4 8 5 00	190 7 7 0 00	190 7 7 0 00	33

Directions:
1. Prepare a classified income statement for the year ended December 31, 20XX.
2. Prepare a statement of owner's equity for the year ended December 31, 20XX.
3. Prepare a classified balance sheet as of December 31, 20XX.

PROBLEM 10-4B

Objective: To prepare closing entries from a work sheet

Directions: From the work sheet in Problem 10-3B, prepare closing entries on page 1 of a general journal.

PROBLEM 10-5B

Objective: To prepare closing entries from account balances

The following are adjusted account balances of Sue's Variety Store as of December 31, 20X1. Beginning merchandise inventory is $29,210; ending is $25,495.

Account	Adjusted Balance
Advertising Expense	$ 3,275
Sue Ambly, Capital	79,210
Sue Ambly, Drawing	11,650
Depreciation Expense—Delivery Equipment	5,700
Depreciation Expense—Office Equipment	10,200
Depreciation Expense—Store Equipment	12,600
Insurance Expense	7,300
Office Salaries Expense	31,900
Office Supplies Expense	7,210
Purchases	207,645
Purchases Returns and Allowances	17,620
Purchases Discounts	4,155
Rent Expense	14,400
Sales	305,650
Sales Returns and Allowances	11,250
Sales Discounts	6,055
Sales Salaries Expense	65,200
Store Supplies Expense	2,300
Utilities Expense	5,275

Directions: Prepare closing entries on page 2 of a general journal.

PROBLEM 10-6B

Objective: To record adjusting and reversing entries

Directions:
1. In each of the following unrelated situations, record the appropriate adjusting entry as of December 31, 20X3:
   (a) The Office Supplies account shows a balance before adjustment of $17,700. Office supplies of $3,145 are on hand.
   (b) The Prepaid Insurance account shows a payment of $1,680 on April 1, 20X3, for a two-year policy.
   (c) Salaries of $64,000 are paid on Monday for the preceding week. This year, December 31 fell on a Wednesday.
2. Prepare reversing entries as needed.
3. Record the weekly salary payment on Monday, January 5, 20X4, for the week ended January 2, 20X4.
4. Assuming that the company does not use reversing entries, prepare the entry to pay the salaries on January 5, 20X4.

CHALLENGE PROBLEMS

PROBLEM SOLVING

The completed work sheet for Save Mart Department Store is shown on pages 390–391.

Directions:
1. Open a general ledger account for each account listed in the Trial Balance columns. Enter the balances as of December 31, 20X2.
2. Prepare a classified income statement.
3. Prepare a statement of owner's equity.
4. Prepare a classified balance sheet. The notes payable are due in three years.
5. Calculate working capital and the current ratio rounded to the nearest tenth.
6. Journalize and post adjusting entries.
7. Journalize and post closing entries.
8. Prepare a post-closing trial balance.
9. Journalize reversing entries (if needed). Date the entries January 1, 20X3.
10. Comment on the financial condition of the company.

COMMUNICATIONS

Salli Ann Quinlan is an accounting teacher at a local community college. After studying the material in this chapter, several students asked her the same question: Cost of goods sold, operating expenses, and other expenses are all deductions from revenue. Why are they not simply listed in one section called "Expenses" instead of reported separately on the income statement?

In a paragraph, answer the question.

ETHICS

Raymond Collier is a business owner who is very interested in showing a good current ratio. Therefore, he instructs his bookkeeper to list all notes payable on the balance sheet as long-term liabilities. Explain why this is an unacceptable accounting practice.

ANSWERS TO REVIEW QUIZZES

REVIEW QUIZ 10-1

(a) $63,750
(b) $61,600
(c) $124,700

REVIEW QUIZ 10-2

(a) $69,200
(b) $20,900
(c) $48,300
(d) $30,100, income from operations
(e) $28,700, net income

Save Mart Department Store
Work Sheet
For Year Ended December 31, 20X2

	Account Title	Trial Balance Debit	Trial Balance Credit	Adjustments Debit	Adjustments Credit	Adjusted Trial Balance Debit	Adjusted Trial Balance Credit	Income Statement Debit	Income Statement Credit	Balance Sheet Debit	Balance Sheet Credit	
1	Cash	8 3 5 0 00				8 3 5 0 00				8 3 5 0 00		1
2	Accounts Receivable	7 4 2 5 00				7 4 2 5 00				7 4 2 5 00		2
3	Merchandise Inventory	25 4 6 0 00		(b) 30 2 1 5 00	(a) 25 4 6 0 00	30 2 1 5 00				30 2 1 5 00		3
4	Office Supplies	12 3 5 0 00			(c) 7 1 9 0 00	5 1 6 0 00				5 1 6 0 00		4
5	Store Supplies	11 3 0 0 00			(d) 8 4 0 0 00	2 9 0 0 00				2 9 0 0 00		5
6	Prepaid Insurance	3 9 0 0 00			(e) 2 2 0 0 00	1 7 0 0 00				1 7 0 0 00		6
7	Office Equipment	42 0 0 0 00				42 0 0 0 00				42 0 0 0 00		7
8	Accum. Depr.—Off. Eq.		12 0 0 0 00		(g) 3 0 0 0 00		15 0 0 0 00				15 0 0 0 00	8
9	Store Equipment	90 0 0 0 00				90 0 0 0 00				90 0 0 0 00		9
10	Accum. Depr.—Store Eq		28 4 0 0 00		(h) 6 2 0 0 00		34 6 0 0 00				34 6 0 0 00	10
11	Delivery Equipment	32 0 0 0 00				32 0 0 0 00				32 0 0 0 00		11
12	Accum. Depr.—Del. Eq.		18 5 0 0 00		(i) 6 5 0 0 00		25 0 0 0 00				25 0 0 0 00	12
13	Accounts Payable		11 4 2 5 00				11 4 2 5 00				11 4 2 5 00	13
14	Salaries Payable		—		(f) 9 8 5 00		9 8 5 00				9 8 5 00	14
15	Notes Payable		25 0 0 0 00				25 0 0 0 00				25 0 0 0 00	15
16	Doreen Woods, Capital		71 2 6 0 00				71 2 6 0 00				71 2 6 0 00	16
17	Doreen Woods, Drawing	39 0 0 0 00				39 0 0 0 00				39 0 0 0 00		17
18	Income Summary			(a) 25 4 6 0 00	(b) 30 2 1 5 00	25 4 6 0 00	30 2 1 5 00	25 4 6 0 00	30 2 1 5 00			18
19	Sales		524 8 0 0 00				524 8 0 0 00		524 8 0 0 00			19

#	Account	Trial Balance Dr	Trial Balance Cr	Adjustments Dr	Adjustments Cr	Adjusted Trial Balance Dr	Adjusted Trial Balance Cr	Income Statement Dr	Income Statement Cr	Balance Sheet Dr	Balance Sheet Cr
20	Sales Returns and Allow.	22,400.00				22,400.00		22,400.00			
21	Sales Discounts	8,200.00				8,200.00		8,200.00			
22	Purchases	306,500.00				306,500.00		306,500.00			
23	Purch. Ret. and Allow.		20,300.00				20,300.00		20,300.00		
24	Purchases Discounts		5,950.00				5,950.00		5,950.00		
25	Freight In	13,650.00				13,650.00		13,650.00			
26	Sales Salaries Expense	41,000.00		(f) 360.00		41,360.00		41,360.00			
27	Store Supplies Expense	—		(d) 8,400.00		8,400.00		8,400.00			
28	Advertising Expense	6,700.00				6,700.00		6,700.00			
29	Depr. Exp.—Store Equip.	—		(h) 6,200.00		6,200.00		6,200.00			
30	Depr. Exp.—Del. Equip.	—		(i) 6,500.00		6,500.00		6,500.00			
31	Rent Expense	20,000.00				20,000.00		20,000.00			
32	Office Salaries Expense	18,000.00		(f) 625.00		18,625.00		18,625.00			
33	Office Supplies Expense	—		(c) 719.00		719.00		719.00			
34	Utilities Expense	7,800.00				7,800.00		7,800.00			
35	Depr. Exp.—Office Equip.	—		(g) 300.00		300.00		300.00			
36	Insurance Expense	—		(e) 2,200.00		2,200.00		2,200.00			
37	Miscellaneous Expense	1,200.00				1,200.00		1,200.00			
38	Interest Expense	400.00				400.00		400.00			
39		717,635.00	717,635.00	90,150.00	90,150.00	764,535.00	764,535.00	505,785.00	581,265.00	258,750.00	183,270.00
40	Net Income							75,480.00			75,480.00
41								581,265.00	581,265.00	258,750.00	258,750.00

REVIEW QUIZ 10-3

(a) $86,800
(b) $8,000
(c) $78,800
(d) 10.85:1 (or 10.85 to 1)

Yes, the company should be able to pay its current liabilities as they fall due. For every $1 of current liability, Glendale has $10.85 in current assets. A current ratio of 2:1 is considered acceptable.

REVIEW QUIZ 10-4

1			Closing Entries					1
2	20XX Jul.	31	Sales	70 0 0 0 00				2
3			Purchases Discounts	2 9 0 00				3
4			Income Summary			70 2 9 0 00		4
5								5
6		31	Income Summary	55 6 1 6 00				6
7			Sales Returns and Allowances			8 0 0 00		7
8			Sales Discounts			1 2 0 0 00		8
9			Purchases			38 0 0 0 00		9
10			Rent Expense			4 0 0 0 00		10
11			Salaries Expense			9 0 0 0 00		11
12			Depreciation Expense			8 0 0 00		12
13			Supplies Expense			9 5 00		13
14			Telephone Expense			1 9 5 00		14
15			Utilities Expense			1 4 0 0 00		15
16			Miscellaneous Expense			1 2 6 00		16
17								17
18		31	Income Summary	15 8 7 4 00				18
19			T. Massey, Capital			15 8 7 4 00		19
20								20
21		31	T. Massey, Capital	12 0 0 0 00				21
22			T. Massey, Drawing			12 0 0 0 00		22

REVIEW QUIZ 10-5

1			Reversing Entries					1
2	20X4 Jan.	1	Salaries Payable	8 1 0 00				2
3			Salaries Expense			8 1 0 00		3

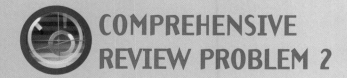

COMPREHENSIVE REVIEW PROBLEM 2

MILLS SPORTING GOODS STORE

GL You have now completed the accounting cycle for a merchandising business and you are ready to try to put it all together in this second comprehensive review problem. You are keeping the accounting records for Cindy Mills, owner of Mills Sporting Goods Store. You begin with the balances in her accounts and go through the accounting cycle for two months.

Directions:

1. Open accounts in the general ledger with the following balances as of January 1, 20X1:

No.	Account Title	Balance
111	Cash	$ 5,560
112	Accounts Receivable	2,955
113	Office Supplies	825
114	Store Supplies	1,915
115	Merchandise Inventory	13,540
116	Prepaid Insurance	750
121	Office Equipment	9,500
121.1	Accumulated Depreciation—Office Equipment	2,600
122	Store Equipment	16,600
122.1	Accumulated Depreciation—Store Equipment	4,000
123	Delivery Equipment	13,000
123.1	Accumulated Depreciation—Delivery Equipment	7,000
211	Accounts Payable	3,880
311	Cindy Mills, Capital	47,165
312	Cindy Mills, Drawing	
313	Income Summary	
411	Sales	
412	Sales Returns and Allowances	
413	Sales Discounts	
511	Purchases	
512	Purchases Returns and Allowances	
513	Purchases Discounts	
514	Freight In	
611	Salaries Expense	
612	Rent Expense	
613	Utilities Expense	
614	Office Supplies Expense	
615	Store Supplies Expense	
616	Insurance Expense	
617	Depreciation Expense—Office Equipment	
618	Depreciation Expense—Store Equipment	
619	Depreciation Expense—Delivery Equipment	

2. Open accounts in the accounts receivable ledger with these balances as of January 1, 20X1:

Customer Name	Balance
H. Galvin	$1,025
Lee Maddox	755
Neagle Co.	1,175
Smitz, Inc.	-0-

3. Open accounts in the accounts payable ledger with these balances as of January 1, 20X1:

Creditor Name	Balance
W. Bedford Co.	$1,365
Jones Co.	-0-
Lemke Brothers	1,540
Wohlers, Inc.	975

4. Record the January transactions in a general journal (page 12), a one-column sales journal (page 26), a purchases journal (page 10), a five-column cash receipts journal (page 11), and a four-column cash payments journal (page 9). All credit sales carry terms of 2/10,n/30. Freight on all purchases is charged to the Freight In account.

20X1

Jan.   2   Paid rent for the month, $1,070; Check No. 234.

      2   Sold merchandise to Smitz, Inc., $765, Invoice No. 176.

      4   Collected the balance due from H. Galvin, less 2% discount.

      5   Sold merchandise to H. Galvin, $1,670, Invoice No. 177.

      6   Collected the balance due from Neagle Co., less 2% discount.

      7   Issued a credit memo to H. Galvin for the return of defective merchandise sold on the 5th, $210.

      7   Purchased merchandise from Lemke Brothers, $1,045; terms 2/10,n/30; Invoice No. 187.

      8   Paid W. Bedford Co. the balance due, less 2% discount; Check No. 235.

      9   Paid Wohlers, Inc. the balance due, less 1% discount; Check No. 236.

    10   Returned defective merchandise purchased on the 7th from Lemke Brothers, receiving a credit memo for $105.

    10   Collected the balance due from Lee Maddox, less 2% discount.

    11   Paid Lemke Brothers the January 1 balance; no discount; Check No. 237.

    12   Received a check from Smitz, Inc. for the amount due on the sale of January 2.

    14   Purchased merchandise from Jones Co., $2,550; terms, 2/10,n/30; Invoice No. 188.

    15   Received a check from H. Galvin for the amount due on the sale of the 5th, less the return of the 7th.

    15   Recorded cash sales for the first half of January, $1,665.

    15   Cindy Mills invested an additional $3,000 cash in the firm.

    16   Purchased office equipment from Wohlers, Inc., $4,400; terms, 2/30,n/60; Invoice No. 189.

    17   Sold merchandise to Lee Maddox, $950; Invoice No. 178.

    17   Paid Lemke Brothers the amount due on the purchase of the 7th, less the return of the 10th; Check No. 238.

    18   Purchased office supplies from W. Bedford Co., $860; terms, n/30; Invoice No. 190.

    19   Returned defective office supplies to W. Bedford Co., receiving a credit memo for $110.

    20   Purchased store supplies from Jones Co., $555; terms, n/30; Invoice No. 191.

    22   Cindy Mills invested a used truck valued at $4,700 in the business.

    23   Sold merchandise to Neagle Co., $820; Invoice No. 179.

    24   Paid the balance due to Jones Co. from the purchase of the 14th; Check No. 239.

    24   Cindy Mills wrote Check No. 240 to pay her home phone bill, $205.

    25   Sold merchandise to Smitz, Inc., $1,995, Invoice No. 180.

    26   Sold store supplies to another firm at cost for cash, $110.

    27   Issued a credit memo to Smitz, Inc. for a shortage on the sale of the 25th, $75.

    27   Purchased merchandise from Jones Co., $750; terms, 2/10,n/30; Invoice No. 192.

    29   Paid January's electric bill, $595; Check No. 241.

    31   Recorded cash sales for the second half of January, $2,445.

    31   Paid freight on January purchases, $450; Check No. 242.

    31   Paid salaries for January, $4,450; Check No. 243.

5. Total all special journals.
6. Post all items that need to be posted.
7. Prepare a trial balance on a work sheet as of January 31, 20X1.
8. Prepare schedules of accounts receivable and accounts payable.
9. Complete the work sheet. Adjustment data for January 31 are as follows:

(a) Office supplies on hand, $830.
(b) Store supplies on hand, $750.
(c) Insurance expired, $20.
(d) Depreciation of office equipment, $90.
(e) Depreciation of store equipment, $125.
(f) Depreciation of delivery equipment, $250.
(g) Merchandise inventory (beginning), $13,540.
(h) Merchandise inventory (ending), $12,210.

10. Record and post adjusting entries as of January 31.
11. Record and post closing entries as of January 31.
12. Prepare a January 31 post-closing trial balance.
13. Prepare an income statement for the month of January. All salaries are sales salaries.
14. Prepare a statement of owner's equity for the month of January.
15. Prepare a January 31 balance sheet.
16. Record the February transactions that follow.

20X1

Feb. 1 Paid rent for the month, $1,070; Check No. 244.
2 Purchased merchandise from Lemke Brothers, $740; terms, 2/10,n/30; Invoice No. 193.
3 Returned merchandise purchased from Lemke Brothers on the 2nd, receiving a credit memo for $75.
3 Collected the balance due from Lee Maddox.
4 Collected the balance due from Smitz, Inc., for the sale of Jan. 25 less the credit of Jan. 27 and less the 2% discount.
5 Cindy Mills took home $40 of office supplies for her personal use.
6 Sold merchandise to H. Galvin, $2,140; Invoice No. 181.
6 Paid Jones Co. the balance due on purchases of $555 and $750, less a 2% discount on the $750 purchase; Check No. 245.
7 Collected the balance due from Neagle Co.
8 Issued a credit memo to H. Galvin for damaged merchandise sold on the 6th, $195.
9 Purchased merchandise for cash, $375; Check No. 246.
11 Paid Lemke Brothers for the balance due on the purchase of the 2nd, less the return of the 3rd; Check No. 247.
11 Returned $20 of the merchandise purchased on the 9th, receiving a cash refund.
12 Sold merchandise to Lee Maddox, $1,185; Invoice No. 182.
13 Cindy Mills wrote Check No. 248 for her own expenses, $350.
14 Recorded cash sales for the first half of the month, $3,095.
15 Paid Wohlers, Inc. the balance due, less 2% discount; Check No. 249.
16 Received a check from H. Galvin for the amount due on the sale of the 6th, less the return of the 8th.
17 Sold office supplies for cash, $85.
17 Paid W. Bedford Co. the balance due for the purchase of Jan. 18 less the return of Jan 19; Check No. 250.
19 Purchased store supplies from W. Bedford Co. $340; terms, n/30; Invoice No. 194.
20 Returned $30 of the store supplies purchased on the 19th, receiving credit.
21 Purchased merchandise from Lemke Brothers, $940; terms, 2/10,n/30; Invoice No. 195.
22 Sold merchandise to Neagle Co., $1,095; Invoice No. 183.
24 Purchased merchandise from Jones Co., $1,045; terms, 2/10,n/30; Invoice No. 196.
25 Sold merchandise to Smitz, Inc., $1,755; Invoice No. 184.
26 Purchased store equipment from Wohlers, Inc., $2,700; terms, 2/30,n/60; Invoice No. 197.
27 Paid the electric bill for February, $550; Check No. 251.
28 Recorded cash sales for the second half of the month, $2,985.
28 Paid freight on February purchases, $435; Check No. 252.
28 Paid salaries for February, $4,450; Check No. 253.

17. Total all special journals.
18. Post all items that need to be posted.

19. Prepare a trial balance on a work sheet as of February 28, 20X1.
20. Prepare schedules of accounts receivable and accounts payable.
21. Complete the work sheet. Adjustment data for February 28 are as follows:
    (a) Office supplies on hand, $355.
    (b) Store supplies on hand, $275.
    (c) Insurance expired, $20.
    (d) Depreciation of office equipment, $90.
    (e) Depreciation of store equipment, $125.
    (f) Depreciation of delivery equipment, $250.
    (g) Merchandise inventory (beginning), $12,210.
    (h) Merchandise inventory (ending), $11,780.
22. Record and post adjusting entries as of February 28.
23. Record and post closing entries as of February 28.
24. Prepare a February 28 post-closing trial balance.
25. Prepare an income statement for the month of February. All salaries are sales salaries.
26. Prepare a statement of owner's equity for the month of February.
27. Prepare a February 28 balance sheet.

11

ACCOUNTING

FOR

PAYROLL

Employee Earnings and Deductions

LEARNING OBJECTIVES

After studying Chapter 11, you will be able to:

1. Describe the importance of payroll records.
2. Calculate gross earnings for employees.
3. Explain the nature of payroll deductions.
4. Calculate payroll deductions and net pay.
5. Complete a payroll register and use it to record and pay the payroll.
6. Make accounting entries for employee earnings and deductions and for payment of the payroll.

The people who work for a business are the most important part of that business. Without them, merchandise could not be sold or a service could not be rendered. In paying those people for their services, certain federal, state, and local government rules and regulations must be complied with. Certain taxes must be withheld from payments made to employees, and special records must be maintained. A minimum amount of wage per hour of work must be paid. Employers must also provide insurance to compensate employees if they are injured while working. Employers must pay special taxes to provide unemployment benefits for their employees in the event that the employees are temporarily laid off or lose their jobs. Additionally, some employers voluntarily provide special employee benefits.

Such government regulations, and possibly union requirements, make payroll accounting unique. Rules and regulations are constantly changing and the payroll accountant must be aware of these changes so the employer can, at all times, be in compliance with the various laws and other requirements. This uniqueness makes payroll accounting a specialty, and payroll accountants are always in demand.

— Allan M. Cross, CPA, MBA
Parks Junior College

Our study of accounting has now taken us through the accounting cycles for both a service business and a merchandising business. For each type of business, we recorded salaries earned by employees in an account entitled Salaries Expense. We have also learned that salaries unpaid (accrued) at the end of an accounting period must be recorded to show the proper amount of expenses for the period. We are now concerned with how the amount of earnings is determined. In this chapter, we will learn how to determine and account for the earnings of employees. We will also learn about various taxes and other deductions that are taken from the pay of employees. We will continue our study of payroll in Chapter 12 by looking at the payroll taxes imposed on the employer.

IMPORTANCE OF PAYROLL

LEARNING OBJECTIVE 1

Let us first consider the importance of payroll information. In many companies, the cost of payroll alone amounts to 50% to 60% of all operating expenses. Due to the significant amount of this expense, companies must have an accurate and efficient means of keeping up with payroll information.

There are two primary reasons for maintaining accurate and up-to-date payroll records. First, we must accumulate the information needed to calculate the pay of each employee for each payroll period. Second, we must provide information needed to complete the various payroll reports that are required by federal and state regulations.

EMPLOYER/EMPLOYEE RELATIONSHIPS

Our first task in learning about payroll is to distinguish between an employee and an independent contractor. An **employee** is under the direct control of an employer on a continuing basis. This means that an employer is able to tell an employee when to work, how to work, and where to work. An **independent contractor**, on the other hand, agrees to perform and complete a specific job or task and is left to determine the ways and methods of achieving that job or task. In other words, an independent contractor is hired for a specific purpose and, since there is no permanent working relationship, is not on the payroll of the employer. Examples of independent contractors are architects, certified public accountants, attorneys, plumbers, and exterminators.

Paradigm College Accounting • Chapter 11

The distinction between an employee and an independent contractor is important because payroll accounting applies *only* to the employees of a firm. Most employers are required to deduct taxes and other amounts from the pay of employees; independent contractors are paid on a fee basis and are personally responsible for paying their own taxes.

HOW EMPLOYEES ARE PAID

We can distinguish between different types of employees on the basis of how they are paid. There are generally two types of employees, *salaried* and *hourly*. **Salaried employees** work for a fixed amount (**salary**) for a definite period of time (such as a week, a month, or a year). Examples of salaried employees include managers, teachers, public officials, and administrative service personnel.

Hourly workers work for a fixed hourly rate, which is commonly called a **wage.** In practice, however, the terms *salary* and *wage* are often used interchangeably.

Fair Labor Standards Act

Employees who receive an hourly wage are generally covered by the **Fair Labor Standards Act** (commonly called the **Wages and Hours Law**), which establishes standards for minimum wages, overtime pay, child labor, required payroll record keeping, and equal pay for equal work regardless of sex. The Fair Labor Standards act is administered by the Wage and Hour Division of the U.S. Department of Labor and applies *only* to firms engaged in interstate commerce. Employees covered by the act are guaranteed a *minimum wage* and *overtime pay* if they work more than 40 hours in one week.

The **minimum wage** is raised periodically to reflect cost-of-living increases. At this writing, it is $5.15 an hour. **Overtime pay** means a *minimum* of one and one-half times the regular rate of pay for all hours worked over 40 during a week. The overtime rate is commonly referred to as **time-and-a-half**.

While the Fair Labor Standards Act requires a minimum overtime rate of time-and-a-half, many companies have gone beyond this and pay double time for weekend work and for work on holidays. Some companies also pay overtime if an employee works more than 8 hours in one day, even though total hours for the week do not exceed 40. Let us stress, however, that this is a matter of company policy (or union contract), not the law. Let us also stress that certain workers, such as executive, administrative, and professional employees, are exempt from the minimum wage and overtime provisions of the Fair Labor Standards Act. Thus, when such workers work more than 40 hours in a week, they usually do not receive overtime pay.

Piece-Rate Plans

Some employees (usually factory workers) are paid on a **piece-rate plan**; that is, they receive a certain rate of pay for each unit they complete. For example, assume that a factory worker is paid $.08 for each unit produced. Further assume that during the last workweek the employee produced 4,800 units. The employee's earnings for that week are calculated as follows:

Number of units produced	×	Rate per unit	=	Earnings for the period
4,800	×	$.08	=	$384

CALCULATING GROSS EARNINGS

LEARNING OBJECTIVE 2

Gross earnings are an employee's earnings before any amount is deducted by the employer. The calculation of gross earnings for a salaried employee is rather simple. The employee is usually hired for an annual salary; the annual salary is then divided by the number of pay periods in the year. How many checks the employee receives in the year will depend on the pay period selected by the employer. Pay periods are usually on a weekly, biweekly (every other week), semimonthly (twice a month), or monthly basis. To illustrate, assume that an employee is hired at an annual salary of $18,720. We can calculate gross earnings per pay period as follows:

Type of Pay Period	Number of Pay Periods in a Year	Gross Earnings per Pay Period
Weekly	52	$ 360 ($18,720 ÷ 52)
Biweekly	26	720 ($18,720 ÷ 26)
Semimonthly	24	780 ($18,720 ÷ 24)
Monthly	12	1,560 ($18,720 ÷ 12)

The calculation of gross earnings for an hourly worker is different. We need information about the number of hours the employee worked, the hourly rate of pay, and overtime rates. To illustrate, let's take two examples. For our first example, we will use Sam Morgan, who is an hourly worker earning $9 an hour. During the last workweek, Mr. Morgan worked a total of 40 hours. His gross earnings for the week are calculated as follows (Note: Since Mr. Morgan's total hours for the week did not exceed 40, he will not receive overtime pay for this period.)

Hours worked	×	Rate per hour	=	Gross earnings
40	×	$9	=	$360

For our second example, we will use Anne Sheppard, who is an hourly worker earning $10 an hour. During her last workweek, Ms. Sheppard worked a total of 44 hours. Her gross earnings for the week are calculated as follows:

Regular hours	×	Regular rate		
40	×	$10	=	$400
Overtime hours	×	Overtime rate		
4	×	$15 ($10 × 1.5)	=	60
Gross earnings			=	$460

Another way to calculate Ms. Sheppard's gross earnings is to multiply her total number of hours worked by $10, and then add the overtime pay. This method looks like this:

Total hours	×	Regular rate		
44	×	$10	=	$440
Overtime hours	×	One-half time		
4	×	$5 ($10 × .5)	=	20
Gross earnings			=	$460

REMEMBER

Overtime is paid only for hours worked over 40 in a week. The overtime rate is at least 1.5 times the regular rate.

REVIEW QUIZ

11-1

Joy Jackson worked 45 hours this week. Her hourly wage is $8.00, and she receives overtime pay at a rate of time-and-a-half. Calculate her gross earnings.

CHECK YOUR ANSWER ON PAGE 425.

PAYROLL DEDUCTIONS

LEARNING OBJECTIVE 3

As everyone who has worked knows, the amount paid to employees (take-home pay) rarely equals the amount of gross earnings, because employers are required to withhold amounts from an employee's gross earnings. To **withhold** means to deduct amounts from an employee's earnings before payment is made to the employee.

The federal government requires employers to withhold *Social Security taxes* and *federal income taxes*. The employer is also required to withhold certain taxes for state (and sometimes local) taxing agencies. Also, employers may agree to make additional withholdings for the benefit of employees—such as amounts for insurance premiums, retirement plans, charities, savings bonds, and union dues. Let's look at these deductions to see how they are calculated.

FICA Tax (Social Security)

LEARNING OBJECTIVE 4

Today most workers in the United States are covered by the **Federal Insurance Contributions Act (FICA)**, which is commonly referred to as Social Security. FICA taxes are used to finance (1) the *federal Old-Age, Survivors, and Disability Insurance* program *(OASDI)* and (2) the *Hospital Insurance Plan (HIP)*, or *Medicare*. A unique aspect of the FICA tax is that *both* the employee and the employer contribute equal amounts. We will discuss the employer's share of FICA in Chapter 12. For now, let's concentrate on the employee's share.

The OASDI Taxable Wage Base

The **OASDI taxable wage base** is the maximum amount of earnings during a calendar year that is subject to OASDI taxes. At the time of this writing, the taxable OASDI base is $68,400. Should an employee's earnings reach or exceed this amount, no additional OASDI taxes will be withheld for the remainder of the year. There is no maximum wage base for HIP taxes, however. That is, all earnings are subject to HIP regardless of the amount. To help clarify this, let's assume that Bill Miller is a sales rep whose earnings for 20X1 are $69,600 as of the November 15 payroll. Since Bill has exceeded the OASDI taxable base ($68,400), he will pay no more OASDI taxes for the rest of the year. However, since there is no wage limit for HIP taxes, he will continue to pay this tax for the rest of the year.

The FICA Tax Rates

Under the Social Security Act, as amended, a separate tax rate is used to calculate OASDI and HIP. At this writing, the OASDI rate is 6.2% (of the first $68,400 earned during the year); and the HIP rate is 1.45% of all earnings. To illustrate, let's return to our earlier example of Sam Morgan. Remember that Mr. Morgan earned $360 during his last workweek. Further, Mr. Morgan's earnings have not reached $68,400 during the year. His FICA tax for the pay period is calculated as follows:

$$\begin{array}{lrll}
\text{OASDI} & \$360 & \times \ .062 \ (6.2\%) & = \ \$22.32 \\
\text{HIP} & 360 & \times \ .0145 \ (1.45\%) & = \ \underline{\ \ \ \ 5.22} \\
\text{Total FICA tax} & & & \ \ \ \ \underline{\underline{\$27.54}}
\end{array}$$

REVIEW QUIZ 11-2

Complete the following.

Employee	Earnings before This Pay Period	Earnings This Pay Period	FICA OASDI	HIP
A	$15,400	$412	$_____	$_____
B	68,100	900	$_____	$_____
C	69,300	825	$_____	$_____
D	32,400	618	$_____	$_____

CHECK YOUR ANSWERS ON PAGE 425.

Federal Income Tax

The federal government's main source of revenue is the income tax imposed on personal incomes. Unless specifically exempted, all income (legal and illegal) is subject to the personal income tax. The amount of personal income tax to be withheld depends on three factors: (1) the employee's gross earnings, (2) the employee's marital status, and (3) the number of withholding allowances claimed by the employee. The calculation of gross earnings was discussed earlier. An employee's marital status, for withholding purposes, is either *married* or *single*. Thus, a divorced person who has not remarried is considered to be single, as is a widow or widower who has not remarried.

A **withholding allowance**, also called an **exemption**, is allowed for the employee, for his or her spouse (if the spouse is not also working and claiming an allowance), and for each dependent for whom the taxpayer provides support. An allowance represents an amount of earnings that is not subject to taxation.

At the start of a new job, or when personal information changes, an employee is required to complete an **Employee's Withholding Allowance Certificate (Form W-4)**, which is kept on file by the employer. The Form W-4 indicates the employee's marital status and the number of withholding allowances claimed. Figure 11-1 shows Sam Morgan's Form W-4.

Various methods are available for calculating the amount of federal income tax to be withheld. Many employers use the **wage bracket method**, in which government-issued tax tables are used to determine the amount of the tax. An Internal Revenue Service publication entitled the **Employer's Tax Guide (Circular E)** provides tax tables for weekly, biweekly, semimonthly, monthly, and daily or miscellaneous payroll periods for married and single persons. Two wage bracket tables, *Single Persons—Weekly Payroll Period* and *Married Persons—Weekly Payroll Period*, are shown in Figures 11-2 and 11-3 on pages 404 and 405.

To see how to use the tables, let's return again to our example of Sam Morgan. Mr. Morgan's Form W-4 (Figure 11-1) indicates that he is married and is claiming two exemptions. He is paid weekly and his earnings for this pay period are $360. Therefore, to determine the amount of federal income tax to be withheld, we refer to the Married Persons—Weekly Payroll Period table in Figure 11-3 on page 405. Since Mr. Morgan's earnings fall in the bracket of "At least $360 but less than $370," and he has two exemptions, his federal income tax withholding is $21.

Form **W-4**	**Employee's Withholding Allowance Certificate**	OMB No. 1545-0010
Department of the Treasury Internal Revenue Service	▶ For Privacy Act and Paperwork Reduction Act Notice, see page 2.	**20X1**

1 Type or print your first name and middle initial	Last name	2 Your social security number
Sam L.	Morgan	420 : 58 : 6369

Home address (number and street or rural route) 1244 Oak Street	3 ☐ Single ☒ Married ☐ Married, but withhold at higher Single rate. Note: *If married, but legally separated, or spouse is a nonresident alien, check the Single box.*
City or town, state, and ZIP code Ames, NJ 07003	4 If your last name differs from that on your social security card, check here and call 1-800-772-1213 for a new card . . . . . ▶ ☐

5	Total number of allowances you are claiming (from line H above or from the worksheets on page 2 if they apply) .	**5**	2
6	Additional amount, if any, you want withheld from each paycheck	**6**	$
7	I claim exemption from withholding for 20X1, and I certify that I meet **BOTH** of the following conditions for exemption:		

• Last year I had a right to a refund of **ALL** Federal income tax withheld because I had **NO** tax liability **AND**
• This year I expect a refund of **ALL** Federal income tax withheld because I expect to have **NO** tax liability.

If you meet both conditions, enter "EXEMPT" here . . . . ▶ | **7** |

Under penalties of perjury, I certify that I am entitled to the number of withholding allowances claimed on this certificate or entitled to claim exempt status.

Employee's signature ▶ *Sam L. Morgan*	Date ▶ January 2 , 20 X1

8 Employer's name and address (Employer: Complete 8 and 10 only if sending to the IRS)	9 Office code (optional)	10 Employer identification number

FIGURE 11-1
Form W-4

The OASDI tax has a ceiling; that is, if your earnings reach the taxable wage base ($68,400), you will cease to pay the tax for the rest of the year. However, there is no ceiling on HIP and the federal income tax—the more you make, the more taxes you pay.

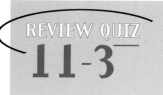

REVIEW QUIZ
11-3

In Review Quiz 11-1, you calculated the gross weekly earnings of Joy Jackson. Now calculate her FICA tax and federal income tax, assuming she is married, claims zero withholding allowances, and has not exceeded the OASDI taxable wage base.

CHECK YOUR ANSWER ON PAGE 425.

State and Local Income Taxes

Most state governments also require an employer to withhold an income tax from the earnings of employees. The rates charged vary so greatly from state to state that it would not be practical to attempt to list them here. The withholding process, however, is very similar to that for federal income tax. The state provides the employer with tax tables similar to the federal tax tables shown in Figures 11-2 and 11-3. And like the federal income tax, the state income tax is also based on an employee's marital status, the amount of earnings, and the number of withholding allowances claimed.

Some county and city governments also require a tax on earnings. Although the tax may be called something other than an income tax (such as an *occupational tax*), such taxes are income taxes, and the withholding process is basically the same as that for the federal and state income taxes.

FIGURE 11-2
Weekly wage bracket table used to find federal income tax withholding for single persons

SINGLE Persons—WEEKLY Payroll Period

If the wages are–		And the number of withholding allowances claimed is—										
At least	But less than	0	1	2	3	4	5	6	7	8	9	10
		The amount of income tax to be withheld is—										
$0	$55	0	0	0	0	0	0	0	0	0	0	0
55	60	1	0	0	0	0	0	0	0	0	0	0
60	65	2	0	0	0	0	0	0	0	0	0	0
65	70	2	0	0	0	0	0	0	0	0	0	0
70	75	3	0	0	0	0	0	0	0	0	0	0
75	80	4	0	0	0	0	0	0	0	0	0	0
80	85	5	0	0	0	0	0	0	0	0	0	0
85	90	5	0	0	0	0	0	0	0	0	0	0
90	95	6	0	0	0	0	0	0	0	0	0	0
95	100	7	0	0	0	0	0	0	0	0	0	0
100	105	8	0	0	0	0	0	0	0	0	0	0
105	110	8	1	0	0	0	0	0	0	0	0	0
110	115	9	2	0	0	0	0	0	0	0	0	0
115	120	10	2	0	0	0	0	0	0	0	0	0
120	125	11	3	0	0	0	0	0	0	0	0	0
125	130	11	4	0	0	0	0	0	0	0	0	0
130	135	12	5	0	0	0	0	0	0	0	0	0
135	140	13	5	0	0	0	0	0	0	0	0	0
140	145	14	6	0	0	0	0	0	0	0	0	0
145	150	14	7	0	0	0	0	0	0	0	0	0
150	155	15	8	0	0	0	0	0	0	0	0	0
155	160	16	8	1	0	0	0	0	0	0	0	0
160	165	17	9	1	0	0	0	0	0	0	0	0
165	170	17	10	2	0	0	0	0	0	0	0	0
170	175	18	11	3	0	0	0	0	0	0	0	0
175	180	19	11	4	0	0	0	0	0	0	0	0
180	185	20	12	4	0	0	0	0	0	0	0	0
185	190	20	13	5	0	0	0	0	0	0	0	0
190	195	21	14	6	0	0	0	0	0	0	0	0
195	200	22	14	7	0	0	0	0	0	0	0	0
200	210	23	15	8	0	0	0	0	0	0	0	0
210	220	25	17	9	2	0	0	0	0	0	0	0
220	230	26	18	11	3	0	0	0	0	0	0	0
230	240	28	20	12	5	0	0	0	0	0	0	0
240	250	29	21	14	6	0	0	0	0	0	0	0
250	260	31	23	15	8	0	0	0	0	0	0	0
260	270	32	24	17	9	2	0	0	0	0	0	0
270	280	34	26	18	11	3	0	0	0	0	0	0
280	290	35	27	20	12	5	0	0	0	0	0	0
290	300	37	29	21	14	6	0	0	0	0	0	0
300	310	38	30	23	15	8	0	0	0	0	0	0
310	320	40	32	24	17	9	1	0	0	0	0	0
320	330	41	33	26	18	11	3	0	0	0	0	0
330	340	43	35	27	20	12	4	0	0	0	0	0
340	350	44	36	29	21	14	6	0	0	0	0	0
350	360	46	38	30	23	15	7	0	0	0	0	0
360	370	47	39	32	24	17	9	1	0	0	0	0
370	380	49	41	33	26	18	10	3	0	0	0	0
380	390	50	42	35	27	20	12	4	0	0	0	0
390	400	52	44	36	29	21	13	6	0	0	0	0
400	410	53	45	38	30	23	15	7	0	0	0	0
410	420	55	47	39	32	24	16	9	1	0	0	0
420	430	56	48	41	33	26	18	10	3	0	0	0
430	440	58	50	42	35	27	19	12	4	0	0	0
440	450	59	51	44	36	29	21	13	6	0	0	0
450	460	61	53	45	38	30	22	15	7	0	0	0
460	470	62	54	47	39	32	24	16	9	1	0	0
470	480	64	56	48	41	33	25	18	10	2	0	0
480	490	65	57	50	42	35	27	19	12	4	0	0
490	500	67	59	51	44	36	28	21	13	5	0	0
500	510	68	60	53	45	38	30	22	15	7	0	0
510	520	71	62	54	47	39	31	24	16	8	1	0
520	530	74	63	56	48	41	33	25	18	10	2	0
530	540	77	65	57	50	42	34	27	19	11	4	0
540	550	80	66	59	51	44	36	28	21	13	5	0
550	560	82	68	60	53	45	37	30	22	14	7	0
560	570	85	71	62	54	47	39	31	24	16	8	1
570	580	88	74	63	56	48	40	33	25	17	10	2
580	590	91	77	65	57	50	42	34	27	19	11	4
590	600	94	79	66	59	51	43	36	28	20	13	5

FIGURE 11-3
Weekly wage bracket table used to find federal income tax withholding for married persons

MARRIED Persons—WEEKLY Payroll Period

If the wages are—		And the number of withholding allowances claimed is—										
At least	But less than	0	1	2	3	4	5	6	7	8	9	10
		The amount of income tax to be withheld is—										
$0	$125	0	0	0	0	0	0	0	0	0	0	0
125	130	1	0	0	0	0	0	0	0	0	0	0
130	135	1	0	0	0	0	0	0	0	0	0	0
135	140	2	0	0	0	0	0	0	0	0	0	0
140	145	3	0	0	0	0	0	0	0	0	0	0
145	150	4	0	0	0	0	0	0	0	0	0	0
150	155	4	0	0	0	0	0	0	0	0	0	0
155	160	5	0	0	0	0	0	0	0	0	0	0
160	165	6	0	0	0	0	0	0	0	0	0	0
165	170	7	0	0	0	0	0	0	0	0	0	0
170	175	7	0	0	0	0	0	0	0	0	0	0
175	180	8	0	0	0	0	0	0	0	0	0	0
180	185	9	1	0	0	0	0	0	0	0	0	0
185	190	10	2	0	0	0	0	0	0	0	0	0
190	195	10	3	0	0	0	0	0	0	0	0	0
195	200	11	3	0	0	0	0	0	0	0	0	0
200	210	12	5	0	0	0	0	0	0	0	0	0
210	220	14	6	0	0	0	0	0	0	0	0	0
220	230	15	8	0	0	0	0	0	0	0	0	0
230	240	17	9	1	0	0	0	0	0	0	0	0
240	250	18	11	3	0	0	0	0	0	0	0	0
250	260	20	12	4	0	0	0	0	0	0	0	0
260	270	21	14	6	0	0	0	0	0	0	0	0
270	280	23	15	7	0	0	0	0	0	0	0	0
280	290	24	17	9	1	0	0	0	0	0	0	0
290	300	26	18	10	3	0	0	0	0	0	0	0
300	310	27	20	12	4	0	0	0	0	0	0	0
310	320	29	21	13	6	0	0	0	0	0	0	0
320	330	30	23	15	7	0	0	0	0	0	0	0
330	340	32	24	16	9	1	0	0	0	0	0	0
340	350	33	26	18	10	3	0	0	0	0	0	0
350	360	35	27	19	12	4	0	0	0	0	0	0
360	370	36	29	21	13	6	0	0	0	0	0	0
370	380	38	30	22	15	7	0	0	0	0	0	0
380	390	39	32	24	16	9	1	0	0	0	0	0
390	400	41	33	25	18	10	2	0	0	0	0	0
400	410	42	35	27	19	12	4	0	0	0	0	0
410	420	44	36	28	21	13	5	0	0	0	0	0
420	430	45	38	30	22	15	7	0	0	0	0	0
430	440	47	39	31	24	16	8	1	0	0	0	0
440	450	48	41	33	25	18	10	2	0	0	0	0
450	460	50	42	34	27	19	11	4	0	0	0	0
460	470	51	44	36	28	21	13	5	0	0	0	0
470	480	53	45	37	30	22	14	7	0	0	0	0
480	490	54	47	39	31	24	16	8	1	0	0	0
490	500	56	48	40	33	25	17	10	2	0	0	0
500	510	57	50	42	34	27	19	11	4	0	0	0
510	520	59	51	43	36	28	20	13	5	0	0	0
520	530	60	53	45	37	30	22	14	7	0	0	0
530	540	62	54	46	39	31	23	16	8	0	0	0
540	550	63	56	48	40	33	25	17	10	2	0	0
550	560	65	57	49	42	34	26	19	11	3	0	0
560	570	66	59	51	43	36	28	20	13	5	0	0
570	580	68	60	52	45	37	29	22	14	6	0	0
580	590	69	62	54	46	39	31	23	16	8	0	0
590	600	71	63	55	48	40	32	25	17	9	2	0
600	610	72	65	57	49	42	34	26	19	11	3	0
610	620	74	66	58	51	43	35	28	20	12	5	0
620	630	75	68	60	52	45	37	29	22	14	6	0
630	640	77	69	61	54	46	38	31	23	15	8	0
640	650	78	71	63	55	48	40	32	25	17	9	2
650	660	80	72	64	57	49	41	34	26	18	11	3
660	670	81	74	66	58	51	43	35	28	20	12	5
670	680	83	75	67	60	52	44	37	29	21	14	6
680	690	84	77	69	61	54	46	38	31	23	15	8
690	700	86	78	70	63	55	47	40	32	24	17	9
700	710	87	80	72	64	57	49	41	34	26	18	11
710	720	89	81	73	66	58	50	43	35	27	20	12
720	730	90	83	75	67	60	52	44	37	29	21	14
730	740	92	84	76	69	61	53	46	38	30	23	15

Other Deductions

In addition to the required withholdings (FICA, federal income tax, and state income tax), an employer may, for various reasons, withhold other amounts from employees' earnings. Examples are union dues, United States savings bonds, insurance, and pension plans. These types of withholdings are for the benefit and convenience of the employee and must be authorized in writing by the employee. Once amounts are withheld, the employer becomes responsible for remitting them to the proper agencies. If union dues are withheld, for example, the employer incurs a legal liability and must remit to the union the amount withheld. We will look at how the employer accounts for these deductions later in the chapter.

CALCULATING NET EARNINGS (TAKE-HOME PAY)

Net earnings (or **net pay**) is the amount of earnings after all payroll deductions have been made; it is the actual amount of the employee's paycheck, the *take-home pay*. To illustrate the calculation of net earnings, let's continue with our example of Sam Morgan. We have calculated Mr. Morgan's gross earnings as $360, his OASDI tax deduction as $22.32, his HIP tax deduction as $5.22, and his federal income tax deduction as $21. In addition to these deductions, assume that Mr. Morgan has a state income tax withholding of $12, medical insurance deduction of $15, savings bonds deduction of $10, and union dues deduction of $5. His net earnings (or take-home pay) is calculated as follows:

Gross earnings		$360.00
Less deductions:		
FICA—OASDI	$22.32	
FICA—HIP	5.22	
Federal income tax	21.00	
State income tax	12.00	
Medical insurance	15.00	
Savings bonds	10.00	
Union dues	5.00	
Total deductions		90.54
Net earnings		$269.46

FIGURE 11-4
Payroll register for Northwest Company

The Status column shows the employee's marital status and the number of withholding allowances being claimed by the employee.

The employee's year-to-date earnings before this payroll are recorded in the Cumulative Earnings column.

Northwest Company
Payroll Register for Week Ended November 18, 20X1

	Name	Status	Cumulative Earnings	Tot. Hrs.	Earnings			Taxable Earnings		
					Regular	Overtime	Total	Unemployment	FICA	
									OASDI	HIP
1	Adams, William	M-2	69 2 0 0 00	40	6 1 5 00	—	6 1 5 00	—	—	6 1 5 00	1
2	Champion, Maureen	S-1	6 5 0 0 00	40	2 4 0 00	—	2 4 0 00	2 4 0 00	2 4 0 00	2 4 0 00	2
3	Jackson, Joy	M-0	17 2 1 0 00	45	3 2 0 00	6 0 00	3 8 0 00	—	3 8 0 00	3 8 0 00	3
4	Kemp, Wilson	S-0	6 9 0 0 00	38	2 0 9 00	—	2 0 9 00	1 0 0 00	2 0 9 00	2 0 9 00	4
5	Morgan, Sam	M-2	17 7 2 0 00	40	3 6 0 00	—	3 6 0 00	—	3 6 0 00	3 6 0 00	5
6	Sheppard, Anne	S-1	29 6 0 0 00	44	4 0 0 00	6 0 00	4 6 0 00	—	4 6 0 00	4 6 0 00	6
7	Totals				2 1 4 4 00	1 2 0 00	2 2 6 4 00	3 4 0 00	1 6 4 9 00	2 2 6 4 00	7

The Unemployment column shows the amount of earnings that the employer will pay unemployment taxes on. Employers pay unemployment taxes on the first $7,000 earned by each employee during the year.

These amounts are not taxes, but amounts subject to the tax rates.

REVIEW QUIZ 11-4

How is Joy Jackson doing? She has gross earnings of $380, a FICA OASDI tax deduction of $23.56, a FICA HIP tax deduction of $5.51, a federal income tax deduction of $39, a state income tax deduction of $15.20, a medical insurance deduction of $15, and a savings bonds deduction of $25. What is the amount of her net earnings?

CHECK YOUR ANSWER ON PAGE 425.

PAYROLL RECORD KEEPING

To provide management with up-to-date payroll information and to comply with various federal, state, and local laws, an employer must maintain payroll records that will supply the following information for each employee:

1. Name, address, and Social Security number
2. The amount of gross earnings for each payroll
3. The period of employment covered by each payroll
4. The year-to-date (*cumulative*) gross earnings
5. The amount of taxes and other deductions
6. The date each payroll was paid

To keep accurate and timely records, a business must have a payroll system that can deal with a large number of employees who have various pay periods, various wage rates, and various types of deductions. This is accomplished by using a *payroll register* and *employees' earnings records*, which we will discuss next.

The Payroll Register

LEARNING OBJECTIVE 5

The **payroll register** is a summary of the gross earnings, deductions, and net pay for all employees for a specific payroll period. The design of the payroll register depends on the number of employees and the method of processing payroll data. The complete payroll register for the Northwest Company—the company for which Anne Sheppard, Joy Jackson, and Sam Morgan work—is shown in Figure 11-4 for the payroll period ending on November 18, 20X1.

	Deductions								Payments		Expense Account Debited		
	FICA		Federal Income Tax	State Income Tax	Medical Insurance	Savings Bonds	Union Dues	Total	Ck. #	Net Amount	Sales Salaries Expense	Office Salaries Expense	
	OASDI	HIP											
1	—	8 92	58 00	24 60	15 00	10 00	5 00	121 52	141	493 48	615 00		1
2	14 88	3 48	21 00	9 60	12 00	—	—	60 96	142	179 04		240 00	2
3	23 56	5 51	39 00	15 20	15 00	25 00	—	123 27	143	256 73	380 00		3
4	12 96	3 03	23 00	8 36	—	—	—	47 35	144	161 65		209 00	4
5	22 32	5 22	21 00	12 00	15 00	10 00	5 00	90 54	145	269 46		360 00	5
6	28 52	6 67	54 00	18 40	12 00	10 00	5 00	134 59	146	325 41	460 00		6
7	102 24	32 83	216 00	88 16	69 00	55 00	15 00	578 23		1685 77	1455 00	809 00	7

These columns show the amounts withheld from the pay of employees.

Take-home pay.

Notice that the payroll register contains *Taxable Earnings* columns. These columns are used to show two things: (1) how much of an employee's earnings for this payroll period are subject to employer's unemployment tax (discussed in Chapter 12), and (2) how much of an employee's earnings for this payroll period are subject to FICA taxes. Remember that there is a taxable wage base for OASDI. By looking in the Cumulative Earnings column, we can see that William Adams's cumulative earnings (before this pay date) are $69,200. As a result, his earnings for this pay period are not subject to OASDI. (Remember that the current OASDI taxable base is $68,400.) No other employee has reached or exceeded the OASDI taxable base.

After all information has been entered in the payroll register, it is totaled, as shown in Figure 11-4. Before payroll checks are prepared, the accuracy of the payroll register should be proved by **cross-footing** the column totals. This can be done as follows:

Total earnings   – Deductions =   Net pay
$2,264.00   – $578.23   = $1,685.77

or

Total earnings –   Net pay   = Deductions
$2,264.00   – $1,685.77   = $578.23

Employee's Earnings Record

As we stated earlier, employers are required to maintain a record of earnings and deductions for each employee. Consequently, a separate **employee's earnings record** is prepared for each employee at the beginning of each calendar year. It is necessary that certain information about an employee be available in the earnings record. Such information includes the employee's name, address, Social Security number, and pay structure. Figure 11-5 illustrates the employee's earnings record that Northwest Company maintains for Sam Morgan.

FIGURE 11-5
Employee's earnings record

Name of Employee	Morgan, Sam				Social Security Number	420-58-6369	
Address	1244 Oak Street				City or Town	Ames, N.J. 07003	
Date of Birth 10-14-58	Married ☒ or Single ☐	Number of Exemptions 2			Phone No. 555-1212		Clock No. 025
Position Clerk	Rate $9.00/hr.	Date 1-1-X1			Date Started 1-1-X1		Date Terminated
Remarks					Reason		

| | | | | FOURTH QUARTER 20X1 | | | | | | | | |

WEEK	Hours Worked		Total Earnings	FICA Taxes		Federal Income Tax	State Income Tax	Union Dues	Savings Bonds	Medical Insurance	Net Pay	Gross Earnings Year to Date
	Reg.	Over Time		OASDI	HIP							
40	40	–	360 00	22 32	5 22	21 00	12 00	5 00	10 00	15 00	269 46	14,235 00
41	40	2	387 00	23 99	5 61	24 00	12 83	5 00	10 00	15 00	290 57	14,622 00
QUARTER TOTALS			4,940 00	306 28	71 63	361 40	249 00	65 00	130 00	195 00	3,561 69	19,562 00
YEARLY TOTALS			19,562 00	1,212 84	283 65	1,641 50	1,020 90	260 00	510 00	780 00	13,853 11	19,562 00

As you can see, the earnings record contains a good deal of information about an employee. The lower portion of the record contains a summary of earnings and deductions for all payrolls during the year. The column headings are self-explanatory; they come from our earlier discussion of gross earnings and deductions. The column heading at the extreme right deserves special notice. The Gross Earnings Year to Date column helps the payroll clerk keep track of total earnings and comply with the maximum amount of earnings subject to the OASDI part of FICA and other maximum wage levels for federal and state purposes.

Don't confuse the employee's earnings record and the payroll register. The payroll register shows payroll data for all employees for a single payroll period; the employee's earnings record shows a summary of payroll data for *each* employee.

PAYROLL SYSTEMS

There are two basic types of payroll systems: manual and computerized. The payroll system we have worked with in this chapter is manual. Many businesses today use electronic equipment to calculate and record the payroll more quickly and efficiently. Let's see how both systems work.

Manual Payroll System

In a manual payroll system, the payroll register is prepared first, and the information is transferred to the employee's earnings record. This is usually done using the "write-it-once" principle. This means that while information is being entered by hand on the payroll register, it is also being entered on an employee's earnings record. This is often accomplished by the use of a *pegboard system* in which one record is placed over the other record, and information is entered on both records (using carbon paper) at the same time. This allows both documents to be completed with "one writing," which saves time and reduces the possibility of errors.

A totally manual payroll system is rare today. Even very small businesses often use machines to at least partially complete their payroll. However, many small businesses process some, or all, of their payroll information by hand.

Computerized Payroll System

Payroll records, and the payroll process itself, are highly repetitive. Pay period after pay period, the payroll clerk records data in the payroll register and transfers the information to the employees' earnings records. This repetitive process lends itself well to computerization. As computers have become faster, cheaper, and smaller, a great number of computerized payroll systems have become available for even the smallest of business firms.

Many payroll software systems available in the marketplace can save the payroll personnel hours of tedious, repetitive payroll calculations. And with improved technology and increased production, the cost of a system—the computer and the software—has become very reasonable. Today we have an array of relatively inexpensive payroll programs that run on desktop computers. Such systems have limited applications, but they are adequate for the needs of many smaller and medium-sized businesses. Larger businesses often own large computers (mainframes) and employ computer programmers who write and maintain the payroll system. Some businesses rent time (*time-shared system*) on a large computer that is owned by another company. This permits the use of a large computer without the heavy investment necessary to purchase the system.

ACCOUNTING ENTRY FOR EMPLOYEE EARNINGS AND DEDUCTIONS

LEARNING OBJECTIVE 6

The payroll register provides all the information necessary to record the payroll. We can use the payroll register as a special journal and post the column totals directly to the ledger. Or we can use the payroll register as an information source for recording the payroll in either the general journal or the cash payments journal. Let's assume that we are using the payroll register as an information source and not as a special journal.

In recording employee earnings and the deductions from earnings, separate accounts should be maintained for the earnings and for each deduction. In previous chapters, we have recorded the earnings of employees in an account entitled Salaries Expense (other commonly used terms are *Wages Expense*, *Payroll Expense*, and *Salaries and Commissions Expense*).

In recording the deductions from employee earnings, it helps to think of the employer as an agent who is responsible for withholding these amounts and then passing them on to the proper agency. In effect, the employer is liable for each amount withheld until it is passed on to the appropriate agency. Thus, *each deduction is recorded in an appropriate liability account.*

To help understand the actual recording of the payroll, let's look at T accounts of the major accounts used in the process.

Salaries Expense

Salaries Expense is an expense account used to record the *gross amount* of the payroll. Sometimes the account is broken down into separate accounts, such as Sales Salaries Expense and Office Salaries Expense. In such a case, the gross salaries in each classification are recorded in the appropriate account. Let's look at the Salaries Expense account in T-account form:

Salaries Expense	
Debit	Credit
+	−
To record the gross amount of the payroll each pay period	

FICA Tax Payable—OASDI and FICA Tax Payable—HIP

Remember that FICA has two parts: OASDI and HIP. The **FICA Tax Payable— OASDI** account is a liability account used to record the amount of OASDI tax withheld from the earnings of employees. It is also used to record the liability for the employer's share of OASDI taxes. The account is credited when OASDI taxes are withheld, and it is debited when OASDI taxes are sent in. In T-account form, we can describe the account as follows:

FICA Tax Payable—OASDI

Debit	Credit
–	+
To record payment of OASDI tax previously withheld from employees or imposed on the employer.	To record OASDI tax withheld from employees or imposed on the employer.

FICA Tax Payable—HIP is a liability account used to record the amount of HIP (Medicare) taxes withheld from the earnings of employees and imposed on the employer. The account is credited when HIP taxes are withheld, and it is debited when the taxes are sent in. In T-account form, it looks like this:

FICA Tax Payable—HIP

Debit	Credit
–	+
To record payment of HIP tax previously withheld from employees or imposed on the employer.	To record HIP tax withheld from employees or imposed on the employer.

Federal Income Tax Payable

Federal Income Tax Payable is a liability account used to record the amount of federal income taxes withheld from the earnings of employees. The account is credited when income taxes are withheld, and debited when the taxes are sent in. In T-account from, we can describe the account as follows:

Federal Income Tax Payable

Debit	Credit
–	+
To record payment of federal income tax previously withheld from the earnings of employees.	To record federal income tax withheld from the earnings of employees.

Other Amounts Withheld

Other amounts withheld should be recorded in an appropriate liability account. For example, state income tax withheld should be recorded in the State Income Tax Payable account. Likewise, union dues withheld should be recorded in the Union Dues Payable account. These accounts, and similar liability accounts, are credited when amounts are withheld and debited when payment is made to the appropriate agency.

Now that we have looked at the major accounts involved in recording the payroll, let's look at the entry to record the payroll. By referring to the column totals of Northwest Company's payroll register (Figure 11-4), we can make the general journal entry shown in Figure 11-6.

FIGURE 11-6
Accounting entry for employee earnings and deductions

	20X1					
1	Nov.	18	Sales Salaries Expense	1 4 5 5 00		1
2			Office Salaries Expense	8 0 9 00		2
3			FICA Tax Payable—OASDI		1 0 2 24	3
4			FICA Tax Payable—HIP		3 2 83	4
5			Federal Income Tax Payable		2 1 6 00	5
6			State Income Tax Payable		8 8 16	6
7			Medical Insurance Payable		6 9 00	7
8			Savings Bonds Payable		5 5 00	8
9			Union Dues Payable		1 5 00	9
10			Salaries Payable		1 6 8 5 77	10
11			Recorded payroll of November 18.			11

The gross amount of the payroll is recorded in the Sales and Office Salaries Expense accounts.

Each amount withheld is recorded in a liability account.

The net amount of the payroll is recorded in the Salaries Payable account. The Cash account would be credited if payment were made immediately. However, recording the net amount in the Salaries Payable account allows the payroll to be recorded before the paychecks are prepared.

This entry would now be posted to the appropriate general ledger accounts. If we were using the payroll register as a special journal, the column totals would be posted directly to the appropriate general ledger accounts. We would then write the number of the account to which a posting was made directly below the column total.

REVIEW QUIZ
11-5

Information from the payroll register of Northwest Company for the payroll period ended February 17, 20X1, is shown below. In general journal form, make the necessary entry to record employee earnings and deductions.

Northwest Company
Payroll Register for Week Ended Feb. 17, 20X1

	Name	Status	Cumulative Earnings	Tot. Hrs.	Earnings			Taxable Earnings			
					Regular	Overtime	Total	Unemployment	FICA		
									OASDI	HIP	
1	Adams, William	M-2	3 2 0 0 00	40	6 1 5 00	—	6 1 5 00	6 1 5 00	6 1 5 00	6 1 5 00	1
2	Champion, Maureen	S-1	9 4 0 00	40	2 4 0 00	—	2 4 0 00	2 4 0 00	2 4 0 00	2 4 0 00	2
3	Jackson, Joy	M-0	2 2 4 0 00	40	3 2 0 00	—	3 2 0 00	3 2 0 00	3 2 0 00	3 2 0 00	3
4	Morgan, Sam	M-2	2 3 8 0 00	40	3 6 0 00	—	3 6 0 00	3 6 0 00	3 6 0 00	3 6 0 00	4
5	Sheppard, Anne	S-1	2 7 1 5 00	44	4 0 0 00	6 0 00	4 6 0 00	4 6 0 00	4 6 0 00	4 6 0 00	5
6	Totals				1 9 3 5 00	6 0 00	1 9 9 5 00	1 9 9 5 00	1 9 9 5 00	1 9 9 5 00	6

CHECK YOUR ANSWER ON PAGE 426.

Making Payment to Employees

Since Northwest has only six employees, each is paid by check out of the company's regular checking account. Larger companies often maintain a special checking account just for the payroll. When this practice is followed, one check for the net amount of the payroll is written on the company's regular checking account. This check is then deposited in the separate payroll account. The individual checks for employees are then written on the special account. When all checks have been cashed by employees, the payroll account should have a zero balance.

Regardless of how employees are paid, however, the entry to record the payment is the same. The following general journal entry was made to record the payment of Northwest Company's November 18 payroll:

	20X1									
1	Nov.	18	Salaries Payable		1 6 8 5 77					1
2			Cash				1 6 8 5 77			2
3			Paid payroll of November 18.							3

In a business that uses special journals, the entry to record payment of the payroll would be made in the cash payments journal.

REMEMBER

The sequence of steps for recording the payroll is:

1. Record the payroll information in the payroll register.
2. Use the payroll register as an information source to record a journal entry for employee earnings and deductions.
3. Record a journal entry for payment of the payroll.

		Deductions							Payments		Expense Account Debited		
	FICA		Federal Income Tax	State Income Tax	Medical Insurance	Savings Bonds	Union Dues	Total	Ck. #	Net Amount	Sales Salaries Expense	Office Salaries Expense	
	OASDI	HIP											
1	3 8 13	8 92	5 8 00	2 4 60	1 5 00	1 0 00	5 00	1 5 9 65	47	4 5 5 35	6 1 5 00		1
2	1 4 88	3 48	2 1 00	9 60	1 2 00	—	—	6 0 96	48	1 7 9 04		2 4 0 00	2
3	1 9 84	4 64	3 0 00	1 2 80	1 5 00	2 5 00	—	1 0 7 28	49	2 1 2 72	3 2 0 00		3
4	2 2 32	5 22	2 1 00	1 4 40	1 5 00	1 0 00	5 00	9 2 94	50	2 6 7 06		3 6 0 00	4
5	2 8 52	6 67	5 4 00	1 8 40	1 2 00	1 0 00	5 00	1 3 4 59	51	3 2 5 41	4 6 0 00		5
6	1 2 3 69	2 8 93	1 8 4 00	7 9 80	6 9 00	5 5 00	1 5 00	5 5 5 42		1 4 3 9 58	1 3 9 5 00	6 0 0 00	6

REVIEW QUIZ

11-6

Referring to the journal entry you made to record Northwest Company's payroll in Review Quiz 11-5, make the entry to record payment of this payroll.

CHECK YOUR ANSWER ON PAGE 426.

WHERE CAN I FIND ANSWERS TO QUESTIONS ABOUT BENEFITS AND COMPENSATION?

You can find information about benefits and compensation at many locations on the Internet. The following sites are some of the most useful:

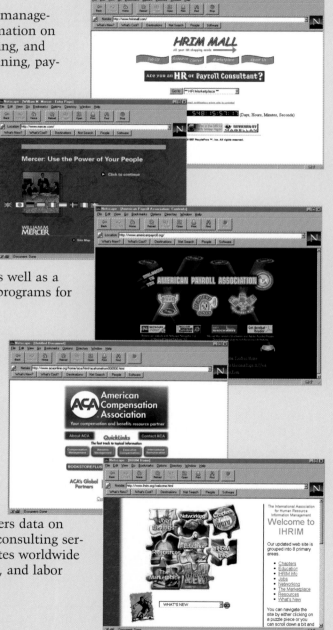

http://www.hrimmall.com
This online human resource information management and technology mall provides information on benefits, compensation, succession planning, and other human resources issues such as training, payroll, and relocation.

http://www.mercer.com
At this site, William M. Mercer offers free information on a variety of benefits issues, including legislative and legal developments.

http://www.americanpayroll.org
This is the home page of the American Payroll Association. It has many links to other compensation sites as well as a "listening room" featuring informational programs for visitors with sound cards.

http://www.acaonline.org
At this site, the American Compensation Association offers information, training, networking, certification, and research tools for the management profession.

http://www.ihrim.org
This is the home page of the International Association for Human Resource Information Management. It offers data on global human resource and management consulting services through links to government Web sites worldwide as well as educational, training, recruiting, and labor resources.

PROCEDURES FOR RECORDING THE PAYROLL

Payroll Register for Week Ended November 18, 20X1

	Deductions								Payments		Expense Account Debited		
	FICA		Federal Income Tax	State Income Tax	Medical Insurance	Savings Bonds	Union Dues	Total	Ck. #	Net Amount	Sales Salaries Expense	Office Salaries Expense	
	OASDI	HIP											
1	—	8 92	58 00	24 60	15 00	10 00	5 00	121 52	141	493 48	615 00		1
2	14 88	3 48	21 00	9 60	12 00	—	—	60 96	142	179 04		240 00	2
3	23 56	5 51	39 00	15 20	15 00	25 00	—	123 27	143	256 73	380 00		3
4	12 96	3 03	23 00	8 36	—	—	—	47 35	144	161 65		209 00	4
5	22 32	5 22	21 00	12 00	15 00	10 00	5 00	90 54	145	269 46		360 00	5
6	28 52	6 67	54 00	18 40	12 00	10 00	5 00	134 59	146	325 41	460 00		6
7	102 24	32 83	216 00	88 16	69 00	55 00	15 00	578 23		1 685 77	1 455 00	809 00	7

The gross amount of the payroll is debited to the Salaries Expense accounts.

Each amount withheld is recorded in an appropriate liability account.

	20X1						
1	Nov.	18	Sales Salaries Expense	1 455 00			1
2			Office Salaries Expense	809 00			2
3			FICA Tax Payable—OASDI		102 24		3
4			FICA Tax Payable—HIP		32 83		4
5			Federal Income Tax Payable		216 00		5
6			State Income Tax Payable		88 16		6
7			Medical Insurance Payable		69 00		7
8			Savings Bonds Payable		55 00		8
9			Union Dues Payable		15 00		9
10			Salaries Payable		1 685 77		10
11			Recorded payroll of November 18.				11

The net amount of the payroll is recorded in the Salaries Payable account.

SUMMARY/RESTATEMENT OF LEARNING OBJECTIVES

1. Describe the importance of payroll records.

Payroll records are important from several perspectives: (1) Payroll is a significant expense of doing business, and accurate records are necessary to maintain control over payroll disbursements. (2) Management needs accurate and timely payroll information for analysis, planning, and decision making. (3) Employers are required to report various payroll data to various government agencies, and records are necessary for this reporting task. (4) Employees of a firm must be paid in an accurate and timely fashion, and records assist in accomplishing this task.

2. Calculate gross earnings for employees.

Gross earnings for **salaried employees** are usually stated by the employer on a weekly, monthly, or annual basis. Gross earnings for hourly workers are calculated by multiplying the hourly rate of pay times the number of hours worked. If an employee works more than 40 hours in one week, the employee is usually paid "time and a half" for hours in excess of 40. For example, Ben Dawson is married, claims two **withholding allowances**, and worked 50 hours last week at a rate of $6.00 an hour. His gross earnings are calculated as follows:

Regular pay	=	$6.00 × 40 hours	=	$240.00
Overtime pay	=	$9.00 ($6.00 × 1.5) × 10 hours	=	90.00
Gross earnings	=			$330.00

3. Explain the nature of payroll deductions.

Payroll deductions are amounts **withheld** by the employer from the earnings of employees for various taxes and other purposes. In this chapter, we discussed three required deductions: (1) **FICA (Federal Insurance Contributions Act)** taxes, (2) **federal income taxes**, and (3) **state income taxes**. We also discussed certain deductions that are not required by law but result from an agreement between the employer and the employee. Deductions of this kind include those for medical insurance, pension plans, savings bonds, union dues, and loan repayments.

4. Calculate payroll deductions and net pay.

We calculate payroll deductions based on the gross earnings of employees. The FICA tax has two components: (1) **OASDI** (Old-Age, Survivors, and Disability Insurance) and (2) **HIP** (Hospital Insurance Plan), or Medicare. The current OASDI rate is 6.2% of the first $68,400 of wages earned during the year. If an employee's earnings exceed this taxable wage base, no additional OASDI taxes are withheld for the rest of the year. The HIP rate is 1.45% of all earnings during the year (no limit).

Federal and state income taxes are found by using tables provided by federal and state agencies. It is very important to use the proper table for single or married persons and for the proper payroll period; that is, weekly, biweekly, semimonthly, or monthly.

Other payroll deductions, such as union dues, pension plans, and medical insurance, are usually fixed at the beginning of a year, and the proper amounts are deducted each pay period. Remember that employers are required to obtain written permission from employees before these amounts can be withheld.

To illustrate how to calculate payroll deductions and net pay, let's return to our earlier example of Ben Dawson. For the workweek ending March 15, 20X1, Ben earned $330. Amounts deducted by Ben's employer were as follows:

FICA:		
OASDI ($330 × 6.2%)	=	$20.46
HIP ($330 × 1.45%)	=	4.79
Federal income tax (table)	=	16.00
State income tax (given)	=	9.00
Medical insurance (given)	=	15.00
Total deductions		$65.25

Ben's net pay for the period is now calculated by subtracting his total deductions from his gross earnings:

Gross earnings − Payroll deductions = Net pay
   $330.00   − $65.25   = $264.75

5. Complete a payroll register and use it to record and pay the payroll.

The **payroll register** is a form that summarizes, for all employees, the number of hours worked and the amount of gross earnings, deductions, and net pay for a single pay period. The payroll register can be prepared manually or with the assistance of a computer. The data provided by the payroll register are used to prepare the entry to record the payroll and to prepare the **employees' earnings records.**

To review how to prepare a payroll register, let's look at the January 17, 20X1 payroll information of Logan's Blades, a comic book and collectible card exchange.

Employee	Status	Hourly Pay	Hours This Week	Earnings
Kaye Merrill	S-1	$8.00	42	$344.00
Lee Mitchell	M-2	9.00	44	414.00
Bill Stanton	S-0	7.65	10	76.50
Dori Winchell	M-1	8.25	40	330.00

Using this information, we can prepare the payroll register shown in Figure 11-7. The Cumulative Earnings column was filled in by looking at each employee's earnings record.

6. Make accounting entries for employee earnings and deductions and for payment of the payroll.

The payroll register prepared by Logan's Blades is not a journal. Thus, it is necessary to use information from the payroll register to make an accounting entry for employee earnings and deductions. This entry appears below in general journal form.

	20X1						
1	Jan.	17	Sales Salaries Expense	8 3 4 50		1
2			Office Salaries Expense	3 3 0 00		2
3			FICA Tax Payable—OASDI		7 2 20	3
4			FICA Tax Payable—HIP		1 6 89	4
5			Federal Income Tax Payable		9 2 00	5
6			State Income Tax Payable		3 4 94	6
7			Medical Insurance Payable		4 5 00	7
8			Savings Bonds Payable		1 0 00	8
9			Union Dues Payable		5 00	9
10			Salaries Payable		8 8 8 47	10
11			Recorded payroll of January 17.			11

Now, assuming that the employees are paid out of the company's regular checking account, we can make the following entry to record the payment:

	20X1					
1	Jan.	17	Salaries Payable	8 8 8 47		1
2			Cash		8 8 8 47	2
3			Paid payroll of January 17.			3

In the two entries we made to record the payroll and its payment, the debit and credit to the Salaries Payable account cancel each other out. Had we chosen, we could have combined the two entries by crediting Cash (rather than Salaries Payable) when the payroll was recorded. However, entering the net amount of the payroll in the Salaries Payable account makes it possible to record the payroll before the checks are actually prepared. If special journals were being used to record payment of the payroll, the entry would be made in the cash payments journal.

FIGURE 11-7
Payroll register for Logan's Blades

Logan's Blades
Payroll Register for Week Ended January 17, 20X1

	Name	Status	Cumulative Earnings	Tot. Hrs.	Earnings			Taxable Earnings			
					Regular	Overtime	Total	Unemploy-ment	FICA		
									OASDI	HIP	
1	Merrill, Kaye	S-1	8 00 00	42	3 20 00	24 00	3 44 00	3 44 00	3 44 00	3 44 00	1
2	Mitchell, Lee	M-2	7 20 00	44	3 60 00	54 00	4 14 00	4 14 00	4 14 00	4 14 00	2
3	Stanton, Bill	S-0	1 70 00	10	76 50	—	76 50	76 50	76 50	76 50	3
4	Winchell, Dori	M-1	3 30 00	40	3 30 00	—	3 30 00	3 30 00	3 30 00	3 30 00	4
5	Totals				10 86 50	78 00	11 64 50	11 64 50	11 64 50	11 64 50	5

KEY TERMS

cross-footing The addition of columns of figures in different ways to check the accuracy of the totals.

employee A person who works under the direct control of an employer on a continuing basis.

employee's earnings record A record maintained for each employee that contains basic employee information and a summary of payroll data for that employee.

Employer's Tax Guide—Circular E An IRS publication containing federal income tax tables for various payroll periods for married and single persons.

Fair Labor Standards Act (also called the **Wages and Hours Law**) An act passed by Congress that established standards for minimum wages, overtime pay, child labor, and required payroll record keeping.

Federal Income Tax Payable account A liability account used to record the amount of federal income taxes withheld from the earnings of employees. It is credited when taxes are withheld and debited when the taxes are sent in.

Federal Insurance Contributions Act (FICA) An act that requires contributions by both the employer and the employee to the federal social security system. The FICA tax has two component parts: OASDI (Old-Age, Survivors, and Disability Insurance) and HIP (Hospital Insurance Plan). OASDI and HIP rates are set by Congress and are revised periodically. The OASDI tax has a wage limit that is usually revised annually.

FICA Tax Payable—HIP account A liability account used to record the amount of HIP taxes withheld from employees' earnings and matched by the employer. It is credited when HIP taxes are withheld (or imposed on the employer) and debited when the taxes are sent in.

FICA Tax Payable—OASDI account A liability account used to record the amount of OASDI taxes withheld from employees' earnings and matched by the employer. It is credited when OASDI taxes are withheld (or imposed on the employer) and debited when the taxes are sent in.

Form W-4 (Employee's Withholding Allowance Certificate) A form filled out by each employee showing marital status and number of withholding allowances claimed.

gross earnings. An employee's earnings before any amount is deducted by the employer.

hourly workers Individuals who work for a fixed hourly rate.

independent contractor A person who agrees to perform and complete a specific job or task and determines the ways and methods of achieving that job or task.

	FICA		Federal Income Tax	State Income Tax	Medical Insurance	Savings Bonds	Union Dues	Total	Ck. #	Net Amount	Sales Salaries Expense	Office Salaries Expense	
	OASDI	HIP											
1	21 33	4 99	36 00	10 32	15 00	10 00	—	97 64	153	246 36	344 00		1
2	25 67	6 00	28 00	12 42	15 00	—	5 00	92 09	154	321 91	414 00		2
3	4 74	1 11	4 00	2 30	—	—		12 15	155	64 35	76 50		3
4	20 46	4 79	24 00	9 90	15 00	—	—	74 15	156	255 85		330 00	4
5	72 20	16 89	92 00	34 94	45 00	10 00	5 00	276 03		888 47	834 50	330 00	5

(Deductions) (Payments) (Expense Account Debited)

minimum wage An amount set by Congress that is the minimum rate that can be paid to workers who are covered by the Fair Labor Standards Act. At this writing, it is $5.15 an hour.

net earnings (net pay) Gross earnings minus payroll deductions.

OASDI taxable wage The maximum amount of earnings during a calendar year that is subject to OASDI taxes.

overtime pay A minimum of one and one-half times the regular rate of pay for hours worked over 40 in a week; commonly called **time-and-a-half**.

payroll register Summary of the gross earnings, deductions, and net pay for all employees for a specific payroll period.

piece-rate plan A method of payment in which workers are paid for each unit they produce, rather than by hours worked.

salaried employees Individuals who work for a fixed amount for a definite period of time, such as a week, a month, or a year.

salary A fixed amount paid to employees for a certain period of time, such as a week or a month.

Salaries Expense account An expense account used to record the gross amount of the payroll. May sometimes be broken down into several accounts, such as Sales Salaries Expense and Office Salaries Expense.

wage A fixed hourly rate paid to an employee.

wage bracket method A method that uses government-issued tax tables to compute the amount of federal income tax to be withheld from employees.

withhold To deduct amounts from an employee's gross earnings.

withholding allowance An amount of earnings that is not subject to taxation. For federal income tax, each person gets one allowance for himself or herself, one for his or her spouse (if the spouse is not working and claiming the allowance), and one for each dependent. Also called an **exemption**.

CONCEPTS AND SKILLS REVIEW

CONCEPTS REVIEW

1. Why are payroll records important?
2. What is the difference between an employee and an independent contractor?
3. What is the difference between a salary and a wage?
4. Distinguish between the terms *gross earnings* and *net earnings*.
5. What are the components of FICA tax?

6. What purpose does Form W-4 (Employee's Withholding Allowance Certificate) serve?
7. Name some deductions that an employee might want to have withheld from a paycheck, in addition to the required deductions.
8. What is the difference in purpose between the payroll register and the employee's earnings record?
9. Is the payroll register a journal? Explain your answer.
10. Why are amounts withheld from employee earnings credited to liability accounts?

SKILLS REVIEW

EXERCISE 11-1

LEARNING OBJECTIVE 2

Objective: To calculate gross earnings

Directions: The following payroll information pertains to four employees of Apex Corporation. Calculate the weekly gross earnings of each person.

Employee	Hours Worked	Hourly Rate	Overtime Rate
Bob Darby	47.5	$ 9.50	1.5
Sam Jones	45.0	10.00	1.5
Joy Smith	40.0	12.00	1.5
Ben White	55.0	7.25	2.0

EXERCISE 11-2

LEARNING OBJECTIVE 2

Objective: To calculate total hours worked and gross earnings

Directions: Tammy Bayto worked the following hours last week: Monday, 8; Tuesday, 10.5; Wednesday, 9; Thursday, 12; Friday, 7. What are Tammy's gross earnings for the week if her hourly rate is $12.50 and she earns time-and-a-half for hours over 40 a week?

EXERCISE 11-3

LEARNING OBJECTIVE 4

Objective: To compute FICA taxes

Directions: Data about four employees are presented below. For each, calculate the OASDI and HIP taxes, using the rates and the taxable limit presented in the chapter.

Employee	Cumulative Earnings	Gross Earnings This Pay Period	FICA OASDI	HIP
D. Mack	$38,500	$ 960	$_____	$_____
J. Caray	61,000	1,820	$_____	$_____
M. Slats	68,800	2,200	$_____	$_____
K. Sharp	68,300	2,050	$_____	$_____

EXERCISE 11-4

LEARNING OBJECTIVE 4

Objective: To determine federal income taxes

Directions: Using the wage-bracket tables presented in this chapter, determine the federal income tax to be withheld from each person's gross earnings for the week.

Employee	Gross Earnings	Status	Withholding Tax
(a)	$328.45	M-2	$_____
(b)	535.00	M-3	$_____
(c)	524.38	S-1	$_____
(d)	335.56	S-0	$_____
(e)	465.00	S-2	$_____

EXERCISE 11-5

LEARNING OBJECTIVE 4

Objective: To calculate net earnings

Directions: LeAnn Brisson is an employee whose hourly rate is $5.60. During the current week, she worked 48 hours. Her time is regulated by the Fair Labor Standards Act. She is married and claims three exemptions. So far this year, she has earned $8,200. She has a medical insurance deduction of $12.50 taken from her paycheck each week. Calculate her net earnings for the week.

EXERCISE 11-6

LEARNING OBJECTIVE 5

Objective: To make journal entries for payroll

Directions: From the following information taken from the payroll register totals for Windsor Company, prepare general journal entries to record (a) employee earnings and deductions and (b) payment of the payroll.

Office salaries	$120,000
Sales salaries	180,000
OASDI tax	18,600
HIP tax	4,350
Federal income tax	55,000
Medical insurance deductions	4,700
Union dues	5,600

CASE PROBLEMS

GROUP A

PROBLEM 11-1A

LEARNING OBJECTIVE 2, 4

Objective: To calculate gross earnings, payroll deductions, and net pay

Directions: Use the wage bracket tables and FICA tax rates presented in the chapter to supply the missing information for each employee listed in this problem. No employee has reached or exceeded the OASDI taxable wage base. Overtime pay is at the rate of one-and-one-half times the regular pay.

Employee	Status	Hours Worked	Hourly Rate	Gross Earnings	FICA OASDI	HIP	Federal Income Tax	Net Pay
H. Arn	M-2	44.0	$ 8.00	$_____	$_____	$_____	$_____	$_____
J. Bell	S-1	39.0	12.00	$_____	$_____	$_____	$_____	$_____
K. Dodd	M-0	46.0	8.75	$_____	$_____	$_____	$_____	$_____
B. Frank	M-4	39.5	9.50	$_____	$_____	$_____	$_____	$_____
A. Gibbs	S-0	42.0	5.15	$_____	$_____	$_____	$_____	$_____
T. Mann	S-2	40.0	8.00	$_____	$_____	$_____	$_____	$_____
H. Ross	M-1	44.0	10.00	$_____	$_____	$_____	$_____	$_____

PROBLEM 11-2A

LEARNING OBJECTIVE 5, 6

Objective: To complete a payroll register and record the payroll

A partial payroll register for Fox Facts, a data processing firm, is presented in the *Study Guide/Working Papers*.

Directions:
1. Complete the payroll register.

2. Use the completed payroll register as an information source to record employee earnings and deductions in general journal form.
3. Make a general journal entry to record the payment of the payroll.

LEARNING OBJECTIVE 4, 5, 6

PROBLEM 11-3A

Objective: To calculate net pay, complete a payroll register, and record the payroll

The following payroll information is for Ron-Ann's, a retail florist and gift shop, for the week ended June 14, 20X3:

Employee	Cumulative Earnings	Earnings This Period	Status	Dept.*	Deductions Medical Insurance	Bonds
John Casper	$ 7,790	$328	S-1	O	$12	$10
George Hines	8,600	355	M-1	S	24	10
Gena Jones	9,200	425	M-2	S	35	25
Jena Miller	6,200	285	S-0	O	0	0
Bill Stokes	6,400	310	S-2	S	24	0
Martha Teal	11,900	510	M-1	O	24	20

*O = Office Salaries; S = Sales Salaries

Directions:
1. Enter the data in a payroll register and complete the register.
2. Record employee earnings and deductions and payment of the payroll in general journal form.

LEARNING OBJECTIVE 5, 6

PROBLEM 11-4A

Objective: To make accounting entries for payroll

Hines Department Store has the following payroll information for the week ended November 21, 20X1:

	Dept.	Name	Cumulative Earnings	Total Earnings	FICA OASDI	FICA HIP	Federal Income Tax	State Income Tax	Medical Insurance	
1	S	Sandra Day	25 2 4 1 00	3 4 0 00	2 1 08	4 93	3 8 00	1 2 92	1 6 00	1
2	O	Ben Ellis	17 2 1 5 00	2 9 0 00	1 7 98	4 21	3 7 00	1 1 02	—	2
3	O	Jan Greene	6 8 2 0 00	2 1 5 00	1 3 33	3 12	1 9 00	8 17	1 2 00	3
4	S	Elisa Iverson	37 2 0 0 00	4 2 0 00	2 6 04	6 09	4 0 00	1 5 96	1 6 00	4
5	S	Robert Tagen	31 6 8 0 00	4 5 8 00	2 8 40	6 64	3 8 00	1 7 40	1 6 00	5
6	O	Tina Watson	4 2 0 0 00	3 1 2 00	1 9 34	4 52	3 4 00	1 1 86	—	6

Directions:
1. Record employee earnings and deductions in general journal form.
2. Record the payment of the payroll in general journal form.

PROBLEM 11-1B

Objective: To calculate gross earnings, payroll deductions, and net pay

Directions: Use the wage bracket tables and FICA tax rates presented in the chapter to supply the missing information for each employee listed in this problem. No employee has reached or exceeded the OASDI taxable wage base. Overtime pay is at the rate of one-and-one-half times the regular pay.

Employee	Status	Hours Worked	Hourly Rate	Gross Earnings	FICA OASDI	HIP	Federal Income Tax	Net Pay
C. Beal	S-1	46.0	$ 8.70	$___	$___	$___	$___	$___
T. Davis	M-3	44.0	13.50	$___	$___	$___	$___	$___
G. Grey	M-2	40.0	9.25	$___	$___	$___	$___	$___
P. Long	S-1	38.5	8.40	$___	$___	$___	$___	$___
K. Norris	M-0	40.0	5.95	$___	$___	$___	$___	$___
H. Reid	M-1	42.0	9.00	$___	$___	$___	$___	$___
G. Steale	S-2	45.0	9.50	$___	$___	$___	$___	$___

PROBLEM 11-2B

Objective: To complete a payroll register and record the payroll

A partial payroll register for Nathan's Bones, a computer and software dealer, is presented in the *Study Guide/Working Papers*.

Directions:
1. Complete the payroll register.
2. Use the completed payroll register as an information source to record employee earnings and deductions in general journal form.
3. Make a general journal entry to record the payment of the payroll.

PROBLEM 11-3B

Objective: To calculate net pay, complete a payroll register, and record the payroll

The following payroll information is for Save-Mart, a small discount department store, for the week ended June 15, 20X4:

Employee	Cumulative Earnings	Earnings This Period	Status	Dept.*	Deductions Medical Insurance	Bonds
Al O'Malley	$ 8,210	$335	M-2	S	$18	$10
Kay Norris	9,600	405	M-0	O	12	0
Joe Peters	7,800	325	S-1	O	12	10
Ted Reeves	1,200	410	M-2	S	18	0
Jay Sparks	11,400	430	M-3	S	25	21
Lori Veal	13,900	530	M-1	S	21	25

*O = Office Salaries; S = Salaries

Directions:
1. Enter the data in a payroll register and complete the register.
2. Record employee earnings and deductions and payment of the payroll in general journal form.

PROBLEM 11-4B

LEARNING OBJECTIVE 6

Objective: To make accounting entries for payroll

Art's Department Store has the following payroll information for the week ended October 22, 20X5:

	Dept.	Name	Cumulative Earnings	Total Earnings	FICA		Federal Income Tax	State Income Tax	Medical Insurance	
					OASDI	HIP				
1	S	William Ashe	21 4 5 6 00	3 1 8 00	1 9 72	4 61	3 4 00	1 2 08	1 2 00	1
2	O	Jason Helmes	5 4 2 0 00	2 7 5 00	1 7 05	3 99	2 8 00	1 0 45	—	2
3	S	Kathy Komendantov	39 6 0 0 00	4 9 0 00	3 0 38	7 11	6 2 00	1 8 62	8 00	3
4	S	Tyler Milkin	24 3 0 0 00	3 1 2 00	1 9 34	4 52	2 3 00	1 1 86	1 2 00	4
5	S	Regina Musselman	18 2 1 0 00	2 7 6 00	1 7 11	4 00	2 4 00	1 0 49	8 00	5
6	O	Mark Pitts	—	3 5 2 00	2 1 82	5 10	2 9 00	1 3 38	—	6

Directions:
1. Record employee earnings and deductions in general journal form.
2. Record the payment of the payroll in general journal form.

CHALLENGE PROBLEMS

PROBLEM SOLVING

Judy Lyle is an account executive for a regional stock brokerage firm. During 20X2, Ms. Lyle received a weekly salary of $650. She also received a commission of 2% on total sales and a year-end 12% bonus that is based on her yearly salary. In 20X2, her yearly sales amounted to $735,000.

Directions: Using the tax tables, OASDI taxable wage base, and other information presented in this chapter, calculate the following:

1. Ms. Lyle's gross earnings for the year.
2. Ms. Lyle's federal income tax for the year. She is married and claims one withholding allowance. Assume a federal income tax rate of 20% on her commission and bonus.
3. Ms. Lyle's FICA taxes for the year.

COMMUNICATIONS

Mike Moore is a new employee of Furtell Industries. When Mike received his first paycheck, he noticed that, in addition to deductions for federal and state income tax, two additional amounts were withheld: OASDI and HIP. Mike has heard of Social Security, but he had never heard of either of these two taxes. Explain to Mike what these taxes are and how they are calculated.

ETHICS

Marie Leclair is a new employee who is in the process of filling in her paperwork for your company. As the human resource manager, you are looking over her employment application and find that she states that she is 19 and single. You then look at her Form W-4 and find that she has listed herself as married with three children. You ask her about the difference between the two forms, and she replies, "Oh yes, I know, but I can save taxes by claiming to be married with three kids. Besides, it's my right to fill out the form as I want to."

Write how you would respond to Marie's reply.

ANSWERS TO REVIEW QUIZZES

REVIEW QUIZ 11-1

$380 (40 × $8 = $320; 5 × $12 = $60; $320 + $60)

REVIEW QUIZ 11-2

Employee	OASDI	HIP
A	$25.54	$ 5.97
B	18.60	13.05
C	-0-	11.96
D	38.32	8.96

REVIEW QUIZ 11-3

FICA:
OASDI = $380 × .062 = $23.56
HIP = 380 × .0145 = 5.51
$29.07

Federal income tax = $39

REVIEW QUIZ 11-4

Gross earnings		$380.00
Less deductions		
FICA—OASDI	$23.56	
FICA—HIP	5.51	
Federal income tax	39.00	
State income tax	15.20	
Medical insurance	15.00	
Savings Bonds	25.00	
Total deductions		123.27
Net earnings		$256.73

REVIEW QUIZ 11-5

	20X1								
1	Feb.	17	Sales Salaries Expense	1 3 9 5 00		1
2			Office Salaries Expense	6 0 0 00		2
3			FICA Tax Payable—OASDI		1 2 3 69	3
4			FICA Tax Payable—HIP		2 8 93	4
5			Federal Income Tax Payable		1 8 4 00	5
6			State Income Tax Payable		7 9 80	6
7			Medical Insurance Payable		6 9 00	7
8			Savings Bonds Payable		5 5 00	8
9			Union Dues Payable		1 5 00	9
10			Salaries Payable		1 4 3 9 58	10
11			Recorded payroll of February 17.			11

REVIEW QUIZ 11-6

	20X1						
1	Feb.	17	Salaries Payable	1 4 3 9 58		1
2			Cash		1 4 3 9 58	2
3			Paid payroll of February 17.			3

12

ACCOUNTING

FOR

PAYROLL

Employer Taxes and Reports

LEARNING OBJECTIVES

After studying Chapter 12, you will be able to:

1. Describe and calculate payroll taxes imposed on the employer.
2. Record the employer's payroll taxes.
3. Record the deposit of employees' federal income taxes and FICA taxes and report these taxes to the government (Forms 8190 and 941).
4. Record and report payment of the employer's federal and state unemployment taxes (Form 940).
5. Report employee earnings and tax deductions to the federal government at the end of the year (Forms W-2 and W-3).
6. Describe and account for workers' compensation insurance.

I n Chapter 11, we looked at the payroll taxes imposed on employees. We learned that employers must calculate and withhold these taxes from the earnings of employees. The taxes, however, were not an expense of the employer. The employer simply had the responsibility of withholding them and then passing them on to the appropriate agency in a timely manner.

In this chapter, we continue our study of payroll accounting by looking at the payroll taxes imposed on employers. We will also look at the journal entries needed when the employer sends in taxes and other amounts that were withheld from the pay of employees.

EMPLOYER IDENTIFICATION NUMBER

Everyone who works must have a Social Security number that identifies that person for federal and state income taxes as well as for Social Security taxes. Likewise, all employers in this country who have at least one employee must have an **employer identification number (EIN)**. This number must be listed on all reports to the government and on all deposit forms that accompany payments of employees' federal income and FICA taxes.

EMPLOYER'S PAYROLL TAXES

LEARNING OBJECTIVE 1

All employers are required to pay certain taxes to federal and state authorities on behalf of employees. The three basic payroll taxes imposed on most employers are FICA (both OASDI and HIP), the federal unemployment tax, and the state unemployment tax. Payroll taxes are a necessary part of operating a business. Consequently, these taxes are recorded in an operating expense account entitled **Payroll Tax Expense**. We can describe this account in T-account form as follows.

Remember
Expense accounts are increased on the debit side.

Payroll Tax Expense	
Debit	Credit
+	−
Used to record the employer's FICA taxes, state unemployment taxes, and federal unemployment taxes incurred during an accounting period	Closed to Income Summary at the end of the accounting period (along with all other expenses)

Now, let's look in greater detail at the payroll taxes imposed on employers.

FICA Tax

Remember from our discussion in Chapter 11 that the FICA tax is a matching tax paid equally by the employee and the employer. Remember also that FICA consists of two parts: Old-Age, Survivors, and Disability Insurance (OASDI) and the Hospital Insurance Plan (HIP), or Medicare.

As we discussed in Chapter 11, the current OASDI rate is 6.2% of the first $68,400 earned in a year, and the HIP rate is 1.45% of all earnings. To illustrate how to calculate these taxes, we will continue with our Chapter 11 example of Northwest Company. Figure 12-1 is the payroll register for Northwest Company, and it provides information for calculating the employer's payroll taxes. In the figure, notice that the FICA columns in the Taxable Earnings section show that $1,649 of employee earnings this pay period are subject to OASDI taxes and that $2,264 are subject to HIP taxes. Using the current rates, we can calculate these taxes as follows:

OASDI taxable earnings × OASDI rate = Tax
$1,649.00 × 6.2% = $102.24

Total earnings × HIP rate = Tax
$2,264.00 × 1.45% = $32.83

If you refer to the taxes withheld by Northwest Company in Chapter 11, you will see that the same amount of FICA taxes withheld from the pay of employees is now being imposed on the employer.

Federal Unemployment Tax

The **Federal Unemployment Tax Act (FUTA)** requires the payment of taxes to provide benefits for workers during periods of temporary unemployment. Unlike FICA, this tax is paid *only* by the employer; it *cannot* be withheld from the pay of employees. The FUTA rate, like the FICA rate, is set by federal legislation. The current rate is 6.2% of the first $7,000 of wages paid to each employee during the calendar year. However, the employer may take a credit of up to 5.4% for timely contributions to state unemployment funds. And since all states have unemployment funds, this leaves an effective FUTA rate of only 0.8% (6.2% − 5.4%).

To calculate Northwest's FUTA tax for the payroll of November 18, refer to the payroll register in Figure 12-1. Look at the total of the Unemployment column in the Taxable Earnings section. This total, $340, is the amount of earnings this pay period that are subject to FUTA. We thus multiply this amount by the effective FUTA rate of 0.8% (.008):

$340 × .008 = $2.72

State Unemployment Tax

All states and the District of Columbia have passed unemployment compensation laws that, along with FUTA, provide benefits to qualified unemployed workers. State unemployment taxes are usually referred to as **SUTA (State Unemployment Tax Act)**. SUTA taxes are paid to the state in which the employer conducts business.

The taxable base for SUTA taxes varies from state to state. For this text, we will assume that the taxable base for SUTA taxes is the first $7,000 earned by each employee in a calendar year. The rate for SUTA, however, can vary from employer to employer, depending on the employer's record of unemployment claims and the state's recent experience with unemployment claims. Most states have a **merit-rating system** that provides a lower rate as an incentive for employers to stabilize employment. Under this system, it is possible for an employer who has laid off few workers to pay considerably less than the maximum rate.

FIGURE 12-1
Payroll register for Northwest Company

	Name	Status	Cumulative Earnings	Tot. Hrs.	Earnings			Taxable Earnings				
					Regular	Overtime	Total	Unemployment	FICA			
									OASDI	HIP		
1	Adams, William	M-2	69 2 0 0 00	40	6 1 5 00	—	6 1 5 00	—	—	6 1 5 00	1
2	Champion, Maureen	S-1	6 5 0 0 00	40	2 4 0 00	—	2 4 0 00	2 4 0 00	2 4 0 00	2 4 0 00	2
3	Jackson, Joy	M-0	17 2 1 0 00	45	3 2 0 00	6 0 00	3 8 0 00	—	3 8 0 00	3 8 0 00	3
4	Kemp, Wilson	S-0	6 9 0 0 00	38	2 0 9 00	—	2 0 9 00	1 0 0 00	2 0 9 00	2 0 9 00	4
5	Morgan, Sam	M-2	17 7 2 0 00	40	3 6 0 00	—	3 6 0 00	—	3 6 0 00	3 6 0 00	5
6	Sheppard, Anne	S-1	29 6 0 0 00	44	4 0 0 00	6 0 00	4 6 0 00	—	4 6 0 00	4 6 0 00	6
7	Totals				2 1 4 4 00	1 2 0 00	2 2 6 4 00	3 4 0 00	1 6 4 9 00	2 2 6 4 00	7

Table heading: **Northwest Company / Payroll Register for Week Ended November 18, 20X1**

For example, Northwest Company is located in New Jersey. At the time of this writing, the employer SUTA rate in New Jersey ranges from a minimum of 0.6% to the maximum of 5.4%. We will assume that Northwest Company's rate is 2.7% (.027). Thus, the SUTA tax for Northwest's November 18 payroll is:

$340 × .027 = $9.18

NOTE

The funds collected by the federal government as a result of the employer FUTA tax are used primarily to pay the cost of administering both the federal and state unemployment programs. The FUTA tax is not used to pay weekly benefits to unemployed workers. Instead, payments are made by each state in accordance with the state's unemployment tax law.

REVIEW QUIZ 12-1

Assuming the current FICA rates, a FUTA rate of 0.8%, and a SUTA rate of 2.7%, calculate the employer's payroll taxes for the following payroll:

Employee	Year-to-Date Earnings	Earnings This Pay Period
Walt King	$14,500.00	$396.00
Bill Todd	5,400.00	215.50
Chuck Wade	6,900.00	200.00
Jill Mimms	33,000.00	675.00
Carol Maris	6,750.00	318.00

CHECK YOUR ANSWERS ON PAGE 455.

RECORDING EMPLOYER'S PAYROLL TAXES

LEARNING OBJECTIVE 2

As stated earlier, the employer's payroll taxes are debited to an expense account entitled Payroll Tax Expense. The journal entry for payroll taxes should be prepared separately from the journal entry for salaries expense. This helps ensure that both salaries expense and payroll tax expense are recognized properly. Let's look again at the payroll taxes imposed on Northwest Company's November 18 payroll:

	FICA		Federal Income Tax	State Income Tax	Medical Insurance	Savings Bonds	Union Dues	Total	Ck. #	Net Amount	Sales Salaries Expense	Office Salaries Expense	
	OASDI	HIP											
1	—	8 92	58 00	24 60	15 00	10 00	5 00	121 52	141	493 48	615 00		1
2	14 88	3 48	21 00	9 60	12 00	—	—	60 96	142	179 04		240 00	2
3	23 56	5 51	39 00	15 20	15 00	25 00	—	123 27	143	256 73	380 00		3
4	12 96	3 03	23 00	8 36	—	—	—	47 35	144	161 65		209 00	4
5	22 32	5 22	21 00	12 00	15 00	10 00	5 00	90 54	145	269 46		360 00	5
6	28 52	6 67	54 00	18 40	12 00	10 00	5 00	134 59	146	325 41	460 00		6
7	102 24	32 83	216 00	88 16	69 00	55 00	15 00	578 23		1685 77	1455 00	809 00	7

Above these columns the spanning headers read: **Deductions**, **Payments**, **Expense Account Debited**.

FICA:
OASDI	$102.24	
HIP	32.83	$135.07
FUTA		2.72
SUTA		9.18
Total		$146.97

The following general journal entry shows the recording of Northwest's payroll taxes for the pay period ended November 18, 20X1.

	20X1					
1	Nov.	18	Payroll Tax Expense	1 46 97		1
2			FICA Tax Payable—OASDI		1 02 24	2
3			FICA Tax Payable—HIP		32 83	3
4			FUTA Tax Payable		2 72	4
5			SUTA Tax Payable		9 18	5
6			Recorded employer's payroll taxes.			6

Notice that, even though all employer payroll taxes are debited to a single expense account, the amount of *each* tax is credited to a separate liability account. This is done to record the employer's obligation to pay the different taxes. For a clearer understanding, let's look at each of the liability accounts.

FICA Tax Payable—OASDI

The FICA Tax Payable—OASDI account is the same account we introduced in Chapter 11 to record the employees' share of OASDI taxes. Since the employer must match the OASDI taxes paid by the employees, the same account is used to record both the employees' and the employer's share. The account is credited to record OASDI taxes imposed on the employer, and debited when the taxes are sent in.

FICA Tax Payable—OASDI
Debit	Credit
–	+
Payment of OASDI taxes previously withheld from employees or imposed on the employer	OASDI taxes: (1) withheld from employees and (2) imposed on the employer

FICA Tax Payable—HIP

As with the OASDI taxes, HIP taxes are shared equally by the employees and employer. Thus, the same account we used in Chapter 11 to record HIP taxes withheld from employees is used by the employer. It is credited to record HIP taxes imposed on the employer and debited when the taxes are sent in.

FICA Tax Payable—HIP	
Debit	Credit
–	+
Payment of HIP taxes previously withheld from employees or imposed on the employer	HIP taxes: (1) withheld from employees and (2) imposed on the employer

FUTA Tax Payable

The **FUTA Tax Payable account** is a current liability account used to record the employer's obligation for federal unemployment taxes. The account is credited when taxes are imposed on the employer, and debited when the taxes are sent in.

FUTA Tax Payable	
Debit	Credit
–	+
Payment of FUTA taxes	FUTA taxes imposed on the employer

SUTA Tax Payable

The **SUTA Tax Payable account** is a current liability account used to record the employer's obligation for state unemployment taxes. The account is credited when taxes are imposed on the employer, and debited when the taxes are sent in.

SUTA Tax Payable	
Debit	Credit
–	+
Payment of SUTA taxes	SUTA taxes imposed on the employer

REVIEW QUIZ 12-2

Using the payroll information in Review Quiz 12-1, make the general journal entry needed to record the employer's payroll taxes.

CHECK YOUR ANSWER ON PAGE 455.

FILING REPORTS AND MAKING PAYROLL TAX PAYMENTS

LEARNING OBJECTIVE 3

As we indicated earlier, employers are responsible for filing reports and making payroll tax payments on a timely basis. Specifically, employers must file reports and make payments in three areas: (1) FICA taxes and federal income taxes, (2) federal unemployment taxes, and (3) state unemployment taxes. In the following discussion, we will examine these three areas and the accounting entries needed when payments are made.

FICA and Federal Income Taxes

The employer's responsibility in this area extends to FICA taxes withheld from the pay of employees, the employer's share of FICA taxes, and income taxes withheld from employees. To summarize the amounts of these taxes, employers must file *Form 941* with the Internal Revenue Service (IRS) at the end of each calendar quarter. If, during the quarter in question, the total of these taxes is less than $500, employers may send payment with Form 941. However, if the total taxes exceed $500, employers are not permitted to send payment directly to the IRS at the end of the quarter. Instead, the taxes must be deposited in a Federal Reserve bank or other authorized bank, and the IRS will send for the taxes.

WHEN TO DEPOSIT TAXES

Employers must deposit FICA taxes and federal income taxes withheld from employees by mailing or delivering a check, money order, or cash to an authorized financial institution or federal reserve bank. There are two deposit schedules—*monthly* or *semiweekly*—for determining when taxes must be deposited. The deposit schedule an employer must use is based on the total tax liability reported during a four-quarter "lookback period." The **lookback period** for any year is the twelve-month period ending on June 30 *of the prior year*. Although this sounds complicated, it's really quite simple. An illustration will help. The lookback period for the year 2002 can be determined as follows:

Keep in mind that the lookback period for the current year is the twelve-month period that ends on June 30 of the year before. Thus, the lookback period for 2002 ends on June 30 of the year before (2001). So, the lookback period is from July 1, 2000, to June 30, 2001.

Now, what would be the lookback period for the year 2003? Go back to June 30 of the year before and you have the end of the lookback period. So, the beginning is simply twelve months earlier than June 30, 2002. Thus, the lookback period would be:

MONTHLY DEPOSIT SCHEDULE

An employer is a monthly depositor for the current year if the total taxes (FICA and withheld income taxes) for the lookback period were $50,000 or less. Under the monthly deposit schedule, taxes must be deposited by the 15th day of the following month. Thus, FICA taxes and income taxes withheld during January must be deposited by February 15.

SEMIWEEKLY DEPOSIT SCHEDULE

If an employer's total taxes during the lookback period were more than $50,000, the semiweekly deposit schedule is required. Under the semiweekly deposit schedule, taxes on payroll payments made on Wednesday, Thursday, or Friday must be deposited by the following Wednesday. Taxes on payroll payments made on Saturday, Sunday, Monday, or Tuesday must be deposited by the following Friday. Figure 12-2 summarizes these rules.

FIGURE 12-2
Semiweekly deposit schedule

Payroll Payment Days/Deposit Periods	Deposit by
Wednesday, Thursday, and/or Friday	Following Wednesday
Saturday, Sunday, Monday, and/or Tuesday	Following Friday

THE $100,000 NEXT-DAY DEPOSIT RULE

If an employer accumulates a tax liability of $100,000 or more on any day during a deposit period, the taxes must be deposited the next business day. For example, a large company such as Coca-Cola or General Motors could easily accumulate a tax liability (employees' and employer's FICA taxes and withheld income taxes) of well over $100,000 in a single payroll. For these employers, the monthly and semiweekly deposit schedules don't apply; they must deposit the taxes the next business day.

ACCOUNTING FOR TAXES DEPOSITED

FIGURE 12-3
Form 8109

When any deposit of taxes is made, the employer should complete and submit to the bank a **Federal Tax Deposit, Form 8109**. Figure 12-3 illustrates this form.

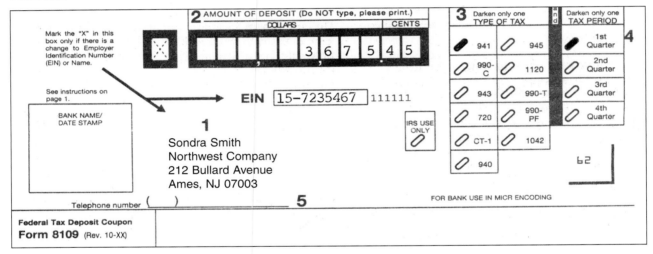

To illustrate the accounting entry for recording the payment of FICA and employees' federal income taxes, let's assume that on April 14, 20X1, Northwest Company deposited the following taxes in a local bank.

Federal income tax withheld from employees		$1,950.00
FICA tax:		
OASDI	$1,398.40	
HIP	327.05	1,725.45
Total amount deposited		$3,675.45

Northwest's accountant made the following general journal entry to record the payment.

	20X1					
1	Apr.	14	Federal Income Tax Payable	1 9 5 0 00		1
2			FICA Tax Payable—OASDI	1 3 9 8 40		2
3			FICA Tax Payable—HIP	3 2 7 05		3
4			Cash		3 6 7 5 45	4
5			Deposited taxes for first quarter.			5

As we mentioned earlier, employers must file **Form 941, Employer's Quarterly Federal Tax Return**, at the end of each calendar quarter. This form is a quarterly summary of FICA taxes (employees' and employer's shares) and federal income taxes withheld. Remember that when the cumulative amount of

FIGURE 12-4
Employer's Quarterly Federal Tax Return (Form 941)

these taxes reaches $500, deposits in an authorized bank are required. As a result, any amount sent with Form 941 should be under $500. Figure 12-4 illustrates the Form 941 prepared by Sondra Smith, owner of Northwest Company, at the end of the first calendar quarter, 20X1.

Form 941
(Rev. January)
Department of the Treasury
Internal Revenue Service (O)

4141

Employer's Quarterly Federal Tax Return

▶ See separate instructions for information on completing this return.
Please type or print.

OMB No. 1545-0029

Enter state code for state in which deposits made . ▶ (see page 3 of instructions).

Name (as distinguished from trade name)	Date quarter ended	
Sondra Smith	3/31/X1	T
Trade name, if any	Employer identification number	FF
Northwest Company	15-7235467	FD
Address (number and street)	City, state, and ZIP code	FP
212 Bullard Avenue	Ames, NJ 07003	I
		T

If address is different from prior return, check here ▶

IRS Use

1 1 1 1 1 1 1 1 1 1   2   3 3 3 3 3 3   4 4 4

5 5 5   6   7   8 8 8 8 8   9 9 9   10 10 10 10 10 10 10 10 10 10

If you do not have to file returns in the future, check here ▶ ☐ and enter date final wages paid ▶

If you are a seasonal employer, see **Seasonal employers** on page 1 of the instructions and check here ▶ ☐

1	Number of employees (except household) employed in the pay period that includes March 12th ▶	**1**	6
2	Total wages and tips, plus other compensation	**2**	11,277 | 42
3	Total income tax withheld from wages, tips, and sick pay	**3**	1,950 | 00
4	Adjustment of withheld income tax for preceding quarters of calendar year	**4**	-0-
5	Adjusted total of income tax withheld (line 3 as adjusted by line 4—see instructions) . . .	**5**	1,950 | 00
6	Taxable social security wages . . . . . 6a $ 11,277 | 42 × 12.4% (.124) =	**6b**	1,398 | 40
	Taxable social security tips . . . . . 6c $ -0- × 12.4% (.124) =	**6d**	-0-
7	Taxable Medicare wages and tips . . . 7a $ 11,277 | 42 × 2.9% (.029) =	**7b**	327 | 05
8	Total social security and Medicare taxes (add lines 6b, 6d, and 7b). Check here if wages are not subject to social security and/or Medicare tax . . . . ▶ ☐	**8**	1,725 | 45
9	Adjustment of social security and Medicare taxes (see instructions for required explanation) Sick Pay $_____ ± Fractions of Cents $_____ ± Other $_____ =	**9**	-0-
10	Adjusted total of social security and Medicare taxes (line 8 as adjusted by line 9—see instructions)	**10**	1,725 | 45
11	**Total taxes** (add lines 5 and 10)	**11**	3,675 | 45
12	Advance earned income credit (EIC) payments made to employees . . .	**12**	-0-
13	Net taxes (subtract line 12 from line 11). **This should equal line 17, column (d) below** (or line D of Schedule B (Form 941))	**13**	3,675 | 45
14	Total deposits for quarter, including overpayment applied from a prior quarter	**14**	3,675 | 45
15	**Balance due** (subtract line 14 from line 13). See instructions	**15**	-0-

16 **Overpayment.** If line 14 is more than line 13, enter excess here ▶ $ _____
and check if to be: ☐ Applied to next return **OR** ☐ Refunded.

● **All filers:** If line 13 is less than $500, you need not complete line 17 or Schedule B.
● **Semiweekly schedule depositors:** Complete Schedule B and check here . . . . ▶ ☐
● **Monthly schedule depositors:** Complete line 17, columns (a) through (d), and check here . . . . ▶ ☐

17	Monthly Summary of Federal Tax Liability.		
(a) First month liability	**(b)** Second month liability	**(c)** Third month liability	**(d)** Total liability for quarter
1,320.03	1,046.24	1,309.18	3,675.45

Sign Here
Under penalties of perjury, I declare that I have examined this return, including accompanying schedules and statements, and to the best of my knowledge and belief, it is true, correct, and complete.

Signature ▶ *Sondra Smith*   Print Your Name and Title ▶ Sondra Smith—Owner   Date ▶ 4-14-X1

For Paperwork Reduction Act Notice, see page 1 of separate instructions.   Cat. No. 17001Z   Form **941** (Rev. 1-97)

Federal Unemployment Taxes

LEARNING OBJECTIVE 4

If the amount of federal unemployment taxes (FUTA) is more than $100 in any quarter, the total must be deposited in an authorized bank by the last day of the first month following the close of the quarter involved. If the amount is $100 or less, no deposit is required. However, this amount must be added to the FUTA tax in the following quarter, and if the cumulative total is over $100, a deposit must be made.

In addition to the quarterly reports that are made when FUTA taxes are deposited, employers also must file **Form 940, Employer's Annual Federal Unemployment Tax Return**, by January 31, following the end of the year. This form summarizes the quarterly reports and deposits. Figure 12-5 illustrates Northwest's Form 940 for 20X1.

FIGURE 12-5
Employer's annual federal unemployment tax return (Form 940)

Form 940

Department of the Treasury
Internal Revenue Service   (O)

Employer's Annual Federal Unemployment (FUTA) Tax Return

▶ **For Paperwork Reduction Act Notice, see separate instructions.**

OMB No. 1545-0028

20X1

T	
FF	
FD	
FP	
I	
T	

Name (as distinguished from trade name)
Sondra Smith

Calendar year
20X1

Trade name, if any
Northwest Company

Address and ZIP code
212 Bullard Ave.
Ames, NJ 07003

Employer identification number
15 7235467

A   Are you required to pay unemployment contributions to only one state? (If "No," skip questions B and C)   [X] **Yes**   [ ] **No**

B   Did you pay all state unemployment contributions by February 2, 20X1? ((1) If you deposited your total FUTA tax when due, check "Yes" if you paid all state unemployment contributions by February 10. (2) If a 0% experience rate is granted, check "Yes." (3) If "No," skip question C.)   [X] **Yes**   [ ] **No**

C   Were all wages that were taxable for FUTA tax also taxable for your state's unemployment tax?   [X] **Yes**   [ ] **No**

If you answered "No" to any of these questions, you must file Form 940. If you answered "Yes" to all the questions, you may file Form 940-EZ, which is a simplified version of Form 940. (Successor employers see **Special credit for successor employers** in the **Instructions for Form 940**.) You can get Form 940-EZ by calling 1-800-TAX-FORM (1-800-829-3676).

If you will not have to file returns in the future, check here, and complete and sign the return   ▶ [ ]
If this is an Amended Return, check here   ▶ [ ]

Part I   **Computation of Taxable Wages**

		Amount paid		
1	Total payments (including payments shown on lines 2 and 3) during the calendar year for services of employees		**1**	128,300 00
2	Exempt payments. (Explain all exempt payments, attaching additional sheets if necessary.) ▶	**2**		
3	Payments for services of more than $7,000. Enter only amounts over the first $7,000 paid to each employee. Do not include any exempt payments from line 2. The $7,000 amount is the Federal wage base. Your state wage base may be different. **Do not use your state wage limitation**	**3** 97,300 00		
4	Total exempt payments (add lines 2 and 3)		**4**	97,300 00
5	**Total taxable wages** (subtract line 4 from line 1) ▶		**5**	31,000 00

Be sure to complete both sides of this return, and sign in the space provided on the back.

Cat. No. 11234O

Form **940** (20X1)

CONTINUES

Paradigm College Accounting • Chapter 12

FIGURE 12-5
Continued

Form 940 (20X1) Page **2**

Part II Tax Due or Refund

1	Gross FUTA tax. Multiply the wages in Part I, line 5, by .062	**1**	1,922 00
2	Maximum credit. Multiply the wages in Part I, line 5, by .054 . . . | **2** | 1,674 00		

3 Computation of tentative credit (Note: *All taxpayers must complete the applicable columns.*)

(a) Name of state	(b) State reporting number(s) as shown on employer's state contribution returns	(c) Taxable payroll (as defined in state act)	(d) State experience rate period		(e) State experience rate	(f) Contributions if rate had been 5.4% (col. (c) x .054)	(g) Contributions payable at experience rate (col. (c) x col. (e))	(h) Additional credit (col. (f) minus col.(g)). If 0 or less, enter -0-.	(i) Contributions actually paid to state
			From	To					
NJ	28677	31,000	1-1-X1	12-31-X1	.027	1,674	837	837	837
3a Totals . . . ▶		31,000						837	837

3b	Total tentative credit (add line 3a, columns (h) and (i) only—see instructions for limitations on late payments) ▶		1,674 00
4			
5			
6	**Credit:** Enter the smaller of the amount in Part II, line 2 or line 3b	**6**	1,674 00
7	**Total FUTA tax** (subtract line 6 from line 1)	**7**	248 00
8	Total FUTA tax deposited for the year, including any overpayment applied from a prior year . .	**8**	224 00
9	**Balance due** (subtract line 8 from line 7). This should be $100 or less. Pay to the Internal Revenue Service. See page 4 of the **Instructions for Form 940** for details . . . . ▶	**9**	24 00
10	**Overpayment** (subtract line 7 from line 8). Check if it is to be: ☐ **Applied to next return** or ☐ **Refunded** . . . . ▶	**10**	

Part III Record of Quarterly Federal Unemployment Tax Liability *(Do not include state liability.)* Complete only if line 7 is over $100.

Quarter	First (Jan. 1–Mar. 31)	Second (Apr. 1–June 30)	Third (July 1–Sept. 30)	Fourth (Oct. 1–Dec. 31)	Total for year
Liability for quarter	198.00	21.00	16.00	13.00	248.00

Under penalties of perjury, I declare that I have examined this return, including accompanying schedules and statements, and to the best of my knowledge and belief, it is true, correct, and complete, and that no part of any payment made to a state unemployment fund claimed as a credit was, or is to be, deducted from the payments to employees.

Signature ▶ *Sondra Smith* Title (Owner, etc.) ▶ *Owner* Date ▶ *1-31-20X2*

To illustrate the accounting entry needed when FUTA taxes are paid, assume that on January 31, 20X2, Northwest Company issued a check for $24 for FUTA taxes that had not been deposited. The following general journal entry records the payment.

	20X2					
1	Jan.	31	FUTA Tax Payable	24 00		1
2			Cash		24 00	2
3			Paid undeposited FUTA taxes.			3

This entry records the payment of undeposited taxes at the end of a year. The same entry is made when quarterly FUTA taxes are deposited during the year.

A streamlined version of Form 940 is now available. This form (940 E-Z) is for employers whose tax situations are not complicated. To use Form 940 E-Z, an employer must meet these three tests:

1. It must have paid SUTA to only one state.
2. It must have made all SUTA payments by the due date of Form 940 E-Z.
3. All of its earnings that were taxable for SUTA must also be taxable for FUTA.

As with all other federal tax forms, Form 940 E-Z can be picked up free of charge at any IRS office, ordered by phone or mail, or found on the Internet.

State Unemployment Taxes

Each state provides its own special forms and specifies how state unemployment taxes are paid. Generally, the amount of state unemployment taxes imposed on employers must be remitted to the proper state office by the end of the month following the close of the calendar quarter in which wages and salaries were earned by employees. To illustrate the accounting entry needed when state unemployment taxes are remitted, assume that on April 27, 20X1, Northwest Company issued a check for $489 to New Jersey in payment of state unemployment taxes on earnings of employees during the first quarter of 20X1. The following general journal entry records the payment.

	20X1					
1	Apr.	27	SUTA Tax Payable	4 8 9 00		1
2			Cash		4 8 9 00	2
3			Paid SUTA for first quarter, 20X1.			3

Form W-2: Wage and Tax Statement

LEARNING OBJECTIVE 5

In the sections above, we discussed the reports that employers must file with the government. Employers must also report to employees. By January 31 of each year, employers are required to furnish copies of **Form W-2, Wage and Tax Statement**, to each person who was employed in any part of the previous year. The employer is also required to send a copy of each employee's Form W-2 directly to the Social Security Administration. This allows the IRS to check on employees and employers as to whether the employees are reporting the proper amount of income on their personal income tax returns and whether the employers are properly reporting and submitting the tax amounts withheld from the earnings of employees. Figure 12-6 shows the Form W-2 that Sam Morgan received from Northwest Company at the end of 20X1. Notice that the information shown on Sam's Form W-2 was taken from his employee's earnings record illustrated in Figure 11-5 on page 408.

FIGURE 12-6
Completed Form W-2

a Control number		Void ☐			
b Employer's identification number 15-7235467			**1** Wages, tips, other compensation $19,562.00		**2** Federal income tax withheld $1,641.50
c Employer's name, address, and ZIP code Northwest Company 212 Bullard Ave. Ames, NJ 07003			**3** Social security wages $19,562.00		**4** Social security tax withhled $1,212.84
			5 Medicare wages and tips $19,562.00		**6** Medicare tax withheld $283.65
			7 Social security tips		**8** Allocated tips
d Employee' social security number 420-58-6369			**9** Advance EIC payment		**10** Dependent care benefits
e Employee's name, address, and ZIP code Sam Morgan 1244 Oak Street Ames, NJ 07003			**11** Nonqualified plans		**12** Benefits included in Box 1
			13		**14** Other

15 Statutory employee ☐	Deceased ☐	Pension plan ☐	Legal rep ☐	942 emp. ☐	Subtotal ☐	Deferred compensation ☐

16 State NJ	Employer's state I.D. No. 28677	**17** State wages tips, etc $19,562.00	**18** State income tax $1,020.90	**19** Locality name	**20** Local wages, tips, etc	**21** Local income tax

Form W-3: Transmittal of Wage and Tax Statements

Along with Copy A of each employee's Form W-2, employers must file **Form W-3, Transmittal of Wage and Tax Statements**, with the Social Security Administration by the last day of February following each year. This form, which is illustrated in Figure 12-7, summarizes the earnings and tax deductions of all employees of the firm for the previous year.

REVIEW QUIZ
12-3

Based on its May 31, 20XX payroll, the Augusta Company owed the following payroll taxes:

FICA:
OASDI	$568.00
HIP	132.00
FUTA	57.00
SUTA	189.00

(a) Record the deposit of the OASDI and HIP taxes, assuming they were deposited on June 15.
(b) Record the deposit of the FUTA tax, assuming a June 30 deposit.
(c) Record the June 30 payment of the SUTA tax.

CHECK YOUR ANSWERS ON PAGE 455.

DO NOT STAPLE

a Control number	33333		For Official Use Only ▶ OMB No. 1545-0008		

b		941	Military	943	1 Wages, tips, other compensation	2 Federal income tax withheld
Kind of Payer ▶		[X]	[ ]	[ ]	$128,300.00	$19,245.00
		CT-1	Hshld.	Medicare govt. emp.	3 Social security wages	4 Social security tax withheld
		[ ]	[ ]		$122,600.00	$7,601.20

c Total number of statements	d Establishment number	5 Medicare wages and tips	6 Medicare tax withheld
6	6	$128,300.00	$1,860.35

e Employer's identification number	7 Social security tips	8 Allocated tips
15-7235467		

f Employer's name	9 Advance EIC payments	10 Dependent care benefits
Sondra Smith		
Northwest Company	11 Nonqualified plans	12 Deferred compensation
212 Bullard Avenue		
Ames, NJ 07003	13	
	14	

g Employer's address and ZIP code		
h Other EIN used this year	15 Income tax withheld by third-party payer	

i Employer's state I.D. No.		
28677		

Under penalties of perjury, I declare that I have examined this return and accompanying documents, and, to the best of my knowledge and belief, they are true, correct, and complete.

Signature ▶ *Sondra Smith*   Title ▶ *Owner*   Date ▶ *1-11-X2*

Telephone number (   )

Form **W-3** Transmittal of Wage and Tax Statements 20X1   Department of the Treasury Internal Revenue Service

FIGURE 12-7
Transmittal of wage and tax statements (Form W-3)

PAYING OTHER AMOUNTS WITHHELD

Earlier we stated that, through agreement between the employee and the employer, deductions other than those required can be made from the earnings of employees. We have seen that when an employer makes such a deduction, an appropriate liability account is credited. For example, Northwest Company's November 18 payroll (Figure 12-1) shows that $55 was withheld from employees' pay to go toward the purchase of U.S. government savings bonds. When enough has been accumulated to purchase a certain amount of bonds, the company will make the purchase and deliver the bonds to the employees. When the deduction was made, the U.S. Savings Bonds Payable account was credited. When the bonds are purchased, this account will be debited, and the Cash account will be credited. To illustrate this entry, let's assume that on February 12, 20X1, Northwest purchased savings bonds for $125, an amount that was withheld during January and the first payroll in February. The following general journal entry records the payment.

	20X1						
1	Feb.	12	U.S. Savings Bonds Payable		1 2 5 00		1
2			Cash			1 2 5 00	2
3			Purchased savings bonds.				3

The sequence of steps for recording the payroll is:

1. Record the payroll information in the payroll register.
2. Use the payroll register as an information source to record accounting entries for employee earnings and deductions and the payment of the payroll.
3. Use the Taxable Earnings columns of the payroll register to calculate the employer's payroll taxes, and then record an accounting entry for these taxes.
4. Record an accounting entry whenever an amount withheld from employee earnings or a payroll tax owed by the employer is paid. Debit an appropriate liability account and credit the Cash account.

WORKERS' COMPENSATION INSURANCE

LEARNING OBJECTIVE 6

Most state governments require employers to carry **workers' compensation insurance** to provide protection for employees who suffer a job-related illness or injury. The entire cost of workers' compensation insurance is usually paid by the employer. The cost depends on several factors, including (1) the number of employees a company has, (2) the company's accident history, and (3) risk factors associated with the job. The third factor, risk, relates to the likelihood that the job will lead to injury. For example, the insurance premium for workers in a steel foundry would probably be higher than for office workers.

Workers' compensation insurance can generally be obtained from private insurance companies or directly from the state in which the company is located. The employer usually pays the premium at the beginning of the year, using estimated payroll figures for the year. At year-end, the actual amount of the payroll is compared with the estimate made at the beginning of the year. An adjustment is then made for the difference between the estimated premium and the actual premium. If the employer has overpaid, a credit is received from the state or private insurance company. If, on the other hand, the employer has underpaid, an additional premium is paid.

To illustrate how to account for workers' compensation insurance, let's assume that on January 2, 20X1, Northwest Company estimates its total 20X1 payroll to be $312,000. Let's further assume that Northwest's insurance premium rate is 0.2% (.002). Accordingly, Northwest's estimated premium is $624, calculated as follows:

Estimated payroll		Premium rate		Estimated insurance premium
$312,000	×	.002	=	$624.00

The following journal entry shows the payment.

1	20X1 Jan.	2	Workers' Comp. Insurance Expense	6 2 4 00		1
2			Cash		6 2 4 00	2
3			Paid estimated premium for the year.			3

Now, let's assume that at the end of the year Northwest's actual payroll was $330,000. Since this amount is more than Northwest's beginning-of-the-year estimate ($312,000), the company owes an additional premium. We calculate the additional premium as follows:

$$\textbf{Actual payroll} \quad \times \quad \textbf{Premium rate} \quad = \quad \textbf{Insurance premium}$$

$330,000	×	.002	=	$660.00

Less estimated premium   624.00
Additional premium due $ 36.00

We now make the following adjusting entry to record the additional expense.

1			Adjusting Entries				1
2	20X1 Dec.	31	Workers' Comp. Insurance Expense	3 6 00			2
3			Workers' Comp. Insurance Payable			3 6 00	3

After this entry is posted, the Workers' Compensation Insurance Expense account appears as follows:

Workers' Compensation Insurance Expense

Debit		Credit
+		–
Jan. 2	624.00	
Dec. 31	36.00	
Bal.	660.00	

In this example, it was necessary to record additional workers' compensation insurance expense because the actual payroll for the year exceeded the amount that had been estimated. But what happens when the reverse is true, that is, the actual payroll is less than the amount estimated? In this case, the company would have overpaid its premium and would thus be entitled to a refund. To illustrate this situation, let's assume that Northwest's actual payroll for 20X1 turned out to be only $300,000. The amount of the refund is determined as follows:

$$\textbf{Actual payroll} \quad \times \quad \textbf{Premium rate} \quad = \quad \textbf{Insurance premium}$$

$300,000	×	.002	=	$600.00

Estimated premium paid $624.00
Less actual premium owed   600.00
  Credit due $ 24.00

We now make the following adjusting entry to record the credit due.

1			Adjusting Entries				1
2	20X1 Dec.	31	Workers' Comp. Insurance Receivable	2 4 00			2
3			Workers' Comp. Insurance Expense			2 4 00	3

The Workers' Compensation Insurance Expense account would then appears as follows:

Workers' Compensation Insurance Expense

Debit		Credit	
+		–	
Jan. 2	624.00	Dec. 31	24.00
Bal.	600.00		

The balance of the account is now $600, which is the correct amount of the expense for the year. This balance will now be closed to Income Summary, along with the balances of all other expense accounts. By the way, this adjusting entry involved a credit to an expense account. This does not happen often, but it was necessary here because too much expense had been estimated (and thus recorded). So, to show the proper amount of expense for the year, the Workers' Compensation Insurance Expense account had to be credited to reduce its balance.

REVIEW QUIZ 12-4

In January 20X2, the accountant for Whitehurst Company estimated its total payroll for the year to be $425,000. At the end of the year, the actual amount of the payroll was $442,000. Assuming a workers' compensation premium rate of 1.5% (.015), record:

(a) The January 2 payment of the estimated premium.
(b) The December 31 adjusting entry showing the additional premium due.

CHECK YOUR ANSWERS ON PAGE 456.

INTERNET ASSETS

WHERE CAN I FIND TAX INFORMATION FOR MY STATE?

If you need to know the minimum wage, the SUTA taxable base, or the income tax rates for your state—or any other state—you can find this information on the Internet. The following locations are good places to start:

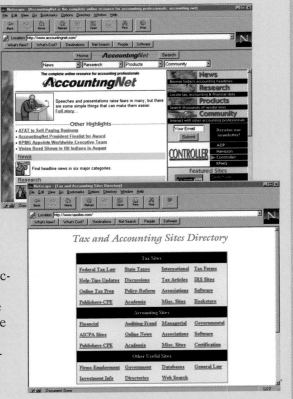

http://www.accountingnet.com
At this site under "Research Library" is a topic entitled "State Resources." It offers many services as well as information. Here you can find the minimum wage for each state, as well as the unemployment (SUTA) taxable base. You can also obtain and file state income tax forms at this location.

http://www.taxsites.com
The home page for this site is entitled *Tax and Accounting Sites Directory*. To find information about individual states, go to a heading in this directory called "Other Useful Sites." Under "Government," you will find the subheading "State Government." Here each state has its own Web site that lists the minimum wage, tax rates, and other valuable information such as the executive and legislative Web sites for that particular state.

JOINING THE PIECES

DEPOSIT RULES FOR FEDERAL TAXES WITHHELD AND FICA TAXES

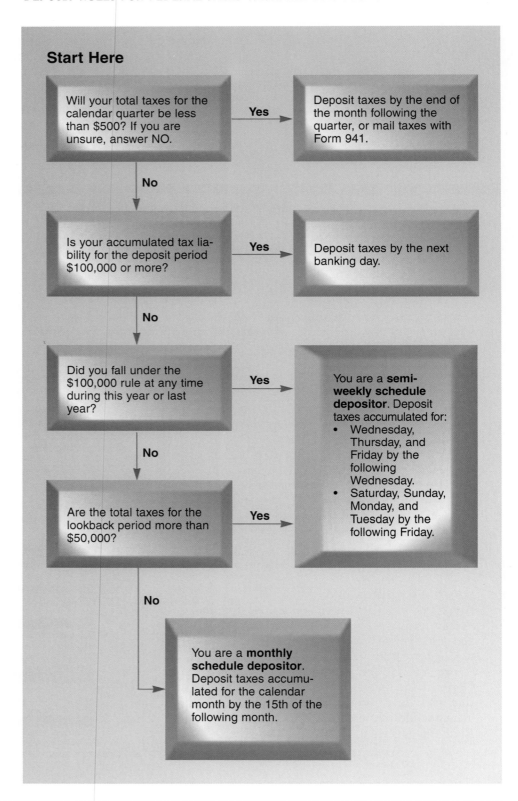

Start Here

Will your total taxes for the calendar quarter be less than $500? If you are unsure, answer NO.

→ **Yes** → Deposit taxes by the end of the month following the quarter, or mail taxes with Form 941.

↓ **No**

Is your accumulated tax liability for the deposit period $100,000 or more?

→ **Yes** → Deposit taxes by the next banking day.

↓ **No**

Did you fall under the $100,000 rule at any time during this year or last year?

→ **Yes** → You are a **semi-weekly schedule depositor**. Deposit taxes accumulated for:
- Wednesday, Thursday, and Friday by the following Wednesday.
- Saturday, Sunday, Monday, and Tuesday by the following Friday.

↓ **No**

Are the total taxes for the lookback period more than $50,000?

→ **Yes** →

↓ **No**

You are a **monthly schedule depositor**. Deposit taxes accumulated for the calendar month by the 15th of the following month.

SUMMARY/RESTATEMENT OF LEARNING OBJECTIVES

1. Describe and calculate payroll taxes imposed on the employer.

Employers are responsible for at least three payroll taxes: (1) FICA (Social Security), (2) federal unemployment taxes, and (3) state unemployment taxes.

Employer FICA Tax. In addition to withholding, reporting, and remitting the FICA (OASDI and HIP) taxes imposed on employees, employers must also match these taxes dollar for dollar. Thus, the Social Security program is funded by equal contributions from employees and employers. To review how to calculate the employer's part of FICA, assume the following payroll data for Gigabite Food Company for the pay period ending October 15, 20X0:

Total payroll for week	$195,000
Part of payroll subject to OASDI	126,000

Notes:

At this writing, the OASDI rate is 6.2% of the first $68,400 of earnings by each employee during the year. Employers pay the same rate based on the same annual wage limit. The current HIP rate is 1.45% of all earnings (no annual wage limit).

Calculations:

OASDI:	$126,000 × .062 =	$ 7,812.00
HIP:	$195,000 × .0145 =	2,827.50
Total FICA		$10,639.50

Federal unemployment taxes. All employers are covered by the **Federal Unemployment Tax Act (FUTA)**, which requires the payment of taxes to provide benefits for workers during periods of temporary unemployment. At this writing, the FUTA rate is 6.2% of the first $7,000 of annual earnings for each employee. A credit of up to 5.4% can be taken against the FUTA rate for state unemployment taxes paid by the employer. This leaves an effective FUTA rate of 0.8% (6.2% – 5.4%).

According to payroll records, there were only four recently hired employees who had not reached the $7,000 annual wage limit when the October 15 payroll was recorded. Their total wages amounted to $2,800. Thus, Gigabite's FUTA taxes for the week are:

$2,800 × .008 = $22.40

State unemployment taxes. All states have passed legislation requiring employers to pay unemployment taxes for the benefit of employees. These taxes are usually referred to as **SUTA (State Unemployment Tax Act)**. The wage base for SUTA taxes can vary from state to state. The SUTA rate also varies from state to state and from employer to employer, depending on the recent experience of the state and the employer with unemployment claims. Most states have a merit-rating system that provides a lower rate as an incentive for employers to stabilize employment. Gigabite Foods has a SUTA rate of 3% of the first $7,000 of annual earnings by each employee. Thus, if the taxable wages are $2,800, the current period's SUTA taxes are:

Same amount as that subject to FUTA
$2,800 × .03 = $84.00

The total of Gigabite's payroll taxes for the current payroll is:

FICA:		
OASDI	$7,812.00	
HIP	2,827.50	$10,639.50
FUTA		22.40
SUTA		84.00
Total		$10,745.90

2. Record the employer's payroll taxes.

Gigabite records its payroll taxes by debiting an operating expense account entitled **Payroll Tax Expense** for the total amount of the taxes. A credit is made to a separate liability account for each tax. Notice that the same liability accounts are used to record both the employees' and employer's shares of the FICA taxes.

	20X0									
1	Oct.	15	Payroll Tax Expense	10 7 4 5 90						1
2			FICA Tax Payable—OASDI			7 8 1 2 00		2
3			FICA Tax Payable—HIP			2 8 2 7 50		3
4			FUTA Tax Payable			2 2 40		4
5			SUTA Tax Payable			8 4 00		5
6			Recorded employer's payroll taxes.					6
7								7

These are the same accounts we used in Chapter 11 to record the employees' part of FICA.

3. Record the deposit of employees' federal income taxes and FICA taxes and report these taxes to the government (Forms 8109 and 941).

If during any calendar quarter the total of employees' income tax withheld and FICA taxes (employee and employer shares) reaches or exceeds $500, the employer does not send the taxes directly to the Internal Revenue Service (IRS). Instead, the taxes must be deposited in a federal reserve bank or other authorized bank. The IRS will then send for the taxes. When a deposit is made, an entry is recorded by debiting the appropriate liability accounts and crediting Cash. To illustrate this entry, assume that on November 7, 20X0, Gigabite Food Company deposited the following taxes in a local bank.

Federal income tax withheld from employees		$15,400
FICA tax:		
OASDI	$6,365	
HIP	1,489	7,854
Total amount deposited		$23,254

The following journal entry shows the payment:

	20X0								
1	Nov.	7	Federal Income Tax Payable	15 4 0 0 00				1
2			FICA Tax Payable—OASDI	6 3 6 5 00				2
3			FICA Tax Payable—HIP	1 4 8 9 00				3
4			Cash		23 2 5 4 00		4
5			Deposited taxes for payroll				5
6			of November 7.				6

Employers must prepare various reports to provide payroll information to the federal government. At the end of each calendar quarter, the employer must prepare and file **Form 941**, **Employer's Quarterly Federal Tax Return**, which summarizes the payment of FICA taxes and federal income taxes withheld. Payment of these taxes can only be made with Form 941 if the total amount of taxes for the quarter is under $500. If the amount of the FICA taxes (employees' and employer's shares) and federal income taxes withheld is $500 or more during any quarter, the taxes must be deposited in an authorized bank. When a deposit is made, the employer fills out a **Federal Deposit, Form 8109.** A copy of this form will go to the IRS, and the IRS will send for the money.

4. Record and report payment of employer's federal and state unemployment taxes (Form 940).

If the amount of federal unemployment taxes (FUTA) is more than $100 in any quarter, the total must be deposited in an authorized bank by the last day of the first month following the close of the quarter involved. If the amount is $100 or less, no deposit is required; however, this amount must be added to the FUTA tax in the following quarter. If the cumulative total is over $100, a deposit is required. The journal entry to record the deposit involves a debit to the FUTA Tax Payable account and a credit to Cash.

Each state provides rules and guidelines for paying state unemployment taxes (SUTA). As a general rule, the amount of SUTA taxes must be remitted to the proper state office by the end of the month following the close of the quarter in which the wages and salaries were earned by employees. The entry to record the payment involves a debit to the SUTA Tax Payable account and a credit to Cash.

To review the accounting entries needed when FUTA and SUTA taxes are sent in, assume the following transactions for Gigabite Food Company:

Transaction:
Nov. 30, 20X0: Deposited FUTA taxes, $156.

Entry:

	20X0							
1	Nov.	30	FUTA Tax Payable		1 5 6 00			1
2			Cash			1 5 6 00		2
3			Deposited FUTA taxes.					3

Transaction:
Jan. 15, 20X1: Mailed a check for $312 to the state government for SUTA taxes incurred during the fourth quarter of 20X0.

Entry:

	20X1							
1	Jan.	15	SUTA Tax Payable		3 1 2 00			1
2			Cash			3 1 2 00		2
3			Paid fourth quarter SUTA taxes.					3

After the end of each year (by January 31), employers must file **Form 940, Employer's Annual Federal Unemployment Tax Return** to summarize the quarterly deposits of FUTA taxes made during the year. Form 940 also shows the amount of SUTA tax that the employer paid to the state in which it is located. A shorter version of Form 940 called *Form 940-EZ* is available for firms that do not have complicated tax situations.

5. Report employee earnings and tax deductions to the federal goverment at the end of the year (Forms W-2 and W-3).

By January 31 of each year, an employer must furnish each employee (who worked any part of the year) with a **Wage and Tax Statement (Form W-2)**, which reports the employee's earnings and taxes for the previous year. The information on the W-2s is summarized on **Form W-3, Transmittal of Wage and Tax Statements**, which is sent to the Social Security Administration along with Copy A of each employee's W-2.

6. Describe and account for workers' compensation insurance.

Most state governments require employers to carry **workers' compensation insurance** to provide protection for employees who suffer a job-related illness or injury. The entire cost of this insurance is usually paid by the employer. The cost depends on the number of employees a company has, its accident history, and overall risk factors associated with working conditions. The employer pays a premium at the beginning of each year, using estimated payroll figures for the year. Recording this payment involves a debit to the **Workers' Compensation Insurance Expense** account and a credit to the Cash account.

At the end of the year, the workers' compensation insurance rate is applied to the actual payroll. If the employer underestimated the payroll and has not paid enough, an adjusting entry is made to show the additional expense and the additional amount that must be paid. If, on the other hand, the employer overestimated the payroll and paid too much, an adjusting entry is made to record the reduction in the expense and the credit to be received.

KEY TERMS

employer identification number (EIN) An identifying number each business must have if, during any part of the year, it employs one or more people.

Federal Tax Deposit, Form 8109 A form that must be filled out when FICA taxes and withheld income taxes are deposited in an authorized bank.

Federal Unemployment Tax Act (FUTA) An act requiring employers to pay into a fund designed to assist workers who are temporarily unemployed.

Form 940—Employer's Annual Federal Unemployment Tax Return Form filed by the employer by January 31, summarizing FUTA deposits during the preceding year.

Form 941—Employer's Quarterly Federal Tax Return A quarterly report that summarizes FICA taxes (employer and employee shares) and income taxes withheld during the quarter.

Form W-2 (Wage and Tax Statement) A form given by the employer to each employee by January 31 that contains a summary of the employee's earnings and deductions for the past year.

Form W-3 (Transmittal of Wage and Tax Statements) An annual form employers file with the Social Security Administration to summarize employee earnings and tax deductions. Copy A of each employee's Form W-2 is filed with Form W-3.

FUTA Tax Payable account A current liability account used to record the employer's obligation for federal unemployment taxes.

lookback period A four-quarter period ending on June 30 of the prior year. Employers look at the amount of FICA taxes (employee and employer share) and withheld income taxes during the lookback period to determine if they are monthly or semiweekly depositors.

merit-rating system A system set up by the states to provide a lower SUTA rate for employers who maintain stable employment.

Payroll Tax Expense account An operating expense account used to record the total payroll taxes imposed on the employer.

State Unemployment Tax Act (SUTA) A law that requires employers to pay unemployment taxes (for the benefit of employees) to the states in which they conduct business.

SUTA Tax Payable account A current liability account used to record the employer's obligation for state unemployment taxes.

workers' compensation insurance Insurance employers must carry to provide protection for employees who suffer a job-related illness or injury.

CONCEPTS AND SKILLS REVIEW

CONCEPTS REVIEW

1. An employee has a Social Security number. What comparable number does an employer have?
2. What is meant by the employer "matching" FICA tax withheld?
3. Why is the FUTA rate said to be an "effective" rate of 0.8%?
4. What is meant by a merit-rating system for state unemployment tax?
5. Why isn't the Salaries Expense account debited for the total of payroll taxes, since these taxes are part of the payroll cost of employees?
6. Explain the meaning of a lookback period.
7. What is the lookback period for the year 2004?
8. What protection is provided by workers' compensation insurance?
9. Why is an adjusting entry always needed for workers' compensation insurance?
10. Indicate when each of the following accounts is (a) debited and (b) credited: Payroll Tax Expense; FICA Tax Payable—OASDI; FICA Tax Payable—HIP; FUTA Tax Payable; SUTA Tax Payable.

SKILLS REVIEW

EXERCISE 12-1

LEARNING OBJECTIVE 1

Objective: To calculate employer payroll taxes

Directions: For each of the following employees, calculate the taxable earnings for FICA—OASDI, FICA—HIP, FUTA, and SUTA for the current week. Then calculate the total taxable earnings and the employer's liability for each of these taxes. Use rates of 6.2% for FICA—OASDI and 1.45% for FICA—HIP and a tax base of $68,400. Assume rates of 0.8% for FUTA and 3.2% for SUTA and a tax base of $7,000.

Employee	Current Week's Gross Earnings	Prior Gross Earnings This Year
Jim Burns	$700	$6,850
Helen Carrol	650	6,200
Barbara Harold	900	8,400

EXERCISE 12-2

LEARNING OBJECTIVE 2

Objective: To record employer payroll taxes

Directions: Using the data from Exercise 12-1, prepare a general journal entry to record the employer's payroll tax expense for the week and the liabilities for FICA taxes and unemployment taxes. The date of the entry is April 3, 20X1.

EXERCISE 12-3

LEARNING OBJECTIVE 1, 2

Objective: To calculate and record employer payroll taxes

PCQ Company had total payroll wages of $16,500 for the week ended March 15, 20X2. PCQ has a FUTA rate of 0.8% and a SUTA rate of 3.0%. All wages during the pay period are subject to both FICA taxes and both unemployment taxes.

Directions: Calculate the taxes and prepare a general journal entry to record the employer's payroll tax expense for the week.

EXERCISE 12-4

LEARNING OBJECTIVE 1, 2

Objective: To calculate and record employer payroll taxes

Portland Company's payroll for the week ended December 14, 20X4, is as follows:

Gross earnings of employees	$138,900
FICA—OASDI taxable earnings	126,300
FUTA taxable earnings	37,000
SUTA taxable earnings	37,000

Directions: Using the FICA rates presented in the chapter, a FUTA rate of 0.8%, and a SUTA rate of 3.5%, calculate the taxes and prepare a general journal entry for the employer's payroll tax expense for the week.

EXERCISE 12-5

LEARNING OBJECTIVE 3

Objective: To record the payment of payroll tax liabilities

On May 12, 20X1, the accountant for Americus Appliance Company deposited the following taxes in a local bank:

Employees' federal income tax withheld	$815
OASDI taxes (employees' share)	318
OASDI taxes (employer's share)	318
HIP taxes (employees' share)	74
HIP taxes (employer's share)	74

Directions: Prepare the general journal entry to record the payment of these taxes.

EXERCISE 12-6

LEARNING OBJECTIVE 6

Objective: To calculate workers' compensation insurance

In January 20X1, the accountant for Quinlan Company estimated its total payroll for the year to be $550,000. The workers' compensation premium rate was 0.6%.

Directions: (a) Calculate the estimated premium for the year. (b) If the actual payroll was $560,000, calculate the amount of additional premium due at the end of the year. (c) If the actual payroll was $530,000, calculate the amount of the credit due at the end of the year.

EXERCISE 12-7

LEARNING OBJECTIVE 6

Objective: To account for workers' compensation insurance

Directions: Use the information given in Exercise 12-6, and prepare general journal entries for (a) the payment of the estimated premium on January 3; (b), an adjustment on December 31 for additional premium due, and (c) an adjustment on December 31 for the credit due.

CASE PROBLEMS

GROUP A

LEARNING OBJECTIVE 1, 2

PROBLEM 12-1A

Objective: To calculate and record employer's payroll taxes

Selected information about six employees follows:

Employee	Current Week's Gross Pay	Prior Weeks' Gross Pay
B. Cassidy	$465.50	$4,900.75
C. Erer	555.75	5,680.30
L. Leung	300.30	3,109.35
H. McMahon	425.80	4,850.10
R. Ramirez	641.90	6,754.70
N. Thomas	790.70	8,010.40

Directions:
1. Calculate the amount of taxable earnings for FICA—OASDI, FICA—HIP, FUTA, and SUTA for each employee and for the total payroll this week. Then calculate the amount of each tax owed by the employer. Use the rates and wage limits presented in the chapter, with a rate of 4.1% for SUTA.
2. Prepare the general journal entry to record the employer's payroll taxes for the week. The date of the entry is March 10, 20X3.

LEARNING OBJECTIVE 1, 2, 3, 4

PROBLEM 12-2A

Objective: To calculate, record, and pay employer's payroll taxes

Marchant Company presents the following data for its payrolls for the months of January, February, and March 20X1:

Month	Gross Salaries	Unemployment Taxable Salaries
January	$25,000	$25,000
February	27,000	27,000
March	32,000	18,000

Directions:
1. Calculate the amounts that the employer owes for both FICA taxes and both unemployment taxes for each month. Assume a SUTA rate of 3.4%. All salaries are subject to FICA taxes.
2. Prepare each month's payroll tax expense entry.
3. Prepare the February 15th entry to deposit the January FICA taxes (employer and employee shares) along with federal income taxes withheld at 20% of the gross payroll.
4. Prepare the April 25th entry to deposit the FUTA tax for the first quarter and the entry on the same date to pay the SUTA tax for the first quarter.

LEARNING OBJECTIVE 1, 2, 3, 4

PROBLEM 12-3A

Objective: To journalize and post employer's payroll taxes

The Wesley Company pays its employees semimonthly. Payroll tax rates for the employer are the standard ones, including a SUTA rate of 2.0%. The balances of certain payroll-related accounts are as follows as of April 1, 20X2:

Number	Title	Balance
215	FICA Tax Payable—OASDI	$1,840.00
216	FICA Tax Payable—HIP	435.00
217	Federal Income Tax Payable	4,500.00
218	State Income Tax Payable	1,500.00
219	FUTA Tax Payable	240.00
220	SUTA Tax Payable	600.00
221	Union Dues Payable	300.00
551	Payroll Tax Expense	1,987.50

Directions:
1. Open the accounts listed and enter the April 1, 20X2 balances.
2. Record the following April transactions in a general journal, page 6, and post only to the accounts that you have opened.

20X2
Apr. 15 Deposited all of the FICA and federal income taxes due for March, according to the April 1 balances of accounts 215, 216, and 217.
15 Prepared the semimonthly payroll as follows:

Gross salaries	$5,000.00
FICA—OASDI	310.00
FICA—HIP	72.50
Federal income tax	750.00
State income tax	250.00
Union dues	500.00

15 Paid the semimonthly payroll.
20 Sent in the union dues withheld through April 1.
25 Deposited the FUTA tax April 1 balance.
27 Sent in the SUTA tax April 1 balance.
30 Sent in the April 1 amount due for state income tax.
30 Prepared the semimonthly payroll. The same amounts apply as on April 15.
30 Paid the semimonthly payroll.
30 Recorded the employer's tax expense for both FICA taxes and both unemployment taxes on the April payrolls.

LEARNING OBJECTIVE 6

PROBLEM 12-4A

Objective: To account for workers' compensation insurance

In January 20X2, the accountant for Scanlon Company estimated that its total payroll for the year would be $798,500. The firm has a premium rate of 0.3% for workers' compensation insurance.

(a) Calculate the estimated premium for the year.
(b) Prepare a general journal entry to record payment of the estimated premium on January 2, 20X2.
(c) If the actual payroll for the year is $805,600, prepare the December 31, 20X2 adjusting entry.
(d) If the actual payroll for the year is $783,600, prepare the December 31, 20X2 adjusting entry.

GROUP B

LEARNING OBJECTIVE 1, 2

PROBLEM 12-1B

Objective: To calculate and record employer's payroll taxes

Selected information about six employees follows:

Employee	Current Week's Gross Pay	Prior Weeks' Gross Pay
E. Delgado	$485.50	$5,200.75
M. Jniene	779.45	7,645.80
K. Minakawa	334.25	3,705.55
R. O'Brien	445.80	4,650.40
A. Sanchez	682.90	6,659.20
S. Zhang	524.30	5,340.10

Directions:

1. Calculate the amount of taxable earnings for FICA—OASDI, FICA—HIP, FUTA, and SUTA for each employee and for the total payroll this week. Then calculate the amount of each tax owed by the employer. Use the rates and wage limits presented in the chapter, with a rate of 2.2% for SUTA.
2. Prepare the general journal entry to record the employer's payroll taxes for the week. The date of the entry is March 6, 20X1.

PROBLEM 12-2B

LEARNING OBJECTIVE 1, 2, 3, 4

Objective: To calculate, record, and pay employer's payroll taxes

Malden Company presents the following data for its payrolls for the months of January, February, and March 20X1:

Month	Gross Salaries	Unemployment Taxable Salaries
January	$35,000	$35,000
February	39,000	34,000
March	42,000	1,000

Directions:

1. Calculate the amounts that the employer owes for both FICA taxes and both unemployment taxes for each month. Assume a SUTA rate of 3.6%. All salaries are subject to FICA taxes.
2. Prepare each month's payroll tax expense entry.
3. Prepare the February 15th entry to deposit the January FICA taxes (employer and employee shares) along with federal income taxes withheld at 20% of the gross payroll.
4. Prepare the April 25th entry to deposit the FUTA tax for the first quarter and the entry on the same date to pay the SUTA tax for the first quarter.

PROBLEM 12-3B

LEARNING OBJECTIVE 1, 2, 3, 4

Objective: To journalize and post employer's payroll taxes

The Albright Company pays its employees semimonthly. Payroll tax rates for the employer are the standard ones, including a SUTA rate of 3.0%. The balances of certain payroll-related accounts are as follows as of April 1, 20X2:

Number	Title	Balance
215	FICA Tax Payable—OASDI	$2,760.00
216	FICA Tax Payable—HIP	652.50
217	Federal Income Tax Payable	6,750.00
218	State Income Tax Payable	2,250.00
219	FUTA Tax Payable	360.00
220	SUTA Tax Payable	1,350.00
221	Union Dues Payable	450.00
551	Payroll Tax Expense	3,416.25

Directions:

1. Open the accounts listed and enter the April 1, 20X2 balances.
2. Record the following April transactions in a general journal, page 6, and post only to the accounts that you have opened.

20X2
Apr.15 Deposited all of the FICA and federal income taxes due for March, according to the April 1 balances of accounts 215, 216, and 217.

  15 Prepared the semimonthly payroll as follows:

Gross salaries	$7,500.00
FICA—OASDI	465.00
FICA—HIP	108.75
Federal income tax	1,125.00
State income tax	375.00
Union dues	750.00

  15 Paid the semimonthly payroll.
  20 Sent in the union dues withheld through April 1.
  25 Deposited the FUTA tax April 1 balance.
  27 Sent in the SUTA tax April 1 balance.
  30 Sent in the April 1 amount due for state income tax.
  30 Prepared the semimonthly payroll. The same amounts apply as on April 15.
  30 Paid the semimonthly payroll.
  30 Recorded the employer's tax expense for both FICA taxes and both unemployment taxes on the April payrolls.

PROBLEM 12-4B

LEARNING OBJECTIVE 6

Objective: To account for workers' compensation insurance

In January 20X2, the accountant for Ruggieri Company estimated that its total payroll for the year would be $825,700. The firm has a workers' compensation premium rate of 0.4% for workers' compensation insurance.

(a) Calculate the estimated premium for the year.
(b) Prepare the journal entry to record payment of the estimated premium on January 2, 20X2.
(c) If the actual payroll for the year is $811,500, prepare the December 31, 20X2 adjusting entry.
(d) If the actual payroll for the year is $829,450, prepare the December 31, 20X2 adjusting entry.

CHALLENGE PROBLEMS

PROBLEM SOLVING

Anna Delmar is an employee with a gross salary of $81,600 for 20X1. She is paid monthly. Calculate the employer's FICA—OASDI (at 6.2%), FICA—HIP (at 1.45%), FUTA (at 0.8%), and SUTA (at 3.7%) taxes for each month of the year. Then prepare the January, February, November, and December 20X1 general journal entries to record the employer's payroll taxes on her salary. Use the FICA rates and wage base presented in the chapter.

COMMUNICATIONS

Ella Hirsch, a new payroll clerk you have just hired, is very confused by the variety of payroll forms that the employer must prepare. Write a brief memo to her to explain the use of the following forms: 940, 941, 8109, W-2, and W-3.

ETHICS

Arthur McNeill is the owner of the Newfound Corporation. The company has experienced a large number of layoffs in recent years and has a high (5.4%) rate for state unemployment tax. As a result, the amount of SUTA tax is substantial. Arthur decides to temporarily save some money and earn some interest by sending in the tax amount annually instead of quarterly.

Explain why, in addition to being in violation of the law by not sending in quarterly payments, Arthur's behavior is unethical, given the purpose of the tax.

ANSWERS TO REVIEW QUIZZES

REVIEW QUIZ 12-1

Employee	FICA—OASDI	FICA—HIP	FUTA	SUTA
King	$ 24.55	$ 5.74	-0-	-0-
Todd	13.36	3.12	$1.72	$ 5.82
Wade	12.40	2.90	.80	2.70
Mimms	41.85	9.79	-0-	-0-
Maris	19.72	4.61	2.00	6.75
Totals	$111.88 +	$26.16 +	$4.52 +	$15.27 = $157.83

REVIEW QUIZ 12-2

	20X1						
1	Nov.	18	Payroll Tax Expense		1 5 7 83		1
2			FICA Tax Payable—OASDI			1 1 1 88	2
3			FICA Tax Payable—HIP			2 6 16	3
4			FUTA Tax Payable			4 52	4
5			SUTA Tax Payable			1 5 27	5
6			Recorded employer's payroll taxes.				6

REVIEW QUIZ 12-3

	20XX						
1	Jun.	15	FICA Tax Payable—OASDI		5 6 8 00		1
2			FICA Tax Payable—HIP		1 3 2 00		2
3			Cash			7 0 0 00	3
4			Deposited FICA taxes.				4

	20XX						
1	Jun.	30	FUTA Tax Payable		5 7 00		1
2			Cash			5 7 00	2
3			Deposited FUTA taxes.				3

	20XX						
1	Jun.	30	SUTA Tax Payable		1 8 9 00		1
2			Cash			1 8 9 00	2
3			Paid SUTA taxes.				3

REVIEW QUIZ 12-4

				Debit	Credit	
1	20X2 Jan.	2	Workers' Comp. Insurance Expense	6 3 7 5 00		1
2			Cash		6 3 7 5 00	2
3			Paid estimated premium for the year.			3

				Debit	Credit	
1			Adjusting Entries			1
2	20X2 Dec.	31	Workers' Comp. Insurance Expense	2 5 5 00		2
3			Workers' Comp. Insurance Payable		2 5 5 00	3

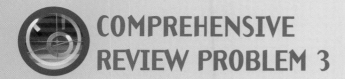

COMPREHENSIVE REVIEW PROBLEM 3

CARLSON COMPANY

CL The purpose of this problem is to follow a payroll system for two weeks. It includes preparing a payroll register and all related accounting entries for payroll.

Assumed tax rates are as follows:

FICA: OASDI   6.2% on the first $68,400
       HIP   1.45% on all earnings
FUTA: 0.8% on the first $7,000
SUTA: 2.4% on the first $7,000
Federal income tax: See tax tables on pages 404–405
State income tax: 5%

Carlson Company pays its employees every week and pays time-and-a-half for all hours over 40 a week. Earnings through the April 12, 20X1 payroll and the classification of the company's workers are as follows:

Sales:

T. Craig	$11,300	M-2
P. Guidry	6,800	S-1
J. Iannone	6,400	M-3

Office:

L. Wesley	14,200	M-4
M. Perez	9,700	S-0

Directions: Record the following transactions in a general journal, pages 46 and 47. Prepare payroll registers as requested, and use them as the basis for some of your accounting entries.

Apr. 15 Deposited March's FICA and federal income taxes in a bank. FICA—OASDI tax amounted to $500, while FICA—HIP tax amounted to $100. Federal income tax withheld amounted to $1,350.
   18 Wrote a check to pay for bonds purchased with March's savings bond deductions, $90.
   19 Recorded and paid the weekly payroll. Prepare a payroll register, journalize the payroll, and record its payment. Use the following data:

Name	Status	Hours	Rate per Hour	Savings Bonds	Union Dues	Ck. No.
T. Craig	M-2	42	$10	$10	$ 5.00	63
P. Guidry	S-1	30	6	-0-	-0-	64
J. Iannone	M-3	45	9	5	5.00	65
L. Wesley	M-4	46	12	10	12.50	66
M. Perez	S-0	40	11	-0-	7.50	67

   19 Recorded the employer's payroll taxes on the April 19 payroll.
   20 Paid March's union dues to the union, $120.
   25 Sent in March's state income tax withheld, $415.
   26 Recorded and paid the weekly payroll. Prepare a payroll register, journalize the payroll, and record its payment. All basic data are the same as for April 19 except for the hours worked and the check numbers. Hours worked are, respectively, 44, 30, 47, 40, and 42. Check numbers continue with No. 68. Remember to calculate the up-to-date cumulative earnings by adding last week's total earnings for each employee to the cumulative earnings the employee had last week.
   26 Recorded the employer's payroll taxes on the April 26 payroll.
   30 Paid FUTA tax for the first quarter. Taxable wages for this tax amounted to $13,000 in the quarter.
   30 Paid SUTA tax for the first quarter. Taxable wages were $13,000.

APPENDIX A

THE VOUCHER SYSTEM

In this appendix, we will focus on another system that is designed specifically to control cash payments. This method, called the voucher system, can result in prompt payment of bills when they are due, including taking advantage of all discounts. In this method of accounting for cash payments, any payment must be authorized in advance, at the same time it is incurred, rather than at the time of payment. With a voucher system, no purchase of a good or a service, and no payment of a liability, may happen without authorization.

COMPONENTS OF A VOUCHER SYSTEM

A typical voucher system has five components: (1) the voucher, (2) the voucher register, (3) the unpaid voucher file, (4) the check register, and (5) the paid voucher file. These are described in the following sections. Figure A-1 shows these components.

The voucher itself is illustrated in Figure A-2.

FIGURE A-1
Components of a voucher system

Component	Description
Voucher	A form used to authorize a purchase or a payment.
Voucher register	A journal in which vouchers are recorded right after they are prepared; similar in appearance to a purchases journal.
Unpaid voucher file	A file of vouchers to be paid, organized by date due so vouchers can be paid promptly.
Check register	A journal in which checks used to pay vouchers are recorded; similar in appearance to a cash payments journal.
Paid voucher file	A file of vouchers that have been paid, organized in numerical order.

FIGURE A-2
A voucher

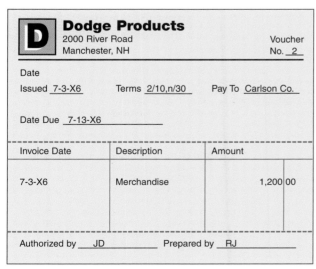

Voucher (Front)   Voucher (Back)

USING THE REGISTERS

To show you how to use the voucher register and the check register, a few sample transactions are presented. Every transaction in the voucher register follows this format:

- Dr. Asset, Expense, or Drawing account
- Cr. Vouchers Payable account

Assume that Dodge Company issued the following five vouchers during July 20X6. Assume also that purchases are made with terms of 2/10,n/30.

Date	Vo. No.	Payee	For	Amount
7/1	1	Acme Realty	Rent	$ 600.00
7/3	2	Carson Co.	Merchandise	1,200.00
7/5	3	Webb Co.	Office supplies	525.00
7/15	4	Jennie Dodge	Drawing	200.00
7/30	5	Payroll	Salaries	5,000.00

Figure A-3 shows how these vouchers would appear in the voucher register. Notice the use of special columns for Purchases Dr., Office Supplies Dr., and Salaries Expense Dr. Notice the use of the Other Accounts Dr. column for Jennie Dodge, Drawing. All credits are recorded in the Vouchers Payable Cr. column.

FIGURE A-3
Voucher register

	Date	Vo. No.	Paid Date	Paid Check No.	Payee	Vouchers Payable Cr.	Purchases Dr.	Office Supplies Dr.	Salaries Expense Dr.		Other Accounts Dr. Account	P.R.	Amount	
1	20X6 Jul. 1	1	7/1	1	Acme Realty	6 0 0 00				1	Rent Expense	611	6 0 0 00	1
2	3	2	7/13	2	Carson Co.	1 2 0 0 00	1 2 0 0 00			2				2
3	5	3			Webb Co.	5 2 5 00		5 2 5 00		3				3
4	15	4	7/15	3	Jennie Dodge	2 0 0 00				4	J. Dodge, Drawing	311	2 0 0 00	4
5	30	5	7/30	4	Payroll	5 0 0 0 00			5 0 0 0 00	5				5
6	31				Totals	7 5 2 5 00	1 2 0 0 00	5 2 5 00	5 0 0 0 00	6			8 0 0 00	6
7						(2 1 1)	(5 1 1)	(1 1 4)	(6 1 2)	7			(✓)	7

Assume next that four of the five vouchers are paid during July—Vouchers 1, 2, 4, and 5. All are paid in their full amounts, except for Voucher 2, for which there is a 2% cash discount. Figure A-4 shows how the checks are recorded in the check register.

FIGURE A-4
Check register

	Date	Ck. No.	Vo. No.	Payee	Vouchers Payable Dr.	Purchases Discounts Cr.	Cash Cr.	
1	20X6 Jul. 1	1	1	Acme Realty	6 0 0 00		6 0 0 00	1
2	13	2	2	Carson Co.	1 2 0 0 00	2 4 00	1 1 7 6 00	2
3	15	3	4	Jennie Dodge	2 0 0 00		2 0 0 00	3
4	30	4	5	Payroll	5 0 0 0 00		5 0 0 0 00	4
5	31			Totals	7 0 0 0 00	2 4 00	6 9 7 6 00	5
6					(2 1 1)	(5 1 3)	(1 1 1)	6

Notice the cross-referencing of voucher numbers in the check register. Each check is written to pay a specific voucher. Notice the entering of check numbers in the voucher register. This procedure enables you to see, at a glance, which vouchers are unpaid. In this case, Voucher 3 remains unpaid at the end of the month.

END-OF-MONTH PROCEDURES

Each register is totaled and posted to the general ledger at the end of the month. It is assumed that all posting has been done in this problem. Vouchers Payable, account number 211, is shown below.

	Vouchers Payable	211
20X6	20X6	
Jul. 31 CR1 7,000	Jul. 31 VR1 7,525	
	Balance 525	

Notice that the Vouchers Payable account has a debit from the check register and a credit from the voucher register. The balance of the account is equal to the amount of the one unpaid voucher—$525.00. Voucher system verification should always end this way: The balance of the Vouchers Payable account should equal the sum of the unpaid vouchers. This check is very much like comparing the balance of the Accounts Payable account with the total of the balances in the accounts payable ledger. Having this final check on the system is one of the reasons why it can properly be called a system of internal control.

Glossary

A

ABA (American Bankers Association) numbers Numbers printed on checks and deposit slips that contain information as to the bank, the area in which it is located, and the like.

Accelerated Cost Recovery System (ACRS) A method of calculating depreciation for federal tax purposes that was introduced by Congress in the Economic Recovery Tax Act of 1981. ACRS allows businesses to write off the costs of assets more quickly than with traditional depreciation methods.

accelerated method of depreciation A depreciation method that allows for larger amounts of depreciation in early years and smaller amounts in later years. The double declining-balance method is an example.

account An individual form or record used to record and summarize information related to each asset, each liability, and each aspect of owner's equity.

accounting The process of recording, summarizing, analyzing, and interpreting financial (money-related) activities to permit individuals and organizations to make informed judgments and decisions.

accounting cycle The steps involved in the recording and summarizing processes of accounting.

accounting equation The equation that expresses the relationship between the accounting elements in a simple mathematical form: Assets = Liabilities + Owner's Equity.

accounting period A period that is typically one year; however, it can be any length of time for which accounting records are maintained, often for a month.

accounts payable The liability that results from purchasing goods or services on credit.

accounts payable ledger A subsidiary ledger that lists the individual accounts of creditors. Also called the *creditors' ledger*.

Accounts Receivable An asset account that shows the total dollar amount due from credit customers.

accounts receivable The asset arising from selling goods or services on credit to customers.

Accounts Receivable—Credit Cards An asset account showing the amount due from nonbank credit card sales.

accounts receivable ledger A subsidiary ledger containing only accounts of credit customers; also called the *customers' ledger*.

accounts receivable turnover A measure that indicates how quickly a firm is collecting its accounts receivable. Calculated by dividing net credit sales by average net accounts receivable.

accrual basis of accounting The basis of accounting that requires that revenue is recorded when earned, no matter when cash is received, and that expenses are recorded when incurred, no matter when cash is paid.

accruals Expenses incurred and revenue earned in the current accounting period but not recorded as of the end of the period.

accrued expenses Expenses that build up or accumulate during the current period but will not be paid until the next period. Also called *accrued liabilities*.

accrued revenue Revenue that has been earned in the current accounting period but will not be received until the next period. Also called *accrued assets*.

accrued salaries (accrued wages) Salaries that are unpaid (and unrecorded) at the end of an accounting period.

accumulated depreciation The total depreciation from the start of the life of a plant asset to any point in time.

acid-test ratio The ratio of quick assets to current liabilities. A yardstick commonly used is a 1-to-1 ratio. Also called *quick ratio*.

addition A capital expenditure that literally adds on to an existing plant asset. The cost of an addition is debited to the plant asset account.

adequate disclosure principle States that financial statements or the explanatory notes and schedules that go with the statements must disclose all relevant data about the financial position of a company.

adjusting entries Entries made at the end of an accounting period to bring the balances of certain accounts up to date.

aging schedule A schedule in which accounts receivable are grouped into age categories and an estimated bad debts rate is applied to each age category.

aging the receivables A way of estimating bad debts expense when using the balance sheet approach.

allowance method A method of accounting for bad debts in which the amount estimated to be uncollectible is established at the end of an accounting period in an adjusting entry. Uncollectible accounts are then written off by debiting Allowance for Doubtful Accounts.

amortization The periodic write-off of the cost of an intangible asset.

apportionment The process of dividing operating expenses among departments.

appropriation of retained earnings A portion of retained earnings earmarked for a specific purpose, such as plant expansion or the retirement of debt. The amount appropriated may not be used for cash or stock dividends.

appropriations The process of authorizing future payments from budgeted income. Only money that is appropriated can be spent.

articles of incorporation An application filed with a state to incorporate a business.

articles of partnership An agreement made between partners that sets forth the terms of their partnership, such as the amount of cash or other assets each is to invest, the amount of time each is to devote to running the business, and how the net income or loss will be divided. Also called a *partnership agreement*.

assets Items with money value that are owned by a business.

asset turnover A measure of the net sales generated by the assets of a firm. Calculated by dividing net sales by total assets excluding investments.

authorized stock The maximum number of shares that a corporation is permitted to sell; this amount appears in the corporate charter.

auxiliary record A business record that is not essential but is helpful in maintaining records that are essential; an example is the petty cash payments record.

average collection period for accounts receivable A rough measure of the length of time accounts receivable have been outstanding. Calculated by dividing 365 days by the accounts receivable turnover.

B

bad debt An account receivable that, for one reason or another, cannot be collected.

balance The balance of an account is determined by footing (adding) the debit side, footing the credit side, and calculating the difference between the two sides.

balance form of account A ledger account form with four amount columns that many businesses prefer to use because the balance is always known and it is easy to see whether the balance is a debit or a credit. Also called the *four-column account form*.

balance sheet A listing of a firm's assets, liabilities, and owner's equity at a specific point in time. Other terms used to describe the balance sheet are statement of financial position and position statement.

balance sheet approach A method of estimating the bad debts expense under the allowance method in which the expense is based on aging the accounts receivable.

bank checking account An amount of cash on deposit with a bank that the bank must pay at the written order of the depositor.

bank discount Interest deducted in advance by a bank.

banker's year A 360-day year used by many companies and financial institutions for ease in calculation of interest. Also called a *commercial year*.

bank reconciliation Making the bank statement balance agree with the checkbook balance.

bankruptcy A condition in which a firm does not have sufficient cash to pay its creditors.

bank statement A monthly report showing the bank's record of the checking account.

beginning merchandise inventory The dollar value of merchandise that is on hand at the beginning of an accounting period.

betterment A capital expenditure that improves a plant asset, such as placing siding on a building. The cost of a betterment is debited to the plant asset account.

blank endorsement An endorsement consisting only of a signature on the back of a check. A check with this kind of endorsement can be cashed or transferred to another by anyone who has possession of it.

board of directors People elected by a corporation's stockholders to oversee the business and appoint the officers.

bond A long-term debt instrument issued in return for a loan of cash.

bond discount Issuing bonds at an amount below the face value of the bonds.

bondholders Those who own bonds issued by a corporation or governmental unit.

bond indenture An agreement, or contract, between the corporation and its bondholders. Also called a *trust indenture*.

bond issue The total number of bonds that a corporation issues at one time. Each bond in the issue usually has a face value of $1,000 (or multiple thereof).

bond premium Issuing bonds at an amount that is above the face value of the bonds.

bond sinking fund A special cash fund that is set up to accumulate cash over the life of the bonds to enable the issuing corporation to pay off the bond issue when it comes due.

bonus to the existing partners A plan for admitting a new partner in which part of the new partner's investment is credited to the existing partners' capital accounts.

bonus to the new partner A plan for admitting a new partner in which a part of the capital of each existing partner is transferred to the new partner.

book of final entry The ledger is referred to as the book of final entry because amounts are transferred (posted) to the ledger from the journal.

book of original entry The journal is referred to as the book of original entry because it is the first place in which transactions are formally recorded.

book value The difference between the cost of a plant asset and its accumulated depreciation.

boot In an exchange of plant assets, the difference between the price of the new asset and the trade-in allowance granted for the old asset.

branches Locations of a business other than its home office.

break-even point The point in operations where total sales dollars exactly equal total fixed and variable costs; the point of zero profit or loss.

budget A formal statement of management's financial plans for the future.

budgeted balance sheet A balance sheet that estimates each element of financial condition at a specified future time.

budgeted income statement An income statement that estimates net income for the next fiscal period, based on all income statement budgets.

business An organization that operates with the objective of earning a profit.

business entity concept The principle that states that, for accounting purposes, a business is a distinct economic entity or unit that is separate from its owner and from any other business.

bylaws A set of policies that act as a corporation's constitution.

C

canceled checks Checks that have been paid by the bank out of the depositor's account.

capital expenditures Expenditures for a plant asset that benefit more than one accounting period. Examples include additions, betterments, and extraordinary repairs. Capital expenditures increase either the value or the life of the asset and are debited to either the plant asset account or its accumulated depreciation account, depending on the type of expenditure.

capital expenditures budget A budget used for long-term planning of when plant assets will need to be replaced.

capital projects funds Government funds that are used for major projects, such as building a park.

capital stock Shares of ownership in a corporation.

cash In its most basic meaning, cash is currency (paper money) and coin. The definition in a business context also includes checks, money orders, traveler's checks, cashier's checks, bank drafts, and receipts from credit card sales.

cash basis of accounting A basis of accounting where revenue is recorded only when cash is received, and expenses are recorded only when cash is paid.

cash budget A budget that estimates the expected cash to be received and spent over a period of time.

cash discounts Discounts offered by a seller to encourage early payment by a buyer. To the seller, cash discounts are *sales discounts;* to the buyer, cash discounts are *purchases discounts.*

cash dividend A dividend paid in cash.

cash equivalents Highly liquid, short-term investments that can be turned to cash with little or no delay.

cash flows Cash receipts and cash payments from operating activities, investing activities, and financing activities.

cash payments journal A special journal used for recording all disbursements of cash. Also called the *cash disbursements journal.*

cash receipts journal A special journal used to record all receipts of cash, regardless of the source.

cash register tape A variation of the sales ticket; the total of the tape serves as the source document for later journal entries.

Cash Short and Over An account used to bring the Cash account into agreement with the actual amount of cash on hand. This account is used in businesses that have many cash transactions and thus often have small amounts of cash over or under what the cash register shows.

centralized branch accounting A system of accounting for branches in which all records for each branch are kept on the home office books.

change fund An amount of money that is maintained in the cash register for making change for cash customers.

Change Fund account An asset account in which the amount of the change fund is recorded.

charges Charges or fees by the bank that are subtracted directly from the depositor's account and appear on the bank statement. Also called *bank charges.*

charter Issued by a state to the incorporators of a company. It is a contract between the state and the incorporators, authorizing the corporation to conduct business. Also called *certificate of incorporation.*

chart of accounts A directory or listing of accounts in the ledger.

check A written order directing a bank to pay a specified sum of money to a designated person or business.

checkbook A bound book of checks with stubs; the depositor's record of the checking account.

check stub Part of a check that remains in the checkbook as a permanent record of the check.

classified balance sheet A balance sheet that divides the assets and liabilities sections into the following subsections: current assets and plant assets, and current liabilities and long-term liabilities.

classified income statement An income statement divided into the following sections: revenue, cost of goods sold, operating expenses, and other income and expenses.

clearing account An account used to summarize the balances of other accounts.

closely held corporation A corporation that is owned by a small group of investors or a family.

closing entries Entries made at the end of an accounting period to transfer the balances of the temporary accounts to the owner's capital account.

closing process The process of transferring the balances of temporary accounts to the owner's capital account.

C.O.D. (cash on delivery) Terms set by the seller that call for payment when the goods are delivered.

combined journal A multicolumn journal used by small businesses to help save journalizing and posting time. It has two special columns for recording debits and credits to cash, various other special columns for recording transactions that occur often, and two general columns for recording transactions that occur less often. Also called a *combination journal.*

common stock Shares of ownership in a corporation. The class of stock that usually has voting rights.

comparative financial statements A side-by-side comparison of a company's financial statements for two or more accounting periods.

compound entry An entry requiring three or more accounts.

consignment A procedure in which one business (the consignee) accepts goods from another business (the consignor) for sale on a commission basis. Consigned goods should be counted in the inventory of the consignor.

consistency The accounting principle that requires a firm to continue to use a method once chosen, rather than switch from method to method arbitrarily or for temporary advantage.

contingent liability A possible liability, such as on a discounted note of a customer, that may become a real liability if certain events occur.

contra asset account An account whose balance is opposite the asset to which it relates. Since asset accounts have debit balances, contra asset accounts (the opposite of assets) have credit balances.

contract interest rate The rate of interest stated on the bond certificate. Also called the *face interest rate*.

contribution margin The excess of sales revenue over variable costs.

contribution margin ratio The percentage of each dollar of sales available to cover the fixed costs and provide operating income.

controlling account An account in the general ledger that summarizes accounts in a related subsidiary ledger.

corporation A form of business that legally exists separate from the investors who own it.

correcting entry An entry used to correct certain types of errors in the ledger.

cost An input into the manufacturing of a product. There are three common inputs in manufacturing: (1) raw materials, (2) direct labor, and (3) factory overhead.

cost accounting The field of accounting that is used to determine the dollar value of goods that are manufactured.

cost accounts Accounts that are presented on the income statement; used to determine the cost of goods sold to customers.

cost behavior The way a cost changes in relation to a change in activity level.

cost of goods manufactured The sum of the elements of cost—raw materials, direct labor, and factory overhead—adjusted for the manufacturing inventories (raw materials and work-in-process).

cost of goods manufactured budget A budget that estimates cost of goods manufactured for the next fiscal period.

cost of goods sold The cost of merchandise sold to customers during the accounting period. The formula used to find cost of goods sold is:

	Beginning Merchandise Inventory
+	Net Purchases of Merchandise
=	Cost of Goods Available for Sale
−	Ending Merchandise Inventory
=	Cost of Goods Sold

cost of goods sold budget A budget that estimates cost of goods sold for the next fiscal period.

cost of production report A report that summarizes all of the units and costs transferred into and out of a production department in a process cost accounting system.

cost percentage In the retail method, the dollar value of goods available for sale at cost divided by the dollar value of goods available for sale at retail.

cost principle The principle that states that, when purchased, all assets are recorded at their actual cost regardless of market value.

cost-volume-profit analysis The study of the relationships among costs, selling prices, production volume, expenses, and profits.

coupon bonds (bearer bonds) Bonds for which the owners are not registered with the issuing corporation; ownership of such bonds is transferred by delivery of the bonds, and interest payments are received by presenting an interest coupon to a bank.

credit The allowance of cash, goods, or services in the present, with payment expected in the future. To credit (Cr.) an account means to enter an amount on the right, or credit, side of the account.

credit balance Occurs when the amount on the credit side of an account is greater than the amount on the debit side.

Credit Card Expense An expense account that is used to record discounts paid when receipts for credit card sales are deposited with the bank that issued the card (such as VISA or MasterCard) or with the credit card company that issued the card (such as American Express).

credit memorandum A document issued to the customer showing the amount of credit granted and the reason for the return.

creditor A business or person to whom a debt is owed.

credit period The amount of time a seller allows a credit customer to pay for a purchase.

credit terms The terms for payment set by a seller of goods or services; includes the amount of time before payment is due and the rate of discount (if any) for paying early.

cross-footing The addition of columns of figures in different ways to check the accuracy of the totals.

cross-reference A way of connecting a journal entry to its corresponding ledger entries so that the transaction can be traced back to its original entry or forward to its final entry.

cumulative preferred stock Preferred stock in which unpaid dividends accumulate from year to year. These unpaid dividends must be paid in full before any amount can be paid to the holders of common stock.

current assets Cash and assets that will be sold, used up, or turned into cash within the current accounting period, usually one year. Besides cash, examples are receivables, supplies, and merchandise inventory.

current liabilities Debts that are due for payment within one year. Examples are accounts payable, salaries payable, sales tax payable, and the current portion of notes payable.

current ratio The ratio obtained by dividing current assets by current liabilities. It is an indicator of a firm's ability to pay its short-term debts as they become due.

D

date of declaration The date on which the board of directors of a corporation formally declares that a dividend will be paid.

date of payment The date on which dividend checks are mailed out to stockholders.

date of record The date associated with reviewing the stockholders' records to determine the ownership of shares outstanding; anyone who buys stock after the date of record will not receive the dividend for that period.

debenture bonds Bonds that are issued based on the general credit of the issuing corporation; no specific assets are pledged as security for the debt.

debit To debit (Dr.) an account means to enter an amount on the left, or debit, side of the account.

debit balance Occurs when the amount(s) on the debit side of an account is greater than the amount(s) on the credit side.

debit memorandum The buyer's written request to a seller for credit for a merchandise return or allowance.

debt securities Investments in debt instruments (bonds and notes) issued by a corporation or a governmental unit.

debt service funds Government funds that provide for the payment of principal and interest of long-term debt.

decentralized branch accounting A system of accounting for branches in which each branch keeps its own records and prepares its own financial statements.

deferrals Expenses and revenue that have been recorded in the current accounting period but are not incurred or earned until a future period.

deferred charges Another name for deferred expenses, usually applying to advance payments that cover more than a year.

deferred credits Another name for deferred revenue, usually applying to amounts received more than a year in advance.

deferred expenses Advance payments for goods or services that benefit more than one accounting period.

deferred revenue The advance receipt of revenue that will not be earned until a future accounting period.

deficit A debit balance in the Retained Earnings account.

departmental margin For a department, gross profit less direct expenses.

departmental margin analysis The determination of the actual financial contribution of a specific department to a firm.

depletion The expense resulting from the using up of a natural resource.

depositor The business or person under whose name a checking account is opened.

deposits in transit Deposits made and appearing in the checkbook but not appearing on the bank statement. Also called *outstanding deposits*.

deposit slip A form that is prepared when coin, currency, or checks are deposited in a bank account. It indicates the depositor's name and account number and summarizes the amount deposited. Also called *deposit ticket*.

depreciation An allocation process in which the cost of a long-term asset (except land) is divided over the periods in which the asset is used in the production of the business's revenue.

depreciation expense The expense that results from the allocation process of depreciation.

depreciation schedule A table that lists for a plant asset the amount of depreciation for each year and the accumulated depreciation and book value of that plant asset at the end of each year.

direct expense An expense that is associated with a specific department; an expense that benefits only that department and that would not exist if the department did not exist.

direct labor The cost of those employees who work directly to produce the product.

direct labor cost budget A budget that estimates direct labor costs for the next fiscal period.

direct labor rate variance The difference between the actual cost per hour and the budgeted cost per hour.

direct labor time variance The difference between the number of direct labor hours used and the budgeted direct labor hours. Also called *labor efficiency variance*.

direct labor variance The difference between actual direct labor costs and budgeted direct labor costs.

direct materials Materials that are an identifiable part of a manufactured product.

direct materials price variance The difference between the actual price paid for direct materials and the budgeted price.

direct materials purchases budget A budget that shows the dollar amount of direct materials that must be purchased to meet production requirements.

direct materials quantity variance The difference between the actual quantity of direct materials used and the budgeted quantity.

direct materials variance The difference between actual direct materials costs and budgeted direct materials costs.

direct method A format for the statement of cash flows that discloses each major class of cash inflow and cash outflow from operating activities. It shows the amount of cash received or paid for revenues and expenses reported on the income statement. This is the method recommended by the FASB.

direct write-off method A method of accounting for bad debts in which the expense is recorded at the time of the write-off of a customer's account.

discounting a note payable Borrowing from a bank on one's own note with the interest being deducted at the time of borrowing.

discount on stock Occurs when a share of stock sells for less than its par value; many states prohibit the practice of issuing stock at a discount.

discount period The time from the date of discounting a customer's note until the due date of the note. Also called *term of discount*.

dishonored note A note that is not paid by its maker on the due date.

distributive share The share of net income or net loss received by each partner.

dividend A distribution of corporate earnings to the stockholders of the company.

dividends in arrears Passed dividends on cumulative preferred stock.

dividend yield A measure of profitability that tells the investor the rate earned on investment. Calculated by dividing the dividend per share of stock by the market price per share.

double declining-balance method A depreciation method that allows greater depreciation in the early years of the life of a plant asset and less depreciation in later years. This is achieved by applying a constant rate to each year's decreasing book value.

double-entry accounting Each business transaction affects the accounting elements in at least two ways. Recording both effects of a transaction is called double-entry accounting.

drawee The bank on which a check is drawn.

drawer The business or person who writes a check.

drawing account A temporary owner's equity account that is used when an owner withdraws cash or other assets from the business for personal use.

dual effect The principle that states that all business transactions are recorded as having *at least* two effects on the basic accounting elements.

due date The date on which a note must be paid. Also called the *maturity date*.

E

earned capital Capital that arises from profitable operations of the corporation; usually called *retained earnings*.

earnings per share on common stock The amount of net income available to the owner of each share of common stock. Calculated by dividing net income (less preferred dividend requirements) by the number of common shares outstanding.

employee A person who works under the direct control of an employer on a continuing basis.

employee's earnings record A record maintained for each employee that contains basic employee information and a summary of payroll data for that employee.

employer identification number (EIN) An identifying number each business must have if, during any part of the year, it employs one or more people.

Employer's Tax Guide—Circular E An IRS publication containing federal income tax tables for various payroll periods for married and single persons.

encumbrances Expected liabilities.

ending merchandise inventory The dollar value of merchandise that is on hand at the end of an accounting period.

endorsement A signature or stamp on the back of a check that transfers ownership of the check to the bank or another person.

enterprise funds A type of proprietary fund similar to a private business, whereby a service is provided and a fee is charged (such as for a transit system).

equipment The physical assets needed by a business in order to operate.

equity securities Investments in stocks issued by corporations.

equivalent units The production work actually done.

estimated revenues budget A budgetary account that lists all anticipated revenues to the governmental unit.

estimated useful life (EUL) The amount of time that an asset is expected to be in use or the amount of output it is expected to produce.

expended When a liability is incurred, per authorization.

expenses The costs of operating a business. Unlike the cost of an asset, the cost of an expense does not provide a future benefit to the business. Therefore, its effect is a reduction in owner's equity.

extension The amount found by multiplying the unit cost of an item by the quantity.

extraordinary repair A capital expenditure that prolongs the life of a plant asset, such as new wiring in a building. The cost of an extraordinary repair is debited to an accumulated depreciation account.

F

factory overhead All costs of running a factory other than raw materials and direct labor; includes utilities, rent, depreciation, and indirect labor.

factory overhead budget A budget that estimates the factory overhead costs for the next fiscal period.

factory overhead variance The difference between the actual factory overhead costs and the budgeted factory overhead costs.

Fair Labor Standards Act (or Wages and Hours Law) An act passed by Congress that established standards for minimum wages, overtime pay, child labor, and required payroll record keeping.

favorable variance A variance that exists when actual costs are less than budgeted costs.

Federal Income Tax Payable account A liability account used to record the amount of federal income taxes withheld from the earnings of employees. It is credited when taxes are withheld and debited when the taxes are sent in.

Federal Insurance Contributions Act (FICA) An act that requires contributions by both the employer and the employee to the federal social security system. The FICA tax has two component parts: OASDI (Old-Age, Survivors, and Disability Insurance) and HIP (Hospital Insurance Plan). OASDI and HIP rates are set by Congress and are revised periodically. The OASDI tax has a wage limit that is usually revised annually.

Federal Tax Deposit, Form 8109 A form that must be filled out when FICA taxes and withheld income taxes are deposited in an authorized bank.

Federal Unemployment Tax Act (FUTA) An act requiring employers to pay into a fund designed to assist workers who are temporarily unemployed.

FICA Tax Payable—HIP account A liability account used to record the amount of HIP taxes withheld from employees' earnings and matched by the employer. It is credited when HIP taxes are withheld (or imposed on the employer) and debited when the taxes are sent in.

FICA Tax Payable—OASDI account A liability account used to record the amount of OASDI taxes withheld from employees' earnings and matched by the employer. It is credited when OASDI taxes are withheld (or imposed on the employer) and debited when the taxes are sent in.

fiduciary funds Monies held by the government, which is acting as a trustee or as a collecting and disbursing agent.

financial statements Summaries of financial activities.

financing activities Transactions that involve cash receipts or payments from changes in long-term liabilities and stockholders' equity—such as selling stock to stockholders and paying dividends, and borrowing from creditors and repaying these loans.

finished goods inventory The inventory of goods that are completed but unsold at the end of an accounting period.

finished goods inventory records Subsidiary records of finished goods kept as a perpetual inventory.

first-in, first-out method (FIFO) An inventory costing method that assumes that the first goods purchased (first-in) are the first goods sold (first-out), leaving the most recent goods purchased as the ending inventory.

fiscal period The period of time that covers a complete accounting cycle. A *fiscal year* is a fiscal period covering twelve months; it does not necessarily coincide with the calendar year.

fiscal year A 12-month time period that may or may not be from January 1 to December 31.

fixed costs Costs that do not change as production changes; costs that occur even without any production.

flexible budget A budget that is actually a series of budgets for different levels of production activity.

FOB destination A shipping term that means that the seller is responsible for all freight costs until the goods reach their destination.

FOB shipping point A shipping term that means that the buyer is responsible for all freight costs while the goods are in transit.

footing The total of the debit column or credit column of an account.

Form 940—Employer's Annual Federal Unemployment Tax Return Form filed by the employer by January 31, summarizing FUTA deposits during the preceding year.

Form 941—Employer's Quarterly Federal Tax Return A quarterly report that summarizes FICA taxes (employer and employee shares) and income taxes withheld during the quarter.

Form W-2 (Wage and Tax Statement) A form given by the employer to each employee by January 31 that contains a summary of the employee's earnings and deductions for the past year.

Form W-3 (Transmittal of Wage and Tax Statements) An annual form employers file with the Social Security Administration to summarize employee earnings and tax deductions. Copy A of each employee's Form W-2 is filed with Form W-3.

Form W-4 (Employee's Withholding Allowance Certificate) A form filled out by each employee showing marital status and number of withholding allowances claimed.

Freight In account A general ledger account in which charges for freight on incoming merchandise are recorded. Also called *Transportation In*.

full endorsement Uses the phrase *Pay to the order of*, followed by the name of the business or person to whom the check is being transferred. Only the specified business or person can cash the check.

fund A fiscal and accounting entity with a self-balancing set of accounts.

FUTA Tax Payable account A current liability account used to record the employer's obligation for federal unemployment taxes.

G

general accounting for manufacturing A system in which costs are gathered throughout the year and transferred periodically to a summary account.

general expenses Expenses related to (1) running a firm's office or (2) any other operating activities that do not involve the sale of merchandise. Also called *administrative expenses*.

general fund The basic, main fund for governmental units, which contains the bulk of the monies, and through which most of the services are paid.

general journal The basic form of journal that has two money columns.

general ledger A ledger containing the financial statement accounts.

goodwill An intangible asset made up of such factors as an excellent reputation, a fine location, a superior product line, or outstanding management skills. Used to give a partner a greater capital credit than the amount of assets invested.

gross earnings An employee's earnings before any amount is deducted by the employer.

gross profit The profit before we subtract the expenses of doing business; it is obtained by subtracting cost of goods sold from net sales.

gross profit method A method for estimating the cost of the ending inventory by using a modified version of the cost of goods sold equation.

H

high-low method A method of separating the variable and fixed cost components of mixed costs by using the highest and lowest activity levels (and the cost at each level).

home office The main location of a business.

horizontal analysis The comparison of each item in a company's financial statements in the current period with the same item from a previous accounting period or periods.

hourly workers Individuals who work for a fixed hourly rate.

I

income from operations Gross profit minus operating expenses. Also called *operating income*.

income statement A summary of a business's revenue and expenses for a specific period of time, such as a month or a year. Other terms used to describe the income statement are earnings statement, operating statement, statement of operations, and profit and loss statement.

income statement approach A method of estimating the bad debts expense under the allowance method in which the expense is based on a percent of credit sales.

Income Summary account A clearing account used to summarize the balances of revenue and expense accounts. It is used only at the end of an accounting period and is opened and closed during the closing process.

incorporators A group of persons who file an application to form a corporation.

independent contractor A person who agrees to perform and complete a specific job or task and determines the ways and methods of achieving that job or task.

indirect expense An expense of operating a business that is not associated with a specific department; an expense that benefits an entire business and would continue to exist even if a specific department were eliminated.

indirect labor The cost of those employees who work in the factory, but not on the product itself.

indirect materials Materials that are used in the production process, but are not an identifiable part of the finished product.

indirect method A format for the statement of cash flows that adjusts the net income figure in order to calculate net cash flows from operating activities.

individual job sheets Records that show the costs accumulated for each job.

intangible assets Long-term assets used in a business that lack physical substance. Examples include patents, copyrights, trademarks, and franchises.

interest The charge for credit; calculated as principal × rate × time.

interest allowances A method of sharing net income that recognizes differences in partners' investments.

interim statements Statements that are prepared during the fiscal year for periods of less than 12 months—such as monthly, quarterly, and semiannually.

internal control The procedures used within a company to protect its assets.

internal service funds Funds that account for activities provided by one governmental unit to another, such as a print shop, on a cost reimbursement basis.

internal transactions Transactions, such as adjustments, that occur within a company and do not affect parties outside the company.

inventory A count taken of the merchandise on hand at the end of an accounting period.

inventory sheet A form on which a physical inventory is recorded.

Inventory Short and Over account An account used to record differences between the inventory value shown on the perpetual records and the value determined by the period-end physical count.

investing activities Transactions that increase and decrease the assets that a business owns.

invoice A business document that contains the names and addresses of the buyer and the seller, the date and terms of the sale, a description of the goods, the price of the goods, and the mode of transportation used to ship the goods. The seller calls the invoice a *sales invoice*; the buyer calls it a *purchase invoice*.

issued stock Shares that have been issued to stockholders.

issuing a note on account Giving a note to a creditor for an extension of time to pay an invoice.

J

job order cost accounting A cost accounting system in which costs are kept track of by job or batch of similar items being produced at one time.

journal A form in which transactions are recorded in chronological order (by order of date).

journalizing The process of recording transactions in a journal.

Just-In-time (JIT) Inventory System An inventory system designed to reduce storage costs and improve efficiency by ordering just enough raw materials to meet daily production needs and finishing just enough goods to be shipped to customers at the end of each day.

L

Land Improvements The title of an account to which the cost of improvements to real estate, such as sidewalks, driveways, fences, and parking lots (all of which have a limited life), are debited.

last-in, first-out method (LIFO) An inventory costing method that assumes that the last goods purchased (last-in) are the first goods sold (first-out), leaving the earliest goods as the ending inventory.

ledger A collective grouping of accounts.

legal capital The amount of earnings that a corporation must retain before a dividend can be paid to stockholders; usually equals the par value of the stock outstanding.

leverage The use of borrowed funds to earn a greater return than the cost of the borrowed funds.

liabilities Debts owed by the business.

limited liability Means that stockholders of a corporation are not personally liable for the debts of the company.

liquidation The process of winding up a business.

liquidation schedule A table that shows the three steps in liquidation.

liquidity Refers to how quickly an asset can be turned into cash, used up, or expire; used in reference to assets, which are listed on the balance sheet in the order of their liquidity.

list price The price appearing in a price catalog issued by the seller.

long-term investments Investments that management intends to hold for more than one year.

long-term liabilities Debts that will not come due for payment within one year. Examples are long-term notes payable and mortgages payable.

lookback period A four-quarter period ending on June 30 of the prior year. Employers look at the amount of FICA taxes (employee and employer shares) and withheld income taxes during the lookback period to determine if they are monthly or semiweekly depositors.

lower of cost or market (LCM) rule An alternate way to value an inventory in which the cost of the merchandise is compared with the market price (current cost to replace) and the lower value is used.

M

maker The person who has received credit and issues a note.

manufacturing business A business that produces a product to sell to its customers.

margin of safety The amount of sales above break-even sales.

market interest rate The prevailing rate of interest in the bond market. Also called the *effective interest rate.*

matching principle Requires that revenue earned during an accounting period be offset by the expenses that were necessary to produce that revenue, so that the accurate net income or net loss for the period can be reported.

materials ledger records Subsidiary records of raw materials kept as a perpetual inventory.

math errors Errors made in addition or subtraction.

maturity date The date on which the principal must be repaid to bondholders.

maturity value The principal plus the interest on a note; the amount that must be paid to the payee on the maturity date of the note.

memorandum entry A notation in the journal that is used to report the effect of a stock split.

Merchandise Inventory An asset account that shows the value of goods (inventory) on hand at a given moment (usually at the beginning or end of the accounting period).

merchandise inventory Goods held for sale to customers in the normal course of business. Also called *stock in trade*.

merchandise inventory turnover A measure of the number of times a firms average inventory is sold during the year. Calculated by dividing cost of goods sold by the average inventory.

merchandising business A business that earns its revenue by buying goods and then reselling those goods. Also called a *trading business*.

merit-rating system A system set up by the states to provide a lower SUTA rate for employers who maintain stable employment.

minimum wage An amount set by Congress that is the minimum rate that can be paid to workers who are covered by the Fair Labor Standards Act. At this writing, it is $5.15 an hour.

mixed costs Costs that have both variable and fixed characteristics.

Modified Accelerated Cost Recovery System (MACRS) A revision of ACRS introduced by the Tax Reform Act of 1986. This method adds new categories of property and the half-year convention.

modified cash basis of accounting A basis of accounting where revenue is recorded only when cash is received and expenses are recorded only when cash is paid. However, adjustments are made for expenditures for items having an economic life of more than one year—such as equipment, prepaid insurance, and large purchases of supplies.

N

natural business year A fiscal year ending at a business's lowest point of activity.

natural resources Long-term assets that are acquired to extract or remove resources from the ground. Examples are oil wells, coal mines, and forests. Also called *wasting assets*.

negotiable Able to be transferred by endorsement to another party.

net earnings (net pay) Gross earnings minus payroll deductions.

net income Occurs when revenue earned during an accounting period exceeds the expenses of the same period.

net loss Occurs when expenses exceed revenue during an accounting period.

net realizable value The difference between the balance in the Accounts Receivable account and the Allowance for Doubtful Accounts account; the actual amount of receivables that the firm expects to collect.

net receivables Another name for net realizable value.

net sales The amount obtained by subtracting the amount of sales returns and allowances and the amount of sales discounts from the amount of sales.

noncumulative preferred stock Preferred stock in which undeclared dividends do not accumulate; in a year in which the board of directors does not declare a dividend, it is lost forever.

noninterest-bearing note A note that has no interest charge.

nonoperating expense An expense, such as interest expense, that is not related to the everyday process of doing business.

nonoperating revenue Revenue, such as interest income, that is earned from a source other than the normal operations of the business.

nonparticipating preferred stock Preferred stock in which the dividend is limited to a fixed amount; most preferred stock is issued as nonparticipating.

no-par value stock Stock without a fixed dollar amount assigned to each share.

normal balance The normal balance of an account is always the same as the increase side of that account; it is where you would expect to find the balance of that account.

note payable A formal written promise to pay a specified amount at a definite future date.

NSF check (nonsufficient funds check) A check drawn against an account in which there are *nonsufficient funds*; a bad check.

number of days in merchandise inventory A measure of the number of days that it takes a firm to sell its inventory. Calculated by dividing 365 days by the merchandise inventory turnover.

O

OASDI taxable wage The maximum amount of earnings during a calendar year that is subject to OASDI taxes.

operating activities Transactions that enter into the calculation of net income; operating activities affect the income statement.

operating expenses Expenses incurred in the normal operation of the business.

operating expenses budget A budget that estimates operating expenses for the next fiscal period.

Operating Transfers In An account that details monies received from other departments.

Operating Transfers Out An account that details monies paid to other departments.

other financing sources Revenue received from interfund transfers and debt issue proceeds.

other financing uses Money spent for interfund transfers.

other income or expenses Income or expenses that are not directly associated with the normal operation of the business, such as vending machine sales, interest income, and interest expense.

outstanding check A check that was recorded in the checkbook but does not appear on the bank statement. In other words, a check that has been written and entered in the checkbook but has not reached the bank's accounting department.

outstanding stock The number of shares actually in the hands of the stockholders. Also called *outstanding shares.*

overapplied overhead When factory overhead charged to production is greater than actual factory overhead charges. When factory overhead is overapplied, the Factory Overhead Control account has a credit balance.

overtime pay A minimum of one and one-half times the regular rate of pay for hours worked over 40 in a week; commonly called *time-and-a-half.*

owner's equity The excess of assets over liabilities (also called capital, proprietorship, and net worth).

P

paid-in capital Capital that comes from stockholders through the purchase of the company's stock.

Paid-In Capital in Excess of Par—Common A paid-in capital account used to record sales of par value common stock for more than par value.

Paid-In Capital in Excess of Par—Preferred A paid-in capital account used to record sales of par value preferred stock for more than par value.

par value stock Stock for which a fixed dollar amount is designated in the corporate charter as the face value of each share.

participating preferred stock Preferred stock that is allowed to receive dividends of *more than* the fixed rate if a sufficient amount remains after both preferred and common stockholders have received a dividend.

partnership An association of two or more persons who co-own a business for profit.

partnership agreement Another name for articles of partnership.

payee The business or person to whom a check or promissory note is made payable.

payroll register Summary of the gross earnings, deductions, and net pay for all employees for a specific payroll period.

Payroll Tax Expense account An operating expense account used to record the total payroll taxes imposed on the employer.

periodic inventory system An inventory system in which the Merchandise Inventory account shows the value of the most recent inventory count, usually at the beginning of the accounting period. No attempt is made to adjust the balance of this account until the next inventory is taken.

permanent accounts Assets, liabilities, and owner's capital are permanent accounts in the sense that their balances will be carried into the next accounting period. Permanent accounts are also called *real accounts.*

perpetual inventory record A record used in the perpetual system to record purchases and sales of an item of inventory and to keep a running balance of that item.

perpetual inventory system An inventory system in which the Merchandise Inventory account is debited each time merchandise is purchased and credited each time merchandise is sold in order to keep a running balance of the entire inventory.

petty cash fund A small amount of cash kept in the office for making small payments for items such as postage and office supplies.

petty cashier The person designated to disburse money from the petty cash fund.

petty cash payments record An auxiliary record, one that is used to record payments from the petty cash fund. At the end of the month, the record is summarized and used as a basis for a journal entry.

petty cash voucher A voucher used when payment is made from the petty cash fund. It shows the amount of the payment, the purpose, and the account to be debited.

piece-rate plan A method of payment in which workers are paid for each unit they produce, rather than by hours worked.

plant assets Assets that (1) have a useful life of more than one year, (2) are acquired for use in the operation of a business, (3) are not intended for resale to customers in the normal course of business, and (4) are tangible—that is, capable of being touched. Examples are land, buildings, cars, machinery, and equipment. Also called *fixed assets, capital assets,* and *property, plant, and equipment.*

post-closing trial balance A trial balance prepared after closing entries have been posted. The post-closing trial balance is also called an *after-closing trial balance* and consists only of permanent accounts.

posting The process of transferring amounts from the journal to the ledger.

posting errors Errors that result from incorrect transfers from the journal to an account or from the ledger to the trial balance.

preemptive right The right of common stockholders to maintain their proportionate ownership share of the corporation if the corporation issues additional shares of stock.

preferred stock A class of stock that a corporation can issue in addition to common. Such stockholders have special rights or privileges that are not available to the holders of common stock: they have a prior claim to dividends and a prior claim to assets if the corporation were to cease operations and liquidate its assets.

premium A fee paid for insurance coverage that will benefit the business in the future.

premium on stock The amount by which the issue price of stock exceeds the par value.

prepaid expenses Another name for deferred expenses, usually applying to advance payments that cover a year or less.

price/earnings (P/E) ratio A measure of the future prospects of a stock. Calculated by dividing the market price per share of stock by earnings per share.

principal The amount of money borrowed or the amount of credit extended. Also called the *face value.*

principle of materiality States that proper accounting procedures have to be strictly followed only for events and transactions that would have an effect on a business's financial statements.

principle of objective evidence States that source documents should form the foundation for recording business transactions.

proceeds The difference between the maturity value of a discounted note and the bank discount charged.

process cost accounting A system in which costs are gathered and assigned to a stage or a department in the manufacturing process.

production budget A budget that estimates the number of units to be produced in the upcoming fiscal period.

profitability The ability of a business to earn a reasonable return on the owners investments.

profit center Any segment of a business that incurs expenses while producing revenue.

promissory note A written promise to pay a sum of money at a definite time in the future. Also called a **note**.

protest fee A fee charged by a bank to the payee of a note when the note is dishonored by its maker.

publicly held corporation A corporation whose ownership is spread over many investors and whose stock is usually listed on an organized stock exchange.

purchase order A written order from a buyer of goods to the seller, listing items needed and a description of the goods.

purchase requisition A written request for goods to be purchased. It is usually prepared by a department head or manager and sent to a firm's purchasing department.

Purchases account A temporary owner's equity account that is used to record the cost of merchandise purchased for resale. Other possible titles include *Merchandise Purchases* or *Purchases of Merchandise.*

Purchases Discounts account A contra purchases account that records discounts received for prompt payment of merchandise (purchases discounts).

purchases journal A special journal used only to record credit purchases of merchandise. (Some businesses design a multicolumn purchases journal that is used to record all credit purchases, not just merchandise.)

Purchases Returns and Allowances account A contra purchases account that is used to record returns and allowances on merchandise purchases.

Q

quasi-external Interfund transfers are called quasi-external because they are similar to receiving money from an outside source.

quick assets Current assets that can be converted to cash right away, such as receivables and marketable securities.

R

rate The annual percent charged on the principal.

ratio A fractional relationship of one number to another.

ratio of owner's equity to total liabilities A measure of the position of a company in the eyes of its creditors. Calculated by dividing owners equity by total liabilities.

ratio of plant assets to long-term liabilities A measure of the margin of safety for those who hold notes and bonds of a company. Calculated by dividing plant assets by long-term liabilities.

Raw and In-Process Inventory An asset account (used in a just-in-time, or JIT, inventory system) to record the cost of raw materials purchased and issued to production.

raw materials Materials used in the manufacturing process.

raw materials inventory The inventory of goods not yet put into production at the end of an accounting period.

realization The step in liquidation in which all noncash assets are converted into cash.

realization principle The principle that states that revenue should be recorded when it is earned, even though cash may not be collected until later.

receiving report A report prepared by the receiving department to indicate what goods were received and in what quantity.

reciprocal accounts Accounts in sets of interrelated records, such as those for a home office and a branch, that match in dollar amount but have opposite balances.

recording errors Errors made in journal entries.

registered bonds Bonds for which the names and addresses of the bondholders are registered with the issuing corporation.

reinstate To reopen a customer's account when a bad debt is recovered.

replenishing the petty cash fund *Replenish* means to fill up. When applied to the petty cash fund, this term means to bring the amount of the fund back up to the level it was at the beginning of the month.

responsibility accounting A management tool that uses the organization's accounting system to hold people responsible for their work.

restrictive endorsement An endorsement on the back of a check that specifies the purpose for which the money is to be used. *For deposit only* is a common one. It means that the check cannot be cashed—it can only be deposited.

retail businesses Those who own businesses such as grocery stores, drugstores, and restaurants, which sell directly to consumers.

retail method A method for estimating the cost of the ending inventory by using a cost percentage derived from cost and retail prices of the goods available for sale.

retained earnings Past earnings that have not been paid out as dividends to stockholders.

retained earnings statement A statement that shows the changes that have taken place in retained earnings over a specific period of time, such as a month or a year.

return on stockholders' equity A measure of the return on each dollar invested by stockholders. Calculated by dividing net income by average stockholders equity.

return on total assets A measure of the profitability of a firm's assets. Calculated by dividing the sum of net income and interest expense by average total assets.

revenue Income earned from carrying out the activities of a firm.

revenue expenditures Expenditures for a plant asset that benefit only the current accounting period. Examples include repairs and maintenance expenses. Revenue expenditures are debited to expense accounts.

reversing entry An entry made at the start of a new accounting period to reverse an adjusting entry made at the end of the previous period. A reversing entry is the exact opposite of the adjusting entry.

revolving charge plan Payment system in which customers pay a percentage of their account plus finance charges on a monthly basis.

S

salaried employees Individuals who work for a fixed amount for a definite period of time, such as a week, a month, or a year.

Salaries Expense account An expense account used to record the gross amount of the payroll. May sometimes be broken down into several accounts, such as Sales Salaries Expense and Office Salaries Expense.

salary A fixed amount paid to employees for a certain period of time, such as a week or a month.

salary allowances A method of sharing net income that recognizes how much work was done by each partner.

Sales account A revenue account used only to record sales of merchandise.

sales budget A budget that estimates the total dollar volume of sales revenue for the upcoming period.

sales discount A cash discount on the books of the seller, which is recorded as a reduction of sales revenue.

Sales Discounts account A contra revenue account with a normal debit balance. It is used to record cash discounts granted to credit customers for prompt payment.

sales invoice Document prepared by a seller of goods and shipped with the goods (or a few days after the goods). It describes the goods and identifies credit terms, price, and the mode of transportation.

sales journal A special journal used only to record credit sales of merchandise.

sales order A document prepared when an order is received from a customer.

Sales Returns and Allowances A contra revenue account with a normal debit balance. It is used to record returns from and allowances to customers.

sales tax A tax on the retail price of goods sold. It is collected by the merchant and paid to the governmental body that levies the tax.

sales ticket A form prepared by the seller when a cash sale is made. It describes the goods sold, identifies the customer, and serves as a source document for recording the sale.

salvage value The amount that an asset is expected to be worth at the end of its productive life. Also called *scrap value*, *trade-in value*, and *residual value*.

schedule of accounts payable A listing of the individual creditor balances in the accounts payable ledger.

schedule of accounts receivable A listing of the balances in the accounts receivable ledger.

secured bonds Bonds that have a specific asset (or assets) pledged as security for the debt. Also called *mortgage trust bonds*.

segmentation The division of an organization into parts.

selling expenses Operating expenses related to the sale of a firm's merchandise.

serial bonds A bond issue in which the bonds mature periodically over a number of years.

service business A business that performs services for customers to earn a profit.

shift in assets Occurs when one asset is exchanged for another asset, such as when supplies are purchased for cash.

signature card Lists personal information and contains the signature of the person(s) authorized to write checks on a bank account. The bank keeps these cards on file to help identify possible forgeries.

slide An entry with an incorrectly placed decimal point, such as entering 100 for 1,000 or 24.50 for 245.

sole proprietorship A business owned by one person.

source documents Various types of business papers used as a basis for recording business transactions.

special journals Journals used by businesses to record transactions that are similar in nature; examples are the purchases journal and the cash payments journal. Also called *special-purpose journals*.

special revenue funds Government funds that contain restricted monies that must be used for specific purposes.

specific identification method An inventory costing method in which units are identified as coming from specific purchases and are assigned a cost based on the price of those purchases.

stability Refers to how long an asset will last. Plant assets are usually listed on the balance sheet according to their stability.

standard cost accounting A system in which costs are assigned to manufactured products in advance and adjusted periodically to the actual costs. This system can be used as part of a job order or process cost accounting system.

standard form of account A form of account with separate debit and credit sides.

stated value stock A value that is sometimes assigned to no-par stock. There is little difference between accounting for par value stock and for stated value stock.

statement of cash flows A financial statement that provides information about the cash flows from operating activities, investing activities, and financing activities during an accounting period and the net increase or decrease in cash that occurred.

statement of cost of goods manufactured A statement used by a manufacturer in a general accounting system to show the costs of manufacturing for an accounting period.

statement of owner's equity A summary of the changes that have occurred in owner's equity during a specific period of time, such as a month or a year. Another term used to describe the statement of owner's equity is capital statement.

State Unemployment Tax Act (SUTA) A law that requires employers to pay unemployment taxes (for the benefit of employees) to the states in which they conduct business.

stock certificate A document issued to a purchaser of stock when the stock has been paid for in full.

stock dividend A proportional distribution of additional shares of a corporation's own stock to stockholders of record.

stockholders Those who own shares of stock in a corporation. Also called *shareholders*.

stockholders' equity The owners' claim against the assets of the corporation; it represents the excess of total assets over total liabilities. It can be divided into *paid-in capital* and *earned capital* (or *retained earnings*). It is also called *shareholders' equity*.

stock split Occurs when corporations call in their stock and issue two, three, or more shares in place of each old share; usually declared to reduce the market price of shares outstanding.

straight-line method A popular method of calculating depreciation that yields the same amount of depreciation for each full period an asset is used.

straight-line rate The annual percent of depreciation in the straight-line method. It is calculated by dividing 100% by the estimated years of life.

subsidiary ledgers Ledgers that contain only one type of account; the example in this chapter is the accounts payable ledger.

sum-of-the-years'-digits method An accelerated depreciation method that uses a fraction to calculate depreciation. The constant denominator of the fraction is the sum of the digits of the years making up the estimated useful life of the asset. The numerator of the fraction changes each year and is the number of years remaining in the useful life of the asset.

supplies Short-term physical assets needed to operate a business.

SUTA Tax Payable account A current liability account used to record the employer's obligation for state unemployment taxes.

T

T account The T account, so named because it looks like a capital letter T, is a skeleton version of the standard form of account.

tangible All physical assets used by a business are tangible (capable of being touched).

temporary accounts Revenue, expense, and drawing accounts are temporary accounts used to show changes in owner's equity during a single fiscal period. When that period is over, the balances of all temporary accounts are summarized, and the information is transferred to the owner's capital account. Temporary accounts are also called *nominal accounts*.

temporary investments Investments that can be turned into cash with little delay. Also called *marketable securities*.

temporary owner's equity accounts Expense accounts, revenue accounts, and the owner's drawing account are called temporary owner's equity accounts because their balances will be transferred to the owner's capital account at the end of the accounting period.

term bonds A bond issue in which all of the bonds mature at one point in time.

time The number of years, months, or days for which interest is charged. Also called the *term*.

times interest earned A measure of a company's ability to meet its interest payments. Calculated by dividing the sum of net income, interest paid, and income taxes by interest paid.

trade discount A percentage reduction from the list price of merchandise.

transaction Any activity that changes the value of a firm's assets, liabilities, or owner's equity.

transposition The reversal of digits, such as entering 240 for 420.

treasury stock Shares of a company's stock that have been (1) issued as fully paid, (2) later reacquired, and (3) not retired or reissued.

trend percentages Measures used to compare financial data over a period of years, in which one year is selected as the base year, and every other year's amount is expressed as a percent of the base year's amount.

trial balance A listing of all ledger accounts with their balances to test the equality of debits and credits; it is usually prepared at the end of each month.

U

uncollectible account Another name for bad debt.

underapplied overhead When factory overhead charged to production is less than actual factory overhead charges. When factory overhead is underapplied, the Factory Overhead Control account has a debit balance.

unearned revenue Another name for deferred revenue, usually applying to amounts received a year or less in advance.

unfavorable variance A variance that exists when actual costs exceed budgeted costs.

unit contribution margin The sales price of an item minus the variable cost per unit.

units-of-production method A depreciation method in which cost is allocated over the estimated productive life of a plant asset. Life is expressed by such measures as hours, units, or miles.

V

variable costs Costs that vary in total as production varies, but remain the same per unit regardless of how many units are produced.

variance The difference between an actual and a budgeted (standard) cost.

vertical analysis The expression of each item in a company's financial statement as a percent of a base figure, in order to see the relative importance of each item. For the balance sheet, the base is total assets; for the income statement, the base is net sales.

voucher A method of accounting for cash payments in which all payments are authorized in advance and kept track of internally through five components: voucher, voucher register, unpaid voucher file, check register, and paid voucher file.

voucher system A method of accounting for cash payments in which all payments are authorized in advance and kept track of internally through five components: voucher, voucher register, unpaid voucher file, check register, and paid voucher file.

W

wage A fixed hourly rate paid to an employee.

wage bracket method A method that uses government-issued tax tables to compute the amount of federal income tax to be withheld from employees.

weighted-average method or **average cost method** An inventory costing method in which it is assumed that all units have the same average price. The weighted average is calculated by dividing the total cost of goods available for sale by the total units available for sale.

wholesalers Those who purchase goods in bulk from manufacturers and sell them to retailers, other wholesalers, schools and other not-for-profit institutions, and, at times, directly to consumers.

withdrawal The removal of business assets for the owner's personal use.

withhold To deduct amounts from an employee's gross earnings.

withholding allowance An amount of earnings that is not subject to taxation. For federal income tax, each person gets one allowance for himself or herself, one for his or her spouse (if the spouse is not working and claiming the allowance), and one for each dependent. Also called an *exemption*.

workers' compensation insurance Insurance employers must carry to provide protection for employees who suffer a job-related illness or injury.

working capital The excess of a firm's current assets over its current liabilities. A strong working capital means that the firm is likely to be able to carry on its current operations.

work-in-process inventory The inventory of goods that are partially completed at the end of an accounting period.

work sheet An informal working paper used by the accountant to organize data for the financial statements and lessen the possibility of overlooking an adjustment.

Z

zero proof test A test performed using the plus and minus bars of a calculator—*zero proof* means that two equal columns have a zero difference.

INDEX

Boldface indicates a key term and the page where it is introduced and defined.

A

ABA numbers, 197
  purpose of, 198
account, **38, 39**
  balance, 47
  contra, 114
  normal balance of, 49
  rules for debit and credit, 39–40
  standard form of, 38–39
  trial balance, 47–49
account form of balance sheet, 16
accounting
  elements of, 4–5
  users of, 2–3
accounting cycle, **68**
  step 1: analyzing transactions from
    source documents, 68, 81
  step 2: recording transactions in
    journal, 68–75, 81
  step 3: posting from journal to
    ledger, 75–81
  step 4: preparing trial balance of
    ledger, 80–81
  step 5: determining needed
    adjustments, 111–117
  step 6: preparing work sheet,
    117–120
  step 7: preparing financial
    statements from completed
    work sheet, 120–124
  step 8: journalizing and posting
    adjusting entries, 124–125
  step 9: journalizing and posting
    closing entries, 146–155
  step 10: preparing a post-closing
    trial balance, 156–157
  summary of steps, 157
accounting equation, **5**
  business transactions and, 7–12
  dual effect and, 6–7, 38
accounting methods
  accrual, 158
  cash, 158
  hybrid, 158
accounting period, **13**
Accounts Payable, **5**
accounts payable ledger, **230**
  posting, 232
  posting to, 238–239
  proving, 239, 242–243
  schedule, 239
  uses of, 289
Accounts Receivable, **4, 272**
  schedule of, 282–283
Accounts Receivable Credit Cards,
  287–288
accounts receivable ledger, **273**

posting from sales ledger, 274–275
  uses of, 289
accrual basis of accounting, **158**
  characteristics of, 158
  uses of, 158
accrued salaries, **325**
accrued wages, **325**
adjusted trial balance columns, end-
  of-period work sheet, 326, 328
adjusting entries, **112.** *See also*
  adjustments
  journalizing, 124–125, 361
  posting, 124–125
adjustments
  depreciation expense, 323–325
  depreciation of office equipment
    and office furniture, 113–115
  determining, 111–117
  insurance expired, 112–113, 323
  matching principle of accounting,
    116–117
  merchandise inventory, 321–322
  for office supplies used, 323
  store supplies used, 322
  supplies used, 112
  unpaid salaries, 115–116
adjustments columns, end-of-period
  work sheet, 326–332
administrative expenses, **354**
after-closing trial balance, **156**
allowance, **234.** *See also* sales
  returns and allowances
  purchase returns, 234–235
American Accounting Association
  Web site, 17
American Institute of Certified
  Public Accountants Web site,
  17
assets, **4.** *See also* plant assets
  classified balance sheet and, 358
  current, 358
  fixed, 358
  liquidity of, 358
  long-term, 358
  plant, 358
  rules of recording debits and
    credits, 40–41
  stability of, 358
  types of, 4
auxiliary record, **190**

B

balance, 7, **47**
balance form of account, **76**–77
balance sheet, **15,** 15–17
  classified, 358–359
  from completed work sheet, 122

forms of, 16
bank checking account, **194**–198
  bank statement for, 198–203
  endorsements, 197
  maintaining, 196–198
  making deposit, 196–197
  signature card, 196
  writing checks, 197–198
bank credit cards, recording sales by,
  287
bank reconciliation, **200**–203
bank statement, **198**–199
  reasons bank balance and
    checkbook balance disagree,
    199–200
  reconciling, 200–203
beginning merchandise inventory, **321**
blank endorsement, **197**
bonds, savings, 440
book of final entry, **80**
book of original entry, **69**
book value, **114**
business, **2**
  organization of, 3
business entity concept, **6**
business transactions
  accounting equations and, 7–12
  dual effect of, 6–7

C

canceled checks, 199
capital, 5
capital statement, 15
cash, **4, 180.** *See also* bank checking
  account; petty cash
cash basis of accounting, **158**
  characteristics of, 158
  uses of, 158
cash disbursements journal,
  237–238
cash discounts, **225**–226
cash payments journal, **237**–238
  posting, 238–239
  uses of, 289
cash receipts journal, **279**–281
  posting, 279–281
  uses of, 289
cash sales, procedure for, 270–271
cash short and over, **194**–195
change fund, **193**–194
charge, **39**
chart of accounts, **75**–76
checkbook, **197**
checking account. *See* bank checking
  account

checks, **197**
  ABA numbers, 198
  canceled checks, 199
  endorsement of, 197
  not sufficient funds, 200
  outstanding, 199
  writing, 197–198
check stubs, **197**
checkwriters, 198
Circular E, **402**
classified balance sheet, 358–359
  assets, 358
  liabilities, 358
classified income statement, 350,
    352–356
  cost of goods sold section,
      352–353
  operating expenses section, 354
  other income and expense section,
      355–356
  revenue section, 352
clearing account, 146
closing entries
  journalizing, 150
  for merchandising business,
      361–367
  objectives of, 361
  posting, 152–155
  steps in, 361–367
closing process
  in accounting cycle, 146
  diagram of, 151
  objectives of, 146
  post-closing trial balance, 367
  reversing entries, 367–370
  steps in, 146–150
closing the books, 151
combination journal, **181**
combined journal, **181**–187
  benefit of, 181
  designing, 183
  posting, 186–187
  proving, 186
  recording business transactions in,
      184–186
  uses of, 181
  zero proof test, 186
compensation. *See* payroll
compound entry, **73**–74
computerized payroll system,
    409–410
contra account, 114
controlling account, **230**
corporations, **3**
correcting entry, **83**
Cost accounts, **227**
  as Purchase account, 227
cost of goods sold, **352**–353
cost principle, **8**
credit, **39**
  abbreviation for, 39
  Accounts Receivable, 272
  for assets, 40–41
  common payment terms for,
      268–269
  for drawing account, 45–47
  for expense account, 43–45

  for liability, 40–41
  for owner's equity, 40–41
  posting, 78
  procedures for sales on, 269–270
  for revenue accounts, 43–45
  rules of, 39–40
  in standard form of account, 38–39
  summary of rules for, 50
  uses of, 47
credit balance, **48**
Credit Card Expense, **287**
credit cards, 287–288
  bank, 287
  by businesses, 288
  private companies, 287–288
credit memorandum, **235**
  sales return, 276
creditor, **5**
creditors' ledger, **230**
credit period, **268**
credit terms, **268**
cross-footing, **408**
current assets, **358**
current liability, **358**
current ratio, **360**
  importance of, to business, 360
customers' ledger, **273**

D
debit balance, **48**
debit memorandum, **235**
debits, **39**
  abbreviation for, 39
  for assets, 40–41
  for drawing account, 45–47
  for expense account, 43–45
  for liability, 40–41
  for owner's equity, 40–41
  posting, 77
  for revenue accounts, 43–45
  rules of, 39–40
  in standard form of account, 38–39
  summary of rules for, 50
  uses of, 47
deposit in transit, **199–200**
depositor, **196**
deposit slip, **196**
deposit ticket, **196**
depreciation, **113**
  adjustment for expense of,
      323–325
  and book value, 114
  land, 115
  purpose of, 113
  straight-line method, 113–115,
      324–325
discounts
  cash, 225–226
  purchasing, 225
  sales, 225, 277–278
  trade, 225
double-entry accounting, **38**
drawee, **197**
drawer, **197**
drawing accounts, **45**–47
  closing process and, 149, 365
  recording transactions in, 45–47

  rules of debits/credits, 45
dual effect, **6**, 38
  accounting equation and, 6–7

E
earnings statement, 15
employee, **398**
  vs. independent contractor, 398–399
  types of, and payroll, 399
employee's earnings record, **408**–409
Employee's Withholding Allowance
    Certificate, **402**
employer identification number
    (EIN), **428**
Employer's Annual Federal
    Unemployment Tax Return,
    Form 940, 436–438
Employer's Quarterly Federal Tax
    Return, 434–435
Employer's Tax Guide, **402**
ending merchandise inventory, **321**
end-of-period work sheet, 326–332
  completing, 332
  financial statement columns, 328,
      332
endorsement, **197**
  types of, 197
equipment, **4, 358**
errors
  correcting, 82–85
  errors that do not cause trial
      balance to be out of balance,
      85
  math, 82
  posting, 82
  recording, 82
exemption, **402**
expense account, **43**
  closing process and, 148
  recording transactions in, 43–45
  rules of debit and credit, 43
expenses, **9**
  administrative, 354
  general, 354
  selling, 354

F
Fair Labor Standards Act, 399
fares earned, 8
federal income tax
  calculating amount to be withheld,
      402
  filing and making payments for,
      433–435
Federal Income Tax Payable, **411**
Federal Insurance Contribution Act
    (FICA), **401**
  filing and making payments for,
      433–435
  tax rates for, 401
Federal Tax Deposit, Form 8109, **434**
Federal Unemployment Tax Act
    (FUTA), **429**
  filing and making payments for,
      436–438
  purpose of, 430
  Tax Payable, recording, 432

fees earned, 8
FICA Tax Payable—HIP, **411**
  recording, 432
FICA Tax Payable—OASDI,
  410–411
  recording, 431
financial statement, **13**–19
  balance sheet, 14–17
  income statement, 13–15
  interim statements, 371
  statement of owner's equity, 14, 15
financial statement columns, end-of-
    period work sheet, 328, 332
fiscal period, **157**–158
fiscal year, **157**–158
  natural business year, 158
fixed assets, **358**
FOB destination, **243**
FOB (free on board) shipping point,
  243
footing, **47**
Form 940, Employer's Annual
    Federal Unemployment Tax
    Return, 436–438
Form 940 E-Z, 438
Form 941, Employer's Quarterly
    Federal Tax Return, 434–435
Form 8109, Federal Tax Deposit, 434
Form W-2, Wage and Tax
    Statement, 438–439
Form W-3, Transmittal of Wage and
    Tax Statements, 439, 440
Form W-4, **402**
four-column account form, **76**–77
  advantages of, 77
freight charges, on incoming
    merchandise, 243–244
full endorsement, **197**

G

General Dr. column, posting
    individual entries, 239
general expenses, **354**
general journal, **69**
  features of, 69
  recording sales in, 272
  uses of, 289
general ledger, **230**
  posting, 232–233
  posting from sales journal,
    274–275
  posting individual entries, 239
  posting Special Column Totals, 239
  uses of, 289
gross earnings, **400**
  calculating, 400
gross profit, **352**

H

Hospital Insurance Plan (HIP), 401
  rate of, 429
hourly workers, **399**

I

income from operations, **352,**
  354–355

income statement, **13**–15
  classified, 350, 352–356
  from completed work sheet, 120
  for merchandising business, 350,
    352
Income Summary, 147–149
  as clearing account, 146
  closing, 364–365
  purpose of, 146
income tax
  federal, 402
  state and local, 403
independent contractor, **398**
  vs. employee, 398–399
insurance
  expiration of and adjustments,
    112–113, 323
  workers' compensation insurance,
    441–443
interim statements, **371**
internal control, **180**
  common steps for, 180–181
internal transactions, **112**
Internet
  accounting mailing lists on, 86
  accounting terms on, 159
  AICPA site, 333
  benefits and compensation
    information on, 414
  Bookmarks, 245
  management and supervisory
    skills, 372
  minimum wage and SUTA taxable
    base for individual states,
    443
  multimedia product vendors, 290
  national accounting association
    sites, 17
  remote banking, 204
  security measures for, 125
  uses of, as accountant, 51
inventory, **321**
invoice, **224**
invoice sales, 269–270

J

journal, **69**
  advantages of using, 75
  as book of original entry, 69
  cash payments, 237–239
  combined, 181–182
  compound entry, 73–74
  general, 69
  making entries in, 69–73
  posting from journal to ledger,
    75–80
  purchase invoices as, 244
  purchases, 228–229
  purpose of, 69
  recording transactions in and
    accounting cycle, 68–75
  sales, 272
  special, 228
journalizing, **69**–73
  adjusting entries, 361
  closing entries, 150
  as step in accounting cycle,
    124–125

L

land, depreciation and, 115
ledger, **39**
  accounts payable ledger, 230
  as book of final entry, 80
  chart of accounts, 75–76
  creditors' ledger, 230
  four-column account form, 76–77
  general, 230
  posting from journal to ledger,
    75–80
  standard form of account, 38–39
  subsidiary ledger, 230
  T account, 39–42
liabilities, **5**
  classified balance sheet and, 358
  current, 358
  long-term, 358
  rules of recording debits and
    credits, 40–41
liquidity, **358**
list price, **225**
long-term assets, **358**
long-term liability, **358**
lookback period, **433**

M

manual payroll system, 409
manufacturing business, **3**
matching principle of accounting,
  116
  adjustments and, 116–117
materiality concept, **84**
math errors, **82**
  correcting, 82, 85
Medicare, 401
  rate of, 429
merchandise, **222**
merchandise inventory, **222**
  adjustments, 321–322
  beginning, 321
  ending, 321
Merchandise Inventory account, **321**
Merchandise Purchases, **226**–227
merchandising business, **3, 222**
  accounts payable subsidiary ledger,
    230–231
  closing entries for, 361–367
  credit card sales, 287–288
  determining needed adjustments,
    318–326
  end-of-period work sheet, 326–332
  freight charges on incoming
    merchandise, 243–244
  interim statements, 371
  journalizing adjusting entries, 361
  posting cash payments journal,
    238–239
  posting from sales journal, 274–275
  posting purchases journal, 231–233
  preparing financial statements for,
    350–361
  proving accounts payable ledger,
    239, 242–243
  purchase invoices as journal, 244
  purchases returns and allowances,
    234–235

purchasing procedures, 222–225
recording cash payments, 236–238
recording cash receipts, 278–281
recording purchases, 226–229
reversing entries, 367–370
sales activity, 268–273
sales discounts, 277–278
sales tax, 283–286
trade discounts, 225
merit-rating system, **429**
minimum wages, **399**
modified cash basis of accounting, **158**
characteristics of, 158

N

natural business year, **158**
net earnings, **406**
calculating, 406
net income, **13**
net loss, **13**
net pay, **406**
net sales, **352**
net worth, **5**
nominal accounts, **146**
normal balance, **49**
note payable, **5**
NSF (Not Sufficient Funds) checks, **200**

O

objective evidence, **68**
source documents and, 68
office equipment, depreciation of and
adjustment, 113–115
office supplies used, adjustment, 323
Old-Age, Survivors, and Disability
Insurance (OASDI) program, 401
rate of, 429
taxable wage base, 401
operating expenses, **354**
operating income, **354**–355
operating statement, 15
other expenses, **355**–356
other income, **355**–356
outstanding checks, **199**
outstanding deposits, **199–200**
overtime pay, **399**
owner's capital account, 365
owner's drawing account, **45**–47
owner's equity, **5**
classified balance sheet and, 358
revenue and, 8, 12
rules of recording debits and
credits, 40–41
statement of, 15
temporary accounts, 42–47
transactions that affect, 12
withdrawal and, 10, 12

P

Pacioli, Luca, 4
P & L statement, 15
partnerships, **3**
payee, **197**
payroll
calculating gross earnings, 400
calculating net earnings, 406
deductions from, 401–406

entries for employee earnings and
deductions, 410–413
Fair Labor Standards Act, 399
importance of, 398
making payment to employees,
412–413
paying other amounts withheld,
439–440
piece-rate plans, 399
types of employees and, 399
workers' compensation insurance,
441–443
payroll record keeping, 407–409
employee's earnings record,
408–409
information needed for, 407
payroll register, 407–408
payroll register, **407**–408
payroll systems
computerized, 409–410
manual, 409
payroll taxes
Federal Income Taxes, 433–435
Federal Unemployment Tax Act
(FUTA), 429, 432, 436–438
FICA tax, 429, 431, 432, 433–435
filing reports and making
payments, 432–439
form W-2, Wage and Tax
Statement, 438–439
form W-3, Transmittal of Wage and
Tax Statements, 439, 440
recording employer's, 430–432
State Unemployment Taxes,
429–430, 432, 438
Payroll Tax Expense, **428**
pencil footings, 48
permanent account, **150**
petty cash, **187**–193
auxiliary record, 190–191
establishing, 190
making payments from, 190
purpose of, 187
replenishing, 191–193
petty cashier, **190**
petty cash payments record,
190–191
petty cash voucher, **190**
piece-rate plans, **399**
plant assets, **358**
position statement, 16
post-closing trial balance, **156**, 367
posting, **75**
accounts payable ledger, 232,
238–239
cash payments journal, 238–239
cash receipts journal, 279–281
closing entries, 152–155
combined journal, 186–187
general ledger, 232–233
purchases journal, 231–233
from sales journal, 274–275
as step in accounting cycle, 124–125
steps in, 77–80
posting errors, **82**
correcting, 84–85
premium, **110**

prepaid expenses, recording,
110–111
profit, gross, 352
profit and loss statement, 15
property, **358**
proprietorship, **5**
purchase invoice, **224**
journal, 244
purchase order, **223**
distribution of, 223
purchase requisition, **223**
purchases
in merchandising business,
226–229
recording, 227–229
Purchases account, **226**–227
in expanded accounting equation,
227
purchases discounts, **225**
purchases discounts account,
236–237
purchases journal, **228**
posting, 231–233
recording purchases in, 229
uses of, 289
Purchases of Merchandise, **226**–227
purchases returns and allowances,
234–**235**
recording, 235
purchasing agent, 222
purchasing procedures, in
merchandising, 222–225

R

real account, **150**
realization principle, **11**
receiving report, **224**
reconciling bank statement, **200**–203
recording errors, **82**
correcting, 83–85
rent income, 8
replenish petty cash fund, **191**–193
report form, 16
restrictive endorsement, **197**
retail business, **222**
return, **234**
purchase returns, 234–235
returns. *See also* sales returns and
allowances
sales returns involving sales tax, 286
revenue, **8**
owner's equity and, 8, 12
revenue account, **43**
closing process and, 147
recording transactions in, 43–45
rules of debit and credit, 43
reversing entries, 367–370, **369**
revolving charge plans, **268**

S

salaried employees, **399**
Salaries Expense, **410**
salary, **399**. *See also* payroll
adjustments for salaries owed but
unpaid, 115–116, 325–326
sales, 8
credit card sales, 287–288

posting from sales journal, 274–275
procedures for, 270–271
procedures for credit sales, 269–270
recording cash receipts, 278–281
recording sales of merchandise, 271–273
sales tax, 283–286
terms of payment, 268–269
sales account, **271**
closing, 363
sales discounts, **225, 277**–278
recording, 278
sales invoice, **224, 269**–270
sales journal, **272**
posting, 274–275
recording sales in, 272–273
recording sales tax in, 284–286
uses of, 289
sales order, 269
sales returns and allowances, 275–277, **276**
recording, 276–277
sales slip, **270**–271
sales tax, **283**–286
recording in sales journal, 284–286
reporting collected, 284
sales returns involving, 286
sales ticket, **270**–271
savings bonds, 440
schedule of accounts payable, 239
schedule of accounts receivable, 282–283
selling expenses, **354**
service business, **3**
service charge, **200**
shift in assets, **7–8,** 184
signature card, **196**
slide, **82**
Social Security, 401
sole proprietorship, **3**
source documents, **68**
objective evidence principles and, 68
special journals, **228**
special purpose journals, **228**
stability, **358**
standard form of account, **38–39**
statement of financial position, 16
statement of operations, 15
statement of owner's equity, **15**
from completed work sheet, 120–121

as link between income statement and balance sheet, 356
showing additional investments on, 122–123
State Unemployment Tax (SUTA), **429**–430
filing and making payments for, 438
Payable, recording, 432
stock in trade, **222**
store supplies, adjustment for used, 322
straight-line method of depreciation, **113**–115, 324–325
book value and, 114
subsidiary ledger, **230**
Summa Mathematica (Pacioli), 4–5
Supplies, **4**
used and adjustments, 112

T

T account, **39**–42
take-home pay, calculating, 406
tangible, **4**
taxes. *See also* income tax; payroll taxes; sales tax
federal income, 402
Federal Unemployment Tax, 429
FICA, 401, 429
local income, 403
OASDI, 401
state income, 403
State Unemployment tax, 429–430
temporary accounts, **146**
temporary owner's equity account, 42–47, **43**
closing process and, 146
drawing account, 45–47
expense account, 43–45
reason for, 43
recording transactions in, 43–45
revenue account, 43–45
rules of debit and credit, 43
time-and-a-half, **399**
trade discounts, **225**
trading business, **222**
transactions, **6**
dual effect of, 6–7
Transportation In, **243**–244
transposition, **82**
trial balance, **47**
end-of-period work sheet, 326–332

errors that do not cause trial balance to be out of balance, 85
post-closing trial balance, 367
preparing as step in accounting cycle, 80–81
steps in preparing, 47–49

V

voucher system
components of, 459
end-of-month procedures for, 461
using registers, 460–461

W

Wage and Tax Statement, Form W-2, 438–439
wage bracket method, **402**
wages, **399**
Fair Labor Standards Act, 399
piece-rate plan, 399
wholesalers, **222**
withdrawal, **9**
in expanded accounting equation, 9, 18
owner's equity and, 10, 12
withhold, **401**
withholding allowance, **402**
workers' compensation insurance, 441–443
working capital, **360**
formula for, 360
importance of, to business, 360
work sheet, **117**
as accountant's scratch pad, 110, 117
Adjusted Trial Balance columns, 117, 119
Balance Sheet columns, 119
end-of-period, 326–332
Income Statement columns, 119
preparing financial statements from completed, 120–124
steps in completing, 117–120
ten-column, 118
Trial Balance columns, 117
uses of, 117

Z

zero proof test, **186**